MW01044477

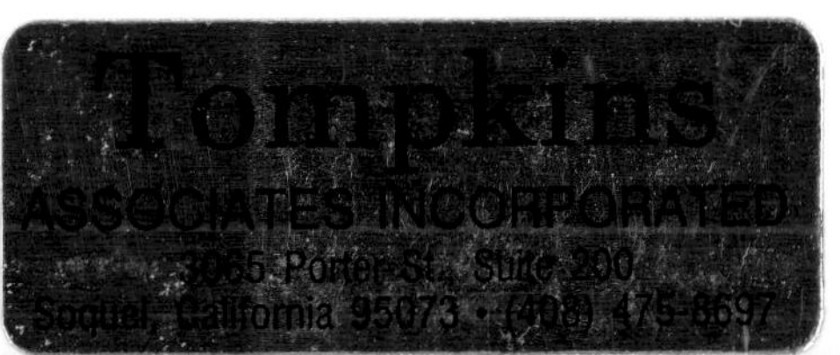
Tompkins
ASSOCIATES INCORPORATED
Porter St., Suite 200
Soquel, California 95073 • 475-8697

The Warehouse Management Handbook

The Warehouse Management Handbook

James A. Tompkins and **Jerry D. Smith**
Editors in Chief

Tompkins Associates, Inc.
Raleigh, North Carolina

McGraw-Hill Book Company

New York St. Louis San Francisco Auckland
Bogotá Hamburg London Madrid Mexico
Milan Montreal New Delhi Panama
Paris São Paulo Singapore
Sydney Tokyo Toronto

Library of Congress Cataloging-in-Publication Data

The Warehouse management handbook.

Includes index.
1. Warehouses—Management. I. Tompkins, James A.
II. Smith, Jerry D.
HF5485.W35 1988 658.7′85 87-16885
ISBN 0-07-064952-9

234567890 DOC/DOC 892109

ISBN 0-07-064952-9

The editors for this book were William A. Sabin and Marlene Hamerling, the designer was Naomi Auerbach, and the production supervisor was Richard Ausburn. This book was set in Baskerville. It was composed by the McGraw-Hill Book Company Professional & Reference Division composition unit.

Printed and bound by R. R. Donnelley and Sons, Inc.

Contents

Editors in Chief

James A. Tompkins, Ph.D., *is one of the most respected practitioners in the field today and is the founder and president of Tompkins Associates, Inc., the internationally known consulting firm specializing in facilities planning, material handling, warehousing, and integrated automation. He has published over 150 works and given more than 1000 talks, seminars, and industrial short courses. Moreover, he has received over 30 awards and citations, including the prestigious Reed-Apple Award from the Material Handling Education Foundation, Inc.*

Jerry D. Smith *is executive vice president of Tompkins Associates, Inc. He has managed over 100 warehousing, material handling, and facilities design consulting projects with major corporations, including General Electric, RJR Nabisco, General Mills, and IBM. He is a senior member of the Institute of Industrial Engineers.*

Contributors

Kenneth B. Ackerman *President, The Kenneth B. Ackerman Company, Columbus, Ohio* (CHAPTER 5)

James M. Apple, Jr. *Partner, Systecon, A Coopers & Lybrand Division, Duluth, Georgia* (CHAPTER 23)

Randall M. Ballard *Consultant, Systecon, A Coopers & Lybrand Division, Duluth, Georgia* (CHAPTER 23)

S. M. Bhardwaj *Vice President, J. George Gross & Associates, Woodbridge, New Jersey* (CHAPTER 2)

Edward J. Budill *Vice President, Tompkins Associates, Inc., Raleigh, North Carolina* (CHAPTER 14)

Richard D. Bushnell *President, Bushnell Consulting, Chalfont, Pennsylvania* (CHAPTER 19)

James M. Cahill *Regional Manager, Rapistan, Oakbrook, Illinois* (CHAPTER 16)

Thomas F. Cecich *Manager of Safety, Health & Environmental Affairs, Glaxco, Inc., Research Triangle Park, North Carolina* (CHAPTER 29)

Michael A. Cramer *Senior Engineer, Tompkins Associates, Inc., Raleigh, North Carolina* (CHAPTER 13)

Thomas Cullinane, Ph.D. *Professor, Department of Industrial Engineering, Northeastern University, Boston, Massachusetts* (CHAPTER 3)

J. Henry Donnon *Vice President (Retired), Artco Corporation, Hatfield, Pennsylvania* (CHAPTER 12)

Michael S. Erwin *Manager, Marketing, Harnischfeger Corporation, Milwaukee, Wisconsin* (CHAPTER 18)

Robert B. Footlik *Executive Vice President, Footlik & Associates, Evanston, Illinois* (CHAPTER 27)

John W. Fowler *Research Associate, Department of Industrial Engineering, Texas A&M University, College Station, Texas* (CHAPTER 9)

J. George Gross *President, J. George Gross & Associates, Woodbridge, New Jersey* (CHAPTER 2)

Ted Hammond *President, Conveyor Logic, Inc., Dutton, Michigan* (CHAPTER 12)

John R. Huffman, Ph.D., P.E. *President, John R. Huffman, P.E., Glendale, California* (CHAPTER 25)

Adolph S. Kannewurf *Director of Marketing, Harnischfeger Engineers, Inc., Milwaukee, Wisconsin* (CHAPTER 17)

Alexander Keeney, Jr., PCMH *Manager, Industrial Engineering, Random House, Inc., Westminster, Maryland* (CHAPTER 7)

Bruce Ketchpaw *Director of Marketing, Rite-Hite Corporation, Milwaukee, Wisconsin* (CHAPTER 11)

Karl E. Lanker, P.E., C.M.C. *Vice President, Engineering, The Sims Consulting Group, Inc., Lancaster, Ohio* (CHAPTER 15)

Eugene L. Magad *Associate Professor and Coordinator, Materials Management Program, William Rainey Harper College, Palatine, Illinois* (CHAPTER 4)

David C. Morrison *Offset Program Manager, Frito-Lay, Inc., Dallas, Texas* (CHAPTER 20)

William L. Morton *Manager, Ernst & Whinney, Washington, D.C.* (CHAPTER 28)

Raymond A. Nelson *President, Raymond Nelson Distribution Consultants, Stamford, Connecticut* (CHAPTER 21)

J. Eric Peters *Senior Engineer, Tompkins Associates, Inc., Raleigh, North Carolina* (CHAPTER 6)

Don T. Phillips, Ph.D., P.E. *Professor, Department of Industrial Engineering, Texas A&M University, College Station, Texas* (CHAPTER 9)

Donald G. Reid *Principal, Donald Reid and Associates, San Francisco, California* (CHAPTER 24)

E. Ralph Sims, Jr., P.E., C.M.C. *Chairman of the Board, The Sims Consulting Group, Inc., Lancaster, Ohio* (CHAPTER 8)

Jerry D. Smith *Vice President, Tompkins Associates, Inc., Raleigh, North Carolina* (CHAPTER 6)

James A. Tompkins, Ph.D. *President, Tompkins Associates, Inc., Raleigh, North Carolina* (CHAPTERS 1 and 3)

Richard E. Ward, Ph.D., P.E. *Director of Education, Material Handling Institute, Charlotte, North Carolina* (CHAPTER 26)

Thomas L. Ward, Ph.D., P.E. *Professor, Department of Industrial Engineering, University of Louisville, Louisville, Kentucky* (CHAPTER 10)

Donald J. Weiss *President, White Storage & Retrieval Systems, Inc., Kenilworth, New Jersey* (CHAPTER 13)

Mickey R. Wilhelm, Ph.D., P.E. *Chairman, Department of Industrial Engineering, University of Louisville, Louisville, Kentucky* (CHAPTER 10)

William Wrennall, C. Chem., C.M.C. *President, The Leawood Group, Ltd., Richard Muther & Associates, Leawood, Kansas* (CHAPTER 22)

Preface

In the mid-1970s, the editors began a crusade which has been most rewarding. This crusade focused on the importance of warehousing and could best be summarized by our belief that *warehousing is a profession.* When we began the crusade, we often found ourselves speaking with small, unenthusiastic groups. However, things have changed. The interest—in fact, the demand—for warehousing knowledge is huge and growing at an ever-increasing rate.

During this same period, the editors have seen the demand for warehousing consulting skyrocket. The publications, conferences, and trade shows in the warehousing field have similarly gone through a metamorphosis of unparalleled magnitude. All signals clearly point to the fact that today warehousing is accepted as a vital and important profession. Only one thing has been lacking: a broad-based handbook that documented the science of the warehousing profession. The objective of this handbook is to fulfill this one last requirement. With the publication of this handbook, it is now clear that warehousing is a profession.

The Warehouse Management Handbook is organized into four integrated parts. The first part (Chapters 1 to 4) introduces the subject of warehousing and provides the context for warehousing. The second part (Chapters 5 to 11) covers the topic of warehouse planning. The third part (Chapters 12 to 20) deals with the subject of warehouse equipment, and the last unit (Chapters 21 to 29) describes the functions of the warehouse operating systems. The index is organized to provide an easy reference on topics of specific interest to warehouse managers.

The editors are indebted to the authors of the handbook chapters. Obviously, without the authors' support, this handbook would not exist. The editors are also appreciative of the patience of Bill Sabin, our publisher, and the entire McGraw-Hill Book Company. A special word of thanks goes to the staff of Tompkins Associates, Inc. Of particular note are the other two partners of Tompkins Associates, Inc., Rickey B. Barnhill and John C. Spain, the vigilant proofreading of Jerry Jackson and the dedicated typing support of the office staff: Janice Millhouser, Krystal Neville, Chris Hutchinson, and Geri Clifton. Finally, the editors would like to thank their wives, Shari and Fran, and their children, Tiffany, Jamie, and Jim Tompkins and April, Jason, Lora, and Daniel Smith, for their support, understanding, and love throughout this project.

JAMES A. TOMPKINS, Ph.D.
JERRY D. SMITH
Tompkins Associates, Inc.
Raleigh, North Carolina
October 7, 1987

1

The Challenge of Warehousing

James A. Tompkins, Ph.D.

President and Chairman, Tompkins Associates, Inc., Raleigh, North Carolina

Introduction

The profession of planning and managing warehouse operations is a critical part of maintaining a profitable business. With more than 300,000 large warehouses and 2.5 million employees in the United States, the cost of American warehousing is more than 5 percent of the gross national product. In the past few years, the field of warehousing has begun to receive the attention that it deserves. However, the warehouse manager has been asked to increase customer service, reduce inventories, increase productivity, handle a large number of stockkeeping units, and improve space utilization. The warehouse manager has realized that these conflicting objectives require a much more professional approach than previously adopted. The purpose of this handbook is to support this more professional approach. It is critical that today's warehouse manager follow this approach to achieve the results expected by today's upper management.

Warehousing Defined

The functions performed by a warehouse are:

1. Receiving the goods from a source
2. Storing the goods until they are required
3. Picking the goods when they are required
4. Shipping the goods to the appropriate user

Oftentimes, a distinction is made between a finished goods warehouse and a raw materials storeroom. The fact is, however, that the functions performed in a finished goods warehouse, receive-store-pick-ship, are identical to the functions performed in a raw materials storeroom. Consequently, both are warehouses. The only true distinctions between the two are the source from which the goods are received and the user to whom the goods are shipped. A raw materials storeroom receives goods from an outside source, stores the goods, picks the goods, and ships the goods to an inside user. A finished goods warehouse receives goods from an inside source, stores the goods, picks the goods, and ships the goods to an outside user.

Likewise, an in-process inventory warehouse receives goods from an inside source, stores the goods, picks the goods, and ships the goods to an inside user, while a distribution warehouse receives goods from an outside source, stores the goods, picks the goods, and ships to an outside user.

The differences among these various warehouses are restricted to the perspectives of the sources, management, and users of the warehouses. If the primary functions of an activity are receive-store-pick-ship, then the activity is a warehouse, regardless of its position in a company's logistics. The tools and techniques presented in this handbook can be successfully used to plan and manage that activity.

History

Warehousing for the purpose of commercial gain is at least as old as recorded history. In early writings, man was described as having stored excess food and kept animals for emergency surplus. As civilization developed, local warehouses were introduced. Merchandise was stored in connection with shipping, trading, and manufacturing activities. When transportation branched out from local to cross-country, warehouses became more than local storehouses. When major trade points developed during the middle ages, warehousing was established to handle the storage of shipped items. The first major commercial warehouse was built in Venice, a center of major trade routes. Warehouses in that area were operated for profit by a brotherhood of merchants known as *guilds*. As trading activity expanded beyond the Mediterranean area, each port city developed its own terminal warehouse. Warehousing at the port city reduced the amount of time a ship was detained in port and improved overseas transportation.

Warehousing in America

In the late 1800s in the United States, the railroad industry provided the most responsive transportation by connecting port cities to inland cities. Freight cars began to be used as warehouses on wheels, especially during the grain harvest season, but freight-car shortages induced the railroad companies to separate the transportation and warehousing functions. With the railroad companies having a monopoly on both warehousing and freight, they were able to favor larger corporations, giving them free warehousing services with the use of the railroads.

In 1891, independent warehouses organized the American Warehousesemans Association (AWA). One of its first activities was to urge carriers, primarily the rail carriers, to discontinue free warehousing. The AWA succeeded in pushing through the Hepburn Act of 1906, which ended freight depot warehousing by the railroads. This legislation defined "storage and handling of property transported" as part of the railroading functions and required the application of published tariff rates for all such services furnished by railroads. The Hepburn Act brought railroads under government control and helped steer the development and rapid growth of the common carrier in the proper direction.

Mass Production

The industrial revolution brought about the combining of craft shops into factories. This resulted in mass production and manufacturing facilities that were complete, from receiving to shipping. Mass production, in turn, created new aspects of warehousing. When mass production first began, goods were typically produced according to a sales forecast. The finished goods and raw materials that were necessary to meet the forecast were usually placed in the factory warehouse. However, when distribution patterns began developing, companies moved warehouses closer to their target market areas. With the use of private and public warehousing services both close to the factory and in the marketplace, customer service levels increased.

In the early days, warehousing was offered as a supplemental service to transportation, and the facility was a part of the clearance terminal. The word *terminal* implies that the warehouses were located in the center of the city, usually close to the railroad depot and the wholesale market district. As the demand for storage space increased and land value rose, multistory buildings were erected to provide more storage space on a minimum amount of land.

Before the end of World War I, the most common materials handling method in warehouses involved the use of hand trucks. Stacking was performed by hand, and, in most buildings, stacking heights were designed in the 8- to 12-foot range. During World War II, the forklift truck and wooden pallet were introduced. Mass production of the forklift truck allowed the practical stacking height of merchandise to be increased to 30 feet, a 300 percent increase. In addition, it allowed a faster movement of merchandise within the warehouse. With the advantage of increased stacking height and the disadvantage of forklifts in multistory facilities, the use of single-story buildings replaced multistory facilities. Since the amount of land necessary for single-story warehouses was not available in the city, relocation to the outskirts of cities took place. The single-store warehouse typically had ceiling heights that ranged from 20 to 30 feet, allowing maximum use of the forklift.

Warehousing systems have progressed throughout history; they have advanced from local storehouses during the middle ages to multimillion-dollar facilities. Yet, during this time, the fundamental principles of warehousing have remained the same. The reasons for storing goods in Venice, the location of the first commercial warehouse, are the same as exist today. Warehousing has advanced over the years with such improvements as forklifts, automated storage/retrieval systems (AS/R systems), and computers. This obviously shows our technologic advancement; however, from a hidden viewpoint, the efforts made in developing these advancements show how much value we place on having a warehousing function.

The Value of Warehousing in the Economy

It is important for all warehouse managers to ponder the question, Does warehousing add value to a product? The traditional school of thought has concluded that, no, warehousing does not add value to a product; in fact, warehousing is strictly a cost-adding activity that is a necessary evil. In firms that follow this school of thought, warehousing costs are typically classified as indirect costs. Often, these cost categories are spread over the direct costs of the firm in such a way that the cost of warehousing is not distinguishable.

To convince yourself of the value of warehousing, consider the value of the refrigerator in your home. Your refrigerator is essentially a warehouse. You purchase food at the supermarket, deliver the food to your refrigerator, store it in the refrigerator, pick the food from your refrigerator as you need it, and ship the food to some location where it will be processed or consumed. What is the value of your refrigerator? What is the value of having milk where you want it, when you want it? If the answer is not yet clear, consider the costs you would incur if you did not own a refrigerator. What are the "costs" of not having milk in your home for cereal at breakfast? Some of the costs are hunger from not eating, indigestion from eating dry cereal, the inconvenience of having to go to the supermarket before breakfast, and the actual expense of going to the supermarket daily.

The true value of warehousing lies in having the right product in the right place at the right time. Thus, warehousing provides the time-and-place utility necessary for a company to prosper.

Without a complete and accurate understanding of its value, companies have failed to give warehousing the same scientific scrutiny as the other aspects of their business. For a profession as important as warehousing, this is not acceptable, and a more scientific approach to warehousing must be taken.

Scientific Approach to Warehouse Planning

Warehouse planning is not simply pouring a concrete slab, installing some racks, and tilting up some walls. Nor is it a static, one-time activity. The changing, dynamic environment within which warehouses are planned quickly renders existing plans obsolete. Therefore, warehouse planning must be a continuous activity in which the existing plan is constantly being scrutinized and molded to meet anticipated requirements. For a warehouse to accomplish its objectives, warehouse managers must consider the variable warehouse resources and mold them into an effective plan. A successful warehouse maximizes the effective use of the warehouse resources while satisfying customer requirements.

Objectives

The resources of a warehouse are space, equipment, and personnel. The cost of space not only includes the cost of building or leasing the space, but also the cost of maintaining the space. Typically, the cost of space in a warehouse is $0.20 to $0.30 per cubic foot per year for taxes, insurance, maintenance, and energy. A company which is ineffectively using its available cubic space is incurring excessive operating costs.

The equipment resources of a warehouse include data processing equipment, dock equipment, unit load equipment, material handling equipment, and storage equipment, all of which combine to represent a sizable capital investment in the warehouse. To obtain an acceptable rate of return on this investment, the proper equipment must be selected and be used properly.

Oftentimes, the personnel resource of the warehouse is the most neglected, even though its cost is usually the greatest. Approximately 50 percent of the costs of a typical warehouse are labor-related. Reducing the amount of labor and pursuing higher labor productivity, good labor relations, and worker satisfaction will significantly reduce warehouse operating costs.

Customer requirements are simply the demand to have the right product in good condition at the right place at the right time. Therefore, the product must be accessible and protected. If a warehouse cannot meet these requirements adequately, the warehouse does not add value to the product and, in fact, very likely subtracts value from the product.

Therefore, the following objectives must be met for a warehouse to be successful:

1. Maximize the effective use of space.
2. Maximize effective use of equipment.
3. Maximize effective use of labor.
4. Maximize accessibility of all items.
5. Maximize protection of all items.

The two distinct types of continuous warehouse planning needed to produce an efficient and effective warehouse operation are *contingency planning* and *strategic master planning*. The differences between the two relate to defensive versus offensive planning.

Contingency Planning

Contingency planning is a defensive tool used to guard against a predictable future change in warehouse requirements, the timing of which is extremely difficult, if not impossible, to anticipate. One example would be the bankruptcy of a primary supplier of goods to the warehouse. While difficult to anticipate, such events do occur, and a contingency plan is needed to locate an alternative supplier to maintain service to the warehouse customers. In other words, contingency plans are needed to efficiently and effectively address the question: "What course of action is required if a given unanticipated change in requirements or circumstances occurs?"

Contingency planning is distinctly different from the common nonplanning approach to addressing such sudden changes in requirements or circumstances. The nonplanning approach, often called "crisis management" or "putting out fires," entails development of plans *after* a change in requirements or circumstances occurs.

Proper contingency planning develops the contingency plan to the fullest extent possible *before* the change occurs. Consequently, proper contingency planning can significantly reduce the lead time required to implement a plan of action. You do not wait until after a fire starts in the warehouse to install a sprinkler system; instead, the sprinkler system is installed long before as a contingency against a fire that may or may not ever take place. Likewise, why not establish formal contingency plans for other predictable circumstances characterized by unanticipated timing?

Strategic Master Planning

Strategic master planning is an offensive tool designed to guard against a predictable change in warehouse requirements, the timing of which can be anticipated. Strategic master planning is directed at forecasting future warehousing needs sufficiently in advance of the actual requirements to allow enough lead time to efficiently and effectively meet those needs.

The approximate timing of many changes in warehousing requirements can be predicted. Warehouse space shortages, labor deficiencies, equipment obsolescence, product-line changes, material control problems, and so on, do not develop overnight. Future inventory levels and product mixes typically can be forecast years in advance based on historical and future business plans. Granted, forecasting with long planning horizons is a risky business, and warehouse plans based on such forecasts often prove unworkable. Nevertheless, the forecast is the best available information concerning the future, and it is foolhardy not to use that information to advantage. In fact, in view of rapidly accelerating investment and operating costs, more and more decision makers are demanding good strategic master plans that express future warehouse space, labor, and equipment requirements.

Contingency planning and strategic master planning are complementary. Strategic master planning without effective contingency plans will subject the warehouse to having to cope with unanticipated problems for which no plan of action is readily apparent. Contingency planning without a strategic master plan makes the contingency planning process that much more difficult and will inherently result in the crisis management philosophy returning to the warehouse. Without a warehouse strategic master plan, a firm runs the risk of not sufficiently anticipating problems and failing to develop contingency plans until well into the lead time required to implement a solution. In either situation, the absence of one planning mode severely limits the effectiveness of the other.

Qualities of a Master Plan. A warehouse strategic master plan is a set of documents describing what actions must be accomplished and when they must be accomplished to satisfy the warehousing requirements of an enterprise over a given planning horizon. A closer examination of this definition reveals the important attributes of a good warehouse strategic master plan.

First of all, a good warehouse strategic master plan should not consist simply of ideas, thoughts, possibilities, and desires that are casually recorded "somewhere" if at all. A good plan is a *formal set of documents* which has been created, collected, edited, and so on, specifically as a strategic master plan of action. Common components of this set of documents include an implementation plan, a descriptive narrative, scaled facility drawings, and supporting economic cost and justification data.

Second, a good warehouse strategic master plan is action-oriented and time-phased. Where possible, the plan should set forth very specific step-by-step actions to be taken to meet requirements rather than simply stating the general alternatives available to meet those requirements. The strategic master plan is established based upon a set of premises concerning future production volumes, inventory levels, staffing levels, available technology, and other factors.

The comparison of alternative actions based upon these premises should already have been performed as a part of developing the strategic master plan. As long as these premises are clearly stated as a part of the strategic master plan, and understood, problems should not arise with regard to implementing actions that prove to be based upon false premises.

This is not to say, however, that a set of warehouse master plans based on a set of different future scenarios of production volumes, inventory levels, staffing levels, available technology, and so on is unacceptable. On the contrary, such a set of plans would represent the ultimate in warehouse master planning.

The strategic master plan should be time-phased to indicate when each recommended action should be implemented. Typically, scaled facility drawings should accompany each recommended action to illustrate what the facility will look like after implementation of a given action.

Finally, a good warehouse strategic master plan should encompass a specified planning horizon. It should have a definite beginning point and a definite ending point. Typically, the planning horizon is stated in terms of years; often a 5-year planning horizon is used. Occasionally, however, the use of milestones other than the passing of years, such as production volumes or inventory levels, may prove more beneficial. For example, a warehouse strategic master plan for a foundry operation might describe the plans of action required to meet the foundry's changing warehouse requirements as production output increments from a level of 250 tons per day to 1000 tons per day.

Developing the Master Plan. The general methodology for developing a warehouse strategic master plan consists of the following seven-step procedure:

1. Document the existing warehouse operation.
2. Determine and document the warehouse storage and throughput requirements over the specified planning horizon.
3. Identify and document deficiencies in the existing warehouse operation.
4. Identify and document alternative warehouse plans.
5. Evaluate the alternative warehouse plans.
6. Select and specify the recommended plans.
7. Update the warehouse master plan.

The first step involves obtaining or developing scaled drawings of the existing warehouse facilities and verifying their accuracy. The accuracy of existing drawings should never be assumed. It should always be physically verified on the warehouse floor.

Existing warehouse equipment should be identified and documented. The labor complement of each area of the warehouse should be determined and the general responsibilities of each person documented. Existing standard operating procedures should be scrutinized and compared with what actually takes place on the warehouse floor. This first step of the master planning process establishes a baseline against which recommendations for improvement can be compared.

Step two involves defining what materials will be stored in the warehouse and the volume anticipated during the planning horizon. Items to be stored in the warehouse should be classified into categories according to their material handling and storage characteristics.

Forecasts or production schedules should then be used to predict the storage volumes and turnover rates of each category of material over the specified planning horizon. Ideally, these volumes would be stated in terms of the unit loads in which the materials would be stored and handled.

The third step involves identifying potential areas of improvement in the existing warehouse operations. The potential for improvement may exist because the operation lacks sufficient capacity to handle future requirements or because existing facilities, methods, equipment and/or labor forces are not the most efficient or effective available.

Step four deals with identifying alternative facility, equipment, procedures and/or personnel plans that will eliminate or minimize the deficiencies identified in the existing warehouse operation. From these alternative plans of action, a specific time-phased plan of action should be recommended for meeting the warehouse requirements over the given planning horizon.

The fifth step of the master planning process involves performing both an economic and qualitative assessment of the alternative plans of action. The economic evaluation should consist of an after-tax, time-value-of-money assessment of the total life-cycle costs of competing alternative plans of action.

The qualitative assessment of alternatives requires a subjective comparison of attributes such as personnel safety, flexibility, ease of implementation, maintainability, and potential product damage. This subjective, qualitative evaluation can often be beneficially quantified by using one of a number of good multiple-objective decision-making models.

Step six involves the selection of the best alternative plan of action implied by the economic and qualitative evaluations, and specifying the recommended warehouse strategic master plan. The master plan will document the space, equipment, personnel, and standard operating procedure requirements of the warehouse over the planning horizon. In addition, scaled facility drawings should be included showing the recommended warehouse layout for all revisions recommended by the plan of action.

The first six steps of this procedure will result in a warehouse strategic master plan. The strategic master planning process, however, will not be complete. In fact, it will never be completed, since strategic master planning is a continuous activity.

The seventh step in the process, therefore, is updating the master plan. By its very nature, a strategic master plan is inaccurate. Since it is based to a large extent on predictions of the future, the warehouse strategic master plan will require updating as better information concerning the future is obtained. Consequently, it should never be used as a precise tool, but only as a guideline for planning future warehousing operations.

Trends in Design

In today's uncertain environment, it is extremely important that the systems installed in warehouses have the ability to adapt to future requirements. This is just as true for automated systems as it is for conventional systems. Guidelines that should be followed to establish systems capable of meeting future requirements are:

1. *Flexibility.* The greater the flexibility, the easier will be long-term integration. For this reason, systems should be "soft" and "friendly" as opposed to "hard" and "rigid." Soft and friendly systems have the capability of addressing a wide variety of circumstances. Material handling systems should be capable of operating at a variety of speeds and should be able to handle a variety of loads. A good deal of standardization should exist throughout the facility. All unit load sizes, configurations, capacities, and "special" equipment should be very closely reviewed. Warehouses are not deterministic, but rather, must be able to accommodate changes in product mix. Material handling systems should be designed to be easily expanded or contracted in order to accommodate higher or lower production volumes.
2. *Top-Down Design.* The suboptimization of material handling systems for a move is not nearly as important as the optimization of the total warehousing material handling system. Therefore, it is only after the overall system is planned that handling systems within the warehouse should be planned within the context of the overall system.
3. *Selectively Operable.* A material handling system in a warehouse must be able to operate in segments and should allow implementation of one segment at a time. Once a segment is implemented and debugged, it should be integrated with other segments. Each segment should have a back-up operating mode.
4. *Automation Supportive.* All material handling systems within a warehouse must interface with other systems for total automation. The system must provide the proper material orientation and alignment. In this regard, a faulty material handling system can quite easily result in quality problems. The system must also be able to report

to the control system all move transactions. There is no control in a warehouse if the material handling system does not support the control system.

5. *Economically Progressive.* In a warehouse, a real problem exists if we take too seriously the traditional industrial engineering approach to economic decision making. Many companies have been over "task-forced" and economically analyzed. In many companies, the entrepreneurial spirit has been killed by the "numbers people" who don't understand that with every large opportunity there is risk. If one analyzes risk from a conservative perspective, the economic analysis will not lead to progressive, forward-thinking decisions.

Equipment Considerations

Equipment will continue to play a major role in the advancement of warehousing. Mechanized and automated equipment are increasing the efficiency and effectiveness of warehouse operations. Some of the equipment which may merit your attention is briefly described below:

Modular Tote Material Handling Systems. The tote pan is the basic handling block on which the material handling system is often going to be built. The tote can be used from the point of entry in a system, to an intermediate point, or to the last step in the system. For example, a system can consist of receiving the product, detrashing it, and putting it in a tote to store in various storage locations until shipping. Totes can be used in conjunction with carousels, AS/R systems, shelves, and other material handling equipment.

It is very important that the tote pan selected is capable of being subdivided. A standard size is crucial to the tote being capable of being combined with other tote pans to create unit loads of several tote pans. The tote pan should be codable to allow an interface with control and information systems.

Carousels. A carousel consists of horizontal or vertically aligned bins that revolve to an operator who is located at a fixed picking station. Carousels are not new; however, vertical carousels have only recently been accepted for warehousing in the United States. Another technological advancement is the placement of storage and retrieval robots at the picking stations to replace the operator. The robot can retrieve and store bins. Robots are usually interfaced with take-away conveyors and computer controls. Various carousels have lock and dust-free options in order to prevent damage to expensive small parts. Typical throughput in a carousel is one store or retrieval cycle per minute. (See Chapter 16 for more information.)

AS/R Systems. Automated storage/retrieval systems are also not new to most people. A wide variety of man-aboard, unit-load, miniload, and deep-lane systems are in operation today. What possibly is new is the transition of AS/R systems from distribution and warehousing to manufacturing. In fact, probably the greatest future application of AS/R systems is as the central handling and storage mechanism for raw, in-process, and finished manufactured goods. (For more information, see Chapter 17.)

AGV Systems. Automatic guided vehicle (AGV) systems are battery-powered, driverless vehicles that are equipped to follow either wire guide paths or a reflective tape placed on the floor while either towing or carrying a load. AGV systems can be designed to carry a variety of sizes and weight capacities. However, consideration must be given to traveling speed in relation to the force required to start and stop the load. The AGV systems control system allows for virtually unlimited computer-controlled operation of the AGV. The AGV systems may be programmed to load, unload, accelerate, deliver, stop, start, block, and select travel paths, all without human intervention. The AGV systems are versatile, allowing easy expansion and adaptation within an existing facility. (Chapter 11 discusses AGV sytems in more detail.)

SPMC. A self-propelled monorail carrier consists of either a top or floor-mounted track with power control buss bars and individually powered, roller-suspended carriers that ride the rail and pick up power and control signals from the buss bars. The flexibility available via SPMCs is excellent. Carriers can be given the capabilities of forward and reverse operation, multiple speeds, shortest-path routing, and system blocking. This very noiseless system can climb or descend grades up to 15° unassisted and even higher with chain drives as helpers. Accumulation in front of a workstation or other location is possible on SPMCs. Although SPMCs do not compete with power and free conveyors in high-volume applications, in low- to medium-volume areas, the flexibility of the SPMC makes it a viable option for the automated factory and warehouse.

Automatic Identification Systems. These systems combine machine-readable encoding and code readers for the purposes of accounting, tracking, and movement control. An automatic identification system consists of:

1. A subject—the item to be identified
2. A code—the label to be read to identify the subject
3. A reader—the device which is to read the code
4. The control—the device to which the code is to be sent

It is clear that a critical activity in the automated warehouse is the replacement of the human who provides input to the control system. Today, this is being accomplished by automatic identification systems. (See Chapter 22 for more information.)

Conclusion

This chapter has presented the evolution and the challenge of warehousing. Because warehousing is crucial to all companies, the time has come to give it the same scrutiny as is given to manufacturing. Good planning, both contingency and strategic, will go a long way toward ensuring that a warehouse will meet it's objectives. In a nutshell, the challenge to warehousing is to meet its objectives through planning by using its resources to fulfill the customer's requirements. A warehouse manager who keeps all this in mind will have a successful operation. Consideration must be given to automating with computer control systems. If a computer in a warehouse can assist a manager in meeting the challenge, then, *go for it*!

Bibliography

Ackerman, K. B.: *Warehousing: A Guide for Both Users and Operators,* Traffic Service Corp., Washington, 1977, chaps. 1–2.

"Considerations for Planning and Installing Automatic Guided Vehicle Systems," *MHI,* Pittsburgh, 1980.

Schwind, G.: "Self-Powered Monrail Carriers; When and Where to Use Them," *Material Handling Engineering,* February 1983, pp. 48–53.

Tompkins, J. A., and J. D. Smith: "Keys to Developing Material Handling System for Automated Factory Are Listed," *IE,* September 1983, pp. 48–54.

Tompkins, J. A., and J. D. Smith: "Optimal Approach to Warehousing Calls for Strategic and Contingency Planning, *IE,* June 1982, pp. 70–74.

Tompkins, J. A., and J. D. Smith: *Warehousing: A Critical Profession,* American Management Association, Watertown, Mass., 1982, chap. 1, pp. 1–6.

Tompkins, J. A., and J. D. Smith (eds.): *Automated Material Handling and Storage,* Auerbach, Pennsauken, NJ, 1983.

2
Warehousing and Physical Distribution

J. George Gross

President, J. George Gross & Associates, Woodbridge, New Jersey

S. M. Bhardwaj

Vice President, J. George Gross & Associates, Woodbridge, New Jersey

What Is Physical Distribution?

In the past few decades, industrial management in the United States has recognized a vital new discipline. It has been called physical distribution, business logistics, logistics management, transportation and distribution, distribution engineering, or materials management. Although these terms are used interchangeably and generally describe the same subject area, there are subtle differences. The three key terms are:

1. Logistics
2. Materials management
3. Physical distribution

Logistics describes the entire process of materials and products moving into, through, and out of the firm. *Materials management* describes the movement of materials and components into the firm. *Physical dis-*

tribution is concerned with outbound movement of material from point of manufacture to point of consumption.[1] Figure 2.1 shows the relationship among these key terms.

The physical distribution activities of United States' businesses currently account for more than 20 percent of our gross national product. That translates to over $400 *billion,* a staggering amount. The distribution cost component for various industries according to the United States Department of Commerce is shown in Table 2.1.

Table 2.2 illustrates the physical distribution costs as percentages of total sales revenues by industry. The range lies between 5 and 30 percent of the sales dollars. If transportation and labor costs continue to rise, physical distribution costs will account for an even greater share of sales dollars. Companies increasingly view physical distribution as a prime area in which to make improvements that will enhance company profitability. An ideal distribution network is one that provides the best customer service level at the least total cost, and warehousing is an important part of this network.

In today's economy, all sections of the distribution chain should understand the others' functions. This gives a firm the best chance to make

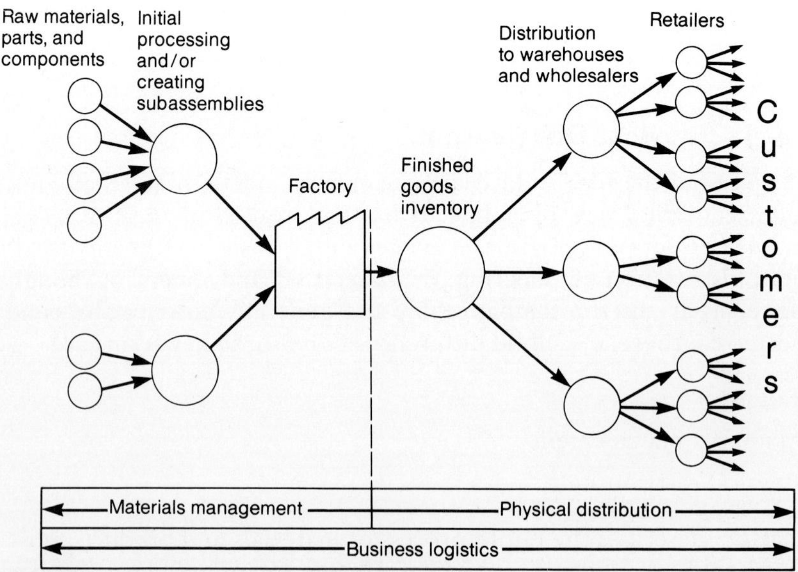

Figure 2.1. Control over flow of inbound and outbound movements. *(From James C. Johnson and Donald F. Wood,* **Contemporary Physical Distribution and Logistics, 2d ed.,** *PennWell Books, 1982, p. 5.)*

Table 2.1. Distribution Cost as a Percent of Total Cost, Including Advertising

Type of industry	%
Food	18
Auto parts	27
Department store (chains)	43
Variety store (chains)	49

competitive, cost-effective use of the cooperative efforts of its warehousing and transportation facilities and personnel.

Until recently in the United States, management's perception of physical distribution had been that of storing materials in a warehouse and somehow getting it to the consumer. It was not considered as important as the other areas of business, such as marketing and finance. But physical distribution, neglected in the past, has been receiving much more attention in recent years. This is related closely to the history of U.S. business. In the early 1800s, the emphasis was on *production.* A firm stressed its ability to decrease the cost to produce each unit. In the early

Table 2.2. Transportation, Total Physical Distribution Costs, and Sales Revenue, 1976

Industry classification	Transportation percentage of sales revenue	Total physical distribution percentage of sales revenue	Transportation percentage of physical distribution
Manufacturing:			
Chemicals and plastics	6.3	14.1	45
Food	8.1	13.4	60
Pharmaceuticals	1.4	4.4	32
Electrical	3.2	13.3	24
Paper	5.8	11.2	52
Machine tools and machinery	4.5	10.0	45
Subtotal—all manufacturing	6.2	13.6	46
Merchandising:			
Consumer goods	8.1	24.2	33
Industrial goods	5.9	25.9	23
Subtotal—all merchandising	7.4	26.6	28
Grand total	6.5	14.8	44

NOTE: Data do not appear to include inbound raw materials transportation

SOURCE: La Londe and Zinszer, *Customer Service: Meaning and Measurement,* NCPDM, Ann. Conf. Proc., 1976.

1900s, production started to catch up with demand, and businesses began to recognize the importance of *sales.*

During World War II, military forces made good use of logistics models and forms of systems analysis to make sure that supplies were at the proper places when needed. Many of these techniques were temporarily ignored during the postwar surge in economic activity. Yet, marketing managers had to fill the postwar demand for goods, and the recessions of the 1950s pressed them to examine their physical distribution networks. Business people, searching for more effective cost control systems, realized that the costs of some items had never been carefully studied and coordinated. Also becoming apparent were other trends that made it necessary to focus attention on product distribution. Here are six of them:

1. *Transportation costs rose rapidly.* Traditional methods of distribution had become more expensive. In the 1970s, fuel prices soared and spot shortages occurred. Higher-level management became involved in transportation-related aspects of logistics at both operating and policy levels. New decisions had to be made in order to adapt to rapid changes. Recent *deregulation* of common carrier transportation has changed many of the long-established "rules of the game." Sophisticated understanding is needed to take advantage of the new laws and regulations.
2. *Production efficiency had reached a peak.* With the "fat" taken out of production, what could be done to produce more cost savings? Attention turned to physical distribution and logistics, still relatively untouched areas.
3. *There was a fundamental change in inventory philosophy.* In earlier business days, retailers and wholesalers-manufacturers usually halved finished product inventories. Sophisticated control techniques now have increased that ratio to a 90 percent distributor, 10 percent retailer balance.
4. *Product lines proliferated.* This was a direct result of the marketing concept of giving each customer the exact product desired. Now style, color, size, and function must be matched to buyer preferences and needs.
5. *Computer technology developed dramatically.* Management of the physical distribution/logistics approach involves a tremendous amount of detail and data. A company must know:

   - The location of each customer
   - The size of each order

- The location of production facilities, warehouses, and distribution centers
- The transportation costs from each warehouse or plant to each customer
- The available carriers and the service levels they offer
- The location of the suppliers
- The inventory levels currently available in each warehouse and distribution center

Manual analysis is virtually impossible. Luckily, just as the physical distribution and logistics concepts were being developed, along came the mathematical beast of burden—the computer—which allows those concepts to be put into practice. Without the development of the computer at that point, logistics and physical distribution concepts would have remained interesting theories with few "real-world" applications.

6. *Increased use of computers by a firm's vendors and customers.* It became possible for firms to systematically study the quality of service they received from their suppliers. They were then able to pinpoint suppliers who consistently offered substandard levels of physical distribution. Many firms were rudely awakened by this and realized the need to upgrade their distribution systems.

Physical distribution has now gained increased importance and recognition in corporate planning. It is no longer treated as an afterthought, something to be considered only after the important work of producing, promoting, and selling a product has been accomplished. Today it is at the center of most planning decisions, and, as a result, physical distribution departments interact with all other major functional departments of their firms.[1]

Definition of Physical Distribution

The National Council of Physical Distribution Management (NCPDM)[2] states that:

> Physical Distribution is the integration of two or more activities for the purpose of planning, implementing, and controlling the efficient flow of raw materials, in-process inventory, and finished goods from the point of origin to the point of consumption. These activities may include, but are

> not limited to: customer service, demand forecasting, distribution communications, inventory control, material handling, order processing, parts and service support, plant and warehouse site selection, procurement, packaging, return goods handling, salvage and scrap disposal, traffic and transportation, and warehouse and storage.

Cumulatively, these constitute logistics, since they include activities related to inbound materials as well as those related to outbound movement.

One of a number of other definitions of physical distribution is:[3]

> An integrated strategy aimed at managing flows of product and information, and related activities in a manner consistent with achieving the goals and objectives of the organization.

These definitions indicate that distribution managers must be prepared to undertake the management of a variety of diverse yet related activities.

Components of Physical Distribution

Figure 2.2 shows the various components of a physical distribution system. Not all of these functions are always treated as a part of physical distribution. Packaging, for example, is considered a function of phys-

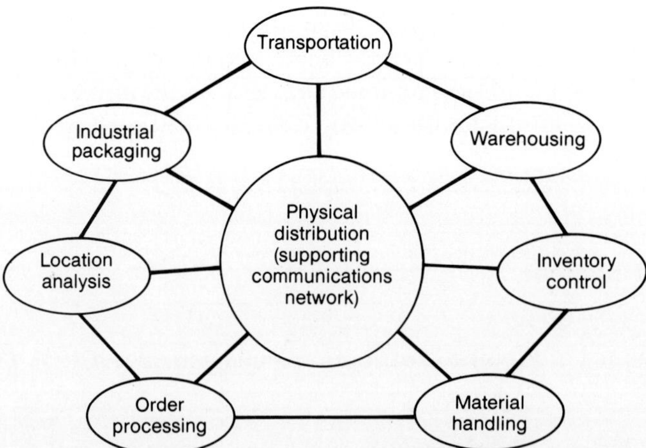

Figure 2.2. Components of a physical distribution system. (*From Charles A. Taff,* **Richard D. Irwin, Mannagement of Physical Distribution & Transportation,** *6th ed., Homewood, Ill., 1978, p. 10.)*

ical distribution by some companies, while others, such as cosmetics and toiletry firms, may consider it a part of manufacturing. Material handling is considered a subcomponent of warehousing by some companies; others have an independent materials handling department.

A typical firm's physical distribution organization is illustrated in Figure 2.3. It may vary greatly both in composition and manpower depending on the policies, nature, and size of the firm.

Figure 2.4 shows the average apportionment of physical distribution costs. Since transportation and warehousing account for almost 70 percent of these costs, they are the most significant components of any physical distribution system. Inventory carrying costs, at about 20 percent, also become a significant factor in distribution network design, especially in determining the number of distribution centers in the system.

Traffic and Transportation

An industrial society cannot develop or operate without efficient transportation to make accessible geographically distant resources and markets.

Essential transportation services are divided into two major categories:

1. Movement of material and products (freight)
2. Movement of people (passengers)

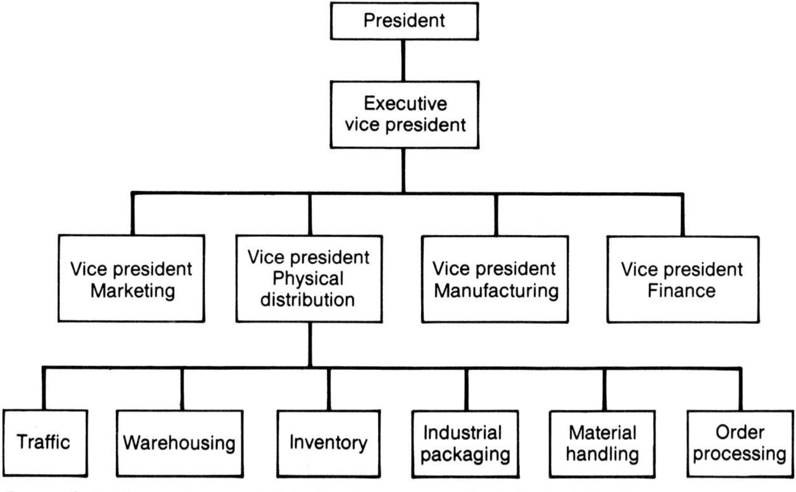

Figure 2.3. Corporate organization showing components of physical distribution management **(*From Charles A. Taff,* Richard D.Irwin, Management of Physical Distribution & Transportation, *6th ed., Homewood, Ill., 1978, p. 39.)***

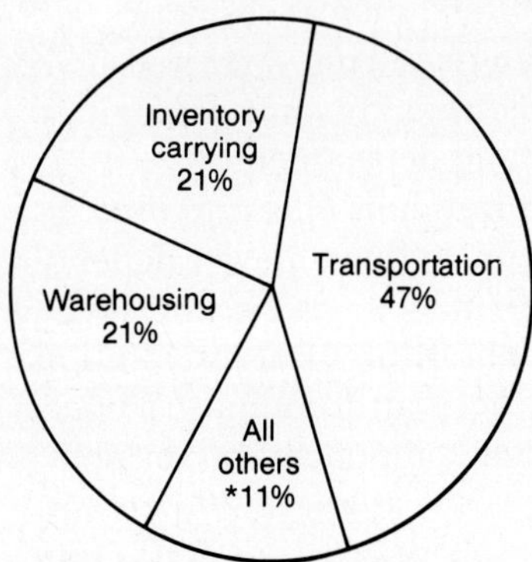

*Order processing, administration, etc...

Figure 2.4. Breakdown of distribution costs. (*From Andre J. Martin and Oliver Wright,* **Distribution Resource Planning,** *Limited Publications and Prentice Hall, Englewood Cliffs, NJ, 1983, chap. 1, p. 8.)*

This discussion deals only with freight transportation.

What is its significance to the economy? In the United States in 1982, $237.5 billion, or 7.8 percent of the gross national product, was spent on freight transportation. Table 2.3 shows this progressive increase in U.S. freight costs since 1960.[4]

Table 2.3. The U.S. Freight Bill Relative to the GNP, Selected Years 1960-1980

Year	Freight costs,* in billions of dollars	% GNP
1960	46.8	9.3
1965	61.1	8.8
1970	83.8	8.4
1975	115.5	7.5
1977	150.4	7.8
1978	174.0	8.1
1979	192.9	8.0
1980	204.7	7.8

* Includes domestic and international transportation, operation of traffic departments, and shipper loading and unloading costs.

SOURCE: Transportation Association of America (now defunct).

The important common element in any definition of transportation is *movement: changing the physical location of freight or passengers*. Products must be moved to the locations where they are needed and wanted, such as groceries moved to a supermarket. Consumers must use some form of movement to get to the supermarket to buy those groceries.

Freight transportation is defined as the "economic movement of commodities and products and the effect of such movement on development and advancement of business." The function of transportation management in a company is referred to as *traffic management*, the terms being used interchangeably.[5]

Structure of Transportation Industry

The five basic modes of transportation are:

1. Rail
2. Highway
3. Water
4. Air
5. Pipeline

Their share of the nation's freight bill in 1982 is shown in Table 2.4.

The structure of the transportation industry is based on these five modes plus a number of variations and subgroups derived from:

Table 2.4. Modal Share of U.S. Freight Bill in 1982

Mode	Amount, in billions of dollars	Percent
Trucking	183.4	77
Rail	27.1	12
Water	14.8	6
Air	4.4	2
Pipeline	7.8	3

SOURCE: Transportation Policy Associates, Washington, D.C., Willis W. Bixby & Frank A. Smith. (From *Dun's Business Month*, January 1984, p. 95.)

- Their several legal forms
- The number of auxiliary users of transportation
- Various modal combinations (coordinated systems)

The relationships among these groups are shown in Figure 2.5.

Legal Forms. The term *legal form* refers to the manner in which a transportation operation is regarded for regulatory purposes. There are four basic legal forms of transportation:

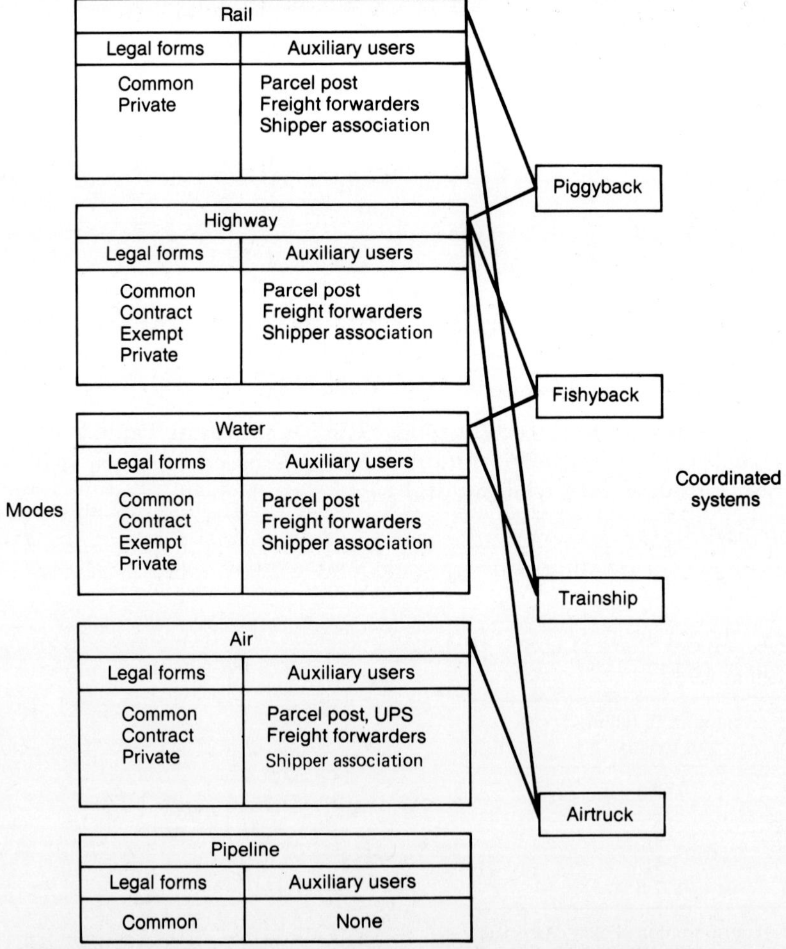

Figure 2.5. Relationship of nodes, legal forms, auxiliary users, and principal coordinated systems of transportation. (*From James L. Heskett, Nicholas A. Glaskowsky, Jr., and Robert M. Ivie,* **Business Logistics**, *2d ed., Ronald Press, New York, 1973, p. 94.)*

1. *Common carriers.* The backbone of the transportation industry, they accept responsibility for carrying goods at any time, to any place, and for all shippers on an equal basis. They have been highly regulated in terms of their authority to operate and the rates they may charge. In recent years, a great deal of deregulation has taken place making this industry highly competitive.
2. *Contract carriers.* These conduct business on a selective basis and can charge different rates to different customers for the same service. The regulatory environment of contract carriers has been less restrictive than that for common carriers.
3. *Private carriers.* Firms using their own fleets to transport their products are private carriers. Such transportation, if incidental to the primary business of the firm, does not face regulation at the state or national level.
4. *Exempt carriage.* This legal form of transportation of a wide range of products, such as agricultural and fishing products, is exempt from federal and state regulation. Some other examples of exempt carriage are newspaper delivery trucks and hotel limousines.

Auxiliary Users. These are defined as transportation agencies that purchase a major portion of their transportation from other carriers via one or more of the basic modes. Auxiliary users include the United States Postal Service (parcel post), United Parcel Service (UPS), freight forwarders, and shippers' associations.

Parcel Post and UPS. These usually transport small shipments with size and weight limitations.

Freight Forwarders. These utilize the services of other common carriers for their long-distance shipments, accepting responsibility for shipments tendered to them by shippers. Their major function is the consolidation of small shipments into large ones.

Shippers' Associations. These perform the same functions as freight forwarders, but are voluntary organizations composed of several members, each of whom uses the service to take advantage of consolidation economies.

Coordinated Systems. These are defined as those offering point-to-point shipment through movements by means of two or more modes of transportation. Modal combinations are shown in Table 2.5. Each of the five modes of transportation is matched against the other modes to illustrate the maximum number of combinations that, theoretically, can be established. Each box contains a term that is used or might be used to denote that particular combination of modes.[6]

Transportation Regulation and Deregulation

The U.S. transportation industry has been under strict government regulation since 1887, when the Interstate Commerce Commission (ICC) was created under the Act to Regulate Commerce. The Act was intended to control and regulate railroads, and the ICC was created to administer it. Key provisions of the Act were:

- All rates must be just and reasonable and be published.
- The same rates and service must be provided to all shippers when the transportation is performed under similar conditions.
- There must be no undue preference or prejudice to any person, locality, or product.

Since 1887, many other laws have been enacted to remove deficiencies in existing regulations or to broaden the sphere of regulations to other segments of the transportation industry. The Motor Carrier Act of 1935 brought trucking under federal safety and economic regulations. The 1938 Civil Aeronautics Act, 1940 Transportation Act, and Freight Forwarder Act of 1942 brought domestic air carriers, some inland water carriers, and freight forwarders under government regulations. In general, the period between 1950 and 1975 was one of strict regulations and vigorous enforcement for the transportation industry.

The movement for transportation deregulation started in the early 1970s when consumer advocate groups started perceiving regulations as protection for the carriers and not the users. They argued that com-

Table 2.5. Transportation Coordination Possibilities

Modes of transportation	Highway	Rail	Water	Air	Pipeline
Highway	X	Piggyback	Fishyback	Air-truck	n.d.*
Rail	Piggyback	X	Train-ship	(Sky-rail)†	n.d.
Water	Fishyback	Train-ship	Ship-barge‡	(Air-barge)†	n.d.
Air	Air-truck	(Sky-rail)†	(Air-barge)†	X	n.d.
Pipeline	n.d.	n.d.	n.d.	n.d.	X

* Does not ordinarily meet the requirements of the definition of Coordinated Transportation Service.

† These combinations do not exist at the present time, and it is unlikely that they could be developed as regular commercial services.

‡ Defined as ship-to-barge or barge-to-ship, *not* barge-to-barge or ship-to-ship.

SOURCE: Heskett, Glaskowski, and Ivie, *Business Logistics*, 2d ed., Ronald Press, New York, 1973, p. 98.

petition, replacing regulations, would enable the industry to function more efficiently. In 1977, the government started the process of deregulation with All-Cargo Aircraft Deregulation. Deregulation of passenger airlines came about in 1978. The most significant deregulatory steps were the enactment of The Motor Carrier Act of 1980 and the Stagger's Rail Act of 1980.

The goal of such legislation, as stated in the revised National Transportation Policy, was to "promote competition and efficient transportation services to meet the needs of shippers, receivers and consumers, and to allow a variety of quality price options to meet the changing market demands and diverse requirements of the shipping public."

Major provisions of the new laws are:

- *Liberalized carrier entry.* Truckers can now obtain operating rights by proving that they are fit, willing, and able to operate in interstate commerce. To receive a common carrier certificate, they must provide some evidence of public need. This has increased the number of licensed truckers to about 28,000, up from about 16,000 in 1979. This increased competition puts shippers in a better bargaining position.
- *Elimination of restrictions on rights.* Truckers may now drop inefficient or energy-wasting operations, such as gateways, circuitous routes, and one-way trips.
- *Greater freedom for contract carriers.* There are now no limits on geographic coverage or on the number of shippers with whom the carriers may contract. Commodity descriptions are broadened.
- *Private carriage expansion.* Private carriers may now haul for subsidiaries and receive compensation provided they are fully owned by the parent organization.[4]

Figure 2.6 shows the regulatory-deregulatory cycle in the transportation industry.

Traffic and Transportation Management

Management of the transportation system falls into two general categories:

1. Those who sell transportation (carrier management)
2. Those who buy transportation (traffic management)

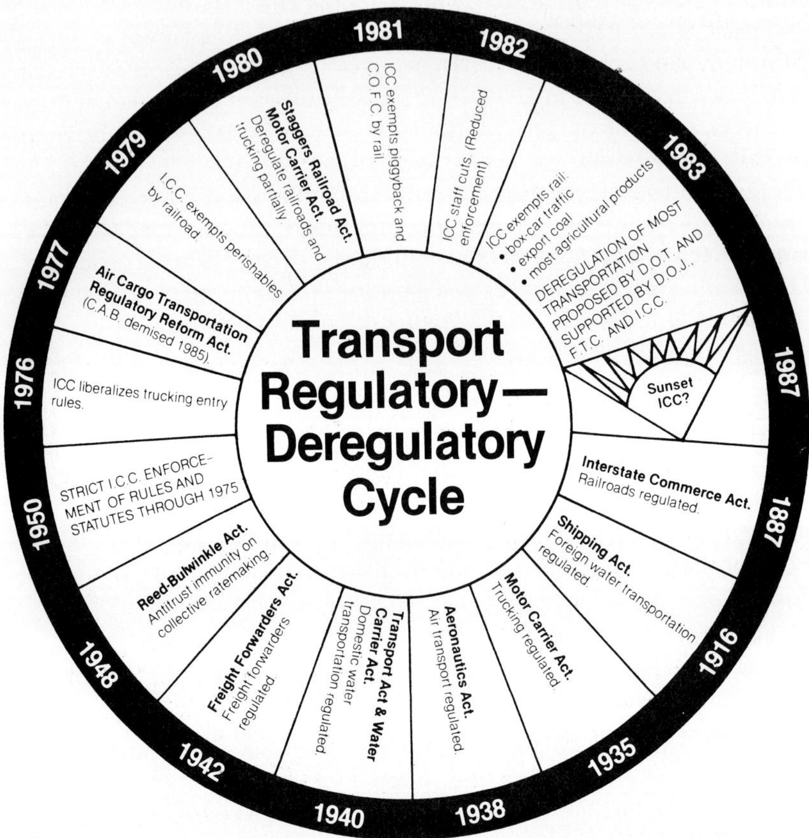

Figure 2.6. Transportation regulatory/deregulatory cycle. (*From* **Traffic Management Magazine,** *December 1983.*)

The sellers, or carrier management, are responsible for operating transportation companies. They obtain freight for their firms, plan the time and method of movement, and negotiate charges for their services.

The buyers, or traffic management, are responsible for arranging transportation for their firms to ship or receive freight.[5] Their functions include:[7]

- Rate negotiation
- Selecting routing and carriers, including mode, special and terminal services, and service responsibility
- Dealing with regulatory matters affecting company operations
- Operating company transportation

- Cooperating with carriers to develop technology for enhancing transportation productivity
- Administering international transportation
- Analyzing transportation costs and services

There are many choices available in the deregulated transportation environment. There are "free-for-all" rates and service plans, long-term arrangements, and many transportation companies from which to choose. The traffic manager *must* function in a world of negotiation.[4]

The Role of Distribution Centers in the Physical Distribution Network

The distribution center is a facility that receives material from a firm's plants or vendors, stores it, and then distributes the material to its customers. The important difference between a conventional warehouse and a distribution center is that the distribution center emphasizes product flow and the warehouse emphasizes storage.

Distribution centers could be market-positioned, production-positioned, or intermediately positioned, depending on the nature of the business of the firm. *Market-positioned distribution centers* are located near the point of final production consumption. They provide the most economical transportation from distant shipping points with relatively short product movements in local delivery areas. Good examples of such market-oriented distribution centers are found in the food industry. *Production-oriented distribution centers* enable manufacturers to give maximum service to their customers. These are located close to production plants. They act as collection points for many products from various plants, and from them, customer orders in desired product mixes are filled. Distribution centers located between customer locations and production locations are referred to as *intermediately positioned.*[8]

Distribution Network Planning

The number, location, and mission of distribution centers in a firm depends on its size, nature of business, and customer service policies. Key elements to be considered in any distribution network planning are:

- Transportation costs
- Warehousing costs

- Inventory carrying costs
- Order processing and administrative costs
- Customer service levels

An ideal distribution network is one that provides the best customer service level at least total cost. The distribution configuration can be centralized or decentralized. *In a centralized configuration,* the number of distribution centers is relatively small (sometimes only one), each covering larger market areas and product lines. *In the decentralized system,* a larger number of distribution facilities are involved. They are either closer to production facilities and handle limited product lines or are closer to markets covering smaller territories.

Figure 2.7, in simplified form, illustrates the relationship between distribution costs and number of distribution centers. Figure 2.8 shows the relationship between distribution costs and customer service.

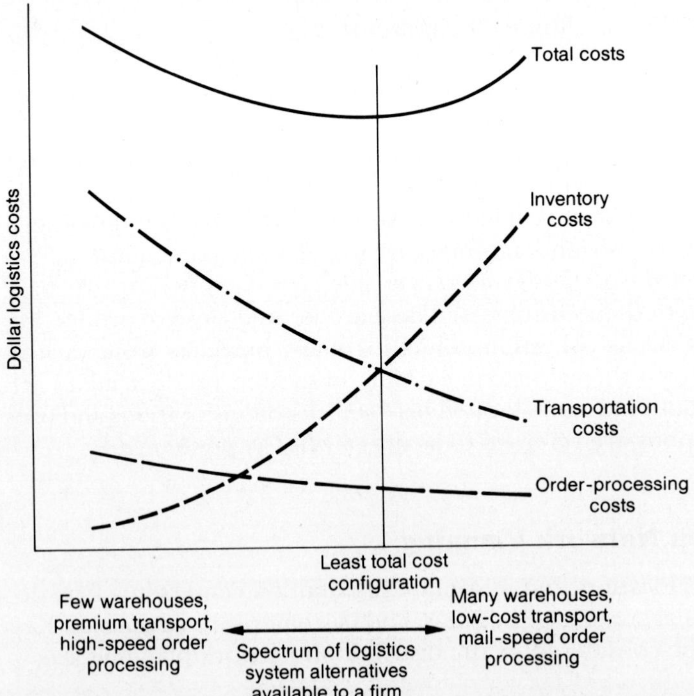

Figure 2.7. Simplified illustration of the total cost concept, showing hypothetical trade-offs among transportation, inventory, and order-processing costs. (*From James L. Heskett, Nicholas A. Glaskowsky, Jr., and Robert M. Ivie,* **Business Logistics,** *2d ed., Ronald Press, New York, 1973, p. 94.*)

A centralized distribution configuration with fewer distribution centers tends to have lower warehousing and inventory carrying costs. This is due to economies of scale in warehousing operations and lower safety stocks. A decentralized configuration with a larger number of distribution centers can offer lower transportation costs and better customer service.

The objective of a distribution network study is to answer the following:

- How many distribution centers should be used?
- What should be their location and size?
- Which market should each distribution center serve?
- Which plant should serve which distribution center?
- What customer service levels are desired?

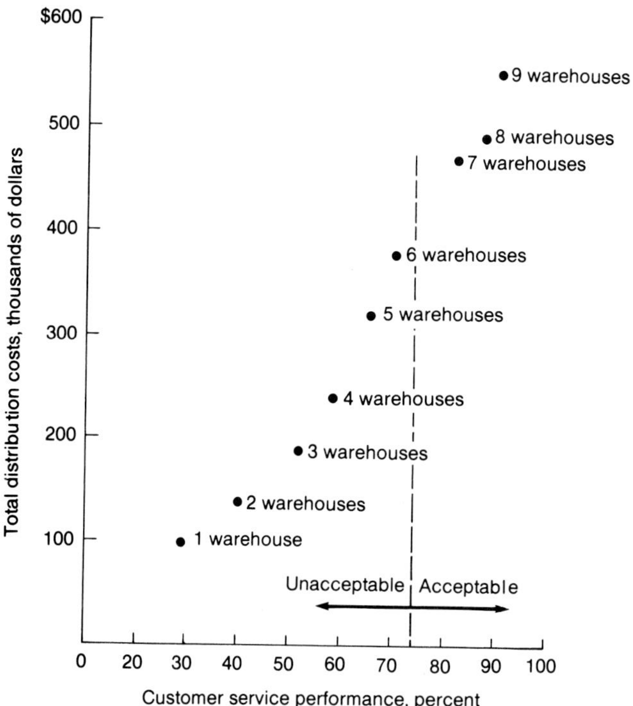

Figure 2.8. Cost of distribution versus customer service. (***From Charles A. Taff, Richard D. Irwin, Management of Physical Distribution & Transportation, 6th ed., Homewood, Ill., 1978, p. 173.***)

To determine this, vast amounts of data and analyses are needed. These include:

- Market areas
- Demand by area
- Alternative distribution center locations
- Shipments and sizes
- Freight costs, inbound and outbound
- Inventory carrying costs
- Warehousing costs[7]

Alternative distribution configurations must be defined and total distribution costs determined in light of the required level of customer service. The configuration that provides the best service at the least cost is most desirable.

To manually conduct a distribution network analysis is an extremely difficult task. There are a number of variables and a large body of data involved. A number of computer-oriented distribution models have been developed that can perform such analyses quickly and economically. Such an analysis can assist in determining the optimum number of distribution centers and their locations depending on the needs of the company.

Warehouse Operating Alternatives

Once a determination as to the number and locations of the distribution centers is made, a firm must determine who will operate them. Two basic alternatives are available:

1. Company-operated distribution centers—owned or leased
2. Public warehouses—short-term or long-term (contract)

In a privately owned facility, a firm owns its building. It may have special requirements and constructs its building for special purposes. A good example would be an automated storage/retrieval system in a rack-supported structure. In a privately leased warehouse, a firm leases a building for a period of time and doesn't necessarily make substantial equipment investments. Neither of the above is always true. The decision to own or lease is essentially financial.

A public warehouse is in the business of performing warehouse services for others. It receives, stores, ships, and performs other related services. Its warehousing services are sold at rates intended to result in a profit to the warehouse.[9]

The contract warehouse is a form of public warehousing with, generally, a longer time commitment in which to perform specialized services. Longer commitments are required, as special equipment may be needed by the warehouser and there must be an opportunity to amortize it. One example is a contract warehouse used by a pharmaceutical distributor that sells in broken lots. To design an efficient operation, the warehouser may have to make an investment in flow racks, pallet racks, conveyors, UPS scales and meters, and computer equipment. When added to space and labor cost, such an investment obviously requires a longer-term contract than the usual 30 days in most public warehousing agreements.

Types of Public Warehouses

Commodity Warehouses. These store products such as cotton, wool, and tobacco, and include other agricultural product facilities.

Bulk Warehouses. These provide tank storage of liquids and open or sheltered storage of dry products, such as coal, sand, salt, stone, and chemicals.

Household Goods Warehouses. These are used for storage of household effects and other personal possessions. They are normally operated by moving companies.

Field Warehouses. These are public warehouses established on the premises of business concerns. They allow warehousers to acquire custodianship of commodities, enabling them to issue warehouse receipts to be used as collateral security by depositors.

Refrigerated Warehouses. These are for temperature-controlled storage and distribution of perishable products.

Merchandise Warehouses. These are public warehouses for the storage and distribution of a great variety of products.

Many public warehouses offer combinations of the above operations[9].

A distribution public warehouse performs four specialized services:

- Stock-spotting
- Complete line assortment
- Break-bulk
- Intransit mixing

Stock-Spotting. Spot-stock capabilities of public warehouses are most often used by manufacturers in their physical distribution systems, particularly those with limited product lines. Rather than storing inventories in facilities near production plants, they can substantially reduce delivery time by pretransaction movement to strategic cities. A consolidated carload of the firm's product line is "spot-stocked" in a public warehouse from which customer orders are filled. Public warehouse facilities utilized for spot-stocking allow inventories to be placed in a wide variety of markets adjacent to key customers.

Complete Line Assortment. A public warehouse used for complete line assorting may be employed by either a manufacturer, wholesaler, or retailer. In this case, the public warehouse performs the complete range of functions for distribution warehouses. Products are stocked in anticipation of customer orders, with customized assortments being grouped upon demand.

The difference between stock-spotting and complete line assortment is one of degree. A firm following a stock-spotting policy will normally have a narrower product line and will place stocks in a wider range of markets than one using public warehouses for complete line assortment.

Break-Bulk. Break-bulk public warehouse service represents a form of assistance in a distribution system that does not involve any storage. Public warehouse concerns often operate local delivery equipment which can be hired by firms distributing in the general market area. A manufacturer can combine into one pooled shipment the orders for different customers located in the market area and send the entire combined shipment to a public warehouse. The public warehouse then separates the individual orders and performs a local delivery. Utilizing the services of a public warehouse in a break-bulk capacity allows the advantage of consolidated freight rates. It also reduces the difficulty of controlling a number of individual small shipments to a given market.

Intransit Mixing. Intransit mixing is similar to break-bulk services; however, it can reduce overall transportation charges as well as overall warehouse requirements when product plants are geographically separated. Intransit mixing may involve shipments to one or more consignees. Solid carloads or truckloads are shipped from production plants to the public warehouser who provides the mixing service. Each large shipment enjoys the lowest possible transportation rate. The loadings of each product are designated to be mixed for specific customers at the public warehouse.

Upon arrival at the public warehouse, the solid trailers or cars are unloaded and the proper customer requirements of each product assorted. Shipment is then made to each individual customer. This total process of intransit mixing is illustrated in Figure 2.9.[8]

Public Warehousing Charges

Traditionally, the public warehouse has three charges:

1. *Handling.* This charge is to receive and ship the merchandise. It is generally invoiced when the material is received. The charges can be by weight, cube, or piece, and there can be a minimum charge.
2. *Storage.* This charge is generally for each month that the material remains in storage. It can also be charged for by weight, cube, or piece, and have a minimum charge.
3. *Paper Handling.* There may be additional charges for preparing bills of lading, marking and labeling merchandise, inventory record keeping, coopering damaged merchandise, sorting, and a myriad of other services that the public warehouse performs

In *contract warehousing*, there may be many ways to charge, depending on the circumstances. One common way, which reduces paper handling, is to charge a percentage of the invoice sent to the firm's customer. This percentage varies according to volume, value of the merchandise, size of merchandise, size of shipment, repackaging, and so on. The percentage would be lower for a pharmaceutical customer than for a customer who has inexpensive bulky furniture.

Legal Liability of Public Warehouses

Generally stated, a public warehouser is liable for damages from loss of, or injury to, the goods caused by a failure to exercise such care in regard to them as a reasonably careful person would exercise under like circumstances. Unless otherwise agreed, the warehouser is not liable for damages which could not have been avoided by the exercise of such care. (U.C.C. 7-204-1)

While liability cannot be limited in any way, the dollar amount of damage can be limited, and agreements to averaging overages and shortages or to a shrinkage allowance can be made. The ability to do this enables the warehouser to lower his or her costs, thus, provide better service more inexpensively.

Private versus Public Warehousing[6]

Figure 2.10 illustrates some of the major considerations involved in determining whether a company should use private warehousing, public warehousing, or a combination of both.

"There are advocates of both public and private warehousing, just as there are for common carrier and private transportation. The following are advantages and methods of engaging in both.

Private Warehousing

The construction, purchase, or lease of a private warehouse offers a firm advantages comparable to the operation of privately owned transportation equipment.

- *First, it is likely to provide greater flexibility in design to meet the specific needs of the owner.* This is especially important if the storage of a firm's products involves special problems such as those of temperature control, the handling of outsized objects, or other special installations not likely to be provided by the public warehouseman.
- *Second, the operation of a private warehouse can provide the using firm greater control of the operation to ensure that warehousing is conducted efficiently.*

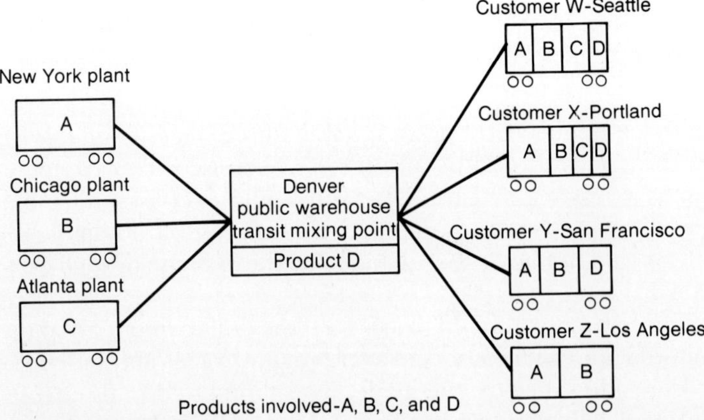

Figure 2.9. Public warehouse intransit mixing. (*From Donald J. Bowersox, Edward W. Smykay, and Bernard J. LaLonde* **Distribution Management**, *rev. ed., Macmillan, New York, 1968, p. 267.*)

- *Private warehousing will, to a reasonable degree, guarantee a given service rate (cost) over a period of time.*

Although operating costs may rise or fall from time to time, the owning or leasing user is likely to have greater advance warning of possible changes. In general, the average cost to handle a unit through a private warehouse is less when the product moves through in a constant, high volume. However, in attempting to increase volume (warehouse throughput), some firms owning or leasing warehouses have *overextended* market territories served by the warehouse. In these situations, they frequently incur *greater* transportation costs per unit than the savings in warehousing costs traded for it.

Owned or leased warehousing space may also be an advantage if it is used to house the local sales or field purchasing organization. This may require the installation of special communications equipment to handle purchase or sales orders. The location of the sales staff at the warehouse location *can* create supervisory and organizational problems. This must be balanced against the savings that can be achieved.

Finally, the use of owned or leased warehousing space may be required if a firm wants to provide warehousing facilities near its manufacturing plant. Most storage space immediately adjacent to the production line is either owned or leased by the operating firm.

Public Warehousing

Public warehousing requires no investment in such facilities. Operating problems assumed by the public warehouser also free the company's executive talent for other activities. The public warehouser is often well equipped to deal with problems of labor, insurance, and other matters related to warehouse design and operation.

The per-unit cost for public warehouse service is probably less than private or leased facilities when the volume of operations is low or the level of operations fluctuates greatly from time to time. The cost per unit handled is a known factor when a public warehouse is used. This makes future cost planning easier for the user. Also, in some localities, no personal property tax is assessed on inventory stored in public warehouses.

Perhaps the *greatest* advantage in the use of public warehousing facilities is the great flexibility allowed in inventory location. This is particularly important when rate relationships among various modes of transportation or localities are subject to considerable change. A firm utilizing public warehousing facilities can shift the location of its inventories to reflect changes in the transportation rate structures that make existing warehouse locations comparatively uneconomical. Because it is purchased and paid for, public warehousing offers a precise documentation of warehousing costs not possible for most private warehousing operations.

Finally, because it is available on a short-term basis, public warehousing may lend itself to test-marketing activities, in which the need for warehousing support is uncertain and perhaps temporary."

Conclusion

The preceding discussion has attempted to give the reader a brief understanding of the physical distribution system, its components, and the role of warehousing in the system.

Warehousing accounts for about 20 percent of the total distribution costs and is the physical embodiment of the distribution system. Top management is aware of how an efficient and productive warehousing operation can improve a company's image and profitability.

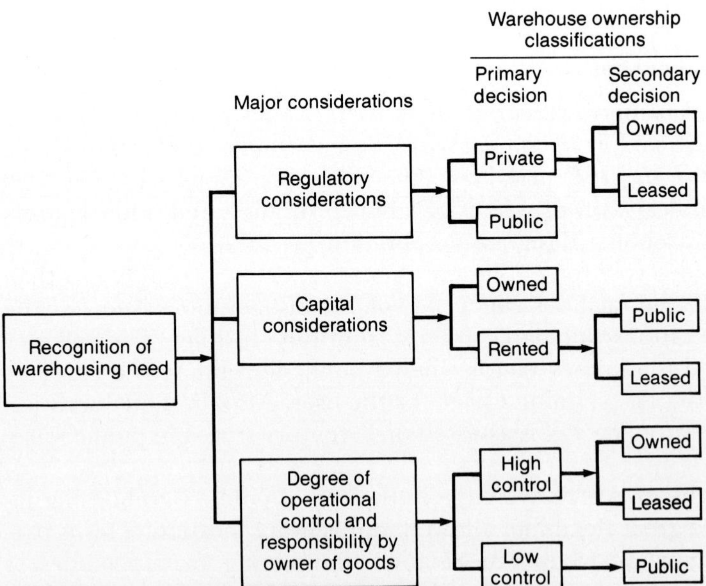

Figure 2.10. Major considerations in evaluating warehouse ownership alternatives. (*From James L. Heskett, Nicholas A. Glaskowsky, Jr., and Robert M. Ivie,* **Business Logistics**, *2d ed., Ronald Press, New York, 1973, p. 62.*)

It is doubly important in these changing, competitive business times, that warehousing and transportation executives realize their *interdependent* partnership. A healthy physical distribution system is a combination of the best in transportation *and* the best in warehousing.

References

1. James C. Johnson and Donald F. Wood, *Contemporary Physical Distribution and Logistics,* 2d ed., Pennwell, 1982, pp. 3–7, 29.
2. Definition of Physical Distribution—NCPDM.
3. C. John Langley, Jr., "Physical Distribution Management: A Strategic Perspective," *NCPDM,* vol. II, October 10–13, 1982.
4. Steve Tinghitella, "What Transportation Deregulation Means to Shippers and Carriers," *Dun's Business Month,* January 1984, pp. 95–98.
5. Bowersox, Calabro, and Wagenheim, *Introduction to Transportation,* Macmillan, New York, 1981, pp. 4–8.
6. James L. Heskett, Nicholas A. Glaskowski, and Robert M. Ivie, *Business Logistics,* 2d ed., Ronald Press, New York, 1973, pp. 93–98, 607–609.
7. Charles A. Taff, *Management of Physical Distribution and Transportation,* 6th ed., Richard D. Irwin, 1978, pp. 105, 171.
8. Donald J. Bowersox, Edward M. Smykay, and Bernard J. LaLonde, *Physical Distribution Management,* rev. ed., Macmillan, New York, 1968, pp. 246, 250–252, 264–267.
9. Creed H. Jenkins, *Modern Warehouse Management,* McGraw-Hill, New York, 1968, pp. 28–29.

3
Warehousing and Manufacturing

Thomas P. Cullinane, Ph.D.

Professor and Chairman, Department of Industrial Engineering and Information Systems, Northeastern University, Boston, Massachusetts

James A. Tompkins, Ph.D

President and Chairman, Tompkins Associates, Inc., Raleigh, North Carolina

Introduction

A key element in any manufacturing system is the warehouse function. Well-managed raw materials warehouses, work-in-process warehouses, and finished goods warehouses are critical support functions of a manufacturing system. Without efficient and effective manufacturing warehouses, the material supply lines for manufacturing cease to function, and the manufacturing system grinds to a halt.

Traditionally, manufacturing warehousing has been viewed as an overhead and not seen as contributing to the profitability of the manufacturing enterprise. Manufacturing management frequently regarded the warehouse as a necessary but noncritical element of the manufacturing system. However, as manufacturing warehouses became the bottleneck in the manufacturing system, more emphasis was placed on their proper planning and management. Today, manufacturing warehousing is typically viewed as an important portion of the manufacturing system.

The basic warehousing functions in the manufacturing environment are:

1. Receiving raw materials
2. Storing raw materials
3. Kitting raw materials
4. Releasing raw materials
5. Receiving work-in-process
6. Storing work-in-process
7. Kitting work-in-process
8. Releasing work-in-process
9. Receiving finished goods
10. Storing finished goods
11. Picking finished goods
12. Shipping finished goods

The first four functions define the raw materials warehouse. Functions five through eight represent the work-in-process warehouse. The last four functions define the finished goods warehouse. The material flow through a facility is as shown in Fig. 3.1.

No attempt is made in this chapter to duplicate the warehousing topics covered elsewhere in this handbook. Therefore, topics such as planning the receiving function, order-picking, storage methodologies, and so on are not covered in this chapter. This chapter addresses only the unique aspects of manufacturing warehouses. Topics to be covered are:

1. Receiving in manufacturing warehousing
2. Storing in manufacturing warehousing
3. Kitting in manufacturing warehousing
4. Integrated warehousing
5. Computer-Integrated Manufacturing (CIM)

Receiving in Manufacturing Warehousing

The receiving point for goods within a warehouse is the point at which the responsibility or the control of the goods is given to the warehouse. For raw materials, this transfer of ownership or control takes place in the receiving department and is identical to the receiving function in a

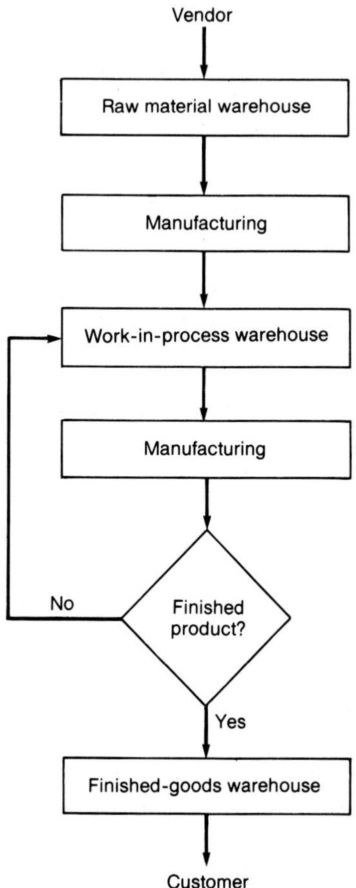

Figure 3.1. Material flow through a facility.

distribution warehouse. However, when work-in-process or finished goods are being placed into the warehouse, the transfer of control is not nearly as well defined. Therefore, a key to effective inventory control is to have clearly defined operating procedures which specify at which point work-in-process belongs to the work-in-process warehouse and at which point finished goods belong to the finished goods warehouse. The interface between manufacturing control and warehouse control is where receiving occurs. The same procedures that are implemented for raw materials receiving should be implemented for work-in-process receiving and finished goods receiving. When this is not properly done, inventory control and material audit trails will not support an efficient or effective manufacturing system.

One additional issue which applies to receiving in manufacturing warehouses is applicable primarily in assembly manufacturing facilities. Often, inventory levels can be reduced if materials are received just in time for assembly. It is, therefore, most desirable to receive goods as close to the time of use as possible. From a receiving perspective, it is important also to receive these goods as close to the *point* of use as possible. This may often result in a desire to have distributed receiving. Under these circumstances, it is seen to be cost effective to have the carrier move to a receiving dock close to the point of use. One advantage is that this enables the carrier to make several short trips from the distributed dock to the point of use rather than several long trips from centralized receiving to the point of use. Another advantage is that moving the carrier once to a distributed dock minimizes internal plant material handling; whereas having all carriers unload at a centralized receiving area considerably increases internal material handling.

Storing in Manufacturing Warehousing

In theory, the storage functions would not have to exist in manufacturing systems. That is, raw materials would arrive from the vendor just in time to be put into the manufacturing process. The shop floor would be scheduled such that there would be no work-in-process between operations, and, as units were completed, the customer would take immediate delivery. Unfortunately, to achieve an acceptable level of machine utilization and labor productivity, this theoretical desire for zero inventory is not workable.

A review of the material flow cycle in any manufacturing system reveals that materials are stored as they arrive in the form of raw materials, work-in-process materials are repeatedly stored as they are being processed, and finished goods are stored awaiting consolidation for a customer order. While it is true that, as manufacturing companies strive to make demand more uniform, lead times more predictable, quality more controllable, and vendors more cooperative, the "just-in-time" type of philosophy will allow for the reduction of the quantitates of raw materials to be stored. However, raw materials storage will still need to exist. Similarly, as production levels become more uniform, equipment reliabilities increase, and set-up times are reduced, the "stockless" production philosophy will allow for the reduction of the quantities of work-in-process to be stored. However, work-in-process storage will still need to exist.

Space utilization in the raw materials manufacturing warehouse and the finished goods manufacturing warehouse is typically viewed as an important issue and addressed appropriately. Unfortunately, the same cannot be said of the work-in-process warehouse. Because of the high cost and value of manufacturing space and the reality that the work-in-process warehouse typically is located on the manufacturing floor, this is not only incorrect; it is totally unacceptable. It is critical that the work-in-process warehouse be viewed in the same manner that all other warehouses are viewed. It is critical that space-efficient and materials handling–efficient equipment be applied to work-in-process warehouses.

Similarly, there are manufacturing storage locations that are not within the purview of raw material, work-in-process, or finished goods warehouses. These storage locations (quality control holds, inspection buffers, department hold areas, etc.) must also be scrutinized from the perspective of good space utilization. The application of the storage equipment presented in this handbook can be just as readily applied to these areas as they can be to actual warehouse areas.

Kitting in Manufacturing Warehouses

The task of filling a customer order by seeking out warehoused units and accumulating them for shipment is called *picking*. In manufacturing, the picking of warehoused units to form a unit of items to be assembled is called *kitting*. Kitting, like picking, can be done according to three general procedures: sequential kitting, batch kitting, or zone kitting. As the name implies, sequential kitting requires the kitter to move through the raw material warehouse or the work-in-process warehouse selecting units until all units that form a kit have been picked. This method of kitting requires excessive travel time and thus results in poor labor utilization. Except when used to pick only a low volume of kits, sequential kitting is unacceptable. Batch kitting allows the kitter to create several kits at the same time. This method aims first at getting the units picked, and second at sorting them for a specific manufacturing kit. In operations where a wide variety of products are being produced and a large number of orders are kitted, batch picking is usually preferred. Zone kitting requires that a kitter stay in a specific zone of the raw materials or work-in-process warehouse. Each zone kitter then picks the units for a kit from that zone. The kits are only completed after all zones have kitted the production order. Just as for quality order-picking systems, an efficient kitting system requires accurate inventory records and a well-thought-out kitting document. Designing a kitting system should be done much in the same way as designing a picking system.

Integrated Manufacturing Warehousing

Stated in this chapter thus far is the approach traditionally taken to raw materials warehousing, work-in-process warehousing, and finished goods warehousing. However, when one restructures the functions of manufacturing warehousing in the following manner, a potential for innovation is presented.

It is clear from Table 3.1 that the functions of the three manufacturing warehouses are all basically the same. Further, consider the following observations:

1. The raw materials warehouse, work-in-process warehouse, and finished goods warehouse typically report to different sections of the manufacturing organization: the raw materials warehouse reports to purchasing or inventory control; the work-in-process warehouse reports to manufacturing or production control; and the finished goods warehouse reports to marketing or distribution.
2. The raw materials warehouse, work-in-process warehouse, and finished goods warehouse each have a separate location, have separate staffs, utilize their own handling and storage equipment, and often utilize different computers and information systems for inventory control.
3. The raw materials warehouse, work-in-process warehouse, and finished goods warehouse have drastically different slow and busy

Table 3.1. Functions of the Three Manufacturing Warehouses

Function of raw materials warehouse	Function of work-in-process warehouse	Function of finished goods warehouse
Receive	Receive	Receive
Store	Store	Store
Kit	Kit	Pick
Release	Release	Ship

periods. For example, the raw materials warehouse is busy in the morning and slow in the afternoon, whereas just the opposite is true for the finished goods warehouse. The raw materials warehouse is busy at the beginning of the month and slow at the end of the month, whereas just the opposite is true for the finished goods warehouse. The work-in-process warehouse is relatively constant over a day and throughout a month.

4. The management of manufacturing inventory levels does not seem to understand that the levels of raw materials, work-in-process, and finished goods are related. For example, if in one month the raw materials inventory is thought to be too high, a mandate is passed to reduce it, and the mandate is implemented by releasing inventory to manufacturing. It should not, therefore, be a surprise when next month's work-in-process inventory increases. Obviously, the reduction of raw materials inventory directly results in the increase in work-in-process inventory. This relationship must be understood, and a manufacturing company's total (raw materials, work-in-process, and finished goods) inventory must be managed.

A conclusion that may be reached by reviewing these observations is that, given that these three manufacturing warehouses are performing the same function, does it not make sense to integrate them into one manufacturing warehouse? By integrating the three, not only would a firm be in a better position to utilize space, equipment, labor, and computer systems, but they would also be able to:

1. Better manage the total manufacturing inventory, and
2. Due to the synergism of combining the functions, better justify automated systems.

Thus, although the concept of integrated manufacturing warehousing is nontraditional, there are significant reasons to consider such an approach.

Computer-Integrated Manufacturing

Computer-Integrated Manufacturing (CIM) is the integration or joining of many manufacturing functions through computer databases. For true integration to take place, all manufacturing functions must be able to communicate. Therefore, CIM will have an important impact on all manufacturing functions, including the warehouse function. In a CIM environment, warehouse operations and manufacturing operations must allow for the tracking of all materials from the time they arrive on a manufacturing site until they are shipped. This typically occurs through the use of compatible computers, common data structures, and a single, integrated database. The process control computers in the warehouses (for automated guided vehicle systems, automated storage/retrieval systems, automatic identification equipment, etc.) must be compatible with the manufacturing management systems to integrate fully the material flow through a manufacturing facility, and establishing this compatibility may very well require a total rethinking of the warehouse systems. This rethinking must provide for the integration of the warehouse into the manufacturing systems.

Conclusion

In this chapter, warehousing in the context of manufacturing was explored. Virtually the entire remainder of the handbook has relevance to manufacturing warehousing. Given the few unique issues raised in this chapter, with the rest of the handbook and good common sense, the task of planning and operating manufacturing warehouses should be under control.

Bibliography

Tompkins, James A., and J. A. White: *Facilities Planning,* John Wiley, New York, 1984.
Tompkins, James A., and J. D. Smith: *How to Plan and Manage Warehouse Operations,* American Management Association, Watertown, Mass., 1984.

4

Warehousing and Materials Management

Eugene L. Magad

Associate Professor and Coordinator, Material Management Program, William Rainey Harper College, Palatine, Illinois

The term *materials management* is relatively new in business vocabulary. However, the basic activities performed by this function are found in all organizations and in all industries, whether the company is organized for profit or nonprofit, manufacturing or nonmanufacturing, or for government or the private sector. The primary objective is to coordinate all activities within an organization as they relate to the materials cycle.

This chapter is devoted to discussing the basic philosophy of materials management and its varied relationships to warehousing activities. Warehousing is an essential group within a materials management organization. Well-organized and efficient warehousing performance is critical to the effectiveness of this activity. In order to perceive the relationship between warehousing and materials management, it is important to have a basic understanding of total materials management—the concept's background, definition, and approach.

Introduction to Materials Management

Basic to all materials groups is the objective of optimizing all company resources while providing good customer service. These resources include materials, labor, money, and facilities. The inventories controlled by materials management represent a high percentage of total product costs and include: raw materials, supplies, work-in-process, and finished goods.

Definition, Scope, and History

The rapid growth of materials management organizations has prompted questions concerning its function. People at various levels of management would like to know more about its activities, scope, and the history of its emergence as an integral group.

Definition. *Materials management* can be defined as, "an organizational concept which fosters a total systems approach to plan, acquire, store, move and control materials, in order to optimize all company resources and provide customer service consistent with company policy."[1]

Scope. In terms of scope, Dean S. Ammer describes materials management as, "In the broadest sense, . . . concerned with activities involved with the flow of materials from suppliers' plants, through the manufacturing process, into finished goods warehouses and on to the ultimate use of the product."[2] Figure 4.1 represents a typical flow of materials from supplier to customer.

Lamar Lee, Jr. and Donald W. Dobler group materials management into three basic functions: planning and control, purchasing, and physical distribution. The planning and control functions include inventory control, production control, and scheduling. Purchasing functions consist of buying, subcontracting, value analysis, and expediting. Distribution functions encompass receiving, shipping, packaging, transportation, and warehousing (Ref. 3, p. 23).

The following subfunctions tend to be included in the materials management group when companies incorporate the total materials organization approach.

1. Planning
2. Inventory control

3. Production control
4. Purchasing
5. Receiving and stores
6. Materials handling
7. Physical distribution

Not all companies have accepted the concept of an integrated materials organization. Varying reasons include "company politics," individual personnel capabilities, management philosophies, and ignorance of the materials management concept. Other descriptions may be used to define this function, such as logistics and physical distribution; however, despite the various terms used by companies to describe a total materials group, the trend in recent years is to adopt the title *materials management.*

History. From the prehistoric age until today, people have directed their efforts toward obtaining, moving, and controlling materials. During the late 1800s, Frederick W. Taylor, known as the father of scientific management, made major contributions in the areas of time study, job design, personnel selection, and training. Scientific management's primary efforts were directed at the lower level of organization—the shop floor, foreman, superintendent, and lower management.[4] Taylor recognized the need for functional specialists, such as those found in materials management.

Total materials management as an organizational concept started its growth during the 1950s, following World War II. Fluctuating domestic and international market requirements, economic conditions, and increased competition were some of the contributing factors which stimulated interest. The 1970s were a period of further growth as U.S. industries, confronted with problems such as scarcity of money, ecological control, inflation, and so on, began to adopt this organizational structure to improve their overall cost-efficiency and effectiveness.

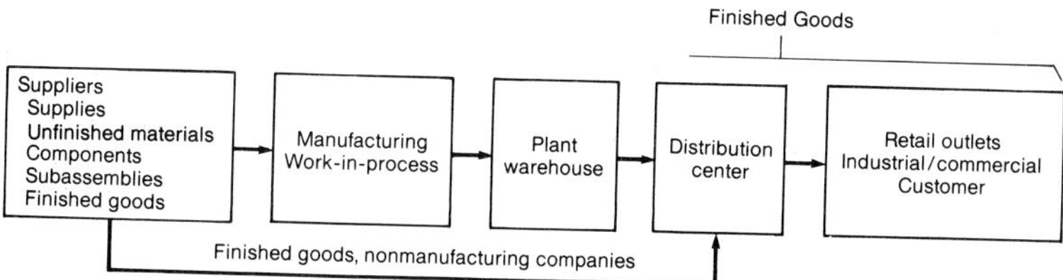

Figure 4.1. Typical materials flow. (***From Eugene L. Magad and John M. Amos, Total Materials Management, Dryden Press, Hinsdale, Ill., 1985.***)

Professional Societies. Various professional societies are active throughout the world in educating their members to the materials management concepts and applications. Most of these groups in the United States concentrate efforts on a particular portion or subfunction, such as production control, inventory control, purchasing, and physical distribution. In recent years, there has been a trend to broaden this scope of interest. These societies have made a valuable contribution to the education of practitioners. Listed below are some of the professional organizations that are active in the United States and other countries.

American Production and Inventory Control Society (APICS)

American Society of Traffic and Transportation (ASTT)

Delta Nu Alpha (DNA)

International Material Management Society (IMMS)

National Association of Purchasing Management (NAPM)

National Council for Physical Distribution Management (NCPDM)

Society of Logistics Engineers (SLE)

Organization

Why are some companies more successful than others? There are numerous reasons for a company's success. Management experts agree that one of the primary contributors to a flourishing business is a good organization. Organization provides the building blocks for an entire company. Peter Drucker indicates that organizational design should be based upon an "ideal organization," a conceptual framework. Individual company environments will demand some concessions, compromises, and exceptions; however, it is critical that these exceptions be infrequent and confined to purely local situations.[5]

Ideal Organization. Companies must cope with increasing costs and control problems related to materials. Substantial benefits can be realized by organizing individual groups related to materials into one functional entity. The rapid increase in the number of companies adopting a materials management organization is typified by the manufacturing industries. In a 1979 survey done by Jeffrey Miller and Peter Gilmour,[6] they reported, "Nearly half the manufacturers who responded to our survey now have materials managers playing important corporate and/or divisional roles, compared with a scant three percent reported in a 1966 survey."

The ideal organizational structure, which Peter Drucker indicates is a contributor to management, can be developed for the materials group. One example of an ideal organization, shown in Figure 4.2, reflects the desirable integrated format. This organizational chart would be similar for either a manufacturing or nonmanufacturing environment. Some activities may be removed or changed; however, the basic structure would remain the same. The executive responsible for the materials group reports to top management, which in this company example is the president, as do the other key departments, such as engineering, finance, and marketing.

Line and Staff Functions. As companies expand, there is a need to establish centralized and decentralized materials management organizational relationships through line and staff functions. Line activities are those activities performed by the personnel, typically working in a plant or distribution center, that support the everyday functions of the operating unit. Staff responsibilities consist of those activities performed to assist and/or support the functions of the overall company or a division of the company.

The central staff, headed by a materials management executive (often referred to as corporate staff), reports to the president or executive vice president (Figure 4.3) and is responsible for the overall company materials management functions. This group has no direct responsibility for operating-unit activities but does have staff authority. The line-materials manager reports to the head of an operating facility (i.e., general manager or plant manager).

Central staff materials groups develop policies and procedures which relate to all materials management functions. This provides for uniform

Figure 4.2. Desirable organization for a totally integrated materials management group. (*Eugene L. Magad and John M. Amos,* **Total Materials Management,** *Dryden Press, Hinsdale, Ill., 1985.*)

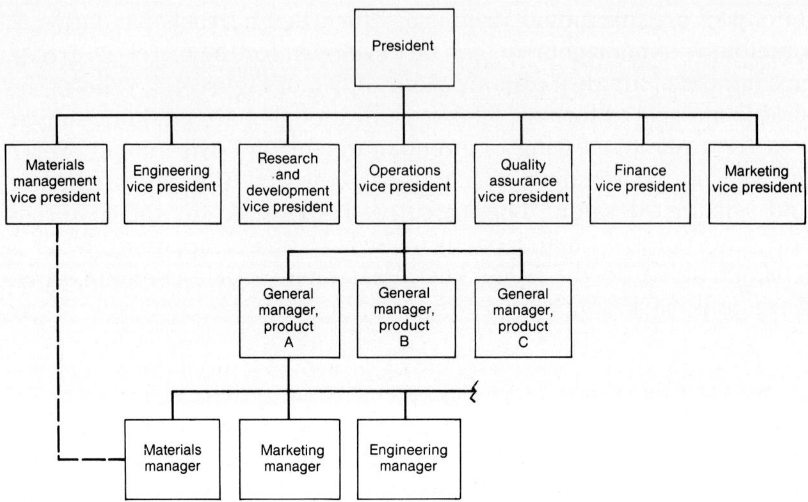

Figure 4.3. Decentralized organization based upon product groups.

performance of various activities. The central staff executive is responsible for the functional performance of line materials management activities. This responsibility is referred to as *dotted-line authority*. Centralized staff activities also decrease the duplicated costs often generated by various decentralized operating units. Other activities that normally would be performed by central staff personnel include the following:[1]

- *Systems development.* An important activity is assisting in the design and development of systems (manual and computer) that will be beneficial to more than one operating facility. This responsibility sometimes includes debugging of the system.
- *Communication.* Central staff personnel provide a clearing-house for information that will be beneficial to various operating facilities. This may take the form of bulletins or informational papers containing specialized knowledge. The staff will communicate worthwhile experiences from one unit to another and information on savings related to individual materials management activities.
- *Centralized purchases.* The central staff can identify materials that are purchased by different operating units. Negotiating contracts for consolidated purchases can provide significant cost savings.
- *Training.* Training is an essential and continuing central staff function. It can be performed by conducting seminars/meetings at central locations or in individual operating units.
- *Measurement.* Measuring performance of all activities is critical to assessing and improving individual group effectiveness. The central

staff should provide standard formulas/ratios which can be used by all groups to develop goals and objectives, measure performance, and identify areas requiring improvement. This information can also be useful to management for evaluating various operations.

- *Consulting.* Consulting services similar to those available from management consulting firms can be provided by the central staff. One of the advantages of having internal personnel performing this function is that they possess valuable knowledge of company products, policies, procedures, and personnel.

Benefits

Lamar Lee, Jr., and Donald W. Dobler reflect on the number of companies adopting a materials management organization. They refer to a *Business Week* management-section report which discusses the rapid growth of this management concept (Ref. 3, p. 2). Companies which have instituted integrated materials groups recognize the benefits which can be derived. Some of the major benefits are discussed by Eugene L. Magad and John M. Amos and are summarized below.[1]

Maximum Company Profits. Reducing costs contributes significantly to increased profits. The potential for cost reduction with a total materials group is considerable in many industries. Because this group relates to the control of company resources, it has high potential for providing profit improvement programs. Examples of areas which can contribute to reduced costs would include the following:

1. Decreased parts shortages resulting in more efficient use of labor, machines, and material
2. Reduced inventory levels through improved controls
3. Lowered transportation costs as a result of using minimum-cost shipping methods
4. Reduced materials obsolescence through greater control of inventory and timely processing of engineering change notices
5. Lowered purchase prices and total acquisition costs through the use of quantity buying and other techniques

Improvement of Customer Service. *Customer service* can be defined as a customer-oriented company philosophy that integrates and manages all elements of customer relations within a predetermined optimum cost-service mix. Good customer service is certainly a key element in any company's plans to grow and prosper. The concept that a customer should be fully satisfied has merit in today's competitive economy.

It is important that total materials management provide upper management with information regarding trade-offs that may be necessary as a company increases customer service levels. For example, it will have to forego minimum inventory levels in favor of maintaining safety stock to ensure meeting higher-than-normal product demand and/or compensating for late delivery of purchased materials. A company's desire for no lost sales or a minimum backlog of orders will require a relaxation of its attempt to obtain high inventory turnover [normally computed by dividing annual cost of sales by the average inventory level (Ref. 7, p. 14)].

Integration of Organization. One of the primary benefits of total materials management is the establishment of an integrated organization that will work as a team to accomplish company goals and objectives. Each group works together without voids, overlap, or friction. The International Material Management Society depicts this close relationship between the subfunctions as a "planetary gear" concept (Figure 4.4).

Let us review a typical scenario in a company that has not consolidated all materials subfunctions under one administrator. A meeting is called to determine why a customer's order wasn't shipped on Friday. The shipping supervisor denies responsibility, claiming that the order pickers did not pick the order on time. The finished goods warehouse supervisor says that it was not the order pickers' fault because production control did not produce the products on time. The production control supervisor places the blame on a shortage of parts. This meeting then continues with each group indicating it was not at fault. After two or three hours of discussion, everyone leaves the meeting with a knotted stomach, secure in the feeling that they were not at fault. However, the fact remains that the customer did not receive the order on time! Meetings similar to the one depicted in this classic story are being held by companies throughout the world, all of which have fragmented materials management responsibilities. Buck-passing can be reduced through an integrated materials organization that ensures that all subordinate supervisors assume their proper share of coordinated responsibility. Management and user departments can look to one central individual for both answers and action.

Interaction of Individual Manager Objectives. Each manager has a responsibility to meet the overall objectives of the company. However, each manager also recognizes that future success with the company is dependent upon the achievements of the department. A fragmented materials organization contributes to a situation in which individual supervisors concentrate on achieving their own immediate objectives, at the sacrifice of long-term objectives and cooperation with other groups. Total materials management motivates supervisors to accomplish individual departmental objectives while encouraging communication and cooperation among departments to achieve both the short-term and long-term objectives of the entire company.

Mr. John J. Davin, Vice President Materials and Facilities of GTE, discusses the problem of conflicting objectives, as follows:

> There is a natural tendency for functional departments—purchasing, production and inventory control, physical distribution—to look inward to accomplish their objectives. The purchasing manager prepares his budget,

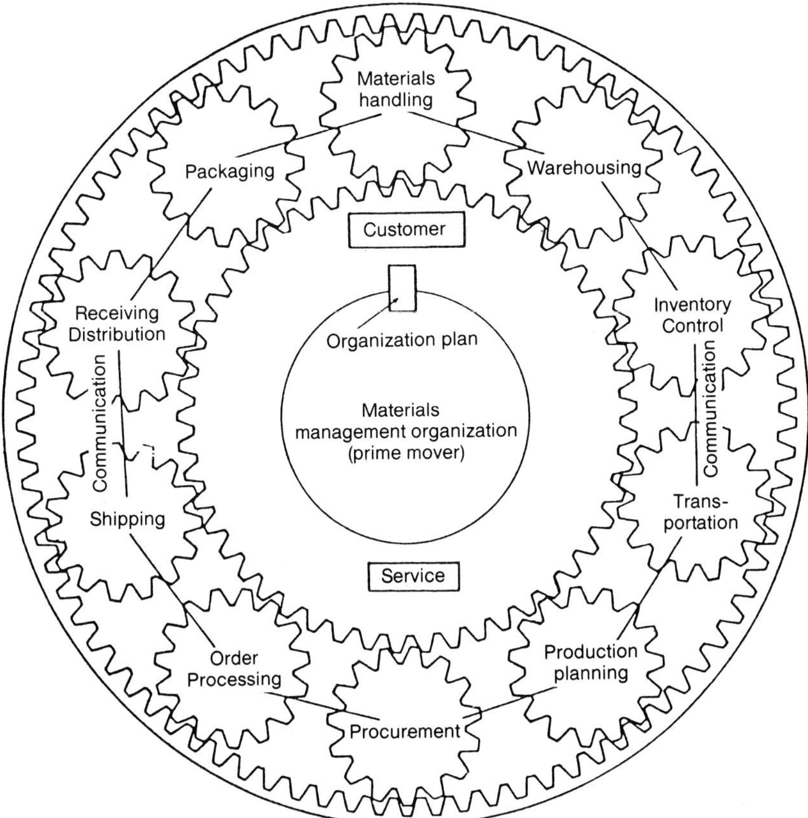

Figure 4.4 Planetary gear concept. (***From International Material Management Society, Lansing.***)

plans, and objectives each year and is held accountable for his accomplishments. Likewise, the inventory manager is expected to improve turns in order to make his profit contribution. Without coordination, these two managers may end up working against each other—one trying to bring materials into the plant on a volume basis, the other trying to prevent material from accumulating ahead of production. Materials management is a natural solution to the dilemma. Instead of two managers reporting to different supervisors with dissimilar goals, a materials manager becomes the sole decision maker for materials as they flow through the organization. Here is where the potential is greater than if the functions remained separate. Being able to see the entire breadth of a situation, the correct emphasis can be placed in order to accomplish the objective.[8]

Improvement of Credibility. An important factor in the day-to-day operations of a company is the reliability and accuracy of each group's performance and activities. Company activities are similar to a fine orchestra. Each individual and group within the company (or orchestra) is dependent upon others for correct timing and performance. If anyone falters, the overall performance is affected. In some respects, company activities become even more complex. Individual departments begin to take safety precautions when they are forced to work with others who are not as dependable. Days or even weeks are added to "cushion" projected requirement dates when working with a group who has a history of missed deadlines. Supervisors begin to hoard materials because they cannot rely on the warehouse group to maintain inventories. With a total materials management organization, various functions (marketing, manufacturing, etc.) find that they get better, more reliable service. This organization provides credibility of performance, which contributes to reduced costs and less confusion. It also contributes to an atmosphere of mutual trust and cooperation.

Improvement of Resource Control. A goal of any organization, whether it is a profit-oriented company or a nonprofit organization, is the control of the organization's resources, and materials managers have successfully contributed to this goal. Generally, these resources are referred to, and easily remembered, as the "four Ms": materials, machines, manpower, and money. All subfunction activities are related to the control of these four resources, sometimes as individual elements, and often several at one time. The four Ms are expanded upon as follows:

1. *Materials.* Control of materials resources is certainly a key element of any organization having a materials management function. This control relates to all areas. Companies with multiple divisions and/or facilities may have various materials organizations. When this occurs,

a company can compare the diverse results. For example, Motorola, Inc. has some divisions within a major product group with similar products and customers, common problems, and identical management systems that have an integrated materials management organization, and some which do not. Inventory turnover is consistently at least 25 percent higher with the integrated materials management structure, with all other business evaluation factors being equal or better.

2. *Machines (facilities).* Materials management is a major force contributing to the control of company facilities. Capacity requirements planning, both for the short term and long term, will aid in determining the need for building new plants and warehouses. Planning must be an ongoing activity in order to ensure capacity availability when required. At the same time, every effort must be expended to optimize use of existing facilities by efficient techniques (i.e., good scheduling of machines, manpower, and overtime hours, and improved facilities planning can contribute significantly to the maximum use of company capacity). The need for new buildings and equipment can be eliminated or minimized by effective control of operations.
3. *Manpower.* Human resources of a company are critical to achieving success. No company can grow and prosper without capable and conscientious employees. Usually, with a fragmented materials management organization, individuals in each group have fewer opportunities to develop and broaden their knowledge and skills. As members of an integrated materials organization, employees have more opportunities to broaden their knowledge and understanding. Personnel can be rotated and promoted among the subfunctions. The materials organization can also contribute to minimizing operating department personnel requirements and increasing manpower efficiency by reducing time-consuming materials-related problems, such as excessive expediting, downtime due to lack of materials, and poor scheduling.
4. *Money.* Materials management provides a systems-oriented structure for minimizing monetary expenditures and controlling the management of money. Picture a typical, frustrating situation for the controller or treasurer of a company. The executive may be busy in the morning arranging for a bank to provide needed capital. Walking through the facility that same afternoon, instead of seeing materials in different shapes and forms, the executive visualizes the materials as money. The question that might then be asked is, "Why was I devoting so much time and effort trying to obtain money when it is

sitting around everywhere in the facility?" This may appear to be an oversimplification, but in many companies the materials management organization has decreased monetary problems by minimizing inventories, reducing total costs of procurements, and diminished costs of materials handling an physical distribution.

Reduction of Duplicated Efforts. The fragmented materials organization has a natural duplication of various activities built into it. Since all of the materials subfunctions are interrelated, it is inevitable that overlapping of activities will contribute to repetition of efforts by various groups. Duplications are not unusual in records and data, in which each group maintains its own information. Also, this commonly occurs when several people in the company are expediting the same orders.

Improvement of Morale. The total materials management organizational philosophy contributes to a winning team spirit. Such a team spirit provides both harmony and a feeling of accomplishment. This type of structure also affords people greater intracompany mobility. For example, the fragmented organization approach contributes to groups such as shipping, receiving, and warehousing often being limited in specific career opportunities. However, in an integrated organization, individual identity and importance are upgraded. The increased mobility of personnel within subfunctions is an important factor in improved individual employee morale.

Enhancement of Communication. Instituting a total materials organization will contribute to improved communication among the various materials subfunctions, as well as between materials management and other major company functions, such as marketing, manufacturing, and engineering. The concept provides a communication network that reacts quickly and more rationally throughout the system. By combining the various fragmented groups into one cohesive management structure, a company will shorten the message channels by allowing use of common data.

Relationship with Warehousing

Materials management is an umbrella type of organization that integrates all material-related activities of a company. As materials are received, they flow through to all operations, until final shipment to the customer.

Warehousing is responsible for storing goods until they are needed.[9] To some degree, warehousing is related to all facets of the materials management function. It is an integral part of the overall materials group as well as each subfunction within the materials management structure.

Planning

Both short- and long-range planning are vital activities in every company. The primary objective of this materials subfunction is to maximize long-range planning in order to optimize use of company resources and provide for customer demand. Some of the relationships between planning and warehousing activities are as follows:

- Planning must correlate sales forecasts with operating and support requirements for periods of 1 to 10 years.
- Warehousing contributes critical information to planning related to its projected requirements for manpower, money, and facilities.
- Planning will provide some of the basic information to be translated into budgetary controls for warehousing operations (i.e., inventory, supplies, equipment, etc.).
- Warehousing requires planning information to aid in developing justifications for any major innovative changes involving capital equipment, future expansion, relocation, and so on.

Inventory Control

The inventory-control subfunction includes all activities and techniques required to maintain materials at desired levels. These materials generally include raw materials, work-in-process, and finished products. Some of the relationships between inventory control and warehousing are as follows:

- Accuracy of inventory control records are dependent upon warehousing data integrity. Any major discrepancies by stores personnel that contribute to lost material, inaccurate cycle counts or stocking/picking quantities, and unknown material damage will result in inventory control problems. These discrepancies cause operating company complications in scheduling material availability and, eventually, delivery performance and credibility.

- Inventory control can cause difficulties for warehousing with incessant requests for check counts of various stored items. This substantiates the need for credible inventory records being maintained by the warehouse.
- Suboptimum warehouse space utilization and congestion can occur if appropriate warehousing unit load quantities are not considered in material ordering activities.
- Errors by inventory control, such as duplication of orders, excess material order quantities, and incorrect due-date requirements, can result in congested warehouse conditions. This can adversely affect employee and equipment productivity.

Production Control

Production control is the materials subfunction responsible for directing or regulating the movement of materials through the entire manufacturing cycle, from the raw materials stage through all operations, to the finished product stage. Some of the relationships between production control and warehousing are as follows:

- Production control prepares schedules for production parts, subassemblies, and products. A manufacturing warehouse must issue the correct material, in the correct quantity, at the correct time, and to the correct location. Anything less than this can result in problems for production control, such as downtime for production personnel and machines, duplication of production control efforts, and late delivery to customers.
- Warehousing depends upon production control to develop reasonable, realistic schedules. Errors in manufacturing schedules can cause warehousing to have excess overtime costs and chaotic conditions.
- Production control relies upon good communication with warehousing to avoid or detect material problems that may result in schedule variations.
- Production control can minimize warehouse materials by employing efficient systems. Current systems, such as Material Requirements Planning (MRP) and Distribution Requirement Planning (DRP), have been instrumental in reducing warehouse activities through better control of material quantities and improving purchasing and production schedules.

Purchasing

Purchasing is responsible for procurement of materials from outside suppliers, in accordance with purchase requisition requirements. Some of the relationships between purchasing and warehousing are as follows:

- Good-quality supplies and equipment should be procured by purchasing according to schedule requirements to provide warehousing with items needed to perform its activities.
- Warehousing can avoid duplication of purchased materials by maintaining accurate control of all stored items. Lost materials results in additional and wasted purchasing activities.
- Purchasing can contribute to efficient warehousing operations by obtaining from suppliers unit loads that are conducive to maximizing space utilization and minimizing equipment and personnel requirements.
- Purchasing can increase warehouse order-picking productivity by arranging for materials to be received in packages containing quantities that relate to those ordered by customers and/or operating departments. For example, if there are frequent orders for ten screws or multiples of ten, it may be cost-effective to obtain packages containing ten screws, rather than bulk containers. This could eliminate the time-consuming counting by an order picker.

Receiving and Stores

Receiving is the group responsible for unloading materials from incoming carriers. It verifies the accuracy of all information and prepares reports. *Stores* is one of the terms used to describe warehouse activities. Some of the relationships between receiving and stores are as follows:

- Receiving is the first materials management subfunction to provide input regarding incoming materials. It is important that all data related to these items be accurate. Any discrepancies, such as incorrect quantities or material identification, will result in additional problems and work for other materials management subfunctions, including the stores group.
- Stores depends upon the receiving group to be alert and inform them as soon as "hot items" are received. Promptness in supplying this information will allow stores to disburse the material expeditiously.
- Communication between the two groups can affect stores employee and equipment productivity levels. For example, if receiving informs

stores of anticipated deliveries, stores management can improve scheduling of its group's activities.

- Cooperation between receiving and stores regarding application of automated operations will benefit both groups. For example, supplier-applied coded labels will allow receiving to use scanners to check incoming materials automatically and provide for automated transfer of these materials to designated stores locations.

Materials Handling

Materials handling involves both design and physical movement. Its primary responsibility is developing and implementing appropriate manual, mechanized, and automated systems to provide optimum movement of materials throughout the company. Some of the relationships between materials handling design and warehousing are as follows:

- Materials handling designers are responsible for support of warehousing by reviewing and analyzing all operations to determine areas that require improvement.
- Warehousing depends upon materials handling engineers to design and justify new materials handling systems, which will provide increased storage capacity, reduced labor costs, improved material flow, and safer working conditions.
- Materials handling designers should involve warehousing personnel in the development of any new systems, to be sure that the end result is user-oriented.
- Warehousing personnel can contribute to the attainment of new materials handling systems objectives by adhering to prescribed methods and procedures. Prior to instituting any changes, suggested improvements to operations should be discussed with the materials handling group. This is critical to the achievement of planned activities. The materials handling group has an overall view of the entire system, and if warehousing implements changes without consulting the designer, the results can be negative.

Physical Distribution

Physical distribution encompasses all of the operations involved in the movement and flow of finished products, from the time the goods are received to the time they are shipped to the customer. Chapter 2, "Warehousing and Physical Distribution," describes in detail the interaction between these two groups. Finished goods warehousing is an integral part of physical distribution operations, which also encompasses other activities, such as packaging, shipping, and transportation. Some of the relationships between warehousing and other physical distribution activities are as follows:

- Warehousing, shipping, and transportation cooperate to identify and process materials that should be returned to suppliers, scrapped, or sold as surplus. Control of these materials is essential to a company's total materials management program in order to improve cashflow, provide additional storage space, and reduce potential losses in material values.
- In manufacturing companies, raw materials and work-in-process warehousing operations have a critical effect upon efficiency and distribution. Ineffective management of these warehousing activities will result in problems for physical distribution, such as lower employee and equipment productivity, additional paperwork processing, and congestion of shipping staging areas.
- Optimum customer service is an essential objective of materials management. However, there is an extra emphasis concerning customer service related to the physical distribution subfunction. One reason is that this group is the last involved in the total cycle that provides the customer with required products. Finished goods warehousing is a critical link in the physical distribution "chain" that supplies optimum customer service.
- Transportation of both incoming and outgoing materials is part of the physical distribution group's responsibilities. It is essential that the method of transportation minimize shipping damages to materials. Damaged materials and/or loads result in numerous problems for warehousing, including material stock-outs, unsafe employee working conditions, increased paper work, and so on.

Role of the Computer

The computer is an essential and integrating link that connects all materials management subfunctions and relates their activities to other company functions. During the 1960s and 1970s, materials groups in both large and small companies accelerated their use of computer applications to aid in coping with the increasing complexity of materials-related problems. This was made possible by the significant progress in the development and enhancement of both hardware (e.g., memory, terminals, and data links) and software packages. Greater utilization was further achieved by the reduced cost of computer systems.

Introduction

Computers allow materials personnel to cope with a multitude of information in an orderly and systematic manner and to flow the information to users in a desirable time frame: data needed for reports can be collected, analyzed, and printed by the computer in minutes; previously it would have taken days or even weeks to accomplish the same task. This permits the discovery and interpretation of a significant trend or potential problem area while it is still in the formative stage. Since time is often an important factor in operating a business, the fact that computers can provide accurate decision-making information quickly has made them a significant tool.

Materials management is one of the business functions which has critically needed the development of software for its various activities. The types of software presently available range from simple programs to perform addition and subtraction (i.e., for maintaining inventory counts), to advanced analytical programs that use mathematical modeling to perform experimental analysis of alternative plans (i.e., for determining how many warehouses are required, what to stock, and how much to stock).

Many companies have experienced the benefits of successful computer applications. Those companies which do not have internal computer expertise (some smaller companies prefer to forego these increased costs) have access to computer service firms. Terminals at the user location can feed data to and receive data from the computer service firm's equipment.

Typical Computer Applications

Several of the many potential examples of materials management computer applications are as follows:

Material Requirements Planning (MRP). One of the primary reasons for maintaining warehouses in a manufacturing environment is to provide for fluctuating demand by production departments. This increased demand and resultant higher inventories is often caused by the type of inventory control and production control system. One of the most common systems is based upon an order-point–order-quantity ordering technique. The order-point system uses historical information to compute required material quantities. Usually this employs an Economic Order Quantity (EOQ) calculation. The order-point system has as part of its basic philosophy a dedication to stock maintenance.

MRP is a system that uses bills of material, inventory and open-order data, and master production schedule information to calculate requirements for materials (Ref. 7, p. 18). MRP systems normally employ computers to process the myriad amounts of data. The computer program provides recommendations for the release of material orders on an as-needed basis, as opposed to the maintenance of inventories found in an order-point application. MRP results in less inventory and warehousing. Also, MRP considers future product demand and the resultant assemblies, parts, and materials requirements, as opposed to the averages based upon historical data utilized by order-point systems.

Since MRP is a time-phased system, it makes recommendations to reschedule open orders when due dates and need dates are not in phase. This system recognizes, in advance, when an assembly will not be available because one or more components will not be completed on time. For example, a perennial problem in production is having eight parts produced and one part missing on the date planned to complete an assembly. Either the eight parts should have been scheduled for later production (thereby possibly making available for other needed orders all resources utilized to make the parts) or the one late part expedited for completion on time. MRP addresses this problem with its time-phased system.

MRP can considerably reduce the amount of time devoted to "fire fighting" and expediting. Most manufacturing companies that do not utilize an MRP system and those that implement an ineffective MRP program have continual problems that cause imbalances among materials, personnel, money, and facilities. Although problems can occur with computer systems, MRP systems allow easy input of changes to adjust for the many variables involved. This results in revised schedules that are available for immediate implementation. Anyone experiencing the frequent chaos that occurs in manufacturing companies when all the "white shirts" (from the president on down to lower positions) are expediting an order, can appreciate the potential benefits achieved by a properly implemented MRP system.

Many MRP system installations have incurred serious and sometimes fatal problems related to the various stages of implementation. Some of the factors which are crucial to success are as follows:[10]

1. *Commitment.* The commitment of all levels of management is a prime requirement. The top executive (e.g., president or general manager) cannot approve the program and then ignore it. A sustained, dynamic leadership role is required. All members of manage-

ment must understand their roles and those of their groups in accomplishing a successful MRP program.

2. *Task force.* A full-time task force that includes key personnel from various departments should be used. The number of members will vary depending on the company size, operations, and so on. A task force supervisor should be selected from the production control and inventory control groups. Task force members should be good communicators and known for accomplishing required tasks.
3. *System design.* It is critical to program success that a total systems design approach is used. After developing system specifications, determine whether the software will be purchased or developed in house. It is better to purchase an existing package, if one that suits the company is available. An important consideration in ensuring successful implementation is "tailoring" any purchased software to individual company requirements.
4. *Education and training.* This activity has proven to be one of the most important phases in MRP program implementation. Some companies allocate one-third of total system costs to this area. Personnel can only perform to the level of their competence and understanding. Therefore, education and training must be directed to all functions in the company, including materials management groups (i.e., purchasing, warehousing, inventory control, and production control), as well as other key functions (i.e., data processing, marketing, manufacturing, and engineering).
5. *Pilot test.* Everyone may be anxious to begin using the new system, but it is essential that time be devoted to running a pilot test of the system. This test will allow various personnel to become more familiar with MRP activities as related to their particular tasks. It will also provide a debugging period to determine and correct any deficiencies in the system. Communication channels must be "fine-tuned" during this time, as they are essential to accomplishing desired results. Do not discontinue an existing system until the new MRP system is in full, satisfactory operation.

Computerized Purchasing. Computers have a critical role to play in purchasing activities because of the enormous amount of clerical work that is performed by this materials management subfunction. Requisitions, purchase orders, change orders, and expedite lists are just some of the "mountain" of paperwork transactions required for purchasing operations. Data accumulation and report development are also important purchasing activities that require repetitive clerical work. Most of this clerical paperwork can be automated to minimize labor requirements and provide accurate, timely information for decision making.

Improving purchasing operations by the use of computer technology will have considerable impact upon warehousing. If purchasing can provide an uninterrupted flow of materials to satisfy company requirements, the warehousing activity will be able to improve user department service, reduce stock-outs, improve employee productivity, and reduce hot-list expediting. Improved receipt of purchased materials can reduce the often-times chaotic conditions found in a stores department. Automation of purchasing activities can result in both tangible and intangible benefits. Purchasing communication with warehousing and other materials management subfunctions, as well as with other company functions, can be improved. Direct gains can be obtained in the form of reduced inventory investment due to faster clerical response time. This can be accomplished by having critical information at the touch of a finger. Available information can include part/product identification, supplier name, supplier history, projected delivery dates, price quotations, historical usage and projected needs, and open orders. Other computer-related purchasing benefits include:

1. Reduction or elimination of all manual filing.
2. Automatic generation of information and reports, such as expedite lists and letters to remind suppliers of promised delivery dates.
3. Multifacility operations can be serviced by reviewing comparable purchased items and determining if national contracts can achieve cost reductions. Benefits can accrue even from informing individual facilities of price discrepancies.
4. Automated preparation of purchase orders, where feasible, will eliminate personnel efforts.
5. Vendor evaluation, both individually and in comparison to multiple suppliers, can be improved through readily available data in a format that allows fast decision making.
6. Computer assistance will result in minimizing the time required for the clerical and professional staff to perform their tasks, which can result in reduced numbers of personnel and/or increasing the scope of purchasing operations.
7. Reduction in the purchase order aging time (lead time required from date of requisition to date of supplier receiving purchasing order).
8. Improved ability of purchasing management and executive management to review purchased materials investments in detail and pinpoint potential savings areas.

9. Provide a scorecard for measurement and control of purchasing effectiveness. Individual buyers and the entire department can be analyzed regularly, using information such as material lead-time analysis, inventory levels, cashflow, supplier evaluation systems, and so on.

Summary

Companies in various industries are faced with many of the same problems related to control of materials. These include rising material and labor costs, pressure to provide improved customer service, increased complexity of products and operations, and difficulties related to cashflow. Total materials management is an organizational solution which can aid firms in coping with these problems. The objective of this philosophy is to coordinate within the business all activities that relate to the materials cycle, from supplier, through all company operations, to shipping and, ultimately, to the customer, in order to achieve better customer service, control of materials, and higher profits.

Warehousing is an integral part of the materials management function. It has close association with all materials subfunctions, including planning, inventory control, production control, purchasing, receiving and stores, materials handling, and physical distribution. Warehousing is responsible for control of all materials, including raw materials, supplies, work-in-process, and finished goods, which are vital to the accomplishment of the materials function objectives. Total materials management cannot be achieved without capable warehousing operations.

The computer has become an essential and integrating link in achieving materials management objectives. Good computer systems can provide materials personnel with accurate, up-to-date information in order to make better decisions. The current business environment, with its many variables and pressures, makes the use of computer technology a necessity. Examples of just a few of the many uses of computer systems in total materials management include Materials Requirement Planning, automated warehouses, and computerized purchasing.

References

1. Eugene L. Magad and John M. Amos, *Total Materials Management,* Dryden Press, Hinsdale, Ill., 1985.
2. Dean S. Ammer, "Materials Management," *Guide to Purchasing,* National Association of Purchasing Management, 1971.

3. Lamer Lee, Jr., and Donald W. Dobler, *Purchasing and Materials Management,* McGraw-Hill, New York, 1977.
4. Norman Gaither, *Production and Operation Management,* Dryden Press, Hinsdale, Ill., 1980, pp. 7–9.
5. Peter F. Drucker, *Management: Tasks, Responsibilities, Practices,* Harper & Row, New York, 1974, pp. 599–600.
6. Jeffrey A. Miller and Peter Gilmour, "Materials Managers: Who Needs Them," *Harvard Business Review,* July–August 1979, pp. 143–44, citing Gregory V. Schultz, "The Real Low-Down on Materials Management," *Factory,* December 1967, p. 49.
7. Thomas F. Wallace (ed.), *APICS Dictionary,* American Production and Inventory Control Society, Washington, 1980.
8. National Association of Purchasing Managers, *Aljian's Purchasing Handbook,* 4th ed., P. V. Farrell and G. W. Aljian (eds.), McGraw-Hill, New York, 1982, p. 19–6.
9. Creed H. Jenkins, *Modern Warehouse Management,* McGraw-Hill, New York, 1968, p. 1.
10. Jerry D. Rose, "Craters Along the MRP Road," *1978 National Conference Proceedings,* American Production and Inventory Society, Washington, 1979, pp. 211–17.

5
Site Selection

Kenneth B. Ackerman

President, The K. B. Ackerman Company, Columbus, Ohio

Choosing the location for a warehouse is certainly one of the most important corporate decisions made in physical distribution management. Real estate professionals have worn out a proverb that claims that the three most important qualities for any parcel of real estate are location, location, and location. Without question, a warehouse that is located in the wrong spot can deal a costly and possibly even mortal blow to the life of a corporation heavily involved in physical distribution.

The task of site selection involves art as well as science. Judgment decisions usually involve a weighing of priorities, a determination of which features are critical, and a process of elimination. Since every location has both advantages and disadvantages, the final selection of a site is likely to involve some compromises.

Reasons for Site Seeking

First, consider why you are looking for a new warehouse site. The following are four common reasons:

1. It is necessary to relocate an existing warehouse operation.
2. The business is expanding and must move inventory into a new market.

3. More warehouse space is needed to accommodate a growing inventory.
4. Contingency planning requires some decentralization of existing warehousing—in other words, there are too many eggs in one basket.

Depending on which of the above reasons is the motivator for seeking a new warehouse, the site search can take many different forms.

Geography

Both man-made and geographical factors can substantially affect the utility of a warehouse site. Consider one man-made factor illustrated in Figure 5.1. A site may have beautiful visual access to a major freeway, thus offering image and advertising value. However, that visual access may have negative value for physical distribution purposes if trucks moving to and from the distribution center must take a circuitous route to reach the nearest access ramp of the highway.

Access conditions can be even more critically governed by geography when a distribution center requires access to several modes of transportation, such as rail, highway, and water. While roadways offer possibilities for the most extensive geographical coverage, the ability to extend waterways and railways is usually strongly governed by geography.

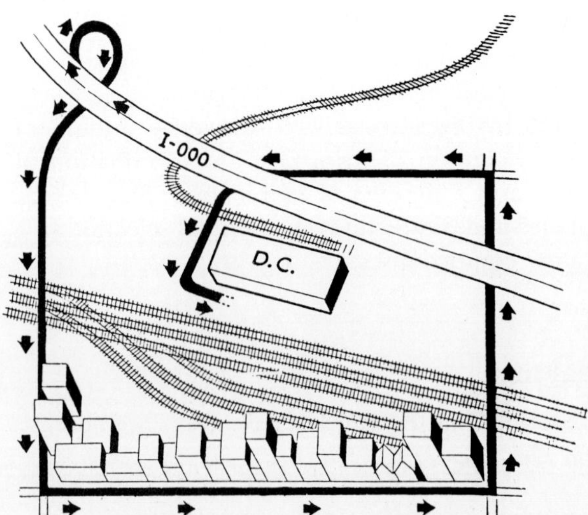

Figure 5.1. So Near and Yet So Far: The fact that a distribution center is located within a few hundred feet of a superhighway means little if trucks have to run miles to find the nearest access ramp. (*Distribution Centers, Inc.*)

Obviously, waterway access is changed only by construction of canals or dredging, which are both extremely costly operations. Similarly, railway extension can be limited by topography, since locomotives cannot climb steep grades.

Climatic aspects of geography have become an increasingly important factor with the rise of energy costs. The U.S. Department of Commerce publishes the *Climatic Atlas of the United States*, which lists annual mean heating degree days. A heating degree day is an average temperature one degree below a given temperature base, usually calculated as 65°F. A sample map from this government source is shown in Figure 5.2. While heating degree days may not be a critical factor in locating a warehouse, the possibility that climate will disrupt access to transportation modes is a consideration. If air freight service is critical to the operation, the service record of the nearest airport under consideration should be analyzed.

Location Theories

Consideration of location theory is a useful exercise in picking the spot for a new warehouse. Whether you accept or reject any of the theories which follow, at least consider them as helpful guidelines to the location decision. First, move from a "macro" to a "micro" decision. Following this theory, we might first determine that the new warehouse must be someplace within the continental United States. Second, we might determine that the facility should be in the southwestern region of the United States. Third, we determine that it must be in the state of Texas; fourth, that it be in the Dallas-Ft. Worth metropolitan area; fifth, that it be in the southwest area of the city of Dallas; and finally that it be on a specific site on Duncanville Road.

More than a century has passed since J. H. Von Thunen wrote about the advantages of growing the bulkiest and cheapest crops on land closest to the city that needed that commodity. The same principle can certainly be applied to all kinds of manufactured products: location of inventory is most critical for those that have the least value added. An inventory of gold or diamonds, for example, can be economically kept in one spot and moved by air freight all over the world, but the producer of bagged salt may find it necessary to place inventories close to the market.

The theory of postponement also has an impact on site selection. *Postponement* is the delay of the final formation or commitment of a product until the last possible moment. Postponement was practiced long before marketing theorists became interested in it. One early example in industry—Coca Cola—goes back to the beginning years of the twen-

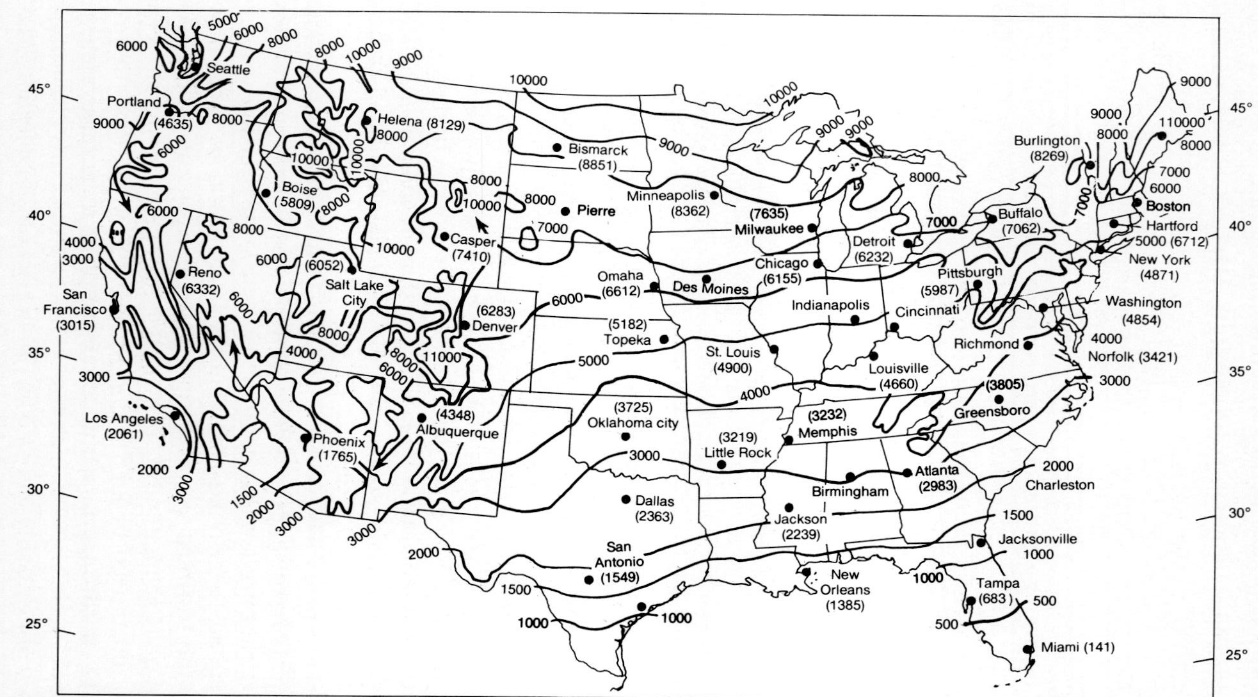

Figure 5.2. Annual mean heating degree-days below 65°F. A heating degree-day is an average temperature 1°F below a given temperature base (in this case, 65°F). A day with an average temperature of 60°F thus has 5 degree-days. The map gives the degree-day totals for all days of the year with average temperatures below the base 65°F. (*From* **Climatic Atlas of the United States,** *Department of Commerce, Washington, D.C. June 1986, p. 70.*)

tieth century. Soon after Coca Cola was established, its management realized that it would be far more economical to ship concentrated syrup to field locations, adding water and carbonation in glass bottles at points relatively close to the market. Coca Cola thus postponed the final blending and packaging of the product to create substantial economies for consumers. Postponement was described as the opposite of speculation. A speculative inventory is put in a distribution center whenever the cost of that inventory is less than the profit derived from using the inventory to stimulate purchases. Conversely, placement of inventory may be postponed when there is an economic incentive to do so.

Some products can be manufactured in a semifinished state, or finished but not given the final brand or identification. Inventory of postponed goods can be held until specific customer orders are received, at which time the goods are finished or branded to the customer's specifications. The postponement warehouse then becomes an assembly center as well as a distribution center. The need for these assembly capabilities could affect its location.

How Many Warehouses?

Conceptually, the least speculative way of providing warehousing services is to have a single finished goods warehouse located directly at the end of the assembly line. If finished goods are staged at the point of manufacture, presumably they can never be in the wrong place. As multiple locations are added at greater distances from the assembly site, the user runs a constantly increasing risk that goods committed to storage in Los Angeles will subsequently be needed in New York, necessitating a cross-country move that presumably would have been avoided if they had never left the production site. Therefore, in considering number of warehouses, one starts by assuming that one exists at point of manufacture. Presumably the second is needed when the first is either full or is unable by reasons of geography or capacity to satisfy consumer needs in other regions of the country. If geography and capacity do not cause establishment of a second warehouse, customer service pressures or transportation costs may force the issue.

The justification for a warehouse is frequently made by showing that the cost of bulk transportation from factory to field warehouse is less than the cost of multiple small shipments, and a mathematical analysis can be constructed to show these savings. On the other hand, inventory as a percentage of sales will presumably go up every time a remote warehouse is established, and one runs the earlier-mentioned risk of committing inventory in the wrong place. Therefore, any warehouse must reflect the negative factors of increased inventory cost and inventory commitment risk. These are measured against resultant savings in transportation or improvements in customer service. The same process is used every time another remote location is considered, and this analytical process should also be used from time to time to check the validity of existing warehouse locations. In many cases, such an analysis may show that the user will save money by closing the remote location and serving its territory from another existing warehouse.

Economic Factors

Perhaps the most important economic factor to measure in site selection is the cost versus the value of a new warehouse site. There is one thing that nearly all industrial buildings have in common: the physical life of the structure will probably outlast the useful life of the building for its present user. Therefore, every site or building should be considered as an investment which will eventually be resold, hopefully on favorable terms. Some locations are likely to increase in value, and others, predictably, will decrease in value. The future value of a site may be influenced by emotional as well as rational factors. Certain areas gain a reputation as high-growth locations, and others, however undeserved, are considered to be depressed. Perhaps the best way to test the future value of a site is by extensively interviewing people who understand neighborhood trends and can analyze them in an unbiased fashion. For example, the area development department of one power company maintains records on crime, number of unsold houses, population migration, and other statistics that could reflect economic distress in each of the villages and suburbs of its metropolitan area.

One important economic factor is the local tax on inventories, primarily because this cost can vary significantly from one location to another. In a few cases, states or other taxing authorities have used the presence of inventory in storage as the basis for levying franchise, income, or other taxes on the owner of property. Radical changes in tax policy have frequently caused manufacturers to shift inventories from a state in which there is a significant tax burden. As transportation has improved, manufacturers have gained the ability to provide reasonable delivery service to their customers and still avoid those states and municipalities that have created conditions of tax harassment.

States differ widely in their approach to inventory taxes. At the same time, rates of taxation within states or even within counties or towns can also show significant differences. Because state and local tax situations change frequently, expert advice should be sought when comparing tax policies of individual states or communities.

One economic factor which is rising in importance is a federal privilege known as a *foreign trade zone*. Such zones provide exemption from normal customs duties for products while they remain within the zone. For example, the Port of Houston has developed a zone of more than 1700 acres which includes 32 separate sites in the Port area. More than a third of these are public warehouse buildings, and raw land is also available for new construction within this zone.

Site Layout

In looking for a plant site, it is usually more effective to find one that fits a general construction plan than to attempt to adapt construction to the site. Warehouse buildings with odd-shaped walls designed to fit a railroad curve or some other site constraint are usually costly to build and even more costly to operate. It is nearly impossible to create an orderly warehouse layout in a building that lacks rectangular walls.

The ability of your company to grow on this site is a critical factor in the planning process and should preceed site selection. This planning is likely to govern selection standards and priorities. For example, is the warehouse facility one that must be designed for future conversion to manufacturing? If so, labor, floor load, and power specifications will probably be substantially different from a site that would never be converted to production. If production conversion is a consideration, planning should allow for the projected density of people per acre found in various manufacturing operations. Table 5.1, an illustrative table of industrial densities taken from a U.S. Department of Commerce study, will aid you in determining whether your industry is intensive or extensive in the density of employees per acre.

For example, assume that you as distribution director for a manufacturer of refrigerators are analyzing a site. Your product is one that is notably easy to store and handle in a high-volume situation. Materials handling attachments are available that will carry as many as six refrigerators down the floor at a time, and the product can typically be stacked to heights of 20 to 30 feet. Therefore, in selecting a site in which to store refrigerators, you might prefer planning a building with a practical pile height of 30 feet and an employment density as low as one worker per 10,000 square feet of space, or about four employees per acre. Such planning could be well supported by those experienced in warehousing this commodity. But if the planned building must eventually be converted to production of refrigerators, the number of employees per acre will probably increase to more than 30. Can the high cube storage space be effectively used in production? Should it be adapted by adding mez-

Table 5.1. Illustrative Table of Industrial Densities

Industry land-use group	Type of major industry group and SIC codes	Acres per 1000 employees	Employees per acre
I	Intensive	30	33
	23 Apparel and related products		
	36 Electrical machinery		
	38 Instruments and related products		
II	Intermediate-intensive	40	25
	27 Printing and publishing		
	37 Transportation and equipment		
III	Intermediate-extensive	90	11
	20 Food and kindred products		
	24 Lumber and wood products		
	25 Furniture and fixtures		
	26 Pulp, paper, and products		
	28 Chemicals and products		
	30 Rubber products		
	33 Primary metal industries		
	34 Fabricated metal products		
	35 Machinery, except electrical		
	39 Miscellaneous manufactures		
IV	Extensive	375	3
	29 Petroleum and coal products		
	31 Leather and leather goods		
	32 Stone, clay, and glass products		
	All industry not included above	125	2
	Public utilities	200	5

SOURCE: U.S. Department of Commerce, Office of Area Development, *Future Development of the San Francisco Bay Area, 1960–2020,* U.S. Government Printing Office, 1959.

zanines, or can the overhead space be profitably used for the conveying of work-in-process? If employment density increases from 4 to more than 30 people per acre, will the site support the additional parking required? Will the sanitary sewer requirements be expandable to handle the far greater use when employee density grows?

All of these planning factors are typical of the kinds of things that are considered when a site is analyzed for its future reuse as well as its immediate planned use.

Outside Advisors

It is difficult to pick a spot for a new warehouse without eventually turning for advice to people outside your organization. For this reason, you should consider six commonly used sources of such advice.

Real Estate Brokers. Real estate brokers are often involved in any search for new property. One aspect of selecting a broker is knowing that, while multiple listing services are available for many brokers, they are not available to all. However, the most important thing to remember about real estate brokerage is that the broker's compensation for this activity is based upon successful completion of a transaction. Therefore, it is normal for the broker to be motivated to complete a commissionable sale. Furthermore, commission arrangements that may not be known to the prospective buyer could make it difficult for the broker to maintain objectivity as a source of outside advice. Not all real estate brokers are biased, of course, but the user should be aware of the fact that the commission system for brokerage tends to create pressures which could affect the execution of the site search. When the broker's time invested in the search starts to approach the value of the commission, the broker would be foolish not to abandon the search activity.

Warehouse Sales Representatives. If existing warehouse space is sought, the use of a warehouse sales representative could be useful. The public warehouse industry has several national marketing chains, each of which has representation in the Chicago and New York metro areas. Typically, the chain sales representative is not paid a sales commission, though a few may work on a commission as well as a salary basis. Since the chain sales agent normally cannot represent competing warehouses, each chain has only one outlet in each major city.

Railroads. Major railroads are a source of advice on sites for new buildings as well as existing warehouses. Railroad representatives do not work on a commission basis, but they naturally will want to have the new warehouse located on their railroad rather than a competing railroad. If railroad competition is not a factor in the decision, the railroad representative can be a reliable source of advice. If only two railroads are under consideration, the use of two competing railroad development agents may be a valuable exercise.

Utility Companies. The area development departments of electric and gas utilities are excellent sources of outside advice, once the general area for the facility has been determined. With a few exceptions, there is usually just one electric or gas utility to service a city and its suburbs. Therefore, the representatives of that utility should be unbiased in recommending sites in the entire metro area. Utility people try to work with local real estate brokers to become a clearinghouse of information on available buildings and land within the service area.

Government Agencies. State and local government development agencies, as well as local chambers of commerce, are also reliable information sources once the decision as to community has been made. Some large metro areas have several chambers of commerce or government development officers. Since these people are motivated to attract new industry into their own area, make sure the area is where you really want to be before relying on this source of advice.

Consultants. Finally, a consultant may provide an unbiased source of advice. In selecting a consultant, one important consideration is whether the individual is truly independent and objective. Some individuals who use the term *consultant* are also involved in other activities, such as real estate brokerage, which may affect their objectivity in handling the site search.

There are three reasons to bring in an outside consultant. First, and most importantly, is objectivity. Second, the consultant may have extensive experience in site seeking, and this experience will save time. Finally, the consultant represents a source of executive time without a long-term commitment. A detailed site search takes many hours which may not be available from members of your organization, and hiring new executives to handle the job would be foolish if the activity will end when the site has been selected.

In looking at the cited alternatives, the most objective sources of outside advice are either a public utility representative or a consultant. Whatever the case, be sure that the outside advisor is truly independent and objective.

Requirements Definition

Your search for a location must be modified and directed by your specific requirements as a warehouse user. Therefore, to prepare for a successful site search, you need to define these requirements carefully.

Transportation. Since transportation has traditionally had a ham-and-eggs relationship with warehousing, the transportation requirements for the new warehouse are of utmost importance. Consider which modes of transportation are required. (All warehouses need trucks, and some depend heavily upon rail, water, air, or a successful combination of these modes.) While delivery zones become less important in these deregulated times, the user must also consider zones and costs of transportation to specific sites.

To the extent that a warehouse is a marketing tool, it is important to consider the relationship of the proposed site to the locations of the planned users. Beyond just looking at locations, consider transportation costs and order-cycle times to serve various potential users. The warehouse user should not really care where the inventory is held, as long as product can be delivered in a timely fashion and at a reasonable price.

Labor. The labor market is probably less important for most warehouses than for the typical manufacturing plant. The degree of importance of the labor market depends upon the nature of the warehousing operation. If the proposed operation has a high degree of automation and relatively little touch labor, the availability of well-motivated workers may be of minor importance. On the other hand, labor can be of critical importance in other warehousing operations.

Inventory Tax. There can be wide variations in taxes, particularly those affecting inventory, in some metropolitan areas. Taxes can be a critical competitive factor when the warehouse inventory has high value.

Community Attitudes Community attitudes toward the new warehouse should be carefully studied by every site seeker. In most communities, a clean and quiet warehouse development is considered preferable to the many manufacturing operations that cause pollution, congestion, or other conditions that are detrimental to the quality of life. Yet, some communities are opposed to any new industrial development, even warehousing. If such opposition exists, it is best to recognize it and look elsewhere. A sample requirements definition for a wholesaler/distributor is shown in Table 5.2.

New versus Existing Space. A requirements definition should certainly consider whether or not a new building is necessary or whether an older one could be adapted for this use. In the past, it was generally assumed that the best locations for future growth were the undeveloped suburban areas where good rehabilitation opportunities are not easily found and new construction was necessary. Therefore, a new building in the suburbs was seen as a better business investment than a reconditioned older building located closer to the center of the city. Also, tax regulations, including those covering depreciation, tended to treat most favorably a warehouse user who constructed a new building rather than reconditioned an old one.

Table 5.2. Wholesaler Distributor Site Requirements Definition

1. The corporation should own that real estate which is used to perform its distribution function.
2. The company should look for a facility of approximately 30,000 square feet with ample land for truck parking and expansion, a site ranging from three to five acres.
3. The location should be within Franklin County, preferably on the east side of the county.
4. The only transportation mode necessary is trucking, with ample land for parking of trailers. Rail service could be an interesting option for resale, but it should not be a requirement.
5. The building should have characteristics which suggest a high-quality image for sales people and employees. It should also project an image of distribution efficiency.
6. The function of the building is primarily as a fast-turn distribution center. Storage space is incidental, since space for dead or slow-moving items can be readily acquired from public warehouse sources.

However, this is changing. New tax legislation has provided impetus for increased interest in the preservation, conversion, and adaptive reuse of older buildings.

The 1978 Revenue Act was the first law to offer incentives for rehabilitation. The Economic Recovery Tax Act of 1981 altered those incentives. This act provided no tax credits for buildings less than 30 years old. A 15 percent credit is granted for a building between 30 and 39 years old, and a 40-year-old building will qualify for a 20 percent tax credit. Today there are many still-usable 30-year-old buildings that have high ceilings and were designed for materials handling systems.

Financial decisions are an important part of a requirements definition. How important is the availability of mortgage financing at favorable rates?

Fluctuating Space Requirements. If space needs are somewhat volatile, the availability of overflow space, either from the public warehouse market or from short-term lease space, is an important consideration. It is difficult to construct or to purchase a building which is the right size on a year-round basis. Therefore, the warehouse user may find it best to develop a relatively small permanent building, utilizing overflow space within the community for seasonal requirements.

A Summary of the Selection Process

The first step in the selection process is to determine the macro location and reduce it to the micro location. It is important to do this, since it forces the analyst to go through certain processes of elimination. First, determine the largest possible universe that could be considered in picking the site. Then systematically narrow this down, sometimes using the process of elimination as certain alternatives are considered and for good reason are rejected. In moving from macro to micro, the analyst must bear in mind the reasons why the organization is looking for a new site. Four common reasons for seeking a new warehouse were previously outlined, and if the reason for choosing or rejecting certain criteria does not tie in with the organization's original reason for making the search, clearly something is wrong.

As sources of information are checked, an important warning is to believe nothing anyone says. If one informant states that a specific site has never had any history of flood, look for a second opinion from another party who cannot possibly be influenced by the first informant. Only if multisource checking produces consistent answers should one have confidence in the information.

In moving through the site analysis, there are several general areas that must be carefully considered to be sure they do not present problems for the intended use. These are zoning, topography, existing buildings or other improvements on the site, landscaping, access to the site, storm and sanitary sewage, water, sprinklers and other fire protection systems, power, fuel, and taxes.

It is also very valuable to have contingency plans. If site A is the preferred site, it is wise to have selected a site B which is almost as good and equally available. Then, in the event that the bargaining for site A should break down, it is well to let the seller discover that there is a fallback site.

The process of dealing with the site selection decision cannot be discussed too often. Other distribution decisions are correctable, but a poor choice for a warehouse site is a decision which, while not irreversible, is often very costly to correct. For this reason, finding a location for a new warehouse is one of the most challenging business decisions the average distribution executive is ever likely to make.

A checklist which can be a useful aid in analyzing a location follows.

1. General information
   a. Site location (city, county, state):
   b. Legal description of site:
   c. Total acreage:
   Approximate cost per acre:
   Approximate dimensions of site:
   d. Owner(s) of site (give names and addresses):
2. Zoning
   a. Current:
   Proposed:
   Master plan:
   Anticipated:
   Is proposed use allowed? [ ] yes [ ] no
   b. Check which, if any, is required: [ ] rezoning [ ] variance [ ] special exception
   Indicate approximate cost and time required:
   Probability of success: [ ] excellent [ ] good [ ] fair [ ] poor
   c. Applicable zoning regulations (attach copy):
   Parking/loading regulations:
   Open space requirements:
      Office/portion:
      Maximum building allowed:
      Warehouse/DC portion:

Percent of lot occupancy allowed:
Other:
Setbacks, if required:
Height restrictions:
Noise limits:
Odor limits:
Are neighboring uses compatible with proposed use?
[ ] yes [ ] no

d. Can a clear title be secured? [ ] yes [ ] no
Describe easements, protective covenants, or mineral rights, if any:

3. Topography
   a. Grade of slope:
   Lowest elevation:
   Highest elevation:
   b. Is site: [ ] level [ ] mostly level [ ] uneven [ ] steep
   c. Drainage: [ ]excellent [ ] good [ ] fair [ ] poor
   Is grading necessary? [ ] yes [ ] no
   Cost of regrading:
   d. Are there any: [ ] streams [ ] brooks [ ] ditches [ ] lakes [ ] ponds [ ] marshlands
   Are they: [ ] on site [ ] bordering site [ ] adjacent to site
   Are there seasonal variations? [ ] yes [ ] no
   e. What is the 100-year flood plan?
   f. Is any part of site subject to flooding? [ ] yes [ ] no
   g. What is the groundwater table?
   h. Describe surface soil:
   i. Does site have any fill? [ ] yes [ ] no
   j. Soil percolation rate: [ ] excellent [ ] good [ ] fair [ ] poor
   k. Load-bearing capacity of soil: ____lb/ft^2
   l. How much of site is wooded?
   How much to be cleared?
   Restrictions on tree removal:
   Cost of clearing site:
4. Existing improvements
   a. Describe existing improvements:
   b. Indicate whether to be: [ ] left as is [ ] remodeled [ ] renovated [ ] moved [ ] demolished
   Cost:

5. Landscaping requirements
   a. Describe landscaping requirements for building parking lots, access roads, loading zones, and buffer if necessary:
6. Access to site
   a. Describe existing highways and access roads, including distance to site (include height and weight limits of bridges and tunnels, if any):
   b. Is site visible from highway? [ ] yes [ ] no
   c. Describe access including distance from site to:
      (1) interstate highways
      (2) major local roads
      (3) central business district
      (4) rail
      (5) water
      (6) airport
      Describe availability of public transport:
   d. Will access road need to be built? [ ] yes [ ] no
      If yes, who will build?
      Who will maintain?
      Cost?
      Indicate:
      (1) curb cuts
      (2) median cuts
      (3) traffic signals
      (4) turn limitations
   e. Is rail extended to site? [ ] yes [ ] no
      Name of railroad(s):
      If not, how far?
      Cost of extension to site:
      Who will maintain?
      Is abandonment anticipated? [ ] yes [ ] no
7. Storm drainage
   a. Location and size of existing storm sewers:
   b. Is connection to them possible? [ ] yes [ ] no
   c. Tap charges:
   d. Where can storm waters be discharged?
   e. Where can roof drainage be discharged?
   f. Describe anticipated or possible long-range plans for permanent disposal of storm waters, including projected cost to company:
8. Sanitary sewage
   a. Is public treatment available? [ ] yes [ ] no
      If no, what are the alternatives?

b. Is sanitary sewage to site? [ ] yes [ ] no
Location of sewer mains:

c. Cost of laterals (from building to main)—include surface restoration if necessary:

d. Tap charges:

e. Special requirements (describe fully):

f. Describe possible or anticipated long-range plans for permanent disposal of sewage, including projected cost to company:

9. Water

a. Is water line to site? [ ] yes [ ] no

b. Location of main:
Size of main:

c. Water pressure:
Pressure variation:

d. Hardness of water:

e. Source of water supply:
Is supply adequate? [ ] yes [ ] no

f. Capacity of water plant:
Peak demand:

g. Who furnishes water meters?
Is master meter required? [ ] yes [ ] no
Is submetering permitted by code? [ ] yes [ ] no
Preferred location of meters: [ ] outside [ ] inside

h. Are fire hydrants metered? [ ] yes [ ] no
If yes, who pays for meter installations?

i. Attach copy of water rates, including sample bill for anticipated demand, if possible:

10. Sprinklers

a. What type of sprinkler system does code permit?

b. Is there sufficient water pressure for sprinkler system?
[ ] yes [ ] no

c. Is water for sprinkler system metered? [ ] yes [ ] no

d. Is separate water supply required for sprinkler system?
[ ] yes [ ] no

e. Where can sprinkler drainage be discharged?

11. Electric power

a. Is adequate electric power available to site? [ ] yes [ ] no
Capacity available at site:

b. Describe high-voltage lines at site:

c. Type of service available:

d. Service is [ ] underground [ ] overhead

e. Reliability of system: [ ] excellent [ ] good [ ] fair [ ] poor
f. Metering is [ ] indoor] [ ] outdoor
g. Is submetering permitted? [ ] yes [ ] no
h. Indicate if reduced rates are available for:
(1) heat pumps [ ] yes [ ] no
(2) electric heating [ ] yes [ ] no
i. Indicate applicable electrical code (attach copies if possible):
j. Attach copy of rates, including sample bill for anticipated demand, if possible:

12. Fuel
a. Gas:
(1) Type of gas available:
(2) Capacity:
Present:
Planned:
(3) Peak Demand:
Present:
Projected:
(4) Location of existing gas lines in relation to site:
(5) Pressure of gas:
(6) Metering is [ ] indoor [ ] outdoor
(7) Is submetering permitted? [ ] yes [ ] no
(8) Is meter recess required?
(9) Who furnishes gas meters?
(10) Indicate limitations, if any, on new installation capacity requirements:
(11) Attach copy of rates, including sample bill for anticipated demand, if possible:
b. Coal:
(1) Source of supply:
Reserves:
(2) Quality of coal available:
Cost (per million Btu) delivered:
(3) Method of delivery:
c. Oil:
(1) Source of supply:
Volume available:
(2) Quality of oil available:
Cost (per million Btu) delivered:
(3) Method of delivery:
d. Taxes
(1) Date of most recent appraisal:

(2) Real estate tax-rate history, last 5 years:
(3) History of tax assessments, last 5 years:
(4) Proposed increases, assessments, and tax rates:
(5) Are any abatement programs in effect? [ ] yes
[ ] no
If yes, describe.
(6) Is site in an Enterprise Zone? [ ] yes [ ] no
Duty-free zone? [ ] yes [ ] no
(7) Have any special taxes been assessed? [ ] yes [ ] no
If yes, describe:
(8) Indicate anticipated or possible major public improvements:
(9) Services provided for taxes paid:
Local:
County:
State:
(10) What is state policy on inventory tax, floor tax, etc.?
Is it a free port state? [ ] yes [ ] no
If no, describe assessment dates, procedures, and tax rates:
(11) Indicate rates for:
Personal income tax:
Corporate income tax:
Payroll tax:
Unemployment compensation:
Personal property tax:
Sales and use tax:
Worker's compensation:
Franchise tax:
Other taxes:
(12) Indicate taxation trends:
(13) Are industrial revenue bonds available? [ ] yes
[ ] no

6
Warehouse Space and Layout Planning

Jerry D. Smith

Vice President, Tompkins Associates, Inc., Raleigh, North Carolina

J. Eric Peters

Senior Engineer, Tompkins Associates, Inc., Raleigh, North Carolina

Space is a primary, finite resource common to all warehouses. The amount of space available, the physical nature of the space, and the arrangement, or layout, of the space are critical to the operating efficiency and effectiveness of the warehouse. Consequently, proper planning of warehouse space and layout requirements is needed to ensure that all the objectives of the warehouse are adequately met. This chapter addresses proper space planning and layout planning for the warehouse.

Warehouse Space Planning

Space planning is the part of the science of warehousing concerned with making a quantitative assessment of warehouse space requirements. As is true of any science, space planning possesses a very specific methodology, and it consists of the following general steps:

1. Determine what is to be accomplished.
2. Determine how to accomplish it.
3. Determine space allowances for each element required to accomplish the activity.
4. Calculate the total space requirements.

The first two steps of the space planning process define the activity and the techniques, equipment, information, and so on, to be used in performing that activity. Step three involves determining the space requirements of each element that goes into performing the activity. In warehousing, these elements might include personnel and personnel services, material handling and material storage equipment, maintenance services, and utilities. Finally, step four combines the space requirements of the individual elements to obtain total space requirements.

Two major activities in a warehouse require space planning: receiving and shipping activities, and storage activities. The following sections of this chapter transform the general space planning methodology outlined above into very specific methodologies for the receiving and shipping activities, and for the storage activities.

Space Planning for Receiving and Shipping

The most important functions of a warehouse occur on the receiving and shipping docks. Unfortunately, these are also the most neglected areas of a warehouse. The transfer of control of merchandise from the source or carrier of the merchandise to the warehouse usually takes place on the receiving dock. On the shipping dock, the transfer of control of merchandise from the warehouse to the user or carrier of the merchandise usually takes place. If these transfers of control are not accomplished efficiently, safely, and accurately, the warehouse cannot possibly meet its objective of satisfying customer requirements, regardless of the quality of the other aspects of the warehouse. An important prerequisite of efficient, safe, and accurate receiving and shipping activities is enough space in which to perform them. The following methodology should be followed to determine the space requirements of receiving and shipping activities.

Define the Materials Received and Shipped. The first step in space planning for receiving and shipping operations is to define what is to be accomplished, that is, to define the materials to be received or shipped. An excellent tool for this is the Receiving and Shipping Analysis Chart

(RSAC). A completed RSAC appears in Figure 6.1. The first five columns of the RSAC define what is to be received or shipped, and column 7 shows when the receipts and shipments will occur. For an existing warehouse, the information for the first seven columns of the RSAC can be obtained by reading old receiving reports or shipping releases to determine what has actually been received or shipped in the past. This historical data can then be tempered, based on projections of future business activity. For a new facility, historical data is not available; consequently, base the information requirements of the first seven columns of the RSAC on forecasts of the types and volumes of material that will be received or shipped.

It is seldom practical to have a separate entry on the RSAC for each individual stock-keeping unit, and, in fact, it is usually undesirable to do so. It is impractical because most warehouses store thousands of different stock-keeping units and completing the RSAC for each would be an extremely time-consuming job. It is undesirable because the forecasts from which the information is obtained are inevitably wrong. Consequently, planning a warehouse based on specific item requirements will result in an inaccurate warehouse plan.

A much better strategy for completing the RSAC is to establish generic categories of items and then to complete the RSAC for each generic category. The items in a given generic category should have similar characteristics with respect to type of item and unit load received, stored, or shipped. Developing generic categories reduces the number of entries on the RSAC to a manageable level. Another advantage is that fluctuations in requirements for individual stock-keeping units will have less impact because they will affect a generic category, not just one unit.

Columns 8 and 9 of the RSAC list the types of carriers that might handle each generic category of material. The important characteristics include the length, width, height of the carrier bed off the roadway, and the clearance height of the top of the carrier. This information can be readily obtained for an existing warehouse by contacting the freight carriers used in the past or, for a new warehouse, by contacting the carriers projected for use in the future. The freight carriers should be able to predict the types and characteristics of carriers that will be used over the next 5 to 10 years, for the types and quantities of materials that will be warehoused.

The last two columns of the RSAC deal with the methods and time required to unload the carrier on the receiving dock or to load the carrier on the shipping dock. This information will prove valuable in determining labor and material handling equipment requirements to perform the receiving and shipping activities.

Company A.R.C., Inc. Date March 18, 1986 Raw Materials ____ In-Process Goods ____

Prepared by J. Smith Sheet 1 of 1 Plant Supplies ____ Finished Goods ____

	Unit Loads				Size of Shipment (Unit Loads)	Frequency of Shipment	Transportation		Material Handling	
Description (1)	Type (2)	Capacity (3)	Size (4)	Weight (5)	(6)	(7)	Mode (8)	Specs (9)	Method (10)	Time, hr (11)
Steel pipe plug, 1.00 in diameter × 0.50 in	Wooden crate	3200 pcs.	2 ft × 2 ft × 4 ft	825 lb	12 crates	Quarterly	Truck	34 ft × 8 ft × 7 ft	Fork truck	0.75
Aluminum bar 2.75 in × 250 in × 16 ft	Bundles	25 bars	12.5 in × 14 in × 6 ft	1625 lb	25 bundles	Quarterly	Open-bed truck	34 ft × 8 ft	Crane	5.00
Stainless steel bar, 0.875 in × 12 ft	Bundles	36 bars	6 in × 6 in × 12 ft	900 lb	7 bundles	Semiannual	Open-bed Truck	34 ft × 8 ft	Crane	1.00
Rubber O ring, 0.75 in diameter	Cartons	40,000 O rings	12 in × 18 in × 3 ft	125 lb	2 cartons	Semiannual	Truck	20 ft × 8 ft × 7 ft	Handtruck	0.25
Brass bar, 0.75 in diameter × 12 ft	Bundles	36 bars	6 in × 6 in × 12 ft	720 lb	14 bundles	Semiannual	Open-bed truck	34 ft × 8 ft	Crane	2.00

Figure 6.1. Receiving and shipping analysis chart.

Determine Dock Requirements. After the materials to be received or shipped have been defined, the next step is to determine the requirements for the receiving or shipping dock bays. Two questions must be addressed: (1) How many dock bays are required? and (2) How should the dock bays be configured?

The number of dock bays required is a function of the time intervals between carrier arrivals at the dock and the time required to service the carriers upon arrival, and simulation is the proper tool for determining this requirement. (Refer to Chapter 9 for more information on the use of simulation in the warehouse.)

Two basic dock configurations exist: 90° docks and finger docks. With a 90° dock, Figure 6.2*a*, the truck is positioned at the dock so that the angle between the truck and the dock is 90°. At a finger dock, the angle between the truck and the dock is less than 90°. For example, for a 45° finger dock, shown in Figure 6.2*b*, the angle between the truck and the dock is 45°. The differences between 90° docks and finger docks lie in the amount of space required for dock operations inside and outside the warehouse. Figure 6.2 shows that a 90° dock requires less width (the distance parallel to the building) and more depth (the distance perpendicular to the building) than a finger dock. Therefore, a 90° dock requires less inside warehouse space and more outside space than does a finger dock. The amount of inside space required by finger docks decreases as the angle of the finger dock increases, but it is always greater than the space required by a 90° dock. As the angle of the finger dock increases, the outside space required also increases, but it is always less than the space required by a 90° dock.

Typically, space inside a warehouse is more expensive than space outside a warehouse; therefore, 90° docks are more popular than finger

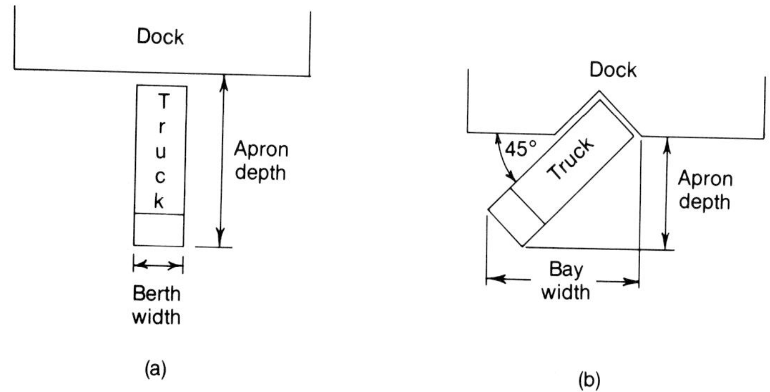

Figure 6.2. Basic dock configurations. (*a*) **90° Dock** (*b*) **45° Finger dock**

docks because they require less inside space. When outside space is at a premium, however, because of the shape of the warehouse site or the need to expand, finger docks are a much more attractive dock configuration.

Tables 6.1 and 6.2 give general guidelines for required dock bay widths and apron depths for 90° docks and finger docks, respectively. It should be noted that the apron depths for 90° docks given in Table 6.1 are for an unobstructed dock. Where trucks must back into the dock alongside other trucks, the apron depths given in Table 6.1 should be increased by the length of the truck.

Additionally, the apron depths given in Tables 6.1 and 6.2 assume clockwise backing by trucks into the dock area. Trucks should enter a receiving or shipping dock area in a counterclockwise direction of travel to allow the truck to back into the dock berth in a clockwise direction of travel. Clockwise backing enables the truck driver to clearly see the rear of the truck as it turns into the dock berth. However, when backing counterclockwise, truck drivers must rely on rearview mirrors to guide their approach to the dock. At first glance, this issue may appear trivial; however, experience has shown that counterclockwise backing requires that the apron bay depth be approximately 20 feet greater than that required for clockwise backing. In those instances in which counterclockwise travel about a warehouse is not possible owing to site configuration or location, either a truck turnaround area should be provided or 20 feet should be added to the apron bay depths given in Tables 6.1 and 6.2.

Table 6.1. Space Requirements for 90° Docks

Truck length, ft	Dock width, ft	Apron depth, ft
40	10	46
	12	43
	14	39
45	10	52
	12	49
	14	46
50	10	60
	12	57
	14	54
55	10	65
	12	63
	14	58
60	10	72
	12	63
	14	60

Table 6.2. Space Requirements for Finger Docks for a 65-Foot-Long Truck

Dock width, ft	Finger angle, degrees	Apron depth, ft	Bay width, ft
10	10	50	65
12	10	49	66
14	10	47	67
10	30	76	61
12	30	74	62
14	30	70	64
10	45	95	53
12	45	92	54
14	45	87	56

For additional information on planning dock facilities and vehicle interface requirements, refer to Chapter 8, "Facilities Planning," and Chapter 11, "Dock Design."

Determine Maneuvering Allowances Inside the Warehouse. The maneuvering space required on a receiving or shipping dock consists of the space needed to enter and exit the carrier and to travel between the carrier and the buffer area, into which incoming material is deposited, or the staging area, from which outgoing material is retrieved (Figure 6.3). The first component of the receiving or shipping dock maneuvering space is the area occupied by the dock leveling device. The amount of space required will vary according to the type of leveling device used. Generally, temporary inside dock leveling devices will occupy 3 to 7 feet, measured from the dock face, while permanent inside dock leveling devices will require 4 to 10 feet of inside warehouse space. Other types of dock leveling devices are installed outside the warehouse or on the truck itself and require no inside warehouse space allowances. (See Chapter 8, "Dock Design," for more details.)

The second component of the receiving or shipping dock maneuvering space is an aisle located between the back edge of the inside dock leveling device and the receiving buffer area or shipping staging area. This aisle allows unloading/loading personnel and equipment to enter and exit the carrier and to travel to the appropriate buffer or staging area. The dock maneuvering aisle should not be a main warehouse aisle; travel in this aisle should be restricted to dock personnel and equipment actively servicing carriers. The existence of other traffic within the dock maneuvering aisle will inevitably result in injuries to both dock personnel and the other traffic. The required width of the dock maneuvering

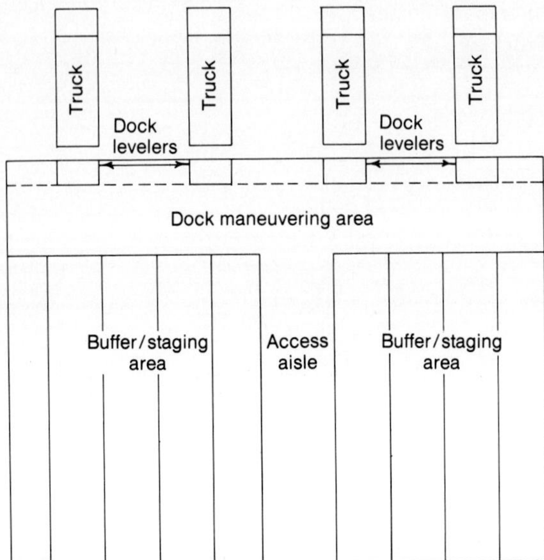

Figure 6.3. Receiving/shipping dock space requirements.

aisle depends on the type of material handling equipment used to service the carriers. Generally, 6 to 8 feet are recommended for manual handling and nonpowered material handling equipment, whereas 8 to 12 feet are sufficient for powered material handling equipment.

Determine Buffer and Staging Area Requirements. A buffer area for a shipping dock should be located behind the dock maneuvering aisle (Figure 6.3). The receiving buffer area serves as a depository for the materials unloaded from the carrier. The receiving buffer area allows the dock personnel to concentrate on unloading the carrier for fast receiving "throughput." Fast receiving throughput is essential for companies with large investments in their own trucking fleets. For companies without their own trucking fleets, it avoids demurrage, or detention, charges. Once the carrier is unloaded and released, a more thorough check-in and inspection of the merchandise can be performed within the receiving buffer area.

The shipping staging area serves as an accumulation point for the merchandise that comprises a shipment. Various levels of accumulation may be established within the shipping staging area. For example, individual line items that make up a customer order, the customer orders that comprise a shipment, or the shipments for a particular region can be accumulated. Activities performed within the staging area might include packing, unitizing, or verifying that the entire customer order or shipment is ready for loading onto the carrier.

Specifying accurately the optimum amount of receiving buffer space or shipping staging space is a very difficult task. Unfortunately, an incorrect amount of space will reduce greatly the efficiency and effectiveness of the receiving or shipping operation. The impact will be particularly severe if too little buffer space or staging space is provided. Too little buffer or staging space will lead to dock congestion that will inevitably cause lost material, damaged material, split shipments, and erroneous shipments. Determining the amount of buffer or staging space required is largely a matter of the degree of control which exists over the work load of the dock area. The more uncertain the receiving or shipping work load is throughout the day, the more flexible the receiving buffer area or the shipping staging area must be. For example, if a warehouse has the ability to schedule carrier arrivals, and if that schedule is adhered to, then chances are good that the receiving buffer area or shipping staging area can be limited to one truckload of material per dock bay. However, if carrier arrivals are not controlled, and if they are extremely heavy during certain parts of the day and extremely light during other parts of the day, the amount of buffer or staging area must be based on how much area is required during the surge periods of the day. Requirements for buffer area or staging area in existing warehouses should be determined by analyzing historical shipping patterns to identify the surge periods and volumes. For new facilities, the anticipated suppliers and users of the warehouse should be asked for estimates of when and in what quantities their materials will be received or shipped; then, the buffer and staging area allocations can be based on the anticipated surges in activity.

Aisle space must be provided within the buffer or staging area. This aisle space is not intended for use in placing materials in or taking them out of the buffer or staging area. Instead, it provides access to and egress from the dock area to other parts of the warehouse. Materials should be placed in the buffer and staging areas from one end and taken out from the other end; therefore, intrabuffer-area and intrastaging-area aisles should be kept at a minimum. The width of a buffer or staging area aisle depends on the type of traffic that will use the aisle. Powered equipment traffic will require a wider aisle than predominantly pedestrian traffic. Likewise, aisles with bidirectional travel need to be wider than for single-direction travel.

Determine Dock-Related Space Requirements. Several dock-related space requirements exist which support the receiving and shipping functions. These include:

1. Office space
2. Receiving hold area
3. Trash disposal
4. Empty pallet storage
5. Truckers' lounge

Office space must be provided for receiving and shipping supervision and for clerical activities. Approximately 125 square feet of office space should be provided for each dock employee who will regularly work in the office. Oftentimes, the supervisor's office space will be located within the dock area, and many of the receiving and shipping clerical and data-processing activities will be combined with similar activities in the remainder of the warehouse.

A receiving hold area is essential for accumulating received material that has been rejected during a receiving or quality-control inspection and that is awaiting either return to the vendor or some other form of disposition. Rejected material should never be allowed to accumulate in the receiving buffer area. To do so will surely cause unsatisfactory merchandise to be accepted by the warehouse. A separate and distinct receiving hold area must be allocated. The amount of space required for the receiving hold area depends on the type of material likely to be rejected, the specific inspection process followed, and the timeliness of disposition of the rejected merchandise.

Dock operations, particularly receiving functions, generate a tremendous amount of trash, including corrugated boxes, binding materials, broken and disposable pallets, bracing, and packing materials. Space must be allocated within the receiving and shipping areas for disposal of these items. Failure to do so will result in poor housekeeping, congestion, unsafe working conditions, and a loss of productivity. Oftentimes, receiving and shipping functions are planned without concern for trash disposal and so must sacrifice space allocated for some other function to hold the trash. Dock operations generate trash; therefore, be prepared.

In most warehouses, loads often arrive unpalletized or on pallets with odd dimensions and require palletizing or repalletizing. A store of empty pallets must be readily available to the dock area so that this activity can be accomplished.

A truckers' lounge is an area to which truck drivers are confined when not servicing their trucks. The truckers' lounge should include seating, magazines, and, ideally, refreshment facilities, telephones, and private toilet facilities to provide everything the trucker needs while waiting for his or her truck to be serviced. General space requirements for a basic truckers' lounge are approximately 125 square feet for the first trucker, and an additional 25 square feet for each additional trucker expected in the lounge at the same time. Consequently, a truckers' lounge designed for an average of three truckers would require approximately 175 square feet.

The purpose of the truckers' lounge is to effectively control the movements of the trucker while on site. Doing so will eliminate many potential problems related to trucker safety, theft and pilferage, labor-union campaigning, and warehouse employee productivity.

Space Planning for Storage Activities

The second major area in a warehouse that requires space planning is the storage activity. Storage space planning is particularly critical because the storage activity accounts for the bulk of the space requirements of a warehouse. Inadequate storage space planning can easily result in a warehouse that is significantly larger or smaller than required. Too little storage space will result in a world of operational problems, including lost stock, inaccessible material, poor housekeeping, damaged material, safety problems, and low productivity. Too much storage space will breed poor use of space so that it appears that all the available space is really needed. The result will be high space costs in the form of land, construction, equipment, and energy.

To avoid these problems, storage space planning must be approached from a quantitative viewpoint as opposed to a qualitative assessment of requirements. The following sections present the scientific methodology of storage space planning, that, when followed, will generate a quantitative and defensible assessment of storage space requirements.

Define the Materials to Be Stored. The first step in storage space planning, as in receiving and shipping planning, is to define what is to be accomplished; that is, to define the materials to be stored. A useful tool in defining the materials to be stored is the Storage Analysis Chart (SAC) given in Figure 6.4. The first five columns of the SAC define what materials are to be stored, columns 6 through 8 specify how much is to be stored, and columns 9 through 12 define how the materials are to be stored.

If a receiving and shipping analysis chart (Figure 6.1) has been completed, the information in the first five columns can likely be used in

Company A.R.C., Inc. Date March 18, 1986 Raw Materials ____ In-Process Goods ____

Prepared by J. Smith Sheet 1 of 1 Plant Supplies ____ Finished Goods ____

	Unit Loads				Quantity of Unit Loads Stored			Storage Space			
Description (1)	Type (2)	Capacity (3)	Size (4)	Weight (5)	Maximum (6)	Average (7)	Planned (8)	Method (9)	Specs (10)	Area, ft^2 (11)	Ceiling Height Required, ft (12)
Steel pipe plug, 1.00 in diameter × 0.50 in	Wooden crate	3200 pics.	2 ft × 2 ft × 4 ft	825 lb	14	8	12	Pallet rack	25 ft × 10 ft × 3 ft	66	9
Aluminum bar, 2.75 in × 2.50 in × 16 ft	Bundles	25 bars	12.5 in × 14 in × 16 ft	1625 lb	30	17	30	Two cantilever racks	Four-arm dual rack, 5 ft × 16 in × 8 ft	160	8
Stainless steel bar, 0.875 in × 12 ft	Bundles	36 bars	6 in × 6 in × 12 ft	900 lb	7	4	7	Cantilever rack	Four-arm dual rack, 4 ft × 12 in × 10 ft	48	10
Rubber O ring, 0.75 in diameter	Cartons	40,000 O-rings	12 in × 18 in × 3 ft	125 lb	2	1	2	Storage shelf	Metal frame, 12 ft × 2 ft × 8 ft	24	8
Brass bar, 0.75 in diameter × 12 ft	Bundles	36 bars	6 in × 6 in × 12 ft	720 lb	15	8	14	Cantilever rack	Four-arm dual rack, 4 × ft 12 ft × 6 ft	48	6

Figure 6.4. Storage analysis chart.

the first five columns of the SAC. Changes might be necessary only if the unit load to be stored is different from the unit load received or shipped. However, the generic categories of materials that are on the RSAC should also be recorded on the SAC. If an RSAC has not been completed (which might be true if one is analyzing the storage space requirements in an existing facility where the dock requirements are not under investigation), the information requirements for columns 1 through 5 of the SAC can be obtained by physically surveying the existing storage areas. The survey would proceed by identifying, generically classifying, measuring, and weighing the unit loads presently in the storage areas.

Columns 6 and 7 of the SAC list the maximum and average number of unit loads of each category of material that should be on hand. In most firms, determination of inventory policy falls outside the control of warehouse management and into the realm of production and inventory control. Consequently, the inventory control department should be queried for the maximum and average inventory levels for each category of material listed in column 1 of the SAC.

Column 8 of the SAC cites the planned inventory level of each type of material for which storage area will be planned. Determining the proper inventory level is directly related to the storage philosophy that will be used for each category of materials. The different storage philosophies and the decision process one should use to determine the proper planned inventory level will be discussed in the next section of this chapter.

The last four columns of the SAC define the physical characteristics of the storage area being planned. These physical characteristics include the method of storage and the space requirements of that method.

Determine Storage Philosophy. Once the maximum and average inventory levels have been recorded, the inventory level that will be used as a basis for planning required storage space must be determined. The planned inventory level depends on the philosophy followed in assigning material to storage space. There are two major material-storage philosophies: fixed, or assigned, location storage; and random, or floating, location storage. In fixed-location storage, each individual stock-keeping unit is always stored in a specific location, and no other stock-keeping unit may be stored in that location, even though that location may be empty.

With random-location storage, any stock-keeping unit may be assigned to any available storage location. A stock-keeping unit in location A one month might be stored in location B the following month, and a different stock-keeping unit stored in location A.

The amount of space planned for a stock-keeping unit is directly related to the method of assigning space. If fixed-location storage is used, a given stock-keeping unit must be assigned sufficient space to store the maximum amount of the stock-keeping unit that will ever be on hand at any one time. For random-location storage, the quantity of items on hand at any time will be the average amount of each stock-keeping unit. In other words, when the inventory level of one item is above average, another item will likely have an inventory level that is below average; the sum of the two will be close to the average.

Oftentimes, the storage philosophy chosen for a specific stock-keeping unit will not be strictly fixed-location storage or random-location storage. Instead, it will be a combination of the two. A grocery store is an excellent example of combination, or hybrid, location storage. Fixed-location storage is used in the sales area of a grocery store where the consumers shop. Pickles are assigned a fixed location, and only pickles are stored in that location. Pickles will not be found in any other location in the sales area of the grocery store. In the back room, or storeroom, of the grocery store, however, the excess, or overstock, merchandise is usually stored randomly. Pickles may be found in one location one week and in a different location the next week. Because combination-location storage is based on a mixture of fixed-location storage and random-location storage, its planned inventory level falls between the fixed-location quantity and random-location quantity. At what point between the fixed-location and random-location quantity the planned inventory level falls is dependent upon the percentage of inventory to be assigned to fixed locations.

To summarize, the planned inventory level recorded in column 8 of the storage analysis chart in Figure 6.4 should be equal to the maximum inventory level (column 6) for fixed-location storage, the average inventory level (column 7) for random-location storage, or a value between the maximum and average quantities for combination-location storage.

Determine Alternative Storage Method Space Requirements. The space requirements of a storage alternative are directly related to the volume of material to be stored and to the use-of-space characteristics of the alternative. The two most important use-of-space characteristics are aisle allowances and honeycombing allowances. Aisle allowance is the percentage of space occupied by aisles within a storage area. Aisles are necessary within a storage area to allow accessibility to the material being stored. The amount of aisle allowance depends on the storage method, which dictates the number of aisles required, and on the material-handling method, which dictates the size of the aisles. Expected aisle allowance must be calculated for each storage alternative under consideration.

Honeycombing allowances are the percentage of storage space lost because of ineffective use of the capacity of a storage area. The unoccupied area within the storage location is honeycombed space. Honeycombing occurs whenever a storage location is only partially filled with material and may occur horizontally and vertically. For example, Figure 6.5*a* presents a plan view of a bulk storage area in which material can be placed four units deep. Because the bulk storage area is full, no honeycombing occurs. In Figure 6.5*b,* however, two units of product A and one unit of product B have been removed, leaving three empty slots. No other items can be placed in these slots until the remaining units of A and B have been removed (otherwise, blocked stock will result), so

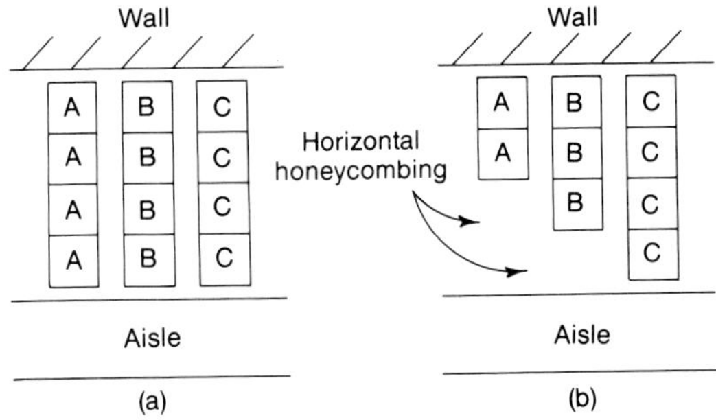

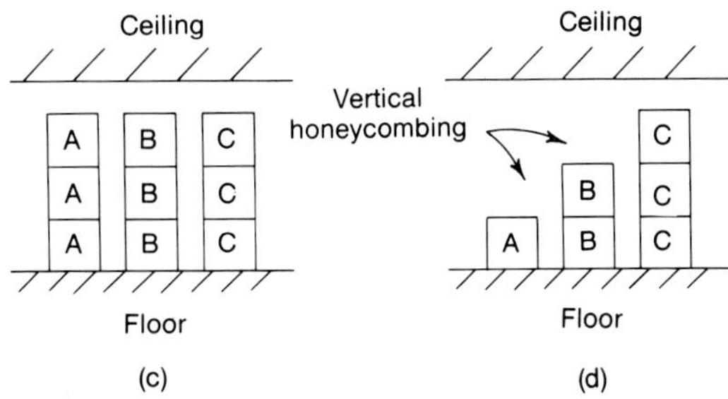

Figure 6.5. Horizontal and vertical honeycombing. (a) Plan view of bulk storage area—no honeycombing. (b) Plan view of bulk storage area showing horizontal honeycombing. (c) Elevation view of bulk storage area—no honeycombing. (d) Elevation view of bulk storage area showing vertical honeycombing.

these slots are horizontal honeycombing losses. Figure 6.5*c* is an elevation view of a bulk storage area in which material can be stacked three units high. Here again, the storage area is full and no honeycombing occurs. In Figure 6.4*d*, however, two units of product A and one unit of product B have been removed, leaving three empty slots. To avoid blocked stock or poor stock rotation, no other units can be placed in these slots until the remaining units of A and B have been removed. Consequently, the empty slots are vertical honeycombing losses. Horizontal and vertical honeycombing losses will occur. Efforts to totally eliminate honeycombing may improve space utilization but will assuredly result in increased material handling costs related to double handling loads, material damage, and lost productivity. Honeycombing, while it should be minimized, must be considered a natural and allowed-for phenomenon of the storage process. For each storage alternative under consideration, the expected honeycombing allowance must be estimated.

Once the aisle and honeycombing allowances for a storage method alternative have been determined, a space standard can be calculated for that storage method. A space standard is a benchmark which defines the amount of space required per unit of product stored. Given the space standard and the total inventory of a class of items to be stored, the total space required for that class of items can then be calculated. Figure 6.6 presents an example illustrating the calculation and use of space standards.

Warehouse Layout Planning

Objectives of a Warehouse Layout

Before layout planning can begin, the specific objectives of a warehouse layout must be determined. In general, the objectives of a warehouse layout are:

1. To use space efficiently
2. To allow the most efficient material handling
3. To provide the most economical storage in relation to costs of equipment, use of space, damage to material, and handling labor
4. To provide maximum flexibility in order to meet changing storage and handling requirements
5. To make the warehouse a model of good housekeeping

Item A requires special environmental control. A special storage area must be established to house the maximum quantity of Item A expected ever to be on hand. The maximum storage requirement for Item A is 300,000 cases. Item A is to be stored on pallets, four pallets high. In a bulk storage-analysis chart, how much space should be allocated for the storage of Item A?

- Case size = 2 ft × 1 ft × 1 ft (height) = 2 ft^3
- Palletized = 48-in × 48-in × pallet 4 tiers high = 64 ft^3 (32 cases/pallet)

Step 1. The aisle allowance (AA) has been estimated from a proposed layout to be 10%. The honeycombing allowance (HA) has been estimated to be 25%.

Step 2. The pallet height is 6 in, and the clearance between stacks is 4 in. The total space required for one four-pallet-high stack of Item A is therefore:

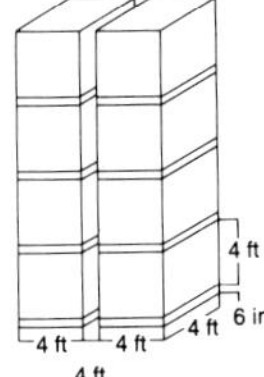

Stack width × stack depth × stack height = (4 ft + 0.33 ft) × 4 ft × [(4 ft + 0.5 ft) × 4] = 312 ft^3 for 128 cases of Item A

Step 3. The inclusion of allowances for aisles and honeycombing results in the following space standard:

$$\frac{312 \text{ ft}^3}{(1 - \text{AA})(1 - \text{HA})(128 \text{ cases})}$$

$$= \frac{312 \text{ ft}^3}{(1 - 0.10)(1 - 0.25)(128 = \text{cases})} = 3.61 \text{ ft}^3/\text{case}$$

Step 4. The total storage space required for the maximum anticipated volume of Item A, using the proposed storage method, is:

Total storage space required = 300,000 cases × 3.61 ft^3/case
= 1,083,000 ft^3 or 60,167 ft^2 having a clear stacking height of 18 ft

Figure 6.6. Example of space standard calculation for storage area.

The astute observer will notice that the first three objectives above are essentially identical to the overall objectives of a warehouse. Recall from Chapter 1 that the objectives of a warehouse are:

1. To maximize effective use of space
2. To maximize effective use of equipment
3. To maximize effective use of labor

4. To maximize accessibility of all items
5. To maximize protection of all items

It is true that the objectives of both a warehouse itself and of the warehouse layout are almost redundant. This shows the importance of layout planning to warehouse planning. Without a good warehouse layout, it is impossible to have a good warehouse. The objective of layout planning is to arrange and coordinate the space, equipment, and labor resources of the warehouse. Poor layout planning can undermine superior space, equipment, and personnel planning. Put another way, accomplishing the objectives of warehousing depends on having a good layout. If the warehouse layout is bad, the warehouse as a whole will be bad; and if the warehouse as a whole is bad, chances are the warehouse layout is bad.

The fourth objective of a warehouse layout recognizes the fact that warehousing exists not within a static, unchanging environment, but within a dynamic, ever-changing environment. If the mission of a warehouse changes, the warehouse layout should very likely change, too, to adapt to the new mission. However, a good warehouse layout possesses the flexibility to absorb minor variances in expected storage volumes and product mixes with few or no alterations required. This flexibility allows the warehouse to function even if the forecasts on which it was planned prove to be wrong, as they inevitably do.

The last objective of warehousing follows the principle that there is efficiency in order. Good housekeeping is essential to good warehousing; a good warehouse cannot exist without good housekeeping. Yet good housekeeping by itself will not ensure a good warehouse. If the space, equipment, personnel, and layout are not properly planned, all the housekeepers in the world could not get a warehouse to function. But poor housekeeping will surely undermine good space, equipment, personnel, and layout planning.

Layout Planning Methodology

Warehouse layout planning methodology consists of two steps:

1. Generate a series of warehouse layout alternatives.
2. Evaluate each alternative against specific criteria to identify the best warehouse layout.

These two steps are discussed in the following sections.

Generate Alternative Layouts. Generating alternative warehouse layouts is as much art as it is science. The quality of the layout alternatives will largely depend on the skill and ingenuity of the layout planner. This fact is crucial to the most common approach to generating layout alternatives: template juggling. The word *juggle* means to skillfully manipulate a group of objects to obtain a desired effect. Consequently, template juggling is the skillful manipulation of a group of templates, models, or other representations of warehouse space, equipment, and personnel in order to obtain a warehouse layout that meets objectives. In other words, template juggling is a trial-and-error approach to finding the proper arrangement and coordination of the physical resources of the warehouse.

The quality of the alternatives created from template juggling depends on the creativity of the layout planner. Unfortunately, layout planners often either lack creativity or do not attempt to express their creativity. Many layout planners approach the problem with a preconceived idea about what the solution should be. They tend to bias the layout planning process toward that preconceived solution. As a result, creativity is stifled. Oftentimes, the layout chosen for a new warehouse looks exactly like the layout used in the old warehouse. The generation of layout alternatives thrives on the creativity of the layout planner, yet many layout planners withhold this basic and essential ingredient.

The generation of warehouse layout alternatives should be accomplished by the following procedure:

1. *Define the location of fixed obstacles.* Some objects in a warehouse can be located only in certain places, and they can have only certain configurations. These objects should be identified and placed in the layout alternative first, before objects with more flexibility are located. Some fixed obstacles are building support columns, stairwells, elevator shafts, lavatories, sprinkler system controls, heating and air-conditioning equipment, and, in some cases, offices. Failure to consider the location of these types of items first will prove disastrous. The warehousing corollary to Murphy's law states, "If a column can be in the wrong position, it will be." Don't be the layout planner who designs a warehouse and buys the storage and material handling equipment only to find that, when the equipment is installed, the location of the building columns makes an aisle too narrow for the handling equipment.

2. *Define the location of the receiving and shipping functions.* Oftentimes, the configuration of the warehouse site will dictate the location of the receiving and shipping functions. When this is not true,

however, the receiving and shipping location decision becomes an important one. Receiving and shipping are high-activity areas and should be located so as to maximize productivity, improve material flow, and properly utilize the warehouse site. The location of access roads and railroad tracks, if rail service is required, are important considerations in locating receiving and shipping. The question of whether receiving and shipping should be located together or in different areas of the warehouse must be addressed. Common receiving and shipping docks can often result in economies of scale related to sharing space, equipment, and personnel. Separate receiving and shipping areas may, on the other hand, be best to ensure better material control and reduce congestion. Energy considerations are important. Where a choice exists, receiving and shipping docks should not be located on the side of the building that faces north. Avoiding this location reduces the amount of heat loss in the winter from northerly winds entering the warehouse through open dock doors. The preferred location of the receiving and shipping docks is the south side of the warehouse, with east and west as second and third choices. The particular weather patterns around each warehouse site should be examined, however, to identify the prevailing wind direction at that particular site, and the docks should be located away from the prevailing wind.

3. *Locate the storage areas and equipment, including required aisles.* The types of storage areas and equipment to be used will dictate to some extent the configuration of the storage layout and the aisle requirements. Be sure to make allowances for the fixed obstacles in the facility. Main warehouse aisles should connect the various parts of the warehouse. The cross aisle at the end of the storage area may need to be wider than the aisles within the storage area, depending on the type of material handling equipment used. For example, a sideloading fork truck that can operate with a 7-foot-wide storage aisle may require 12-foot-wide cross aisles at the ends of the storage aisles to allow maneuvering into and out of the storage aisle.

4. *Assign the material to be stored to the storage locations.* This step in the generation of layout alternatives ensures that storage allowances have been made for all the items to be stored. In addition, it allows the performance of a mental simulation of the activities expected within the warehouse.

5. *Repeat the process to generate other alternatives.* Once a warehouse layout alternative has been established following the four steps just outlined, the process must be repeated many times to generate additional layout alternatives. Different layout configurations, build-

ing shapes, and equipment alternatives should be used. The creativity of the layout planner should be taxed to ensure that each succeeding layout alternative is not essentially identical to the first.

Evaluate the Alternative Layouts. A number of warehouse layout philosophies exist to serve as guidelines for the development of an effective warehouse layout. Each warehouse layout alternative should be evaluated against the specific criteria established for each of these warehouse layout philosophies.

1. *Popularity Philosophy.* An Italian economist named Pareto once stated that 85 percent of the wealth of the world is held by 15 percent of the people. On closer examination, Pareto's law actually pertains to many areas other than wealth; one of these areas is warehousing. In a typical warehouse, it is not unusual to find that 85 percent of the product throughput is attributable to 15 percent of the items, that another 10 percent of the product throughput is attributable to 30 percent of the items, and that the remaining 5 percent of the product throughput is attributable to 55 percent of the items. Consequently, the warehouse contains a very small number of highly active items (often called *A items*), a slightly larger number of moderately active items (often called *B items*), and a very large number of infrequently active items (often called *C items*). The warehouse layout philosophy on popularity suggests that the warehouse should be planned around the small number of highly active items that constitute the great majority of the activity in the warehouse. The popularity philosophy maintains that the materials having the greatest throughput should be located in an area that allows the most efficient material handling. Consequently, high-turnover items should be located as close as possible to the point of use.

The popularity philosophy also suggests that the popularity of the items help determine the storage method used. Items with the greatest throughput should be stored by methods that maximize the use of space. For example, if bulk storage is used, high-turnover items should be stored in as deep a space block as possible. Because the items are moving into and out of storage at a relatively high rate, the danger of excessive honeycombing losses is reduced, and excellent use of space will result from the high-density storage. Low-throughput items in deep bulk storage blocks will cause severe honeycombing losses because no other items can be stored in that location until the low-throughput item is removed.

2. *Similarity Philosophy.* Items that are commonly received and/or shipped together should be stored together. For example, consider a retail auto parts distributor. Chances are that a customer who requires

a spark plug wrench will not buy, at the same time, an exhaust system tailpipe. Chances are good, however, that a customer who buys the spark plug wrench might also require a condenser, points, and spark plugs. Because these items are typically sold (shipped) together, they should be stored in the same area. The exhaust system tailpipe should be stored in the same area that the mufflers, brackets, and gaskets are stored. Sometimes, certain items are commonly received together, possibly from the same vendor; they should be stored together. Similar types of items should be stored together. They will usually require similar storage and handling methods, so their consolidation in the same area results in more efficient use of space and more efficient material handling.

An exception to the similarity philosophy arises whenever items are so similar that storing them close together might result in order-picking and shipping errors. Examples of items that are too similar are two-way, three-way, and four-way electrical switches; they look identical but function quite differently.

3. *Size Philosophy.* The size philosophy suggests that heavy, bulky, hard-to-handle goods should be stored close to their point of use. The cost of handling these items is usually must greater than that of handling other items. That is an incentive to minimize the distance over which they are handled. In addition, if the ceiling height in the warehouse varies from one area to another, the heavy items should be stored in the areas with a low ceiling, and the lightweight, easy-to-handle items should be stored in the areas with a high ceiling. Available cubic space in the warehouse should be used in the most effective way while meeting restrictions on floor loading capacity. Lightweight material can be stored at greater heights within typical floor loading capacities than heavy materials can.

The size philosophy also asserts that the size of the storage location should fit the size of the material to be stored. Do not store a unit load of 10 cubic feet in a storage location capable of accommodating a unit load of 30 cubic feet. A variety of storage location sizes must be provided so that different items can be stored differently. In addition to looking at the physical size of an individual item, one must consider the total quantity of the item to be stored. Different storage methods and layouts will be used for storing two pallet loads of an item than will be used for storing 200 pallet loads of the same material.

4. *Product Characteristics' Philosophy.* Some materials have certain attributes or traits that restrict or dictate the storage methods and layout used. Perishable material is quite different from nonperishable material, from a warehousing point of view. The warehouse layout must encourage good stock rotation so that limitations on shelf life are met.

Oddly shaped and crushable items, subject to stocking limitations, will dictate special storage methods and layout configurations to effectively use available cubic space. Hazardous material such as explosives, corrosives, and highly flammable chemicals must be stored in accordance with government regulations. Items of high value or items commonly subject to pilferage may require increased security measures, such as isolated storage with restricted access. The warehouse layout must be adapted to provide the needed protection. The compatibility of items stored close together must also be examined. Contact between certain individually harmless materials can result in extremely hazardous reactions and/or significant product damage. Specific steps must be taken to separate incompatible materials. Oftentimes, the easiest way to accomplish this objective is through the warehouse layout.

5. *Space Utilization Philosophy.* This philosophy can be separated into four areas:

a. Conservation of space
b. Limitations on use of space
c. Accessibility of material
d. Orderliness

The conservation-of-space principle asserts that the maximum amount of material should be concentrated within a storage area, the total cubic space available should be effectively used, and the potential honeycombing within the storage area should be minimized. Unfortunately, these objectives often conflict. Increased concentration of material will usually cause increased honeycombing allowances. Therefore, determining the proper level of space conservation is a matter of making trade-offs among the objectives that maximize use of space.

Limitations on use of space must be identified early in the layout planning process. Space requirements for building support columns, trusses, sprinkler-system components, heating-system components, fire extinguishers and hoses, and emergency exits will affect the suitability of certain storage and handling methods and layout configurations. Floor loading capacities will restrict storage heights and densities.

The warehouse layout should meet specified objectives for material accessibility. Main travel aisles should be straight and should lead to doors in order to improve maneuverability and reduce travel times. Aisles should be wide enough to permit efficient operation, but they should not waste space. Aisle widths should be tailored to the type of handling equipment using the aisle and the amount of traffic expected.

The orderliness principles emphasize the fact that good warehouse housekeeping begins with housekeeping in mind. Aisles should be well marked with aisle tape or paint; otherwise, materials will begin to infringe on the aisle space and accessibility to material will be reduced.

Void spaces within a storage area must be avoided, and they must be corrected when they do occur. If a storage area is designed to accommodate five pallets and, in the process of placing material into that area one pallet infringes on the space allocated for the adjacent pallet, a void space will result. Because of this, only four pallets can actually be stored in the area designed for five pallets. The lost pallet space will not be regained until the entire storage area is emptied.

To evaluate the alternative warehouse layouts, each should be compared against specific expectations relative to the layout philosophies as discussed. The layout planner must determine which layout philosophies are most important under the specific circumstances and attempt to maximize the extent to which the recommended layout adheres to these philosophies. Remember, however, that warehousing exists within a dynamic environment; therefore, the layout chosen as best today may not be so as conditions change. The extent and timing of changing requirements in the future should be forecast and a warehouse master plan established to effectively compensate for the changing mission of the warehouse.

7
Personnel Planning

Alexander Keeney, Jr., PCMH

Manager, Industrial Engineering, Random House, Inc., Westminster, Maryland

Labor Standards

In order to plan for the staff of a warehouse, it is necessary to identify and establish standards for the tasks to be performed and the amount of time each task should take. This includes each and every function, from receiving to shipping. As the activities grow in size, the standards of a department or activity may multiply and become more complex, but certain standards are basic in each of the warehouse activities.

Basic Warehousing Activities. A warehouse has 10 basic activities that must be executed to move an item accurately and expeditiously from receiving to shipping, and all functions must be available on site at each warehouse. These activities are as follows:

1. Receiving
2. Inspection
3. Inventory control
4. Storage
5. Replenishment
6. Order-picking
7. Checking
8. Packing and marking

9. Staging and consolidating
10. Shipping

Receiving. The basic function of the receiver is to unload the incoming material; count the material; and record any overage, shortage, or damage on the receiving ticket and driver's copy of the freight bill. The receiver also records on a receiving form the name and address of the supplier, date, name of item received, part number, quantity received, purchase order shipped against, discrepancies in quantity, and/or notation of possible damage. Purchasing and Inventory Control receive documents of this receipt.

Inspection. The purpose of the inspection is to determine if the product meets the specifications and drawing requirements of the purchase order. Documents are prepared to notify Purchasing and Inventory Control as to the status of the material. Some businesses eliminate incoming warehouse inspection by having source inspection. However, a sample check of the inventory should still take place during order fulfillment to discover in-house damage. The degree of inspection is relative to the methods and frequency of handling in the warehouse.

Inventory Control. Materials are moved from the inspection area to one of two points: (1) the picking location (in the case of a picking outage) or (2) a storage location (i.e., a bin, shelf, or rack). To control the location and quantities of materials on hand, it is important that the responsibility for routing materials to the proper locations be assigned. This is a clerical function.

Storage. The physical act of moving materials from inspection and placing them in storage is generally a lift-truck operator's function. In very small operations, a manual lift truck might be used for the horizontal move, then the product hand-transferred from the pallet to the storage shelf.

Replenishment. When warehouse management assigns a special area for picking stock, it is necessary to move cartoned stock from general storage to the prime picking area. This is the replenishment function.

Order-picking. With an invoice or customer order ticket, the order picker goes about selecting the items in the quantity requested and unitizing them in a container, on a pallet, or at a station. The most critical part to this function is the document on which the order is written. The document must be a legible copy; preferably a typed original, well-spaced, and of characters large enough to see under warehouse lighting conditions.

Checking. Each order should be checked for accuracy of item, quantity, and condition. If experience dictates, a sampling checking plan can be put into effect. The level of sampling is determined by the incidence of damage.

Packing and Marking. Less than full-carton quantities of products have to be packaged and packed for shipment. In some warehouse operations, split-case handling is avoided by shipping the next full case if the order for a broken case lot is 50 percent or more of a carton or by shipping short if the order for a broken case lot is less than 50 percent of a carton. This technique is generally practiced within the same firm, as when a central warehouse ships stock to a regional warehouse. The marking or labeling of a container must contain the consignor, consignee, invoice number, purchase order, account number, quantity, and description. There are variations of this data, such as bar code labeling, industry marking practices, governmental marking requirements, and international symbology.

Staging and Consolidation. This function is necessary for gathering together the various orders for a single customer. The orders may have entered the cycle at different times; or, if entered into the cycle as a group, may have been held up within the cycle for several legitimate reasons. Orders are also staged by carriers that service different regions of the distribution area that the warehouse serves.

Shipping. The actual loading of the carrier is generally accomplished by one of four methods or a combination thereof: hand-pallet truck; forklift truck; mobile containers, such as are used in grocery and retail drug distribution; and "bricklayering," i.e., hand-stacking cartons, much the same as laying bricks on one another when building a wall.

Defining Daily Routine Tasks. With the 10 basic warehouse functions described, the next step in establishing standards is to determine the tasks performed within a given function. Some are performed with a degree of frequency during any given work period or shift. Other tasks are performed only a few times per day or week. When establishing work standards for a given function, the frequently performed tasks should have a time value assigned, expressed as an amount of time per unit or cycle, or a number of units per hour. The infrequently performed duties can be summarized as a total amount of time per day or week. Such nonroutine tasks found in a warehouse could include:

1. Obtaining supplies, such as carton tape
2. Totalizing receiving reports
3. Writing inspection summaries
4. Replacing missing or damaged merchandise on order

As shown in Table 7.1, identifying the repetitive and nonrepetitive duties of each department enables department supervisors and ware-

Table 7.1. Repetitive and Nonrepetitive Tasks

Weekly Functions	
1. Receive 800 pallets @ 0.05 hr/pallet	40.00
2. Receive operating supplies @ 1.0 hr/day	5.00
3. Move 800 pallets to Inspection Department @ 0.02 hr/pallet	16.00
4. Deliver operating supplies @ 1.0 hr/day	5.00
5. Take receiving bills to office @ 0.25 hr/day	1.25
6. Clean up work areas @ 0.25 hr/day	1.25
7. Obtain and deliver lift truck to Maintenance for service @ 0.25 hr/day	1.25
8. Obtain operating supplies @ 0.50 hr/week	.50
	70.25

Normal Calculations

$$\frac{\text{70.25 hr weekly workload}}{\text{40 hr/week/employee}} = \text{1.75 employees required}$$

Recommended Calculation

$$\frac{\text{70.25 hrs. weekly workload}}{\text{37.5 available hrs/week/employee}} = \text{1.88 employees required}$$

house management to determine the approximate crew size or staffing requirement for each warehouse function.

From such a basic summary, one can better manage people and time, and evaluate the impact of any changes in procedure or work assignment. If you are in a warehouse situation in which employees can be assigned to departments as needed, it can be seen by the example that if the function has two employees, one can work in another area for 9.75 hours (normal) during the week. Any change in procedure can be identified and the impact noted. If freight bills are to be taken to the office more frequently, an employee's availability to another department will be reduced. If obtaining operating supplies is taking longer, it can highlight the need to investigate the cause and reschedule the trip to the supply center, if necessary.

Document Nonproductive Activities. In addition to having standards that define the tasks in each warehouse activity and the time to perform them, it is also important to know about and control employee activity that is not warehouse oriented. It is surprising what an analysis reveals of normal, justifiable actions that occur daily. Supervisors are responsible for a given number of employees. Management expects these employees to be productive during their 40 hours per week, with reasonable allowances for fatigue, personal time, and uncontrollable delays in the work process. Yet, there are legitimate daily occurrences that reduce the number of hours the employee is available for productive work. In establishing work standards, some managements use a 7.5-hour shift per worker. This recognizes the two-coffee-break system so popular in American industry, as well as a shift start-up and clean-up allowance. Expected productivity is then measured against the 7.5 hours of "productive time" per employee, and the crew size for the expected work to be produced is determined accordingly. The frequently made management error is, for example, to consider 800 hours of work to be done at 8 hours per employee per day. This calculation requires 100 employees. This is not a pragmatic approach to staffing an operation. More correctly, 800 hours of work to be done at 7.5 hours per employee indicates that 107 employees are required. This more nearly reflects the reality of the situation.

Figure 7.1 illustrates a typical situation that occurs in industry. It would serve supervision and management well to analyze how employees legitimately spend time away from the job during the work shift. In the exhibit, there are 10 employees. Each is paid for 40 hours during the week being analyzed, except for Carter who went home ill one day (36 hours). It is important to note that the supervisor does not have the employees available to work for the full 396 hours in the example.

Column 1 represents the clocked hours, which is the number of hours normally said to be available to do an assigned amount of work. It is the number of hours for which an employee is paid (excluding sick pay). Column 2 is the amount of time lost each 40-hour work week due to a 10-minute start-up, two 10-minute coffee breaks, and a 10-minute clean-up–time allowance. This will vary with local warehouse practice. Column 3 is the time an employee requires, from the moment work stops until it is resumed, for dispensary aid, be it a cut finger, fever, headache, dizziness, lift-truck operator eye examination, or a company-required physical. Column 4 represents time lost due to personnel visits or programs. Column 5 concerns union business, which, depending on company practice, could be conducted on company time. Column 6 documents time employees are temporarily loaned to another department. Column 7 documents unmeasured work for a work assignment outside the normal duties of a worker. Column 8 documents no-fault lost time during which one or several group members cease productive functions through no fault of their own, such as for a machine malfunction. Column 9 represents the total of columns 2 through 8. Column 10 is the total amount of work theoretically assigned for this example and completed. Column 11 is the net amount of worker time available to do the work. The percent effective to payroll is found by dividing Column 10

Labor Utilization Index													
Employee	Payroll, hours (1)												
Adams	40	2.5	.6						3.1	40.0	36.9		
Brown	40	2.5				12.0			14.5	28.0	25.5		
Carter	36	2.3	1.5	1.2			5.5		10.5	22.0	25.5		
Davis	40	2.5			2.7				5.2	31.0	34.8		
Ewell	40	2.5		.8					3.3	35.0	36.7		
Fox	40	2.5	.2					.7	3.4	38.0	36.6		
Grey	40	2.5	.2			4.0	2.0		8.7	31.5	31.3		
Howe	40	2.5			.4				2.9	38.0	37.1		
Inn	40	2.5						3.1	5.6	35.0	34.4		
Joy	40	2.5	.5						3.0	40.0	37.0		
Summary	396.0	24.8	3.0	2.0	3.1	16.0	7.5	3.8	60.2	338.5	335.8	85.4	100.8

Figure 7.1. Labor utilization index.

by Column 1. It indicates that the group was only 85 percent effective. The percent effective to availability is found by dividing Column 10 by Column 11. It indicates the group was 100.8% effective.

If warehouse managers and supervisors do not perform some sort of record keeping and have some standards to measure against, it will be very easy to go astray in not recognizing employee efforts for what they are. Also, if nonproductive activities are not recorded, it will be difficult to spot trends in accident- or health-related incidents, excessive socializing when legitimately excused to visit other areas, or similar situations that affect the effective utilization of warehouse labor.

Establishing Labor Standards. Labor standards are important if one expects to have control of any given operation. Somewhere it was said that one must measure to manage. Managerially speaking, one must have benchmarks to determine if progress is being made and whether at an acceptable pace. The benchmark must be consistent to be a valid reference of measurement. Labor standards are the benchmarks. They are determined or established based on a given sequence of events. First, the warehouse must establish the basic functions of warehouse activity. For each function, management must determine the duties to be performed and how they are to be performed. This includes such characteristics as:

1. Frequency of an action, such as once per stock-keeping unit (SKU) or once per three SKUs or twice per SKU.
2. Degree of detail in performing a given duty. This could vary from tossing SKUs into totes, to requiring the exact placement of the SKU into cell #1 in the tote or, in the case of paperwork, "print in block letters only."
3. Quality consciousness should be considered. Receiving functions should require alertness to damaged incoming materials. A packer's standard may require a cursory examination of items being packaged for shipment.
4. Impositions of weight handling and limitation of weight being handled by a person or machine. This can include volume limits and limits on the mass of an item. In many warehouse activities, there are SKUs that are within the prescribed weight limits of an individual's lifting range, but the mass of the SKU dictates that either two or more employees or powered equipment is necessary to lift it safely. For example, a 35-pound item may be packed in a carton 75 inches by 75 inches by 5 inches. This would indeed be difficult for one employee to manage.

After the task has been described to management's satisfaction, it must be measured in terms of time to become a labor standard.

Labor Measurement

Labor measurement can be an excellent tool in controlling the costs of warehousing. However, the measurement must be acceptably accurate, and the administration of the labor measurement program must be within acceptable cost constraints. Before any further comment on warehouse labor measurement, let us consider the environment of the warehouse relative to work measurement. Work measurement began in the repetitive production environment. Consequently, emphasis was placed on very precise time measurements of highly repetitive tasks or actions. Tasks had to be identical to the activity units that were time studied if one expected the same time values to apply. The industrial engineers who were the time-study observers would question an elemental time if it varied by 3 percent from the arithmetic mean. It is very difficult to obtain this precision in warehousing activity and, for this reason, the industrial engineering "purist" avoided the warehouse as an area of practice. Since the measured work concept grew and flourished in the assembly area, it seems to have been tagged as a management tool for production areas only, and both labor and management avoided its use in warehousing. Education in business, economics, commerce, accounting, and industrial engineering focused the student's attention on production problem solving and control of direct costs (labor and material); indirect costs, such as warehouses, were ignored as areas in which traditional industrial engineering management techniques could be applied.

Measures of Warehouse Productivity. In a recent survey (February 1983) conducted by this author, it was found that warehouse management was using several methods to measure warehouse productivity. Eight "systems" in all are generally in use.

1. Cases per man-hour
2. Lines per man-hour
3. Pounds shipped
4. Lines per day
5. Orders per day
6. Dollar volume per day

7. Unit loads per hour
8. Hours actual versus hours standard

The first seven systems of measurement are not very reliable because too many variable factors affect an employee's performance. (1) The weight, size, and shape of cases and the variability of these physical features drastically affect the productivity of the worker. (2) Lines per man-hour does not reveal the (3) volume per line, which is a significant factor. For example, a line item of 100 pounds of steel is quickly and easily moved with a lift truck. However, moving 100 pounds of feathers could be a time-consuming, voluminous job. (4) Lines per day and (5) orders per day similarly do not take into account the physical variables. (6) Dollars per day does not correlate with the physical energies expended. Any price changes would require a mathematical analysis to plot and compare past and current activity to establish a performance standard. (7) Unit loads per hour would also be similar to (2), in which variables in the task go unrecognized.

The hours actual versus hours standard system is the most effective means of measuring warehouse labor. Time values are developed for the various general elements of the task, and a sum value is assigned to each invoice or to a batch of job tickets. In establishing the time values, one cannot be an industrial engineering purist. While each act of picking a box of pencils, a box of ball-point pens, and a box of felt-tip markers has a slightly different value, the warehouse industrial engineer should take the practical and realistic approach of establishing one value for all three items. The value could be based on average weight or on the most frequently occurring event. Hands-on experience in a particular environment should indicate the proper course of action. Time-studying the various warehouse functions is time-consuming and can be expensive, but the managerial control that results and the savings realized are worth the cost. With accurate measurement techniques management can, with a high degree of accuracy:

1. Determine staffing levels for a given level of activity
2. Plan personnel changes well in advance of need
3. Budget realistically and accurately and eliminate generalizations for warehouse budgets
4. Develop long-range warehouse forecasts based on long-range production and sales forecasts
5. Use work measurement in model simulation for analyzing, altering, or expanding warehouse activity

Sources of Labor Standard Systems. The United States Department of Agriculture and the Department of Defense have both published basic standards for warehousing and the steps for establishing warehouse standard costs systems. This data includes elemental descriptions, basic time values, and allowances. This data along with other useful charts, formulae, and analytical forms can be obtained in a booklet entitled, "Digest of Warehouse Cost Calculations and Handling Standards."[1]

For those interested in developing their own standards or gaining a working knowledge of applying work measurement to the warehouse activity, there is a comprehensive dissertation in Chapter 4 of the *Handbook of Industrial Engineering.*[2] There are also several consulting firms that will accept a company's employees as students for two- and three-week accelerated courses or will send staff members on site to conduct an on-site program of time-study analysis and work-standards development.

Benefits of Labor Measurement. Once labor measurement is in effect, there are several benefits to be gained:

- Both the worker and supervisor should have a clear understanding of how long any task should take.
- Incidents that cause delays in meeting the standard can be noted, isolated, and corrected.
- Staffing requirements can be easily determined when man-hours are related to product activity.
- Analytical charting is easier when working in hours per unit or hours per 1000 units.
- Management can predict, with reasonable accuracy, the consequences of changes in warehouse loading, software, methods, or layouts.

A word of caution! The use of measured labor alone is not sufficient to judge changes in operational schemes. Seasonal peaks and valleys must also be reckoned with as legitimate and very influential characteristics of planning and evaluation. Warehouse management in some cases must also be aware of where a product is in its life cycle to make judgments about its volume of activity.

Labor standards must also be prudently used by management and,

[1] Published by Marketing Publications Inc., National Press Building, Washington, DC 20045.

[2] Gavriel Salvendy (ed.), *Handbook of Industrial Engineering,* John Wiley, New York, 1982.

especially, first-line supervisors. Labor measurement is a guide to what can be reasonably expected as a consistent daily effort of output. One must recognize that the work environment and the employee's personal psyche affect daily performance. Good employees have bad days and fall below the established standard. Employees will also accept the challenge and exceed or "beat" the standards with some frequency. Supervisors must learn to recognize a periodic versus a patterned decline in productivity. The work standard must never become a device for enforcing continuously higher achievement as a means of the supervisor gaining management recognition. Productivity is increased and recognition is gained through improving the method, simplifying the process, or changing the layout. The cliché of "working smarter not harder" applies. Management must intelligently lead the workers to increase productivity; not threaten, bully, or deceive to obtain improved results.

Labor-Standard Maintenance. To be a meaningful management tool, labor-measurement values must be kept current. In the dynamics of daily routine and the pressing nature of everyday business, the maintenance of time values is often forgotten. If job conditions change so that there is difficulty in meeting the standard, time-value maintenance will be self-policing; there will be complaints. However, creeping changes may go unnoticed and unreported. The labor-measurement system then becomes valueless and can also be costly.

An actual case involved a standard that was not reviewed in total for 25 years. The time values for various subassemblies were changed individually as methods and equipments were improved. However, the formulae for some major components were ignored. This resulted in the company paying for more work than the shop actually had to do.

Administration of Labor-Measurement Systems. The administration costs of a labor-measurement system are the second reason for a lack of work measurement in the warehouse environment. It is simply not practical to undertake a program the benefits of which are exceeded by the cost of its administration. Warehouse operations are frequently so varied that a large pool of clerical help would be necessary to apply time-values to each order or invoice. However, some manual systems have been developed whereby orders or invoices are identified by zones of like activity, and a time value is applied per frequency of occurrence in a particular zone. This helps reduce administrative clerical labor. For example:

- Value *A* would be for picking all 24-count cartons of dry cereal. (Time value × number of cartons)

- Value *B* would be for picking all 24-count cartons of #303 cans of fruit, vegetables, and soups. (Time value × number of cartons)

Computerized Administration of Standards. The use of computers and computer-generated invoices or picking documents has opened the field of applying time values to the documents. It can be done in a fraction of a second by the computer. This eliminates the problem of excessive clerical help for a manual time-value program. A computerized time-value program requires an in-depth study of the order-picking program so that the industrial engineer knows each basic function of picking. Then the elemental data have to be grouped in natural and logical order. The data must be kept as simple as possible. Variable elements of a like nature should be combined to keep the program formula simple. This is where the work measurement purist must give way to reality in order to have a workable and manageable program. A sufficient number of observations have to be made to be sure that what is observed is representative of the work being done over a long time period.

To computerize time values, a detailed breakdown of the time values is of the essence. But, the most important consideration is to know how the computer identifies specific products. The computer logic must be thoroughly understood in order to organize time-study observations and develop standard data tables. If the computer has no way of recognizing a keg of nails, per se, or differentiating between a keg of nails and a box of carpet tacks, there are significant problems ahead. The computer recognition of commodities must be categorized so that basic standards can be developed for like items. In one case, the problems exist in weight per stock-keeping unit to be handled, cubic volume to be handled, and the dexterity with which both weight and volume are handled. As weight and cube vary, the time value by category will vary. There are many ways to categorize products in computers. Be sure each category or sphere of activity is organized and identified logically so that programmed time values will be properly indexed and applied to the picking document.

In a particular case of computer-generated work standards, the computer customized the picking standard as each invoice was generated. There were four basic order-picking concepts. As each invoice was being generated, the computer totaled the order by each picking concept and held these four totals in memory. The criteria of "picking concept by category" was determined by the total number of items per order and the total weight. Once volume and weight were determined, the correct standard was selected from memory and printed on the invoice. Such a technique saves many clerical hours, is relatively easy to maintain, and results in a standard tailored to each invoice.

Short Interval Scheduling. In addition to establishing work standards for historically indirect activities—warehouses, distribution centers, store rooms, receiving, and shipping—two additional tools are required to measure work effectively. The work must be scheduled and all time must be accounted for during the shift.

Short Interval Scheduling (SIS) or a variation of this scheduling technique should be used to allow for close supervisory control. Twenty-minute batches of assigned work for each order picker keeps the supervisor current with orders picked and picking problems or time delays encountered. The problem may be people, documents, stock-outs, or equipment. If these problems, as well as accomplishments, are reported on by each worker in 20-minute intervals, the involved supervisor will be more aware of the work situation than most counterparts in other warehouses. If work measurement is to be meaningful, management must act or react to that which affects measured work.

Supervision

The supervisor is the primary managerial contact with the worker. Generally, this is the level at which is set the tone of conduct regarding hourly employees attitude toward both production and the company in general. The supervisor's attitude toward the employees, personality, leadership capability, technical competence, comprehension of changing social conditions, awareness of currently developing situations, and constant focus on the future will determine his or her success. Warehouse supervision is basically the same as supervision in an assembly or production operation. The most important function is the proper utilization of people. This is brought about by the supervisor influencing the opinions, attitudes, and behavior of the workers to result in optimum productivity. The only two areas in which warehousing supervision differs from supervision in the production and assembly environment are the technical knowledge peculiar to warehousing and the ability to supervise employees who are frequently out of sight of the supervisor (spread throughout various storage and picking aisles).

Warehouses vary in physical size and in the size of staff. Since this handbook is intended to cover all warehouses, the comments must be taken in line with the size of the reader's organization and the degree of development of the organization. Larger businesses generally have a human resources or personnel department which can assist in training and developing supervisors and provide help and guidance in the complex areas of labor relations, human behavioral science, and understanding and complying with various employment regulations and laws.

Dynamics of Warehouse Supervision. The position of supervisor has changed dramatically during the 20th century. The age of authoritarian supervisor has passed. Modern supervisors must execute through good leadership. Those chosen to be supervisors must continue to develop leadership skills. Occupying a position of authority does give one authority but does not make one a leader. Leadership skill must be learned and developed; and the development is on-going. The dynamics of the work force require changing managerial attitudes. Supervisors should take advantage of any supervisory, labor relations, human relations, industrial psychology, or like programs being offered by the company, community and four-year colleges, industrial management clubs, or technical societies. Even degreed supervisors should take courses in the above to reinforce and remain current with concepts and trends in these areas. The relationship that develops between the supervisor and the work force is most critical. This relationship frequently determines if there will be an adversarial, "we-they" attitude or a harmonious "we-are-one" attitude. The worker and company are interdependent on each other. The company cannot function without employees, and employees cannot achieve economic goals without an employer. Working together in an harmonious atmosphere is what the supervisor must establish as a general goal.

Good supervision is a learned skill. The subject is very broad and has much depth. If a supervisor intends to progress through the ranks of management, the development of leadership skills is very important. The further one progresses into middle management, the more one needs to know how to accomplish company goals through the leadership of people.

Supervisory Responsibilities. A supervisor is responsible for knowing, understanding, and working with a variety of tasks, situations, and problems. The following is a list of duties, responsibilities, and concerns that a supervisor faces either daily or at some less frequent interval:

Planning. This includes setting present and future goals, and establishing procedures and policies to meet them. In some organizations, a production control function sets the daily production goal; in other organizations the supervisor must do this.

Organizing. This involves assigning workers to tasks.

Staffing. This includes selecting and training workers. Some businesses have a human relations department to assist in recruiting, selecting, and training workers. In less structured organizations, a supervisor may be responsible for recruiting workers. This is one of the areas in which the responsible supervisor must be aware of all the laws and regulations that govern the acts of the employer. The text of a help-wanted ad could be in violation of a law or regulation regarding discrimination as to age, sex, and/or physical ability. The employment application form may be in violation of a law. For example, "date of birth" is a legitimate piece of employment information *after* a person is hired. However, on an employment application it is considered to be age discrimination unless there is a bona fide reason for asking, e.g., when the company doubts the majority age of the applicant in reference to child labor laws or for valid insurance considerations.

Directing. This includes the daily supervision of employees as well as providing needed training to individuals or groups.

Controlling. This involves determining the priorities of the work tasks to accomplish the goals.

Technical Competence. This is the ability to operate the machinery and comprehend the operations and processes of the department.

Developing Employee Loyalty. This involves creating an atmosphere of trust between the workers and company. Create a we-are-one outlook. Earn the respect and approval of the employees by being firm but fair, being worthy of their trust, and helping them as well as allowing them to help you.

Praising Good Work. Constructively criticize errors. Praise is a public acclamation; criticism is personal and private.

Providing Opportunities. Give employees a chance to function with a minimum of supervision. However, be able to recognize and give close support to those who need it and seek it out.

Building Morale. Help develop your employee's attitude or frame of mind, be it toward the work task or the company.

Discipline. Be fair, firm, and keep a record of disciplinary actions signed by the employee and, if represented, by the shop steward.

Drugs and Alcohol. Be able to identify the problem and handle it in accordance with company policy.

Unionism. If the workers are under contract, be sure you know and understand the contract. Check and be sure that you are interpreting it in the same manner as other members of management.

Motivation. Understand what motivates employees to produce and how motivational factors will fluctuate.

Off-the-Job Influence. Be able to recognize, understand, and deal with nonwork factors that influence production, such as employee problems with finance; health; marriage; illness of other family members; children's welfare, behavior, and well-being; and similar categories that worry people. You are not expected to counsel in these areas, but by all means recognize that these factors affect employee attitude and performance and be ready to recommend that your human resources personnel talk with the employee.

Absenteeism. Learn its causes and corrective actions to take.

Adjusting to a Changing Work Force. Work forces change for many reasons, and the supervisor must be aware of these changes and respond accordingly. Laws and regulations as well as population mobility and immigration can affect a work force. As the make-up of the work force changes, the supervisor must come to understand the needs, desires, and social nature of the emerging majority of workers in order to maintain the necessary leadership skills. The work force may change as to age, sex, race, ethnic origin, and education.

Handling Grievances. Be it a union or nonunion shop, the supervisor must learn how to handle an employee grievance. The nature of the grievance may be such that it needs to be resolved at a higher level.

Budgeting. Be aware of operating costs and function within the established cost limits, keeping track of that which interferes with cost containment.

Quality. Meet the standards of performance established for the task.

Accident Prevention and Safety. Identify practices and conditions that could lead to accidents. Thoroughly investigate the circumstances of any accident, recording facts and not conjecture. Be an example; be safety conscious.

Terminations. A properly handled termination can be beneficial to both the employer and employee. It should be done with an explanation of the reason(s) for termination and should be done only after the emotions of the moment have subsided and the situation has been clearly thought out.

Preventing Theft. The warehouse environment, with its availability of finished goods, makes it a prime area for theft. The supervisor in the warehouse must be more aware of theft possibilities than supervisors in areas where the product is of little or no value to potential thieves.

Communications. Frequently, the art of listening and reading body language are emphasized as ways to improve communications. These are beneficial techniques. However, warehouse communications are frequently carried on by telephone and/or memo. The person originating the communication already knows the problem and circumstances. The difficulty is in conveying this knowledge to another party. Use proper shop terminology and be specific.

Laws and Regulations Important in Supervision. Supervisors in small warehouses generally do not have the staff support found in larger firms. Consequently, they must personally gain a working knowledge of laws and regulations affecting employment. There are at least 15 areas of concern.

1. State employer's liability and compensation act
2. Unemployment insurance
3. Social Security
4. State old-age and assistance programs
5. Fair Labor Standards Act
6. Acts governing the employment of females and minors
7. Walsh-Healy Act
8. Taft-Hartley Act
9. Veterans' Reemployment Rights Act
10. Equal Employment Opportunity Commission
11. Vocational Rehabilitation Act (governs employment of handicapped)
12. Civil Rights Act
13. Occupational Safety and Health Act (OSHA)
14. State-level OSHA
15. Employee Retirement Income Security Act (ERISA)

Basic Knowledge Requirements. Supervisors that function in warehouses without staff services should also expand their background to include a functional knowledge of methods analysis, work simplification, warehouse layout, equipment evaluation techniques, space utilization analysis, and materials handling principles.

Modern-day supervisors need a very broad background to meet all the responsibilities of the position. Continuing education in the various categories of supervisory duties and responsibilities is necessary to keep skills current.

Personnel

The personnel or human resources department is a highly developed staff function that handles many facets of a warehouse, as well as other types of businesses. This section deals only with those subjects that pertain especially to warehousing.

Safety. A safety program should be part of the warehouse operation, and the personnel department should either spearhead the program or actively monitor and guide the warehouse management in this area.

Lift-Truck Operator Training. By OSHA regulations, only trained and authorized operators shall be permitted to operate powered industrial vehicles. Source material can be obtained from the published OSHA regulations and ANSI B56.1, 1975.[3] A complete training and testing program including slides, test-course layout, and reference materials that can be purchased from the International Materials Management Society (IMMS).[4] Lift-truck manufacturers have also been a source of these programs. Industrial-truck operator training is important. Remember, possession of a motor vehicle driver's license *does not* qualify an employee as a powered industrial-truck operator. The training section of the personnel department should coordinate this program.

Physical Examinations. Personnel should also arrange for periodic examinations of powered industrial-truck and crane operators. Good natural or corrected vision as well as good depth perception are important. Good hearing is also necessary, especially for crane operators who use a system that combines audible communication and visual signals.

Training. Personnel may be responsible for employee training. For example, employees will need training when converting from a paper-and-pencil transaction system to an on-line, or microcomputer, system of records keeping, or from mechanical lift-truck operation to those using on-board microprocessors.

Testing. Lift-truck operators must be able to read load tickets and move tickets and shelf or pallet locations. They must be able to read and comprehend the address system used in a warehouse. The personnel department should establish a battery of tests to evaluate candidates for warehouse positions.

Unions

People are very conscious of unions and union activity, but surprisingly only about 20 percent of the industrial work force in the United States is union-represented. Employees' attitudes concerning unions vary geographically as well as demographically (e.g., urban vs. rural, skilled vs. unskilled workers). Probably the greatest influence concerning unions is whether the employees see themselves in a we-are-one environment or in a we-they situation.

Actions During Union Organizing. If the warehouse is nonunion and there is an indication that there is organizing activity, management

[3] American National Standards Institute, 345 East 47th Street, New York, NY 10017.

[4] International Materials Management Society, 3900 Capital City Blvd., Suite 103, Lansing, MI 48906.

should quickly obtain the services of a professional specialist or labor-lawyer for advice and direction. There are laws and rulings that specifically deal with the allowed and nonallowed activities of management, the employees, and the organizing union during the organizing period.

Labor law is a very complex subject and negotiations should not be undertaken by nonprofessionals. Management that has had proper counsel should be able to properly advise its employees and answer their questions concerning an organizing campaign. It is essential to have professional advice in such a critical matter and to have it early.

If the warehouse is functioning under a union contract, it is important for management to remember that all management rights and policies stand except as limited or prohibited in the contract. Actions and expectations are governed by a specific contract. What happens in labor relations at other warehouses may be note-worthy, but each company's obligations and rights are established in its own contract. What may have been done under one labor contract may in no way be applicable to another situation.

Discipline in a Union Environment. Management—especially first-line supervisors—should be trained. This training in dealing with disciplinary procedures should also be frequently reviewed. Such acts as fighting, drinking, drug use, gambling, stealing, and refusing a legitimate order require immediate supervisory action. It is important that this action be swift and correct, but it is just as important not to overreact. When possible, the supervisor should allow for tempers to cool before making a disciplinary decision. Cooling a temper can be as simple as going to the personnel manager or to the next echelon of management to discuss the situation and the intended disciplinary action. A rash action can be detrimental to the morale of the department if there is a "we-they" attitude and the supervisor has to back down on an impulsive decision. Such incidents contribute to polarizing attitudes.

The most frequent union situation a supervisor will probably deal with is a grievance. There can be several steps or levels a grievance can travel through; there is the potential for the grievance to be resolved at any of these levels. The first step is an informal one-on-one discussion in which a represented employee cites to the supervisor what is believed to be a violation of the existing labor agreement. The supervisor explains to the worker his or her understanding of the administration of the contract. If the disagreement cannot be resolved, a process as spelled out by the contract begins, whereby different levels of management and union officers attempt to resolve the issue. The contract frequently provides that if an issue cannot be resolved between the parties of the contract, the issue is submitted to arbitration for a third-party determination of a solution. Arbitration is expensive and both parties share the expense of the arbitrator's fee. It does bring an outsider's view into a situation which is really the business of two parties. Precedent has very little to do with an arbitrator's decision. Each case is evaluated independently based on the contract and included agreements. Even though one case may very closely parallel a previous case, the decision in the former may not be the same. Labor law is a field unto itself and differs from other law. Criminal law is based on guilt beyond a reasonable doubt. Tort law is based on the preponderance of evidence. Labor law is based on contract and intent of the parties.

Management and supervision should take advantage of every opportunity to improve their knowledge and understanding of unions and labor relations. As mentioned before, management needs labor to be able to engage in economic activity, and labor needs business in order to realize its monetary goals. We should strive to bring about an atmosphere in which both parties can achieve their goals to their mutual benefit.

Incentive Systems

Incentive systems can be utilized effectively in warehouses when customized to the conditions of the warehouse environment. The incentive system is a means of rewarding increased skill and effort with increased pay. This differs from management-directed work simplification, acquisition of technically advanced machinery, changes in product design, changes in shop and workplace layout, and changes in tooling that affect productivity potential. In these cases, benefits generally accrue to the employer and constitute a methods change. Historically, the incentive system was based solely on employee skill and effort. To earn incentive pay, the employee would have to expend more energy in performing the task, become more skillful, utilize time better during the shift, and develop better personal methods (workers are generally entitled to the benefits of their own methods improvements unless they are shared through the suggestion system).

In production operations, the repetitive nature of the work contributes to the justification of personal incentive programs. The implementation and administration of individual incentive programs has been profitable. However, the diversification of work, the broad base used to establish standards in a warehouse, plus the costs of administering such a program make an individual incentive program very difficult. In such a situation, group incentive is the more practical approach.

Before any incentive system is placed into operation, there should be a firm commitment by management to back the plan and follow through with the administration of the program. The plan should be thoroughly explained to the workers. The benefits that are to be realized by both management *and* the worker should be explained. The explanation should cover the effects on the system when new methods, new equipment, and/or new products enter the picture.

A problem with incentive wages is that too often the employees adjust their standard of living to the inflated rate. Then, when some economic influence necessitates a change that reduces take-home pay to the base level, the employees become unhappy. Some of the more modern plans that are more productivity oriented eliminate this problem. For productivity to be considered improved, there must be a permanent increase, rather than one based on a fluctuation. Once a new level of productivity is achieved, it is expected to be maintained, and the economic benefits are permanently shared between employees and employer. Since the beginning of the 20th century, there have been about 10 popular incentive plans that centered around individual skill and effort. These plans have all but passed away. The three most popular productivity plans are the Scanlon Plan, the Rucher Plan, and IMPROSHARE (IMproved PROductivity through SHARing)®.[5] These plans provide an incentive to improve productivity in which both the employees and employers gain. Rather than measure the results of individual skill and effort, the work force is evaluated as one. The gains are derived more from the permanent methods improvements than from fluctuating skill and effort improvements. Hence, the improvement in productivity is more constant.

Developing an incentive system for a particular warehouse should be done by people with expertise in the field. It is necessary to analyze the work site and attitude of the employees and develop what is best-suited to the type of warehouse operation under consideration.

Almost hand in hand with any productivity program must be an awareness of product quality. Quality must be maintained. Whether in warehousing or production, the goal is three-pronged. Deliver a *quality* product at an established *cost* within the allotted *time.* The framework of a warehouse incentive system or productivity measurement system should include factors to evaluate timeliness of orders fulfilled, shipping damage versus handling damage, and the cost of doing all this at an acceptable level of performance. One must be constantly aware of all three areas of responsibility. A supervisor can excel in one category while neglecting one or both of the other goals. The task is to coordinate all three in an harmonious relationship.

[5] IMPROSHARE was developed by Mitchell Fein, New Rochelle, NY. For more information contact: Industrial Engineering and Management Press, Institute of Industrial Engineers, 25 Technology Park, Norcross, GA 30092.

8
Facilities Planning

E. Ralph Sims, Jr., P.E., C.M.C.

Chairman of the Board, The Sims Consulting Group, Inc., Lancaster, Ohio

General Management Considerations of Facility Planning

A warehouse building is basically a weather protection device to store invested capital in the form of goods, and to provide work space for the people and equipment who must handle these goods and deliver them to customers or to manufacturing operations. Often, managers look upon the building as the key element in warehouse design because its high cost dominates the total facility investment. The traditional architectural viewpoint that the building must be beautiful and well located before its function is clearly defined often distorts the relationship among the cost of the building, the cost of the equipment within it, the value of the material to be stored, and the cost of the operation. As a result of these economic and attitude postures, management often retains the architect who, although competent as a building designer, constructs a building before defining its internal configuration. In such cases, column spacing, overhead clearances, door arrangement, floor loading, sprinkler and lighting patterns, and many other structural features are often designed without adequately coordinating these with the functional characteristics of the operation. The resulting conflicts can be costly in long-range labor expense, reduced facility capacity, operating limitations, and operating flexibility.

When designing a warehouse building, one must first establish the characteristics of the operation to be placed within it. If the building is a speculative design for public warehousing operations, forecasting the internal work pattern or transport interface requirements may be difficult or impossible. While it is essential to avoid "putting the cart before the horse" if one is to avoid designing a structure that inhibits operations and dictates performance patterns, this chapter nonetheless concentrates on the construction of the building itself.

Certain standard features must be included in the layout. The arrangement of the building on the site must also be considered. Very few warehouses are large enough the day they open. They must usually be expanded within a very few years. This mistake is based upon capital limitations, ultraconservative sales projections, overoptimistic inventory turnover estimates, and Parkinson's Law, which says that "the inventory grows to fill the available space."

For these and many other reasons, the arrangement of the building on the site is a critical design factor that must be addressed at the outset. Arrangement affects the external and internal traffic patterns, the building's expandability, and the character of the structural design. The existence of related facilities often dictates arrangement and constrains adjustment. These issues force the designer to recognize other operating characteristics as dominant over structural economics.

The recognition of energy as a major economic factor has introduced another element into warehouse design. Many warehouses operate with low temperatures or with no heat at all, depending upon both climate and the nature of the merchandise stored. The ultimate option in energy conservation is either to dress the workers for arctic temperatures or automate the system and ignore the need to heat the facility for human comfort. The ultimate option in comfort is air conditioning, which requires careful design of the building for energy and heat conservation. Thus, the structural configuration and the cost and use of energy, coupled with management's policy toward employee comfort, are significant design factors.

In summarizing this background, then, one must approach the building design from the point of view of the operation within it, the labor-relations factors involved, the site arrangement, the availability of capital, and the overall function of the facility. After these management and policy issues are settled, many structural and architectural options remain. Each should be evaluated in relation to the functional requirements of the installation. Once the optimum system has been designed to meet the needs of the operation and its configuration has been identified, cost considerations should be reviewed. The system concept can then be modified to optimize the relationship among the building design, system function, and capital expenditure.

Building Configurations and Design Elements

Two basic classes of warehouse buildings exist: the conventional, free-standing building within which warehousing operations are performed; and, the single-purpose, rack-supported structure, which, because it is designed as a machine or integrated system to perform a single task, is generally not considered reusable for other operations.

Many of the peripheral elements of a rack-supported structure are common to a conventional warehouse. The site arrangement, office space, employee services, truck and rail docks, and so on are similar. However, the structural considerations in these two types of buildings are significantly different.

First, let us identify some basic design elements and parameters of warehouse buildings that respond to operational requirements and govern the configuration of the building. These are:

1. Floor design
2. Overhead clearances
3. Column spacing
4. Rack-supported structures
5. Roof and wall design
6. Truck and rail dock design
7. Supporting services
8. Security and fire defense

In high rack-supported structures, such special design considerations as wind/soil factors, foundation stability, and rack stability, among others, must be addressed separately.

Floor Design

The floor of the warehouse is the working surface of the building. While the number of columns, the character of the walls, and the type of roof can all be varied depending upon structural and economic considerations, a badly designed floor affects the operation in many critical ways. *Thus, it is well to examine some of the characteristics of floor design which are significant to warehouse operations.*

Floor-Load Requirements. The floor design must meet specific load requirements which include:

Static Load Capacity. Static load capacity sufficient to support the stacks of merchandise and/or the legs of pallet racks with a safety factor of not less than 1.95–2.00.

The floor can be designed on a compacted earth base as an independent bridge-type structure, as a raft structure, or in many other design configurations. However, the design must provide an adequate safety factor to prevent significant cracking, tilting, flexing, or wearing.

Flexing and Loading Design. Compacted earth fill stabilized with soil cement or oil, with an overlay of compacted gravel and stone, is a common method of warehouse floor design. Such floors normally use reinforcing bar grids to provide additional strength. While a 6- to 8-inch floor slab is normal, heavier slabs are quite common when very high or heavy storage operations are involved. These warehouse floors often use a highway-type construction design and are frequently laid with paving machines.

Cost-consciousness may inhibit the fail-safe design of a warehouse floor. Over the long run, overdesign would probably be a good investment.

Types of Floor Designs. The most common floor designs are:

Compacted Fill. Heavy vehicular travel on a compacted fill floor flexes it imperceptibly each time a vehicle rolls over it. The net result is a further compaction of the fill and the eventual development of an air-gap between the bottom of the concrete slab and the top of the supporting gravel or sand fill. If this flexing does not exceed the elastic limit of the structure, the floor will not crack or break. However, continual flexing over time will generate fatigue failure and the concrete will develop progressive cracks. The precaution against this type of problem involves the use of heavy reinforcing bars to limit flexing and the appropriate floor design to ensure its ability to handle live loads without exceeding its limits.

Structural Floors. In situations in which compacted fill is not practical because of soil conditions, other floor designs are often used. The structural floor is built like a bridge. In this case, the column footers, which may be mounted on pile clusters or single piles, support the corners of a floor panel. The floor, then, functions as a membrane, or bridge.

The span between the columns is critical to the thickness and design of the floor structure. Again, in this situation, the reinforcing bar grid carries the tension load, and the concrete carries the wear and compression load. In this type of floor, precast soil beams are often poured or placed between the column footers, and the floor is poured on top of these beams to give added strength to the structure. The condition of the soil below the floor is often irrelevant. The column footer and the piling or other support structure that carries the building-structure load also carries the full working load of the floor.

Since this type of floor is more vulnerable to flexure failure, it is usually poured in sections with expansion joints along the column lines. This allows repairs to be made in segments and reduces the maintenance cost problem. It also limits the spread of cracking. Saw cuts placed in the floors control crack patterns.

Raft Floor Design. A third design configuration is the raft-type floor, so called because it is designed to "float" on an unstable soil base. This type of construction is quite expensive and is used only in situations in which compaction is not practical or available and where very wide column spacings limit the ability to use a membrane or bridge-type design.

The raft floor literally floats on the base. It is constructed with a series of soil beams and a multiple layer of flooring to add strength. The hazard in this type of design is not normally in cracking; the major risk is in the tilting of the whole slab. If the supporting soils and the floor loadings are not consistent, errors in projecting support from the soil and/or changes in the consistency of the soil due to underground water or other natural causes can cause the whole floor slab to tilt. This failure is very difficult to correct. Attaching the raft-type structure to the footers and pile caps which support the main building's structural frame usually prevents tilting. However, in extreme situations, the building footers may also move and take the floor slab with them.

Soil Studies. The most commonly omitted step in the design of a warehouse facility is geological analysis of the site. Before purchasing any site, the prospective owner should arrange for deep borings in a fairly inclusive pattern to make sure that the underground features of the location will support the live and dead loads of the facility to be built. Surprises can be expensive and disastrous! Many times people have purchased land and later found it to be useless for their intended purpose because of underground features which made construction too expensive or even impossible. The presence of caverns, old mine shafts, underground lakes or rivers, unstable soils, and many other geological features can block development of a safe and economical warehouse building or raise the cost beyond acceptable limits.

Floor Surface. Another factor in floor design involves the floor surface itself. The use of floor hardeners, special extra-hard concrete, and surface sealers prolongs the life of the floor, reduces the generation of dust in the warehouse, and limits the wear grooves developed by wheels passing over the same track in aisles, as is a common practice in narrow-aisle storage systems. The hardener is usually cast into the floor and reduces the effect of wear. When using sealers, it is essential to cure the floor first using a muriatic acid wash, and to vacuum and scrub it before applying the seal. Floor seals must be cared for and replaced periodically.

In the final analysis, then, the design of a warehouse floor or any industrial building floor has two primary criteria to meet. It must be compatible with the geological structure upon which it rests and it must be capable of dealing with the operating characteristics of the system which rests upon it.

Overhead Clearances

The overhead clearances in a warehouse are affected by the stack height of the stored merchandise, the design of any racking or shelving systems, the use of automated storage systems, and the configuration of wheeled vehicles.

The Product. Selection and development of storage height must be based upon the load-supporting structure of the product to be stored. For example, with proper pallets, steel drums can usually be stored 6 to 8 pallets high and, on occasion, 10 high. Paper rolls are often stacked 30 to 40 feet high using roll-clamp fork-lift equipment. Conversely, grocery products in plastic bottles can seldom be stacked more than four pallets high without structural failure of the packages at the bottom of the stack and the resulting tilting or collapsing of the storage pile. If a warehouse is to be designed entirely on the basis of bulk storage, the design and structural strength of the package are the controlling criteria in deciding on the height of the building.

Storage Equipment. The storage-system design or concept defines the type of storage equipment that will be used. In turn, the choice of pallet racks, shelving, and storage machines add a new consideration to calculating the height of the building. The rack configuration eliminates structural strength of the package from the dimension analysis. At that point, the relationship between the vehicle used and the rack becomes the controlling criterion. If narrow-aisle storage vehicles are used, machines normally stack pallets up to 40 feet high in racks divided by a 5- or 6-foot aisle. The choice of pallet or unit load size and storage vehicle or storage/retrieval machine impacts on the column spacing and building dimensions. Thus, the dimensional limits of the storage system are controlled by the height of the top pallet load on the top rail of the racks; or, if order-picking is to be conducted at that elevation, the height of the overhead guard on the order-picking vehicle and the size of the unit load and vehicle aisle. This is demonstrated in Figure 8.1.

Crane Clearance. The use of an overhead bridge crane in a facility adds additional design criteria. When a bridge crane is used, the height of

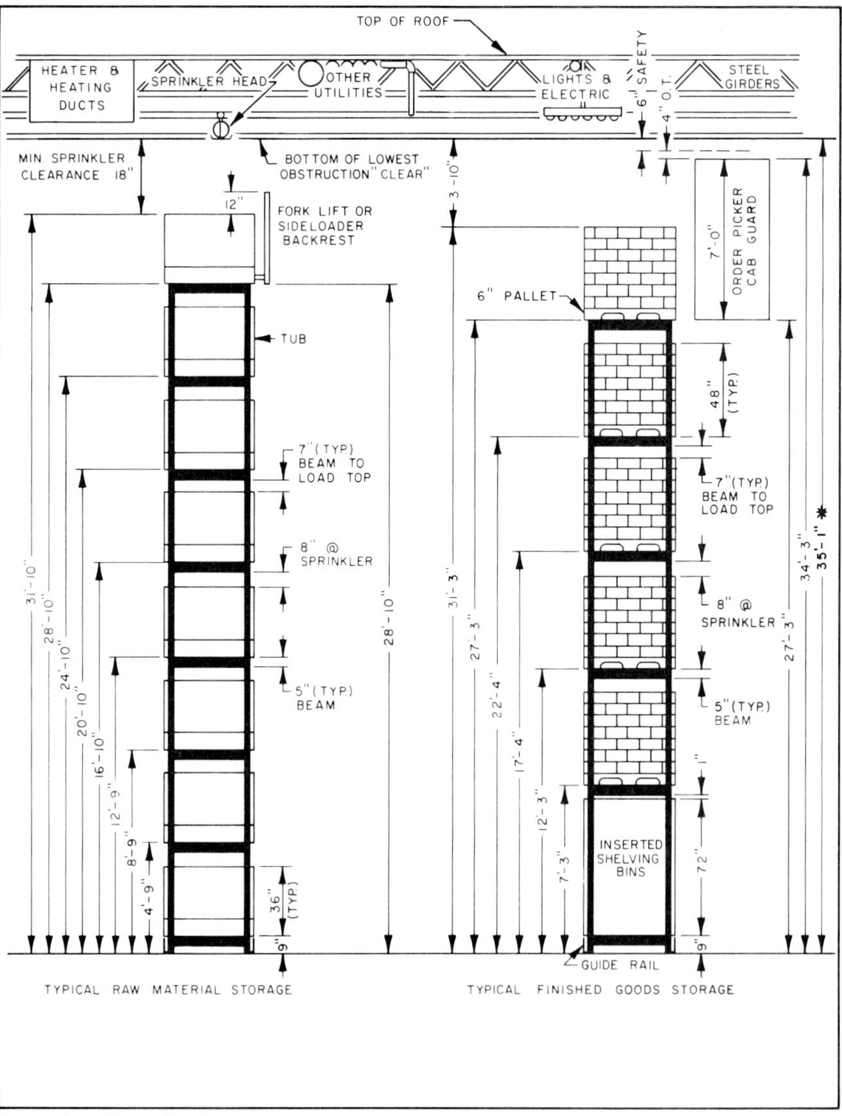

Figure 8.1. Typical building elevation requirement (with full-height order-picking). * Clear Height. (*The Sims Consulting Group, Inc.*)

the building must be based upon the sum of the required hook height, the depth of the crane structure, and the clearances between the top of the crane's running gear and any roof-supported devices or structures.

The Definition of Clear Height. In warehouse design, the *clear height* is the dimension from the floor to the bottom of any device hanging from the ceiling. This includes the clearance under the drain tube of a steam-unit heater, the bottom of a light fixture, the legal clearance under sprinkler heads, the clearances under pipes, and so on (Figure 8.1).

Generally, the *operating height* of a warehouse should be the maximum clearance height of the equipment or storage system, plus 12 inches for safe clearance under all obstructions, plus the dimension from the bottom of the lowest obstruction to the bottom of the lowest member of the roof structure, such as the bottom chord line of a bar joist or girder.

The depth of the roof structure depends upon the span between columns, the local roof loading codes and the type of structure used. This will be discussed in a later section of this chapter.

The guideline for conventional pallet warehouses storing 2000- to 4000-pound unit loads of conventional products on four-high pallet racks should be a minimum clearance under all obstructions of 28 feet 6 inches. This clearance allows for high order pickers with 7-foot overhead guards on the picking platform, unit heaters suspended from the ceiling, the 18-inch under-sprinkler legal requirement, roof-supported lighting, 4-foot pallet loads in racks with 6-inch clearance above the load, and 4- to 6-inch pallet-rack rails with in-rack sprinklers. It also permits the use of large-wheel reach trucks and/or solid guide rails for turret-type equipment. This 28 foot 6 inch dimension reaches the bottom of the steel and assumes that sprinklers will be above the chord line of the trusses and that lighting hung between the trusses will not protrude below. Figure 8.2 demonstrates these dimensions.

In a rack-supported structure, the design of any storage retrieval machine affects these overhead clearances. If the machine connects to the structure at the top or has top-running electrical connections, the requirements of the running gear in its contact with the roof define the roof structure dimensions. If the machine is operated entirely from the floor, however, the top of the moving element of the crane in the fully extended position and the top of the uppermost load become the controlling dimensions. In any case, a minimum of 12 inches of safety clearance above the most extreme position of either the crane or the load should be allowed, and sprinklers within the roof structure should not protrude below the steel.

Generally, then, the definition of the overhead clearance in a warehouse facility depends upon the operational design, the type of material

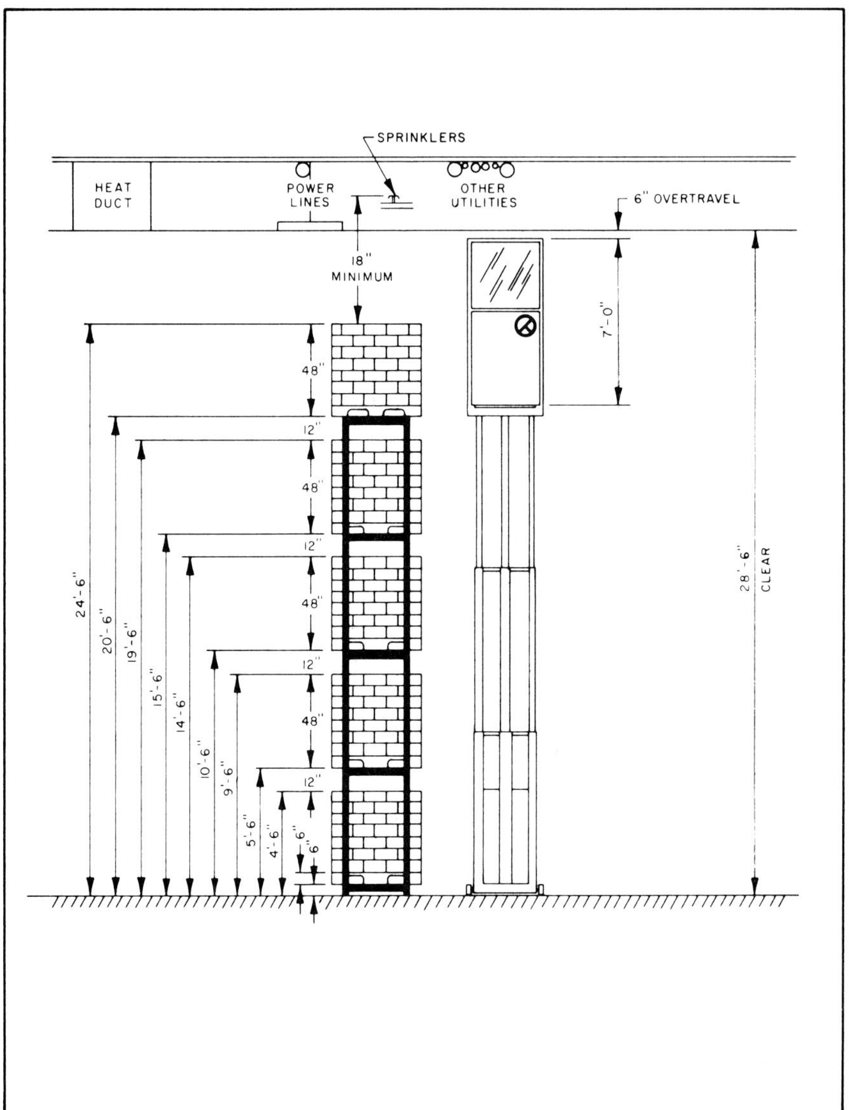

Figure 8.2. Picking building elevation and rack height dimension (5 pallets high). (*The Sims Consulting Group, Inc.*)

stored, and the materials handling system used within the facility. In addition, a major consideration that affects the basic system design is the cost of land and the cost of buildings.

High storage facilities require less land cover and typically provide more additional capacity at a lower cost per unit of storage. Increasing height to the limits of the handling system capacity in any system increases efficiency, and is more cost-effective than extending the ground cover of the building. It is, therefore, desirable—once the basic storage system has been defined—to maximize its practical operational height. To achieve a given capacity, it is significantly less expensive in terms of cost per cubic foot to increase height than to increase floor cover. This may not, however, necessarily apply when automated storage/retrieval systems have faster horizontal travel speeds than vertical travel speeds. In such cases, there may be a breakeven point between height and aisle length, beyond which it may be more economical to increase capacity by adding length rather than height.

Column Spacing

Rack/Column Fit. One of the most common errors in the design of warehousing facilities is the use of building cost criteria to define column spacings. Steel mills generally produce structural members in 20- and 40-foot lengths. Architects and structural engineers habitually use these lengths in designing building configurations. However, when designing a storage system, the clear spacing between columns must be compatible with the storage system. The structural dimensions of the steel or other structural members are secondary.

If, as shown in Figure 8.3, a 48- by 40-inch pallet is used and normal 4-inch clearances are allowed between pallets and between uprights and pallets, a minimum of 92 inches clear distance is required between the faces of the uprights in a pallet rack. If the pallet rack is a conventional four-high unit capable of carrying 2000-pound unit loads, the uprights will normally be 4 inches square. Thus the overall width of the pallet rack is 100 inches, or 96 inches centerline to centerline of the columns.

Carrying this analysis a step further, a typical 26-foot clear storage building will require 12-inch heavy wall pipe columns or 12- by 12-inch-wide flange beam or box columns. If pallet racks are to be used and three sections of pallet racks are to be placed between each pair of columns, the clear space between the faces of the columns must be 292 inches, or 24 feet 4 inches. A four-unit bay would require 32 feet 4 inches. Placement of six double-pallet-width units requires a clear space of 49 feet 8 inches. Thus, in a typical warehouse design, a 33- by 51-foot center-to-center bay spacing with 12-inch columns would probably accommodate rack storage in either direction and provide optimum flexibility of layout with elimination of column loss.

Bay Alignment. In such a design pattern, arranging the 33-foot bay parallel with the truck docks provides further advantages. The place-

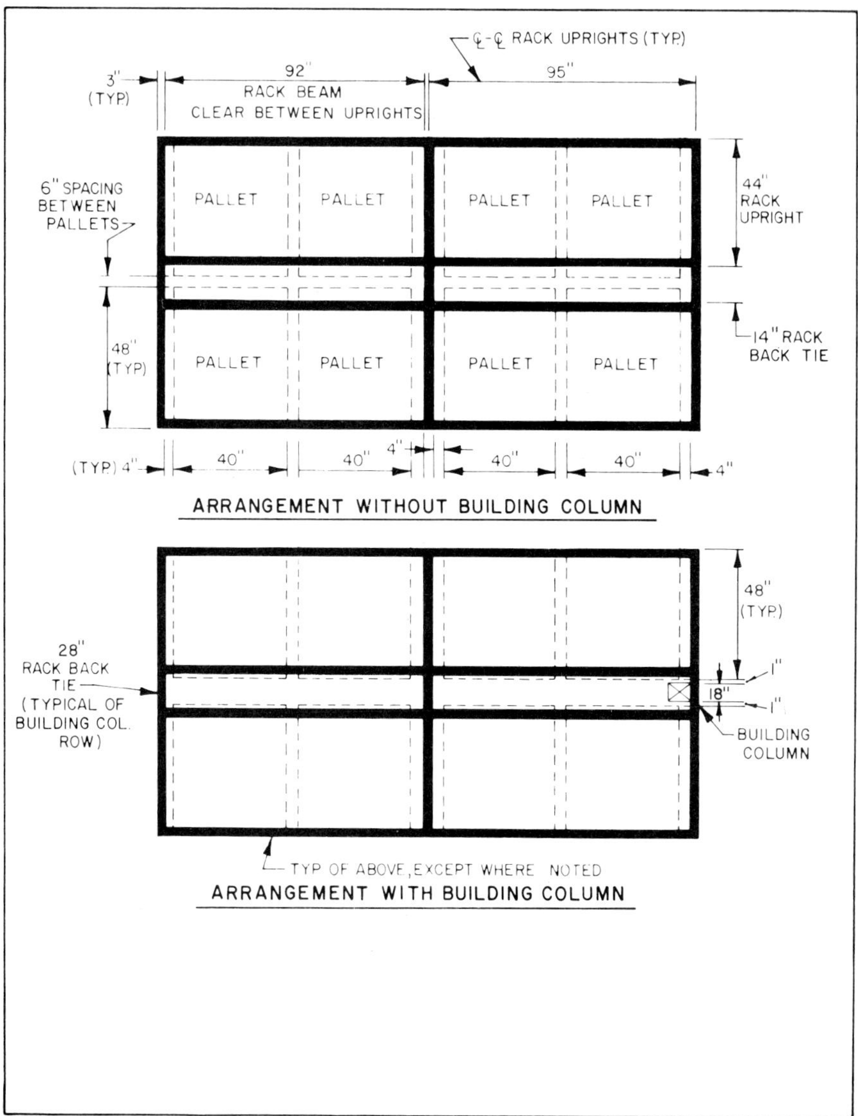

Figure 8.3. Typical plan view rack detail. (*The Sims Consulting Group, Inc.*)

ment of the truck docks on 15-foot centers places two docks in each bay, and the 51-foot span allows a column-free truck service area behind the docks (Figure 8.4). If, as is normally recommended, the truck docks and the rail docks are at right angles on one corner of the build

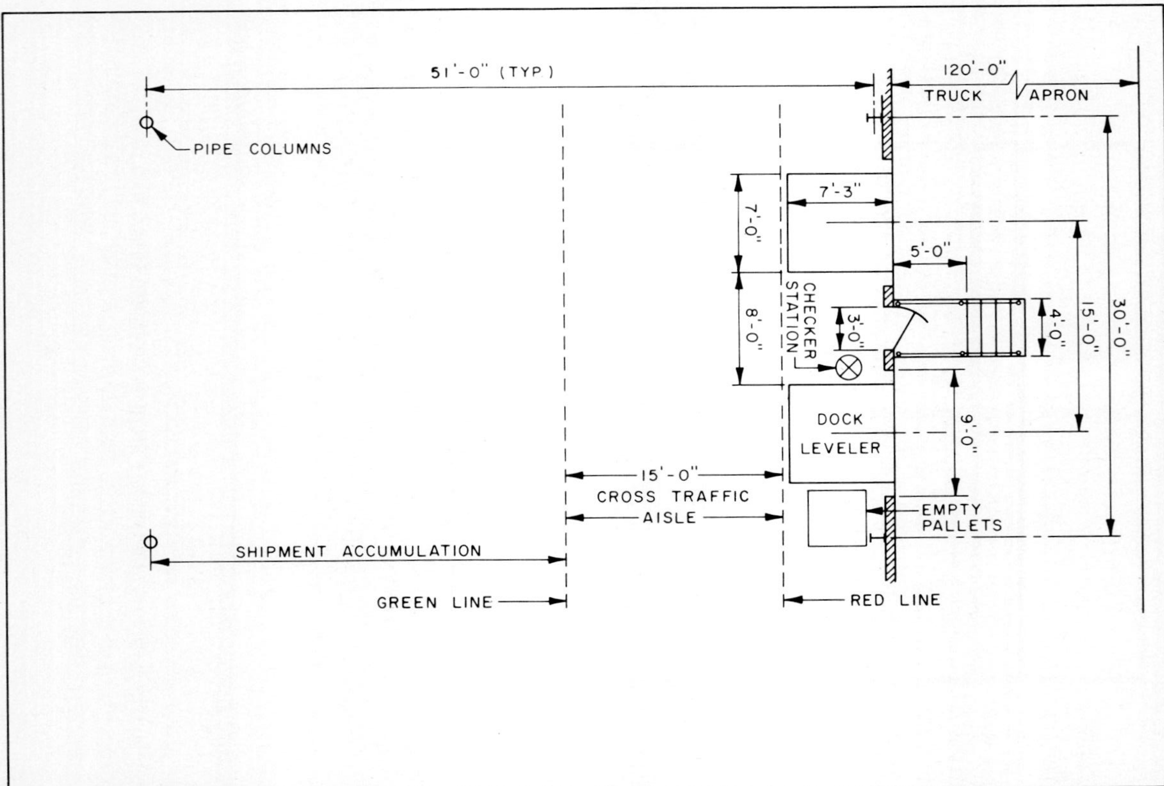

Figure 8.4. Basic dock layout. *The Sims Consulting Group, Inc.*)

ing, the 51-foot span along the rail docks would allow optimum flexibility for placement of cars varying in length from 40 to 60 feet or even 90 feet. The 33-foot bay would provide approximately 20 feet from the face of an inside rail dock to the column line, or 33 feet from the outer wall with clear spacing if building face doors were used.

Needless to say, different pallet sizes affect the dimensions of the racks, and rack dimensions further affect the column spacing dimensions. Thus, before designing a building, it is essential to determine what is to be stored within it. Since the 48- by 40-inch pallet is the Grocery Manufacturers Association's standard and the most commonly used size in consumer and many industrial distribution systems, the dimensional analysis above will probably provide a suitable basis for most warehouse designs where conventional rack systems are to be used. This dimensional pattern eliminates the need to modify the building in accordance with vehicle dimensions, since the racks will fit between the columns in either configuration and aisle spacing is at the option of the layout designer. In the event that a different aisle width is required by the storage machine or forklift truck, a modification in column dimensions may be appropriate.

In this analysis, the size and character of the columns must also be considered. Heavy-wall round or square tubular columns should be used in warehouses. These types of columns eliminate rodent and vermin nesting places, ensure easy maintenance and cleanliness, provide the ability to place downspouts within the columns, and minimize the effect of denting on column strength. Such columns are a little more expensive than H beams, but in the long run provide a much better facility. They also eliminate the corners that can pull packages from pallets when fork operators move too close to the column. In an all-concrete structure, a square column is normally preferable. Square columns are also normal in timber construction.

Rack-Supported Structures

When storage/retrieval machine systems demand extremely high clearance, consideration must be given to rack-supported buildings, since the column size grows to abnormal dimensions and takes up a lot of floor space in very high conventional structures. In a built-for-purpose storage facility with storage racks at the 40-foot or higher level, rack-supported structures are quite common and eliminate the issue of column design. In such instances, the storage rack system itself becomes the roof support structure and the external covering of the building is attached as paneling. The advantages of this type of structure are both economic and functional. A rack-supported structure offers some economic advantages under current tax codes. However, the main economic advantage is in the normally lower construction costs. The disadvantage lies in the single-purpose design.

The dimensioning of a rack-supported structure is based entirely upon the type of equipment and system to be installed. The aisles and the storage racks are dominated by the unit load size and vendor's requirements concerning clearances, power supply, running gear, and so on.

The column design in the rack suffers from a very real weakness in the application of codes. Although the rack-supported building is a building structure, the Internal Revenue Service and many building code agencies consider it a machine and, therefore, do not enforce structural safety factor codes in rack-supported buildings or, for that matter, in pallet racks. The Rack Manufactures' Institute rack standards call for a 1.95 factor of safety in the columns and 1.65 in the beams, with no safety factor for the integrated rack structure itself. Conversely, most building codes require a factor of safety of 1.95 to 2.00 for the structure and all of its members.

One of the economies of a rack-supported building is the reduction in the required steel. This, however, creates an additional hazard in the event of overload, windloads, and other factors. Because of its height, the arrangement of a rack-supported structure in relation to prevailing winds and storms is a critical design issue. Nonetheless, the design of racks within the building are not normally covered by codes that require wind load stability considerations, and unless the local building code agency enforces standard building design codes, it is not uncommon for a rack-supported building to be underdesigned from a construction point of view.

In summary, then, to provide a fail-safe facility when a rack-supported structure is considered, the design should be based upon building code standards, not materials handling equipment standards. This rule should also be applied to racking within a building, since impact loading from placement of pallets can damage and collapse a rack system, with disastrous effect.

Roof and Wall Design

A number of configurations are possible in the design of a warehouse. Some of the basic considerations in selecting a roof structure, or for that matter the structural system of the warehouse, involve the economics of local construction operations. In some parts of the United States and Canada, steel construction is normal because of the availability of steel components, the common use of these components, and the skills pattern of contractor personnel.

Where steel is more difficult to acquire, precast concrete is more common. This is also true in Europe, Latin America, Asia, and Africa. The capital facilities necessary to produce precast concrete components for construction are less expensive than those required to produce structural steel. Therefore, concrete construction is more common in underdeveloped countries, in iron curtain countries, and in many locations in Europe where highway limitations make delivery of steel members difficult.

Where lumber is abundant, timber construction is common. This is particularly true in the northwestern United States, where chemically treated, laminated redwood is used for columns and trusses. Each of these systems has a variety of advantages. If we accept that local construction and economic considerations have great weight, it is worthwhile to discuss some of the advantages and disadvantages of the different kinds of construction.

Roof Construction. In all warehouse designs it is desirable to have the roof self-supporting. The perimeter of the building should be supported with columns, and the walls should not be load supporting. Load-supporting walls limit expansion and modification of the building. In this discussion, we will ignore masonry walls with pilaster columns supporting the outer perimeter of the roof.

The roof support system can be a preengineered structure with continuous stress beams. The disadvantages of this type of structure lie in the tapered shape of the columns that inhibit storage operations close to the wall, the normally sloped roof that increases the amount of cube to be heated or air conditioned with no particular advantage to the user, and the standard dimensions that sometimes are not compatible with storage layout requirements. The primary advantages of this type of structure are its relatively low cost, rapid erection, and, in some cases, ability to be relocated.

Preengineered Building Roofs. In preengineered buildings, the roof is normally designed as a panel structure with either steel pans, concrete slabs, or synthetic roof slabs placed on top of the roof beams. When steel pans are used, the pan is often designed as a roof beam and functions as the purlin as well as the roof deck. In most cases, the designer places some form of insulating panel on top of this deck. This panel can be synthetic, concrete, plywood, fiberglass, or of some other material which insulates against both the sun and heat loss. In low-cost buildings, the covering on top of this material is normally tar paper with a brushed-on asphalt-and-gravel or sand coating. Recently, rubber or plastic sheeting has been used instead of brushed-on coatings. This type of material is more durable and less vulnerable to damage. In some locations, corrugated steel or aluminum sheets are used as a roof panel.

Bar Joist Roofs. The second most common type of structure is the bar joist design. In this case, straight columns along the perimeter and within the building are connected with I-beam girders, heavy-duty bar joists, or trusses. Bar joists are used as purlins between the beams. The roof deck is normally steel pan or concrete slabs. In some instances, the steel pan is filled with concrete but, more often, insulated paneling is placed on top of it. The same type of roof covering as described earlier for the preengineered building is used. The column spacing, the depth of the truss or girder, and the depth of the bar joist or purlin in each case depend upon the codes and building loads required. In northern climates where heavy snow loads and winds are expected, the depth of the roof structure will approach 3 or 4 feet. In warmer climates where snow loading is not a factor and the building is not in a hurricane area, the depth of structure may be as low as 2 feet, depending upon the design of the steel.

Steel Roof Hazards. One hazard of steel building construction is fire defense. Regardless of sprinkler protection, a fire in a steel building usually damages the structure. Steel softens at about 900°F. Flame temperatures at the top of a pile of merchandise are very high, often in the 1500 to 2500°F range. Consequently, a fire in a warehouse can soften the roof structure and cause it to collapse, even though it will not actually burn. This will occur if the sprinkler system does not douse the fire completely or limit it until the fire fighters can get it under control. Roof damage occurs more often than not in any fire in a steel building.

Precast Concrete Roofs. Precast concrete construction is quite popular in the southwest and in many foreign countries. The most effective concrete construction method uses precast, prestressed members with steel connecting plates and welded connections. The design is very similar to steel. The columns are usually square with steel caps on top and bolt plates at the bottom. They are bolted to cast-in-place footers, and the concrete floor is poured right to the column.

The steel connector at the top of the column is made of cast-in-place angles and butt plates. Concrete beams and girders are placed on the columns and welded in place. In such structures the roof is normally concrete pan construction topped in many cases by an inch of sealing concrete.

Precast roof pans or flexicore-type decking is often used to eliminate the need for purlins. In other cases, a poured-in-place waffle construction is used. This process involves placing a form between the columns and pouring the roof in place. The waffle ridges serve as purlins. Normally, a brushed-on tar or a rolled-on membrane surface of rubber, tar paper, or other impervious material covered with gravel or sand provides the top coating of concrete roofs. In addition to their economic advantages, some precast concrete structures offer fire resistance and ease of construction. Generally they will not collapse in a fire. They require less maintenance because they do not rust, and their design can include precoloring of the concrete and decorative shape casting.

Wood Roofs. Laminated wood structures are common in the northwest. Their construction features are similar to steel and concrete with the exception that the roof framing is usually designed as either a bow string or a triangular truss. Flat-roof timber buildings are generally not capable of as wide a span as that achieved with steel or concrete. When they do have this wide span, the roof depth is much greater.

Timber construction provides two advantages if the facility is in an area where timber is economical. They are generally easier to repair and, contrary to common belief, less vulnerable to fire damage than steel. A properly designed wood structure will usually survive a fire with heavy charring; if the fire is controlled early, collapse of the structure is unlikely.

Wall Design. The design of the walls for the warehouse depend on a combination of climatic and economic issues with a touch of architectural asthetics. Four basic types of warehouse walls are common:

1. Concrete block and other types of masonry, such as brick, are perhaps the oldest traditional sidings.
2. Concrete panel is used in either precast or tilt slab form.
3. Walls of single-faced, prepainted steel panels have insulation mounted on the inside.
4. The typical sandwich panel is composed of two prepainted steel panels with insulation material between them.

Brick Walls. A brick warehouse is the most expensive to build. It is often the most beautiful and more often than not considered only when the building is to be attached to an existing brick building or is in an area where building style is governed by the terms of a deed or local codes. These masonry walls should be constructed as curtain walls and should not be load-supporting structures.

Many old warehouses have brick walls. These were built when labor was cheaper and bricks were more commonly used. In these older warehouses brick pilasters often replaced perimeter columns. As a result, the removal of a wall, the expansion of the warehouse, and changes in the structure are more difficult. When pilasters are used, they should contain a concrete core with centered steel reinforcing bars to provide maximum strength. They also should have a steel slip plate on the top so that roof movement from varying temperatures does not apply bending load to the pilaster and crack it.

Block Walls. Nearly as labor-intensive and expensive is a block-walled warehouse. The same problems of a load-supporting structural wall with pilasters and the difficulty in changing walls apply here. While concrete block is an appropriate medium for interior walls, on the outside it generates such problems as a need for painting, pointing, and frequent sealing. It is also less attractive than some other types of construction.

Concrete Panel Walls. The best way to build a beautiful, fire-resistant warehouse is to use either precast or tilt-up, poured-on-site concrete panels. These panels can be poured in varying colors using decorative molds which present a beautiful appearance. They are relatively easy to install and generally less labor-intensive to construct than a block or brick wall. They have the major advantage of being almost burglar proof.

Metal Panel Walls. Because of its lower cost, the most common warehouse design uses metal panels with or without insulation, depending upon the location and climate. These prepainted panels are normally corrugated and bolted onto the steel framing of the building. A beautiful building can also be designed with this wall construction. Their disadvantages include the fact that they can be penetrated from the outside in a burglary and they offer little fire resistance.

In each case, the warehouse wall is designed primarily for appearance and weather protection. The walls should not support the roof. Walls should be removable so that the size and shape of the warehouse can be altered as necessary for growth and rearrangement. When fire walls are required it is best to use concrete block.

An exterior wall is often designed as a fire wall between a first stage of construction and a planned future expansion. In such cases, door jambs and lintels are often placed in the wall during initial construction and plugged with block or paneling. This allows expansion without major changes in the existing building.

This technique also provides for dock expansion. Often, dockleveler pits, door jambs, and lintels placed in the original construction are temporarily plugged and sealed with paneling. As dock capacity requirements increase, the plugs and panels are removed. Though docklevelers and doors must be installed, no major construction is required.

Figure 8.5 shows a section through a typical panel-type warehouse building. In each instance, the architect or building designer uses techniques appropriate to the local climate and construction trade practices to achieve the optimum balance between aesthetics, function, and costs.

Truck and Rail Dock Design

A critical element in the design of a warehouse facility is the truck and rail dock configuration and the relationship of the building to the environment. Chapter 6 addresses the selection of the warehouse site, and Chapter 12 discusses truck and rail dock design. However, from a building design point of view, the spacing, arrangement, location, and characteristics of rail and truck docks are significant considerations.

Figure 8.4 shows the general arrangement and spacing of truck docks, and Figure 8.6 shows a section through an inside truck dock with some related building features.

Rail docks are another consideration. Outside rail docks are common and less expensive, especially when car sizes are uniform and climate is favorable. However, modern practice brings the rail car inside the building because of the variety of boxcar sizes and lengths and the difficulty of spacing external docks. Allowable interior clearances vary from one railroad to another; however, the dimensions shown in Figure 8.5 generally accommodate them all.

Truck dock and yard dimensions are critical, and the arrangement of the building on the site is very important. In general, trucks should back in with a left turn so that drivers can see the dock as they turn the trailer in. Figure 8.7 shows the desired yard dimensions for smooth operation.

Supporting Services

The design of a warehouse must include consideration of personnel support services, offices, heating, air conditioning, security, parking, and often food facilities. The warehouse designer must provide adequate space for the anticipated number of people and functions in such a manner that this service space will not interfere with operations.

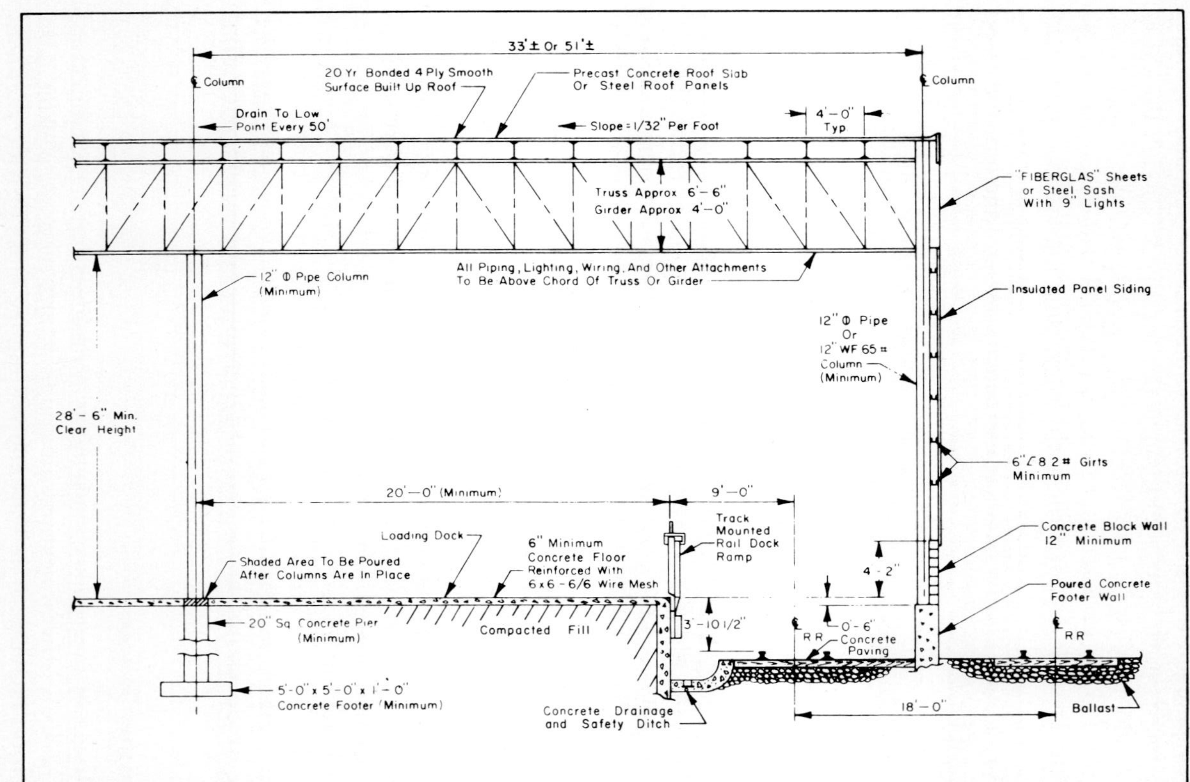

Figure 8.5. Steel frame and panel construction: typical warehouse design features and rail siding dimensions. (*The Sims Consulting Group, Inc.*)

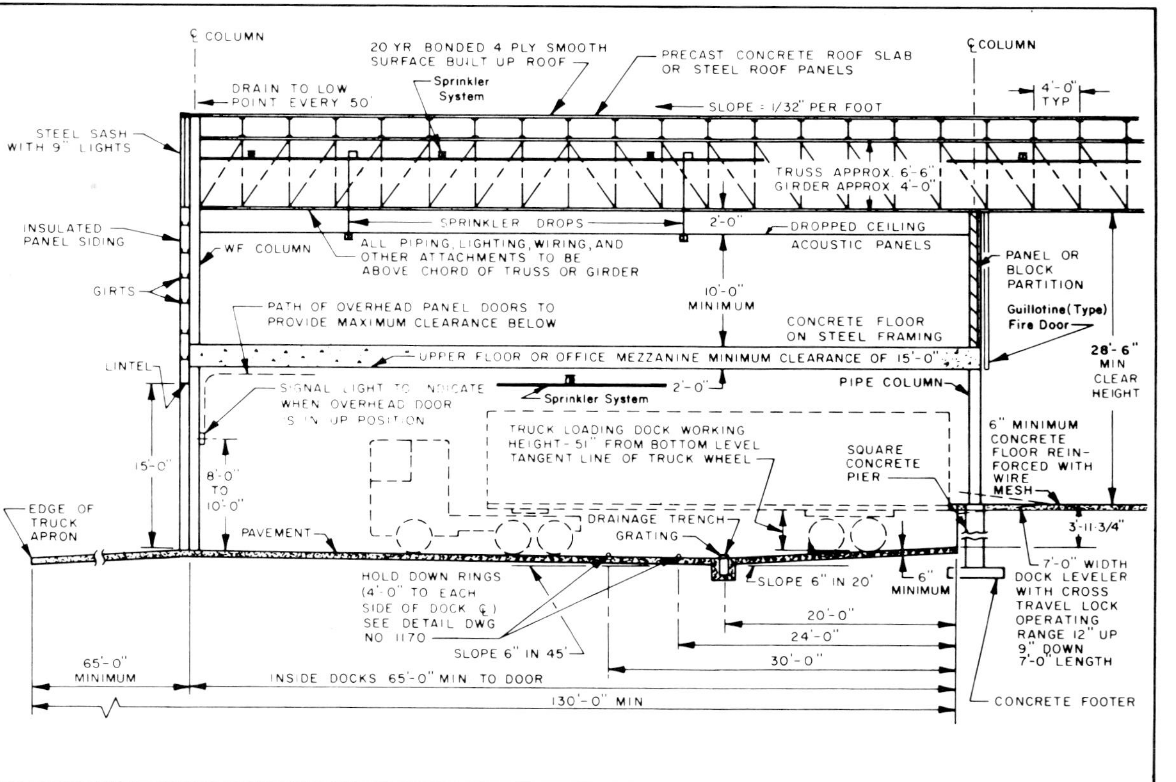

Figure 8.6. Steel frame and panel construction: typical warehouse design features and truck dock dimensions. (*The Sims Consulting Group, Inc.*)

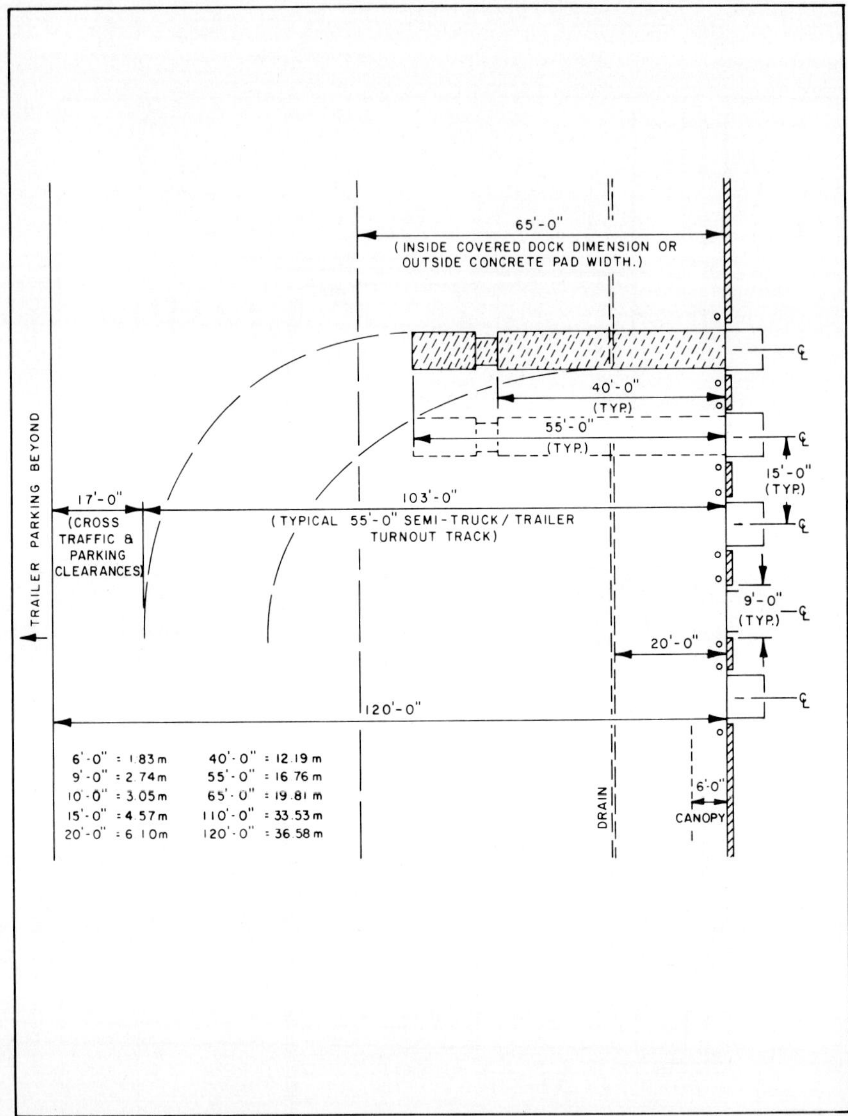

Figure 8.7. Typical truck apron layout. (*The Sims Consulting Group, Inc.*)

Generally, the best place for supporting services is on a mezzanine above the truck-dock work area. This high cube area is useless above 12 or 14 feet. Stepping down the design of the roof causes additional building cost and, in snow territories, difficulties from drifting snow and other weather. A single roof height continuing over the truck and rail docks can provide sufficient cube for food services facilities, offices, computer rooms, toilets, and in some cases, even tenant office space on the mezzanine. The cost of such facilities varies directly with the additional floor and column footer capacity required, since no additional roof is needed. Putting services on the mezzanine also prevents interference with operations at the working level. Modern communications facilities, remote computer terminals, radio, squawk boxes, and other devices make it unnecessary for working personnel on the floor level to make frequent visits to the mezzanine.

Regulations require elevators to permit handicapped people to work on upper levels and dual stairways to provide for fire exits. Although

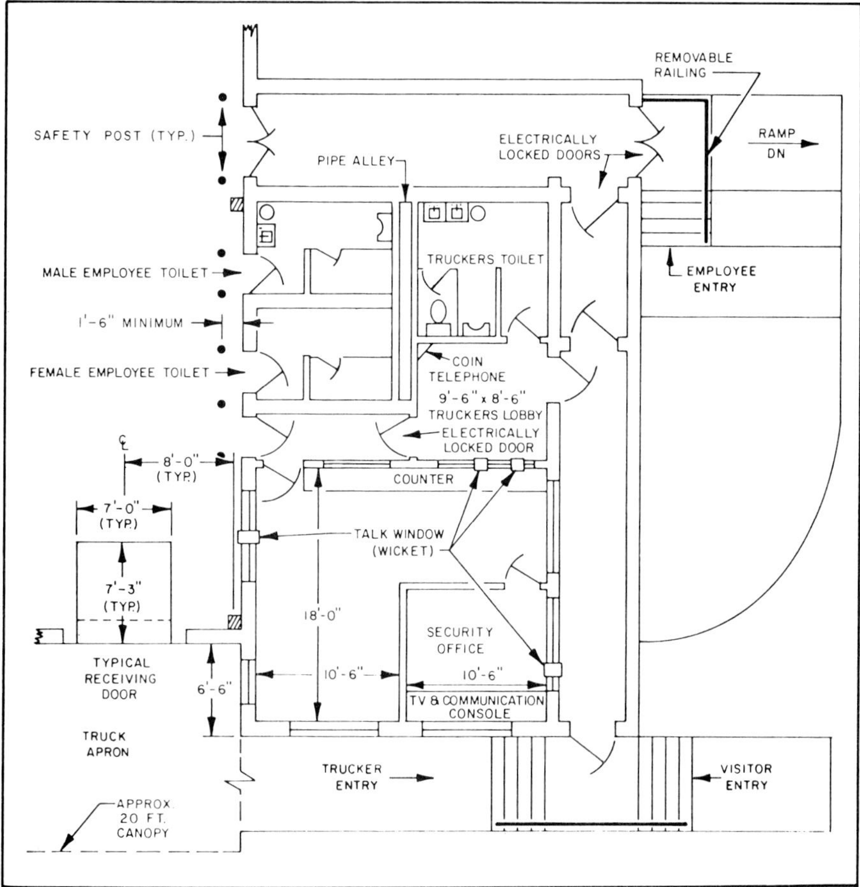

Figure 8.8. Typical receiving office arrangement (functional dimensions). (***The Sims Consulting Group, Inc.***)

these items add to the cost, the savings in overall floor space by double use of ground cover more than compensates for this expense. The facilities on the main floor should be limited to necessary office space for receiving and shipping clerks, and dock foremen. A truckers' room and toilet and any required security facility should also be provided.

All sedentary and support operations should be placed on the mezzanine to limit their impact on operations. Island and peninsula layouts in working areas should be minimized. Figure 8.8 shows a typical dock office arrangement which includes security space adjacent to a truck dock.

Security and Fire Defense

One key issue in warehouse security involves the level of security required. If the whole facility is secure, the need for guards and gates is limited. Controlling access and egress, keeping parking areas away from the immediate vicinity of the building, and designing the building to be difficult to penetrate limit the cost of security. Alarm systems are useful as a deterrent, but the professional burglar can bypass them.

In any case, most warehouse losses come from internal theft. Control of egress and access coupled with a document system which is difficult or impossible to forge can limit loss risks.

A good fire defense usually provides suitable structural security. Protection at the truck dock requires isolation of outside drivers from the merchandise. Figure 8.8 shows the use of a truckers' room to achieve this isolation.

9
Simulation

Don T. Phillips, Ph.D., P.E.

Professor of Industrial Engineering, Texas A&M University, College Station, Texas

John W. Fowler

Research Associate, Department of Industrial Engineering, Texas A&M University, College Station, Texas

Warehouse management engineering involves the full integration of men, materials, resources, and facilities. It presents a complex environment of realistic parameters, system dependencies, multiple product mixes, and heterogeneous system components (conveyors, AGV systems, AS/R systems, robotics, etc.). The most attractive alternative for systems modeling appears to be digital systems simulation. This chapter will provide an overview of the need for systems simulation and present some of the related philosophical issues. Available commercial simulation languages will also be categorized and reviewed.

Simulation of Warehouse Systems

Throughout recorded history, man has sought to predict the future. From Merlin to modern oracles, the desire to obtain information about events that might occur has dominated the thoughts of conquerors, kings, and the inquisitive mind. Closely related to the development of large-scale digital computers, systems simulation is the engineer's answer to this age-old quest.

Through the use of modern systems simulation tools, techniques, and methodologies, the systems analyst can accurately predict the behavior and operational characteristics of complex systems before they are actually installed. Of particular interest, and the area to which we will now focus our attention, is the analysis of modern warehouse systems and the operational behavior of such systems within the larger manufacturing environment.

In recent years, there has been a tremendous explosion of warehouse technology; high-rise storage retrieval systems, computerized picking systems, microcomputer-controlled conveyor systems, and stacker-crane unit load systems. All have been accepted as necessary components in the development of more cost-effective and productive systems. Closely correlated to the development of these material handling components, we currently see a corresponding interest in MRP, group technology, piece-part coding and classification, and WIP planning and operational concepts. By and large, the levels of the technological advances in the warehousing area have come from industry, with primary focus on hardware configuration and control algorithms. The integration of the materials handling system to the operation planning concepts, along with the attendant logistics of manufacturing-system integration, have lagged far behind hardware development. In particular, development of realistic systems analysis procedures, operations research techniques, and predictive-optimization algorithms are virtually nonexistent.

The two primary reasons for the lack of development of analysis and predictive tools by academicians in relation to the warehousing arena are: (1) such systems, either in isolation or in relationship to the larger manufacturing environment, are extremely complex, and (2) the high cost of procuring, maintaining, and up-dating warehousing hardware for physical experimentation, an issue which may not be resolvable in light of current academic funding deficiencies.

The need for academic involvement in both warehouse research and the broader arena of manufacturing systems analysis is evidenced by the $50 million IBM funding program to establish centers of excellence in manufacturing systems engineering, announced in the spring of 1984.

However we choose to rationalize the obvious lack of academic involvement in warehouse research, there is great need for the academic community to become involved in this area.

In order to cope with stochastic, highly interactive, exogenously driven warehouse systems, the tools and techniques of digital systems simulation analysis seem to be the most desirable and often the only available systems analysis technique. Within the context of analyzing complex warehouse material handling environments, the following advantages are unique to systems simulation:

- Simulation makes it possible to study and experiment with the complex internal interactions of a specified or existing system.
- Through simulation, one can study the effect of certain informational changes on the operation of a warehousing system by altering the simulation model rather than experimenting directly on the system itself. Simulation enables the analyst to observe the effect of these alterations on the system's behavior.
- The experience of designing a computer simulation model may be more valuable than the actual simulation itself. The knowledge obtained in designing a simulation study frequently suggests changes in the system being simulated. The effects of these changes can then be tested via simulation before implementing them on the actual system.
- Simulation of complex systems can yield valuable insight into which variables are more important than others in the system and how these variables interact. This knowledge may result in a possible new (analytical) approach or simplified analysis.
- Simulation can be used to experiment with new situations about which there is little or no information, so as to prepare for what may happen. Simulation can be used to answer "what if" questions in analysis and design.
- Simulation can serve as an "experimental test" to try out policies and decision rules for operating a system, before running the risk of experimenting on the real system.
- Simulation enables one to control time. Time can be easily compressed, expanded, and changed from one experiment to the next.
- When new machines or product lines are introduced into a system, simulation can be used to point out bottlenecks and other problems that may arise during system operation.

The remainder of this overview will deal with two important aspects related to the simulation of warehousing problems: (1) What are the characteristics of a warehouse-manufacturing–material-handling system that necessitate digital simulation analysis? (2) How would one choose a suitable simulation methodology for systems analysis? The second objective will be dealt with by presenting a comparison of simulation software currently available to the industrial sector.

When to Use Simulation

Do the Activities Exhibit a Wide Range of Time Variability? Perhaps the most significant difference in systems analysis between using digital simulation techniques and operations-research–mathematical-modeling techniques is the use of stochastic parameters. By and large, analytical planning tools used in industry utilize only *point estimates* or *expected-value statistics.* Systems design analysis and performance measures are characterized by the use of *deterministic* or *pseudodeterministic* models. Notable exceptions are the use of queueing theory, Markov processes, and/or certain inventory control models. However, use of stochastic models in industry for planning and control are the exception rather than the rule. Computer simulation models address a stochastic world that is described by probabilistic measures: empirical density functions, probability density functions, or process-dependent state equations.

Systems designed and/or controlled by expected values are often doomed to failure, to overdesign, or both. The reason is clear: *The long-run acceptability of a system is more dependent upon system surges or variabilities than any other factor.* This observation is more clearly evident in the behavior of in-process storages, queueing phenomenon, and random failures than any other areas. Simulation allows an analyst to both incorporate these factors into the model and study the behavior of the system under their influences.

Are Activities-Functions Highly Dependent Upon One Another? Most analytical models and virtually all mathematical stochastic models (Markov chains, linear programming models, etc.) assume independence of random phenomena or short-term dependencies. The "real world" might be assumed to operate in this manner, but *in practice it rarely does.* As in the old southern spiritual, "The hip bone's connected to leg bone, the leg bone's connected to the foot bone, the foot bone's connected to the toe bones . . . now hear the word of the Lord! " Warehousing-manufacturing systems are much the same – an unusual or catastrophic event often has far-reaching effects. Complex system dependencies, cause-and-effect phenomena, are routinely reflected in digital simulation models.

Have You Real-Time Operating Experience with the (Proposed) System or System Changes? A major factor in the acceptance of digital simulation as a systems analysis tool is the ability to experiment with a wide range of physical phenomena and observe related system behavior. The ability to perform such analysis is particularly important in a system's design or reorganization phase. In the system design phase, one is typically faced with the problem of specifying or postulating system operating procedures, and these are often based upon intuitive rules or prior perception of "theoretical" system operation. In cases in which system operating parameters and/or rules are being developed concurrently with the system design phase, systems simulation is a powerful and dynamic analysis tool.

Is There a High Degree of Human-Machine Interface? In the vast majority of analytical models, the problems of human-machine interface and the direct influence of human decision making and/or control is virtually ignored, or at best absorbed in the time-consumptive factors of the model. Systems simulation allows the analyst to real-time interface the human element. Typically, this influence is in the arena of stochastic influence on the model (changes in operating procedures, stochastic decision points, or lack of human resources), and this influence often triggers entirely different operating parameters and/or procedures.

Are There Strong Possibilities for "Resource Blocking"? It would be rare to imagine a warehouse of any size or complexity which is not severely influenced by the availability of scarce resources. These resources might be in the form of raw materials, required paperwork, physical manpower, or materials handling equipment. In any case, the direct treatment of resources and resource requirements are seldom found to any great extent in analytical models. This is unfortunate, since in most materials-handling–warehousing functions, the influence of direct or indirect resources is often the major influence on warehousing requirements and operations planning. In general, the use and influence of resources within a simulation model or simulation environment are well within the scope of the simulation analyst. Some simulation languages provide automatic resource control and resource blocking. These capabilities will be subsequently addressed in the section dealing with computer simulation languages.

How Predictable Are Your Warehousing Storage Requirements? A major advantage in using digital systems simulation to study the behavior of existing or proposed warehousing-handling systems is to characterize the behavior of warehouse storage. The design and operation of warehouse storage areas are highly dependent upon the influence of many factors. Arrival rates, service rates, types of picking equipment, picking equipment failures, limited manpower and/or resources, and many other elements of the integrated system greatly influence the fluctuating size and requirements of the warehousing storage area. In general, only a detailed, integrated systems simulation model can reflect the true and accurate steady state as well as time the varying behavior of the warehousing/picking environment.

How Sensitive Is System Performance to Queueing Phenomena? There are classes of manufacturing systems which may not require the use of digital simulation analysis to accurately predict their behavior. Such systems are characterized by fixed cycle times, constant activity times, and fixed, highly predictable materials handling and manufacturing components. Statistically, such systems are composed of components or subsystems that exhibit very little *variance* from one operation time to the next. Such systems will usually develop *no queues* or *infinite queues* depending upon the nature of the arrival and service rates to each component of the system. In general, even if highly automated AS/R systems or NC/DNC systems comprise the manufacturing environment, there will be a wide range of activity durations. This phenomenon develops due to the human interactions to the system, limited resources, changing arrival and/or service rates in other connected operations, and many other factors. Queueing phenomena is very sensitive to both changes in the *average* rates and the *variance* of those rates. In most complex manufacturing systems, queueing phenomena will dictate whether or not the system will function or become hopelessly congested. Simulation analysis can be used to study all forms of queueing phenomena, and in most models relate these statistics to cause and effect parameters.

Do Sequences of Activities Depend upon Product-Specific or Random Influences? In most applicable analytical models, which are those that can address stochastic performances, the influence of randomness on the system is handled through use of specified and limited probability density functions in the particular model being applied. Simulation analysis frees the analyst from these binding assumptions. One is free to choose any probability density function desired, and time varying parameters are easily incorporated. The latter capability is very important if the warehousing and supply functions are to be related to flexible manufacturing systems, since the flow of a wide range of products, each with its own processing characteristics and supply rates, must be modeled.

Do You Consider Equipment Reliability and Availability to Be an Integral Part of the System? A powerful capability of digital simulation analysis is directly to incorporate into the systems model the effect of catastrophic or status-disturbing events. In most product or production-intensive systems, the real-time failure of machine or product lines can have a devastating effect on normal operating procedures. Systems failures can place extreme demands upon an in-process storage or warehousing system, and these imbalances should be considered in the design process. A realistic model should allow one to dynamically change the operating procedures and parameters of the system when those events occur. Systems simulation allows the analysts to incorporate power failures, machine breakdowns, repair activities, and other status-disturbing events directly in the systems model. It should also be noted that a good simulation model will allow for the study of both steady-state and transient system behavior. In cases in which the system is "shocked" by catastrophic behavior, the transient analysis is usually more important than the system steady-state results.

Is the System Product-Dependent, or Flexible? Product-dependent, or flexible, manufacturing systems have become important concepts in modern systems design. The effect of flexible manufacturing is often a demand for opportunistic, or flexible, warehousing. Unfortunately, unless model decomposition is possible, these systems are very difficult to analyze. Exceptions are those systems that behave in a relatively deterministic fashion and to which linear programming can be applied. Transient or composite data on system operation for warehousing and manufacturing systems of any size and complexity are most easily obtained through the use of systems simulation.

How Should One Simulate?

Once it has been determined that simulation is a tool that should be used to analyze a complex warehousing system, the analyst must address the issue of which vehicle should be used to simulate the system. Unfortunately, this choice is often no choice at all, but is often determined by the analyst assigned to perform the work and/or the simulation software currently residing in the computer system to be used. Typically, once the decision has been made to simulate, the simulation methodology is often selected from the following structural languages for the reasons given:

1. GPSS V/GPSS P/C—since the host computer is IBM, or the analyst already understands the language
2. SIMSCRIPT II.5—since "we have a SIMSCRIPT compiler" and Joe Whiz has used SIMSCRIPT before

3. FORTRAN IV, PL-I, COBOL—since Dan College has had a course in simulation methodologies and he is an expert in those languages
4. SIMAN or SLAM II—since Professor John Q. Simact presented the concepts of these languages in an academic program

All of the above choices happen every month, somewhere, and all are sometimes as inefficient as mowing the lawn around your house with a Caterpillar tractor. Simulation technology and software have experienced tremendous technical growth in the past five years, and simulation software alternatives have become available to the general public and general host computers at minimal costs. Initially, it should be agreed that GPSS, SIMSCRIPT, SLAM II, and other major languages are comprehensive, complete simulation languages, and are properly utilized daily in major simulation exercises. However, the message to be heard is that there are now powerful alternatives which should be explored, particularly since several simulation languages can now run on microprocessors. At the time of this writing, there are several specialized languages which provide modeling capabilities directed toward warehousing systems (GEMS, MAST, SEE-WHY, MAP-I, etc.). When applicable, those specialized languages offer orders-of-magnitude increases in simulation modeling efficiency. The point is more clearly revealed by referring to the linear programming problem in two variables which was solved by MPSX because the operations analyst had never been exposed to the graphical solution procedure. In general, the selection of simulation methodology depends upon the nature, complexity, and basic characteristics of the proposed study. Often, the selection is dictated by the computer hardware available to the analyst, rather than the best available tool.

Advantages of Simulation Languages

The development of simulation languages has been an evolutionary process that began in the late 1950s. At first, the languages used in simulation were general-purpose languages. After programming a number of models, analysts recognized that many of the situations being simulated could be categorized broadly as systems involving the flow of items through processes. Since many of the programs had functionally similar processes, several groups of researchers in the late 1950s and the early 1960s almost simultaneously had the idea of developing special-purpose languages. These developed gradually from assembly-language programs with special features, through extended commercially available problem-oriented languages, to sophisticated special-purpose simulation languages. Any algorithmic programming language can be used for simulation modeling. But those languages designed specifically for the purpose of computer simulation provide certain useful features. These include:

1. Reduction of the programming task
2. Provision of conceptual guidance
3. Aid in defining the classes of entities within the system
4. Flexibility for change
5. A means of differentiating between entities of the same class by characteristic attributes or properties
6. Relating the entities to one another and to their common environment
7. Adjusting the number of entities as conditions vary within the system

Emshoff and Sisson[1] believe that all simulations require certain common functions, which make a simulation language different from a general algebraic or business programming language. Among these are the need to:

1. Create random numbers
2. Create random variates
3. Advance time, either by one unit or to the next event
4. Record data output
5. Perform statistical analyses on recorded data
6. Arrange outputs in specified formats
7. Detect and report logical inconsistencies and other error conditions

Further, they state that for simulation in which discrete items are processed by specific operations, the following common processes are additionally present:

1. Determining type of event (after retrieval from an event list)
2. Calling subroutines to adjust the state variables as a result of the event
3. Identifying specific state conditions
4. Storing and retrieving data from lists (tables or arrays), including the event list and those that represent the state

Some of the simulation languages are *languages* in the more general sense that, beyond linking the user with the computer as a means of conversing, they afford the user an aid to problem formulation. Having a vocabulary and a syntax, they are descriptive, and consequently their users tend after some utilization (as with other languages) to think in them. Thus, Kiviat[2] believes the two most important reasons for utilizing simulation languages as opposed to general-purpose languages are programming convenience and concept articulation. Concept articulation is important in the modeling phase and in the overall approach taken to system experimentation. Program convenience points up its importance during the actual writing of the computer program. Other advantages of the simulation languages are their use as communication and documentation devices. By writing in English-like languages, simulations can more easily be explained to project managers and other nonprogramming-oriented users. A major cited disadvantage of using simulation languages is that most were developed by individual organizations for their own purpose and released to the public more as a convenience and intellectual gesture than a marketed commodity. More and more, however, well-documented simulation languages are commercially available.

Factors Pertinent to Language Selection

Before a programming language is selected, the computer to be used (both as to type and model) must be determined. Ideally, this selection is one of the decision options open to the analyst.

In actual practice, the user probably has available a particular hardware configuration and little latitude as to modification or choice. Once the computer to be used is known, one is ready to select the language. This selection should be a two-phased screening process. The initial phase can be accomplished at any time, even before a particular problem arises. In this phase, language possibilities are examined for their operational characteristics relative to the user's environment and capabilities. The second phase, which is related to the specific problem, must be accomplished after subsystem modeling and computer selection.[3]

In the first phase of the selection process, we are concerned with the availability of references, documentation, and software compatibility. We are basically trying to screen the multiplicity of available languages to find those that make good sense for us to consider later when we have a specific problem. The type of questions to be answered deal with the general environment in which the analyst is working. Among the questions we need to explore are:

1. Are intelligibly written user's manuals available?
2. Is the language compiler compatible with available computer systems?
3. Is this language available on other computer systems on which the user's problem might be run?
4. Does the language translator provide documentation and extensive error diagnostics?
5. When the organizing, programming, and debugging time is combined with the compiling and running time, does the efficiency appear attractive?
6. What is the cost of installing, maintaining, and updating the software for the language? (Since some languages are proprietary, there may be an explicit charge for these services.)
7. Is the language already known or easily learned?
8. Are a sufficient number of simulation studies anticipated for the future to justify the cost of learning and installing the new language?

In the second phase, we must deal with the characteristics of the specific problem at hand. Several different languages have probably survived the phase I screening and are now available for possible use. Phase II, therefore, deals with choosing the specific language to be used on the specific problem at hand with the specific computer to be used. Among the issues to be dealt with in this phase are:

1. What are the range and applicability of the world view of the language? (*World view* is defined as the conceptual manner through which the language represents real-world activities.)
   a. What are its time advance methods?
   b. Is it event, activity, or process oriented?
   c. What is its random number and random variate generation capability?
2. How easily can state and entity variable data be stored and retrieved?
3. What is the flexibility and power provided by the language to modify the state of the system?
4. How easily can it be used to specify dynamic behavior?
5. What are the forms of output available, what are their utility, and what statistical analyses can be performed on the data?
6. How easy is it to insert user-written subroutines?

Table 9.1 shows some of the operational characteristics of several of the most widely used discrete simulation languages; the following is some elaboration.

Both GPSS and SIMSCRIPT require the use of a special compiler, but both can be purchased to run on almost any mainframe and are now available for a limited number of microprocessor models. It is safe to say that neither is as universally portable as FORTRAN-IV, PC/I, or C-based programming languages tend to be. All simulation languages utilize a structured input, and all provide for use of individual, tailor-made output. Most now provide interactive, user-friendly, graphic modes of prompted input. SIMSCRIPT II.5, SLAM II, and SIMAN provide maximum flexibility to the user, but the trade-off is between the ease of learning the language and the additional necessity of writing subroutines to achieve this flexibility. Generally, in complex simulations, one programs internal logic using these languages. However, SIMAN and SLAM II are "hybrid" languages, which provide a "no-programming" environment for a limited (but flexible) subset of problems. GPSS, Q-GERTS, GEMS II, SIMAN, SPEED, MICRONET, MAP-1, PSIM, Interactive, and IDSS 2.0 adopt the philosophy that the user should not engage in a true "programming" activity but, rather, use a standard set of symbols or commands to model environments. However, most support this philosophy with the capabilities to write external code (the GPSS help block, for example). SIMAN and GPSS utilize a "block diagram," logical command structure; Q-GERTS, uses an activity-on-arc network representation; MICRONET and GEMS-II utilize an activity-on-box/node network representation. SPEED, MICRONET, MAP-1, PSIM, and SEE-WHY use reserved commands and syntax. IDSS 2.0 is basically forms-driven with front-end interactive use and has a directory of commands and syntax. IDSS 2.0, SIMAN, SEE-WHY, SIMSCRIPT P/C and GPSS P/C provide front-end interactive graphics packages. SLAM II interactive input, along with extensive database management and output options, is provided through a program called TESS. When applicable, the network-based and symbol-driven languages can provide orders-of-magnitude savings when building a simulation model. The world view that each language embodies is important, and will be briefly discussed.

Language World Views. As previously stated, the *world view* of a simulation language is the conceptual manner through which the host language represents real-world activities. The implication of a language's world view is that, when utilizing a particular language, the user is forced to view the world in the same manner and accordingly restrict the applicable arena of language application. Three world views are prevalent:

Table 9.1. Operational Characteristics of Popular Simulation Languages

Simulation language	Language base	Event monitors	Arithmetic	Modeling base	Microhardware	Graphic input	Application areas
GEMS II	FORTRAN	Discrete	Real	Network	—	No	Manufacturing systems
GPSS/H	GPSS	Discrete	Integer	Block diagram	—	No	General purpose
GPSS/PC	GPSS	Discrete	Integer	Block diagram	IBM PC	No	General purpose
IDSS 2.0	FORTRAN/Machine 1	Combined	Real	Network	CAD-LINK	Yes	General purpose
INTERACTIVE	PASCAL	Discrete	Real	Network	Apple, IBM PC[b]	No	General purpose
MAP-1	FORTRAN	Discrete	Real	Statements	—	No	Batch manufacturing systems
MAST	FORTRAN	Discrete	Real	—	IBM PC[b]	No	Design of FMS
MICRONET	FORTH	Discrete	Integer	Network	Apple, IBM PC[b]	No	General purpose
PC SIMSCRIPT II.5	SIMSCRIPT	Discrete	Real	Event	IBM PC[b]	No	General purpose
PSIM	PASCAL	Discrete	Real	Event	Apple, IBM PC[b]	No	General purpose
Q-GERTS	FORTRAN	Discrete	Real	Network	—	No	General purpose
SEE-WHY	FORTRAN	Discrete	Real	Event	Cromemco or System[c]	No	Manufacturing systems
SIMAN	FORTRAN	Combined	Real	Block diagram	—	No	General purpose
SIMAN P/C (for micro)	FORTRAN	Combined	Real	Block diagram	IBM PC[b]	Yes[d]	General purpose
SIMSCRIPT II.5	SIMSCRIPT	Discrete	Real	Event	IBM PC[b]	No	General purpose
SLAM II[a]	FORTRAN	Combined	Real	Network	—	Yes[e]	General purpose
SLAM II PC	FORTRAN	Combined	Real	Network	IBM PC[b]	No	General purpose
SPEED	FORTRAN	Discrete	Real	Statements	—	No	Manufacturing systems

[a] IDSS 2.0 must be run on a VAX 11/780, VAX 11/750 or CAD-LINK microprocessor.
[b] Software that will run on an IBM PC may run on IBM compatibles.
[c] The necessary hardware to run SEE-WHY can be purchased with the software.
[d] BLOCKS, available from Systems Modeling Corp., can be used to graphically input the block diagram.
[e] TESS (The Extended Simulation System), available from Pritsker and Associates, Inc., can be used to graphically input the network.

1. Event orientation
2. Activity scanning
3. Process orientation

Event Orientation. Using an event-oriented world view, the system to be modeled is described in terms of status-disturbing events. The analyst constructs a simulation model by:

1. Defining each event which can occur in the system.
2. Specifying the cause and effects of each event.
3. Creating mechanisms to execute event change within the simulation model.
4. Logically linking the events to one another.
5. Updating time and statistics at each status-disturbing event.
6. Collecting statistics of interest. SIMSCRIPT, SIMAN, and SLAM II allow models to be built using the event orientation.

Activity Scanning. In some simulation models, events which are known to occur cannot be scheduled. However, it is usually possible to define the event mechanism in terms of those physical influences which trigger the event at an (unknown) time. For example, when the temperature of a particular cutting tool reaches a predetermined level, the cutting process must be interrupted for cooling. The event, "stop for cooling" can be defined but not scheduled in the simulation model. The rate of change of temperature might be represented by a difference or a differential equation, the value of which must be continuously monitored. The mechanism by which events of this nature are monitored is called *activity scanning.* Activity scanning may occur either indirectly or directly. Direct activity scanning is automatically provided by MICRONET, SIMAN, and SLAM II. (World Dynamics and System Dynamics are also examples of activity scanning simulation languages.)

Process Orientation. Using a process orientation, the simulation language views the world as being composed of sequences of events which occur in a definite pattern. For example, a single-channel queueing model possesses a waiting line, a service mechanism, and structured rules as to how items move through the service system. The entire sequence of activities can be combined into a single simulation "command" which executes a fixed set of processing rules. Although queue disciplines (FIFO, LIFO, random, etc.) and service time distributions (exponential, normal, gamma, etc.) may vary, once they are specified, the sequence of events is uniquely determined. GPSS, Q-GERTS, and GEMS models are built using the process orientation. SIMSCRIPT, SLAM, and SIMAN also allow models to be built using this orientation. The fundamental and direct influence of this world view is the ability to model complex, real-world systems in a "no-programming" environment.

Many writers find it convenient to further classify simulation models into two major categories: (1) continuous-change models or (2) discrete-change models. Continuous-change models use fixed-increment, time-advance mechanisms and are appropriate when the analyst considers the system being studied as consisting of a continuous flow of information or items counted in the aggregate, rather than as individual items. In discrete-change models, the analyst is interested in what happens to individual items in the system. Most discrete-change models, therefore, utilize the next-event type of timekeeping. Some problems are clearly described best by one type or other, whereas either type might be used for other problems.

One of the most interesting recent developments is the appearance of simulation languages which allow combined discrete-continuous models. GASP IV was the first well-documented language of this type. SLAM II and SIMAN also have this capability, and there is a version of SIMSCRIPT II.5 which can also accommodate combined models.

Conclusion

In conclusion, one should be aware of the simulation alternative currently available to the systems analyst. For a wide variety of real-world models, computer programming may be entirely unnecessary, and simulation results produced in a matter of hours. (GEMS II, MICRONET, IDSS 2.0, SIMAN, MAP-I, MAST, SEE-WHY, SLAM II, etc.) For some complex models, process-oriented languages may not provide the necessary framework, and higher-level languages (event oriented) should be used (SLAM II, SIMSCRIPT II.5, etc.). Some languages provide for fast no-programming modeling of queueing phenomena (GEMS II, IDSS 2.0, Q-GERTS, SLAM, GPSS, MICRONET, MAST, SEE-WHY, SIMAN, etc.) while others provide a more specialized capability for modeling complex material handling or manufacturing systems (MAP-1, SPEED, GEMS II, SIMAN). In any case, simulation must now be viewed as a powerful systems analysis tool for which there are several modeling alternatives. The modern and educated systems analyst will choose the most desirable or applicable simulation language for the problem at hand. Also, it should be noted that, based upon experience in modeling material handling and warehousing systems, either as stand-alone models (AGVS/ASRS/MINI-LOAD) or as part of a broader model, the process-oriented simulation languages can be used effectively in gross modeling exercises. For detailed models, the standard options available in the no-programming environment often fail to provide the necessary machinery. In particular, detailed modeling of long conveyor runs, complex interference models, picking logic, AS/R systems and conveyor interfaces, and merge/sort lines often require auxiliary (user-interface) programming. The intelligent user, properly schooled in the arts and sciences of simulation, will undoubtedly find the proper path to effective, representative simulation models. The industrial community should continuously be attentive to recent developments, since this field is evolving rapidly.

References

1. J.R. Emshoff and R.L. Sisson, *Design and Use of Computer Simulation Models,* MacMillan, New York, 1970.
2. P.J. Kiviat, "Development of Discrete Digital Simulation Languages," *Simulation,* vol. VII, no. 2, 1967.
3. R.E. Shannon, *Systems Simulation: The Art and Science,* Prentice-Hall, Englewood Cliffs, NJ, 1975.
4. D.T. Phillips, A. Ravindran, and J.J. Solberg, *Operations Research: Principles and Practice,* John Wiley, New York, 1978.
5. D.T. Phillips, "Future Shock in Simulation Languages," IIE National Convention, Chicago, 1984.

Simulation Software Sources

Lodestone II, Inc.
3833 Texas Avenue, Suite 460
Bryan, TX 77802
(409) 846-4171

Wolverine Software Corporation
7630 Little River Turnpike, Suite 208
Annadale, VA 22003

Minuteman Software
P.O. Box 171
Stow, MA 01775
(617) 897-5662

Pritsker and Associates, Inc.
P.O. Box 2413
West Lafayette, IN 47906
(317) 463-5557

Micro Simulation
50 Milk Street, Suite 1500
Boston, MA 02109
(617) 451-8448

CMS Research, Inc.
945 Bavarian Court
Oshkosh, WI

C.A.C.I.
12011 San Vincente Blvd.
Los Angeles, CA 90049
(213) 476-6511

BLSL, Inc.
83 Cambridge Street
Burlington, MA01803
(617) 272-7333

Systems Modeling Corp.
Calder Sq. P.O. Box 10074
State College, PA 16805
(814) 238-5919

Horizon Software, Inc.
460 Totten Pond Road
Waltham, MA 02154
(617) 890-6665

10
Economic Analysis

Thomas L. Ward, Ph.D., P.E.

Professor, Department of Industrial Engineering, University of Louisville, Louisville, Kentucky

Mickey R. Wilhelm, Ph.D., P.E.

Chairman, Department of Industrial Engineering, University of Louisville, Louisville, Kentucky

Introduction

Economic analysis is an aid for choosing between alternatives. Such choices arise frequently in warehousing. In the case of existing operations, the question may be one of retirement and replacement: should an old industrial truck be retained one more year, or should it be replaced with a new improved model? When new facilities are being planned, the decisions are usually complicated by a large number of alternative designs that must be evaluated. The basic principles of economic analysis can be applied in both cases.

As an example, consider a firm that is evaluating several designs for a large warehouse. One alternative is a 20-aisle, 98-bay, 10-high automated storage/retrieval (AS/RS) system. A preliminary consideration of costs has yielded the following data:

First Costs	
Building	$3,150,000
Racks	2,100,000
S/R machines	2,300,000
Aisle hardware	320,000
Controls	1,530,000
One-time expense	800,000
Land	200,000

Annual Operating and Maintenance Costs	
Labor	$65,000
Electrical power	28,000
Fuel oil	17,000
Miscellaneous	72,000

Other Data	
Expected life	20 years
Salvage value	$1,000,000
Incremental tax rate	40%
Discount rate	19.7%
Inflation rate	5%

For an economic analysis of this design, see Table 10.1.

Since this example will be elaborated on in subsequent sections, take a closer look at its features. All first costs appear in the first two rows (year 0) of column (2) of Table 10.1. They are shown as negative cashflows since they are costs or disbursements. The $9,600,000 total cost of land, building, and equipment is shown separately from the $800,000 one-time expense, since these two amounts are treated differently for tax purposes. All annual operating and maintenance costs are combined and shown as negative cashflows in the entries for years 1–20 in column (2). The magnitudes of these costs increase each year due to the effects of inflation and price escalation. The $1,000,000 salvage value is shown as a positive cashflow in year 20 of column (2), since it is a benefit or receipt. The depreciation in column (3) was based on the U.S. Tax Reform Act of 1986. The balance of the columns are obtained as described in the table notes.

The −$9,111,620 amount at the bottom of column (9) is called the "present worth" (PW) of the project. When two or more projects that satisfy the same need are being compared, the benefits may be equal or unknown. In such cases, it is customary to drop the minus sign and refer to $9,111,620 as "present cost" (PC) or "present worth-cost" (PW-C). In either case, the project with the lowest cost is selected. It is also common to compare projects on the basis of equivalent uniform annual cost (EUAC). Using techniques to be described later, the EUAC for this project is $1,375,727 in constant year-0 dollars. If the benefits are known or can be estimated, they may be added to the before-tax cashflows (BTCF) in column (2) of Table 10.1. If the benefits are sufficiently great, a positive BTCF will result for all or most of years 1–20. When the benefits are explicitly included in this way, the PW is sometimes called the "net present worth" (NPW). When the NPW is positive, the project is said to be economically feasible or profitable. In this case, it will usually be possible to determine the discounted cashflow internal rate of return (IRR).

Table 10.1. Economic Analysis of Sample Design for a Large Warehouse

End of year n (1)	Before-tax cashflow $U(n)$ (2)	ACRS depreciation $D(n)$ (3)	Effect on taxable income $V(n)$ (4)	Effect on income tax $T(n)$ (5)	After-tax cashflow $X(n)$ (6)	Present-worth factor $(P/N,i,n)$ (7)	Present worth $P(n)$ (8)	Cumulative present worth P_n (9)
0	− 9,600,000				− 9,600,000	1.0000	− 9,600,000	− 9,600,000
0	− 800,000		− 800,000	320,000	− 480,000	1.0000	− 480,000	− 10,080,000
1	− 193,920	1,295,833	− 1,489,753	595,901	401,981	0.8354	335,824	− 9,744,176
2	− 206,655	2,100,000	− 2,306,655	922,662	716,007	0.6979	499,722	− 9,244,454
3	− 220,264	1,300,000	− 1,520,264	608,106	387,841	0.5831	226,137	− 9,018,317
4	− 234,809	820,000	− 1,054,809	421,924	187,115	0.4871	91,145	− 8,927,172
5	− 250,356	820,000	− 1,070,356	428,142	177,786	0.4069	72,348	− 8,854,824
6	− 266,978	460,000	− 726,978	290,791	23,813	0.3400	8,096	− 8,846,728
7	− 284,751	100,000	− 384,751	153,900	− 130,850	0.2840	− 37,163	− 8,883,891
8	− 303,759	100,000	− 403,759	161,503	− 142,255	0.2373	− 33,753	− 8,917,644
9	− 324,090	100,000	− 424,090	169,636	− 154,454	0.1982	− 30,616	− 8,948,261
10	− 345,840	100,000	− 445,840	178,336	− 167,504	0.1656	− 27,739	− 8,975,999
11	− 369,113	100,000	− 469,113	187,645	− 181,468	0.1383	− 25,105	− 9,001,104
12	− 394,018	100,000	− 494,018	197,607	− 196,411	0.1156	− 22,701	− 9,023,805
13	− 420,675	100,000	− 520,675	208,270	− 212,405	0.0966	− 20,509	− 9,044,314
14	− 449,211	100,000	− 549,211	219,684	− 229,526	0.0807	− 18,515	− 9,062,828
15	− 479,763	100,000	− 579,763	231,905	− 247,858	0.0674	− 16,703	− 9,079,531
16	− 512,479	100,000	− 612,479	244,992	− 267,488	0.0563	− 15,059	− 9,094,590
17	− 547,519	100,000	− 647,519	259,007	− 288,511	0.0470	− 13,569	− 9,108,160
18	− 585,052	100,000	− 685,052	274,021	− 311,031	0.0393	− 12,221	− 9,120,381
19	− 625,263	100,000	− 725,263	290,105	− 335,158	0.0328	− 11,002	− 9,131,382
20	− 668,349	54,167	− 722,515	289,006	− 379,343	0.0274	− 10,403	− 9,141,785
20	1,000,000	1,250,000	− 250,000	100,000	1,100,000	0.0274	30,165	− 9,111,620

NOTES: (numbers refer to columns)
(1) Cashflows are assumed to occur at end of year n.
(2) See Table 10.6.
(3) See Table 10.11.
(4) Effect on taxable income $V(n) = U(n) - D(n)$. Negative cashflow indicates a decrease in income.
(5) Effect on cashflow for income tax, $T(n) = -tVn$, where t is the combined incremental tax rate, 40% in this example. Positive cashflows indicate a reduction in the outflow for taxes.
(6) After-tax cashflow $X(n) = U(n) - T(n)$.
(7) Single-payment present-worth factor, $(P/F,i,n) = (1 + i)^{-n}$ where i is the minimum attractive rate of return, 19.7% in this example.
(8) Present worth $P(n = (P/F,i,n)X(n)$
(9) Cumulative present worth $P_n = \Sigma P(n)$

Life-Cycle Costs and Consequences

Cost estimation was required to generate the before-tax cashflows for column (2) of Table 10.1. This is frequently the most time-consuming part of the economic analysis.

Listing of Project Consequences. The first step in the estimation process is to attempt to prepare a list of all the consequences that will result if the project in question is selected. At this stage, a list of categories is prepared. Detailed estimating comes later. In addition to categories of costs and benefits associated with acquisition, operation, and retirement, there will be consequences that are difficult or impossible to quantify in dollars.

Irreducibles. Irreducibles are of two types: (1) factors that cannot readily be reduced to dollar amounts even though it may be conceptually possible to do so. Examples might be an increase in production due to worker job satisfaction, or an improvement in material flow due to the reduction of congestion on the floor. (2) Factors such as ethical considerations that are intangibles. Identifying irreducibles is useful prior to making a categorical list of cost areas. Not only will it help ensure that all important decision criteria are considered, but it may suggest associated costs that would have been overlooked.

Table 10.2 is a list of qualitative factors frequently of importance in the selection of equipment and/or warehousing systems. The table is not a complete list of irreducibles. Rather, it should be used as a checklist to aid in the identification of categories of project specific irreducibles. Since most qualitative factors involve people and operations, their early consideration may assist in planning for implementation.

First Cost. First costs include land, depreciable property, and one-time expenses that should be considered separately because of their differing tax treatment.

Land is neither depreciable nor can it be taken as a deductible expense. In the example in Table 10.1, the $200,000 cost of land was included in the $9,600,000 entry for column (2), year 0. It was not considered in calculating depreciation, column (3), nor did it affect taxable income, column (4). The cost of site preparation directly associated with the construction of buildings and roadways is part of their costs and is depreciable.

Buildings, machinery, equipment, and vehicles used for business are depreciable property. In Table 10.1, the total of $9,400,000 for the building, racks, S/R machines, aisle hardware, and controls is depreciable and is added to the $200,000 cost of land to form the −$9,600,000 entry in column (2), year 0. Like land, the cost of depreciable property did not affect the taxable income in column (4). Unlike land however, the $9,400,000 was considered in calculating the depreciation charges in column (3). In fact, the entries in that column total $9,400,000. Table 10.3 is a list of typical costs associated with the purchase and installation of depreciable property.

One-time expenses are costs incurred before or during the time that equipment or a system is readied for service and are tax-deductible. In

Table 10.2. Quantitative Aspects to Be Considered When Evaluating Warehouse Systems

1. Ability to pace, or keep pace with, production requirements
2. Aesthetic considerations
3. Automatic weighing, counting, and verification capabilities
4. Availability of equipment needed
5. Availability of repair parts and/or contract maintenance services
6. Availability of trained operators
7. Avoidance of construction projects
8. Capability of handling less than unit loads
9. Compatibility with the materials handling operating organization
10. Cubic space (volume) utilization
11. Degree of automation desirable
12. Degree of inventory control afforded
13. Ease of future expansion of the handling methods
14. Ease of maintenance and rapidity of repair
15. Ease of supervision and control
16. Effect of natural conditions: land, weather, and ambient temperature
17. Effect on in-process time
18. Empty-pallet handling systems and slave-pallet handling (dispensing)
19. Flexibility (ease of changing or rearranging the installed methods)
20. Frequency and seriousness of potential breakdowns
21. Increased systems productivity
22. Insuring of FIFO discipline
23. Integration with and ability to serve process operations
24. Integration with external storage facilities
25. Interruption or disruption of production and related confusion during installation and start-up
26. Limitations imposed by the handling methods on the flexibility and ease of expansion of the layout and/or buildings
27. Personnel problems: availability of skilled workers, training capability, disposition of redundant workers, job description changes, union contracts, and work practices
28. Potential delays from required synchronization and peak loads
29. Promotional or public relations value
30. Quality of product and risk of damage to materials
31. Release of storage on manufacturing floor
32. Safety and housekeeping
33. Shrink wrapping, strapping, and load stabilization
34. Space utilization
35. Supporting services required
36. Tie-in with external transportation
37. Tie-in with scheduling, inventory control, and recordkeeping
38. Time required to get into operation: installation, training, and debugging
39. Versatility and adaptability of the handling methods to day-to-day fluctuation in products, quantities, and delivery times
40. Volume of spare parts required in stock
41. Working conditions and employee satisfaction

Table 10.3. First Costs of Warehousing Equipment and Systems Including Expenditures Necesary to Ready for Service

1. Buildings
2. Docks
3. Electrical installation
4. Erection
5. Fire-protection systems
6. Foundations and flooring
7. Heating, ventilating, and air-conditioning systems
8. In-warehouse transportation equipment: fork trucks, conveyors, automatic guided vehicles, etc.
9. Installation
10. Instrumentation: bar-code readers, sensors, information-gathering devices, computers, software, controllers, etc.
11. Invoice price of equipment
12. Landscaping
13. Modification of existing equipment
14. Rearrangement of existing facilities
15. Roads
16. Security equipment
17. Site preparation
18. Supports, racks, etc

Table 10.1, the one-time expenses give rise to the separate −$800,000 entry in column (2), year 0. This expense is not involved in the calculation of depreciation charges in column (3). It does result in a corresponding −$800,000 entry in column (4), taxable income. Table 10.4 lists costs that may occur near the time the property is placed in service and still, under certain conditions, be treated as expenses.

Table 10.4. Vendor-quoted Items that May, Under Certain Circumstances, Be Expenses Rather than Part of First Cost

1. Consulting fees
2. Debugging
3. Engineering
4. Expenditures incurred after warehousing equipment and systems are placed in service, including:
   a. Advertising
   b. Labor
   c. Maintenance
   d. Materials
   e. Operating expenses
   f. Rental and leasing expenses
   g. Utilities
5. Implementation
6. Materials that are to be used after warehouse and/or its systems are placed in service
7. Normal system modification

Operation and Maintenance. Costs of operation and maintenance (O & M) are expenses and enter the analysis in exactly the same way as one-time expenses. The only difference is that O & M costs are continuing expenses that are incurred over the life of the project. Table 10.5 is a partial list of O & M costs typical to warehousing.

Salvage. When equipment is retired or a system is removed from service, it is ordinarily sold. The salvage value is the net difference between the income received from this sale and the costs of removing it from service. Typical costs of removing property from service include modification and repair of the building upon removal of large machines, elimination of hazards remaining after removal, and site repair required by zoning laws or lease provisions.

Cost Estimations. After preparing lists of costs, actual dollar amounts are estimated. In some cases, estimation must be preceded or accompanied by further liaison with the vendor to unbundle quotes.

Unbundling Quotes. Quotations are unbundled by separating the total cost into capital and expense items. The goal is to identify costs that can be treated as one-time expenses. The costs in Table 10.4 are likely candidates if incurred after the equipment or system is placed in service. Each instance should be reviewed with the company's tax accountant. Computer software is frequently a large cost and its tax treatment should be considered carefully. If the software is developed by the warehouse owner, costs can either be treated as an expense or as a depreciable amount, as long as the policy is consistent companywide. Purchased software is ordinarily considered depreciable. The treatment of software

Table 10.5. Operating and Maintenance Costs

1. Actual costs attributable to absenteeism
2. Actual costs of injuries and illness
3. Coal, fuel oil, and gasoline
4. Contract maintenance services
5. Direct and indirect labor overtime
6. Electrical power
7. Labor turnover
8. Maintenance tools and supplies
9. Maintenance, supervision, and other indirect labor
10. Natural gas
11. Operating and other direct labor
12. Operating materials
13. Other utilities
14. Property taxes and insurance
15. Training
16. Working capital

cost prepared to the user's specification by an outside vendor or consultant should be discussed with the analyst's tax consultant.

First Costs. The invoice price of depreciable property can be based on proposals and quotations from vendors, architects, and contractors. However, the cost of these items must also include shipping charges, installation costs, and all other costs necessary to ready the property for service. A list of such costs is shown in Table 10.3. At least some of these costs may not be a part of the vendor's quote and must be estimated by the analyst.

Operation and Maintenance. Most O & M costs listed in Table 10.4 can be categorized as labor, purchased material and supplies, and purchased services. Labor should be estimated in terms of the number of workers or the number of work-hours per year. Annual costs are obtained by multiplying by current labor rates, including fringe benefits. Only incremental costs should be considered. Overhead or burden should ordinarily not be applied to labor costs. Only the actual dollar amount of the change in overhead cost attributable to the project under consideration should be included. Estimates of the cost of purchased supplies and materials should also be based on estimates of the physical quantity required multiplied by current prices. Purchased services are usually supplied under contract and can be estimated on vendor quotations.

In the case of large projects or when electronic spreadsheet templates or specialized computer programs are being written, it may be desirable to treat the above process more formally. Here is one model.

The year n cost of the mth good or service is given by:

$$C_{m,0}(n) = p_m(0)q_m(n) \tag{10.1}$$

where $q_m(n)$ = the quantity required in year n and $p_m(0)$ = the price in today's dollars. Similarly, the subscript 0 in the cost, $C_{m,0}(n)$, indicates that the cost is measured in present dollars. The question of price escalation and inflation will be considered below.

In the example outlined in the introduction, let labor be commodity 1, electrical power commodity 2, etc. Four full-time workers are required. The cost of one worker, including fringes but excluding overhead, is \$16,250 per year. Electrical power costs \$0.05 per kilowatthour, and 560,000 kilowatthours are required. Thus,

m	$q_m(n)$	$p_m(0)$	$C_{m,0}(n)$
1	4	\$16,250.00	\$65,000
2	560,000	0.05	28,000

and so on for as many commodities, m = 1, 2,...M, as required. Thus, the number of workers and the usage of electricity are assumed constant over the 20-year life, so $C_{m,0}(n)$ is constant for n = 1 to 20.

Salvage. The salvage value of equipment at the end of the project life is usually based on historical records or the judgment of persons with extensive experience trading in similar items. There is greater uncertainty in the estimation of salvage values than in the case of first costs and O & M costs. However, the fact that salvage occurs in the future reduces the importance of estimation errors. For example, in Table 10.1 the $1,000,000 salvage value at the end of 20 years only affects the present cost by $30,814. Salvage values are usually estimated in terms of actual dollars current at the time of retirement.

Price Escalation. For the foreseeable future, most prices can be expected to escalate at rates high enough to be important in the economic analysis of warehouse equipment and systems. Separate estimates of the escalation rate should be made for the price of each commodity, that is, for each labor grade, material, supply, and service that enters into the annual cost of O & M. Such escalation rate estimates are also required for benefits. For commodity m, the price in year n is given in terms of the year-0 price by:

$$p_m(n) = p_m(0) \prod_{j=1}^{n} [1 + s_m(j)] \tag{10.2}$$

where $s_m(j)$ = effective price escalation rate for commodity m in year j. It is frequently assumed that the price escalation rate is constant for a particular analysis, that is, $p_m(n) = p_m$ = constant, so that Equation (10.2) becomes

$$p_m(n) = p_m(0)\,(1 + s_m)^n \tag{10.3}$$

Sometimes a differential escalation rate, $s_m{}'$, is defined by

$$s'_m = (s_m - f)/(1 + f) \tag{10.4}$$

where f = general inflation rate (to be defined in the next section). The differential escalation rate is zero if the price of commodity m is exactly responsive to inflation, negative if it is underresponsive, and positive if it is overresponsive. Things undergoing rapid technological improvement, such as microcomputers in recent times, are frequently underresponsive. Depletable resources such as strategic metals may be overresponsive.

Some firms subscribe to the services of organizations that make projections of economic activity on the basis of managed econometric models. Such services usually include estimates of the general inflation rate and of the escalation rates of important sources of energy. Trade publications, the opinion of suppliers, and the firm's own historical records are other sources of price escalation data.

After determining the cost of each commodity in today's dollars $C_{m,0}(0)$, and the corresponding price escalation rate s_m, the cost in actual year n dollars is calculated from:

$$C_{m,n}(n) = C_{m,0}(m)\,(1 + s_m)^n \tag{10.5}$$

where the subscript n in $C_{m,n}$ is a reminder that the cost is measured in actual year-n dollars. The total cost for year n is then given by:

$$C_n(n) = \sum_{m=1}^{M} C_{m,n}(n) \tag{10.6}$$

where M = total number of commodities. Again, the subscript n in $C_n(n)$ indicates that the total cost for year n is measured in actual dollars.

In the case of the example in the introduction and Table 10.1, there are $M = 4$ commodities as follows:

m	$C_{m,0}(0)$	S_m
1	\$65,000	7%
2	28,000	8%
3	17,000	9%
4	72,000	5%

It must be emphasized that these price escalation rates s_m are illustrative and apply only to this example. In actual analyses, values must be estimated as described below. Table 10.6 shows how these costs were escalated using Equation (10.5) and combined using Equation (10.6). Thus, for example, the labor entry for year 1 is (1.07) (65,000) = 69,550 and the miscellaneous entry for year 20 is $(1.05)^{20}(72,000) = 191{,}037$. The total cost from column (6) of Table 10.6 was then entered into column (2) of Table 10.1.

General Inflation. The economist considers inflation to be a rise in the price level of all goods and services. Usually, this is measured by the rise of prices of all the goods and services in the gross national product (GNP). In engineering terms, it can be considered to be part of the conversion factor that relates two different units of measurement: *actual* dollars (A\$) and *real* dollars (R\$). Actual dollars, also called *current* dollars, or *then-current* dollars, are the monetary units of day-to-day life. Real dollars, also called *constant* dollars, are the monetary units used to measure prices at a particular reference time.

The relation between actual dollars in year n and real dollars based on reference year k is:

$$A\$ = R\$ \prod_{j=k+1}^{n} [(1 + f(j)] \qquad (10.7)$$

where $f(j)$ = general inflation rate for year j. If $f(n) = f$ = constant, then Equation (10.7) becomes:

$$A\$ = R\$(1 + f)^{n-k} \qquad (10.8)$$

Values of f used in economic analysis are frequently based on the predictions of economists, for example, as obtained from managed econometric models. Inflation rates of 5 to 7 percent are commonly estimated for the United States for the balance of this century. The general inflation rate of 5 percent used in the introductory example did not enter directly into the preparation of Table 10.1. Only price escalation rates were used (see the previous section). The general inflation rate was required for the calculation of the EUAC in constant year-0 dollars. This will be discussed in a subsequent section. Notice that the escalation rate for miscellaneous costs of $72,000 was assumed to be 5 percent. When

Table 10.6. Illustration of Total Cost Calculation Based on Four Cost Components, Each with Its Own Price Escalation Rate

End of year n (1)	Labor $C_{1n}(n)$ (2)	Electrical power $C_{2n}(n)$ (3)	Fuel oil $C_{3n}(n)$ (4)	Miscellaneous $C_{4n}(n)$ (5)	Total cost $C_n(n)$ (6)
0	65,000	28,000	17,000	72,000	
1	69,550	30,240	18,530	75,600	193,920
2	74,419	32,659	20,198	79,380	206,655
3	79,628	35,272	22,015	83,349	220,264
4	85,202	38,094	23,997	87,516	234,809
5	91,166	41,141	26,157	91,892	250,356
6	97,547	44,432	28,511	96,487	266,978
7	104,376	47,987	31,077	101,311	284,751
8	111,682	51,826	33,874	106,377	303,759
9	119,500	55,972	36,922	111,696	324,090
10	127,865	60,450	40,245	117,280	345,840
11	136,815	65,286	43,867	123,144	369,113
12	146,392	70,509	47,815	129,302	394,018
13	156,640	76,149	52,119	135,767	420,675
14	167,605	82,241	56,809	142,555	449,211
15	179,337	88,821	61,922	149,683	479,763
16	191,891	95,926	67,495	157,165	512,479
17	205,323	103,601	73,570	165,025	547,519
18	219,696	111,889	80,191	173,277	585,052
19	235,074	120,840	87,408	181,940	625,263
20	251,529	130,507	95,275	191,037	668,349

no other data is available, or when costs are made up of a large variety of common goods and services, it is not uncommon to assume that the price escalation rate equals the general inflation rate.

Cost of Capital. The discount rate or minimum attractive rate of return (MARR) used in economic analysis is usually based on the firm's cost of capital. Frequently it is exactly the cost of capital. At other times, it is an arbitrary rate that is established by fiat and that is required to be used for all economic analyses in a particular organization. Even in the latter case, the analyst should make a rough estimate of the cost of capital. If there is substantial disagreement between the analyst's estimate and the value generally used by the firm, specific consideration of this fact is required. In particular, one should test to see if the recommended decision is *sensitive* to the difference in interest rates. Sensitivity analysis is discussed in the section on risk and uncertainty.

Calculation of the cost of capital is controversial. In engineering economic analysis, the combined weighted cost of capital is almost invariably used. This figure takes into account the cost of debt capital and equity capital. For a profitable firm growing at an approximately constant rate, a working estimate of the cost of capital can be based on data in the firm's annual report. Table 10.7 is an example of such a calculation. Cost of capital estimates should be made for several recent years. If there is substantial variation, a value representative of the performance expected over the life of the project should be selected.

Depreciation

The following discussion is an analysis of the U.S. Tax Reform Act of 1986. It was based on a staff report of the joint Congressional committee on taxation (see references) that was made prior to the availability of applicable publications from the Internal Revenue Service (IRS). A current tax guide and IRS publications should be consulted to determine if there have been any subsequent changes or clarifications.

Depreciable property has been previously defined in connection with the discussion of life-cycle costs. It can be further subdivided into personal property and real property.

Personal Property. For depreciation purposes, personal property consists of machinery, equipment, and vehicles, used in business or held for the production of income. Such property may be depreciated by either of two methods: *accelerated-cost recovery system* (ACRS) depreciation, or *straight-line* (SL) depreciation. One method is selected at the time the property is placed in service and that method must be retained for the life of that property. It is not possible to switch back and forth, except as specifically provided for in the definition of ACRS depreciation. Profitable firms usually select ACRS. Start-up firms that are not expected to make profits in the early life of the firm as well as those that have sustained recent losses may elect to use straight-line depreciation.

ACRS Depreciation for Personal Property. A life of 3, 5, 7, 10, 15, or 20 years must be used. Guidelines for selecting the ACRS life are given in Table 10.8. When the life has been selected, the annual depreciation charges for 3-, 5-, 7-, and 10-year life property are calculated using double declining balance (DDB) depreciation with an optimum shift to SL depreciation, assuming zero salvage value. Depreciation charges for 15- and 20-year properties are calculated in the same way, except that 150 percent declining balance depreciation replaces DDB depreciation. There are no statutory tables of ACRS depreciation charges as there were from 1981 to 1986, although the IRS may prepare tables and include them in a future issue of Publication 534.

Table 10.7. Approximate Calculation of the Average Cost of Capital for a Stable Profitable Firm, in Thousands of Dollars*

Net profit (current year)	$47,750	
Depreciation (current year)	28,000	
Increase in deferred taxes (current year)	1,000	
Total cashflow		$76,750
Total stockholder equity (previous year)		305,600
After-tax equity rate: 76750/305600 = 0.2511 (25.11%)		
Interest expense (current year)		$17,000
Long-term debt (previous year)†		$136,000
Before-tax debt rate: 17000/13600 = 0.1250 (12.50%)		
Combined incremental tax rate: 0.40 (40%)‡		
After-tax debt rate: (1 − .40) × (12.50%) = 7.5%		
Stockholder's equity	$305,600	
Total debt	136,000	
Total capital		$441,600
Equity ratio: 305600/441600 = 0.6920 or 69.2%		
Debt ratio: 136000/441600 = 0.3080 or 30.80%		
Average monetary cost of capital (including inflation):		
(0.6920) × (25.11%) + (0.3080) × (7.5%) = 19.69%§		
General inflation rate: 0.05 or 5%‡		
Approximate adjustment to find real cost of capital:		
(1 + 0.1969)/(1 + 0.05) − 1 = 0.1399 or 13.99%¶		

* Based on illustrative data from Merrill Lynch, Pierce Fenner and Smith (1983).

† Only long-term debt was included because interest expense on short-term debt was not known.

‡ Assumed for examples in this chapter.

§ For convenience, 19.7% was used in Table 10.1.

¶ For convenience, 14.0% was used in examples elsewhere in this chapter.

Half-Year Convention. With the exception to be discussed under "Half-Quarter Convention," it is assumed that all personal property is placed in service at the middle of the year. Thus, there is a half-year depreciation taken in the first year ($n = 1$) and a half-year depreciation taken in the $N +$ 1st-year ($n = N + 1$), where N is the ACRS property class life. If $B(0)$ is the total first-cost, an algorithm for calculating the nth-year depreciation $D(n)$ and end-of-year book value $B(n)$ is: (1) Set $n = 1$ and calculate $D(1) = B(0)R/2$, and $B(1) = B(0) - D(1)$. (2) Increment n by 1 and calculate $D_R(n) = B(n - 1)R$, $D_S(n) = B(n - 1)/(N - n + 1/2)$, $D(n) = \max[D_R(n), D_S(n)]$, and $B(n) = B(n - 1) - D(n)$. (3) IF $n > N$ THEN loop back to step 2, ELSE $D(N + 1) = B(N)$, $B(N + 1) = 0$, and

Table 10.8. ACRS Depreciable Lives for Personal Property

Three-Year Class
Property with an ADR midpoint of 4 years or less, excluding automobiles; light, general-purpose trucks; and property used in connection with research and experimentation.
Five-Year Class
Property with an ADR midpoint of more than 4 but less than 10 years, including automobiles; light trucks; qualified technological equipment; computer-based telephone central office switching equipment; research and experimentation property; geothermal, ocean thermal, solar, and wind energy properties; and biomass properties described in section 48(1) that are used in connection with qualifying, small, power-production facilities.
Seven-Year Class
Property with an ADR midpoint of at least 10 years but less than 16 years, including single-purpose agricultural or horticultural structures and property with no ADR midpoint that is not classified elsewhere.
Ten-Year Class
Property with an ADR midpoint of at least 16 years but less than 20 years.
Fifteen-Year Class
Property with an ADR midpoint of at least 20 years and less than 25 years, including municipal wastewater treatment plants and telephone distribution plant, as well as comparable equipment used for two-way exchange of voice and data communications.
Twenty-Year Class
Property with an ADR midpoint of 25 years and more, other than section 1250 real property with an ADR midpoint of 27.5 years and more, and including municipal sewers.

NOTE: Asset depreciation range (ADR) midpoints for selected asset guideline classes are given in IRS Publication 534. A more extensive list is given in Revenue Procedure 83–85. Some assets that do not have ADR midpoint lives are specifically included in a class (*e.g.*, computer-based telephone central-office switching equipment in the *five-year class*). Assets that do not have ADR midpoint lives and are not included elsewhere are considered seven-year class property.

STOP. The results of these calculations for $B(0) = 1$ are shown in Table 10.9. In order to use the table, the total first-cost (including shipping, installation, and other costs of placing the property into service) are simply multiplied by the percentages shown. The salvage is not considered in calculating the yearly depreciation charges. In fact, the percentages in each column of Table 10.9 total 100 percent within the limits imposed by rounding errors. This ensures that, at the end of its depreciable life, the property will have a book value of zero. The same charges are used regardless of the time of year (month or quarter) that the property is placed into service.

Half-Quarter Convention. When more than 40 percent of newly acquired personal property is placed in service during the last quarter of the corporate tax year, the half-year convention cannot be used. Rather, it must be assumed that asset is placed in service at the midpoint of the quarter in which the property was actually placed in service. If $B(0)$ is the total first-cost of a property placed in service during the kth quarter, an algorithm for calculating the nth year depreciation $D(n)$ and end-of-year book value $B(n)$ is: (1) Set $n = 1$and calculate $D(1) = B(0)R(9 - 2k)/8$, and $B(1) = B(0) - D(1)$. (2) Increment n by 1 and calculate $D_R(n) = B(n - 1)R$, $D_S(n) = B(n - 1)/[N + (2k - 1)/8 -$

Table 10.9. ACRS Depreciation Percentages

Year	Three-year class	Five-year class	Seven-year class	Ten-year class	Fifteen-year class	Twenty-year class
1	0.33333	0.20000	0.14286	0.10000	0.05000	0.03750
2	0.44444	0.32000	0.24490	0.18000	0.09500	0.07219
3	0.14815	0.19200	0.17493	0.14400	0.08550	0.06677
4	0.07407	0.11520	0.12495	0.11520	0.07695	0.06177
5		0.11520	0.08925	0.09216	0.06926	0.05713
6		0.05760	0.08925	0.07373	0.06233	0.05285
7			0.08925	0.06554	0.05905	0.04888
8			0.04462	0.06554	0.05905	0.04522
9				0.06554	0.05905	0.04462
10				0.06554	0.05905	0.04462
11				0.03277	0.05905	0.04462
12					0.05905	0.04462
13					0.05905	0.04462
14					0.05905	0.04462
15					0.05905	0.04462
16					0.02953	0.04462
17						0.04462
18						0.04462
19						0.04462
20						0.04462
21						0.02231

$n]$, $D(n) = \max[D_R(n), D_S(n)]$, and $B(n) = B(n-1) - D(n)$. (3) IF $n < N$ THEN loop back to step 2, ELSE $D(N+1) = B(N)$, $B(N+1) = 0$, and STOP. The uncertainty associated with the time a property is placed in service suggests that most engineering economy studies will be made using the half-year convention.

SL Depreciation for Personal Property. If straight-line depreciation is elected, the property is depreciated over its ACRS class life (Table 10.8). Once the SL depreciable life, N, is selected, the annual depreciation charge, $D(n)$, is calculated from:

$$D(n) = B(0)/2N \qquad \text{for } n = 1, n = N + 1 \tag{10.9a}$$

$$D(n) = B(0)/N \qquad \text{for } n = 2, 3, \ldots, N \tag{10.9b}$$

For example, a \$9000 light-duty truck with a 5-year ACRS life could be depreciated based on 5-year SL depreciation using the following depreciation charges: \$900 in year 1, \$1800 in years 2, 3, 4, and 5, and \$900 in year 6. Apportioning one-half of a normal year's depreciation to the first and last years is called the "half-year convention."

Real Property. Depreciable real property generally includes buildings and any site preparation necessary for construction. Such property is depreciated by the SL method using a life of 27.5 years for residential rental property and 31.5 years for nonresidential real property. The half-month convention is used to calculate the depreciation as follows:

$$D(1) = [B(0)/N][(25 - 2m)/24] \tag{10.10a}$$

$$D(n = B(0)/N \qquad \text{for } n = 2, 3, \ldots, [N] \tag{10.10b}$$

$$D([N] + 1) = [B(0)/N\{N - [N] + [(2m + 1)/24]\} \qquad \text{for } m = 1, 2, \ldots, 6 \tag{10.10c}$$

$$D([N] + 1) = B(0)/N \qquad \text{for } m = 7, 8, \ldots, 12 \tag{10.10d}$$

$$D([N] + 2) = 0 \qquad \text{for } m = 1, 2, \ldots 6 \tag{10.10e}$$

$$D([N] + 2) = [B(0)/N]\{N - [N] - 1 + [(2m - 1)/24]\} \qquad \text{for } m = 7, 8, \ldots, 12 \tag{10.10f}$$

where $[N]$ is the integer function; for example, $[31.5] = 31$. Values for $N = 31.5$ are shown in Table 10.10.

Alternative Depreciation

When property is (1) to be used predominantly outside the United States, (2) leased to a tax-exempt entity, (3) financed by tax-exempt bonds, and in certain other cases, an alternative form of depreciation *must* be used. The alternative requires the use of SL depreciation over the ADR midpoint life rather than the ACRS class life.

Example of a Depreciation Calculation. The depreciation charges that appear in column (3) of Table 10.1 were based on the 31.5-year ACRS depreciation of the $3,150,000 building and 5-year ACRS depreciation of the $6,250,000 total for racks, S/R machines, aisle hardware, and controls. In order to illustrate the half-month convention for real property, it is assumed that the warehouse is placed in service in month 7 of year 1, and removed from service in month 7 of year 20. The SL depreciation charge for the building is $3,150,000/31.5 = $100,000. This is the charge shown for years 2 through 19. For the first year, the building is in use for 5.5 months, so that the charge is (5.5/12) ($100,000) = $45,833. In the last year, the building is in use for 6.5 months and the charge is $54,167, leaving an end-of-year book value of $1,250,000. It is assumed that the firm owning and operating the warehouse is a distributive trade and service firm and engages in wholesale and retail trade. This places the racks, S/R machines, aisle hardware, and controls in asset guideline class 57.0 according to Revenue Procedure 83-85. Class 57.0 has an ADR midpoint life of 9 years. Thus, from Table 10.8, that property should be depreciated using ACRS 5-year class life. The resulting charges are shown in Table 10.11. The total charges from Table 10.11 were then transferred to column (3) of Table 10.1.

Corporate Income Taxes

Corporate income taxes are important in the economic analysis of warehouse equipment and systems because the particular depreciation

Table 10.10. ACRS Depreciation Percentages for 31.5-Year Real Property

Month placed in service	Year 1	Years 2 to 31	Year 32	Year 33
1	0.03042	0.03175	0.01720	0.00000
2	0.02778	0.03175	0.01984	0.00000
3	0.02513	0.03175	0.02249	0.00000
4	0.02249	0.03175	0.02513	0.00000
5	0.01984	0.03175	0.02778	0.00000
6	0.01720	0.03175	0.03042	0.00000
7	0.01455	0.03175	0.03175	0.00132
8	0.01190	0.03175	0.03175	0.00397
9	0.00926	0.03175	0.03175	0.00661
10	0.00661	0.03175	0.03175	0.00926
11	0.00397	0.03175	0.03175	0.01190
12	0.00132	0.03175	0.03175	0.01455

method used affects the timing of after-tax cashflows. It is also through these mechanisms that the effects of inflation are felt.

Federal Taxes. Although many state and local governments have income tax laws, it is the federal tax that has the highest rates, and hence is of greatest importance.

Tax Rates. For federal tax purposes, the first \$325,000 of taxable income for domestic corporations is divided into four steps as follows:

Taxable income V	Tax rate
$\$0 < V \leq \$50{,}000$	0.15
$\$50{,}000 < V \leq \$75{,}000$	0.25
$\$75{,}000 < V \leq \$100{,}000$	0.34
$\$100{,}000 < V \leq \$335{,}000$	0.39
$\$335{,}000 < V$	0.34

Thus, a corporation with a taxable income of \$1,000,000 would pay (.15) (50,000) + (.25) (25,000) + (.34) (25,000) + (.39) (235,000) + (.34) (665,000) = \$340,000 income tax. All income over \$335,000 is taxed

Table 10.11. Example of Depreciation Calculations

End of year n (1)	Building book value $B_1(n)$ (2)	Depreciation $D_1(n)$ (3)	Equipment book value $B_2(n)$ (4)	Depreciation $D_2(n)$ (5)	Total depreciation $D(n)$ (6)
0	3,150,000		6,250,000		
1	3,104,167	45,833	5,000,000	1,250,000	1,295,833
2	3,004,167	100,000	3,000,000	2,000,000	2,100,000
3	2,904,167	100,000	1,800,000	1,200,000	1,300,000
4	2,804,167	100,000	1,080,000	720,000	820,000
5	2,704,167	100,000	360,000	720,000	820,000
6	2,604,167	100,000	0	360,000	460,000
7	2,504,167	100,000			100,000
8	2,404,167	100,000			100,000
9	2,304,167	100,000			100,000
10	2,204,167	100,000			100,000
11	2,104,167	100,000			100,000
12	2,004,167	100,000			100,000
13	1,904,167	100,000			100,000
14	1,804,167	100,000			100,000
15	1,704,167	100,000			100,000
16	1,604,167	100,000			100,000
17	1,504,167	100,000			100,000
18	1,404,167	100,000			100,000
19	1,304,167	100,000			100,000
20	1,250,000	54,167			54,167

at a rate of 34 percent. If a corporation has a taxable income of over \$335,000, and if the acceptance or rejection of the warehousing alternative being analyzed does not cause the income to drop below this figure, then every dollar that the alternative brings in will result in \$0.34 for taxes, and every dollar of cost will result in \$0.34 less taxes. For this reason the 34 percent tax rate is called the *incremental* tax rate, and is the one used in economic analysis. The tax rate of 39 percent from \$100,000 to \$335,000 was selected so that the average tax rate on taxable income above \$335,000 is also 34 percent. State and local income taxes may not have such equal incremental and average rates.

Investment Tax Credit. Prior to the Tax Reform Act of 1986, depreciable property was eligible for investment tax credit (ITC) if used in the production of income. This powerful incentive to capital investment was eliminated by the 1986 law. All the texts shown under "References" discuss the ITC and can be consulted if the ITC is restored.

Combined Federal, State, and Local Income Tax Rates. State and local income tax laws are frequently modeled on the federal law. The incremental state rate and incremental local rate should be determined, if they apply. Usually, local taxes are deductible for both state and federal tax purposes and state taxes for federal purposes. When this is true, the *combined* incremental tax rate, t, is given by:

$$t = t_f + t_s + t_l - (t_f t_s + t_f t_l + t_s t_l) + t_f t_s t_l \qquad (10.11)$$

where t_f, t_s, and t_l = federal, state, and local incremental tax rates. If, for example, these rates are 34, 7, and 2 percent respectively, then the values 0.34, 0.07, and 0.02 are substituted into Equation (10.11) to yield 0.398, or about 40 percent.

After-Tax Cash-Flow Analysis

A tabular computation, such as that reflected in columns (1) through (6) of Table 10.1, is called an after-tax cash-flow analysis. In order to form that table, the before-tax cashflows (BTCF) were estimated taking into account the effects of inflation, and placed in column (2). The yearly depreciation charges were calculated and placed in column (3). Depreciation is a noncash amount and its only importance in the analysis is that it is subtracted from BTCF to obtain the effect on taxable income (ETI). This quantity is called ETI because it is not the total income of the firm. It merely indicates how the firm's taxable income would be affected if this alternative were adopted. Thus, in the first year, the total taxable income of the firm would be decreased by $800,000. And, because the combined incremental tax rate is 40 percent, the effect on income tax (EIT) would be to reduce the tax bill by $320,000. Notice that EIT is obtained by multiplying ETI by *minus* the tax rate. This is because a positive taxable income results in a negative cashflow for income taxes (since taxes are a disbursement). Finally the EIT, column (5), due to this project, is added (algebraically) to the BTCF, column (2), to obtain the after-tax cashflow (ATCF), column (6).

The ATCF is plotted as a cash-flow diagram in Figure 10.1. The large initial cashflow due to first costs that flow at the end of year 0 are not shown to scale. The positive cash flows due to this project in years 1 through 6 are due to the effects of ACRS depreciation of the equipment. The increasingly negative cashflows in years 7 through 19 are due to the effects of costs increasing because of price escalation. In year 20, the salvage value causes a positive cashflow.

Analysis Methods

In order to permit alternative projects to be compared, the after-tax cashflows [e.g., column (6) of Table 10.1] must be evaluated. The theoretically correct techniques that take explicit account of the time value

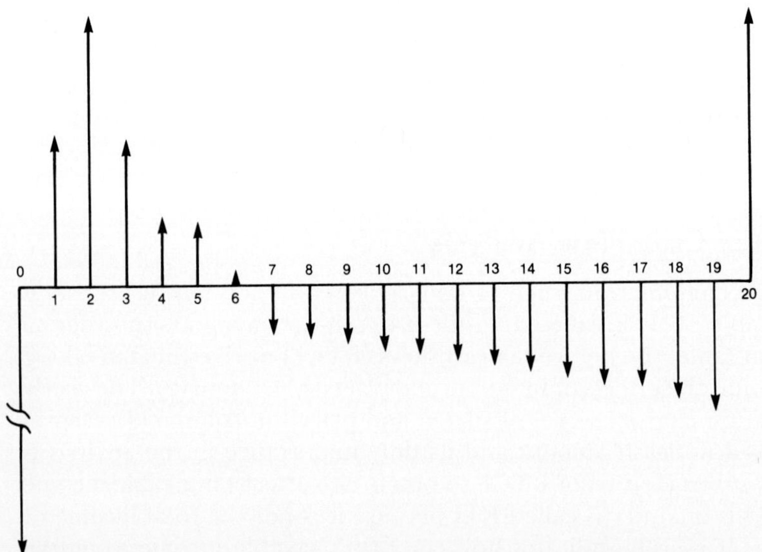

Figure. 10.1 After-tax cash flow.

of money make use of discounted cash-flow (DCF) calculations. There are also a variety of approximate and/or incorrect methods in use.

Discounted Cash-Flow Methods. Discounted cash-flow methods use an appropriate interest rate (also called the *discount rate*) together with discount factors to transform the sequence of cashflows to be evaluated to a common reference time. By this means, all alternatives are compared using a common measure.

Present Worth. In the present-worth method, the ATCF is transformed to an equivalent single amount at $t = 0$ (i.e., at the "present" time). In this method, the present amount, $P(n)$, that is equivalent to the year n after-tax cashflow, $X(n)$, is calculated by means of:

$$P(n) = (P/F,i,n)X(n) \tag{10.12}$$

where

$$(P/F,i,n) = (1 + i)^{-n} \tag{10.13}$$

and i = discount rate (e.g., the combined tax-adjusted cost of capital). To arrive at total present worth, all $P(n)$ values are summed:

$$\mathrm{PW} = \sum_{n=0}^{N} P(n) \tag{10.14}$$

or

$$\mathrm{PW} = \sum_{n=0}^{N} (1 + i)^{-n}X(n) \tag{10.15}$$

where N = life of the project.

The computation of Equations (10.12) and (10.14) is illustrated for i = 19.7% in Table 10.1. Column (7) is just the single-payment, present-worth discount factor $(P/F,i,n) = (1 + i)_{-n}$. It should be remarked that Table 10.1 was constructed with an electronic spreadsheet program that maintains 10-place accuracy in all its calculations. The values shown in the table have been rounded, so that it may not be possible to exactly duplicate some of the illustrated calculations using only values from the table. Thus, for year 2 in Table 10.1, 0.6979 is written in place of $(P/F, 19.7\%,2) = 0.697929\ldots$

Multiplying columns (6) and (7) yields in column (8) the amount $P(n)$ that is equivalent to the nth year ATCF. For example, in year 2, \$499,722 is the present amount that is equivalent to the \$716,007 ATCF at the end of year 2. Column (9) is the cumulative present worth of the project calculated from

$$P_n = \sum_{n=0}^{n} P(n) \tag{10.16}$$

where P_n = cumulative PW through year n. The last entry in column (9) is just the total present worth of the project PW = P_N = − \$9,111,620.

In this example, the benefits were not explicitly considered. Rather, it was assumed that several projects, each satisfying the same need, were being compared. These alternatives could be ranked directly by their PW. For example, an alternative with a PW of −\$7,000,000 would be superior to the one shown in Table 10.1 because −\$7,000,000 is larger than −\$9,111,620. Many analysts prefer to use present cost, defined by:

$$\text{PC} = -\text{PW} \tag{10.17}$$

in such cases. One would say then that the project with a present cost of \$7,000,000 is preferred because it has the lower cost.

Annual Cost. In the present-worth method, the ATCFs are transformed to a single equivalent present amount. In the annual cost method, the ATCFs are transformed to an equivalent uniform annual cost (EUAC). The choice of a uniform annual sequence has the appeal that many decision makers are accustomed to thinking of annual amounts as a result of their use of annual financial statements. In addition, the method has certain other real advantages to the analyst, and at least one potential trap.

In elementary treatments of engineering economic analysis, there are numerous simplified techniques for calculating the EUAC. In general, these are only useful when taxes and inflation are ignored. In real problems, such as that in Table 10.1, taxes and inflation should always be considered. In these cases, the EUAC in real dollars R\$ is defined by:

$$\text{EUAC [R\$]} = (A/P,i_r,N)(\text{PC}/[\text{A\$}]) \tag{10.18}$$

where [R\$] indicates that EUAC is measured in real dollars, [A\$] indicates that PC is measured in actual dollars, i_r is real interest rate (as defined in the section on cost of capital) and

$$(A/P,i,n) = i/[1 - (1 + i)^{-n}] \tag{10.19}$$

is the capital recovery factor. It is also possible to calculate the EUAC in actual dollars A\$ using:

$$\text{EUAC [A\$]} = (A/P,i_c,N)(\text{PC}[\text{A\$}]) \tag{10.20}$$

where i_c = combined interest rate that includes the effects of the general inflation rate.

Equation (10.18) returns an equivalent amount that is constant in real terms, whereas Equation (10.20) returns an amount that, in real terms, declines over the life of the project. Projects evaluated with Equation (10.18) must not be compared with projects evaluated with (10.20). This is the trap alluded to above. It is best to consistently use one and one only. Equation (10.18) is recommended since it is universally applicable and there are instances (e.g., in retirement and replacement studies) when Equation (10.20) will fail. In the example of Table 10.1, i_c and f were given as 19.7 and 5 percent respectively, and it was determined that PC and i_r were $9,111,620 and 14 percent, respectively. By substituting the latter two values into Equation (10.18):EUAC [R$] = $(A/P,14\%,20)$ ($9,111,620) = $1,375,727 is obtained.

Required Revenue. Revenue requirements is a method that is closely related to the annual-cost method and is widely used by regulated utilities. It determines gross revenue, or sales, that must be generated in order for the project just to break even. The revenue required, RR, is determined from the EUAC using:

$$\mathrm{RR} = \mathrm{EUAC}/(1 - t) \tag{10.21}$$

where t = required incremental tax rate. For the example of Table 10.1: RR = $1,375,727/(1 − 0.4) = $2,292,878, where RR is in the same units (R$) as the EUAC.

In order to see the role of RR as the break-even sales required by the project, assume that the project described in Table 10.1 generates before-tax benefits of $2,292,878 that escalate at 5 percent per year, so that the actual benefits are $2,407,552 in year-1 dollars, $2,527,898 in year-2 dollars, etc., as shown in column (2) of Table 10.12. Subtracting the total costs of Table 10.6, column (3) of Table 10.12, yields the before-tax cashflows in column (4) of Table 10.12. It will be seen that the PW [the final column (11) entry] is exactly zero.

Rate of Return. If the benefits associated with a profitable project are known, it will almost always have a real positive rate of return. If so, that rate of return can be calculated with the aid of Equation (10.15). In order to emphasize that present worth PW is a function of the discount rate, that equation will be rewritten as

$$\mathrm{PW}(i) = \sum_{n=0}^{N} (1 + i)^{-n} X(n) \tag{10.22}$$

where it will be remembered that $X(n)$ is the after-tax cashflow at the end of year n. The *internal rate of return* (IRR) is defined as the value of $i = i^*$ such that $\mathrm{PW}(i^*) = 0$, that is, it is the break-even interest rate.

As an example of an IRR calculation, assume that the project analyzed in Table 10.1 will result in annual benefits of $3,000,000 that es-

Table 10.12.

End of year n (1)	Revenue $Bn(n)$ (2)	Costs $C_n(n)$ (3)	Before-tax cashflows $U(n)$ (4)	ACRS depreciation $D(n)$ (5)	Effect on taxable income $V(n)$ (6)	Effect on income tax $T(n)$ (7)	After-tax cashflow $X(n)$ (8)	Present-worth factor $(P/N,i,n)$ (9)	Present worth $P(n)$ (10)	Cumulative present worth P_n (11)
0		9,600,000	−9,600,000				−9,600,000	1.0000	−9,600,000	−9,600,000
0		800,000	−800,000		−800,000	320,000	−480,000	1.0000	−480,000	−10,080,000
1	2,407,522	193,920	2,213,602	1,295,833	917,769	−367,108	1,846,495	0.8354	1,542,602	−8,537,398
2	2,527,898	206,655	2,321,243	2,100,000	221,243	−88,497	2,232,746	0.6979	1,558,300	−6,979,098
3	2,654,293	220,264	2,434,029	1,300,000	1,134,029	−453,612	1,980,417	0.5831	1,154,714	−5,824,385
4	2,787,008	234,809	2,552,199	820,000	1,732,199	−692,880	1,859,320	0.4871	905,686	−4,918,699
5	2,926,358	250,356	2,676,002	820,000	1,856,002	−742,401	1,933,601	0.4069	786,858	−4,131,841
6	3,072,676	266,978	2,805,699	460,000	2,345,699	−938,280	1,867,419	0.3400	634,858	−3,496,983
7	3,226,310	284,751	2,941,559	100,000	2,841,559	−1,136,624	1,804,936	0.2840	512,628	−2,984,354
8	3,387,626	303,759	3,083,867	100,000	2,983,867	−1,193,547	1,890,320	0.2373	448,520	−2,535,834
9	3,557,007	324,090	3,232,917	100,000	3,132,917	−1,253,167	1,979,750	0.1982	392,431	−2,143,403
10	3,734,857	345,840	3,389,017	100,000	3,289,017	−1,315,607	2,073,410	0.1656	343,355	−1,800,048
11	3,921,600	369,113	3,552,487	100,000	3,452,487	−1,380,995	2,171,492	0.1383	300,416	−1,499,632
12	4,117,680	394,018	3,723,662	100,000	3,623,662	−1,449,465	2,274,197	0.1156	262,844	−1,236,788
13	4,323,564	420,675	3,902,889	100,000	3,802,889	−1,521,156	2,381,734	0.0966	229,969	−1,006,819
14	4,539,742	449,211	4,090,532	100,000	3,990,532	−1,596,213	2,494,319	0.0807	201,203	−805,616
15	4,766,730	479,763	4,286,967	100,000	4,186,967	−1,674,787	2,612,180	0.0674	176,032	−629,585
16	5,005,066	512,479	4,492,587	100,000	4,392,587	−1,757,035	2,735,552	0.0563	154,006	−475,578
17	5,255,319	547,519	4,707,801	100,000	4,607,801	−1,843,120	2,864,680	0.0470	134,734	−340,845
18	5,518,085	585,052	4,933,033	100,000	4,833,033	−1,933,213	2,999,820	0.0393	117,869	−222,976
19	5,793,990	625,263	5,168,727	100,000	5,068,727	−2,027,491	3,141,236	0.0328	103,113	−119,863
20	6,083,689	668,349	5,415,340	54,167	5,361,174	−2,144,469	3,270,871	0.0274	89,698	−30,165
20	1,000,000		1,000,000	1,250,000	−250,000	100,000	1,100,000	0.0274	30,165	0

calate at 5 percent. These benefits can be added to the costs developed in Table 10.6 as was done with Table 10.12 in the previous section when creating the revenue requirements example. The results are shown in Table 10.13. It should be emphasized that these benefits are assumed to escalate at 5 percent only for computational convenience. In actual practice, the benefits or cost savings should be categorized and obtained by detailed estimating, just as the costs were.

When the ATCF analysis made on the basis of $3,000,000 is analyzed at $i = 19.7\%$, the resulting cumulative present worth is shown in column (11) of Table 10.13. It will be seen that the present worth is $2,810,015. Since this value is positive, the project is economically feasible and it is likely that the IRR is greater than 19.7 percent. The cumulative present worths for discount rates of 25 and 26 percent are shown in columns (3) and (4) of Table 10.14. It is seen that PW (25%) is positive and that PW (26%) is negative. This indicates that the IRR must be between 25 and 26 percent. These values were obtained by trial and error. An improved estimate of the IRR can be obtained by linear interpolation as follows:

i	PW(i)
25%	$34,714
IRR	0
26%	− 366,983

$$\frac{\text{IRR} - 25\%}{26\% - 25\%} \approx \frac{0 - 34{,}714}{-366{,}983 - 34{,}714}$$

$$\text{IRR} \approx 25 + (26 - 25)\,\frac{-34{,}714}{-401{,}697}$$

$$= 25.1\%$$

The correct value is 25.083 percent, to five significant places.

Most spreadsheets have an IRR function that will calculate this value directly and eliminate the need for manual interpolation.

There is a relation between the rate of return and the revenue requirements methods. Notice that in the case of the example of Table 10.1, when benefits are exactly equal to RR as in Table 10.12, then PW (19.7%) = 0. This means that RR is just the amount of benefit required to yield an IRR equal to the MARR.

Payback Period Method. There are two types of payback-period analysis. Undiscounted payback analysis can be performed using simple arithmetic. Discounted payback attempts to partially account for the time value of money.

Table 10.13.

End of year n (1)	Revenue $Bn(n)$ (2)	Costs $C_n(n)$ (3)	Before-tax cashflows $U(n)$ (4)	ACRS depreciation $D(n)$ (5)	Effect on taxable income $V(n)$ (6)	Effect on income tax $T(n)$ (7)	After-tax cashflow $X(n)$ (8)	Present-worth factor $(P/N,i,n)$ (9)	Present worth $P(n)$ (10)	Cumulative present worth P_n (11)
0		9,600,000	−9,600,000				−9,600,000	1.0000	−9,600,000	−9,600,000
0		800,000	−800,000		−800,000	320,000	−480,000	1.0000	−480,000	−10,080,000
1	3,150,000	193,920	2,956,080	1,295,833	1,660,247	−664,099	2,291,981	0.8354	1,914,771	−8,165,229
2	3,307,500	206,655	3,100,845	2,100,000	1,000,845	−400,338	2,700,507	0.6979	1,884,764	−6,280,465
3	3,472,875	220,264	3,252,611	1,300,000	1,952,611	−781,044	2,471,566	0.5831	1,441,086	−4,839,379
4	3,646,519	234,809	3,411,710	820,000	2,591,710	−1,036,684	2,375,026	0.4871	1,156,889	−3,682,490
5	3,828,845	250,356	3,578,489	820,000	2,758,489	−1,103,396	2,475,093	0.4069	1,007,212	−2,675,278
6	4,020,287	266,978	3,753,309	460,000	3,293,309	−1,317,324	2,435,986	0.3400	828,152	−1,847,126
7	4,221,301	284,751	3,936,550	100,000	3,836,550	−1,534,620	2,401,930	0.2840	682,184	−1,164,943
8	4,432,366	303,759	4,128,608	100,000	4,028,608	−1,611,443	2,517,165	0.2373	597,253	−567,689
9	4,653,985	324,090	4,329,895	100,000	4,229,895	−1,691,958	2,637,937	0.1982	522,898	−44,791
10	4,886,684	345,840	4,540,844	100,000	4,440,844	−1,776,337	2,764,506	0.1656	457,800	413,009
11	5,131,018	369,113	4,761,905	100,000	4,661,905	−1,864,762	2,897,143	0.1383	400,806	813,815
12	5,387,569	394,018	4,993,551	100,000	4,893,551	−1,957,420	3,036,130	0.1156	350,906	1,164,721
13	5,656,947	420,675	5,236,273	100,000	5,136,273	−2,054,509	3,181,764	0.0966	307,216	1,471,937
14	5,939,795	449,211	5,490,584	100,000	5,390,584	−2,156,234	3,334,351	0.0807	268,963	1,740,900
15	6,236,785	479,763	5,757,022	100,000	5,657,022	−2,262,809	3,494,213	0.0674	235,471	1,976,371
16	6,548,624	512,479	6,036,145	100,000	5,936,145	−2,374,458	3,661,687	0.0563	206,146	2,182,517
17	6,876,055	547,519	6,328,536	100,000	6,228,536	−2,491,415	3,837,122	0.0470	180,470	2,362,987
18	7,219,858	585,052	6,634,806	100,000	6,534,806	−2,613,922	4,020,884	0.0393	157,989	2,520,976
19	7,580,851	625,263	6,955,588	100,000	6,855,588	−2,742,235	4,213,353	0.0328	138,305	2,659,281
20	7,959,893	668,349	7,291,544	54,167	7,237,378	−2,894,951	4,396,593	0.0274	120,568	2,779,850
20	1,000,000		1,000,000	1,250,000	−250,000	100,000	1,100,000	0.0274	30,165	2,810,015

Table 10.14.

End of year n (1)	Cumulative present worth $P_n(19.7\%)$ (2)	$P_n(25\%)$ (3)	$P_n(26\%)$ (4)
0	− 9,600,000	− 9,600,000	− 9,600,000
0	− 10,080,000	− 10,080,000	− 10,080,000
1	− 8,165,229	− 8,246,415	− 8,260,967
2	− 6,280,465	− 6,518,091	− 6,559,968
3	− 4,839,379	− 5,252,649	− 5,324,417
4	− 3,682,490	− 4,279,838	− 4,382,123
5	− 2,675,278	− 3,468,799	− 3,602,762
6	− 1,847,126	− 2,830,220	− 2,993,994
7	− 1,164,943	− 2,326,499	− 2,517,600
8	− 567,689	− 1,904,189	− 2,121,370
9	− 44,791	− 1,550,131	− 1,791,814
10	413,009	− 1,253,294	− 1,517,712
11	813,815	− 1,004,432	− 1,289,734
12	1,164,721	− 795,790	− 1,100,118
13	1,471,937	− 620,871	− 942,411
14	1,740,900	− 474,225	− 811,244
15	1,976,371	− 351,283	− 702,153
16	2,182,517	− 248,216	− 611,422
17	2,362,987	− 161,812	− 535,964
18	2,520,976	− 89,378	− 473,209
19	2,659,281	− 28,657	− 421,019
20	2,779,850	22,032	− 377,797
20	2,810,015	34,714	− 366,983

Undiscounted Payback Analysis. Undiscounted payback is the method understood when one speaks of, simply, the payback-period method. It can be applied to either the BTCF or the ATCF. In either case, the cashflows are summed year by year to form cumulative cashflows. The cumulative sums are then examined to determine when they switch from negative to positive. As an example, the BTCF and ATCF from Table 10.13 are shown in Table 10.15. It will be seen that payback based on BTCF occurs between years 3 and 4. Linear interpolation gives a value of 3.3 years. For the ATCF, payback is between years 4 and 5, and the interpolated value is 4.1 years.

This method of analysis does not take into account cash-flow consequences that take place after the end of the payback period or the time value of money. It is quite possible to have two projects that are ranked one way by DCF methods, such as present worth, and the other way by the payback method. Further, payback frequently rejects large, technologically innovative projects that may be important to the long-term economic health and productivity of the firm. Some simulation studies have shown that exclusive reliance on payback may actually be *worse* than

Table 10.15.

End of year n (1)	Before-tax cashflows $U(n)$ (2)	Cumulative BTCF (3)	After-tax cash-flow $X(n)$ (4)	Cumulative ATCF (5)
0	− 9,600,000	− 9,600,000	− 9,600,000	− 9,600,000
0	− 800,000	− 10,400,000	− 480,000	− 10,080,000
1	2,956,080	− 7,443,920	2,291,981	− 7,788,019
2	3,100,845	− 4,343,075	2,700,507	− 5,087,512
3	3,252,611	− 1,090,465	2,471,566	− 2,615,945
4	3,411,710	2,321,245	2,375,026	− 240,919
5	3,578,489	5,899,734	2,475,093	2,234,174

random selection. At best, payback analysis should only be used to supplement other, economically correct DCF methods.

Discounted Payback Analysis. Like undiscounted payback, the discounted method can be applied to either BTCF or ATCF. For illustration, only the ATCF of Table 10.13 will be considered. First, the individual cashflows are discounted to obtain the corresponding equivalent PW for each year. Finally, the present worths are summed to obtain the cumulative PW. For the Table 10.1 example, this is exactly the process shown in columns (8) through (11) of Table 10.13 using a discount rate of 19.7 percent. The sign changes from negative to positive between the ends of years 9 and 10. Interpolation between those values yields 9.1 years for the discounted payback period. The discounted payback period has a special interpretation. It is the break-even life of the project. That is, if the project is kept in service for 9.1 years, it will yield an IRR of 19.7 percent. If it is kept in service for 20 years, it will have an IRR of 25.08 percent as shown in the section on rate of return.

Accounting Method. There are a variety of methods that attempt to approximate true discounted cash-flow cost of capital recovery using straight-line depreciation. To the extent that any attempt is made to justify such methods, it is on the basis that their use, somehow, allows reconciliation of the capital recovery cost with the accounting records of the firm. There are also a number of closely related methods by which rate of return is improperly computed.

Table 10.16 shows an *incorrect* method actually proposed for evaluating material handling and warehousing investments. It is called the *average-book method.* The entries in Table 10.16 can be followed by reference to the cost for the example given in the introduction. The −$800,000 entry in column (2) is the one-time expense. The $2,818,000 income for years 1–10 is the difference between the $3,000,000 annual

Table 10.16. Example of Incorrect Method Proposed for Evaluating Material Handling and Warehouse Investments

Year (1)	Income (2)	Straight-line depreciation (3)	Taxable income (4)	40% income tax (5)	Net return (6)	Investment (7)	Average investment (8)
0	−800,000		−800,000	−320,000	−480,000	9,600,000	
1	2,818,000	940,000	1,878,000	751,200	1,126,800	8,660,000	9,130,000
2	2,818,000	940,000	1,878,000	751,200	1,126,800	7,720,000	8,190,000
3	2,818,000	940,000	1,878,000	751,200	1,126,800	6,780,000	7,250,000
4	2,818,000	940,000	1,878,000	751,200	1,126,800	5,840,000	6,310,000
5	2,818,000	940,000	1,878,000	751,200	1,126,800	4,900,000	5,370,000
6	2,818,000	940,000	1,878,000	751,200	1,126,800	3,960,000	4,430,000
7	2,818,000	940,000	1,878,000	751,200	1,126,800	3,020,000	3,490,000
8	2,818,000	940,000	1,878,000	751,200	1,126,800	2,080,000	2,550,000
9	2,818,000	940,000	1,878,000	751,200	1,126,800	1,140,000	1,610,000
10	2,818,000	940,000	1,878,000	751,200	1,126,800	200,000	670,000
TOTALS:		9,400,000			10,788,000		49,000,000

benefits and the $182,000 annual operating and maintenance costs. The straight-line depreciation amounts in column (3) are simply the $9,400,000 depreciable first costs (one-time expense and land have been excluded) divided by 10. The accounting method rate of return, 10,788,000/49,000,000 = 0.220 or 22.0% is obtained by dividing the average net return from column (6) by the average investment from column (8).

The value of 22.0 percent is close to the true internal rate of return of 25.08 percent obtained in the section on rate of return, but this is only an accident. Note that Table 10.16 ignores the life (the accounting method normally uses a 10-year life), inflation, or ACRS tax depreciation. Extending the life to 20 years, adding the effects of price escalation, and using ACRS depreciation together with the method shown in Table 10.16 lead to rates of return of 28, 53, and 84 percent respectively. The accounting method is not just approximate, it is incorrect.

Electronic Spreadsheets. All numerical steps in the economic justification process—cost estimation, depreciation calculation, after-tax cash-flow tabulation, and final analysis—are greatly facilitated by the use of personal computers and electronic spreadsheets. In the example problem discussed in the introduction, the cost and price escalation calculation were done on one sheet (Table 10.6), the depreciation calculations on another sheet (Table 10.11), and the two were combined in the final after-tax cash-flow tabulation and analysis sheet (Table 10.1). A further, and not insignificant advantage, is the ease with which the individual sheets can be listed on a printer and included in the written report.

Written Reports

The written report serves to document the analysis. It should reflect a level of detail that will permit another analyst, previouly unfamiliar with the project, to understand and follow the path that lead to the recommendation. Here is one possible outline:

Executive Summary. There should be an abstract or executive summary that concisely states the alternatives being considered, the method of analysis used, and the recommendations. The length of this section should not exceed about 10 percent of the length of the body of the report, except in very short reports. For short reports, a minimum of 200 words is recommended.

Introduction. The introduction should be written to explain the circumstances that gave rise to the particular alternatives being considered. The project history should be sufficient to properly place it within the broader context of related operations of the firm or organization.

Estimating Summary. If two or more alternatives having identical annual benefits are being considered, and if one of the alternatives *must* be selected, this section will be a cost summary. If one of the alternatives is to "do nothing," that is, if the analysis is a pure economic justification, then annual benefits must also be estimated and summarized. A general explanation of the estimating methods and sources of data should be provided. Detailed references to data sources and cost calculations should be placed in an appendix.

Irreducibles. This should be a discussion of factors that are important, but that are difficult to quantify. These might include intangible benefits, costs, and risks associated with each alternative. Important political, public relations, and social concerns that are external to the firm may be considered in this section.

Recommendations. This section should present the alternative recommended and the reasons for that recommendation. Attention should be directed to important irreducible factors that might change the weight given to the recommendation. The detailed economic analytical calculations (after-tax cash-flow tables, present-worth calculations, etc.) should be placed in an appendix.

Advanced Considerations

For very large projects, particularly when alternatives are closely ranked by economic analysis, further consideration may be required. Such further analysis might include explicit consideration of such factors as risk, uncertainty, and multiple criteria. Only a general guide is provided here; the details of these methods can be found in the references at the end of this section.

Risk and Uncertainty. Break-even analysis is the most common analytical technique for dealing with risk and uncertainty. Some examples have already been provided. Based on the data from the example in the introduction, the section on required revenue showed that the break-even revenue is \$3,299,001. Thus, even if the estimates of revenue are uncertain, the project will be profitable if one is reasonably certain that this amount of revenue can be obtained. On the other hand, if an annual benefit of $4,000,000 is ensured, but the minimum attractive rate of return is uncertain, the break-even MARR can be found to be 30.48 percent by the method shown in the section on rate of return.

In a similar manner, the break-even value of any benefit, cost, or other parameter can be calculated. It is merely necessary to determine the value of the parameter that will just cause the recommendation to be reversed. For example, preliminary analysis at a given value of percentage system availability may show that system A has a lower EUAC than system B. If system availability is uncertain, the analysis should be extended to determine the percentage system availability (if any) that would just cause system B to have a lower EUAC than system A.

When more than one parameter is judged to be risky or uncertain, simple break-even analysis is not sufficient. In such cases, it is necessary to estimate the probability distributions of the relevant parameters. One can then calculate the expected value and variance of the present worth by analytical means or by using computer simulation. Both methods are discussed in the references.

Multiple Criteria. The most common approach to the noneconomic criteria is simply to attempt to recognize and list them, as discussed in the section on irreducibles. When one or more nonmonetary criteria are judged to be particularly important, more formal methods can be used. These include dominance, feasible ranges, lexicography, effectiveness index, and so on. Attention is directed to the references.

References

Canada, J. R., and J. A. White, Jr.: *Capital Investment Decision Analyses for Management and Engineering,* Prentice-Hall, Englewood Cliffs, N.J., 1980.

DeGarmo, E. P., W. G. Sullivan, and J. R. Canada: *Engineering Economy,* 7th ed., Macmillan, New York, 1984.

Fleischer, G. A.: *Engineering Economy: Capital Allocation Theory,* PWS Engineering, Boston, 1984.

How to Read a Financial Report, 5th ed., Merrill Lynch, Pierce, Fenner and Smith, New York.

Newnan, D. G.: *Engineering Economic Analysis,* 3d ed., Engineering Press, San Jose, Calif., 1988.

Staff of the Joint Committee on Taxation: "*General Explanation of Tax Reform Act of 1986,*" *Prentice-Hall Federal Taxes,* Prentice-Hall, Englewood Cliffs, N.J., May 11, 1987.

11
Dock Design

Bruce Ketchpaw

Director of Marketing, Rite-Hite Corporation, Milwaukee, Wisconsin

Introduction

Loading dock design has entered a new era of sophistication. Just-in-time inventory practices require docks to accept more frequent deliveries from trucks of many sizes. Management has traded 90-day inventories for 2-hour, 8-hour or 24-hour supplies. Some of these supplies are delivered in light-duty vans. Others arrive on trucks that are longer and wider than regulations have allowed in the past. So today's loading docks must be more flexible and efficient than ever before.

The dock designer must understand materials handling, inventory control, safety requirements, and interstate trucking regulations. Ideally, a team composed of plant owners and managers, the architect, the building contractor, and a loading dock specialist should determine how docks contribute to the overall operation. With these considerations in mind, they should design the docks in the early stages of facility planning.

This chapter reviews the steps in designing a loading dock, considering each stage of material movement. The dock designer must plan for safe, efficient movement of vehicles and materials from the time the trucks enter the compound, through material movement across the dock, to the trucks' departure from the plant site.

Follow these guidelines to design a loading dock that will contribute to the safety, efficiency, and profitability of the entire operation:

1. Position the facility and its docks on the site and design the approach so trucks can leave the highway, enter the compound, and maneuver to the dock quickly and safely.
2. Specify dimensions of the loading dock to allow trucks of all sizes to service it efficiently.
3. Select dock equipment to help dock workers load and unload trucks safely.
4. Plan the staging area inside the loading dock so material flows efficiently to and from its in-plant destination.

Begin Dock Design by Positioning the Facility on the Site

The designer's first goal is to get the trucks off the highway safely. So the first step is determining where the facility and docks should be positioned on the building site and designing safe access roads to the dock area. Before positioning the building and docks on the site, consider these factors:

- Where is the material needed or produced in the plant?
- How much space will the dock and maneuvering area require?
- Will the operation need more dock positions soon?
- What type of dock will best serve the operation?
- What is the safest design for access roads?
- Will the operation receive or ship deliveries by rail?
- How will site topography affect traffic and dock operations?
- What are the dimensions of a safe approach?

Consider Material Flow When Determining Dock Location

Before locating the plant and docks on the site, determine where the docks should be located. This depends on where deliveries are needed or where shipments originate in the plant. The in-plant destination of the material influences whether the facility will have one central dock or several point-of-use docks. Each would require different clearances from the boundaries of the building site.

Traditionally, buildings had one dock area. In small facilities, shipping and receiving were combined, and in large plants, shipping and receiving might have been separate but adjacent. The central dock reduced supervision costs and efficiently used material handling people and equipment. The external maneuvering and parking area for this type of dock has to accommodate the most trucks serving the operation at any moment. It also has to serve both the largest and smallest trucks.

Point-of-use docks are becoming more popular as just-in-time inventory demands efficient flow of material or components to production departments (Figure 11.1). With this arrangement, several docks are located around the plant perimeter. Each is designed to serve a particular production line or operating area. One might receive frequent, small deliveries from light-duty vans. Another might receive deliveries from trucks that are longer, lower, and wider than previous state or federal

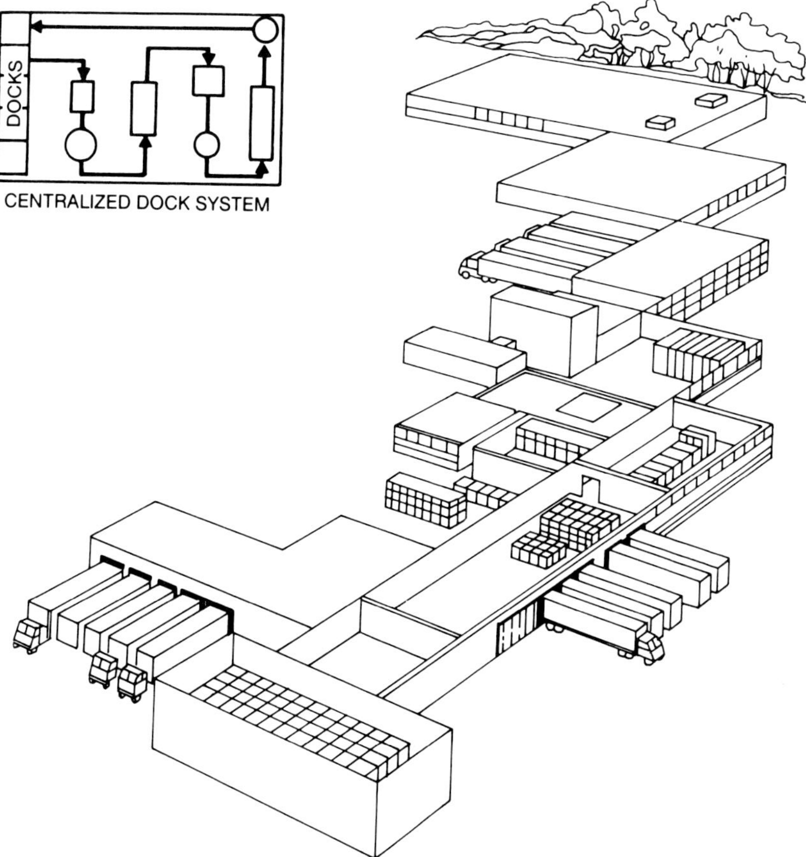

Figure 11.1. Traditional centralized docks are being replaced by point-of-use docks in some operations. (*Rite-Hite Corp.*)

transportation regulations ever allowed. The design decisions for each type of dock are clearly different and affect placement of the building and docks on the plant site.

Calculate the Number of Dock Positions Before Siting the Building

Before determining the location of loading docks on the plant site, the designer must know how much space to dedicate for the dock and maneuvering area. This is determined by how many dock positions are needed, the size of trucks delivering to the operation, and the largest number of trucks serving the dock at any time.

When determining the number of dock positions, consider dock-traffic needs for the next five years. Most firms make a reasonably good forecast for that length of time, and careful planning can avoid costly remodeling soon after the building opens. Remember that at least one year might pass before the building you are planning is constructed. To determine the number of dock positions, estimate the number of trucks that will serve the dock.

To estimate truck activity at a new facility, follow these steps:

1. Review the number and location of suppliers that will ship to the operation and the volume of shipments from the plant.
2. Establish the mode of transportation, the typical shipment size or volume.
3. Predict which carriers will deliver and how many carriers will deliver.
4. For each carrier, estimate the expected arrival time to the nearest hour, which shipments will be carried on scheduled or dropped vehicles and which shipments will be random arrivals.
5. Determine how long it takes to load or unload the average truck. Allow adequate time for parking and restraining the truck, check-in, loading or unloading, and leaving the dock.

When determining the number of dock positions, adjust for daily, seasonal, or other peaks. Unmanaged peak loading can present expensive problems. It can result in demurrage charges or close down a line that depends on just-in-time deliveries. Plan enough dock positions to handle any regularly occurring peaks. But recognize that designing a facility for the absolute peak day five years from now could result in costly overbuilding. Adjust to provide for a continuous peak period and not necessarily the highest day's activity.

The Management Council of the American Trucking Association has prepared mathematical formulas for calculating the optimum number of truck positions. These formulas appear in the *Shipper-Motor Carrier Dock Planning Manual.* Additional help is available from some manufacturers of dock equipment who will assist in calculating the number of dock doors needed.

The number of positions or doors required for each dock clearly affects how much area must be dedicated to the docks and the position of the building on the site.

Allow Enough Maneuvering Area for the Largest Trucks

Before positioning the facility and docks on the site, plan for adequate maneuvering area to extend from the docks. The size of maneuvering areas depends on the size of the trucks serving the operation.

Different methods of controlling material handling costs have prompted two very different trends in truck delivery. The just-in-time inventories call for small quantities, sometimes a three-hour supply, to be delivered frequently throughout the day.

On the other hand, economies of scale have always been recognized. So the same docks that receive from the smaller trucks making just-in-time deliveries might receive deliveries from huge trailers. New regulations have allowed trailer widths to increase from a maximum of 96 inches to 102 inches. They now allow single trailers to be 48 feet long, double (tandem) trailers to be 28 feet long, and gross vehicle-weights to reach 80,000 pounds.

Dockyard design must allow the full range of trucks to maneuver as safely and quickly as possible. So the area must be designed to accommodate the largest trucks that could serve the facility.

For example, if three of the largest trucks delivering to the building were parked next to each other at the dock and the center truck were ready to depart first, there would have to be adequate room in the maneuvering area for it to pull straight forward, beyond the front of the other trucks so it could turn to leave the yard. When designing the dockyard , the length of the dock approach should be at least twice the length of the longest tractor-trailer combination.

Plan for Future Dock Operations

Traditionally, docks were placed in the back of the building for aesthetic reasons, and in some cases, a green lawn in the front of the building was considered more important than a buffer area for growth around the dock. But extensive remodeling requires too much time and money. Production lines and budgets will not tolerate the inefficiencies of a dock that cannot accommodate the widening range of truck sizes or the growing demands of an operation.

Before positioning a building and its docks on the site, look for opportunities to expand the dock area. Expansion will be necessary if larger or longer trucks begin serving the operation, and additional dock positions might be required in the future. So before positioning the building on the site, evaluate land adjacent to planned docks to see if it is suitable for expansion.

Also, design the dock so it can be expanded efficiently and relatively inexpensively. Build in knock-out panels for doors and knock-out pits for docklevelers in the initial construction. Pave the approach to these future positions in the initial construction.

Select the Type of Dock that Will Best Serve the Operation

Select the style of dock that has features critical to the entire operation (Figure 11.2). For example, staggered sawtooth docks are useful when a site does not provide sufficient maneuvering area between the dock and the nearest obstruction or street. The major disadvantage of this dock type is that it uses twice as much building space while reducing dock space. If the sawtooth is constructed at less than a 45-degree angle, it will use twice as much space per position as a 90-degree dock. In addition, the space between positions is lost because it is wedge-shaped.

The use of space is just one consideration when selecting the type of dock. Other factors are weather protection, energy use, security, and construction cost.

Enclosed Dock. If cost and use of space were not primary factors, the ideal dock would be enclosed like a large garage. In some operations, the high initial cost and use of space for an enclosed dock is justified because it offers the most security from theft or vandalism. The enclosed dock also protects loading operations from the weather. It keeps out cold, heat, rain, and snow and protects merchandise that is sensitive to temperature or moisture. As with any dock, the enclosed dock has disadvantages as well. It offers climate control but runs up energy costs. Its operations are never interrupted by weather, but it requires exhaust systems to remove fumes from truck engines and adequate drainage to divert run-off of rain or melted snow.

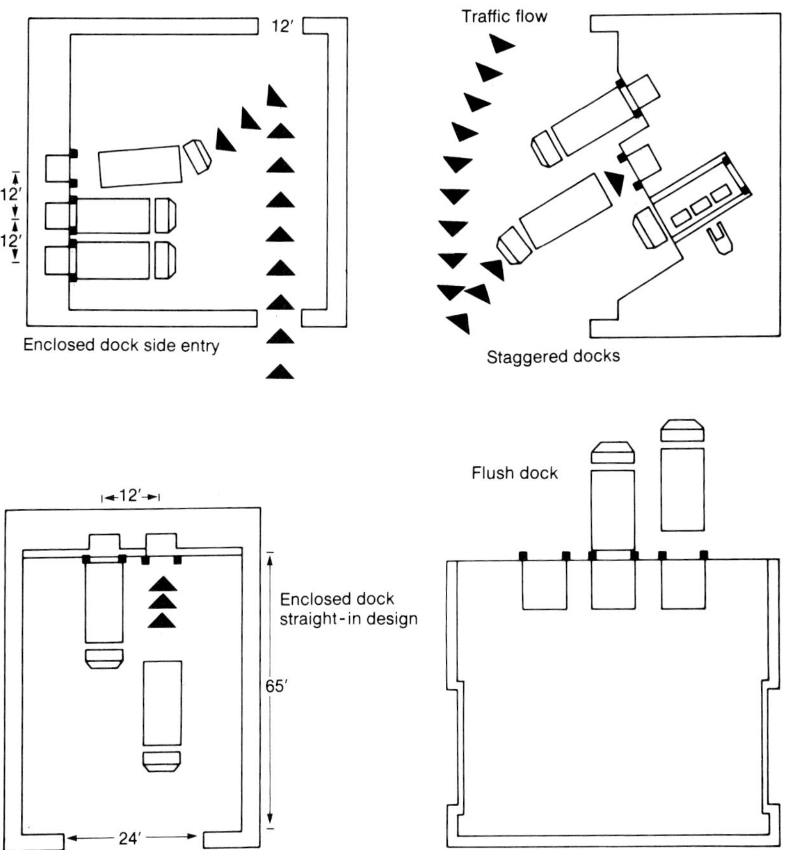

Figure 11.2. Dock types. (*Rite-Hite Corp.*)

If the dock is completely enclosed, each dock position should be a minimum of 12 feet wide. The clear height in the vehicle docking area should be a minimum of 15 feet. More clearance should be allowed if overhead lift equipment would be useful for the loading and unloading of open tops and flatbed trucks.

The back-in enclosure is the most frequently designed enclosed dock. Each berth has its own door, or one door can serve two berths. Each berth should be at least 12 feet wide, with a wider end berth to provide additional maneuvering room. The distance from the edge of the dock to the inside of the doorway where the vehicle enters the dock should be 5 feet longer than the longest vehicle combination.

Flush Dock. Most modern docks are flush docks. The outside wall of the building is flush with the face of the dock. Its main advantage is that both the dock and the building wall use a common foundation. The flush design completely encloses the interior dock areas and provides an ideal support for dock seals and canopies, which control the effects of weather. The dock becomes part of the facility, which discourages vandalism or pilferage of dock lights, skids, docklevelers, portable plates, and other equipment, plus permits easy heating or cooling of the entire dock.

Disadvantages of flush docks emerge if the building is placed on grade and the only way to achieve proper dock height is by depressing the driveway. The creation of a slope causes the top of the truck or trailer to lean toward the building. If the slope is too steep, the dock must be extended or the building wall recessed, so the top of the truck does not strike the building wall before the bottom contacts the dock bumpers. This damages the building wall, the trailer, or both. Flush docks provide installation of overhead doors with locks for each truck berth.

Open Docks. Open docks are the least desirable, and rising crime rates have made them nearly obsolete. But if conditions dictate their use, provide a canopy that extends a minimum of 4 feet beyond the dock. The greater the extension, the better. The outer edge of the canopy must be a minimum of 15 feet high. The dock should be sufficiently deep to handle two-way cross traffic. To determine the proper width for forklift traffic, multiply the width of the material being handled by 4 and add the length of the docklevelers. This minimum width does not allow for storage. So if temporary storage is needed, increase the dock width to accommodate it.

Design Service Roads for Safe Traffic Flow

Once you've determined the number of docks, the type of dock, and the area required for maneuvering, you can determine the position of the building, docks, and access roads on the site. Proper dock placement allows convenient access from a major thoroughfare and protection for pedestrians from truck traffic.

To design a safe access road, place the buildings on the site so trucks can drive straight in, especially if the facility is bordered by a boulevard or one-way street. Backing in from this type of roadway requires a blind right-hand back, which results in blocked traffic in both lanes. If the building site requires trucks to enter from a narrow street, reduce the angle to the access road. Consider a Y approach with an off-ramp from the road to the entrance gate measuring twice as long as the length of the longest truck (Figure 11.3). This design allows entrance and exit from both directions at a single point, which in turns allows a centralized gate operation for security. The Y approach also routes truck traffic safely away from pedestrians with an economical use of land.

Place the building and docks on the site so roads can be wide enough to accommodate all traffic safely. If funds and space permit, specify one-way service roads. They provide better traffic circulation and are far safer. These should be a minimum of 12 feet wide. Two-way service roads should be no less than 26 feet wide to give drivers at least 2 feet of clearance between passing vehicles and adequate side clearance. Mixed traffic and pedestrian roads are least desirable. But if space limitations dictate, make them a minimum of 16 feet wide and separate the 4-foot-wide pedestrian lane by a 4-foot-high barrier.

Make every effort to establish a counterclockwise traffic pattern. It provides the best visibility, so it is safer and more efficient. It is easier for drivers to make left-hand turns with large vehicles, and this pattern allows drivers to use their mirrors to maneuver and back into docks with a direct view of the dock and trailer.

Specify Adequate Clearance from Railway

Another factor affecting building-placement decisions is whether the operation receives any deliveries by rail. At least one dock must be placed on the site near the railroad tracks. Railroad, state, and local codes specify a minimum distance from the center of the track to the face of the

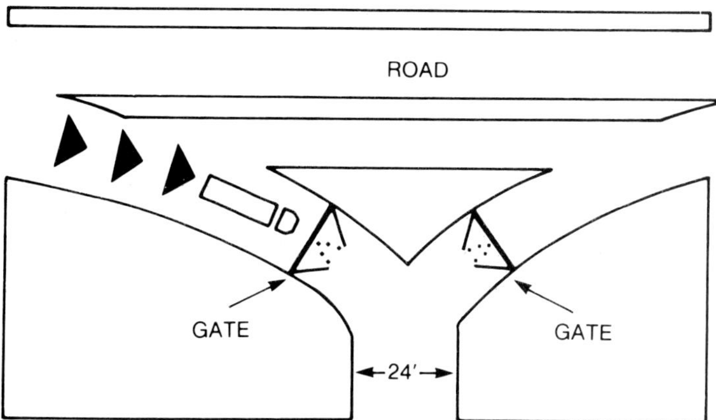

Figure 11.3. A Y approach provides a safe access with economical use of land. (*Rite-Hite Corp.*)

building. This is to provide clearance for a person between the boxcar and the building when the train is moving. Check with the railroad that serves the area for exact requirements. Then position the dock for the shortest gap legally allowable between the building and track, allowing at least 8 feet of clearance to accommodate permanent rail ramps.

Consider How Site Topography Will Affect Traffic and Dock Operations

Careful consideration of the site's topography when positioning the plant can lead to better traffic flow and more efficient dock operations. Avoid a sizable slope to the dock area and select long, level tracts for service roads to eliminate unnecessary hills and corners. Study how inclines could promote proper drainage to keep the road's surface level and dry and help control erosion of the subbase supporting access roads.

When positioning the facility on the site, take advantage of any windbreak provided by hills, trees, and nearby buildings. Designate an area of snow removal, if necessary, and consider whether low-lying dock areas might be subject to flooding.

Specify Adequate Dimensions for a Safe Approach

A greater range of trucks serve docks than ever before. Both light-duty pickup trucks and enormous supervans must back to the same dock, pause for unloading, and leave the yards as quickly and safely as possible. The total servicing time for one truck might be 10 minutes; the other might be dropped for hours. Meanwhile other trucks are arriving and departing and maneuvering around them.

Several design considerations can make the dock approach more convenient, more efficient, and safer. For example, the width of truck berths should never be less than 12 feet. Scrimping on the width of the berth results in sprung doors, scratched equipment, and loss of time because of more difficult maneuvering. Tighter tolerances can also result in more accidents. Using the space created by the increased width for storage or staging can offset the cost, and the additional space can provide a margin of safety for drivers and workers in a busy dock area.

Depressed driveways can be both efficient and safe with careful design. Grades should be less than 10 percent in areas where ice and snow could collect and severely reduce traction. Consider heating these driveways with electric cable or hot water pipes in the concrete. Ideally, the grade should not exceed 3 percent to avoid "start-up" resistance of a full load pulling away from the dock on a depressed driveway. A truck resting on a severe incline can encounter several problems: loads can topple out, loading and unloading is difficult, and handling equipment is more difficult to maneuver. This is neither safe nor efficient.

One solution is to design 4 to 10 feet of level area directly ahead of the dock, before beginning the slope. This approach lessens the incline angle of the truck when in position. It permits easier loading and unloading and lessens the danger of material falling from the truck.

When the dock is higher than grade, plan a forklift ramp to provide a means for forklifts to get from the building to the driveway. If this is not practical, consider a lift for these vehicles. To assist truck drivers who must enter the dock area, construct steps or a ladder from the driveway to the dock. Provide steel ladders from the driveway to the dock. Provide steel ladders or concrete steps with safety tread and hand rails. Place steps at each end of the dock or, on long docks, every fifth truck position.

Once you have established the size of the dock area, the building position and the dock approach, move to the second step in designing efficient loading docks.

Arrange the Loading Dock to Accommodate Trucks of All Sizes

One challenge facing the dock designer is planning for an increasing range of trucks serving today's operations. To arrange the most efficient dock positions, carefully determine these dimensions:

- The size of the dock door
- Dock height
- Location of the landing strip

Specify the Optimum Door Size

In the past, trucks were standard sizes, but as regulations allow variations in truck width, length, and depth, only one truck measurement should remain constant. Because it is unlikely that the United States will raise every highway overpass, trucks will not be taller than 13 feet 6 inches in the foreseeable future. So the distance from the driveway to the top of many dock doors can be 14 feet.

But several factors affect truck height. Snow and ice build-up on the driveway raise the height of the trailer. Depressed driveways essentially lower the height of the truck. On the other hand, truck lifts and ramps used to bring the low-slung, high-cube trailers to dock height essentially raise the height of the truck. Tire pressure and profile, spring set and listing, and load weight also affect the height of the truck. At one time, an 8-foot-high door on a 4-foot-high dock was adequate to service most trucks because the trailer was rarely packed to the last 1 foot 3 inches of space.

But emphasis on efficiency now requires higher loads, so a 9-foot-high door is quickly becoming the standard. For docks that will receive deliveries frequently from high-cube trailers, consider one dock position with a permanent concrete ramp or trailer lift to raise the trailer to dock height. For such dock positions, doors should be at least 10 feet high. Doors 11 or 12 feet high provide maximum flexibility.

The primary disadvantage of a door that is too big is that it loses conditioned air to the outside. Dock seals and shelters help keep in the air, but if they are too tight, they are easily damaged. So designers must plan door sizes as close as possible to the measurements needed.

Door width depends on the frequency of deliveries from 102-inch-wide trucks. These wider trucks are becoming standard. Doors or docks that serve these trucks should be 9 feet wide with shelters to seal the gap around smaller trucks. The advantage of the high-cube vans is the volume of goods they can deliver. Doors that are too small to permit ease of unloading quickly erode the savings from the efficiency of these large carriers. The operation also loses if maneuvering time is increased in order to spot a wide truck precisely on a narrow dock.

Select the Optimum Dock Height

Dock-height range has always been an issue, but most docklevelers could extend the full range required by most trailer heights. However, as industries require larger trucks that cannot get taller than clearances of highway overpasses, the trucks are getting wider, longer, and lower. The lower trailers are requiring special dock design. A standard trailer height is 50 to 52 inches from the ground to floor level. A refrigerated truck averages 54 to 60 inches high. The high cube or supervan is 36 inches to floor level, and a Lo-Boy® is 30 inches to floor level. These dimensions are also affected by tire pressure and loads.

There are four recognized methods for bringing low trailers up to the standard 48-inch dock height.

Some operations raise low trailers by backing the trailers onto portable ramps. These ramps are inexpensive but cumbersome, limited to a fixed height, and may be unsafe—especially in winter.

Other operations install a trailer lift in the truckwell; these are flexible and safe. Some operations use extra-long levelers (up to 12 feet) to allow servicing of trailers above and below dock with minimum leveler slope.

The final method is to dedicate at least one dock to serving lower trailers. Build the dock with either a permanent concrete ramp or a lower dock height. The remaining dock positions could be designed to accommodate the majority of the trucks serving the operation.

Place the Landing Strip to Support All Trucks Serving the Operation

If you plan on an asphalt surface, build flexibility into the landing strip. Place this concrete strip in the drive approach to support the trailer and prevent it from sinking into the asphalt when a tractor is not attached. Again, consider the range of trailer lengths when designing this concrete strip. Plan the strip to support landing gear of trailers ranging from 27 to 45 feet long.

Equipping the Loading Dock

The third step in dock design is specifying dock equipment. Efficient material flow is the goal of the well-designed dock. Today's production processes are especially vulnerable to delays from down-time at the dock. An efficient operation depends on facilities that fit the trucks and equipment. It is essential that individuals familiar with dock operations participate in selection of dock equipment. Contractors might degrade specifications for equipment on the basis of cost. So it is imperative that those responsible for material flow through the docks judge equipment on the basis of safety, capacity, and flexibility.

Primary considerations when selecting dock equipment include:

- What equipment contributes to safety on the dock?
- How can dock equipment protect the facility?
- How should frequency of use and weight of material handling equipment determine adequate equipment capacity for low maintenance and lowest lifetime ownership costs?

- Which dock equipment can handle a range of truck sizes?
- How can dock equipment assist with quality control?
- Can dock equipment contribute to sanitation?
- How can dock equipment enhance security?

Specify Safety Equipment for Every Dock Position

According to the Bureau of Labor Statistics, the trucking and warehousing industry is the second most dangerous industry in the United States. In fact, it is more dangerous than coal mining. Reliable equipment selected for each operation can reduce the number and severity of accidents on the dock.

When specifying a dockleveler, consider that dock attendants cross over the dangerous gap between dock and truck between 25,000 and 50,000 times a year. Any dockleveler will bridge the gap between truck and dock, but some dock systems have features to keep that gap closed. The busier the dock, the greater the chances that accidents will occur unless designers build in some safety measures that work even at the busiest times.

The National Safety Council reports that the most severe loading-dock accidents occur when a forklift truck either overturns or falls off the dock into the driveway approach. Several precautions can be taken to avoid this type of accident.

Any time a low truck pulls up to a dock it can create a hazard. If the dockleveler platform has to be lowered to meet the truck, it creates a void in the warehouse floor. The depressed ramp becomes especially hazardous if it isn't repositioned after the truck departs. Any cross traffic over a depressed leveler could result in a forklift truck tipping.

Where cross traffic over levelers occurs, designers should specify docklevelers that automatically recycle to cross-traffic position after the truck departs. This reduces the chances of a forklift operator driving onto a depressed platform.

Only individuals who have worked with dock operations know how easily accidents can occur. Many of these accidents can be prevented with safety equipment. Four of the most common dock accidents result from:

1. *Trailer creep.* The impact of a lift truck on a parked trailer, with or without the tractor, causes the trailer to inch forward imperceptibly, until it is beyond the reach of the leveler's lip. The lip then

falls to the pendant or vertical position. Forward momentum of the lift truck propels it into the void or topples it sideways into the driveway.

2. *Unscheduled departure.* This occurs when the trailer makes an unexpected departure while the lift truck is entering or backing out of the trailer. The unsecured lift truck topples off the truck with the operator in grave danger.
3. *Reluctant passenger.* This occurs when the lift truck is in the trailer and the trailer pulls away without warning. The forklift and driver may be tossed about inside the trailer.
4. *Landing gear collapse.* Semitrailers are often parked at loading docks detached from the tractor, with the nose supported by a landing gear. The impact of a load and lift truck crossing the leveler pushes the trailer forward, rocking the landing gear. Eventually the landing gear collapses, pitching the lift truck and the driver into the nose of the trailer.

The U.S. Occupational Safety and Health Administration (OSHA) prescribes the use of wheel chocks to prevent trailer creep and to avoid premature departure of a truck. However, truck drivers do not always remember to set the chocks in place even when they are available. Also, wider trucks parked closer together make setting chocks more difficult, which discourages their use.

A much more effective method of restraining trucks is available. A device has been developed for locking the truck to the dock (Figure 11.4). This restraint device consists of an assembly that mounts on the dock face. It locks to the underhung protective bumper, or ICC bar, required on trucks by the U.S. Department of Transportation.

When a truck is backed into its final parked position at the dock, a heavy-duty steel hook rises and locks on to the horizontal cross member of the underhung bumper. The hook is electrically or manually powered. It prevents forward inching of the trailer as it is loaded or unloaded by a lift truck. It also restrains the truck if the driver tries to pull away before servicing is finished.

When not in use, the hook is in a lowered position. At this time, a red-light display inside the building indicates that the trailer is not secured and should not be entered. At the same time, a green-light display outside the building signals the truck driver that he or she is free to move the trailer.

When the hook is engaged and the trailer secured, the light display inside the dock changes to green to indicate that the trailer can be en-

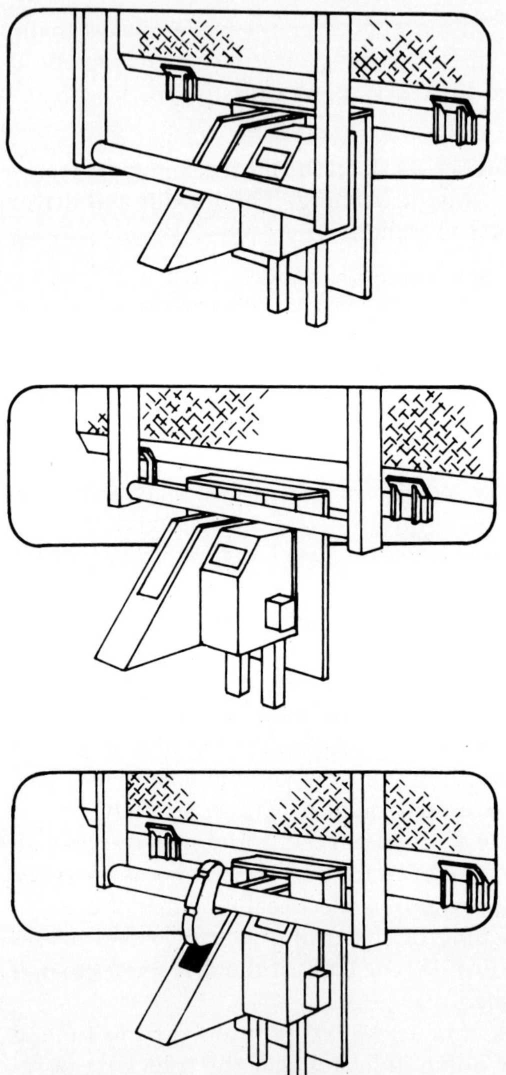

Figure 11.4. A truck restraint device ensures the safety of material handling personnel crossing the critical safety gap between truck and dock. (***Rite-Hite Corp.***)

tered from the dock. The outside light turns red to signal the truck-driver not to pull away. These light signals do not change until the operator inside the building depresses the button to disengage and lower the hook after the loading or unloading operation is complete and all dock personnel have safely left the trailer.

It is best to use two outside caution signs in addition to outside lights. One of the signs should be in conventional print, and the other in mirror-image print that the truck driver can read in the rearview mirror. The signs should explain the light display code.

If the ICC bumper is bent or missing or, for some reason, proper securement cannot be made, an inside alarm should be provided to indicate that the trailer is not restrained and is therefore unsafe to enter.

Other lighting considerations make a dock area safer as well. Provide a minimum of 30 footcandles of overhead lighting throughout the dock and specify dock loading lights to illuminate the inside of the trailers. Mount these loading lights on columns between truck positions or from above the dock openings. They should shine from the outer corners of the dock openings into the trailer. Some lights are equipped with swivel mountings, so light can be directed into the truck where needed.

Protect the Facility with Dock Equipment

When designing a building, the cost of the facility is painfully evident. It is a prime time to protect the investment by specifying equipment to protect the building from the force of backing trucks. A loaded semi-trailer weighing 40,000 pounds backing at a rate of 4 miles per hour would hit the dock with 150,000 pounds of force. This tremendous impact would tear apart even a steel-reinforced concrete dock. It would also damage the trucks and their cargoes. But adding 1 inch of cushioning to the front of the dock would lower the impact from 150,000 to 15,000 pounds. Bumpers installed on the dock would absorb this shock and protect the building.

Select laminated bumpers to absorb more impact. For additional protection, install cement-filled posts to guard the inside door and building walls.

Specify Dockleveler Capacity for Lowest Lifetime Ownership Cost

The single most important piece of dock equipment is the dockleveler system, and both frequency and weight of shipments should determine its capacity. The leveler bridges the critical gap between dock and truck.

The dock worker and all the material delivered to the operation or shipped from the operation travels over this gap.

Docklevelers should be permanently installed to provide a secure base for travel. They should be adjustable to accommodate varying truck heights. Select docklevelers with the capacity to withstand the heaviest loads from the most frequent deliveries for the life of the facility.

Specify docklevelers after considering these factors:

1. Number and nature of loads handled into and out of vehicles
2. Greatest height difference between the dock and bed of trucks or trailers serviced
3. Type of material handling equipment used

A forklift, operator, and load driving into the back of a truck can create a tremendous impact force. Dockleveler capacity should be based on the greatest impact force predicted in the operation based on frequency and grade. A 20,000-pound-capacity dockleveler should absorb 20,000 pounds of impact. However, that impact force can be generated by as little as 7,000 pounds, depending upon speed of the forklift and grade of the ramp.

Typical Forklift Weights, in pounds

Capacity	Gas/LP	Electric
3,000	6,000	7,000
4,000	6,900	8,000
5,000	8,700	10,000
6,000	10,600	12,500
7,000	12,700	13,500
8,000	13,500	14,000

Speed of the lift truck, ramp incline, and frequency of use are some of the variables that can reduce the life of the equipment. Also consider that three-wheel fork trucks have a concentrated area of weight that require a higher capacity dockleveler.

The capacity rating standards that apply to the dockleveler industry as issued by the U.S. government and the American National Standards Institute (ANSI) are based on minimum-use situations and do not take into account the variables presented by each leveler application. The dock designer receives the most accurate guidance in determining capacity of equipment from dockleveler manufacturers who have compiled performance data from thousands of installations. The manufacturer helps designers select equipment based on the weight of the heaviest load, the number of operating shifts, the number of loads per shift, the speed of the forklifts, and the predicted leveler grade for most operations.

Select Dock Equipment that Can Handle a Range of Truck Sizes

The nature of deliveries influences the carriers that will serve the dock, and the trailer height of these carriers dictates the length of docklevelers. Short levelers, 5 or 6 feet long, are adequate when truck heights are fairly constant and within 6 inches of the dock height. Similarly, the edge-of-dock leveler is used primarily with captive truck fleets.

When trucks with a range of trailer heights serve a dock, a longer leveler is critical. Levelers that are too short create these problems:

- Material handling equipment can hang up on ramps, because the crown is too great to negotiate.
- Loads can spill, become unstable, or damaged when operators are forced to negotiate severe inclines into the truck.
- Severe grades impose more wear on tires, clutches, and drive trains. They also shorten battery life of electric fork trucks.

Typically, the longer the dockleveler, the longer its life. The more gentle the slope, the less impact-force generated on the ramp, which results in less wear. The most popular length is 8 feet, but longer levelers will help reduce the grade of the ramp when truck heights vary substantially from dock height.

Percent of Grade for Material Handling Equipment

Type of equipment	Allowable percent of grade
Powered handtrucks	3
Powered platform trucks	7
Electric fork trucks	10
Gas fork trucks	15

Width of the dockleveler also depends on the types of loads at the facility, the type of material handling equipment, and the nature of the deliveries. The 6-foot-wide dockleveler has always been the most common, because the inside of most trailers measured 7 feet 6 inches. With the increasing frequency of trailers loaded completely to the end, 7-foot-wide levelers were employed to gain access to end loads. The lips of the 7-foot-wide levelers are tapered to accommodate imprecise trailer spotting.

An excellent compromise is the 6-foot 6-inch–wide leveler without a tapered lip. This provides access to end loads and serves the wider 102-inch-wide trailers. Because the lip is not tapered, the possibility of forklift wheel drop-off is eliminated (Figure 11.5). The safety of the platform is unsurpassed.

Levelers that are too narrow create problems for forklifts. Tires can be damaged and loads can spill when wheels travel too close to the sides of a narrow ramp. In addition, access to some loads is severely limited. Just imagine unloading a 102-inch-wide trailer, loaded to the doors with 48- by 40-inch pallet loads handled from the 48-inch side of a 6-foot-wide dockleveler. The economy of the large load could be lost in the amount of time required to unload the truck.

Specify Dock Equipment for Environmental Control

Some commodities present obvious requirements for climate control. Dairy products require refrigeration. Chemicals might require both temperature and humidity control. Most material requires some protection

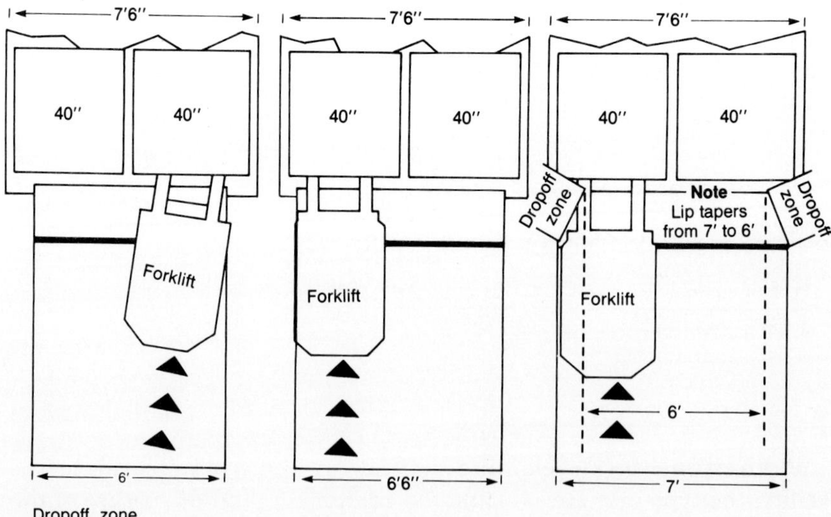

Figure 11.5. The 6-foot 6-inch-wide dockleveler serves wider trucks without creating spotting problems or dangerous drop off zones. (*Rite-Hite Corp.*)

from the weather. Dock areas should be designed to maintain conditioned air, whether the air is cooled or heated, for the welfare of the commodity or the dock workers. Dock seals and shelters help restrict the loss of conditioned air.

Shelters are available in a variety of types and sizes. Some are fabric over an extended housing or metal framework that surround the truck. Others consist of large foam pads covered with heavy, coated fabric. They can be protected from wear with a series of flaps fastened to the front to withstand the abrasion caused by truck movement during loading and unloading. Some can adjust to different truck sizes.

The range in truck sizes is complicating selection of dock seals and shelters. Manufacturers of shelters are responding with wider side curtains that accommodate larger truck bodies and move out of the way on contact. Dock pads—solid foam cushions that seal up against the rear of the truck—are presenting a tougher design challenge. If they are placed to seal the back of a 96-inch-wide truck, they will block the doorway of 102-inch-wide truck. Manufacturers have developed pads that seal up against the sides of the truck as the body pushes in between them. When specifying or installing dock pads and shelters, keep in mind the outside dimensions of the trucks that serve the operation. A 102-inch-wide truck with the doors open has a total body width of 108 inches. Refrigerated trucks can be as wide as 120 inches with doors open. These wider trucks with doors open will cause greater wear.

Dock pad and shelter manufacturers will gladly assist any dock designer in determining and specifying the actual dimensions of this equipment for a specific dock.

Another important equipment feature for containing conditioned air is the weather seal on docklevelers. Flush docks, equipped with docklevelers, should have weather seals applied to the full length and rear width of the dockleveler. This minimizes the loss of cool or warm air in loading areas. For long-range economy, be sure that these weather seals can be replaced quickly and inexpensively, because they wear out with use. Docklevelers can also be insulated with foam to reduce condensation and frost in frozen food operations.

Extreme temperature control can be accomplished by constructing a vestibule. This allows the dock to be partitioned off from sections of the building which have controlled temperatures. The vestibule can be equipped with several different types of doorways to permit efficient forklift traffic. Types include: sliding doors, bumper doors, and clear plastic-strip doors. They are available in different styles and combinations. Another method of controlling air flow is to mount air curtains over the doorways.

Determine Whether the Operation Requires Sanitation Equipment

Many industries have special requirements for sanitation in all phases of material movement. Some dock equipment helps to maintain sanitary conditions.

If the operation requires constant cleaning, specify galvanized docklevelers so the pit can be washed out without premature rusting of the equipment. Some manufacturers have a line of docklevelers designed for frequent, easy cleaning as required in the food and beverage industry. They have built-in, water-spray nozzles and removable debris pans.

Keep windblown dirt from entering the plant by specifying docklevelers with side and rear weather seals. Similarly, a 20-inch-long dockleveler lip section covers the face of the pit when closed and keeps out dirt and debris.

Remember that all loading-dock operations produce some refuse. Place a trash container or compactor at an end dock position to keep the busy dock area clear.

Select Dock Equipment that Enhances Security

Security equipment on the dock must include locks on all doors of enclosed or flush docks, but special features of other dock equipment can further enhance security.

Docklevelers with hinged lips can present a security problem unless equipped with night locks. If the lip of the dockleveler is not secured, it is easily lifted. Some docks have been damaged when vandals gain access into the dock through these openings. But if the docklevelers are stored in lip keepers, the leveler is essentially locked to prevent building break-in through the dock area.

Another piece of dock equipment, designed for safety, also enhances security. Truck restraints lock the trailer to the dock to prevent it from separating before dock personnel have finished servicing the vehicle. The restraints can also lock the trailer to the dock at night to prevent highjacking of theft of valuable cargo.

Shippers of commodities with high street-values such as cigarettes, alcoholic beverages, and blue jeans have installed vehicle restraints not only for their safety value, but also for the protection they provide against trailer theft.

Planning the Staging Area Within the Dock

The final step in effective dock design is arranging the staging area within the dock. Every loading dock is different, just as every operation is unique. Several factors will determine the format and influence the efficiency of the staging area. When designing the inside of the dock, consider:

- How can the staging area enhance material flow?
- Can careful design enhance the safety of the material handling operation?

Enhance Material Flow with Staging Area Design

Design a minimum area inside the plant behind the edge of the dock to be kept clear and unobstructed for the movement of freight and materials handling equipment. The width of the area must allow for maneuverability of materials handling equipment in and out of vehicles and for two-way cross traffic behind the dock. Allow an area four times the width of the material handled and the length of the leveler. If conveyors move goods directly from production to truck, the requirement for a clear distance behind the dock edge does not apply.

Some dock areas must accommodate temporary or long-term storage areas for commodities. Others serve just-in-time operations that require the docks to serve as conduits for material flowing directly to production lines. Establish the destination of materials before designing the loading dock.

If the operation requires temporary storage areas, estimate the amount of space needed with this formula: A 40-foot-long trailer that is 8 feet wide has 320 square feet of storage area, usually loaded to a height of 6 feet. If you store freight 12 feet high, you will need 160 square feet per trailer. If it is stored 3 feet high, you will need 640 square feet per trailer, and so on.

If several variables make a more accurate projection of space needs necessary, follow the steps for computing accumulation space from the *Shipper-Motor Carrier Dock Planning Manual.*

Accumulation space might be needed to stage shipments so they are ready for the pickup vehicle and for storing materials or components until they are ready for production. Accumulation space might contain storage racks, bins, or shelves. It might collect pallets, skids, carts, or other containers.

Determine the space needed for total shipment accumulation for the peak hour of the day. The warehouse picks orders at a certain rate and loads trucks at certain times. So the accumulation space must allow storage for the total of orders picked during the day minus the total of orders loaded out. Estimate these total volumes by the hour to determine both what the peak is and when the peak occurs. Generally, the peak accumulation for most facilities occurs in the early afternoon, just before the peak arrival period for carriers.

To calculate the space needed, convert the maximum volume for the peak into cubic feet. Establish conversion factors for converting pounds or cases into cubic feet. However, remember that finished goods might not be accumulated in one easily stacked or measured mass, so provide additional space for access and for separation of shipments by carrier. For most conditions, allowance for additional space is usually about two and one-half to three times as great as the actual cube of the product. So, multiply the finished goods cubic feet by 2½ or 3 to obtain the total storage cubic feet required.

To prepare a layout, determine the number of square feet for accumulation space by:

1. Determining the overall stacking height for the shipment to be stored, and by
2. Dividing the total storage cubic feet by the stacking height

The result is the storage area in square feet.

If the storage is not a primary issue because the operation requires just-in-time delivery of material or components to a production line, investigate whether conveyors or robotics will transport materials from the dock. This will significantly influence dock layout.

Whether the material is headed for storage or production, design the inside of the dock to allow straight-in-and-out forklift travel from the docklevelers. Making sharp turns while on the leveler will slow loading operations and could cause the forklift to drop off the side of the leveler.

Design the Staging Area with Safety in Mind

As with all aspects of dock design, safety is a primary consideration when laying out the inside dock area. Remember that in a warehousing operation, up to 60 percent of the work force could be on the dock at one time. Provide adequate ventilation, especially if internal combustion trucks are used on the dock or highway vehicles are parked inside.

Provide adequate trash containers for the inside dock area to collect packing materials that could impair forklift traffic or present a safety hazard.

Insist on safety communications for the inside dock area. Mark forklift lanes with yellow lines and specify a schedule for inspecting the markings for wear. Require rotating or flashing warning lights on all powered mobile equipment on busy docks.

Enhance the safety of the loading area by training all truck drivers and dock workers to recognize the light-display messages of truck restraint systems. The flashing light displays will serve as a constant reminder to dock personnel that they are in a dangerous environment.

Plan dock areas so that you can add a mezzanine over the dock area. A mezzanine can become a driver waiting area, room for storage, or warehouse supervisor's office.

Providing a drivers' lounge will enhance the efficiency, safety, and security of a dock. The lounge location should provide separate washroom facilities for men and women and possibly vending machines for refreshments. To assist with prompt completion of shipping documents, provide tables and chairs in the lounge and consider placing the area next to the dispatcher's office—separated by Dutch doors—to restrict the drivers from the rest of the operation but provide access to shipping and receiving personnel.

Conclusion

Each stage of truck movement, from the time it enters the plant compound until it arrives at its destination, requires careful considerations of dock design. Review each design decision with the plant's safety, efficiency, security, and ultimately, profitability in mind.

For assistance specific to your operation, contact manufacturers or distributors of dock equipment. They have a special interest in providing designers with guidance to construct safe and efficient loading docks for any operation.

Bibliography

Dock Design for the Future, Rite-Hite Corporation, Milwaukee, 1984.

How Big Is A Truck—How Sharp Does It Turn, The Management Council, American Trucking Associations, Inc., Washington, 1974.

Shipper-Motor Carrier Dock Planning Manual, The Management Council, American Trucking Associations, Inc., Washington, 1973.

12
Large-Parts Storage Systems

J. Henry Donnon

Vice President (Retired), Artco Corporation, Hatfield, Pennsylvania

Ted Hammond

President, Conveyor-Logic, Inc., Dutton, Michigan

Types of Racks

Pallet Racks

Steel pallet-rack structures have been designed to facilitate the maximum storage of products placed on pallets in any given warehouse space, as well as provide accessibility for order-picking case lots or individual pallet units, as may be desired. The development of pallet-rack design progressed hand in hand with the development of forklift trucks. As height and load capacity of lift trucks increased, rack size followed to meet these needs. About 35 years ago, average rack heights were 10 feet. New building construction compensated for the advancement of warehouse storage equipment, and currently, some facilities can use lift trucks and storage racks higher than 40 feet.

Selective pallet storage racks consist of upright frames and a pair of load beams for each shelf elevation (see Figure 12.1). It must be kept in

Figure 12.1. Pallet rack. (*ARTCO Corp.*.)

mind that the pallet and the unit load, including weight and overall dimensions, dictate the rack design when properly coordinated with the desired lift-truck equipment to operate the storage area. Common sense tells us that we cannot put a size 12 foot in a size 10 shoe. Establishing the storage-rack dimensions forms the basis of properly determining a warehouse layout. Collection of the fundamental data of the unit load and handling equipment will provide the information required to determine the upright frame size and capacity, corollated with the shelf load-beam span and capacity.

It is of primary importance to determine the type of lift-truck equipment that will be used for rack storage in the warehouse. Counterbalanced (wide-aisle), reach-type (up-and-over), or double-deep equipment or straddle trucks (narrow-aisle) are most common today. Turret-type trucks are also used in narrow-aisle storage operations. Each type of lift truck presents different characteristics that must be considered and accounted for in providing ample operational clearances in the rack design for a sound storage system to function properly.

Normally, two pallets are placed side by side over the rack load beams or shelf. When operating with counterbalanced lift trucks, 4 inches should be allowed between upright frame columns and the load, and 4 inches between the loads. Always allow 4 inches of operational clearance from the top of the load to the underside of the upper rack shelf (see Figure 12.2).

Straddle-type trucks require a minimum of 5½ inches between the upright frame column and outboard side of the pallet stringer. This 5½-inch clearance provides operational space for a 4-inch-wide straddle leg normally provided for straddle lift trucks. Wing-type pallets are generally used with straddle trucks, and pallet construction will provide anywhere from 1 to 4 inches overhang of the face boards over the outside of the pallet stringers. The truck straddle legs, therefore, operate below the pallet wing or overhanging face boards and between the pallet stringer and upright column. It is of fundamental importance to provide 4 inches between the load and the upright columns, with 4 inches between loads and beneath the upper load support beams (see Figure 12.3) as operational clearances. These basic clearances provide truck operator maneuverability and a margin of error when hand stacking loads on the pallet.

The overall height of the storage rack must be compatible with that of the maximum lift height of any lift truck equipment. It is important that the top shelf be 6 inches less than the maximum lifting height of the truck to position a 6-inch-deep pallet. A tilting adaption of the lift-truck mast can assist, especially if the floor and top rack shelf elevation are not level. The bottom of the pallet in this case must be raised above the top of the top-shelf load beams.

These operational clearances may seem fundamental; however, they must be both determined and applied to provide an economical and workable storage-rack system of operation. Here is an example of misapplied data that created a nonworkable system and/or a greater capital outlay.

The owner informs the rack supplier that he or she is purchasing a 4000-pound-capacity counterbalanced lift truck; therefore, the pallet

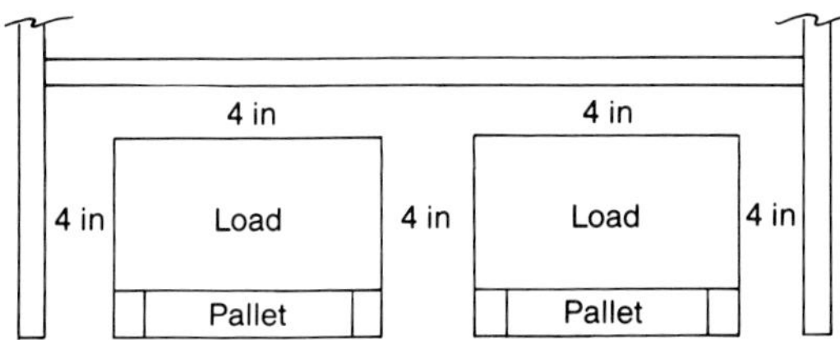

Figure 12.2. Pallet-rack clearance requirements.

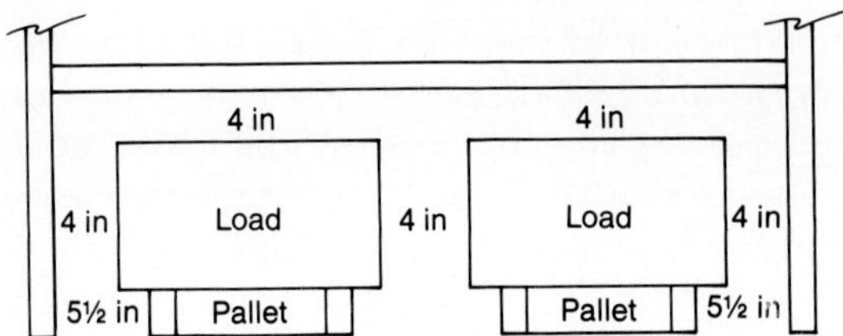

Figure 12.3. Required pallet-rack overhead clearances.

load will weigh 4000 pounds and the contents or product will be placed on 48- by 48-inch pallets, stored two pallets wide per shelf. The rack supplier would provide shelf load beams having a minimum capacity of 8000 pounds with a horizontal clear span of 108 inches between upright frames. This accounts for two 48-inch pallets and 12 inches of operational clearance (4 inches between columns and loads, and between loads). When the equipment is delivered and assembled, it is discovered tha the maximum unit load weight was only 2000 pounds. The best stacking pattern on the pallet added up to a 50-inch-wide load. Result: The owner paid extra to purchase 8000-pound-capacity shelves when only a 4000-pound capacity was really required. Also, the truck operators were restricted to less than 3 inches of operational clearances, increasing the time of operation and the possibility of product damage.

Rack Bay. Similar to the nomenclature of building bays, which is the distance between walls to building columns and between building columns, a rack bay is the space between upright frames or rack supporting columns. Any given rack bay may be one or more shelves high. The connection of two or more rack bays in length constitutes a row of racks; thus, for example, 1 row, 20 bays, 3 shelves per bay would consist of the following parts for assembly: 21 upright frames and 60 pairs of shelf load beams. This basic nomenclature accounts for only the quantity of rack parts. Use the dimensions of the pallet, the overall size of the load (width, depth, and height), weight of the load, and characteristics of the lifting equipment to calculate the required shelf capacity and depth of load beams. Add the operational clearance to load height and beam depth figures to determine the first shelf elevation.

When handling standard pallets, the rack depth over the shelf load beams is usually 6 inches less than the pallet stringer length. This provides 3 inches of front and rear overhang of the pallet on the shelf beams for the truck operator to quickly and safely position the pallet load for storage on the shelf.

The number of shelves that can be used per rack bay is determined by the lifting height of the truck and allowable ceiling height. The number of shelves high and the required load capacities then determine the required supporting capacity of the upright frame. The accumulation of all of the aforementioned information is shown in Figure 12.4. Apply the following data to determine the dimensions for one rack bay:

Counterbalanced lift truck: capacity—4000 pounds; minimum height—162 inches

Ceiling height: 18 feet (216 inches)

Standard pallet size: 48 inches deep by 42 inches wide by 6 inches high

Load: size—48 inches deep by 44 inches wide by 40 inches high; weight—2200 pounds

The rack requirements for Figure 12.4 are as follows:

Two upright frames: size—42 inches deep by 56 inches high; minimum capacity—13,200 pounds

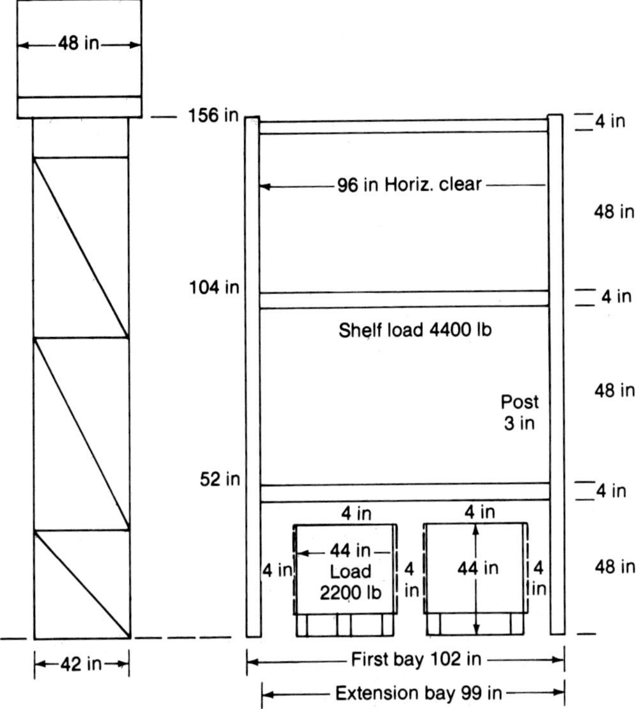

Figure 12.4. Rack bay specifications.

Three shelves, six load beams: span—96 inches; minimum load capacity—4400 pounds

Storage: eight pallet load racks per bay

Figure 12.4 illustrates the necessity of collecting the required data, as mentioned before, to establish the rack sizes and quantities to determine the first bay of racks. Extension rack bays may be added to attain any overall length (down-aisle) of racks you may require, within building limitations.

Consider this illustration for better economy. The ceiling height of 21 feet will permit double stacking (two high in lieu of only one high) on the top shelf. The lift-truck minimum lift must now be 202 inches. The top rack shelf must now carry 8800 pounds, and the frame capacity is proportionately increased to 17,600 pounds minimum. In most cases, you will find the increased cost for the lift truck and the rack equipment minimal. The storage of two additional pallets will reduce the cost of all pallets stored in the rack bay.

The Rack Manufacturers Institute, Inc. safety specifications suggest that the ratio of overall height of the top load to the depth shall not exceed 6 to 1 without anchoring the rack to the building structure. In the above illustration, if double stacking on the top shelf is selected, the single-rack rows must be anchored to the building wall or building columns as the height of the top load exceeds the 6-to-1 ratio. Rack rows installed back to back should be assembled with rigid back-to-back frame ties. The overall rack depth is the measurement from aisle post to aisle post, which, in this case, is within the ratio for safe stability.

Overall height of storage (from floor to top of the top load) must be considered to allow for overhead fire-control sprinklers in determining allowable clear ceiling height of the building. Check with your insurance carrier to find out the required clearance between the top of the load and the sprinkler heads. The combustibility of the products you store also determines if the insurance carrier requires additional in-rack sprinklers. Information regarding fire-control requirements is published by the National Fire Prevention Association. (See the suggested bibliography at the end of this chapter.) The rack supplier may have to provide additional space for in-rack sprinklers when required, especially when rows of racks are installed back to back. Normal spacing between load beams is 8 inches, allowing 3 inches of overhang of each load, and 2 inches of operational space considered a longitudinal flue in the down-aisle direction. Occasionally, insurance carriers want the 2-inch longitudinal flue increased so that when loads are stored back to back they cannot obstruct the flow of air in the flue space between the loads. Advise your rack supplier of this required dimension and be sure to consider this factor in determining your storage floor-plan layout.

Floor-plan layout. There are several requirements to keep in mind when you formulate your floor-plan layout. Among these are: door openings, direction of of down-aisle travel of lift trucks and picking carts, building column locations kept within the confines of the racks, lift-truck-equipment aisle-width requirements, placement of overhead lighting, fire-control sprinklers, loading and floor stacking, cross-aisle requirements, overall length of rack rows, and quantity of load units to be stored in the racks. All of these requirements can be met if all the basic dimensions have been specified so that the data can be applied to establishing a floor-plan layout.

Starting with the unit load, determine the size of one rack bay that provides a multiple length on the floor plan. The overall length of the rack row or number of rack bays can be determined later to fulfill the quantity of pallets for rack storage. The depth of the loads or the stringer length of the pallet is another multiple needed, along with the required aisle width for lifting equipment operation. These factors will determine the overall width of the building and location of building columns. In most instances, building costs can be minimized by providing four rack rows and two aisles between building columns or between walls and building columns, as shown on Figure 12.5. This is particularly true if a new building for rack storage is going to be constructed. Should racks be installed in an existing building, make every effort to keep building columns within the confines of the rack and out of the operating aisles. This can be accomplished by slightly increasing the aisle width to locate

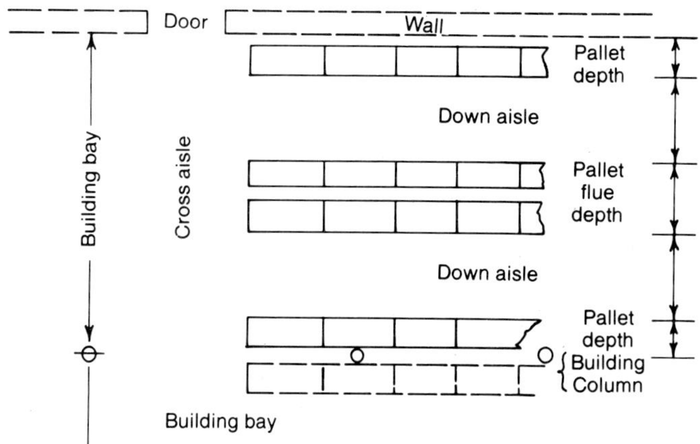

Figure 12.5. Typical pallet-rack arrangement in building bay.

the building column between two rows of racks installed back to back or within a rack bay. In the case of the latter, it is much better to lose the pallet space at the building column location. Building columns in the operating aisle create hazards to the column and to order-picking traffic, and damage to the product being handled. Figure 12.6 shows various options that can be used to keep building columns within the confines of the rack.

Storm-drain plumbing from the roof should be treated in the same manner as building columns and should be positioned to minimize lost space and maximize space utilization of the warehouse.

The basic information can be utilized as input to computer routines to ascertain the required area for any given number of pallet units to be stored. However, the computer summary will only afford data to a drafter-designer who can then formally establish a complete floor-plan layout. Consideration of doorways; floor stacking areas; overhead obstructions, such as lighting, air coolers, and sprinkler systems; and operational cross aisles must be accounted for in the completed floor plan.

Although the aforementioned details apply to pallet storage, the same fundamentals can be applied to establish rack storage for other products of various shapes, weights, and sizes, such as: carpet rolls, 55-gallon drums, unpalletized cartons, rolled-steel coils, steel box skids, and so on. The rack manufacturer can usually provide shelf support beams and accessories to accommodate storage of products having special characteristics. Pallet storage racks afford 100 percent selectivity of any unit content either manually or by lift trucks operating from the aisle.

In recent years, double-deep reach-type lift trucks have been manufactured to store two pallets in depth. To accommodate storage of this nature, pallet racks are then assembled as two rows set back to back to the lift-truck operation from one aisle, placing two pallets deep. Although this type of storage decreases the immediate aisle selectivity by 50 percent, it conserves storage space due to the conservation of an aisle. Consideration of a double-deep storage system should only be undertaken when large quantities of palletized loads of the same items are

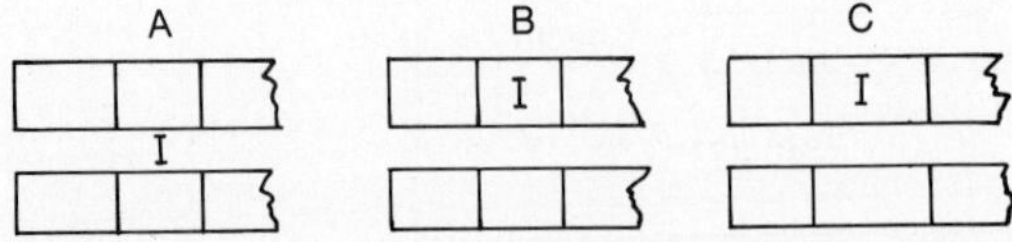

Figure 12.6. Options for locating building columns within pallet rack. (*a*) **Between rack rows set back to back;** (*b*) **Lost pallet space in one rack bay;** (*c*) **Increase horizontal shelf span to accommodate two pallets wide and a building column.**

to be stored. Double-deep storage has the great advantage of increasing pallet unit storage in a minimum of warehouse space. Figure 12.7 illustrates double-deep rack storage as compared to a standard selective pallet-rack installation.

Drive-in/Drive-thru Pallet Racks

Drive-in racks are designed for bulk storage of palletized loads. Only pallets facing the aisle provide selectivity of contents, whereas the in-depth stored pallets provide bulk storage to maximize space utilization. Rack bays are only one pallet wide and are designed and manufactured to store two or more pallets deep as well as multiple pallets high (Figure 12.8).

As the name implies, the racks must be designed to permit entry of the forklift truck so that the truck can "drive in" the rack from the operating aisle and between the rack columns and pallet support rails. Drive-in racks have horizontal shelf beams between adjoining upright frame columns that restrict the "in-depth" travel of the truck. When the shelf beams are omitted, the rack allows the lift truck to "drive thru" the rack structures to the opposite working aisle (Figure 12.9).

When selecting between drive-in and drive-thru rack designs, keep in mind that pallet loads must be stored so as to eliminate any load placement in the rack bay that would restrict the travel of the lift truck. Should such travel restrictions ever occur, the drive-thru design obviously should not be considered. It is possible for drive-thru racks to provide first-in, first-out (FIFO) storage, whereas drive-in racks only function with first-in, last-out (FILO) storage operations.

Design of drive-in/drive-thru rack equipment requires the same basic information as that required for selective pallet racks, *plus* more complete specifications pertaining to the lift truck. The rack-bay opening and first shelf elevation must provide ample space for the lift truck and pallet load to enter the rack. Therefore, the following dimensions of

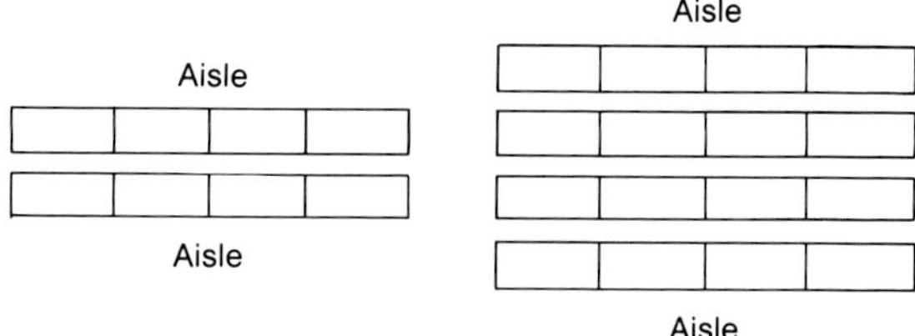

Figure 12.7. Double-deep storage versus single-deep storage.

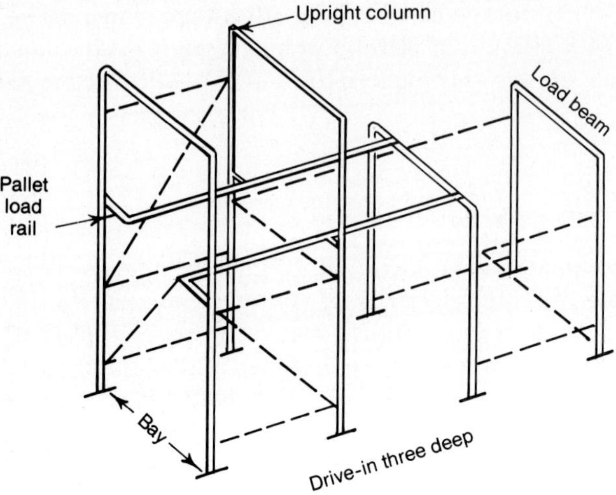

Figure 12.8. Drive-in rack.

the truck must be known: *body width and height, width and elevation of overhead guard, hose reel location, width and collapsed height of mast, and lift height of forks.* It is also important to know the elevation and position of the truck's steering wheel to allow ample clearance for safe steering operation.

The rack bay can only be designed after all of the specification data is collected. Operational clearances between load and upright frame columns should be 4 inches. Four inches should be provided between the top of the load and the underside of the pallet support rails or cantilever rail support arms. A minimum of 4 inches should be allowed between the top of the uppermost load and the top bridge tie. An additional clearance of 1 to 2 inches at the top location allows the truck operator more latitude in loading or unloading the top load. This extra clearance is advisable if the ceiling height permits and does not adversely affect the capacity of the upright frame column.

Figure 12.9. Plan view of drive-in/drive-thru rack.

Figure 12.10 is an illustration of one drive-in/drive-thru rack bay showing the dimensions required to obtain the overall bay width. A plan view is shown to obtain the overall depth of three 48- by 48-inch pallets. These dimensions are required to establish the first rack bay, which can then be extended to fulfill the drive-in storage-rack requirements for both height and length of a row.

For each row of drive-in/drive-thru racks, it is advisable that there be *at least* as many rack bays as pallets to be stored in depth; for example: five pallets in depth of storage should require a minimum of five rack bays in length of row. It is also advisable, particularly with drive-thru racks, to structurally tie the uppermost rack columns to building columns. Never tie any racks to roof supports of the building. Snow loads, wind loads, and vibration of the interaction of the racks can play havoc with roof construction as well as create an overload to the pallet racks.

Figure 12.11 shows a drive-in rack in use with double stacking of pallets on the floor and one guide-rail pallet shelf designed to support four pallets in depth. Each rack bay will provide storage for 12 pallets of merchandise when fully loaded.

Should a secondary fire-control sprinkler system be required, the plumbing of sprinkler heads should be located such that they do not obstruct the storage operational clearances. Keeping the sprinkler heads within the lateral and horizontal confines of the rack structures also aids in protecting the sprinkler head. Confirmation and approval of the secondary sprinkler system should be obtained from your insurance carrier.

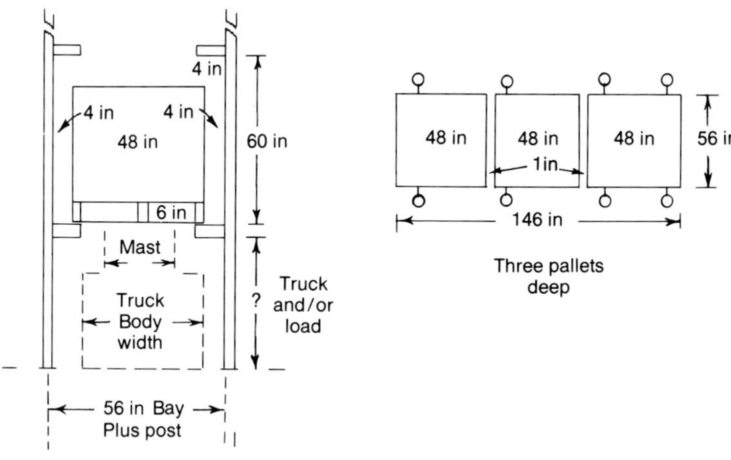

Figure 12.10. Drive-in/drive-thru rack bay.

Figure 12.11. Drive-in rack. (*ARTCO Corp.*)

Pallet support rails of many configurations are available, but will vary from manufacturer to manufacturer. Structural steel angles or inverted formed channels are most common. These rails are connected to cantilever arms protruding from the upright frame columns. Bolted or boltless connectors are used to connect the arms to the frame columns, whereas the pallet-load support rails are bolted to the protruding arms when installed. The support rails can be manufactured not only to support the pallets, but also to be used as guide rails to confine the pallet on the rails. Various types of pallet-load support rails are shown in Figure 12.12.

The clearance between pallet support rails must allow the lift-truck mast to pass between the rails, but must not allow the width of the pallet to fall through this clearance. The Rack Manufacturers Institute recommends that, should a pallet be moved totally to one side of the bay opening, a minimum of 1 inch remain as support under the opposite side of the pallet. For guided-type support rails, a minimum surface of ¾-inch is required to support the pallet when the pallet is moved against the opposite guide rail.

All upright frames or upright rack columns should be anchored to the floor. Floors should be level and the racks should be installed plumb. It is critical to install and maintain the rack columns vertically plumb to avoid increasing or decreasing the bay openings between columns. Floor anchoring assists in maintaining the span clearance between the frame columns, but does not in any manner aid in the stability of rack structure. Anchoring helps prevent lift trucks from pushing the bottom of the columns out of alignment. It is advisable to reinforce the bottom portion of the aisle rack column to help withstand lift-truck or pallet abuse when entering or leaving the rack bay at this location. Most rack manufacturers can provide column guards or can reinforce the upright column facing the aisle as a deterrent to damage. Reinforcing the column from the floor to the first shelf elevation can deter damage from trucks backing across the aisle and striking the columns. Some manufacturers can provide aisle frames that have the aisle column recessed or slanted back toward the interior of the rack, which slightly removes the post obstruction near the floor elevation. Although this construction or rack design tends to minimize damage to the bottom of the aisle column, it does not entirely eliminate the possibility of a pallet striking near the base of the column on entry. Depending on the elevation of the first shelf, it would be possible to create a hazard to the truck operator should he or she back across the aisle into an adjoining or protruding pallet support rail or shelf. The same hazard can occur if the pallet support rails protrude too far into the operating aisle.

There are pros and cons regarding the provision of truck or pallet floor guide rails at the base of drive-in racks. The intent of guide rails,

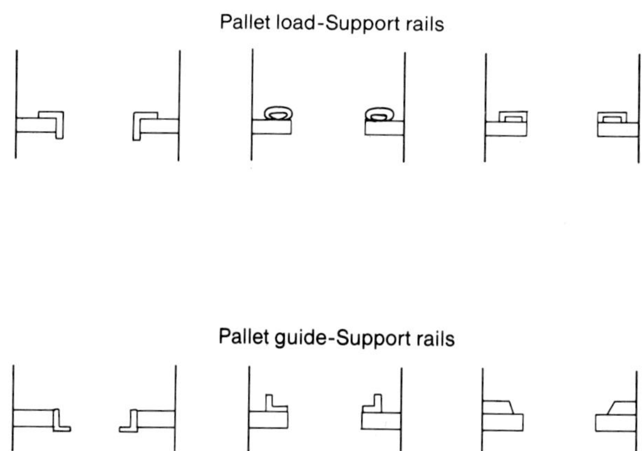

Figure 12.12. Drive-in/drive-thru rack support rails.

of course, is to allow easier operation of fork trucks into and within the racks. Should guide rails be installed, they must be more substantially anchored to the floor to withstand the pressure of the side truss created by the lift truck. Truck operators often rely too much on the presence of guide rails rather than on their own operating abilities, which creates greater maintenance cost in keeping the guide rails in position and repair. The absence of floor guide rails generally gives the operator more maneuvering space to travel within the rack confinement, keeping maintenance to a minimum. Only well-trained truck operators should be allowed to operate in drive-in/drive-thru racks, since accuracy of driving the lift truck into these racks is more stringent than servicing standard selective pallet racks from the aisle.

Cantilever Racks

Cantilever racks are used for the storage of long objects, such as metal extrusions, structural steel bars, tubes, pipe, or cartons of unwieldy sizes and shapes. The common name for this type of racking is a "Christmas tree," which they resemble. In essence, cantilever racks have a center upright column that supports cantilevered arms protruding outward on one or both sides of the main column. Single-sided and double-sided cantilever racks are available.

Heavy-duty cantilever racks are used in steel warehouses or manufacturing facilities that must handle and store long loads of extrusions. When designing a rack for this purpose, it is important to know the handling equipment specifications. Narrow-aisle, side-loader fork-lift trucks seem to be most efficient (Figure 12.13); however, equipment operated from overhead cranes or floor-mounted equipment running on rails is also available to handle trays or bundles 10 to 21 feet long.

The basic frame construction of cantilever racks consists of a load-bearing upright column attached to a base structure. The base distributes the weight over the floor area and aids maintenance of the upright column in a plumb, cross-aisle direction. Two frame sections, joined by installing braces between the columns, keep the uprights plumb. When two sections are joined, they become a rack bay. Additional column sections may be added to extend the overall row length to meet any desired storage requirement (Figure 12.14). The height of the rack is dependent on the limitations of the lifting or handling equipment and ceiling height.

To design a cantilever rack, the fundamental information of the unit load data must be determined (i.e., length, diameter or height and width, and weight). Determine if the bundles will be strapped or if the con-

Figure 12.13. Cantilever rack and sideloading forklift truck. (*ARTCO Corp.*)

tents will be contained and handled in pans or trays. The handling equipment data must also be determined and corrolated with the load data to meet the storage-rack criteria.

The load size and weight determine the length and support capacity of the cantilever arm, which in turn determines the number of arms required to support a load placed on one shelf elevation. Operational clearance between the top of the load and the underside of the cantilever arm must be provided to allow ample room for placement of the load or to lift the load when it is extracted from the rack. The vertical clearance allowed for placement of the load plus the depth of the cantilever arm provides the data for each shelf elevation. The number of shelf elevations depends on the lifting or handling equipment capabilities and the allowable ceiling height.

Figure 12.14. Cantilever rack bays. (*ARTCO Corp.*)

After the total number of shelf elevations are determined, either on a single-sided or double-sided rack, the total maximum weight for each column can be tallied. This data allows the rack manufacturer to determine the size and capacity of the base structure required to support the rack when completely loaded.

Aisle width should be determined by the lift-equipment manufacturer. Maximum and minimum width dimensions from the rack base to the top shelf elevation should be considered to allow for proper operational space. This space may vary due to the load placement on varying shelf elevations at the aisle sides of the rack. The upright columns tend to bend slightly toward the side supporting the maximum weight loads. In other words, it is possible in very high racks to have the columns bend toward each other from opposite sides of the aisle, creating a decrease in the operational space from the rack base to the top shelf elevation. This space may vary due to the load placement on varying shelf elevations. To offset this condition, the rack upright columns can be extended in height and provided with top cross-aisle ties (Figure 12.15). These top-aisle ties will then maintain the clearance required for proper op-

Figure 12.15. Cantilever rack with cross-aisle ties. (*ARTCO Corp.*)

eration of floor running equipment. Consideration given to this condition for overhead handling equipment is to shorten the length of the cantilever arms at the top shelf elevations or to increase the aisle width proportionately.

Smaller versions of cantilever racks that are prefabricated for storage use in maintenance areas or tool bins are available. These racks are only about 8 feet high and are manually loaded or unloaded. Compared to pigeon-hole–type bins, cantilever racks of this design minimize the use of the working area by allowing the materials to be side loaded, rather than being loaded from the ends. They make raw steel stock more accessible in the generally restricted area of the workroom.

Light-duty cantilever racks are designed for use by furniture manufacturers or distribution warehouses storing large, nonpalletized cartons or products. The advantage of cantilevered racks over standard selective pallet racks is the absence of the front aisle post, which provides greater flexibility for storage of cartons of varying sizes.

Cantilever racks of this design consist of upright frame columns attached to the rack base or directly on the floor. Cantilever arms are attached to the columns at predetermined elevations when assembled. The rack arms are generally joined down-aisle with either metal or wooden supports and are covered with plywood or sheet-metal decking. Decking of this nature provides a continuous storage shelf the full length of the back row.

Narrow-aisle platform lifting equipment is used to service the racks, and the unit loads are generally handled manually. Guide rails mounted to the rack base, or preferably mounted on the floor, restrict the handling equipment movement from hitting the rack installation. Heavy entrance guards or bumpers should be floor mounted at the ends of the back row to assist the equipment operator in aligning the lift equipment within the guide rails when entering the operating aisle. The entrance guides or bumpers have to withstand extreme abuse, both during the entrance and exit of the moving equipment. The most substantial entrance guides are those that are constructed having a curved steel wearing surface anchored to the floor and filled with concrete. During recent years, cantilever racks of this nature have been found to be extremely useful in the textile industry, department store warehouse storage, and furniture manufacturers' production and outlet distribution warehouses.

Stacking Frames

Stacking frames should be considered to provide multiple stacking and storage of products that do not normally permit stacking of one pallet load on top of another. The addition of stacking frames to the pallet provides support to allow multiple stacking and prevent crushing of product content. Compared to permanently installed standard pallet racks, stacking frames provide a portable storage unit. In this respect, portable units can be located or readily relocated to any storage area of the warehouse. Stacking racks can be designed to retain those "unstackable" items or products on the pallet, as well as provide the supporting structures to allow multiple stacking (Figure 12.16).

The tire manufacturing industry is a good example of the handling and storage of crushable products on stacking frames so that they can

Figure 12.16. Stacking frames. (*ARTCO Corp.*)

be transported and stacked. Crushable cartoned goods can be palletized and transported to various production stations or to the shipping dock, as required.

Stacking frames are available in various types of construction that vary from manufacturer to manufacturer. Most units are designed so that they can be knocked down for storage when they are not in use. Stacking frames are generally assembled on the pallet prior to loading of the product; therefore, the face width of the pallet must be greater than the total width of the intended load to provide space for attaching or detaching stacking frames. It is important to provide the supplier with the dimensions of the pallet, showing top board size and placement, as well as the size and length of the pallet stringers. Each manufacturer has varying means of attaching the units to the pallet. The use of stacking frames on wing-type pallets should be discouraged if the wing overhangs the pallet stringer by a dimension greater than that of the stacking frame post. The distribution of unit weight should be transferred vertically from the pallet to the stacking-frame upright posts, downward to the floor.

The height of the stacked loads must be determined to obtain the maximum weight capacity of each frame. The capacity of each stacking-frame assembly is based on the total weight that the bottom or floor load must support. As an example, suppose you want to stack 2000-pound loads, four high. Since the bottom unit weight rests on the floor, it must have a capacity of 6000 pounds, which is the total static load it supports. Basically, the minimum information to provide the supplier or manufacturer includes: *pallet dimensions, stringer size, vertical clear load height, unit weight of each loaded pallet, and the number of units to be stacked*. However, to maximize cubic space utilization, consider the lift-height capabilities of the lift truck and the available clear ceiling height of the warehouse. The overall height of a stacking frame unit consists not only of the load height, but also 6 inches for the pallet and 2 inches for the top supporting structure of the stacking frames. In other words, add 8 inches to the load height to obtain the overall height of one assembled unit. This height can then be divided into the allowable clear storage height in the warehouse. Should you find you are losing some of the "air space," consider increasing the unit load height, providing the lift truck will be able to access the top load. The slightly increased cost of the stacking-frame unit will be more than offset by the savings in lost overhead "air rights."

Flow Rack

A flow rack is a series of vertical columns, horizontal load supports, and conveyors that rest on load supports. Figure 12.17 shows a typical flow-rack structure. The uprights and cross arms are very similar in strength and structure to the materials used in other types of rack systems. The conveyor that rests on the cross arms has the same technical specifications as a conveyor that would be used to transport a pallet in a factory or warehouse. A flow-rack system is quite simply a conveyor within a rack structure.

Two factors govern the size of a flow-rack system: lane depth and the number of levels in the rack. There are essentially no restrictions to lane depth. There are, however, two problems with a very deep lane: acceleration and travel distance. When the lane is nearly empty and a pallet

Figure 12.17. Gravity-roller conveyor flow rack. (*Conveyor-Logic, Inc.*)

is placed in the lane, it travels the full length of the lane, accelerating as it moves. The greater the lane depth, the greater the force of the collision between the two pallets at the end of the run. Travel distance is the second problem with a deep lane. The deeper the lane, the greater the chances of having a pallet become blocked or jammed in the lane. It is a very time-consuming process to extract a jammed pallet from a flow-rack system.

The only real restriction on a flow-rack system is the number of levels. Material handling equipment will not be the restricting factor with respect to the number of levels, because there is a storage and retrieval device to service any height of rack. Generally, the restricting factor is the ceiling height. The entry or rear section of the rack is higher than the front section of the rack due to the slope of the conveyor. The deeper the lane, the greater the difference between the front and rear elevations of the rack. The front of the flow rack may fit into the building, but if the lane is too deep, the rear section could be too high.

Each lane of a flow rack is dedicated to a single stockkeeping unit (SKU). Unit loads are placed into the back of the rack and indexed to the discharge end of the rack, typically by gravity. The weight of the unit loads can be as much as 5000 pounds or greater, and can be stored in temperatures ranging from −40 to +130°F. These unit loads can be placed into the rack or taken out of the rack by most industrial trucks and storage/retrieval (S/R) machines. A flow-rack system is a versatile storage technique that lends itself to almost any type of industrial application.

Advantages and Disadvantages. Flow-rack systems have several advantages over other storage systems. First, it is a first-in, first-out storage system. Pallets are constantly being indexed forward, with the first pallet stored in the lane always being the first one picked from that lane. Flow rack is the best storage method to ensure a FIFO storage system. Pallet rack cannot be considered a FIFO storage system because it is hard to ensure that the first pallet stored in the rack will be the one pulled out first. Even with multiple lanes of the same product in a flow-rack system, this problem is minimal when compared to the problems of maintaining FIFO with multiple pallets in a pallet rack. Both drive-in rack and flat storage are last-in, first-out storage systems and cannot be considered where FIFO is a major storage requirement.

A second advantage of flow rack is that it is a high-density storage system. Flow rack provides good space utilization, going many loads deep and many loads high. This minimizes the amount of floor space and the number of aisles required to store the unit loads. Flow rack utilizes the overhead storage space much better than flat storage, because the problem of crushability limits the stacking heights with flat storage. A flow-rack system may also utilize overhead space better than drive-in rack. The lifting capacity of an industrial truck may limit the height of the drive-in rack, not the ceiling height. An automated storage/retrieval (AS/RS) system can be used to store and retrieve product from a flow rack system, whereas an AS/RS system cannot be used with a drive-in rack. This allows for high ceiling heights resulting in increased utilization.

The advantage of flow-rack over pallet-rack systems is the reduced number of aisles required. Pallet-rack systems generally store pallets one load deep, creating many aisles. A flow-rack system can be many loads deep, storing the same number of pallets as the pallet rack, but with fewer aisles.

The third advantage of the flow rack is that it minimizes truck travel distances. Flow rack has one load and one discharge point for each lane. With the loading point of the rack close to the palletizing or receiving area, the rack does the work of moving the pallet toward the shipping area. The deeper the lanes, the more movement done by the flow rack, and consequently, the less lift trucks have to travel. With a drive-in rack, the operator has to drive into the rack and place the load into storage, going to a different location each time a load is stored or retrieved. In a pallet-rack system, the truck operator must also go to a different location each time to store and retrieve loads. An operation that has high labor costs and many lift trucks may find it advantageous to go to a flow-rack system because of the shorter travel times required to store and remove product from storage.

The fourth advantage of flow rack is minimized honeycombing. Flow rack has less honeycombing than both drive-in and flat storage. A flow-rack section four high can have four different SKUs in that section. Once the first pallet is placed in a drive-in rack four levels high, all four levels in that section have to be dedicated to that product. The same holds true for flat storage. By altering the lane depths, it is possible to improve honeycombing with flat storage and drive-in rack. The trade-off, however, is that more aisle space is required than with flow rack, making the overall space utilization of flow rack much better than flat storage or drive-in rack.

Additional advantages of flow rack are reduced pilferage and damage. Storing the product in a rack structure in which only the first pallet in each lane is accessible reduces the pilferage rate; whereas pallet rack allows easy access to every pallet in the warehouse, thus increasing the chances of pilferage over flow rack. In a flat storage environment, loads are stacked one on top of another, causing a crushability problem. Each load in a flow-rack structure is supported by the flow rack, thus reducing potential damage.

Flow rack, on the other hand, is not the solution to all storage problems. There are several disadvantages associated with this storage technique, the biggest of which is cost. Flow rack is typically five to seven times more expensive than pallet rack, and four to six times more expensive than drive-in rack. When a decision is based solely on economic considerations, flow rack may be very hard to justify. Many of the justifications for flow rack are hard to put into monetary terms. To consider the importance of FIFO purely on economic grounds would not provide an accurate analysis of the different alternatives. Economic issues alone should not be used to make a determination on whether or not to purchase a flow rack. If none of the qualitative issues are significant, flow rack is probably not the solution to the storage problem.

A second problem with flow rack is that a higher-quality pallet is generally required for storage. Pallets that have warped or split runners or deckboards are very difficult to use in a flow rack, since they may jam within the lane. The use of higher-quality pallets will result in increased storage costs. Captive or slave pallets are required in some flow-rack systems. Captive pallets require even more additional cost than regular pallets and can require additional handling.

The third problem with flow rack is flexibility. A large shift in product lines or volumes could result in a need to reassess lane depths and the number of lanes required for maximum space utilization. It is extremely expensive to rearrange the lane depths of a flow rack. Flow rack is very inflexible when it is necessary to change the physical layout of the warehouse. If a change in the physical layout had to occur, considerable storage capacity would be lost during the transition period. Pallet rack and flat storage are flexible in comparison. The need to change or reassess lane depths is a minimal problem with flat storage and is not at all a problem with pallet rack.

The fourth problem with the flow rack is the matter of equipment failure. Flow rack, unlike other rack-storage methods, has moving parts. These moving parts are susceptible to mechanical failure. A jammed conveyor track could block a complete lane of product. Though equipment breakdown may be infrequent, it does occur. Neither pallet-rack, drive-in rack, nor flat storage has moving parts, making them more fail-safe alternatives to flow rack.

Types of Flow Racks. There are several different types of flow-rack systems available. The most popular type of flow rack is the gravity roller-conveyor flow rack. The pallet is transported through the flow rack on a gravity conveyor. Plastic wheels, metal wheels, narrow rollers, or wide rollers can be used to move the load forward. A brake wheel or retarder is used to slow the speed of the pallet as it flows to the front of the rack. These brake wheels are spaced about one pallet length apart and provide a constant braking action. Gravity roller-conveyor flow rack is good for general applications in which the load is fairly stable and between 600 and 6000 pounds. Gravity roller-conveyor flow rack is the least expensive of the different flow-rack alternatives.

A special type of gravity flow rack is one that uses rubber wheels. The difference between typical gravity roller-conveyor flow rack and rubber-wheel flow rack is that each rubber wheel contributes to the braking action instead of intermittent brake wheels. Hysteresis is used to control the speed of the pallet. Each wheel absorbs the kinetic energy of the pallet as it moves forward to keep the pallet from going too fast. The result is a fairly uniform speed throughout the flow rack.

A second type of flow rack is an air-speed–controlled flow rack. Two types of air-speed–controlled flow racks are available. Both index the pallet forward by pulses of air. The first type of air-speed–controlled flow rack uses air to lift a conveyor track up into contact with the pallet.

The pallet then moves forward on the conveyor track. When the product has moved forward the appropriate distance, the air is released and the pallet settles back down to the rails. The second type of air-controlled flow-rack system is one in which air actually moves the pallet. The air pulses lift a pallet with special runners and index the pallet forward. The movement of the pallet forward is a combination of gravity and controlled flow. Optical sensors and a controller determine pallet movements.

Air-speed–controlled flow rack moves the pallet with a steady speed and is very good when a fragile product or products of varying weight are to be moved down the flow-rack lane. This controlled flow ensures uniform movement through the flow rack.

A car-in-lane flow rack uses a shuttle car rather than a conveyor to transfer the load forward. The shuttle car is dedicated to the lane and is computer controlled to determine how far the car should move for each load. The load movement forward is at a constant speed, and the loads do not descend down a decline. Since all of the loads do not move forward when the front load is removed or when a new load is stored, the car must constantly index loads in the lane whenever a load is removed. The computer maintains a constant spacing between loads, making car-in-lane storage good for loads that are fragile or that vary in size or weight.

Rack Selection

There are more than 40 rack manufacturers in the United States, and each manufacturer has its own design and engineering standards for production of its equipment. The Rack Manufacturers Institute, Inc. (RMI) has developed a manual called "Design, Testing and Utilization of Industrial Steel Storage Racks." This manual has been developed after many years of research and testing and is considered to be the "bible" for the rack industry. The RMI continues to update this engineering manual to better ensure safety and economy for its customers. A current issue should definitely be part of a warehouse manager's library. (See the reference at the end of this chapter.)

Bottom-line economy always plays an important part in rack selection. However, consideration should be given to the rack structures required to fulfill each particular storage requirement. As an example, upright frames can be purchased to support the rack capacity when completely loaded, but may not withstand lift-truck abuse in a fast-moving warehouse storage operation. The less expensive storage racks may prove to be the most expensive after a few years' use. The best guidelines for acquiring state-of-the-art equipment is to request that pallet racks you purchase be manufactured to conform to the current RMI design specifications. To safeguard your rack purchase, have the rack manufacturer confirm this in writing.

The RMI design specifications apply to standard pallet racks and accessories as well as stacker racks used in AS/RS systems. Specifications for stacking frames have also been adopted. The RMI is currently doing research to develop standard specifications for the design of drive-in/drive-thru racks and cantilever racks.

There are areas in the United States that follow the Uniform Building Code jurisdiction for pallet storage racks. This is particularly true in certain seismic or earthquake zones. Racks should be investigated prior to purchase to make sure the equipment conforms to local or state regulations.

Suggested Bibliography

RMI Rack Manufacturer's Institute, Inc., 1326 Freeport Road, Pittsburgh, PA 15238. (Request material from the Library.) "Design, Testing and Utilization of Industrial Steel Storage Racks." Request current publication.

RMI "Industrial Steel Storage Racks," 1980 ed. Describes and illustrates racks for storage of pallets and unconventional products.

RMI "Portable Rack Specification."

NFPA National Fire Protection Association, Inc., Battery March Park, Quincy, MA 02269. Request current literature. "Rack Storage of Materials," ANSI/NFPA, *Bulletin No. 231-C.*

UBC Uniform Building Code Standards, International Conference of Building Officials, 5360 South Workman Mill Road, Whittier, CA 90601. Request manual, 1982 edition (Reference: Standard No. 27-11, Steel Storage Racks).

13
Small-Parts Storage Systems

Donald J. Weiss

President, White Storage and Retrieval Systems, Inc., Kenilworth, New Jersey

Michael A. Cramer

Senior Engineer, Tompkins Associates, Inc., Raleigh, North Carolina

Small-parts storage systems can be generally classified into two categories: static and dynamic. The distinction between the two is a function of how the stored materials are accessed. With a static small-parts storage system, the warehouse personnel access the storage system by traveling to a stationary storage location. Primary examples of static small-parts storage systems are shelving and modular drawer cabinets. With a dynamic small-parts storage system, the storage system generally moves the material to a fixed personnel location where picking and stocking occur. Primary examples of dynamic small-parts storage systems are carousels and mini load automated storage/retrieval (AS/RS), systems. Static and dynamic small-parts storage systems are discussed in more detail in the following sections.

Static Small-Parts Storage

Static small-parts storage is the safekeeping of goods within a device that is standing or fixed in one place and does not force the movement or flow of the goods within the device. Static small-parts storage systems tend to be fairly simple devices and are, thus, relatively inexpensive compared to other storage methods. Despite the relative lack of automation or sophistication, these systems are often operationally and economically the best storage methods for the application. They are particularly effective where conditions of low to moderate throughput and storage volumes are combined with a wide range of types of products to be stored.

Alternative Static Small-Parts Storage Methods

As previously mentioned, two primary methods that fall within the classification of static small-parts storage are shelving and modular drawer storage.

Shelving. Shelving (Figure 13.1) represents one of the earliest forms of product storage and has changed very little over the years. In its sim-

Figure 13.1. Typical shelving units. (*Republic Steel Co.*)

plest form, shelving consists of four vertical posts that support one or more horizontal shelves. Shelving is generally constructed of light-gauge cold rolled steel, in which a number of different post forms exist, such as: single-angle, double-angle, beaded T, and heavy-duty, each of which is designed to support a wide range of load weights.

Shelving exists in a wide range of standard sizes. Standard shelf widths are generally 36, 42 and 48 inches. Shelf depths vary from 9 to 36 inches, with 3-inch increments. Post heights generally are up to 84 inches, with greater heights available for high-rise shelving. Individual shelf heights are typically adjustable on 1.5-inch centers.

Shelving is a very basic storage method that affords the user significant flexibility in the type and quantity of goods that can be stored, and at a relatively low capital investment. Consequently, shelving is by far the most popular small-parts storage technique in use in warehouses. Most of these applications are well justified. The warehouse planner must not, however, approach the specification of a shelving system with any less care than one would an automated storage/retrieval system. An examination of the shortcomings of typical shelving installations reveals why.

Shelving is not an inherently space-efficient storage technique. Cubic space utilization within a typical shelving installation is often less than 50 percent. Two primary reasons exist for this poor space utilization. First, shelving installations often make poor use of the vertical space available in the warehouse. Installations of 84-inch-high shelving in warehouses with 20 feet of clear stacking height available are all too common. The result is significant wasted overhead space.

The second space utilization problem inherent in shelving is the potential for poor utilization of space in a given shelf opening. It is not unusual to see a typical shelf opening that is 36 inches wide, 18 inches deep, and 12 inches high being occupied by a 6-inch-cubed box. Many shelves are occupied more by air than by product. A portion of this air space is required to allow "reach-in" accessibility to the items stored on the shelf. Another portion of the air space is the result of improperly specifying the shelving for the product to be stored.

These space utilization problems directly result in increased warehouse costs related to the amount of shelving required and the amount of warehouse space required to house the shelving. Additionally, they indirectly lead to employee productivity losses in that warehouse personnel must travel greater distances within the shelving system to access shelf locations. The point of this discussion is that proper shelving specification can minimize such problems. Shelving is a simple storage system, but the warehouse planner must not be simple-minded in its application.

To properly specify shelving, the warehouse planner must evaluate the type of shelving and layout configurations that should be used.

Shelving Configuration. This is the physical structure of the shelving unit. A wide range of shelving configurations can be created, ranging from simple, open shelving to complex combinations of shelf-accessories, such as shelf dividers, inserts, boxes, bins, and so on (Figure 13.2). The addition of shelf accessories to the basic open shelving configuration is accomplished with the objectives of improved space utilization and product accessibility. The shelving accessories effectively compartmentalize the shelf to match the size of the space to the size of the item to be stored. The warehouse planner must carefully evaluate the sizes of the products to be stored and determine the proper shelving accessories required to efficiently utilize the space on the shelf.

Layout Configuration. This is the physical arrangement of the shelving units. Three basic layout configurations exist, each providing a different level of vertical space utilization. These configurations include low-level shelving, mezzanine shelving, and high-rise shelving.

Low-level shelving is simply a single elevation of shelving units resting on the floor. These shelving units are typically no more than 84 inches in height to allow warehouse personnel on the floor level access to the top-most shelf. In some cases, a ladder is used to improve accessibility. Low-level shelving is best applied in areas with low ceiling height. If installed in high-ceilinged areas, consideration should be given to specifying shelving capable of being converted to a mezzanine or high-rise shelving system at a later date, if utilization of the available vertical space proves necessary.

Mezzanine shelving (Figure 13.3) typically consists of two elevations of shelving units bolted together vertically, with a mezzanine walkway in the aisle of the upper elevation. Personnel walk on the aisle mezzanine for access to the upper elevation. The aisle mezzanine is typically located approximately 84 inches above the floor. Stairways are provided to allow access to the mezzanine level. Mezzanine shelving increases vertical space utilization in high-ceilinged areas. Mezzanine shelving is generally found in configurations of two or three levels; however, they are not structurally restricted to three levels. Freestanding mezzanines are occasionally used to provide multilevel shelving systems. The freestanding mezzanine is an unbroken floor grating that relies on a series of columns for support. This variety offers the advantage of utilizing a portion of the elevated space for purposes other than shelving storage.

High-rise shelving consists of extended height uprights that support shelves to heights typically in the 14- to 21-foot range. Unlike mezzanine shelving, the aisles are clear of mezzanines, and the upper elevations of the shelving system are accessed by use of a machine that ele-

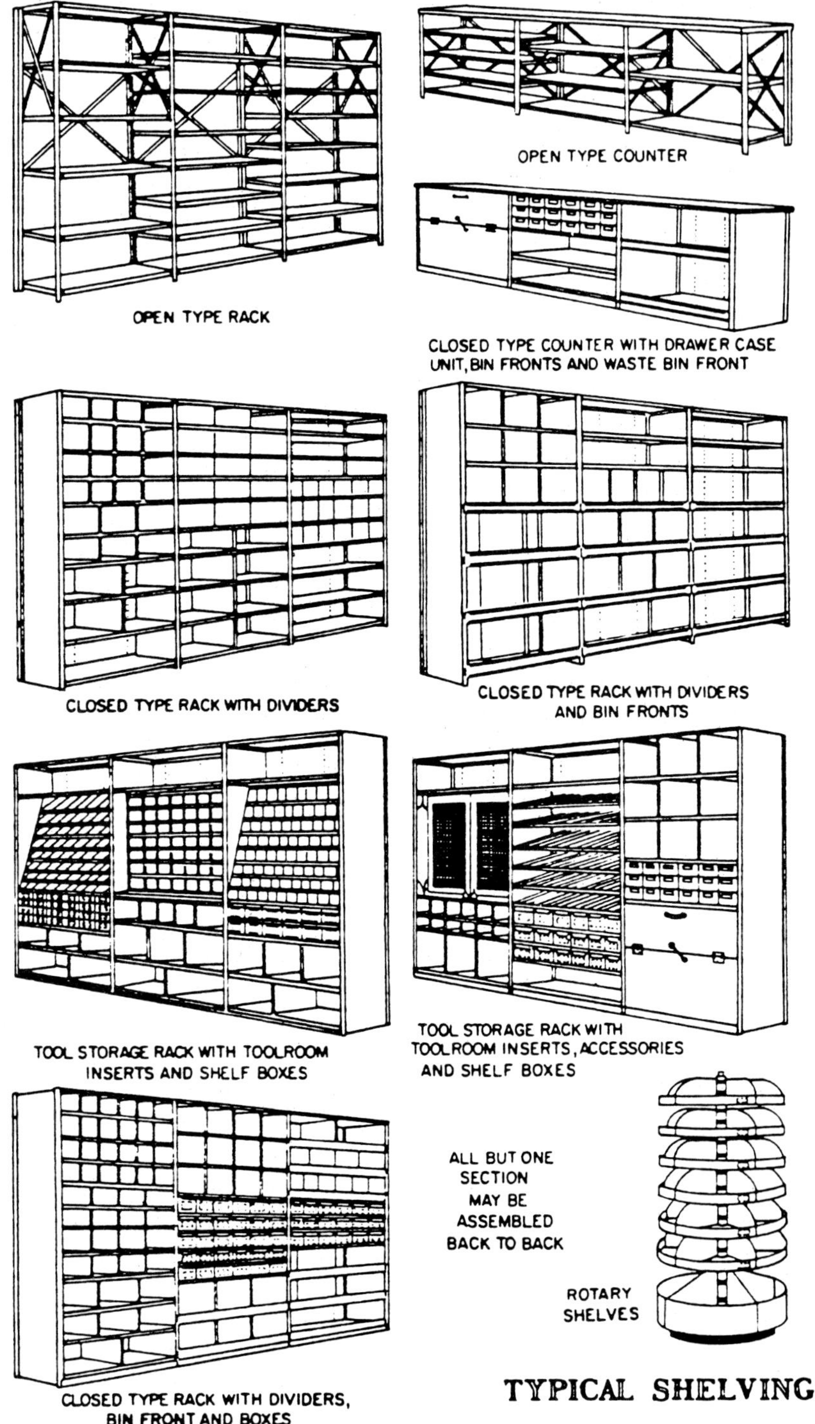

Figure 13.2. Typical shelving configurations. (*Adapted from* Warehouse Modernization and Layout Planning Guide, *Department of the Navy, NAVSUP Publication 529, 1978.*)

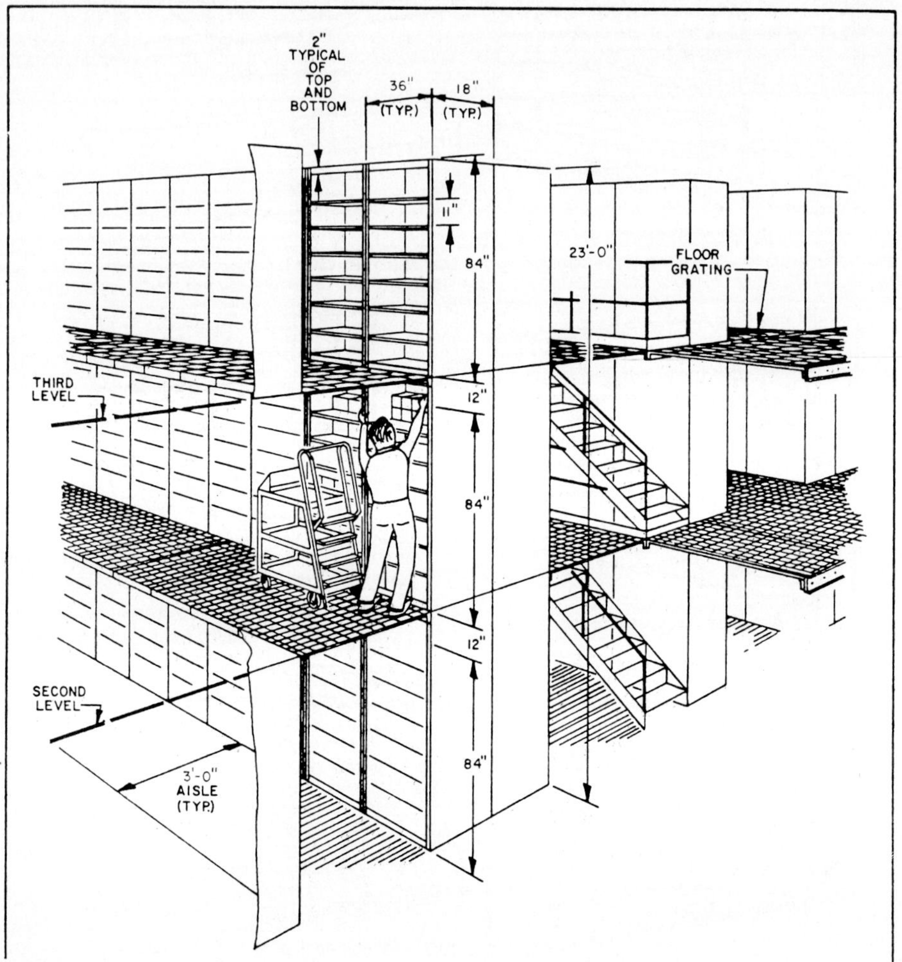

Figure 13.3. Typical mezzanine shelving system. (*Adapted from* **Warehouse Modernization and Layout Planning Guide,** *Department of the Navy, NAVSUP Publication 529, 1978.*)

vates the warehouse personnel to the appropriate level. Two common machines are used to transport personnel through the system: order-picking lift trucks and storage/retrieval (S/R) machines. Order-picking lift trucks are free-path lift trucks with an operator's cab located on the front of the telescoping mast of the truck. As the forks of the truck are raised, the operator's cab raises in kind. The lift-truck operator is thus raised to the elevation required in the shelving to accomplish the storage and retrieval. A storage/retrieval machine (Figure 13.4) is a device that rides on a rail at floor level and a rail above the top elevation of the rack. An operator's cab raises and lowers on a vertical mast attached at either end to the rails.

High-rise shelving provides efficient vertical space utilization and increases labor productivity by increasing the speed with which warehouse personnel move within the system. Walking is replaced by riding. Additionally, the order-picking lift trucks and S/R machines can be equipped with computer terminals to automatically transmit instructions to the operator.

Modular Drawer Storage. As discussed in the previous section, an inherent disadvantage of shelving storage for small parts is the inefficient use of space within a given shelf opening. To improve this space utilization, shelving accessories are added to the basic shelving configuration to compartmentalize the shelf opening. A consequence of this compartmentalization process is a significant increase in the investment cost of the shelving.

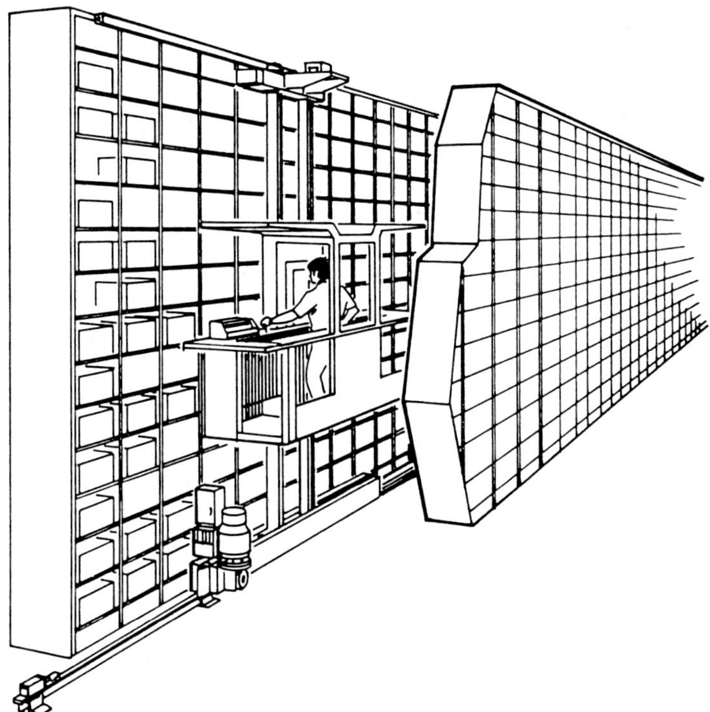

Figure 13.4. High-rise shelving with S/R machine. (*Adapted from* **Warehouse Modernization and Layout Planning Guide,** *Department of the Navy, NAVSUP Publication 529, 1978.*)

The objective of compartmentalization is to fit the size of the space to the size of the items to be stored. The smaller the items, the more difficult and expensive this becomes to accomplish with shelving. Shelving is relatively space efficient and inexpensive for relatively "large" small parts. Conversely, shelving is relatively space inefficient and expensive for relatively "small" small parts. Consequently, where the volume of relatively "small" small parts is high, other storage alternatives may prove to be more efficient and economical than shelving. It is this scenario in which modular drawer storage is best applied.

Modular drawer storage consists of metal cabinets into which metal drawers are placed. A modular drawer cabinet is, in effect, a "chest of

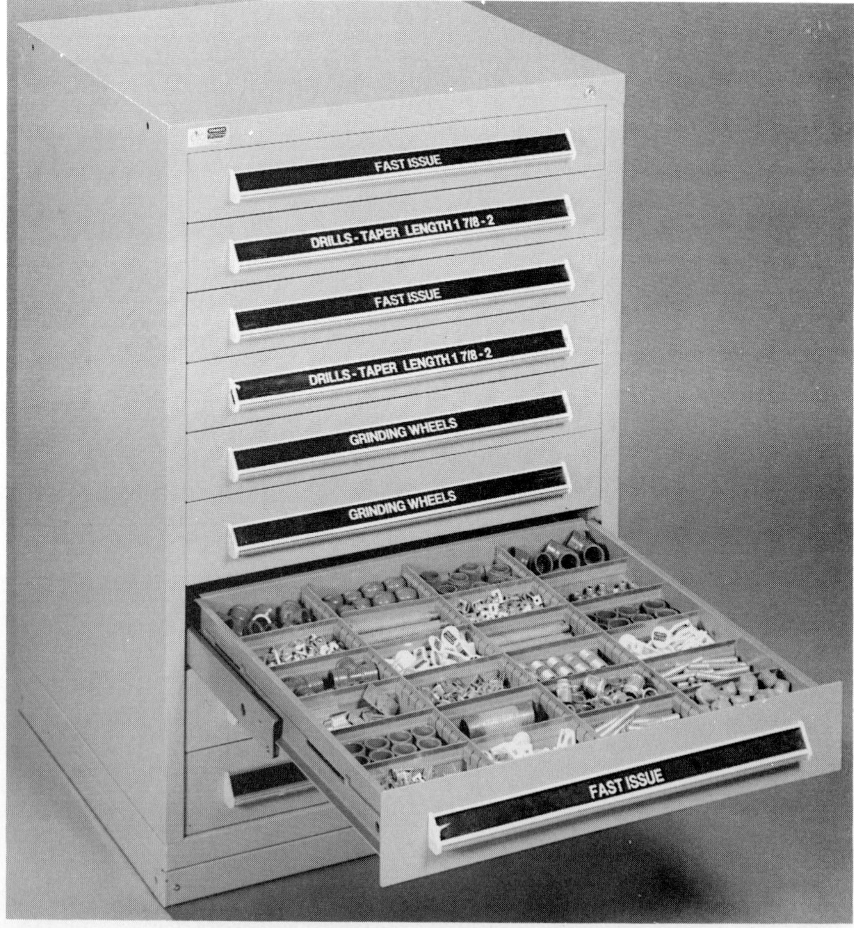

Figure 13.5. Typical modular drawer storage cabinet. (*Stanley-Vidmar.*)

drawers" (Figure 13.5). Modular drawer cabinets typically stand 42 or 60 inches high and contain drawers, the width and depth of which range from 24 to 36 inches. Drawer heights range from 2 to 12 inches. Weight capacity per drawer is approximately 450 pounds. Cabinets can be stacked one on top of another for good vertical space utilization; ladder, order-picking lift trucks, or S/R machines are utilized to access the upper drawer cabinets (Figure 13.6).

Modular drawer storage offers the following significant advantages over shelving:

1. Each drawer can be easily compartmentalized to maximize space utilization within the drawer (Figure 13.7).
2. Reach-in space is eliminated, since the contents of a drawer are accessed by pulling the drawer out into the aisle, instead of reaching into the cabinet.
3. Drawer storage typically results in a reduction of up to 50 percent of the space required for the same inventory in a shelving system.
4. Since total floor space required is less, travel distances are reduced between storage locations and labor productivity is increased.
5. Part cleanliness is improved, since the parts are contained within a closed cabinet.

Figure 13.6. Modular drawer storage system. (*Stanley-Vidmar.*)

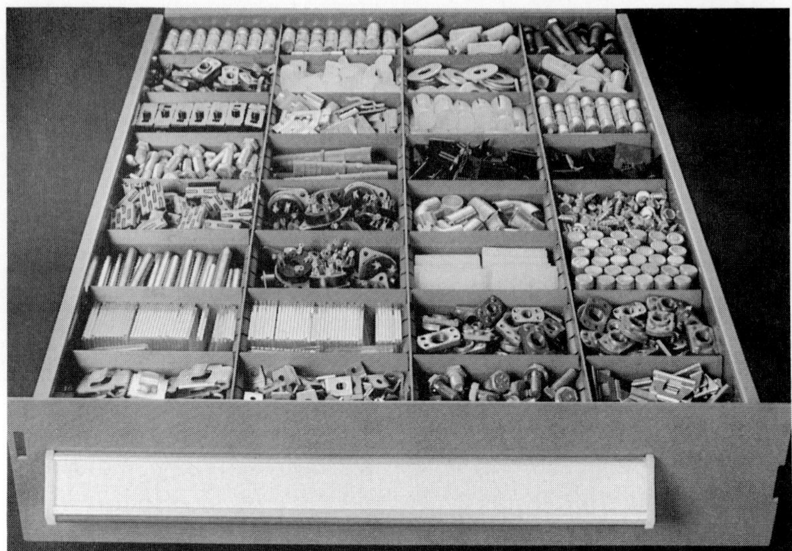

Figure 13.7. Typical modular storage drawer showing compartmentalization. (*Stanley-Vidmar.*)

6. Cabinets can be locked to limit access, thus improving inventory security.

The major disadvantage of modular drawer storage is its relatively high investment cost. The smaller the object to be stored, the more economical modular drawer storage becomes. The larger the object to be stored, the more economical shelving storage becomes. In most applications, the optimum small-parts storage system consists of a mixture of shelving, modular drawer storage, and, perhaps, one or more of the dynamic small-parts storage methods discussed in the following sections of this chapter.

Dynamic Small-Parts Storage

In today's warehouse, there is no activity that is as dynamic as the handling of small parts. The retrieval and storage of small parts, or "broken lot picking," as it is sometimes referred to, has long taken a back seat to unit load or pallet-handling systems for the warehouse. Just a few years ago, in most warehouse applications, one was overwhelmed by the small area and minimal attention that was given to the handling of small parts. However, when one closely examines today's warehouse, it becomes apparent that the amount of labor expended in the small-parts area is inordinate when compared with the dollar value of inventory processed. Today, more and more of management's attention and capital expenditures are being concentrated in the area of small parts because of the tremendous potential savings in labor and reductions of inventory levels.

The arrival of the computer on the warehouse and factory floor has enabled automated storage/retrieval systems to offer benefits many times more significant than realized from stand-alone hardware in the past. The AS/RS system hardware for small parts, which consists primarily of carousels, miniloads, and movable-aisle systems, has not changed drastically in recent years, but the systems used to control them have. The net result has been a tremendous upsurge in the implementation of systems to store and retrieve small parts, making this the hottest segment of AS/RS system business today.

In the pages that follow, carousels, miniloads, and movable-aisle systems, the basic dynamic systems for small parts, are explained, along with their salient applications and benefits.

Carousels

A carousel can be described as a series of bins that are linked together in a continuous chain and mounted on an elongated oval track. The track is generally horizontal, and a drive unit that powers the bins around the track is located in the center of the track. When activated, the entire carousel revolves, bringing the desired bin to the operator (Figure 13.8). The basic theory is that the carousel delivers the bin to the person, instead of the person going to the bin. Carousels are modular in design. By connecting standard drive, idler, and intermediate sections, a final configuration is generated, much in the same way the track sections are put together to make a model train layout. This modular concept enables short lead times, quick installation, and ease of extension or movement.

Carousels are available in an almost unlimited variety of heights, lengths, widths, bin designs, and capacities. This wide range of design configurations has resulted in carousels being used in many different applications in the warehouse and factory. The products stored on carousels can range from tools, hardware, and appliances to drugs, computer parts, and softgoods. The versatility of carousels results in appli cations in a space as small as 5 by 15 feet or as large as the largest miniload AS/RS systems installations. They are found in corporate environments that include shipping, manufacturing, stockrooms, tool cribs, clean rooms, test chambers, warehouses, and even the office and retail stores.

Figure 13.8. Typical horizontal carousels. (*White Storage & Retrieval Systems, Inc.*)

Industrial carousel systems evolved from light-duty, overhead conveyor systems for storing garments or hangers. The first industrial carousels, made in the 1960s, were overhead garment conveyors with suspended wire baskets and shelves mounted on the overhead chain in place of suspended garments. In the 1970s, heavier-duty, bottom-driven versions were introduced that were capable of carrying weights in excess of 1000 pounds per bin. The original versions had simple hand or foot controls that could revolve the unit either left or right. Soon afterward, simple analog controls were added that provide a short-route capability. The operator simply had to press a button for the desired bin, and that bin revolved to the front by the shortest route.

In the 1980s, sophisticated computer and microprocessor controls for carousels were developed, and this enabled carousels to become viable automated storage devices. Robotic load and unload devices have been developed to interface with carousels and eliminate the person-machine interface that had been required until recently. With sophisticated controls and robotic interface, carousels have been integrated into the automated factory.

Types of Carousels Two major types of carousels exist: horizontal and vertical. Horizontal carousels are generally either top-driven or bottom-driven, and may be designed for either intermittent or continuous-run operations. While some multilevel drive carousels are used, they are rather special in nature and limited in field usage.

Top-drive units consist of a tubular track supported by poles or stanchions every few feet on which the conveyor chain is mounted. Wire bins are hung from the chain and loosely guided below on a lower track. Wheels are generally lifetime sealed bearings mounted at a 45-degree angle that support a hinge pin and connecting chain links. The loads to be carried determine the quantity and size of the wheels used. While larger-diameter tracks, wheels, yokes, and hinge pins may be used to carry heavier loads, top-driven units are generally used for lighter loads or continuous-run, slower-speed applications. Drives on top-driven units may be mounted above the track or below and recessed.

Bottom-drive units use the same tubular track but use a larger-diameter concave steel wheel with axial rollers mounted under a steel-bottom plate. The upper guide track is mounted on stanchions and traps the upper guide wheels. Drives are floor-mounted and accessible by removable bin backs. Bottom-drive units are more popular because of their ability to carry heavier weights more dependably. They also eliminate the potential of product contamination from wheel/track wear, require less overall height, are more adaptable to double tiering, and distribute floor load more evenly.

Most carousels are used to store and retrieve items and are activated by manual control, microprocessor, or computer when an item is to be loaded or unloaded. When activated, the carousel revolves and the desired bin is delivered to the operator control point by the shortest route. Manual hand or foot controls may be used to operate the unit in a continuous mode for short periods.

Continuous-run carousels are generally unidirectional and often have manually or electrically variable speed drives. They are generally used in assembly operations where work is stored and transported on the carousel while operators are stationed on one or both sides of the unit. Inventory is removed from the moving carousel by any operator and placed back into the carousel also while moving, generally at slow speeds. Continuous-run units are also used for high-volume sorting or timed-cycle, burn-in applications.

The concept of vertical carousels (Figure 13.9) is the same as that of horizontal carousels previously discussed; however, the units revolve on an elongated oval track in a vertical plane. The short-route control features are nearly identical. Vertical carousels come in heights up to 20 feet but are very limited in the choice of widths, depths, and chain pitches. Attention must be paid to severe unbalanced load conditions, because movement of the carousel requires that the loads be lifted. Some of the features of these units include furniture-finish exterior panels, adjustable movable-height counters, and the ability to lock the entire contents of the unit.

Figure 13.9. Vertical carousel. (*White Storage & Retrieval Systems, Inc.*)

Vertical units are more expensive than horizontal carousels and can generally be justified only in applications in which one operator operates only one unit with high activity, or floor space is of the utmost concern, or security is an overriding consideration. On occasion, vertical units can perform as a vertical lift or dumbwaiter device.

Major Features and Options of Standard Carousels. Carousel drives are typically located at either or both ends of the unit. Most drives consist of an individual motor, speed reducer, roller chain, pulleys, and sprockets. Dual drives are required for heavier loads and longer units.

The supporting structure of top- and bottom-driven carousels consists largely of welded-angle iron and channel iron. The basic concept is that standard drive and idler end sections and standard center sections of different lengths fit together to form a unit of any length. Expansion of the unit is possible at any of the splice joints.

Standard bins and shelves are generally fabricated of wire. Wire is less expensive than sheet metal, lighter in weight, and dust-free. Where heavier weights are involved, standard wire bins must be strengthened by using solid sheet-metal supporting bin backs. The solid backs give the bin rigidity, prevent small items from falling through, and reduce vertigo effect, but most importantly, support the major portion of the weight of each individual shelf. Shelf load is, therefore, distributed down through the solid back and both wire sides.

Shelves are adjustable without the use of hardware, and each shelf forms a rigid box structure by joining the two sides and back of the bin. Where loads in excess of 100 pounds per shelf are required, reinforced shelves should be used. Shelves are generally pitched 5 to 10 degrees toward the rear.

The most standard bin widths are 21, 24, and 30 inches. Other widths can be made, but can be expensive because they generally require a different chain pitch. Bin heights may be anywhere from 2 to 10 feet, but are generally 6, 7, or 8 feet. Standard shelf depths are 14, 18, and 22 inches, but other depths are available. Standard bins offer vertical shelf adjustability on 3-inch or 6-inch centers, but other centers are also offered. Special sheet-metal or angle-iron cantilevered bin designs are quite common.

The major space-saving benefit of carousels occurs when they are placed side by side or multitiered. Units can be placed only a few inches apart if no access is desired along the sides and if the items to be stored are not likely to protrude. In many installations, an emergency service aisle is placed between carousels. For this very limited purpose, a maximum of 18 inches is usually sufficient. On the other hand, if a working service aisle is desired, 2 feet or more may be left between units.

When multitiered units are used to take advantage of available ceiling height, mezzanine design becomes an important consideration. Mezzanines may cover the entire area or may be used in the actual picking area, and not between levels of carousels. When no mezzanine is used between carousel levels, there is generally a savings in lighting and sprinkling costs, but a loss of accessibility.

Carousel Controls. Carousels can be effectively controlled by anything from a simple foot switch to a powerful mainframe computer. While most carousels are controlled by microprocessors of various types, selection of the appropriate control should always take into account both present and future needs. All controls should be plug-compatible for interchangeability and future upgrading. The present range of controls include:

1. Manual Controls:
   - *a. Foot control.* A momentary-contact, bidirectional-type switch usually with OSHA guard.
   - *b. Hand control.* A maintained-type switch that generally mounts on an arm extending from the carousel.
   - *c. Keyboard control.* A digital selector that delivers the desired bin via the shortest route and contains bidirectional jogging capability, lighted display, and emergency stop.
   - *d. Floor mats.* Various-size electrified mats that activate or deactivate carousels at multiple locations.
   - *e. Safety lockouts.* For systems with multiple control points, one operator is able to retain control while locking out others.

2. Microprocessor controls:
   a. *Carousel interface box.* The basic building block for any computer-controlled system. This is an intelligent microprocessor that communicates through a single network cable to other carousels, terminals, and computers. The interface box includes logic to stop the unit accurately, report its status, and take instructions from other devices, plus self-diagnostics.
   b. *Microprocessor with memory.* This type of control can usually monitor from one to six carousels and has the ability to queue and sort several hundred requests. Bin location data is stored in its memory, and a bank of carousels can be activated intelligently. It is ideal for users who are not ready for full computer control, but want to be able to upgrade by simply unplugging a microprocessor and plugging in a computer at a later date.

3. Computer control. Carousels can be controlled by almost any kind of computer, ranging from small personal or home computers to large mainframes. It is generally recommended that a dedicated host (usually a mini) control the carousels because of real-time constraints. Any computer will communicate with the basic carousel interface box described above.

Major Benefits of Carousels. Carousel users have been able to justify the purchase and use of carousels for a very wide range of reasons. What may be important to one user may not even be pertinent or of interest to another. It is always hard to attempt to generalize the major benefits of any product, but certain savings and improvements are more prevalent than others. Not all carousels are computer controlled, and it would therefore be helpful to separately delineate the major benefits of stand-alone carousels and those that are computer-controlled. This separation should also help to emphasize the synergistic benefits of carousels and computers when used together in an integrated system.

The major benefits of stand-alone carousels include the following:

1. *Save labor.* Because the picker never moves, no time is wasted in walking or searching for parts. The operator may be processing paperwork , or weighing or counting parts while the carousel is doing the walking.
2. *Increase throughput.* One person can generally operate two to four carousels with very high efficiency. This means that several parts may be coming to one operator simultaneously, resulting in increased throughput and decreased retrieval time.
3. *Improve control.* Supervision and training of personnel is simplified because the orderliness of carousels reduces the dependency on

memorization and specialized knowledge. Carousel systems permit employees to remain in full view of area supervisors, eliminating wandering employees. Pilferage will drop dramatically in those installations in which it presents a problem, because employees are observable at all times.

4. *Save space.* By placing carousels adjacent to each other, wasted aisle space is virtually eliminated. Typical order-picking applications can result in as much as a 30 to 40 percent space savings over conventional shelving.
5. *Reduce fatigue.* By eliminating the need for operators to walk up and down aisles, employee fatigue is reduced. By placing the most active items on the middle levels of the carousel, it is not really necessary for operators to reach beyond their normal picking range. The presence of automated equipment can be a source of pride and motivation to employees who work with the equipment.
6. *Increase cube utilization.* A fixed ladder or platform, used at either end of a carousel, can result in effective use of single-tier shelving up to 10 feet in height. Even greater gains in space utilization can result from the adjustable nature of carousel shelves and the specially designed parts containers that are available for them. Double- and triple-tiered systems can be used where ceiling height will permit one to take even greater advantage of cube utilization.

The major benefits of computer-controlled carousels include:

1. *Random storage.* With computer-controlled part locations, random storage of parts can be extremely effective. The computer assigns locations and backup locations randomly, and when this is combined with the carousel's ability to easily adjust storage compartments, the assignment of locations based upon product size and quantity will result in further dramatic increases in storage density.
2. *Sequenced picking.* When the computer indexes the carousel by bin location, virtually all waiting time is eliminated. Instead of randomly moving the carousel from left to right to deliver the desired bin, the requests are first sorted by computer, and the carousel is incremented only a very short distance at each new pick. As each part is picked, the computer rotates the carousel to the next appropriate bin while the operator is simultaneously picking parts from other carousels which have already delivered the appropriate bin.
3. *Multiple picks.* When large orders or batch orders are picked, it is possible to get several picks from one carousel bin. A typical carousel bin has 25 cubic feet of storage capacity and, by delivering such

a large amount of inventory to an operator, the chance for multiple picks is increased.

4. *Faster replenishment.* The ability to randomly restock materials results in a significant time savings in the replenishment function, because it is not necessary to search for an available space.
5. *Simplified inventory.* With an on-line perpetual inventory that is truly visible, the task of taking a physical inventory can be reduced to a routine inspection. In fact, with a laser scanner and bar-coded labels, inventory can be taken after working hours without any people required to perform the task.
6. *Lower inventory levels.* By providing accurate and timely inventory data, and with improved visibility, supervision, and increased throughput, both inventory levels and shortages can be reduced dramatically.
7. *Integration.* Only with the use of computers can carousels be integrated into factory systems. Integration can consist of simple downloading of work from a host computer or range all the way to the control of robot picking and loading devices. Integrated systems result in improved accuracy and major labor savings.

Movable-Aisle Systems

In the past few years, movable-aisle systems have found their way from offices to the warehouses and factories of America. Their chief benefit is that they provide more space by simply placing existing racking or shelving on a mobile "carriage" which glides along tracks, thereby eliminating unnecessary and wasted aisle space. Since aisles can typically require greater space than that actually used for storage, the benefits are obviously significant. Claims of doubling storage capacity or, alternatively, decreasing current storage requirements into half the present area can, in fact, be achieved by utilizing movable-aisle systems.

Movable-aisle systems are excellent in areas in which each group of movable carriages are served by a limited number of lift trucks or people, or the activity rates are moderate to low. The aisle-saving principles work well in small-parts storage areas or in massive pallet-racking environments where carriages can be hundreds of feet in length and loads can be in excess of 1,000,000 pounds per carriage.

A movable-aisle system can be described as a group of platforms on which shelving, racking, cabinets, and so on are placed. These platforms consist of a frame made up of side channels stabilized by cross members, or "saddles." Once wheels are placed into these saddles, the platform becomes a carriage that can glide along a number of leveled and

Figure 13.10. Movable-aisle storage system. (*White Storage & Retrieval Systems, Inc.*)

parallel tracks (Figure 13.10). The tracks are installed in such a way as to provide a flush and level floor so that operators or trucks can move in and out of areas without consequence or danger. Usually, a single changeable aisle is provided in a "bay" of such carriages. The single aisle can be created wherever and whenever necessary, so that picking can be accomplished. In conventional storage, an aisle must be provided on all active sides of shelving or racking. As can be seen in Figure 13.11, the before and after benefits of aisle saving is significant, since all the unnecessary aisle space is removed.

In Figure 13.12, the "before" depicts a conventional storage area which is capacity-limited. That is, it is limited if an aisle-saving approach is not utilized. When the existing storage is placed on carriages, a doubling or tripling of capacity generally results.

Types of Movable-Aisle Systems. There are basically four types of movable-aisle systems. Designs are determined by the type of application the system must serve. Lighter-weight systems are usually found in small areas where loading is not a key factor and systems are manually moved. The heaviest-duty systems can be found in warehouses carrying pallet loads; carriages are rarely moved manually but are generally moved by motors. The basic system types include:

1. *Lighter-weight.* These systems carry the lightest loads. Typically, the 3-foot carriage can support 2100 pounds. A bay of these carriages

might only consist of three or four carriages and an aisle. The carriages could have either a manual "pull" handle or a mechanically assisted (gear-reduced) crank to glide the carriage along the tracks. Systems like these rarely exceed 9 to 15 feet in length.

2. *Manual.* For applications requiring heavier loading (i.e., exceeding 700 pounds per linear foot of carriage length, but not much over 1000 pounds) and in which carriage widths grow to 48 inches and lengths near 15 feet, the heavier-duty manual system has been developed.
3. *Mechanical-assist.* Rated for the same loading capacities as the manual version above, the mechanically assisted carriages can approach 30 feet in length (30,000-pound capacity) due to the presence of gear reduction capabilities. With only one pound of force, 6000 to 9000 pounds are easily moved.
4. *Electric.* These systems typically can carry loads of up to 2000 pounds per linear foot of carriage length. Carriage lengths themselves grow to 75 feet. Major person-machine safety features are prerequisites in the installed system.

Equipment Descriptions. High-density movable-aisle systems consist of a carriage with wheels that roll on leveled and parallel track. Aside from the safety features discussed in the next section, the key ingredients in determining which system meets your load, height, width, and length requirements are: carriage structure, track assemblies, and wheel specifications. As a rule of thumb, you can say that the lighter the load, the less substantial these three ingredients have to be. Conversely, as loads

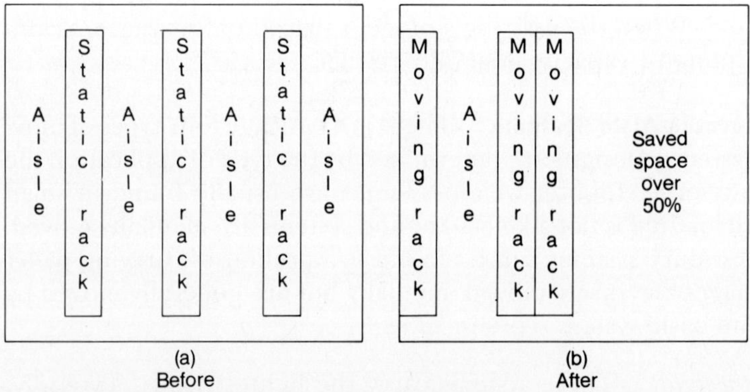

Figure 13.11. Consolidation storage in half the space.

increase, the thickness or gauge of the carriage, the diameter and hardness of the wheels, and the hardness, size, and distributive properties of the track assembly all must increase.

Track assemblies should consist of more than just a rail or bar. They must include an integral base plate that will distribute the load transmitted from the wheels across an area of floor. As loads increase, the importance of comparably hard wheel and track assemblies to prevent wear is essential.

It is important that there are excellent guidance principles used in the design of the system, as well as provisions for a barrier-free, flush floor. Systems that require wide channels, gaps alongside the track, or holes in the floor for carriage guidance actually create potential dangers. Carriages should almost glide on the track. Torquing, twisting, or wrenching of the carriages during movement are serious problems that have been overcome in reputable movable-aisle system designs; all wheels should "bite" at the same time. Carriage movement should be provided at the half-way point of the carriage, and not just at the front wheel.

Units fabricated of metal will last longer than those made of wood. Systems that can be modified after installation (e.g., moving an installation, or making the carriage shorter or longer) provide flexibility and do not become obsolete. Bolt-together carriages are installed with splice plates. Carriages greater than 9 feet in length should be of bolt-together design to facilitate installation.

Equipment Features and Safeties. On the lighter-weight manual and mechanically assisted systems, one should look for slightly inclined walk-up ramps, possible use of security keylocks, barrier-free flush floor de-

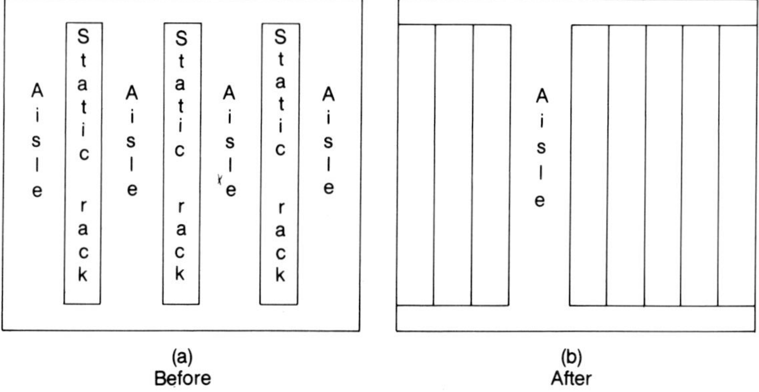

Figure 13.12. Increasing storage capacity in the same space.

signs, and carriage locking capabilities. Better systems include a center drive mechanism that prevents torquing of the carriage and a good safety-latch mechanism to immobilize the carriage while someone is in an aisle.

In electrified systems, the following equipment safety features should be considered:

1. Microprocessor diagnostics on start-up
2. One-button aisle opening
3. Lighted override and reset switch
4. Electrical overload sensor
5. Motor shut-off timers
6. Safety indicator lights
7. Limit to system coast on any safety deactivation of 1½ inches
8. Emergency stop button of each carriage
9. Flanged safety wheels

In the heavier, pallet-carrying electric systems, all of the above should be included, *plus:*

1. Safety-sweep kick plate along both sides of the carriage to deactivate carriage movement on contact
2. Corner reinforcement against lift truck
3. Advanced-alert warning horn to preview carriage movement
4. Rotating beacons to light *before* and *when* carriage moves, to visually highlight carriage movement
5. Antitip devices
6. Two-speed motor slow-down for smooth acceleration and deceleration
7. Truck scrapers
8. Underwriters Laboratories–approved DC drives
9. Double-flanged safety wheels

All of the above features should be standard in movable-aisle systems. Additional and/or more exotic features can be added as options. These include:

1. Passive electric safety floors (in non-lift-truck applications)
2. Electric security locks

3. Steel side panels, which provide a secure cube when carriages are rolled together
4. In-rack sprinkler systems
5. Radio frequency–controlled aisle opening
6. Pressure-sensitive emergency tapes and panic buttons for emergency stops
7. Key-operated override switches
8. Overhead power distribution
9. Automatic aisle lighting
10. Interfaces to building security/cameras
11. Magnetic proximity devices
12. Computer controls
13. Photoelectric scanning devices
14. Emergency operation

Applications of Movable-Aisle Systems. The following applications represent the wide range of uses for movable-aisle systems:

1. *As a storage unit for documents.* While all applications of movable-aisle systems involve storage, by far the greatest acceptance of these systems is wherever "paper" is used. Most applications for documents and other media are found in high-rent space, and often auxiliary warehouse space is used for less active hardcopy, microfilm, and so on.
2. *As a storage unit for data processing tapes and supplies.* Along with the advent of automated offices and factories has come the computer. The paperless society is not upon us yet, but usage of computer tapes, supplies, forms, and printouts has increased significantly. These must be stored, and movable-aisle systems have found their niche.
3. *As a storage unit for spare parts.* Repair facilities stocking replacement spare parts have become more decentralized. Again, they tend to be in high-cost facilities. Since these service companies are highly visible, maximizing stock cube is a necessity.
4. *As a storage facility on the factory floor.* Centralized stores, where inventory is controlled and secured on the manufacturing floor, has become one of the "hot buttons." Manufacturing floor space is critical. Utilizing the cube and having the product *there* are key. With

movable-aisle systems, the cube is maximized, and systems can be rolled together and locked. They not only provide security, but also minimize product deterioration due to contact with the elements.

5. *As a storage facility for supplies or tools.* Many applications are found in back rooms, supply areas, and toolrooms that are in close proximity to warehouse and production floors. Again, security is a key consideration.
6. *For use in vaults, freezers, and explosion-proof areas.* A great number of users of movable-aisle systems find themselves requiring expansion in costly space environments, such as low–flash-point rooms, cold rooms, and vaults. The products, especially the nonelectrically moved systems, are perfect where "sparks" would present serious hazards. Vault space, freezer space, and other special environmentally controlled or secured areas are generally more expensive than conventional storage areas and, consequently, provide an even greater justification for movable-aisle systems.
7. *As a dead-storage unit.* Movable-aisle systems are used for storage of chemicals, prescription, products, solutions, or papers which, by regulation, must be kept "forever." Batches of paint lots, product specimens, and so on, are some of the items that might be found on these systems.

Miniload AS/RS Systems

In recent years, the miniload has been considered a basic AS/RS system. In fact, "AS/RS system" and "miniload" are often erroneously used interchangeably. While a miniload is truly an AS/RS system (or part thereof), an AS/RS system is not necessarily a miniload.

The evolution of the miniload represents one of the industry's first steps toward automating the warehouse. During the late 1960s, the dream of an automated warehouse and concerns of increasing warehousing costs helped the early version of the miniload to evolve. In today's competitive environment, it is no longer a desire to automate, but a necessity. Today's miniload systems are certainly an alternative when considering an AS/RS system.

During the last few years, miniload systems have been finding broader applications. They have moved from the warehouse onto the production floor as a work-in-process storage device. They have also been used as a work-in-process delivery system with through-the-rack feed and discharge. Through imaginative applications, the miniload will continue to grow in its role as an AS/RS system.

Basic Configuration. A miniload AS/RS system is a fully enclosed, automatic storage system that brings parts and materials to an operator for picking, kitting, and so on, and automatically returns the material into the system.

Miniloads are actually the kid brother of the larger unit load systems (see Chapter 14). They bring material to the picker, rather than requiring that the picker go to the material. Materials are stored in uniform totes or containers, and these, in turn, are located on shelves or racks. The shelves are arranged to form two single-depth rows facing each other. A center aisle provides the area in which a mechanical device travels vertically and horizontally, carrying containers in and out of the storage-shelf locations. This device, an automatic insertion and extraction mechanism, is the heart of a miniload AS/RS system. It conveys all the containers within the storage lane to and from the work station, most often located at the end of the lane. The miniload handles only containers; it is at the work station that materials are handled in and out of the containers. The actual picking and replenishing of parts is, therefore, performed at the work station. Stations are most commonly placed at the end of a lane. Dual, fixed work stations allow parts to be picked from one container while the retriever is picking or returning other containers. Off-line, multiwork stations utilize conveyors to move containers between the retriever and the work stations. A variety of controls are available, ranging from simple to sophisticated. Push-button keyboards at the work station provide entry of location commands. The keyboard entry can be enhanced by using a punch-card reader or bar-code scanner. More complex systems, or those integrating a database, require real-time computer control. When a host computer control is used, the movement and positioning of the retriever is performed with local controls. The host computer generates and downloads a put-in/take-from location command to the local control. The local control then performs the operations necessary to insert or extract the container.

History and Development. As indicated earlier, the miniload is actually the kid brother of the larger unit load AS/RS system. The unit load was designed to handle pallet-size loads, and the miniload designed for less-than-pallet loads.

The evolution of the miniload system is easy to trace. In the most basic warehouse operation, a person directly picks the material and places it into a box. The first mechanical aid provided to the picker was a push-cart, or an easy way to transfer the picked material, and a ladder to help the picker safely reach higher levels. The cart or transfer device was then powered with a motor, or a powered conveyor was used. For heavy loads, a fork truck that carried the person picking the material was used.

In later applications, the truck would carry the person not only horizontally, but also vertically. Good cube utilization was now possible for high-density storage. The next step was to design the unit to automatically pick and deliver the material to an operator who could perform other tasks while directing the automatic pick device. Today, we have the capabilities for a computer to completely coordinate the picking activities. Pallet loads are retrieved from the system and then delivered to their destination. With mini- or less-than-pallet loads, a container of material is delivered to a picking station, the required quantity picked, and the remaining material in the container is returned. As you can see, the evolution of the miniload can be traced to the automation of basic picking functions.

The Application and Use of Miniload Systems. It is important to remember how miniloads evolved. Unit load retrievers had already established their benefits when the first miniloads came along. Space, labor, security, and accuracy were already proven returns. Yet, the miniload was intended for loose or split-case items. Consider these basic differences between pallet and loose-goods picking.

Pallet storage represents the vast majority of space in a warehouse. Therefore, the space-savings unit load AS/RS systems offered were applied to most of the warehouse space. In contrast, the total space required for split-case storage might be equivalent to a postage stamp on a letter. A 50 percent savings of floor space is one thing; 50 percent of 5 percent of your total space is not very exciting. Therefore, miniload systems could not be justified on space savings alone, and other factors then become vital. The labor and space cost of storing and picking split-case items is huge in proportion to the volume they generate. A picker may, in a full day, produce a dollar volume equal to only a portion of a pallet load. One answer to this problem would be to eliminate these high-cost/low-yield items. Market demands, customer needs, and competition prevented this option. A way of improving the unfavorable cost of small-parts handling was needed. Additionally, the emerging high-technology market was dramatically increasing the dollar value of small parts, and a new customer emphasis on lowering inventories resulted in smaller, more frequent orders. All these factors were combined to put pressure on small- and split-case handlers to find better ways. The miniload application represented a viable solution.

Miniload systems have found their way out of the traditional warehouse. They are being utilized for manufacturing support in many areas. A miniload in a manufacturing environment can serve both as a work-in-process queue and a delivery system for each work station. Miniloads have also been used for tool and die storage. Coupled with an inventory control system, a miniload helps to ensure an accurate inventory. The very nature of the miniload forces operators to maintain inventory integrity.

Benefits of Miniload Systems. A miniload AS/RS system offers the following major benefits.

1. *Floor space savings.* Since the mechanical picking device requires little area between rows of shelves, loss of wasted area (normally reserved for aisles) is minimized and capacity is increased.
2. *Cube utilization.* Miniload systems can be built to take advantage of all available ceiling areas and, perhaps, can extend above the present roof.
3. *Throughput.* The mechanical picking device can be "continually" moved to store or retrieve containers. While it can be argued that cycle times may be slower than human intervention, this logic cannot be extended past the point when human fatigue would enter into the comparison (i.e., continuous repetitive operations will tilt the calculations in favor of the more reliable and consistent mechanical device).
4. *Manpower, fatigue, and control.* A single operator can control picks. Since the container is brought to the work station, the operator does not have to walk or search for the container. Since the mechanical device retrieves the container, loaded containers may exceed weights normally moved by an operator. Bending, stooping, and stretching are eliminated.
5. *Security.* Miniloads are usually constructed with an "enclosed shell" protecting the contents of the system. This "enclosed cube" is a significant benefit where security is of key concern. The sheet-metal enclosure shields the items from personnel and from dust or other contamination.
6. *Control of parts.* Computerization allows the user to know the random location and parts quantity of every item. It can also arrange for correct sorting or accumulation of containers.

14
Automated Storage/Retrieval Systems

Edward J. Budill

Vice President, Tompkins Associates, Inc., Raleigh, North Carolina

Introduction

Automated storage/retrieval (AS/RS) systems consist of several subsystems, the operations of which are directed by a central control system. The system is designed to meet a specific application in either manufacturing and/or distribution. The designer must be familiar with the different types of equipment and how they may best be applied to satisfy the application's requirements. This chapter will first review the different types of major components used in AS/RS systems and some applications illustrating how these components can be integrated into an overall system. It will then look at some basic economic considerations and, finally, some future system developments.

Types of AS/RS Systems

The most common terminology divides AS/RS systems into unit load and miniload systems. A unit load can be defined as a pallet or standard container, as contrasted with bulk or packaged material (Figure 14.1).

Figure 14.1. A unit load AS/RS handling standard containers of parts in a full load-in/load-out system. (*Hartman MHS.*)

A unit load AS/RS system generally handles loads that weigh 1000 pounds or more. The pallet or container is the most common type of load and may contain all of the same stockkeeping unit (SKU) or may contain a number of SKUs. While the majority of systems have been built to handle containers or pallets, other systems have been built to handle a product, such as truck engines, transmissions, axles, and steel coils directly, without the need for any container.

Miniload systems always have multiple SKUs per container, achieve extremely high storage density, and are normally installed in existing buildings, generally 30 feet high or less. Their containers are usually captive to each storage location (Figure 14.2). Material is retrieved for picking, which usually occurs at the end of the aisle at special picking stations. Sometimes the containers are conveyed out to the order pickers. The containers are subdivided, egg-crate fashion, to accommodate the multiple SKUs, and their size is usually 14 by 48 inches or 18 by 36 inches, with heights ranging from 6 to 12 inches. Capacities are always under 750 pounds, with the majority of systems being 500 pounds or less.

Miniload S/R machines usually have a pin-type extractor that engages an appendage on the container (Figure 14.3). The load is dragged from the rack structure onto the machine. This contrasts with the unit load

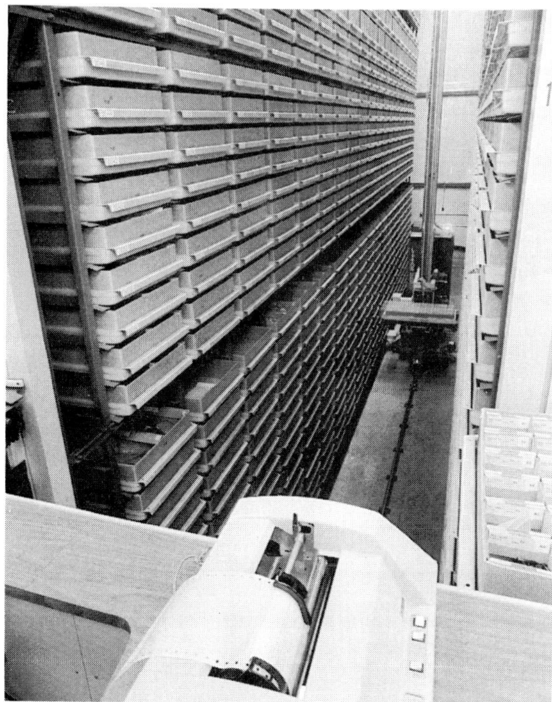

Figure 14.2. Miniload systems achieve high storage density using dedicated containers which are subdivided to contain several SKU s. (*Litton IAS.*)

system in which a shuttle must lift the load from the rack structure. This feature on the miniload permits the characteristic high-density storage (Figure 14.4). There are, however, systems that qualify as miniloads and that use a shuttle similar to the unit load system. The distinguishing attributes of a miniload system are the captive container, multiple SKUs per container, very high density storage, and installation within an existing building. These factors physically differentiate the miniload from the unit load system. In terms of control-system software, there are unit load systems that have multiple SKUs per container, and operate similarly to miniload systems.

Load Storage Characteristics

Many factors affect the design of the storage structure of an AS/RS, but none is more fundamental than the load itself. The most important factor is the size of the load and thus the storage cubicle required to

Figure 14.3. The pin-type extractor is the key to a mini-load's storage density. (*Hartman MHS.*)

accommodate it. The next is whether the pallet or container can be accommodated in the AS/R rack system.

If the container is unsuitable for storage or if containers with widely differing dimensions are used, it may be extremely difficult and expensive to design a rack system that will accommodate all the containers (Figure 14.5). The best solution may be to use a slave pallet. In other cases, the plant container or pallet may be unusable because of damage or nonuniform support surface.

Most S/R machines handle the load with a shuttle table that is raised underneath the load. The load is supported in the rack system on its edges, which are perpendicular to the axis of the aisle. The majority of systems are designed so that all storage cubicles have the same down-aisle dimension and the same dimension into the rack. Systems can have multiple load heights. In rare cases, a system can be designed to accommodate loads that may have different down-aisle and into-the-rack dimensions. The load will determine the storage-rack design and the type of load handling device on the S/R machine.

There are other factors that affect whether one should use slave pallets or whether the load can be handled directly. Although factory containers may theoretically be conveyable and storable in a rack system, they may be so battered from general handling that slave pallets are necessary for practical operation. Slave pallets are captive to the AS/RS system and do not travel around the factory or get shipped to other

Figure 14.4. The end-of-aisle station is designed to maximize the picker's productivity. (*Litton IAS.*)

plants. In some cases, the load may not lend itself to placement on apallet or in a container. It may be advantageous operationally to handle this load as it comes or with a special handling device. Truck axles are being handled directly by S/R machines and stored on cantilever racks, and truck engines are hung from cantilever-rack arms by special handling devices that accommodate movement on power-and-free conveyors through assembly operations.

Certain types of raw materials can be handled directly as they come from metal processing operations, where it would be difficult to handle the load in or on a container. Large farm tractor transmissions are stored is specially designed racks. In all these cases, the operational requirements of either the manufacturing operations or the need to use space effectively dictated that the material be stored and handled in these unique manners. While it does require some extra cost in both engineering and manufacturing, the operational benefits to the user can be considerable. The basic rule is that, within certain limits, the storage-rack system can be custom designed at a moderately increased cost to accommodate a variety of load configurations. In other cases, a small

Figure 14.5. An unusually shaped load is picked up from a special pickup station and stored on slave pallets. (*Hartman MHS.*)

quantity of unusual loads should be excluded from the system or stored in a specially designed aisle(s) to prevent incurring excessive cost to the majority of the system.

Rack Design Factors

The drive-thru–type rack is most usually used in unit load systems. The load is supported on its edges, which are perpendicular to the axis of the aisle. The load is handled by the S/R machine's shuttle table, which is extended underneath the load and picks it up from the rack arms. The rack system is described as follows (Figure 14.6):

1. Bays are the horizontal, down-aisle spaces.
2. Rows are the numbers of rack spaces across the system.
3. Tiers are the number of vertical levels in the system.

Most systems have single-bay spacing, which is a vertical array of loads supported by shelf arms that are connected to the upright columns. The

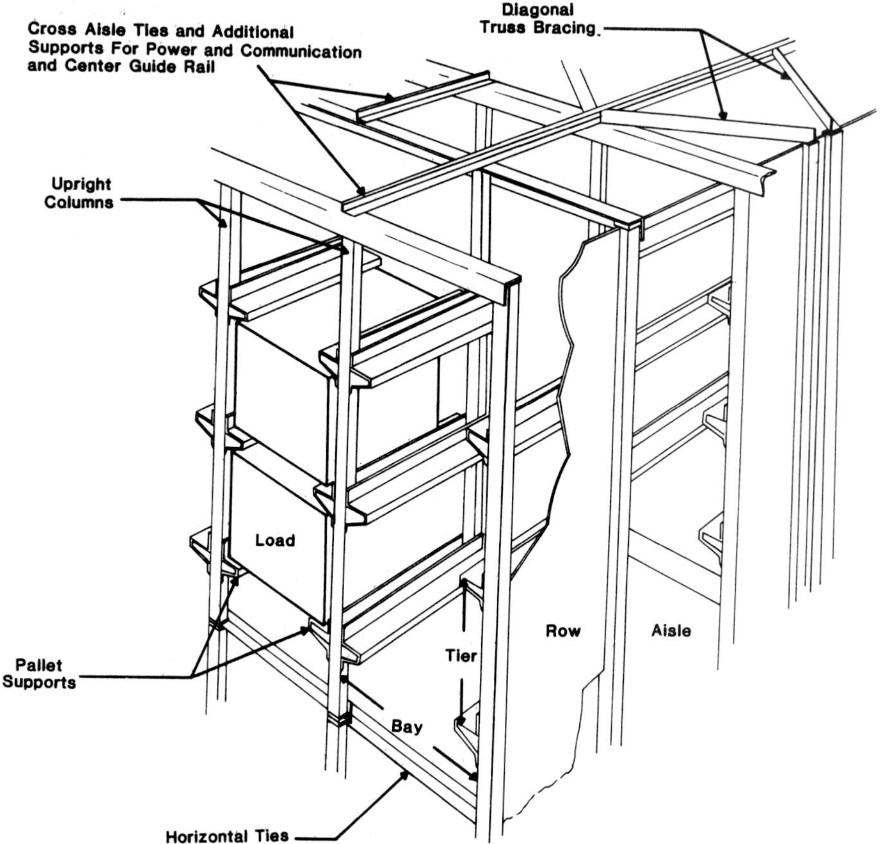

Figure 14.6. The basic features of the drive-thru AS/RS rack system.

vertical array has its first elevation about 24 inches from the floor. Depending upon load depth and capacity, the vertical space between the top of one load and the bottom of the next load is about 7 inches. This consists of 4 inches for the thickness of the shuttle and 1½ inches clearance above and below the shuttle as it extends between the loads. This distance may expand, depending upon the dimension required for the shuttle and the vertical tolerances. From the top load to the top of the rack is generally about 12 to 18 inches.

The side clearance is the dimension between the side of the load on the S/R machine and the load in the racks. This is a minimum of 3 to 4 inches on each side. The clearance required between the loads in back-to-back rows is generally 6 inches, but can be a function of the arrangement of the fire protection system.

Runout Space. At either end of the system, runout space is required. The runout at the front is determined by the length of the S/R machine, which must come clear of the racks in order to pick up and discharge loads. The rear runout area is that length of the S/R machine that extends beyond the last rack column when the S/R machine serves the last bay of storage racks.

Types of Rack Structures. In the late 1960s and early 1970s, almost all AS/RS systems in the United States were built with free-standing racks. The concept of the rack-supported building was not as popular as it was in Europe. Today, three of every four unit load systems are rack-supported.

AS/RS systems can be either part of a factory building or in a standalone facility connected in some way to the manufacturing or distribution operation (Figure 14.7). Where they are integrated into the factory, they can use a free-standing rack structure erected within a raised portion of the factory roof, or the roof can be raised and a rack structure erected that carries the roofing and siding down to the factory roof level. This is a logical approach, even though it may create a somewhat strange appearance for the factory.

Figure 14.7. Free-standing systems are installed in a building from which they are structurally independent. (*Hartman MHS.*)

If the system is to be built outside of the major operational structure, economics can dictate the choice of being free-standing or rack-supported. Today, most systems are higher than 60 feet, which makes a building with free-standing racks more expensive than a rack-supported building. Above 95 feet, floor loadings mount dramatically and may require heavy foundations. The cost of the rack structure as well as the cost of the siding and other building accessories will increase as heights over 95 feet are attained. The cost of the S/R machine will also rise incrementally over 95 feet. However, technology exists to create a system higher than 95 feet, and if factors combine to require it, the high system is practical. Today, there are less than 10 systems over 100 feet in North America.

The height of the systems built over the past five years ranges from 60 to 85 feet. In a rack-supported building, the rack system becomes the framework supporting the roof deck, building siding, the HVAC system, the electric power distribution system, and the fire protection system. The rack system itself is trussed together in all directions to form a highly rigid structure that can support these loads. It generally has a lower capital cost than a building and free-standing racks and can be erected in less time. Figure 14.8 shows rack being assembled and erected while the roofing and siding are being applied to finished portions of the structure. Because the rack-supported building is a single-purpose structure, it can qualify for certain advantages to the owner in the following areas:

Figure 14.8. The ability to perform various construction tasks in parallel permits rack buildings to be finished faster and at a lower cost. (*Hartman MHS.*)

1. Possible exemption from the state sales and use tax
2. Accelerated depreciation
3. Possible exemption from property taxes
4. Possible investment tax credits

Different companies, states, and municipalities have different views concerning the tax treatment for a rack-supported building. Because this is a major part of the AS/RS system, its tax consideration and cashflow generation potential should be carefully reviewed as part of the justification analysis. Expert financial opinion should be sought on how the tax and depreciation issues should be handled.

Storage/Retrieval Machine

While the storage rack itself is the operating environment for the system, the S/R machine is the basic unit of material handling (Figure 14.9). It has three basic motions: horizontal, vertical, and a shuttle subcycle. The shuttle subcycle includes extension, pickup, and retraction and, timewise, is basically a fixed cycle.

Figure 14.9. The S/R machine is a very efficient, but specialized, type of equipment. (*Hartman MHS.*)

Operating Speeds. Today, most systems have vertical speeds of 70 to 100 feet per minute. When lifting speeds exceed that, fairly complex electrical and mechanical drive systems have to be used. Vertical drives may use two-speed AC motors (4 to 1 or 6 to 1) or, in higher-speed applications, may require DC drives. The horizontal motion of the modern S/R machine is typically 400 to 500 feet per minute, rarely exceeding 500 feet per minute. The horizontal acceleration is usually 1.0 to 1.25 feet per second per second. Acceleration can be more important to duty-cycle performance than top speed. An S/R machine cannot achieve its top speed in the aisle length unless it has adequate acceleration. The most common horizontal drive is DC with regenerative braking.

The practical maximum horizontal acceleration is 1.75 feet per second. This is the rate of acceleration at which the wheels will spin on the steel rails.

The AS/RS system product section of the Material Handling Institute (MHI) has developed a formula to compute the duty cycle for both single and dual cycles. For a dual cycle, the S/R machine picks up the load at the home station, travels halfway down the aisle and halfway up the rack to deposit it; it then proceeds half of the remaining distance down the aisle, and half the remaining vertical distance to retrieve a load and return to the home station to deposit it. Users sometimes take this one calculated cycle and extrapolate it to become the specified throughput requirement, but rarely will a unit load S/R machine produce more than 30 dual commands per hour.

System suppliers have developed computer simulation programs in which system dimensional parameters are input with machine performance characteristics. A random number generator usually selects a variety of location combinations, and a program calculates the time to perform dual or single cycles to these selected locations. Because it is more detailed, this simulation usually produces somewhat different results from the MHI method (Figure 14.10). Because specified performance requirements must be based on specific locations, measuring S/R machine performance with the MHI method could only be done by having the machine perform one cycle repeatedly.

System Throughput Factors. Overall system throughput is more complex than the simple sum of the S/R machines' performance. Factors affecting overall system performance include control strategies, the configuration of the input/output system, the purpose of the system (full in/full out, order filling or kitting) plus the performance of the S/R machines. Throughput requirements are often stated simplistically at some highly inflated amount. The system can be greatly overspecified and a design established that does not really suit the intended use. Usu-

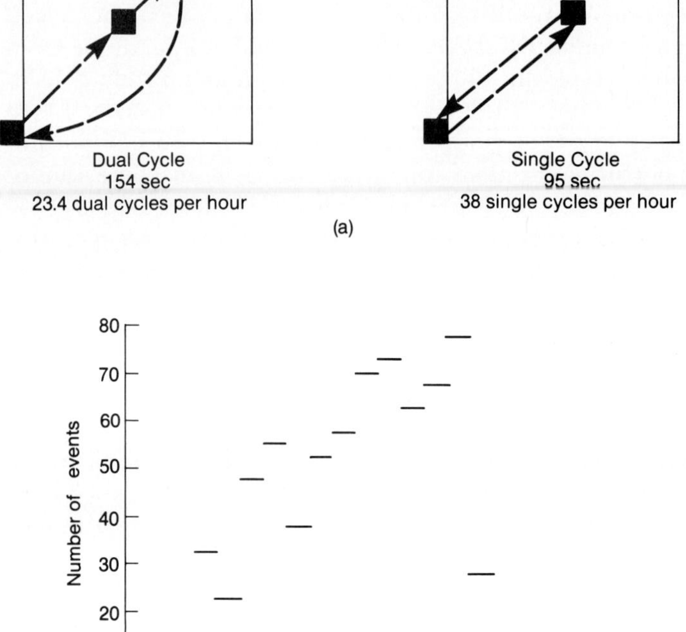

Figure 14.10. Simulation of S/R machine cycles will produce results different than simple calculations. (*a*) **Large-parts storage: S/R machine parameters—simplified calculation cycle; (*b*) large-parts storage: S/R machine performance—discrete event simulated activity.**

ally the throughput is not stated in a manner that really addresses the operational requirements. Systems rarely operate totally on a dual-command basis. In fact, a realistic throughput might state "that the system is required to perform 120 stores per hour combined with 40 retrieves per hour from 7 a.m. to 12 p.m.; 120 retrieves and 40 stores per hour from 12 p.m. to 3 p.m.; and 100 stores and 60 retrieves per hour from 3 p.m. until 11:30 p.m." This might reflect the actual operation of the facility. Careful consideration of how the system must perform in order to serve the facility is the most important first step in establishing performance requirements that are meaningful and that address the needs of the factory and/or distribution center.

Input/Output Systems

While the S/R machine configuration may be similar from system to system, the input/output system is almost always different. In the early days, many systems had simple drop stations on either side of the aisle, which were served by lift trucks. This concept could not provide queuing for the S/R machines, however, this limitation was alleviated by providing conveyorized stations that could queue loads and square and position them prior to pickup. System throughput was controlled by the rate at which lift trucks could serve the system.

Conveyor Systems. Large systems with higher throughput require conveyorization to provide control of flow, positioning, and movement of material to areas where special processes can be performed. Early systems had input and output on different levels and used vertical lifts to move material between them. This approach was primarily used because of the difficulty of implementing control systems that could rapidly and reliably move and track the loads. In multiple-level systems, the vertical lifts determined to a great extent the system's throughput and its reliability.

Where the load is not on a slave pallet, consideration has to be given to its conveyability. Certain pallets or containers are conveyable only in one direction, and the method of direction change, such as turntables, wheel transfers, or chain transfers, must be considered. Some systems require chain-driven live rollers for one direction of travel and chain conveyors for a 90-degree direction change. Figure 14.11 illustrates many of these functions.

In all cases, the conveyor system eventually interfaces with the pickup and discharge spurs. The transverse conveyor (that which goes across the front of the system) may be chain-driven live roller with chain transfers and conveyors bringing the material into the pickup station (Figure 14.12). In almost all cases, a load squaring operation is performed at the point of transfer and a final positioning operation is performed at the S/R machine pickup point. A commonly used approach is a transfer car that lifts the load from the transverse conveyor and moves it into queuing stations or the pickup position. Deposit stations may operate similarly to the input stations but do not perform pallet squaring.

Figure 14.11. Stock lift transfers, lift-truck unload stations, slave-pallet accumulator/dispensers, load size, and weight stations are all part of the input/output system. (*Hartman MHS.*)

Certain components of the conveyor system do specific things required for smooth, overall system operation. A grocery warehouse system has a special load squaring device to ensure that all cases on the pallet are squared and have not shifted prior to entering the AS/RS system. In another system, a tiering device stacks bundles of fiber material to form a larger unit load. Stretch-wrap or shrink-wrap facilities may be included to prepare the palletized loads for shipment or for storage.

Sizing and Weigh Stations. A size check to determine that the load conforms to the length and width limitations of the storage openings is part of all systems. The height check may be either a simple go–no-go or a measurement to determine in which of the different height openings a load can be stored. The sizing station may also determine whether the load exceeds the weight limits of the storage system. A sample weight-count station can be used for inventory control. A section of conveyor is usually mounted on load cells that are interfaced with the instrumentation system. This is usually used when the inventory consists of a large quantity of relatively small items. Several of these items are removed, placed on the sample scale, and the quantity of material in the load is measured. This type of system requires the containers to have a standard tare weight.

Attention must be given to human engineering aspects of order-filling stations. Lift stations may be required to bring pallets to proper work

Figure 14.12. Conveyer pickup/delivery stations interface the S/R machines to the transportation conveyor system. (*Hartman MHS.*)

ing height; there may be rotation to provide access to all sides of the pick-to and pick-from pallets; auxiliary lifting devices will be required if individual parts weigh more than 35 pounds.

Power-and-Free Conveyors. There are other types of input/output equipment to which AS/RS systems are interfaced. Power-and-free systems have successfully been interfaced with AS/RS systems in which the S/R machine picks the carrier or the load directly from the power-and-free system and then stores it in the racks (Figure 14.13). In one system, a power-and-free conveyor engages special bridles that carry diesel engines through final assembly and test operations and into storage in an AS/RS system, where they are "hung" on rack arms by the bridles (Figure 14.14) on the power-and-free conveyor through the engine trim.

Two steel mills that produce bar and rod coils have the banded coils placed on a power-and-free conveyor that takes them to an AS/RS system where they are hung on cantilever-rack arms. Two retail clothing

Figure 14.13. Power-and-free conveyor presents the diesel engine for storage in the AS/RS. (*Harneschfeger Corp.*)

distribution centers have AS/RS systems in which clothes are hung on special carriers that travel on chain conveyors to be stored by semiautomated, operator-on-board, order-picker S/R machines.

In the case of the coils, the power-and-free system serves as a means of load accumulation that absorbs the output of the mill. In the case of engine systems, the downstream operations are enhanced by the movement of the engines on the power-and-free system. In all these cases, the attempt to palletize the material would have been either difficult or inefficient.

AGV Systems. Automated guided vehicle (AGV) systems were first interfaced to AS/RS systems in 1969. Although AGV systems equipment can directly deliver material to the AS/RS pickup stations and take material from the deposit stations, some degree of conveyorization is usually required to permit queueing accumulation, positioning, and other functions necessary for proper inflow and outflow of material. Neither the AS/RS system nor the AGV system performance should be limited by the other.

Tractor-trailer-type systems can be used for simple, point-to-point movement of material (Figure 14.15), such as between shipping and receiving docks and the AS/RS system. The number of destinations is limited, there is usually adequate material to fill the tractor-trailer train, and there is adequate space to permit maneuvering.

The unit load carrier is most applicable where there are a large number of service points in the system. The individual unit load carriers can

Figure 14.14. Diesel engines are hung on cantilever racks by special bridles. (*Harneschfeger Corp.*)

have lift/lower tops for deposit of material on stands or powered roller conveyor tops to interface with conveyor stations. The AGV system control may be a subsystem of the overall AS/RS system control system.

Specialized Systems for Large Storage Volumes

Double-Deep System. There are several specialized AS/RS systems for accommodating large quantities of loads. In the double-deep system, the most common approach has aisles a single load wide. The S/R machines have shuttles capable of extending the load into the second-depth stor-

Figure 14.15. This tractor-trailor AGV system transports material from the AS/RS to production facilities. (*Harneschfeger. Corp.*)

age location. This is generally used where there is a fairly limited number of each. The normal strategy is to put two loads of the same SKU into the double cubicle to minimize the requirement to shuffle loads. Double-deep systems can also be designed with double-width aisles that permit the S/R machine to carry two loads at a time and insert them simultaneously into the double-depth cubicle (Figure 14.16). Double-deep rack systems are economical to design and build. The factor that affects the design of S/R machines is the moment of the extended load into the rack. An S/R machine that can extend a 2000-pound load 8 feet is equivalent to a 4000-pound machine that extends the load 4 feet. The complexity of the shuttle design itself increases as load capacities and extended moments increase.

Tandem Shuttle System. In the tandem shuttle system, the S/R machine has two shuttles and carries the loads one in front of the other. Both this and the double-width aisle system require that two loads always be available for pickup and the machine always be able to retrieve a double load. If the employment of the AS/RS system does not permit this to happen frequently, the unique advantages of the double-aisle width or the tandem load handling machine may not be realized.

Figure 14.16. This double-deep, double-wide storage arrangement is one method of accommodating many loads with few SKUs. (*Hartman MHS.*)

Deep-Lane System. Deep-lane storage is used where there are very few SKUs and a great quantity of each. The prime application is in food storage, and there are several variations. The first uses a gravity flow rack. A specially designed S/R machine picks up loads from a conveyor and transports them to the input side of the flow-through rack, which might be 10 loads deep. A similar S/R machine on the other side is used only for retrieving material (Figure 14.17). The flow-through lane ensures first-in and first-out and provides very high-density storage, but its throughput is limited to that of the two machines. A more logical arrangement might have two machines on the input side and two machines on the output side. There are critical requirements affecting the use of gravity conveyors, such as the conveyability of the load. To alleviate this, some systems have used power conveyors.

In another type of deep-lane system, S/R machines are equipped with a rack entry module (REM) rather than relying on the in-rack conveyors to move the loads. The REM is a powered device, mounted on the S/R machine, which moves off the S/R machine, deposits the load adjacent to the next stored load, and returns to the S/R machine. REMs typically communicate with the S/R machine via radio frequency link. Several of these systems have been applied in the frozen food industry, where throughput may not be great and high-storage density is particularly desirable.

Figure 14.17. Deep-lane systems store several pallets of the same SKU in lanes running perpendicular to the aisle. (*Litton IAS.*)

Pick Tunnel System. There are certain specialized systems in which there are few SKUs, a large quantity of each, and heavy order-filling requirements. The double-deep system and deep-lane storage systems are attempts to accommodate this without requiring an excessive number of aisles and S/R machines. In the pick tunnel system, mezzanines are provided in the rack where order pickers can access all the pallet faces on one level. When the pallet is empty, it is removed and replaced by a full one. Configurations vary, but usually the S/R machine replenishes the lower levels from backup stock stored in the upper levels. The order pickers pick to a conveyor belt or ride mechanized equipment that traverses the length of the pick tunnels.

Control System

Evolution of Controls. The evolution of AS/RS parallels the development of the controls industry. Early systems did not have excessive throughput requirements and were relatively simple to control. The main task was to accurately position the S/R machine at a location and return it to the end of the aisle. Onboard controls in the early 1960s were primarily relay logic and simple AC servodrives. Solid-state electronics became available, and controls evolved into hardwired solid-state systems by the late 1960s and the early 1970s. Address inputs could be made by thumbwheels or punched cards inserted into readers on the machine.

Multiple-aisle systems developed the requirement for centralized control. Hardwired consoles were built that could take cardreader inputs and transmit commands in the S/R machines. S/R machines usually communicated to the central console by a collector bar system or possibly a festoon conductor system.

Programmable logic controllers (PLCs) were applied in the early 1970s. These PLCs were relatively slow and cumbersome to program. They were replaced by microprocessor-based controls. Things are currently going full circle, with some of the manufacturers of the S/R machines going back to PLCs. The modern PLC is built in a variety of capacities. They are microprocessor-based and their size and operating capabilities make them very applicable for S/R machine control. They are standard control products that are well understood by user engineering and maintenance personnel. In certain cases, they are replacing earlier special-purpose microprocessor for on-board control.

Positioning Systems. Positioning systems have evolved from contact, counting systems to absolute systems in which magnetic sensors read binary-coded, decimal-formatted targets. The magnetic systems are based on machine-tool control concepts in which metal target plates with vanes bisect magnetic limit switches on the S/R machine. Another type of position sensing system uses a binary or binary-coded decimal address plate with reflective tape that is read by a series of incandescent retroflective photoeyes.

Incandescent systems are affected by ambient light and just plain dust and dirt. These systems have evolved to binary-coded, highly reflective target plates mounted on the rack, which are read by retroflective, infrared, light-emitting-diode (LED) sensors. The light beams are insensitive to ambient light, dirt, and dust.

Bin Detection Systems. Full-bin–empty-bin detection has also benefitted from changing technology. The original systems had white light-retroflective sensors on the machine and reflective targets at the back of the rack. This evolved to retroscanners, mounted on the carriage of the machine, that bounced light beams off the front of the stored loads.

Linear actuators were also used to physically probe several inches into the space into which a load would be located. The latest development is the use of sonar for detection of full and empty bins. This is particularly important in multiple-load-depth systems and those in which the front of the load can vary several inches from the plane of the nominal load face.

In the development of system reliability, much credit has to be given to the whole area of electronics and sensors. Contact limit switches have largely been replaced by magnetic proximity switches, photoelectric retroscanners, laser scanners for sizing, and other positioning and safety devices. Some of these interface the S/R machine to pickup and delivery stations or other system devices. Great strides have been made in developing compact packaging for this equipment, as well as developing rugged construction and adaptability to the harsh industrial environment.

Communication Systems. Communication is a critical function. Early systems required the machine to go down the aisle and return, regardless of whether it performed a dual or single cycle. All communication took place at the head of the aisle. This was replaced by communications systems that enabled the central control to communicate to the S/R machines by conductor bars. Communication was usually permitted only while the machine was stopped. Some of these early systems required a substantial number of conductors.

The conductor systems were required to provide command and to control communication between the central control system and the onboard system. Systems that used festoon conductors were electrically reliable, but could develop mechanical problems and required space for the conductors.

Today, modems can be used to communicate across a two-collector bar system, from an S/R machine interface panel to the on-board logic. This rapid, reliable communication system is operable while the machine is in motion or while stopped.

Input/Output Controls. Control of feed and discharge systems followed the same path of technological development as the S/R machine controls. The conveyor control system must activate many motor starters and other devices and receive inputs from sensors. In early systems, conveyors were typically controlled by relay logic. Tracking was by sequence only, and loads that got out of sequence threatened the reliable flow of material. Control systems were also expensive to design and difficult to modify in the field. The answer to this was the programmable logic controller. If ever there was an application for which the PLC is suited, it is conveyor control. While S/R machines do have many similarities from application to application, conveyors rarely do. The ease of programming electrical PLCs is an advantage to both designers and users. PLCs are microprocessor-based and have adequate performance for conveyor control

In early systems, the centrally located control cabinets had wires running directly to each individual motor starter and sensor. Today's PLCs have high operating speeds and remote input/output capability that permits the central processor to be located, for instance, in the computer room. The central processor is connected by shielded cables to one or more remote cabinets that are located adjacent to the sections of conveyor that they control. These cabinets contain the motor starters and the input/output modules and are wired at the manufacturer's factory. The remote cabinet is wired from terminal strips out to the motors, the actuators, and the sensors on the conveyor. This is the only area in which complex wiring occurs. This has greatly reduced the field wiring and has speeded the start-up of the conveyor system. The modern PLC can provide a totally independent control subsystem that can positively track the loads.

Minicomputer Control. Since the late 1960s, the development of the minicomputer has profoundly affected AS/RS system design and application. It has done this by permitting these systems to employ central control, which has greatly expanded their size and scope. The early minicomputers had a number of drawbacks, including cost, limited capability, and poor software support from manufacturers. However, they did provide the capability to develop multiaisle systems controlled from a central point.

As the minicomputer capabilities expanded and compatible peripheral equipment was developed, the AS/RS systems grew in size and capability. In the early 1970s, many systems were designed to include inventory record keeping on the AS/RS system computer. Although some attempts were made in the early 1970s to directly control S/R machines and conveyors with minicomputers, the programming was extremely complex because all the automation control had to be resident in one device. This approach was abandoned and distributed control systems have been the rule.

Control-System Hierarchy. As computer prices decreased and functional capability increased, it was natural that more and more functions be placed on the AS/RS system computer (Figure 14.18). As more data

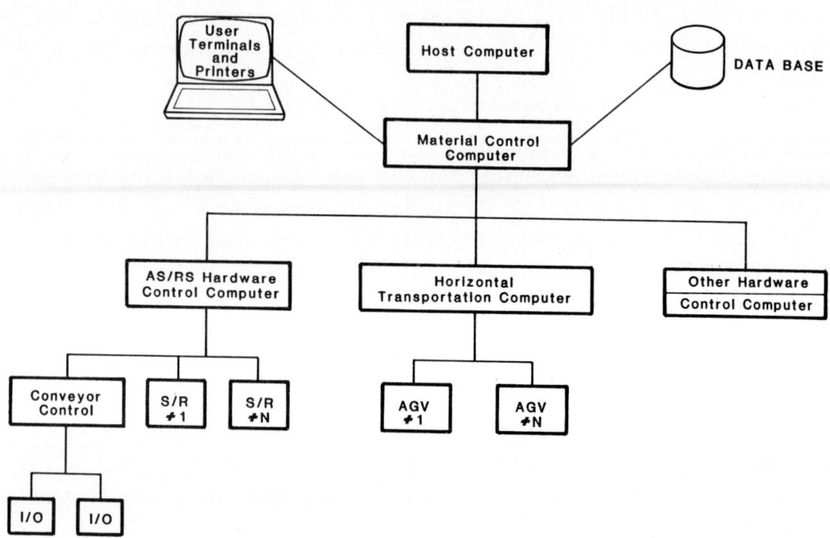

Figure 14.18. Hierarchy used in many manufacturing and distribution control systems.

processing functions were added, system reliability became vital, and the concept of being able to run the system in anything but a fully automatic mode became less and less desirable. Therefore, most current AS/RS systems have redundant computers to provide backup in case of processor failure. Such configurations have two processors and may have totally redundant peripherals (disk controllers, disk files, and certain other key peripherals, such as printers and CRTs). The secondary computer's database is updated by the primary computer. Switchover from the primary to the secondary computer is not automatic but can be quickly accomplished by an operator. The backup capability is particularly important when the AS/RS system computer performs functions that are not performed on the host computer; for example, scheduling retrievals and picking operations or handling verification of receipts on the receiving dock. In fact, many of the minicomputers used for AS/RS systems today have greater capability than mainframe computers of a decade ago (Figure 14.19).

Because of the increasing number of tasks assigned to the AS/RS system computer, plus the decreasing costs of control hardware, it has become desirable to develop the control system with a hardware control computer located between the AS/RS system computer and the machine

Figure 14.19. Material-control computer system of a large distribution center. (*Hartman MHS.*)

controllers. The hardware control computer can be a microcomputer or a small minicomputer, and can handle all the real-time communication with the input/output system, the S/R machines, and the AGV system control. The hardware control computer can handle command and control functions of all subordinate material handling equipment. In addition, it can handle data acquisition from devices such as television-part recognition systems, sample weight-count scales, and scanning systems, thus providing a flow of data to the AS/RS system computer. The AS/RS system computer can then download storage and retrieval commands to the hardware control computer, which can queue operations and provide system operation information through a CRT graphic display. It can also display the identification of loads moving through the system. If the AS/RS system computer is totally down for some reason, the hardware control computer can operate the automated system, but all data must be entered with a keyboard and the database manually updated later.

Data Acquisition. Data acquisition is an important consideration in an AS/RS system design and is performed in a number of ways. Years ago, punched cards, which had to be produced by a computer, were a primary means of data input. The cards were hard to keep track of, became damaged, and were inconvenient to replace. The availability of low-cost CRTs aided data acquisition when the CRT was located at the place where material was ingested into the system. An operator would input the necessary data using the keyboard. This, however, is a process which, regardless of user-friendly software, can be open to errors if many keystrokes are required to enter the data. The operator may make errors in reading data written on the load or simply make mistakes at the keyboard. If manual entry requires more than a few seconds, it may be a limiting factor affecting system performance. This is particularly true in systems that have multiple SKUs on a pallet.

While some manual data entry is part of virtually every system, different methods of load identification have been developed through the use of scanning systems. For instance, an AS/RS system with slave pallets may have a bar-code label attached permanently to each slave pallet. An operator may enter data through a terminal or use a scanner to read bar-code labels on the products on the pallet. A laser scanner may then read the pallet number, and the AS/RS system computer will assign that number as the control number for the pallet, which will identify it as it moves through the conveyor system to the S/R machine input stations.

In other systems, material on the pallet (cartons of products) may be identified with a bar-code label(s). The label may be read by a moving beam scanner with a field of travel that permits it to locate the label. Systems that support receiving functions have to accommodate the acquisition of data from material received from various vendors.

Software Design. Much could be written about software design and its affect on system performance. It is important to stress that software is a factor that affects system performance as does the cycling capability of any of the equipment in the system. In all systems, there are times when data collection, data processing, and material movement must be coordinated to ensure adequate system performance. The data must be collected and decisions made prior to selecting the destination of material and permitting it to proceed. Most user experience with software is based on systems in which the processing of data is an end in itself. The emphasis is on functions and the ability to accommodate a wide range of anomaly conditions. When this experience is carried over to the development of AS/RS software, the emphasis is on the development of function rather than the effect of function on system performance. While these systems are capable of performing a variety of functions, the total emphasis in the design effort must be upon achieving the required performance of the overall system. Software function must be secondary to software performance, and software performance must be part of the system model and simulation. Its performance and its effect on overall system performance must be evaluated in order to achieve system performance objective.

AS/RS Systems Applications

The applications of AS/RS systems can be broken down into distribution applications and manufacturing applications. We will look at a few such applications to get a clear understanding of how these systems fit into the overall operations of the user.

Distribution. A retailer has a number of fairly large stores located in one portion of the country. They purchase merchandise in large quantities in anticipation of the seasons and require a central storage and distribution center. The implementation of a large AS/RS system permitted them to greatly reduce labor and increase service to their retail stores by faster receipt, storage, and reshipment of product to these stores. This system replaced a number of totally manual warehouse operations in leased facilities.

There are several applications in the grocery distribution industry in which AS/RS systems perform the receiving, storage, and distribution functions serving a number of retail stores. The AS/RS system is usually backup storage to some type of case-picking system.

In freezer applications, energy costs are a major factor. In addition, personnel can only work in the freezer for a short period of time. AS/RS systems can be built to provide optimal dimensions for the building, which achieves significant energy savings, and to provide totally automatic storage and retrieval operations, which eliminates the requirement for people to work for sustained periods in the freezer. Modern technology has solved the problem of electronics and mechanical equipment operating in the $-10°F$ environment.

Manufacturing. Manufacturing applications can resemble distribution operations or can be work-in-process applications. There are numerous cases in which systems have been built that handle the receiving and storage of purchased parts in support of manufacturing and assembly lines. Automotive, electronics, and electrical manufacturing are all industries that use these types of systems.

Distribution of service parts has also been an application in which AS/RS systems have been applied. In several firms, multiple manufacturing plants ship parts to a central service part-distribution system that uses both unit load and miniload systems. Parts are then shipped to dealers. Farm equipment, construction machinery, and automotive are typical examples of industries which have used this type of application.

Certain types of industries have a number of small plants, each of which manufactures either a single product or a single product line. In order to get economies of scale in distribution, the smaller plants may ship their product to a central distribution facility, where material is received, consolidated, repackaged, and shipped out to regional distribution centers.

Work-in-process applications require some of the greatest amounts of creative thinking and offer tremendous future applications for AS/RS systems. The work-in-process system may actually be a number of subsystems, each supporting specific types of process operations. For example, a one- or two-aisle system within a conventional factory roof height may support a number of machine tools arranged around its periphery. Material is moved by an AGV system or another horizontal handling system to another module that serves a different type of processing operation, and from there to other modules that support assembly or testing. In these systems, the AS/RS system is really not a storage system, but is actually an extension of the work queue of the process facilities. There are a few systems in which the S/R machine presents the material to the process facility directly. In other cases, the retrieved material may be conveyed a short distance to a module where a robot may feed pieces from specially designed containers to the process operation. The AS/RS system control may provide complete control of the work cell.

Systems have been built to serve multistory factories. The AS/RS system serves not only as a horizontal integrator, but also vertically integrates material by being able to serve the multiple floors of the facility.

Justification of AS/RS Systems

AS/RS systems are major capital investments that develop extremely favorable returns on investment. Most systems pay back their investment in three years, some in less than a year and a half. Because of their size and scope, the development of the financial justification requires creative thinking and thorough research. These systems are purchased for one of two basic reasons. The first is cost avoidance, in which the user can justify the system by reducing documented costs in existing operations. Growth of the business is not a major factor, but elimination of existing costs and maximizing profitability is the major aim. The second reason is growth accommodation, in which the user may see market growth opportunities that require expansion of facilities, new manufacturing processes, or entirely new facilities. An AS/RS system may be the best way to support this growth. In this case, the financial justification is highly dependent on the validity of the forecast of the market growth.

In either case, the major portion of the payback can be determined by addressing the major problems that must be solved in the factory or distribution center. These will generate the greatest payback. However, there are many additional operational savings that can be found. The AS/RS system should be compared to the cost of existing operations and against the cost of alternative new solutions. However, it must be compared based on its own best operating and design characteristics. Do not constrain the AS/RS system to be 20 feet high with 20 aisles if its best operating configuration is 75 feet high with 6 aisles.

While most people will look only at the effect on the operating statement, the effect on the balance sheet should also be considered. The accelerated depreciation permitted by new federal tax laws can quickly return the investment to the owner.

Operational savings from AS/RS systems can come from any areas. Here are some that are typical:

1. Elimination of production delays due to material shortages
2. Reduction of scrap and rework
3. Reduction of cost due to delays in shipping products
4. Enhancement of quality control
5. Increased inventory accuracy
6. Reduced requirement for outside storage
7. Reduced manpower requirements
8. Freeing existing facilities for other uses
9. Reduction of work-in-process inventory with resulting reduction in working capital costs

Future Opportunities and Developments

There are exciting new developments in applications, control systems, and integration of different types of handling equipment with AS/RS systems. The application of work-in-process systems to support flexible manufacturing systems (FMSs) is one of the most exciting things happening today. This has really been a development of the network control system and the interface of material handling to the productive process.

Various developments in control systems have also created exciting opportunities for the applications of AS/RS systems. Television-part recognition systems and new developments in scanning are providing new opportunities in data acquisition to enhance inventory accuracy and system throughput. The rapid development of automated guided vehicle systems with their ability to be closely integrated into AS/RS system operations has also created a dramatic opportunity for serving manufacturing process departments. The integration of robotics with process facilities and serving these robotic cells with material retrieved from the AS/RS system is at its very threshold today.

In conclusion, AS/RS systems are keeping pace with today's demand for greater throughput, lower inventory, and greater flexibility. The use of new computer system capabilities and high-speed data acquisition techniques along with the integration of AS/RS systems with horizontal transportation and robotics will provide systems that are flexible and responsive to changing needs in both manufacturing and distribution applications. Sophisticated design techniques and computer-based control systems will provide the key to realizing the stringent throughput requirements for these systems.

15
Lift Trucks

Karl E. Lanker, P.E., C.M.C.

Vice President, Engineering, The Sims Consulting Group, Inc., Lancaster, Ohio

Introduction

All lift trucks have one thing in common: they are designed to lift and transport loads too heavy for safe, unassisted listing. The trucks discussed in this chapter are limited to those person-operated and controlled designs with a lifting capacity of 10,000 pounds and under.

Typical Lift-Truck Construction

A number of component systems are essential for safe operation of lift trucks. These basic components (Figure 15.1) are discussed below.

The *overhead guard* protects operators from falling objects and is required by the U.S. Occupational Safety and Health Administration (OSHA) in most operating conditions. Trucks that lift loads above the operator's head or operate in high-load stacking areas must be equipped with guards. Low-lift trucks and those used for loading/unloading over-the-road trucks and trailers may be exempted from this requirement. Trucks servicing low-header areas cannot have any elevated part of the truck above 83 inches high. If the guard exceeds that height, powered or manually operated retractable overhead guards are used.

The *mast assembly* consists of a steel upright assembly. Most operate hydraulically, but some have electrically powered lifting devices. The mast's stationary outer channels and telescoping inner channels provide

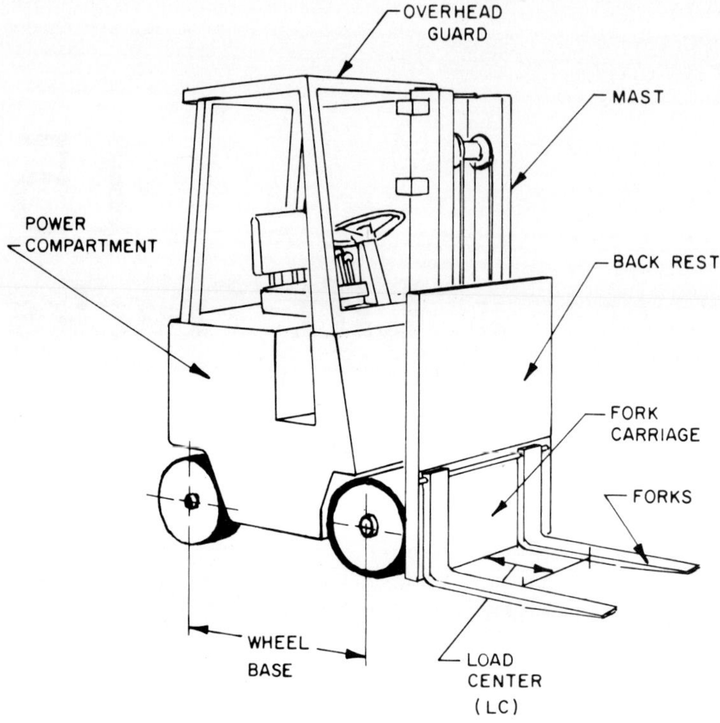

Figure 15.1. Typical lift-truck parts nomenclature. *(The Sims Consulting Group, Inc.)*

for high lifting capabilities and a low collapsed height. Various lift cylinder, mast geometry, and chain configurations are used to equalize reaction to loads, increase stability, and decrease uncontrollable mast deflection. Complex multiple-stage masts require more energy for operation than low, freelift designs.

Single-stage masts have two upright channels. The fork carriage travels within these channels at twice the speed of lifting. These masts have the highest overall lowered height in relation to available lifting height. Used in low-lift or high-lift applications where overall height is not critical, these masts provide the greatest stability of load movement at a given height, because they have the least number of moving or sliding parts.

Two-stage or three-stage masts provide greater lift heights while retaining low overall height. Called "duplex" or "triplex masts," they are equipped with double-acting cylinders and chain reeving. Their fork travel speed varies with the lifting stage of the upright assembly.

Four-stage masts provide the greatest lift height in relation to overall lowered height. The large number of moving parts and the clearances required for movement of each telescoping assembly give this mast the least control over load movement of all mast assemblies. However, *free-lift,* defined as the vertical distance forks can rise before the mast extends from its collapsed height, can be an important operational consideration in low-headroom applications. When high-lift capability is required within the plant but low headroom is available within the truck, quad mast designs solve critical handling problems. The amount of freelift varies widely with mast and truck design. This range extends from a few inches on some models to over 60 inches on man-up turret trucks. This freelift feature is most critical in maneuvering and stacking loads in areas with low head room, such as inside over-the-road trailers. Most manufacturers offer either standard or "high" freelift options.

Fork carriages are classified by the Industrial Truck Association (ITA) according to the capacity of the truck's carriage design. Forks and other attachments are mounted on these carriages, which function as both mounting and lifting bases. Identified as Class 1, Class 2, and Class 3 carriage assemblies, these assemblies often use a backrest to prevent loads from falling apart when the mast is tilted backward and to help align loads vertically. The ITA has standardized the location and pattern of the mounting holes on the bar or frame to ensure interchangeability of attachments and versatility of application.

Forks are the most common loading engagement device used on lift trucks. They are usually 4 to 6 inches wide, 42 to 48 inches long, and 1½ inches thick at the heel. Fork options include chiseled ends, full bottom taper, and spark-resistant materials.

Two popular options are side-shifters and fork spreaders. Side-shifters retain a given fork spacing while providing side-to-side mobility to permit pickup and deposit of loads not perfectly aligned with the truck. Fork spreaders provide the ability to vary the spacing of the forks to accommodate varying load sizes. Both are hydraulically operated from the operator's position.

Wheelbase, the centerline distance between the front and rear wheels, determines, to a great extent, the operating and handling characteristics of the truck. These characteristics include load capacity, turning radius, aisle space required for right-angle load stacking, and the maximum grade down which the truck can negotiate without scraping bottom. This wheel base–maneuverability connection is longest for counterbalanced designs.

Load center (LC) is the distance from the front face of the fork to the center of gravity of the load. It is one of the factors used for determining the lift capacity rating. Most lift trucks with a capacity rated under 10,000 pounds use a 24-inch LC base, which is the industry standard. If the LC of oversized loads exceeds 24 inches, the truck's safe lift capacity will be substantially decreased or derated. This measurement is critical for determining load safety, especially for counterbalanced trucks.

Tires used on lift trucks are either pneumatic, cushion or solid types. These options are discussed in detail in the engineering data section of this chapter.

Power sources for high-lift designs vary. Powered low-lift walkie trucks and narrow-aisle or very narrow aisle rider trucks are electrically powered. Other rider designs are available in a variety of internal combustion options: standard gasoline engines, gasoline engines converted to burn liquified petroleum gas (LPG), or diesel engines. These options are covered in detail in the last section of this chapter.

Lift-Truck Classification

Beyond these general characteristics, lift trucks are divided by lift capability into two primary types: low lifts, which raise loads 4 to 6 inches, and high lifts, which incorporate various special design features that enable them to lift to a nominal height of 40 feet. These two types are subdivided in turn by design features that reflect modifications for special load capacity or applications.

Low-lift trucks use forks or platforms to lift pallets, skids, pans and other types of media 4 to 6 inches above the floor (Figure 15.2). These trucks are either manually or electrically operated. The manually operated variety is commonly called a "pallet jack." Pallet jacks are moved horizontally and vertically by manual effort. Powered models are activated by on-board rechargeable batteries that provide power for the lifting and transporting motions. All powered models can be operated from the floor as walkie-type trucks. If they are equipped with a safe operator platform and hand-grip rail, they can also be operated as rider-type trucks (Figure 15.3).

Because the likelihood of injuries to operators increases with manually operated lifting and pushing of nonpowered transporting devices, the trend is to use powered, low-lift walkie/rider trucks, despite increased vehicle cost. Whether powered or manually controlled, walkies are low- or intermediate-lift trucks.

High-lift trucks use a variety of attachments to stabilize and lift loads to a nominal height of 40 feet. These attachments include forks, platforms, clamps, and shuttle tables. All high-lift trucks are powered, rider models. The few manually controlled, elevated fork-lift walkie trucks are limited to raising loads to an intermediate height of 9 to 13 feet

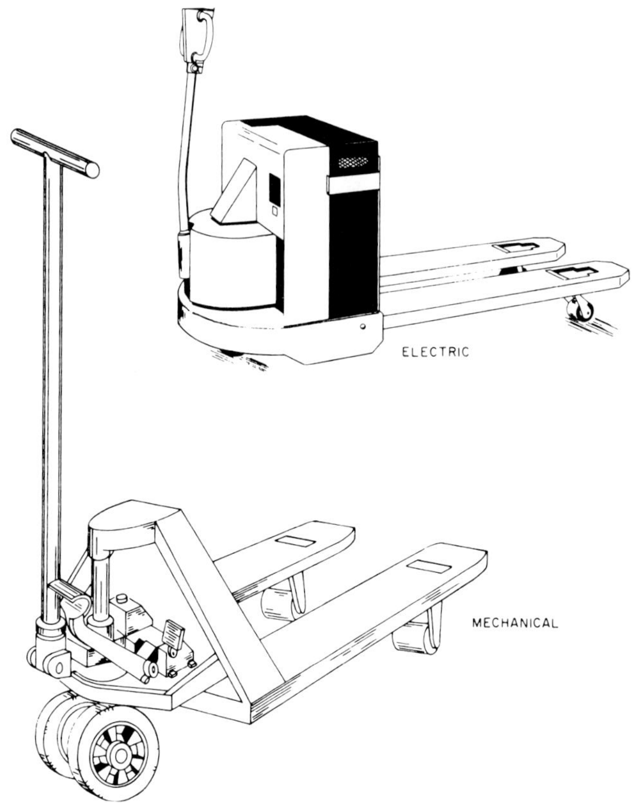

Figure 15.2. Typical low-lift manual and electric truck. *(The Sims Consulting Group, Inc.)*

(Figure 15.4). Beyond this intermediate height, lifting heavy loads with walkie trucks becomes too dangerous.

Because raising loads very high requires complex design modifications, many interesting variations in design have occurred. These variations are quite distinctive and have given rise to several high-lift categories that have become identified as truck types on their own. These include counterbalanced, narrow-aisle, swing-mast, side-loader, turret, and high-lift storage/retrieval (S/R) machines.

The following discussion expands upon the generic characteristics above. The first section begins with walkie trucks. This section includes selection guidelines, control options, and definitions of common low-lift and intermediate-lift walkie designs. It is followed by a discussion of the general characteristics, selection guidelines, and definitions of each of the unique categories of powered high-lift rider trucks. The chapter ends with sections on engineering and power options.

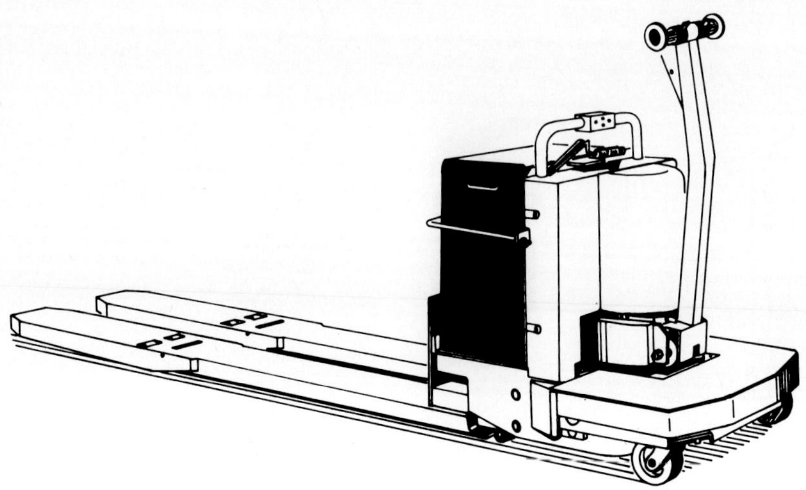

Figure 15.3. Walkie rider (double-length works). *(The Sims Consulting Group, Inc.)*

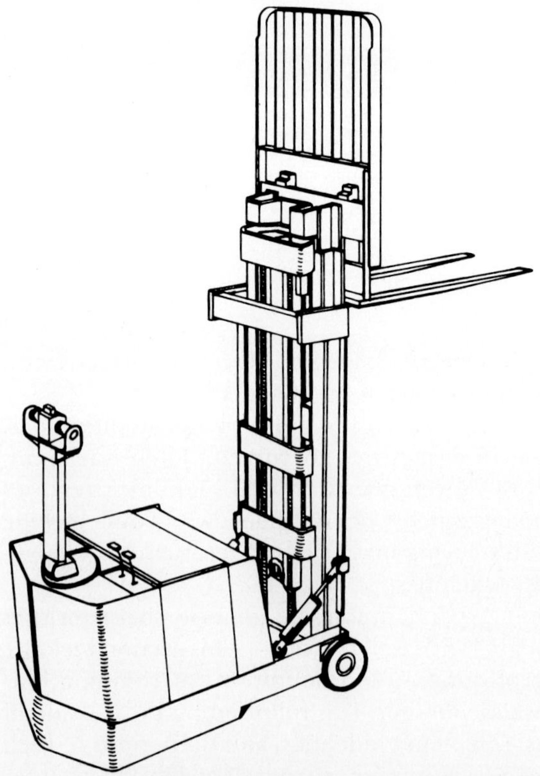

Figure 15.4. Typical walkie intermediate-lift truck. *(The Sims Consulting Group, Inc.)*

Walkie Trucks

The first decision in selecting a walkie truck involves the suitability of a particular type of walkie for a specific application. Options include a series of operational and physical configurations, as well as economies of scale in the application of unit load handling. Figure 15.5 illustrates the general nomenclature of the low-lift truck and the control positions for operating it.

Selection Guidelines

Selection guidelines for walkie trucks must match functional requirements. Because the operating speed of powered walkies is usually limited to 3 miles per hour, one-way travel distance for transporting unitized loads should be limited to less than 200 feet. Frequency of use must also figure in the decision between a walkie and a rider truck. Using walkie trucks for excessive distances and frequencies creates operator fatigue and reduces performance. Density and height of storage are also important selection factors. Low-lift trucks can provide the maneuverability needed in dense, low-level storage configurations.

Aisle and height requirements must be compatible with vehicle choice. These requirements differ with type of walkie truck, as Table 15.1 indicates.

Stacking heights for high-lift walkies are usually limited to a nominal height of 13 feet. The maximum defined stacking height is usually 15 feet. For safety reasons, operating vehicles without overhead guards in high stacking areas is not advisable.

Time requirements for lifting the load-carrying surface 10 feet is about 30 seconds, based on 20 feet per minute (loaded) hoist speed. Time requirements vary with the battery voltage, type of mast, load weight carried, and size of hydraulic lift pump. To assure the best performance, consult manufacturers' specifications.

Unit load requirements must be combined with these general criteria to determine compatibility. These requirements include load height, width, length, and weight, as well as the uniformity of distribution and homogeneity of the load.

To these criteria are added storage/transportation requirements: the type of pallet or skid, the transporting distance and/or stacking height requirements, racks or block storage, type of product, and facility-related considerations. The latter can include ramps and grades to be negotiated, floor loading distribution, elevation limitations, operating clearances, and environmental conditions, such as the presence of hazardous chemicals, humidity, coolers/freezers, and so on.

When powered walkies are considered, support services must include arrangements for battery charging. These include power requirements, location of the charging station within the facility, ventilation, water for washing and drainage, and concrete floors treated to prevent damage from acid spills. Equipment maintenance arrangements will dictate the need for tools, shop equipment, and parts inventory.

Control Options. Control options also impact selection since they affect the total operating efficiency of handling methods. Important walkie truck control issues include speed, lifting, braking, and reversing.

The horizontal traction control—the transporting control—is acti-

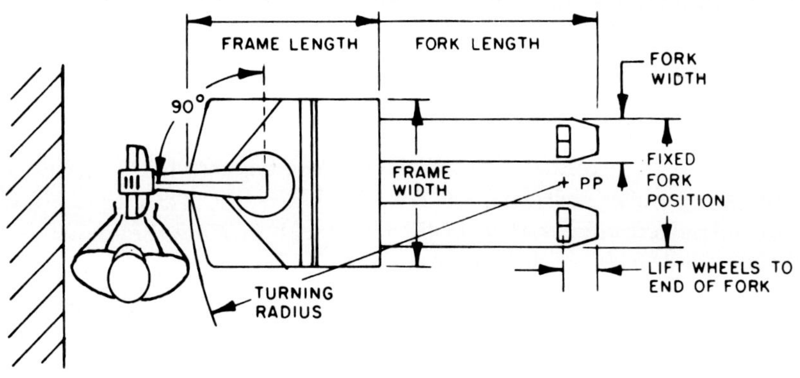

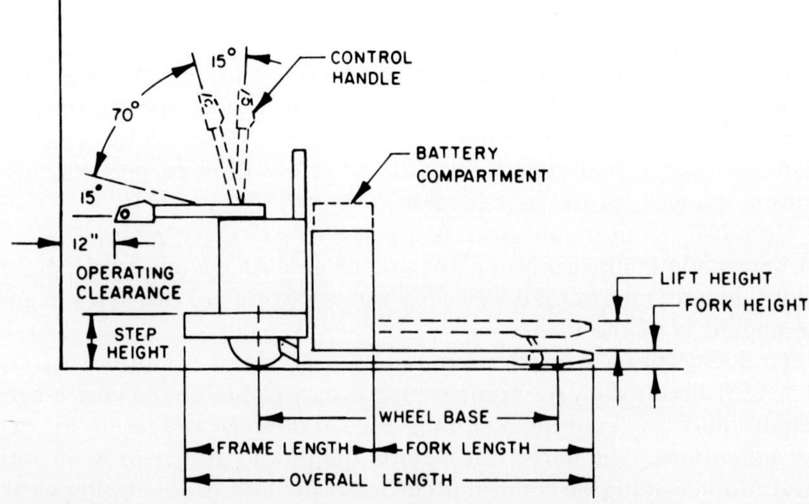

Figure 15.5. Typical low-lift nomenclature. *(The Sims Consulting Group, Inc.)*

vated from the end of the handle. Direction is usually controlled simultaneously with speed. The choice among speed control options depends upon the amount of close maneuvering required and the fragility of the product handled. "Stepped" two- or three-speed forward and reverse options and infinitely variable speed options are available. These variable-speed electronic controls are equipped with transistor or silicon-controlled rectifiers (SCRs).

Lift and lower controls are either electrohydraulically activated through switches or manually hydraulically activated through a level. The electrical switch designs place the switch closest to the speed/direction controls.

Placing the steering handle in a vertical and/or horizontal position on walkie lift trucks activates the brakes. When the handle is in any other position, horizontal travel is possible. When the operator releases the handle, it automatically returns to the vertical position, applying the brakes.

Many models also offer an automatic reversing feature. This feature reverses the truck if the handle encounters a resisting force. It provides additional safety, keeping the operator from being trapped between the truck and stationary objects. To ensure safety, however, operator training is mandatory. The relative simplicity of walkie designs makes training of production workers as part-time operators practical.

Low-Lift Pallet Trucks. The most widely known of the walkie trucks is the low-lift pallet truck. The wheeled forks of this self-loading truck are

Table 15.1. Required Dimensions of Right-angle and Intersecting Aisles for Walkie Trucks*

Walkie truck	Right-angle aisle, ft	Intersecting aisle, ft	Collapsed height, m	Lift height, in
		Low-lift walkies		
Walkie pallet	5–6	5–6	NA	6
Walkie/rider pallet	6–7	6–7	NA	6
Walkie platform	5–6	5–6	NA	6
		Intermediate-lift walkies		
Straddle†	7–8	7–8	94	156
Reach†	7–8	7–8	94	156
Counterbalanced‡	9–11	9–11	94	156

* Load dimension: 48 by 40 in; weight: 3000 lb. Truck load center = 12 in; capacity maximum lift to 6000 lb.

† Based on 12-in clear over rub dimension; depends on battery size, mast type, and clearances between adjacent loads.

‡ Based on two-stage standard lift.

sized to slide between the top and bottom boards of a double-faced pallet. To load the truck, the fork's wheels, which are part of the linkage mechanism, are retracted, allowing the forks to be inserted into the spaces between the bottom boards. For transporting, the wheels are lowered and the pallet raised. Maximum travel speed for loaded walkies is about 3 miles per hour. Specific speeds are proportional to battery voltage.

Nonpowered low-lift trucks are generally used for applications in which travel distance and load tonnage are moderate. These trucks are available in 3000- to 6000-pound-capacity models. Fork spreads are available for use with 30- to 60-inch-wide pallets. The type of pallet must be determined and standardized since these forks are fixed and are not adjustable.

When trucks will be used with double-faced pallets, fork length must correspond to pallet length to ensure that the wheels project beyond the bottom boards of the pallet. Pallet construction and traveling surface can also affect the lift height required for safe, efficient transporting and maneuverability.

Powered low-lift pallet trucks are generally used for applications in which travel distance is relatively short, but load tonnage is moderately heavy. For these uses, they provide an economical alternative to more costly counterbalanced trucks. These trucks can be purchased with permanent extended forks capable of lifting double or quad loads (Figure 15.6).

Walkie/rider low-lift trucks provide a useful alternative when both short-distance and long-distance transporting are required. Again, no

Figure 15.6. Double-load transporter. *(The Sims Consulting Group, Inc.)*

stacking is required. This truck allows the operator to ride on the truck while transporting pallets and to maneuver the truck from the floor while loading or unloading. Because its maximum speed is about 5 miles per hour, the same extended fork applications can be performed by a walkie/rider.

The operator's position on the walkie/rider is either at the front of the truck or in the center. The center position is often used for order-picking applications to position the operator closer to the load (Figure 15.7).

Specialized adaptations or attachments can be used to allow special product handling by low-lift trucks. These include hinged drop frames designed to convert the truck from a fork entry vehicle to a platform truck. A special pantographic grab mechanism allows retrieval and discharge of slipsheet unit loads without requiring pallets.

Low-lift platform trucks are used primarily for transporting skids and bins. These self-loading trucks are available in a variety of platform sizes to ensure compatibility with a variety of skid sizes. Most low-lift platform trucks have a capacity of 4000 to 10,000 pounds. However, some special trucks have capacities much greater than 10,000 pounds.

The wheels are usually affixed to the truck frame. Those wheels under the platform have a larger diameter than the wheels on a pallet truck because they do not have to slide into a double-faced pallet. Seldom are these wheels part of the linkage mechanism used to raise and lower the platform. The minimum lowered height of the platform is usually 6 inches.

Figure 15.7. Order-picking application. *(The Sims Consulting Group, Inc.)*

Two adaptations are common. The platform of these versatile trucks is often modified to accept customized unit loads, such as steel coils, wire and cable reels, bolts of yarn, paper flat stock, or other units with distinctive configurations.

A popular design uses a "skid adapter" to create the platform. This modification permits handling of double-faced pallets with the adapter raised and locked in a vertical position, or single-faced pallets or skids with the adapter resting on the forks.

Intermediate-Lift Walkie Pallet Trucks. Intermediate-lift pallet trucks are self-loading vehicles equipped with an elevating mechanism that permits tiering. They come in powered and nonpowered models. Three basic configurations of this truck are available. These are the regular straddle (outrigger), the straddle with reach forks, and the typical counterbalanced truck. All can be powered or nonpowered.

The few nonpowered, medium-lift walkie truck designs are usually adaptations for specific, nonrepetitive functions. These manually propelled models can be used to raise and transport molds, dies, or other parts that are too heavy to lift and carry in and around a maintenance or repair shop (Figure 15.8). The distances these parts are moved are usually short.

Counterbalanced walkie trucks, like the counterbalanced rider designs, suspend the load forward of the truck's front wheels. The load carried by these trucks is counterbalanced by the chassis weight. These hand-controlled trucks offer intermediate lift capabilities of 9 to 13 feet (Figure 15-4). They can handle single- and double-faced pallets, skids, and bins and can be equipped with many popular rider truck attachments.

Straddle trucks use horizontal members (outriggers) supported on wheels that extend forward from the truck body. The load is carried between these outrigger arms. Since half the load is directly over the straddles, these trucks can have less gross weight than counterbalanced trucks of equal lift capacity. The specifications for this type of truck must provide adequate clearance between straddles for the largest pallet. Otherwise the truck cannot pick up the pallets from the floor.

The *walkie reach truck* can extend and retract its load-engaging forks to pick up or deposit pallets at any level. It can pick up pallets, the widths of which are larger than the clear width between straddles. Normally these straddles extend about 24 inches beyond the retracted position of the forks. When extended, the fork carriage just clears the straddles. In this position, tiered pallets can be positioned without aligning the straddles to clear the floor pallet load.

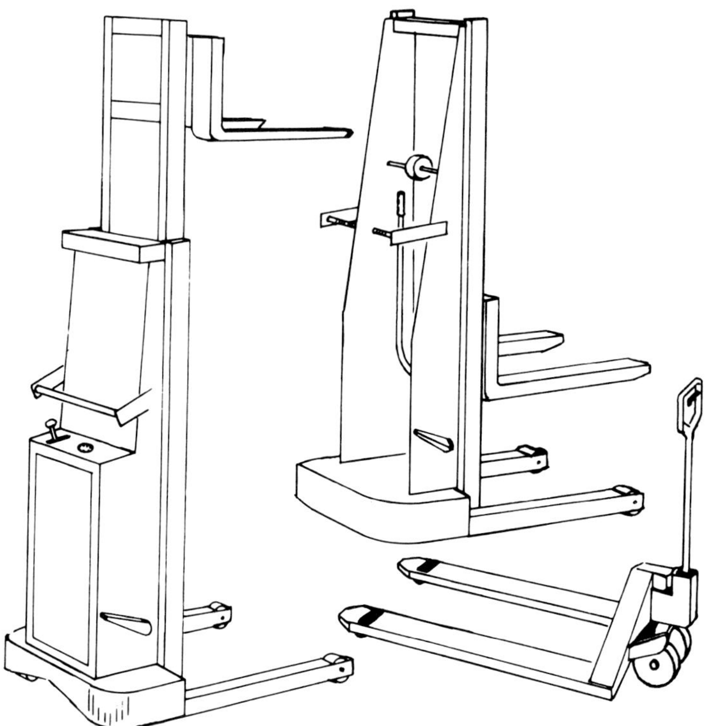

Figure 15.8. Typical manually controlled lifts. *(The Sims Consulting Group, Inc.)*

As with counterbalanced trucks, the lift capacity must be considered when specifying reach trucks. Because the load will extend beyond the front straddle wheels, these wheels become the fulcrum for determining the chassis weight needed to support the full load.

Rider Trucks

When distances to be moved are too great, or when loads are too heavy or must be lifted too high, rider trucks provide a solution to materials handling problems. Though these trucks are more expensive, they are indispensable in most warehouse and manufacturing facilities. Choosing a design that exceeds projected needs is a bit like using an atom bomb to clear a road bed: it is better to choose an appropriate vehicle that will do the job correctly and effectively, ensuring economies of scale within an acceptable budget.

Figure 15.9 illustrates the basic nomenclature of high-lift rider trucks. Though a number of different configurations for high-lift wheeled vehicles are manufactured, these descriptive terms remain the same for all high-lift designs.

Selection Guidelines

Selection criteria for rider trucks must reflect the operating characteristics required for the job to be accomplished. Potential suppliers should demonstrate that their trucks meet these specific job requirements.

Five factors determine the performance characteristics of all lift-truck designs. They are load capacity and dimension, lift height, travel and lift speed, maneuverability, and ramp-climbing capability. All designs represent compromises of these five factors. All are tailored to effectively function within facility and operational constraints. Manufacturers can provide information about the physical characteristics and judgment factors they used in relation to the factors above to determine performance for a specific application. A purchaser must also evaluate the relevance of each of these factors to determine whether a potential design will meet operating needs and perform effectively as well as efficiently.

Load Capacity. Load capacity is usually considered first because the lift truck chosen must be capable of lifting the heaviest-rated load to a specific height. Load capacity is specified at a given load center, calculated as the distance from the vertical fork arm to the center of gravity of the load. The most common LC is 24 inches. Unless stated otherwise, this is the dimension implied in the lift-rate capacity of all lift trucks.

Figure 15.10 graphically illustrates the lift-capacity changes that occur with shifts of the LC. This figure, which includes the method for calculating these capacity changes, is an estimating tool, and not appropriate for engineering verification.

Factors affecting load capacity include variations in the load center and the intended lift height. Attachments must be considered in specifying lift requirements because they can reduce (downrate) truck capacity by extending the load center or adding weight to the front end of the truck.

Figure 15.11 illustrates five definitions of load capacity. Each definition is determined by a specific set of operating characteristics:

1. *Load capacity*, specified at a given load center, is the maximum weight a truck with forks or specified attachments can lift to a stated max-

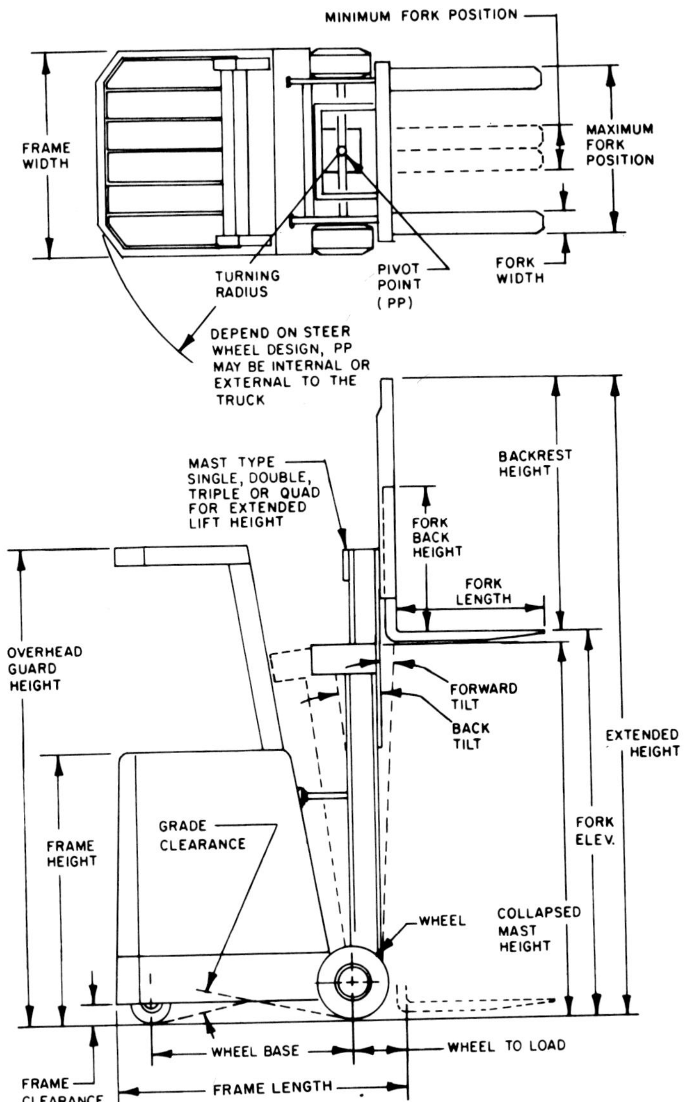

Figure 15.9. Nomenclature of operating parts. *(The Sims Consulting Group, Inc.)*

imum height. At this capacity, the truck must be able to carry and stack loads while maintaining structural strength and stability. This rating is shown on the truck nameplate.

2. *Alternate capacity* establishes the lift capacity at less than maximum elevation for the same load center. This calculation usually exceeds the load capacity calculated at maximum height because the decreased height provides increased stability of the truck.

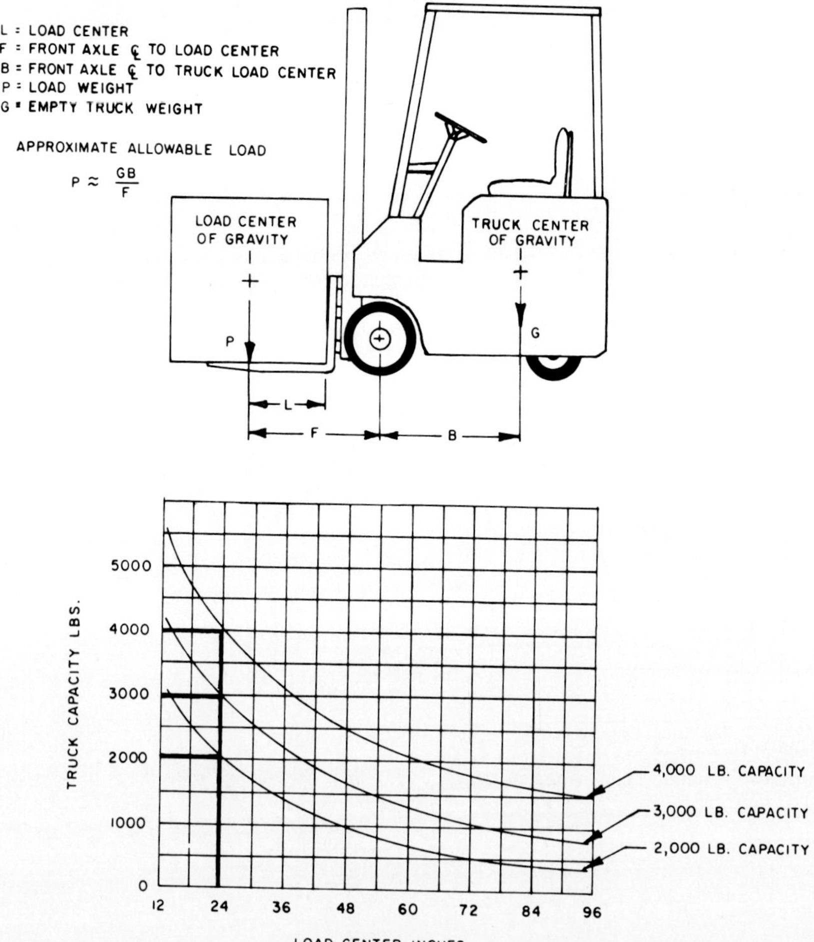

Figure 15.10. Lift capacity changes with shifts in load centers. *(The Sims Consulting Group, Inc.)*

3. *Rated capacity* is established using a homogeneous cube with overall dimensions twice the 24-inch load-center dimensions. This calculation indicates the maximum weight of this cube size that the truck can lift to a height specified by the manufacturer. This rating may be based on structural strength, stability tests, or calculations.
4. *Alternate rated capacity*, like alternate capacity, establishes the weight a truck can carry and stack to an elevation lower than the height originally specified by the manufacturer. The load center and load size used to determine alternate rated capacity may be twice some cube dimension other than the doubled 24-inch dimension used to established rated capacity.
5. *Rated capacity with attachments* is established using a load center and elevation specified by the manufacturer. This rating may be changed by the manufacturer due to increases in maximum elevation or changes in the load center. Such derating reduces the rated capacity to reflect operation at increased lift heights or with changed

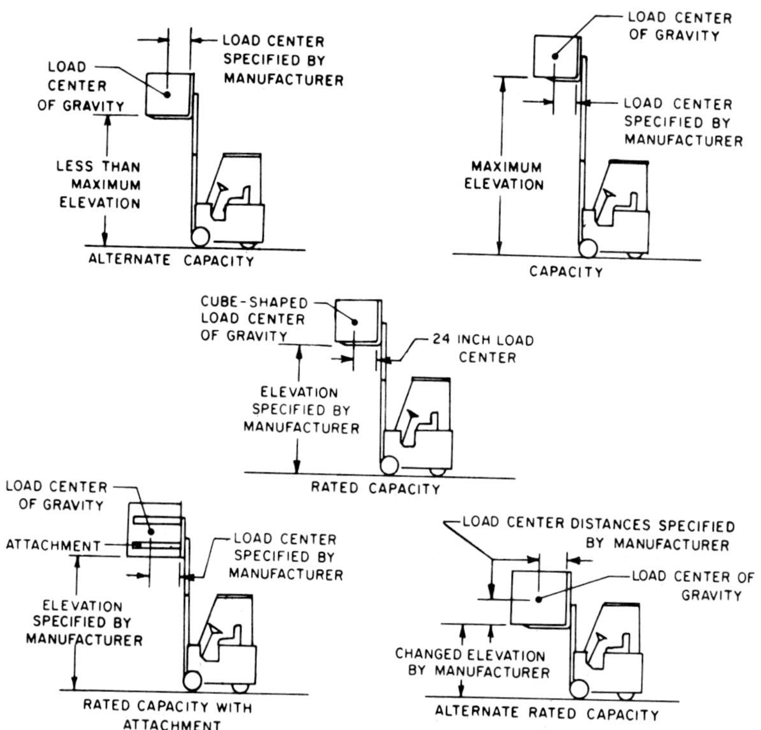

Figure 15.11. Variation and lift effects on lift capacity. *(The Sims Consulting Group, Inc.)*

load centers. This derating results primarily from decreased stability of operation at extended lift heights. Using dual-load wheels, increasing the mast width, and increasing the truck width to increase the footprint of the machine all increase stability.

Because capacity can be specified in any of these ways, actual capacity should be verified with the manufacturer. This can be done by describing the load size, weight, and intended lift height of the application for which the truck will be used. The given lift height used by different manufacturers for rating their trucks generally ranges from 12 to 18 feet.

As the lift height increases, the lifting capacity is downrated. According to the rule of thumb, the lift capacity downrates 100 pounds for every 2-foot increase in lift height above a given vertical lift level (of, say, 15 feet). This downrating must be verified to ensure safe lifting capacity, particularly if the application for which the truck will be used will require heights above the actual height used by the manufacturer in rating the truck's capacity.

Lift. Lift specifications include a variety of dimensions used to determine the overhead clearance dimensions of the truck, the ability to stack loads in low-overhead situations, the maximum lift height available, and the overall stability of the truck (Figure 15.11). The following four common lift ratings are used.

1. *Elevated height* indicates the maximum lift height of the truck. This elevated height should exceed the pallet-level storage height by 6 to 12 inches. This additional height will ensure that loads stacked in the highest storage positions can be lifted clear of the storage rack for pickup or put-away. The load capacity at the desired height should equal or exceed the greatest weight intended for storage.

2. *Extended height*, sometimes called "overall elevated height" (OAEH), indicates the maximum height reached by the top of the mast, fork carriage, load backrest, or operator cage with the mast extended to its maximum elevated height. This height may determine the minimum building clearance needed to operate the truck at maximum height.

At least a 12-inch clearance must be allowed between the extended load height and the lowest building obstruction, such as lights, building beams, joists, pipings, heaters, air make-ups, or other overhead obstructions. For some types of materials, at least 18 inches of clearance between the top load in the static stored position and the ceiling sprinklers is required by law. Before installing racks, the material and clearance requirements should be verified with the National Fire Protection Association, the insurance carrier, and/or OSHA. In no case should clearance requirements be referenced to the bottom of steel (BOS). Clear operating height is a critical issue and must be defined (Figure 15.12).

Very high loads or man-up designs need clearances greater than 12 inches for safe operation. When the backrest, cage, mast, or carriage protrude above the load, the truck configuration is used to determine the building clearance needs. For this reason, the elevated structural height of the truck, including the extended height of the load, must be determined for man-up designs. Depending upon the type of man-up

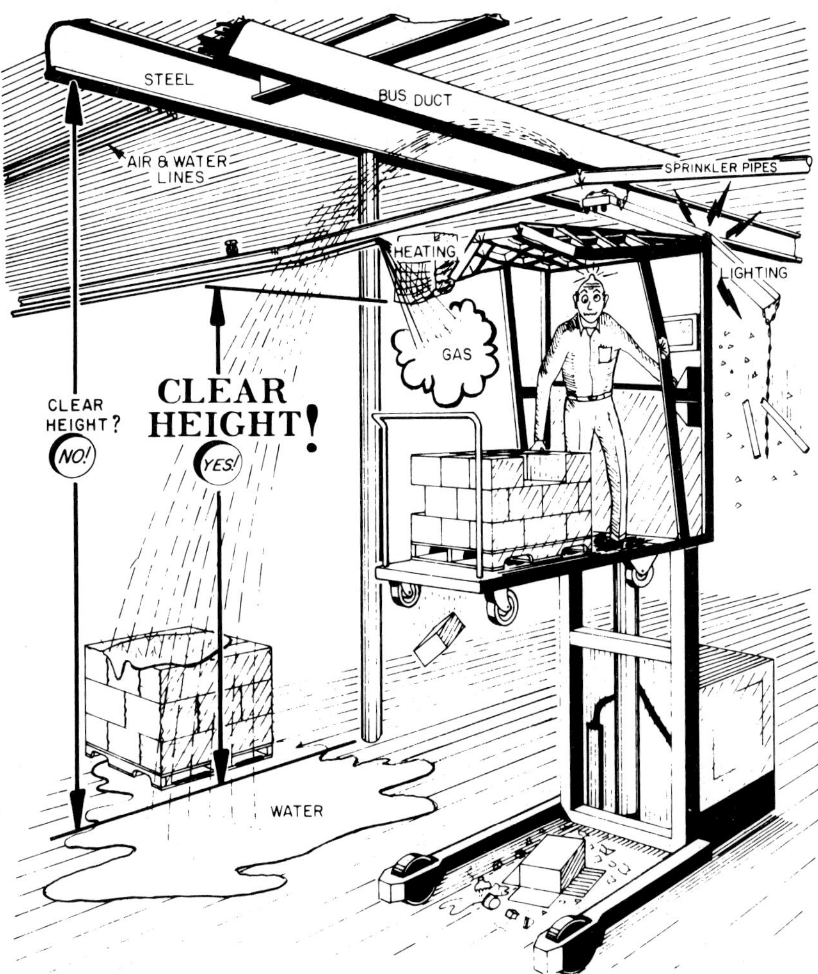

Figure 15.12. Clear height. *(The Sims Consulting Group, Inc.)*

truck, the operator or cab can be this controlling clear-height factor. The cab height can be as much as 7 feet above the elevated fork height. The backrest, load, cage, cab, mast, and attachment must all be checked to determine which is the controlling factor in determining clear operating-height requirements.

3. *Overall collapsed height* may not indicate the overall lowered height of a truck. The overhead guard may be higher than the collapsed mast height, especially on a stand-up rider truck. The overhead guard may determine the minimum operating height of the truck. When the collapsed mast determines overall collapsed height, multiple-stage masts can provide more compact dimensions, retain low collapsed height, and permit high elevated height for operation.

4. *Freelift* indicates the amount of fork elevation possible before the mast moves from its fully collapsed position. This freelift is determined by the mast design. *Low freelift* is the term applied to freelifts of 24 inches or less. *High freelift* is often available nearly to the height of the collapsed mast, about 60 inches. High freelift designs permit loads to be stacked inside boxcars, highway trucks, and other places with low-headroom conditions.

Travel and Lift Speed. Travel and lift speed are basic to every handling cycle. They directly affect the productivity of the lift-truck operator. While manufacturers offer a variety of combinations of travel and lift speed, the combination selected and the maneuverability of the truck together should never be more than the operator can control safely.

The choice of power source usually determines the speed capability for both travel and lift. Improved batteries, motors, and controls have increased travel and lift speeds of most powered lift trucks to those of internal combustion–powered (IC) units. Common maximum travel speeds inside a building reach 6 to 8 miles per hour. Specific speed capabilities depend upon the confinement and adjacent restrictions. Outside (in open areas), these trucks can exceed those speeds.

The design of the truck's hydraulic system determines the lift speed. The pump motor horsepower and the pump volume, rated in gallons per minute, most directly affect this speed. A common means manufacturers use to economize is to undersize the lift-pump capacity to reduce costs. While a truck with an undersized pump can still achieve the desired load capacity, its lifting speed will be decreased enough to make operation inefficient. The truck will take too long to elevate the load. Common speeds for modern electric trucks lifting the design load range from 60 to 90 feet per minute.

Maneuverability. Maneuverability is defined by a truck's ability to operate within a given aisle width. A combination of load length, load spacing, truck size, and outside and inside turning radii determine this aisle requirement. Dimensions that affect maneuverability include width, length, and wheelbase.

The basic index used for maneuverability is the minimum right-angle stacking aisle without clearance. The means of calculating aisle width are discussed in the engineering section at the end of this chapter.

Controls. Controls affect the performance, maneuverability, safety, and service lift of a truck. A variety of standard and optional controls are available. These controls are divided into two major categories:

- Drive controls, which control forward and reverse travel, braking, and raising or lowering of the forks
- Guidance controls, which automatically guide movement in very narrow aisle applications

Drive controls in electrically powered trucks may commonly be either of two types: mechanical, stepped-resistance controls or electronic, silicon-controlled rectifier controls. Stepped-resistance controls mechanically switch a bank of resistors by depressing an accelerator pedal. Only the least expensive trucks or those used occasionally have mechanical controls.

The resistors in mechanical, stepped-resistance controls consume a great deal of power, especially at lower speeds. At full speed, the resistors consume no power, since the battery connects directly to the motor. In operation, the relative values of the resistors and the number of contacts provided by the control determine the amount of power delivered to the motor by each discrete step. The movement is not a smooth transition from one speed level to the next. This relatively inexpensive control is simple to maintain but requires periodic maintenance of the contact assemblies.

Solid-state electronic drive and lift controls are based on SCR technology. These controls have replaced mechanical controls on most fork trucks. They are available in several designs that provide smooth, step-free power. They are efficient and consume little power themselves, making longer working shifts possible and reducing power requirements.

SCR controls deliver full power to the drive motor in short bursts. The accelerator pedal controls the spacing of these bursts of power, directly varying the effective power delivered to the drive motor. By delivering full battery power to the drive motor with each burst of energy, these controls combine high-torque, low-speed capability with smooth speed control.

Reverse polarity, surge currents, and transients generated by reversing direction or plugging do not affect these modern electronic controls. The newest SCR controls employ regenerative energy-recovery techniques. These systems recover some of the energy stored in the vehicle's motion and redirect this energy to the battery, replacing some of the energy used during acceleration or lifting operations. Using regenerative systems increases the amount of working time available during a shift since the battery's usefulness is extended when some energy is restored. Since the hydraulic system and load-lifting functions consume the greatest amount of energy during most material handling cycles, applying these systems to the lift pump motor increases service time most significantly.

Guidance controls have been refined to overcome the effects on maneuverability of aisle size reduction and working-aisle clearances. Both mechanical and electronic automatic guidance systems free the operator from steering while working in the storage aisle. Mechanical systems use guide rails bolted to the floor on both sides of the storage aisle. Guide rollers attached to both sides of the truck passively steer the truck within the aisle through direct contact with these rails. When total aisle length is short and the number of trucks limited, this system is economical. It is easy to install and requires little maintenance.

When the total aisle length or the number of trucks becomes large, electronic guidance systems usually become more economical. These systems use a small guide wire embedded in a shallow, epoxy-filled, saw-cut slot in the floor to actively guide trucks electronically while they operate within the aisle. The epoxy material provides a smooth floor surface. A centrally located driver unit activates the wire, which transmits a low-frequency signal. This signal is picked up by a sensor located on the lift truck. The decoded signal steers the truck.

Most systems use two sensor pickup units, one at each end of the truck, to guide the truck either forward or backward and provide a more positive control. Others may use a single sensor to guide the truck in one direction only; this is not recommended. Sensors are mounted at each end of the frame just above the floor to provide a positive signal contact with the in-floor wire. This wire, driven by a loop driver unit, provides the drive signal used to automatically control the steering motion while the truck is in the guided aisle. This loop driver unit plugs into a standard 120-volt outlet.

Wire-guided systems can be easily modified by saw-cutting the floor to reroute the channel to new locations and by splicing new wires into the loop. These wire systems can also be used to guide travel in other areas of the plant or warehouse. When constructing a new facility to house a wire-controlled storage system, any high-voltage power lines running under the floor must be well protected to eliminate the possibility of an electrical flux interfering with the wire-guided system.

Among the benefits of electronic wire-guided systems is the hands-free steering control, which allows the operator to concentrate on storage, retrieval, or order-picking functions. These systems are unusually safe: they have a variety of safety interlocks that stop trucks that malfunction or lose their guidance signal.

Economically, these wire-guided systems must be justified on a case-by-case basis. Beyond the number of trucks or aisle length, other factors involved include the cost of the trucks and receivers, the number of system driver units or boosters required, and the savings projected through high-rise, very narrow aisle storage.

The benefit of the optional transmission of data both to and from each vehicle must also be considered. Using this technique, the truck receives instructions from a central computer through a receiver unit on the truck. The operator can report to the central computer through the same system, noting abnormal situations such as incorrect stock or insufficient stock. These systems can also provide the base for completely mechanized, computer-controlled order-picking and inventory reporting systems.

Final selection from among those trucks types that meet the operating requirement selected by the purchaser should be made by comparing:

- Truck design features
- Reliability
- Serviceability within the specific plant location
- Price

Though comparing the asking price of specific vehicles within general capacity ranges is somewhat useful, these computations do not reflect total ownership cost. Operating costs, parts prices and availability costs, and service facility costs need to be considered in any purchase-price analysis. These can be more difficult to calculate.

Classification of Rider Lift Trucks

Load-lifting capacity and aisle width requirements divide powered rider trucks into families that serve as primary selection criteria. These classifications are subdivided based on power source and method of control.

Family groupings based on chassis capacity are 1000 to 2000 pounds, 2000 to 5000 pounds, 5000 to 8000 pounds, 8000 to 10,000 pounds, and vehicles with a capacity above 10,000 pounds. This last family, above 10,000 pounds, is not covered in this chapter.

Ratings are certified by manufacturers. However, the ability of each truck to handle a particular load depends upon both the truck's capacity and the relationship of that capacity to the family group chassis capacity. If a truck with a light-duty chassis is used for continuous or heavy-duty operation, operating and repair costs may be accelerated. Operating a truck with a lower-rated chassis at the high end of its load range costs more than operating a truck with a higher-rated chassis at the low end of its load range. Obtaining long life and low operating costs, then, requires knowledge of chassis groupings as well as capacity requirements.

Aisle-width capabilities of rider trucks are divided into three categories:

1. *Conventional-aisle* capability refers to the aisle requirements of the first industrial counterbalanced designs. These vehicles require about 10 to 15 feet for handling a 48- by 40-inch pallet. These conventional-aisle counterbalanced trucks remain the standard for materials handling.
2. *Narrow-aisle* designs resulted from engineering efforts to reduce aisle requirements for handling loads. These trucks, which require about 7- to 9-foot aisles, became known as "narrow-aisle vehicles." The standard chassis for narrow-aisle trucks is a straddle design.
3. *Very narrow aisle* designs can operate in aisles as narrow as 4 to 6 feet. These designs are known as "turret trucks."

Stacking heights for the rider trucks considered in this chapter are limited to a nominal reach of 40 feet. For efficiency reasons, few systems are designed to operate at their maximum-rated stacking height. Lift times vary with power source, chassis design, load capacity, and actual weight of the load. For this reason, it is best to consult individual manufacturers.

Unit load requirements must be combined with the criteria above to determine compatibility. These requirements include load height, width, length, and weight, as well as uniformity of distribution and homogeneity of the load.

To these are added storage/transportation requirements: the type of pallet or skid, the transporting and/or stacking requirements, the type of racks, block storage, or other arrangements, and facility-related considerations such as ramps, grades to be negotiated, floor loading distribution, elevation limitations, and atmospheric conditions.

Support requirements include arrangements for fueling, such as a battery charging station or some other fueling station. Ventilation must be carefully considered in establishing this area. Water and drainage for washing is also needed. Equipment maintenance arrangements will dictate the need for tools, shop equipment, and parts inventory.

Safe operation of lift trucks becomes more complex as truck design becomes more complex. Concern for the operator on rider trucks has led to design features that do not exist on walkie trucks. These include the overhead guard previously discussed, as well as other guards, two-hand controls which prevent the operator's extending his or her hand outside the cab, and speed governors that automatically reduce speed as the cab is elevated. These governors have no effect on travel speed with the cab raised less than 2 feet.

The following provides additional information about the types of rider trucks available in relation to the load size and configuration that each is capable of handling.

Counterbalanced Trucks. Counterbalanced trucks come in two basic designs: the sit-down rider (Figure 15.1) and the stand-up rider (Figure 15.13). If the operator must mount and dismount frequently, the stand-

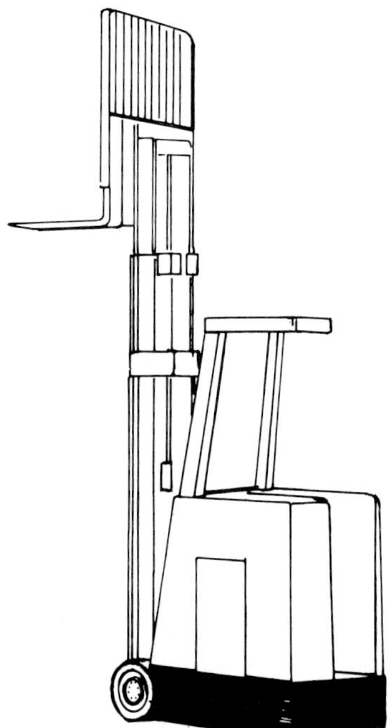

Figure 15.13. Typical stand-up counterbalanced truck. *(The Sims Consulting Group, Inc.)*

up rider is more appropriate, but for long-distance transporting applications, the sit-down rider is best. The longer wheelbase required for sitting down gives sit-down riders greater load capacity than stand-up designs. The shorter wheelbase of stand-up riders allows them to operate in smaller aisles, though their maximum capacity is less than that of sit-down designs.

The loads of all counterbalanced trucks are cantilevered in front of the front load axle and counterbalanced by the weight of the truck chassis. Handling capacity is determined by the relationship of the load center to the truck's center of gravity. Sit-down riders are available with 2000- to 10,000-pound and higher capacities. Stand-up designs are available with 2000- to 5000-pound capacities.

Narrow-Aisle Trucks. Narrow-aisle designs, like the walkie straddle trucks, carry their loads within the wheelbase of the truck, between outrigger arms. This design reduces the need for counterbalancing weight.

Straddle trucks obtain high stability with low vehicle weight because they have a low center of gravity, and half of the load is carried within the footprint of the vehicle.

This small, stable truck is not suited to extremely wide loads, since the straddle spacing would become excessive and the aisle requirements very wide. But straddle trucks can handle conventional-sized loads (i.e., those measuring 48 by 48 inches or smaller in either direction) in less space than counterbalanced designs.

Rider designs are all stand-up designs. Though the length of the straddles may vary, straddle length is commonly 24 inches. These straddles can be as long as 5 or 6 feet to handle long loads or platforms for order-picking in furniture warehouses. The clear width between straddles also varies according to specifications when built. This straddle width determines the stability rating and aisle-width requirements. All straddles are fixed and are not adjustable. When small, heavy loads must be lifted, very high straddle width may result in excessively wide aisle requirements. In such cases, other types of trucks may prove better for the application.

Reach trucks get their name from the pantograph-mounted fork assembly that extends about 2 inches beyond the straddles (Figure 15.14). They are constructed like straddle trucks, with straddles, sometimes called "outriggers," of the same general configuration as those used on straddle trucks. These outriggers do not need to be as wide as the load, since the load need not be suspended between them.

Because the load extends beyond the straddles in a storage/retrieval mode, reach trucks become counterbalanced trucks when in this extended position. When operating in a regular travel mode, the reach truck has the same stability and capacity rating as the standard straddle truck. This is particularly important, since the travel mode is the most critical operating condition.

Two types of handling operations are possible with reach trucks, depending upon the size of the load relative to the outrigger spacing. When a conventional 48- by 40-inch pallet load is used, the minimum straddle width required for stable operation permits the pallet to be retracted within the outriggers. When the load is wider than the outrigger opening, the forks—extended to pick up and raise the load—are withdrawn to a position directly over the outriggers for traveling. This method of retraction is called "up and over." It requires additional maneuvering space and/or first-level pallet-rack opening height to store or pick up pallets. Depending upon load size, the load is positioned approximately over the centerline of the outrigger wheels. When the load

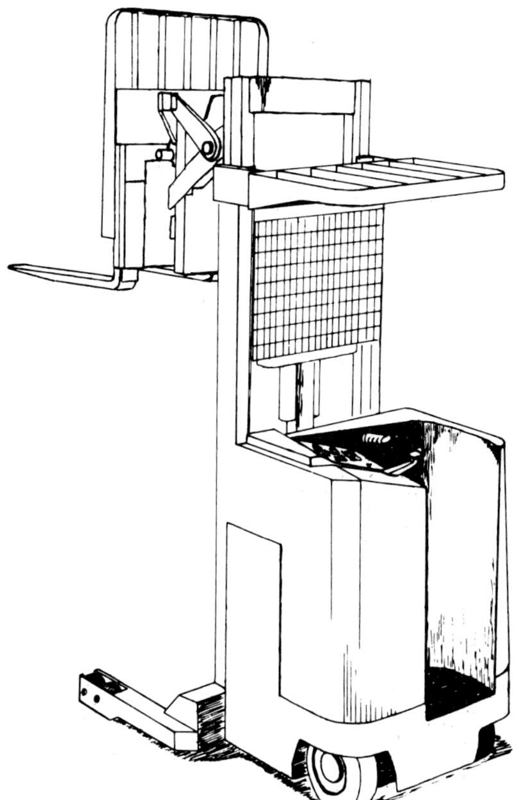

Figure 15.14. Typical reach narrow-aisle truck. *(The Sims Consulting Group, Inc.)*

is extended, the truck's stability depends upon its counterbalance capability and the width of its outriggers.

Two types of outrigger wheels are available. One type uses a single 5-inch-tread by 12-inch-diameter wheel in each outrigger arm. These wheels are suitable for applications where the load will be retracted within the outriggers. Their advantage lies in their ability to negotiate uneven floors and floor cracks better than the second wheel arrangement.

The second type uses dual 4-inch-tread by 5-inch-diameter caster-type wheels in each outrigger arm. These wheels are slightly larger than the height of the outrigger, but they do not extend above the top of the outrigger. The top remains flush. When loads larger than the outrigger spacing make up-and-over retraction necessary, these small dual casters minimize the lift height required to retract a load over the outriggers for traveling.

The major advantage the reach has over the standard straddle truck is that it does not have to straddle the floor load when stacking other loads above it, nor does it require a beam mounted on the floor, as in pallet-rack storage, to raise pallets for insertion of the outriggers.

Double-reach trucks provide additional pantograph extension of a second pallet-load depth beyond the front of the outriggers. This additional extension permits the truck to be used for storing loads two pallets deep (Figure 15.15).

Two dimensions are critical to this double-depth application: the reach distance of the pantograph mechanism and the dimension of the load backrest or pantograph throat. These two dimensions determine the procedure that must be used to execute the double-deep storage procedure.

To handle pallets, the straddles of the double-reach truck must either fit around the bottom of the pallet on the floor, or under a pallet resting on a rack beam mounted 6 to 8 inches above the floor. The front load is stored in the normal manner: the truck is driven to the rack and the load is placed in the first storage position.

To place the load in the second position, however, the double-reach truck must be driven up to the rack with the mast assembly close to the support beam. If the pantograph (scissor) mechanism is designed to extend the second load without a double bite, the load can be placed in the second position by fully extending the forks from this position.

When the pantograph in its fully extended position is not long enough to place the load back far enough on the rack beams to place a second pallet in front of it, a double-bite procedure is used. The operator backs the truck out just far enough to permit the truck to pick up the initial load a second time and position it back an extra 12 inches or less, as needed. To avoid the need for this double-bite procedure, the thrust mechanism must extend two pallet lengths.

The dimension of the backrest affects the storage-rack window. The pallet-rack opening must have enough clearance to permit extension of the pantograph mechanism to the rear position. Storage space not needed to accommodate material dimensions will be wasted because of equipment access requirements if the load height is not at least as high as the backrest dimension.

Swing-mast trucks retain the side-loading and counterbalance features of the turret trucks described under very narrow aisle designs, but they rotate the mast assembly rather than the fork assembly. Because these designs limit rotation to right-hand loading, the operator must exit the aisle and turn the truck for storage or retrieval from the opposite side (Figure 15.16). These trucks closely resemble counterbalanced trucks and can operate in narrow, 5- to 8-foot aisles. However, the additional weight of the rotating mast requires substantially higher truck capacity to achieve the same load-carrying capacity as a counterbalanced truck.

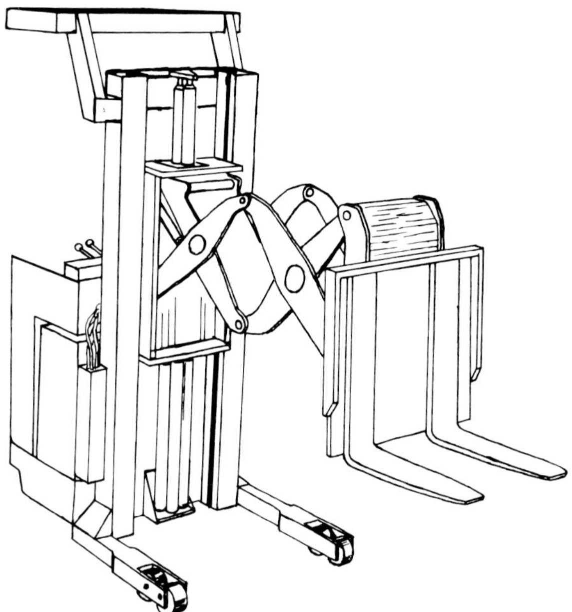

Figure 15.15. Typical double-reach truck. *(The Sims Consulting Group, Inc.)*

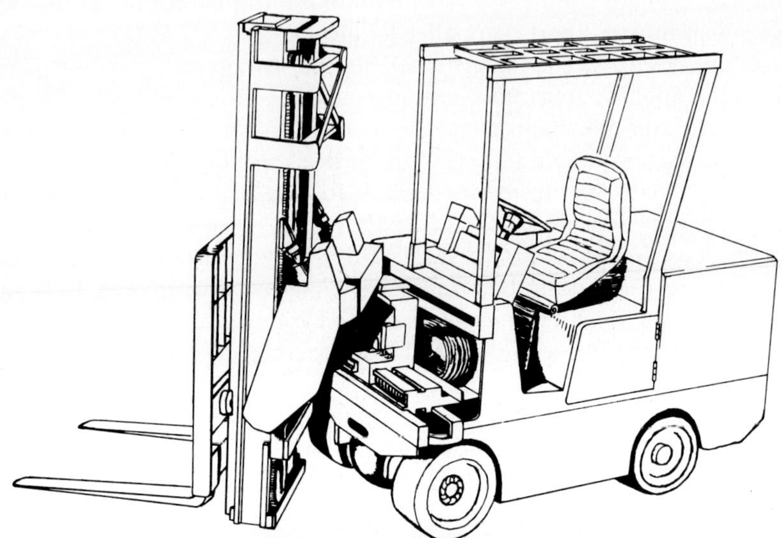

Figure 15.16. Typical swing-mast truck. *(The Sims Consulting Group, Inc.)*

Very Narrow Aisle Trucks. Very narrow aisle trucks use side-loading turret forks that rotate loads perpendicular to aisle travel to store loads. These trucks are used for storing loads at heights of 30 to 42 feet.

Turret trucks combine characteristics of side-loading and counterbalanced trucks. Designed with a long wheelbase for stability, turret designs position the batteries and operator at the rear to counterbalance load weight at high lift heights. The mast width also extends nearly the full width of the truck (Figure 15.17). These trucks perform three basic load movements: lift, which raises the load to the desired height; rotation, which turns the load to face either right or left of the travel direction; and traverse, which moves the load side to side during storage and retrieval in pallet racks.

The turret head comes in two configurations: J and L. The J configuration was designed to facilitate turning loads in working aisles. Its overhead support mechanism restricts the ultimate lift height of trucks using this J mechanism. The throat dimensions of its head also restrict height, and its more massive support structure increases the suspended weight sufficiently to decrease load capacity in comparison with other turret fork designs.

The L-head design has achieved greater acceptance. Its lack of throat restriction makes it suitable for handling variable-height loads. Its lower overall height also permits higher load storage than is possible with J-head designs.

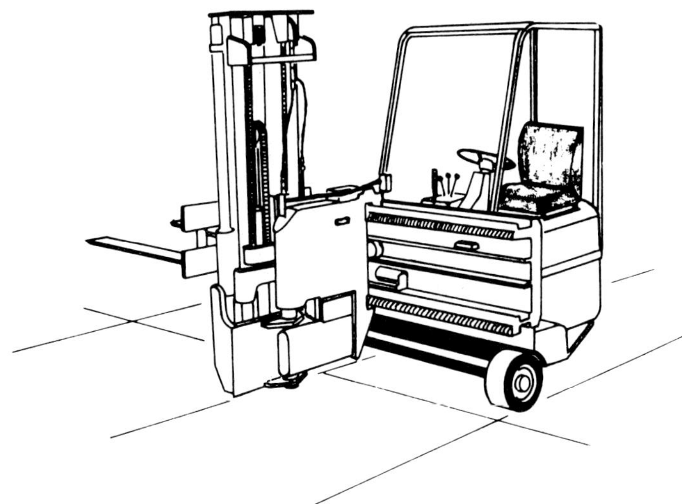

Figure 15.17. Man-down turret truck. *(The Sims Consulting Group, Inc.)*

Rotating loads within aisles requires synchronizing fork rotation and traverse mechanisms. Most truck controls make this synchronization easy. Though it can be done, rotating the load while moving is not advised. Rotating loads within aisles also requires greater aisle width, unless the rotation can be made using a void pallet-rack opening. The actual aisle size needed depends upon the design of the fork rotation and traverse mechanisms, the diagonal dimension of the load, and the relative width and length of the load.

Man-up turret trucks provide an operator platform at the front of the truck. This platform position permits the operator to use the vehicle for order-picking as well as pallet storage and retrieval (Figure 15.18). From his or her position, the operator can observe storage and retrieval operations without relying on guide marks or shelf height selectors to indicate when the pallet is positioned correctly.

To balance the platform and operator weight and to ensure operator safety, the mast designs of man-up trucks use additional bracing to increase stability and reduce uncontrolled deflection. These configurations include mast supports, balanced reaction chains, and changes in mast geometry and construction.

Side loaders are designed primarily for special types of load handling and load configurations (Figure 15.19). The most common side loaders handle long, heavy, metal products such as pipe, bar stock, plate, shapes, sheets, flats, and so on. These vehicles generally operate in guided aisles. They can reach storage heights of 30 to 36 feet (Figure 15.20).

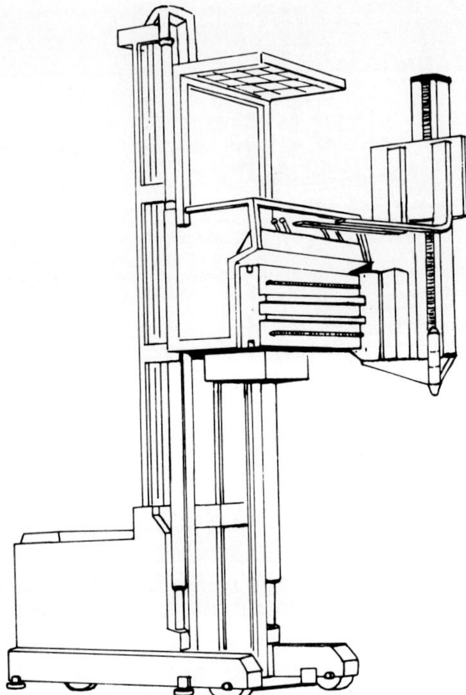

Figure 15.18. Typical man-up turret truck. *(The Sims Consulting Group, Inc.)*

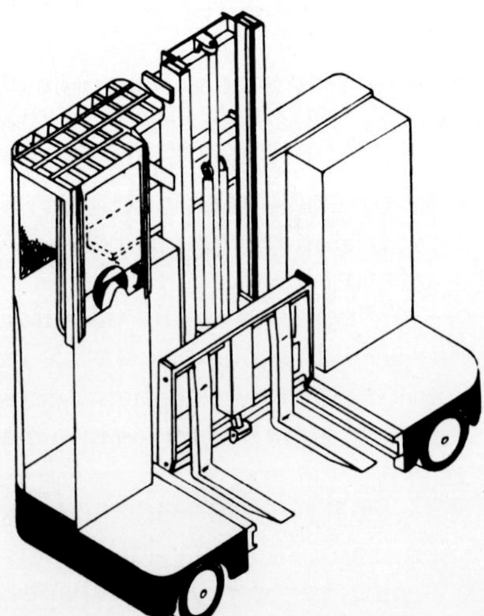

Figure 15.19. Typical side-loader truck. *(The Sims Consulting Group, Inc.)*

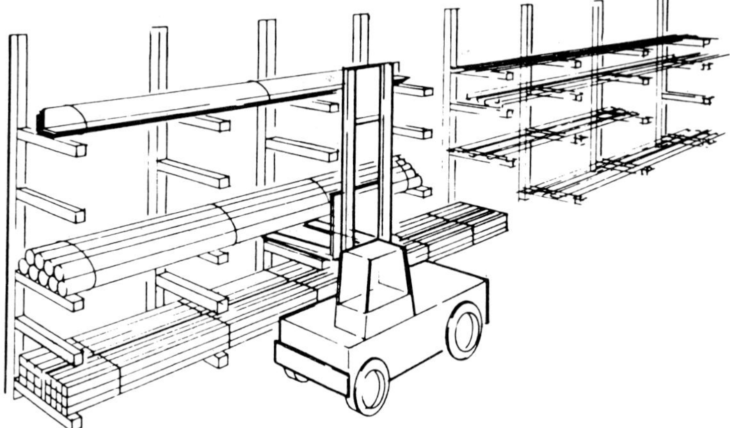

Figure 15.20. Side-loader long-load storage. *(The Sims Consulting Group, Inc.)*

The four-directional (4D) lift truck functions on the same principal as the conventional reach truck and side loader (Figure 15.21). Because these trucks are massive, they use a rail guidance system, rather than a wire system. Their lift capacity ranges from 3000 to 4000 pounds, to well over 10,000 pounds, using either a single-person down or up, or a two-person team-up arrangement for handling individual long-piece storage and retrieval operations (Figure 15.22).

High-lift storage/retrieval machines combine fork truck and automated storage and retrieval technology. They operate on alternating current power-fed through a top guide and collector rail within storage aisles and on self-contained batteries outside these aisles. This guided-

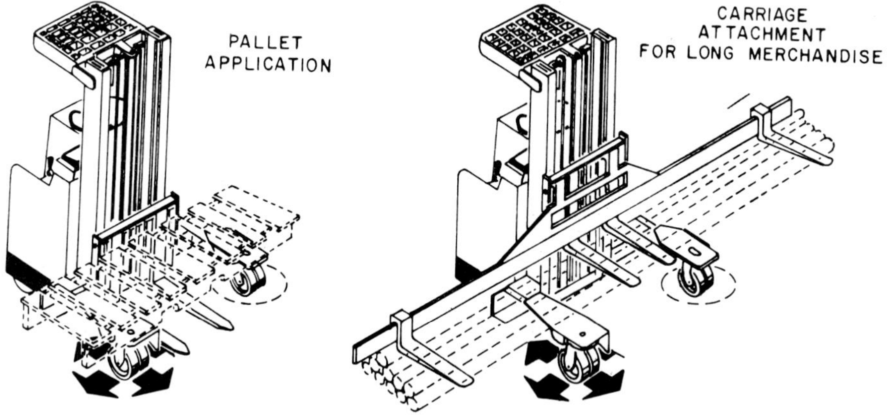

Figure 15.21. Four-directional fork truck. *(The Sims Consulting Group, Inc.)*

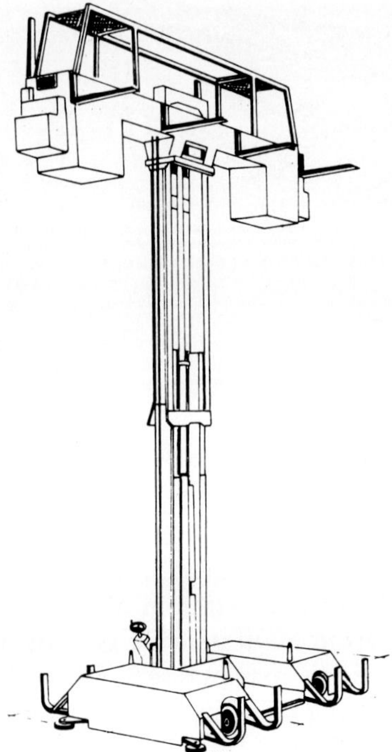

Figure 15.22. Two-operator side loader. *(The Sims Consulting Group, Inc.)*

aisle, AC-powered arrangement permits these trucks to operate at speeds in excess of 400 feet per minute within the aisles. Simultaneous aisle travel and lifting or lowering can be performed in the aisle to reduce cycle time and increase productivity. These simultaneous movement benefits are usually unavailable in turret designs operated at heights above 6 feet.

S/R machine trucks use a shuttle-table mechanism, rather than a fork mechanism inserted into the pallet void, to store and retrieve pallets. This shuttle mechanism simplifies the mechanics of storage and retrieval. It permits direct movement of pallet loads across an aisle without rotation or shifting forks from side to side (Figures 15.23 and 15.24).

Like other man-up designs, S/R machine trucks raise the operator with the load, providing order-picking capability as well as direct visibility and control of storage or retrieval operations. Some designs can handle storage heights up to 60 feet. Yet they are more versatile than dedicated-aisle AS/R machines.

The characteristics of the rider vehicles above are summarized in Table 15.2, which emphasizes their ability to meet the criteria provided in the selection guidelines discussed at the beginning of this section on rider trucks.

Engineering Data

The following engineering information provides the theoretical justification and the formulas needed for making correct engineering choices among the alternative designs discussed above.

Lift Capacity. Technically, *lift capacity* (loadlift) is the moment, created by opposing forces on opposite sides of a fulcrum, expressed in inch pounds. It expresses the weight-distance relationship between the load

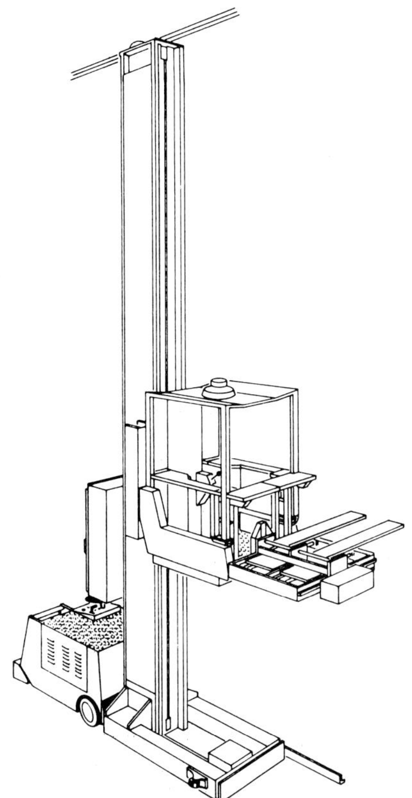

Figure 15.23. High-lift S/R machine (single mast). *(The Sims Consulting Group, Inc.)*

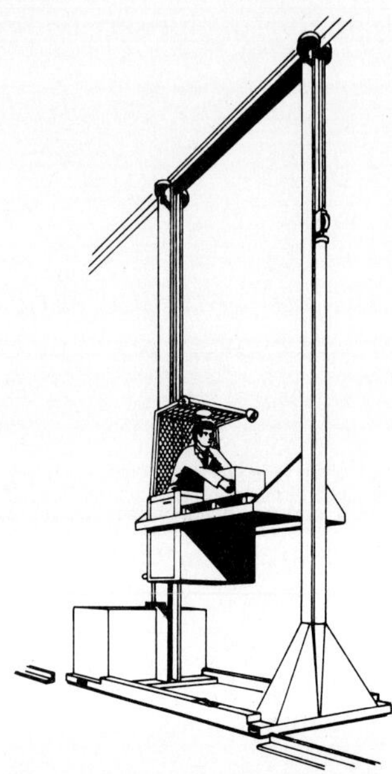

Figure 15.24. High-lift S/R machine (double mast). *(The Sims Consulting Group, Inc.)*

being lifted and the rear, counterbalanced weight of the truck. This fulcrum at the centerline of the front axle is the point about which the load moment resists the forward tipping of the truck.

The manufacturer's calculated lift capacity is not necessarily based on this fulcrum. It is based, instead, upon the load weight and its center of gravity relative to the lifting mechanism of the lift truck. The load center is the distance from the face of the forks to the load's center of gravity. This method of basing lift capacity on LC has become the industrial truck industry's standard.

The LC standard for the industry is 24 inches, which is half the load length of a 48-inch pallet. This standard load configuration affects the manufacturers' design specifications. For this reason, specific load configuration should be discussed with the manufacturer before making purchase decisions. Specific issues to investigate are load weight, load size, truck footprint, lift height, mast fore and aft tilt, and front-end attachments.

The lift capacity specified by manufacturers is the standard LC for the basic truck without attachments and extended high lifts. Using this standard 24-inch LC, a truck with a capacity of 3000 pounds is rated to

Table 15.2. Summary of Powered Lift-Truck Performance Characteristics

	Lift capacity range, lb	Storage-aisle width, ft*	Lift height, in	Lift speed, ft/min	Travel speed, mph	Grade clearance, %
Sit-down counterbalanced	2000–10,000	12–15	264	70	6.0	35
Stand-up counterbalanced	2000–6000	10–12	240	65	5.0	35
Straddle	2000–6000	7–9	252	60	5.3	15
Reach	2000–5000	7–9	360	50	5.5	15
Turret	3000–4000	5–7	480	75	5.5	—†
Man-up turret	3000–4000	5–6	480	50	5.5	—†
Side loader	2000–10,000	5–8	432	50	5.0	20
Swing mast	2000–10,000	5–6	360	50	6.4	15
4-D directional	2000–3000	6	204	40	4.5	12
Hybrid	2000–4000	5	600	60	5.5	—†
Order-picker	2000–4000	4	264	30	2.9	15

* Aisle width determined by specific load size and handling method
† Not designed for use in applications other than super-flat floors

safely lift an evenly distributed weight of 3000 pounds at a 48-inch load length. If the load configuration is increased in weight or size, the capacity should be recalculated to ensure that operation does not exceed the rated stability, creating an operational hazard.

Unless stated, the lifting capacity is based upon single-mast construction, with a fork elevated height (FEH) of 12 to 15 feet. Higher lifts downrate the stated lifting capacity. The data for downrating capacity is covered in a section that follows.

The equation for calculating the effect of load changes on rated lift capacity is based on the moment of the load in relation to the fulcrum:

$$L = WA \tag{15.1}$$

where L = load moment in in·lb
W = weight of load in·lb
A = distance from the fulcrum (centerline of the front axle) to the center of gravity of the load on the fork

As an example, assume a truck rated 3000 pounds using a standard 24-inch load center. The distance from the load's face to the truck carriage is 24 inches, and from the carriage to the center of the front axles (fulcrum) an additional 12 inches.

$$A = 24 \text{ in} + 12 \text{ in} = 36 \text{ in}$$
$$L = WA = 36 \text{ in} \times 3000 \text{ lb}$$
$$= 108{,}000 \text{ in}\cdot\text{lb}$$

If the pallet length is increased from 49 to 60 inches, the safe lifting capacity is changed. This extended load has an LC of 30 inches. Again, the distance from the carriage to the fulcrum must be added.

$$A' = 39 \text{ in} + 12 \text{ in} = 42 \text{ in}$$

Since the allowable capacity of the truck remains 108,000 inch pounds, $L = WA$ must also equal $L' = W'A'$.

$$L = L' = 108{,}000 \text{ in}\cdot\text{lb}$$
$$L' = W'A' \text{ or } WA = 108{,}000 \text{ in}\cdot\text{lb}$$
$$A' = 42 \text{ in}$$
$$L' = 108{,}000 \text{ in}\cdot\text{lb}$$
$$W' = 108{,}000/42$$
$$W' = 2571 \text{ lb}$$

Though the truck is rated to handle 3000 pounds, the safe capacity for this particular load configuration is 2571 pounds. While this moment calculation is acceptable for approximating lift capacity for load changes, it does not compensate for other factors, such as load tilting and extended lift heights. The affects of these factors on stability must be verified with the manufacturer. Figure 15.10 illustrates the affects of downrating on 2000-, 3000-, and 4000-pound lift trucks as the load center is increased.

Many manufacturers do include other stability factors in determining the safety rating of their trucks. These factors include:

1. *Longitudinal running.* The distance required to stop safely while carrying a load 12 inches above the floor
2. *Longitudinal stacking.* The ability to handle elevated loads safely while making sudden stops at low speeds
3. *Lateral running.* The ability to negotiate quick directional changes safely while traveling empty and with a load 12 inches above the floor
4. *Lateral stacking.* The combined factors of the ability to stack high loads safely and of the affects of slightly sloped floors on stability

All possible safety precautions cannot be built into any truck. Other safety considerations include wheelbase, tire tread, size and type of mast and frame, and fork deflection. All these factors must be considered in designing the truck. But if the margin of maneuverability, stability, and capacity is exceeded, the vehicle will be unsafe. The operator remains responsible for safe operation of the truck. Providing proper operating instructions initially and on a continuing basis is extremely important.

Any device other than standard tapered forks and a low carriage backrest attached to or forward from the mast becomes an attachment that must be considered in setting safe operating limits. These attachments—designed for special or improved load handling, placing, or positioning—directly affect the load center and reduce the rated capacity. This effect can be calculated. Purchasing specifications must reflect this downrated capacity or a truck with a standard capacity larger than the required minimum must be purchased.

The following equation can be used as a planning guide to calculate the derated lift capacity of a specific truck:

$$W' = \frac{L - D_1 P_1}{A'} \tag{15.2}$$

where W' = load weight in pounds that can be handled safely with the attachment

L = load moment in in·lb

D_1 = additional distance beyond the original LC from the front axle's centerline to the attachment's center of gravity, in in

P_1 = additional weight of the attachment beyond the weight used in the original calculation in lb

A' = distance from the front axle's centerline to centerline of the load held by the attachment in in

The derating for the same 3000-pound lift truck used in the first derating example, adjusted for a side-shift attachment, which adds an additional 4 inches to the LC and an additional 500 pounds of weight to the truck carriage, is calculated below.

$$L = 108{,}000 \text{ in}\cdot\text{lb (from the first example)}$$

$$D_a P_a = 4 \times 500 = 2000 \text{ in}\cdot\text{lb}$$

$$A' = 40 \text{ in}$$

$$W' = \frac{108{,}000 - 2000}{40} = \frac{106{,}000}{40} = 2650 \text{ lb}$$

The added weight and length of the attachment reduced the truck's capacity from 3000 to 2650 pounds.

Though they may be considered standard equipment, each attachment has a downrating affect upon lifting capacity. Common attachments generally considered standard equipment are: side shifters, fork grippers, rams, revolving carriages, put-and-take devices, push-pull devices, and devices or clamps for handling special goods, such as cartons, drums, paper spools, and bales.

Because many manufacturers use the same frame for a family or series of lift trucks with various capacities, a 2500-pound capacity truck may share the same frame and footprint as a 3500-pound capacity truck. The counterbalanced weight, of course, will be increased to achieve the rated lifting capacity. This results in relative ease in modifying trucks at the low-lift range of a family that shares a chassis with heavier-rated trucks. A truck in the low-lift range of a series may have its lift height modified with a multilift mast without materially affecting the truck's stability as long as the truck is operated within the design safety parameters set by the change. If the truck is in the upper range of a series with a shared chassis, however, the frame of the next larger capacity group should be used for modification.

Right-Angle Stacking. The maneuvering space needed to operate lift trucks effectively is critical in planning and designing materials handling operations in warehouses, assembly plants, and manufacturing facilities. Constraints must be identified early. Making some equipment compromises to gain optimum space utilization and equipment performance may be necessary to achieve effective operations. Major issues in these compromises are right-angle stacking and cross-aisle requirements. In both of these cases, space and performance requirements may be traded to effectively achieve operating requirements without creating barriers and damaging product and equipment.

For planning purposes, right-angle stacking and cross-aisle maneuvering calculations are based on the following three dimensions:

1. Truck turning radii
2. Truck frame configuration
3. Unit load length and width

All trucks have two turning radii, which vary with the type of truck and the steering mechanism. The outside radius is the measure of the overall swing of the truck frame to the furthest part of the rear frame, or extended coupling attachment on the rear frame, in relation to the pivot point of the inside radius. On a two-rear-wheel steering truck, the pivot point of the inside radius is 3 to 4 inches outside the truck drive wheels. These trucks usually cannot pivot within their own footprints. They maneuver slightly around an outside circle.

Both radii should be obtained from the manufacturer when calculating or sizing aisle requirements. Since rear-steering trucks have less wheel weight and, consequently, tend to slip sidewise slightly when maneuvering right-angle turns, the outside radius should be specified for loaded trucks at lift capacity, with the load raised about 6 inches above the floor. Since trucks operate loaded about 50 percent of the time, slippage is a realistic operating condition. Therefore, it should be recognized in specifying right-angle aisle-width requirements.

Calculation of right-angle stacking is influenced by several maneuvering factors in addition to size and space relationships of the area. To ensure effective operation, physical tests should be made to verify calculations.

The calculation in Figure 15.25 uses a double rear-steer-wheel counterbalanced truck. This formula also applies to one-wheel, rear-steer counterbalanced trucks that pivot within their own frame footprint. The inside radius for one-wheel trucks is zero, and E is half the width of the truck.

Since the inside radius impacts right-angle stacking requirements only by a few inches, single rear-steer-wheel designs only marginally affect right-angle aisle requirements. For narrow-aisle reach or straddle trucks, right-angle stacking-aisle requirements are smaller than for counterbalanced trucks. These narrow-aisle requirements may be from 3 to 5 feet less than those required by counterbalanced designs. The amount of this variation depends upon truck design, battery compartment, load size, and operating requirements.

The right-angle stacking clearances specified by most narrow-aisle truck manufacturers are rub clearances rather than operating clearances. True operating clearances seldom are specified. To calculate operating clearances, 12 to 18 inches should be added to the calculated aisle rub width or the stated truck clearance requirement. Clearances greater than this are not usually needed.

There are trade-offs between aisle width and truck productivity. Wider aisles usually improve productivity and minimize damage to goods and equipment. For this reason, operational requirements should be reviewed frequently and aisle allowances tailored accordingly.

Cross-Aisle Requirements. Manufacturers usually base cross-aisle requirements on unloaded truck requirements, also. These dimensions can be misleading, since provisions must be made for safe maneuvering of loaded trucks among aisles. For conventional lift trucks, cross aisles should be slightly wider than right-angle aisles. If the aisle is guided, cross-aisle requirements for turret, swing-mast, and hybrid trucks are directly proportional to the truck length, the load length, and the guidance system. Wire-guided systems require an extra 1 to 2 feet of space

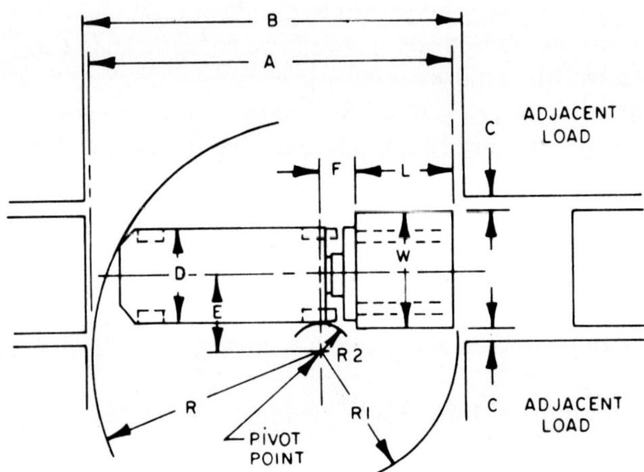

Figure 15.25. Minimum right-angle-stacking aisle requirements calculated for a counterbalanced fork truck. *(The Sims Consulting Group, Inc.)*

Definition:

A = $R + R_1$ = rub aisle width
B = A + 12-in minimum operating aisle width
C = minimum acceptable clearance—4 in between adjacent loads or obstructions
D = overall truck frame width
E = half of D plus R_2
F = centerline of drive/load axle to load against back of forks
R = manufacturer rated outside turning radius from a stop position
$R1 = \sqrt{(F + L)^2 + (W/2 - E)^2}$
$R2$ = manufacturer rated inside turning radius (generally zero for one rear steer wheel
L = pallet load length
W = pallet load width

Example: Given a 4000-lb rated lift capacity of counterbalance truck and a 48-in × 40-in pallet:

E = 24 in
A = 125 in
R = 65 in
$R2$ = 4 in
$R1 = \sqrt{(12 + 48)^2 + (20 - 24)^2} = \sqrt{60^2 + (-4)^2}$
$A = R + R_2 =$ 65 + 60 = 125 in = 10 ft 5 in
B = 125 in + 12 in = 137 in = 11 ft 5 in

at the end of the aisle to align the truck before entering the aisle. Rail systems easily align the truck in the aisle.

Traditionally, cross-aisle systems require 15 to 18 feet to align the truck. Cross and main service aisles should also be wide enough to permit two-way traffic without slowdowns or delays. Two-way aisles should be double the width of the load or truck, whichever is greater, plus a minimum of 18 inches for passing clearance for conventional trucks. Special-purpose trucks often require larger allowances. In any case, the manufacturer should be consulted about proper clearances.

Guided-Aisle Width. In some systems, guided-aisle width requirements may differ depending upon whether the system uses mechanical or electronic control methods. The width requirements and suitability of either system are influenced by the following factors:

1. Physical characteristics of the lift truck, including length, width, and height
2. Type of load handling mechanism used: turret forks, pass-through forks, articulating forks, or carriages
3. Rigidity of the elevated mast assembly
4. Presence or absence of upper-level mast guides
5. Type and size of loads to be stored
6. Storage height
7. Type of guidance system used: mechanical or electronic
8. Compatibility of the vehicle and guidance system voltages
9. Sources of possible electrical interference in electronic guidance systems
10. Flatness and other characteristics of the warehouse floor

Before committing to a guidance system or layout, these factors should be reviewed with both the truck manufacturer and the system supplier. Considering all of these factors in the system design is critical to success. After the guidance system has been installed, operating performance is locked into the system. If the aisles are too narrow or the floor too uneven, trucks cannot operate at design speed. This may reduce performance by 30 to 60 percent. For initial warehouse system designs, only a few of the above factors need to be considered after the guidance system, load size, and type of vehicle have been determined.

Location of guide rails and their relationship to storage racks determine the aisle width of a mechanical system. Rail depth requirements depend upon the type of truck selected and the physical location of the truck guide wheels. If the rails are very large, the base of the pallet rack may need to be recessed to retain a narrow load-handling aisle and ensure rail clearance. The need for and the amount of rack recess in mechanical systems depends upon:

1. Load size
2. Load and mast sway clearance required to travel at the allowable elevated height
3. Upright width and pallet-load overhang of the rack
4. Load traverse or articulation needs

A rule of thumb for rough estimates of aisle width for mechanical systems states that 4 to 6 inches of clearance between the load (or truck) and rack (or load overhang) be provided on each side of the aisle. These same factors apply to selecting an aisle width for electronic guidance systems. However, the clearance on each side of the load preferably should be 6 to 8 inches. This preference for slightly greater clearance in electronic guidance systems stems from the fact that these systems are not rigidly restrained within the aisle as mechanical systems are.

Gradability. *Gradability* is the greatest slope or incline a lift truck can negotiate without considerable loss of forward speed or considerable drain of energy source. This angle of incline, which is stated as a percent, is the tangent of the slope. It is usually between 7 and 25 percent, depending upon the truck design and power source. For a counterbalanced truck, 10 to 12 percent is the accepted grade. For electric reach trucks, the accepted grade is 10 percent or less. Because they have multiple-speed transmissions and more powerful engines, internal combustion–powered trucks can negotiate steeper grader. IC trucks can negotiate inclines between 15 and 25 percent.

Grade Clearance. *Grade clearance* denotes the underframe clearance that controls the degree of change in slope the truck can negotiate without a "hang up" or rub contact between the grade apex and the bottom of the truck frame. This clearance is measured at the lowest part of the frame between the fore and aft wheels. Figure 15.26 shows this truck frame/grade relationship. While this relationship should be verified with the manufacturer, the lowest clearance is directly under the mast. This undermast clearance is usually not as critical as the underframe clearance between the front wheels.

Drawbar Pull. *Drawbar pull* is the amount of effort available to overcome friction and sustain motion when the truck is towing a series of carts. Most manufacturers do not generally recommend using lift trucks to pull carts because the towed weight can pull front wheels of lift trucks off the floor if their forks are not loaded. But loaded trucks do effectively tow carts in a number of warehouse operations.

For regular electric-powered lift trucks, drawbar rating is expressed in nominal capacity loads from 200 to 700 pounds. To convert the nominal weight rating to rolling weight capacity, the drawbar pull is divided by the friction factor, which ranges from 2 to 3 percent. This friction factor varies with the smoothness of the floor and the material composition of the cart wheel tires. Using this formula, the rolling weight capacity ranges from 10,000 to 35,000 pounds.

Tires. Tires for lift trucks come in two basic types: pneumatic and solid. *Pneumatic tires* are inflated with air or filled with a resilient material to provide softer rides and greater traction than solid tires. These industrial tires present an operating casing profile similar to highway truck tires and some passenger car tires. Those tires filled with resilient material resist deflation from puncture while retaining cushion on rough terrain.

Though some pneumatic designs are used for inside operation, most pneumatic industrial tires are for outdoor operation. Those which are used indoors are used where higher speeds are permitted, where cushioning of fragile loads is desired, or where long continuous operation makes driver fatigue a safety and efficiency factor.

Solid tires are made from the same basic materials but have a different structural profile and tread design. Each type and design serves a specific purpose. The two general types are solid cushion and solid. Both

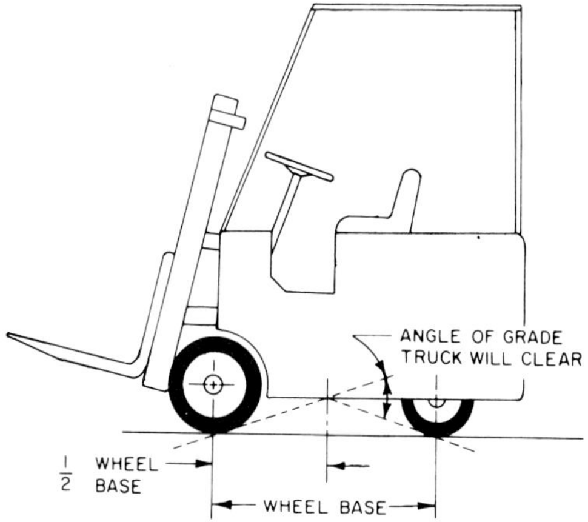

Figure 15.26. Lift truck. *(The Sims Consulting Group, Inc.)*

have a low profile for use with small-diameter tires for which high-stacking truck stability is required. Solid tires are either pressed or cured onto their steel ring, rim, or hub mountings. Bonded to a steel ring, press-on tires are pressed onto the truck wheel. Press-on tires and rings are replaceable. They are used on the drive, steering, and braking wheels, and normally have a tread. Cured-on designs are molded or vulcanized directly to the wheel casing, forming an integral unit that is attached to the axle. When a cured-on tire wears out, the entire wheel must be replaced. They are used for free-rolling wheels and do not normally have a tread.

The following terms are used to identify characteristics of solid tires:

1. *Universal service.* For general-purpose usage, these tires resist chipping and cutting.
2. *Low power consumption with low rolling resistance.* For electric lift trucks to increase battery life.
3. *Oil resistance.* For use where constant contact with oil, grease, or solvent may cause separation, swelling, or excessive cracking of tires.
4. *Static conductors.* For reducing spark hazard in highly explosive environments.
5. *Nonmarking.* For eliminating marks or smudges on floors in special environments, such as showrooms, bakeries, pharmaceutical plants, or hospitals.
6. *Polyurethane.* For its resilience and high resistance to abrasion, this synthetic compound is used in high loading applications.
7. *Shredded wire.* For protection against cutting, chipping, and separation caused by floor hazards, a mixture of short wire lengths are blended with the rubber tread material.
8. *Metal studs.* For improving traction on wet, oily, or icy inclines and ramps.

Motive Power Systems

The two basic power systems for 2000- to 10,000-pound lift trucks are internal combustion engines and electric motors. Trucks with internal combustion power systems are fueled by gasoline, diesel, or liquified petroleum gas. Gasoline engines usually have four or six cylinders and are water cooled. Diesel engines, though similar, are equipped with fuel injection systems, while LPG-powered systems are usually gasoline engines converted to operate using liquified petroleum gas. In all of these systems, the engines are connected to the drive wheels through either a manual transmission or fluid torque converter (automatic transmission).

Electric systems use lead-acid industrial traction storage batteries to power electric motors, which supply drive power. These batteries may be rated both by voltage and ampere-hours, or kilowatthours. Ampere-hours capacity ranges from 200 to 1800 ampere-hours over 6 hours of continuous use. These drive motors may operate on 12, 24, 36, 48, or 72 volts. The 72-volt systems use two 36-volt batteries in series. In all of these designs, the motor's speed is controlled by a motor controller circuit. Additional motors often power other functions, such as the hydraulic, tilting, lifting, steering, and attachment systems.

In evaluating these systems for feasibility in a specific plant application, four factors must be considered:

1. Economy of both purchase price and operating costs
2. Performance
3. Environment
4. Type of truck

Selecting the type of power depends upon the environment and the operating characteristic of the facility. For long, continuous operating periods outside or inside well-ventilated facilities, diesel systems are most economical. Gas- or LPG-powered trucks can also perform the same functions in these same environments. These internal combustion engines are usually used where long runs at high speeds are required. They perform more effectively on rough terrain than electric-powered trucks, especially if 10 percent grades must be climbed regularly.

To size the engine, the gross lifting requirements must be determined. The maximum gross load weight must be matched with the truck's lift capacity to safely meet lifting needs. This figure is used in determining the power required to accelerate and maintain safe speed and maneuverability within the operating environment and to comply with hazardous operating conditions that exist.

Although engines are usually rated in horsepower, the torque output is the prime factor in selecting an engine for an industrial truck. *Torque* is the amount of force the engine can exert upon the flywheel; *horsepower* measures the amount of work the engine can provide in a given period of time. Weight and distance units, such as foot pounds, are used to express torque. An engine rated as having 100 foot pounds of torque exerts 100 pounds of rotational force 1 foot from the center of the flywheel. This torque figure indicates the true amount of energy available to drive the unit after energy losses from friction and cooling are deducted from the operating characteristics.

LPG-Fueled Internal Combustion Engines. Of the internal combustion options, LPG-fueled engines are least well understood. The liquified petroleum gas used is commonly a mixture of propane and butane derived from natural gas. This colorless, odorless fuel weighs about 4.46 pounds per gallon. Odor additives are used to provide a method of easily recognizing escaping gas.

Two types of fuel tanks are available: detachable ICC types and permanently attached ASME types. Quantities of full tanks, equipped with quick-connect fittings, can be delivered to the truck operation area where empty ICC tanks can be quickly exchanged for full ones. Trucks with ASME-type tanks must be driven to a bulk fueling station located, by law, usually a minimum of 50 feet from all permanent facilities. This need for separation causes travel problems, since most trucks need refueling once per shift. Both drivers and trucks are nonproductive during this refueling process, and queueing of trucks at the refueling station can create additional time losses. ASME-equipped trucks that run out of fuel while in service must be towed to the fueling station.

Engines designed originally for LPG have a higher compression ratio than converted gasoline designs. The LPG engine's efficiency results from the fact that vaporized gas directly reaches the air fuel manifold. Gasoline-fueled designs convert liquid fuel into vapor, which is fed into the air fuel manifold—a step eliminated in LPG designs.

LPG systems also have simple carburetion systems and solenoid valves that cut off all fuel when these engines stop. The combined vaporizer-pressure regulator ensures vaporization and controls pressure at the carburetor. LPG systems may be designed for either liquid or vapor withdrawal during operation. When operation occurs over a wide ambient temperature range, the liquid withdrawal designs are best, since the engine heat, rather than air temperature, is used to aid vaporization.

LPG designs have both of these advantages as well as disadvantages. These are shown in Table 15.3.

Battery-Powered Trucks. The low-voltage, direct-current (DC) motor in battery-powered trucks uses a storage battery. The rating of these motors is based upon the torque produced for a given voltage and current draw, rather than upon horsepower. Compared to IC engines, these battery-powered designs provide relatively low horsepower output. The horsepower rating of an electric-drive motor for a 4000-pound truck may be about 4½ horsepower, while a similar-capacity IC truck may provide 40 horsepower.

Only heavy-duty industrial engines with an overload capacity rating of about 500 percent are designed for use in industrial trucks. To ensure sufficient torque for momentary surges, these designs provide more than 10 times the torque needed to move the fully loaded truck on a level grade. A continuously variable silicon-controlled rectifier control system varies the effective power delivered to the motor. This control regulates the torque to produce a much smoother change in vehicle speed than any form of gear shifting.

Electric-Truck Battery Selection. Good battery selection depends largely upon voltage and ampere-hour rating tailored to equipment characteristics and operating environment. Voltage expresses the unit of electrical potential or the pressure from a complete circuit from the battery to the load and back to the battery. Voltage requirements relate directly to truck speed, while ampere-hour rating relates to the length of operating time required. This relationship of volts to amperes needed for a sustained period of rated use may also be shown in kilowatthours. This kilowatthour calculation multiplies the volts times amperes times hours of available use and divides this figure by 1000. However, the most commonly used measure remains ampere-hours.

A typical lead-acid traction battery is made up of cells nominally rated at 2 volts per cell. An 18-cell battery is rated at 36 volts. However, some disagreement exists about the accuracy of this 2-volt rating as a practical measurement, since the operating voltage generally varies from 1.6 to 1.7 volts per fully charged cell. In a discharged state, voltage can drop to 1.2 volts per cell.

Current transfer from the battery through the motor is measured in amperes at a steady draw. Because the rate at which this draw can be sustained depends upon truck activity, battery ratings are stated in terms of 1 ampere flow per hour. If usage requires a battery that discharges at a rate of 125 amperes over a period of six hours, a battery with a

Table 15.3. Advantages and Disadvantages of LPG-Powered Designs

Advantages	Disadvantages
1. More complete combustion because the fuel enters the engine in gaseous state.	1. Increased fuel costs in some areas.
2. Reduction of crankcase oil dilution since no liquid enters the engine.	2. Greater initial equipment costs.
3. Increased engine life and reduced fuel-caused engine deposits.	3. Handling and storage of empty and refueled tanks increase both labor costs and safety hazards.
4. Greater engine efficiency because the fuel is higher octane rated and the combustion more complete.	
5. Reduced fuel costs in some areas.	

750-ampere usable capacity must be used. Effective operating capacity is usually measured to a discharge state not less than 20 percent of capacity. To have 750 amperes usable battery capacity, then, a battery with a 900-ampere rated capacity is needed. A 950-ampere-rated battery is better. Lift-truck manufacturers recommend that batteries not be operated below the 80 percent discharge level. Use below this point can strain the electrical system enough to damage circuits.

Two methods are used to avoid over-discharging batteries. One uses an ampere-hour meter to monitor power consumed and indicate the amount of power remaining above the 80 percent discharge level. At the 80 percent level, a light alerts the driver to take the truck to the battery recharging area for recharging or battery exchange. This meter, which measures battery discharge, operates much like a fuel gauge. The second method involves installing a low-voltage cutout in the lifting circuit that prevents the operator from raising the forks when the battery reaches the 80 percent discharge level. The operator uses the remaining power to return to the battery recharging area.

Battery Chargers. Three types of battery chargers are available: motor-generator (MG), ferroresonant, and pulsed units. MG-type chargers use a drive motor turning a generator to supply the charging voltage and current required. These units are rarely used except for special conditions.

The most widely used units for traction batteries are ferroresonant chargers. These units taper the charge, beginning with an initial high rate of charge that is gradually reduced as the battery becomes fully charged. Until disconnected, these units maintain a trickle charge.

Pulsed units supply maximum voltage until the battery is fully charged, then drop suddenly to a low preset level until the battery is disconnected. These units start again, delivering short bursts of charge on a repeating charge cycle if the battery is not disconnected.

In all cases, charger ratings must be compatible with the battery being charged. Specific chargers or ratings are usually specified by the truck or battery supplier according to application.

Battery Charging Area Planning Requirements. Two basic requirements should be emphasized when designing the battery charging area:

1. What are the equipment requirements?
2. What are the safety requirements?

To answer the first of these questions, the size or projected size of the truck fleet, the shifts of operation, and the locations must all be determined. The issues to consider include:

1. The number of truck positions to park at each charger
2. The number of shifts the trucks will operate
3. The most effective position for battery charge equipment for efficient removal or reinsertion of batteries using carts, cranes, or roll-out/roll-in conveyors if the area must provide service more than one shift
4. Special floor treatment and controlled floor drains to resist acid spill damage or pollution
5. The utilities required to clean the area and maintain the batteries

The answer to the second question requires the following:

1. Proper ventilation to reduce hazardous gas buildup
2. Deluge shower and eyewash equipment
3. Marking of nonsmoking areas
4. Safety clothing and eye protection

Though this last list is short, these items cannot be ignored for ethical as well as legal reasons.

16
Unit Load Conveyors

James M. Cahill, PCMH
Regional Manager, Rapistan, A Lear Siegler Company, Oak Brook, Illinois

Introduction

The most common conveyors found in warehouses are referred to as "unit load handling conveyors" and include roller, wheel, belt, live roller, chain, and others. These conveyors are used to transport a definable shape in a fixed path. The definable shape may be a carton, pallet, or other fixed-dimension article. The selection of which type of conveyor to use is based on both the characteristics of the product or products to be conveyed and the system requirements. In this section, we will concentrate on the equipment selection based on the product carried and the design considerations of the equipment.

Initial Design Considerations

Since unit loads are conveyed with the product surface in contact with the conveyor, the characteristics of the products govern the equipment selection. In both hardware selection and systems design, the first step should always be to describe what is to be conveyed. This description should include dimensions, weight, surface (hard or soft), handling rate, wrap (ties, bands, stretch, etc.), flaps, overhang, center of gravity, and so on. All products should be listed; smallest and largest, heaviest and lightest, sealed and unsealed. As we will see in the discussion of equipment design, it is not always the heaviest or largest product that influences the design: it may be the light product that will not actuate sensors or the small product that influences the selection of belt or roller conveyor. Also, the *range* of product sizes and weights influences equipment designs, particularly in the consideration of gravity versus power; or, in the selection of certain types of accumulation conveyor, the weight range alone has an effect on this decision. Although it may not be practical to design the system or select the hardware to handle all products, they should all be considered at this time. A decision will then have to be made based on the cost of more sophisticated equipment. Remember, the main system does not have to handle all products. It may be more economical to use secondary systems or even manual handling to accommodate unusual or seldom-encountered products. Consideration at this point of all products and their characteristics may result in minor system changes or the use of subsystems that will ultimately provide a more universal warehouse with a better payback.

It is also important to consider future requirements at this point. Check with the marketing department for new product designs or packaging; the sales department for activity rates and storage requirements; the manufacturing department for changes in processes or suppliers; and finally, management for its viewpoint on future implementation of this data and its effect on the warehouse. These future requirements should be considered in two ways: those that affect the basic equipment design and those that will require future modifications or additions. An example of a future requirement that affects the basic design is the characteristic of the product that will require larger or heavier conveyor equipment. As previously described, the conveyor is designed to handle the full range of products, and a larger product or a much smaller product may not be conveyable on the equipment selected. Examples of future hardware and system modifications to be considered are going from nonpowered to powered conveyor, increasing speeds, increasing sortation points or storage lanes, and even reversing the flow of conveyors. All of these can be accomplished when the future requirements are planned in the initial design. Attention to this additional detail at this point may offer better overall system payback in the future and possibly even prevent the initial system from having to be scrapped and replaced by a more sophisticated system.

In this initial planning stage, there are several other factors that must be considered before the actual equipment selection and design begins. Some of these are existing systems (material handling, storage, manufacturing, etc.), environment (temperature, air quality, noise, etc.), energy (availability and conservation), safety, maintenance, and management information systems. In the initial planning phase of the project, it is necessary to gather data in all of these areas. When we discuss the actual hardware features, we will review how this information affects equipment selection. At this point, we will provide only a brief overview of each of these areas.

All new conveyors must interface with some type of existing material handling practices and equipment. In some facilities, that is a simple system of manual interfaces or the use of fork trucks. In more sophisticated facilities, it may be robots, wire-guided vehicles, or stacker cranes. These existing systems will affect both the equipment selection and the system layout, particularly at the interface points. The storage media also affects equipment design. Whether you select simple bin storage or static racks or more complex flow racks and automated storage/retrieval (AS/RS) systems, the new conveyor system must be designed to move product to and from these storage areas within the space allocations and at the rate required. Also, in the manufacturing area, the new conveyor system must move product to and from machines while allowing for operator interfaces, machine maintenance, and so on.

The environment is also a critical concern. Most warehouses operate with limited heat/air conditioning and light. Temperature extremes must be considered in equipment selection, particularly for belting, bearings, and drive units. Although the warehouse is usually a relatively clean environment, the conveyor system may have to interface with a clean room or, at the other extreme, a foundry or other extreme environment. Some products must be quarantined because of health concerns, safety, or security, and this will have to be designed into both the conveyor system and the storage areas. Over the past few years, the effect of continual exposure to higher noise levels has brought about government regulations specifying allowable noise limits. This is always a problem in systems because of the effects of surrounding building features and other equipment that combine to create the final noise level. Although the noise level of the conveyor in a warehouse is usually not as critical as in an office or in operator-intense manufacturing areas such as inspection or assembly, the conveyors still must meet government standards.

Determining the available type and quantity of energy is usually not difficult. However, planning for a new facility or a remodeled existing facility usually includes consideration of energy conservation. This not only includes electricity to operate drive motors, but also for heat and light, which do not have the same high-level requirements in a warehouse as in manufacturing.

Although most conveyors are designed with safety a prime concern, the proper application and selection of equipment is also necessary for a safe conveyor installation. Compliance with safety standards, including those established by OSHA and other federal, state, and local regulatory agencies, is usually the responsibility of the owner of the conveyor equipment. The final determination of guards and other safety equipment is determined by the location of the conveyors and the use of the equipment. Safety should, therefore, be considered in the initial system design to minimize unsafe conditions, then reviewed in the final system design for placement of guards and other safety devices.

All material handling systems require some degree of maintenance. In a gravity system, maintenance usually consists of periodic inspection to make sure that rollers are turning and the product is moving satisfactorily on the conveyor. In the more sophisticated systems, it consists of scheduled preventive actions as prescribed by the manufacturer. Warehouses have historically been a problem maintenance area. Companies recognize the necessity of assigning maintenance personnel to manufacturing in order to keep expensive machines running, but seldom recognize the same requirement in the warehouse. In the initial planning stage, maintenance must be considered and budgeted for as a part of the cost of purchasing a sophisticated material handling system. Maintenance requirements should also be one of the factors considered in the evaluation and selection of the system and the hardware.

The new conveyor system will interface with some sort of management information system. This system may consist of simple move tags that identify the area in which the load is to be manually removed from the conveyor, or it may be a fully computer-controlled system that reports to a central host computer. The level of control sophistication, the source of conveyor decisions, and the quantity of reports generated by the system are all considerations that should be addressed prior to design of the conveyor control system. In many cases, this also affects the choice of vendors for both the design of this management information system and the engineering of the conveyor control system. If there is no in-house capability in these areas, a company may choose to use a consultant to evaluate the requirements and help with these decisions.

Obviously, all the preceding is not necessary to purchase one piece of gravity conveyor, but many of these considerations apply even in that simple example. Most cases in which conveyor purchases have become "white elephants" have been the result of a lack of information, rather than too much information.

Gravity Conveyor

As mentioned previously, our attention will be given to the selection of conveyor hardware and its features, rather than the system design.

According to the "20 Principals of Material Handling," published by the College Industry Council on Material Handling Education, "utilize gravity to move material wherever possible, while respecting limitations concerning safety, product damage, and loss." In addition to the obvious cost advantage of gravity conveyor, it is easy to set up and to add onto or change the layout. As mentioned in the "principal," its major limitations are safety and product damage. Unfortunately, there are two pitches necessary in applying gravity conveyor: the pitch necessary to start the load from stop and the pitch necessary to keep the load moving. Obviously, it is not possible to have two pitches on the same conveyor; therefore, the resulting pitch is usually a compromise between the steeper starting pitch and the less steep running pitch. There are two areas in which this is particularly a problem: (1) when the pitch is set for a light load and a heavier load is placed on a conveyor, or (2) when a second load catches up with the first load because of the lower friction of the rotating rollers, started by the first load. In effect, the combined two loads then act as one heavier load and accelerate on the pitch. These two conditions can result in product damage at the end of the run where the load hits a fixed stop or injury to personnel who encounter the moving loads. One solution to this problem is the use of speed control devices. In this application, the gravity pitch is set at a higher angle and the speed is controlled by devices located along the length of the gravity conveyor. The problems with this solution are the limitation on the range of weights and the additional cost of the speed control devices. If it can be safely applied, gravity should always be the first consideration, but with the previously mentioned limitations in mind.

There are two types of gravity conveyor: wheel and roller. There are advantages and disadvantages to each type of conveyor, and the final selection should be based on several factors, but particularly the load to be handled.

Gravity Wheel

Gravity-wheel conveyors are sometimes called "skate wheel" because of the similarity between their wheels and the wheels on roller skates. Some of the advantages of using wheel conveyor are portable-lightweight sections; differential action of the wheels in curves; low inertia of the wheels for lightweight products; and quick, easy assembly or disassembly of the sections. Some softer surface products, such as heavy wall bags or sacks, convey better on wheel conveyor than roller conveyor. In this type of application, an in-line pattern of wheels is recommended, since the material will form tracks and not be displaced as when passing over rollers. Chimed bottom containers and wire baskets should not be conveyed on wheel conveyor.

Wheel conveyor sections are available with either steel or aluminum frames and steel or aluminum wheels. The aluminum sections are used for lightweight, portable applications, but have less capacity than the steel construction. The wheels are $1^{15}/_{16}$ inches in diameter, with $^{1}/_{4}$-inch-diameter axles. Spaces are used between the wheels to form the various patterns (Figure 16.1). Most manufacturers offer the conveyor in 12-, 18-, and 24-inch widths, with the wheels on multiples of $1^{1}/_{2}$- or 3-inch centers. The standard section lengths are 5 or 10 feet. The steel wheels have a capacity of 25 to approximately 50 pounds, depending upon the manufacturer; the aluminum wheels have a capacity of 10 to 40 pounds. The wheels are supplied lightly oiled or greased and require little or no further lubrication. If the application is in an environment beyond the range of 32 to 100 degrees, the manufacturer should be consulted to prevent problems with the wheel lubricant. Special wheels

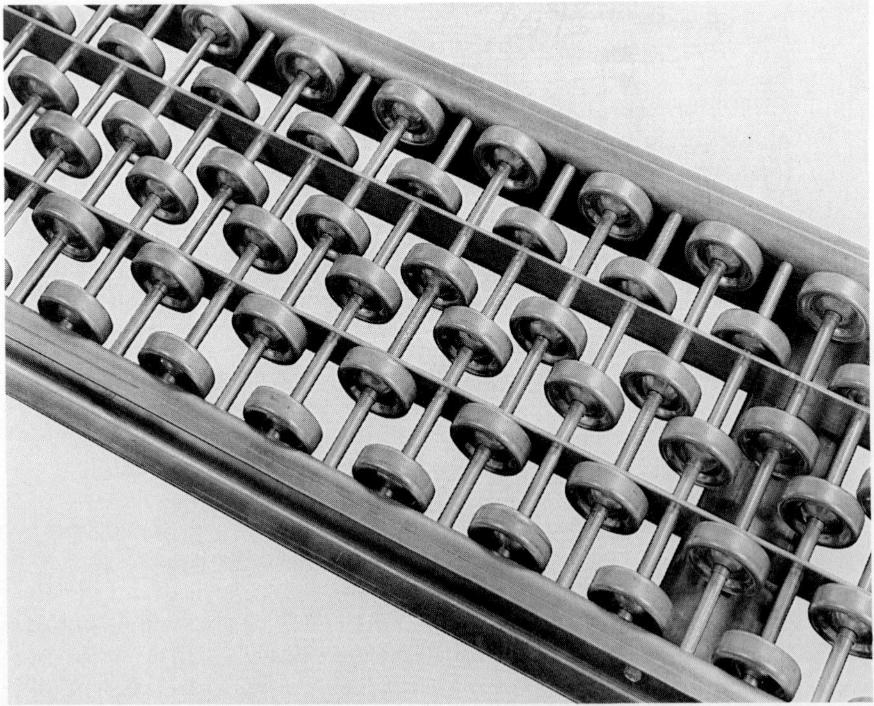

Figure 16.1. Wheel conveyor section.

and wheel coverings are also available for high- or low-temperature applications, moisture conditions, nonmarking of conveyed items, and shock loading.

The standard wheel conveyor frame is two rails of 2½- by 1-inch by 12-gauge formed steel channels, with bolted or welded cross braces. The frames are punched on 1½-inch centers for the wheel patterns. Only experience can determine the proper number of wheels per foot, but in general, the smaller the package, the more wheels are required per foot. The frame capacity is limited by the deflection of the frame, which is a result of the total live load on a conveyor and spacing of the supports. Excessive deflection of the frame causes shock loading and unequal load distribution on the wheels and varying pitch of the section due to the sag between the supports. To avoid these problems, total deflection should not exceed 1/240 of the supported length for horizontal applications and 1/180 of the unsupported length for incline applications. Most manufacturers provide a table of deflections based on loading and distance between supports. In this calculation, if the total frame deflection is more than the allowable, consider the following: use additional supports on closer centers, use a different type of support arrangement, use a different type of conveyor, or contact the manufacturer.

Grades for conveying loads will vary with the weight of the load and the conditions of the surface of the product. The average pitch for cartons is 6 inches per 10 feet. Products with firmer conveying surface require less pitch, and those with softer carrying surface require a greater pitch. Experience and testing are the only proven methods of determining the final pitch requirements. In general, the maximum length of gravity runs without retarders should be 40 to 50 feet, depending upon the weight, size, and conveying surface of the product.

When assembling sections of wheel conveyor, couplings must be compatible with the adjoining sections. Hook and bar-type connectors are the most common for wheel conveyor, but are seldom used in other types of equipment. Therefore, when joining wheel conveyor to powered equipment, the types of connectors must be specified.

Wheel conveyor is available in straight sections, curved sections, spurs, switches, and various other arrangements for complete system layouts. Curves are available in 45 and 90 degrees. The average curved pitch should be approximately one-half the pitch on a 10-foot straight section. Because of the independent rotation of the wheels in the curves, the outer wheels can rotate faster and, therefore, maintain load orientation around the curve. The inside radius of the curve should be at least equal to the length of the longest load to be conveyed. In general, the larger the radius, the better the product will convey. Loads should not be accumulated in curves since they may become interlocked, be bumped out of orientation, or prevented by gravity from starting. Although switches and spurs are available, they should be manually attended for merging of products. Traffic control devices should not be used, since the gravity operation will not provide sufficient force to operate the unit.

Gravity Roller

Gravity-roller conveyor can be designed for a much wider range of applications than wheel conveyor. Although the lighter sections are available in aluminum frames and rollers, it is not as lightweight as wheel conveyor and, therefore, is usually not considered for portable applications or where repeated setup and tear-down are required. In addition to the wider range of capacities, roller conveyor should be considered in applications where wheel conveyor cannot be, such as with wire baskets, recessed-bottom containers, drums, and picture-frame–type pallets. The same general guidelines in regard to the use of gravity conveyor apply for roller conveyor. Gravity should be used whenever possible, but consideration should be given to safety and product damage.

One of the major advantages of roller conveyor is the large variety of combinations of bearings, axles, roller tubing, frame rails, and supports that are available to satisfy a wide range of applications. The selected combination of these components should be based on the product to be conveyed, the environment of the installation, and the cost of the equipment. Most manufacturers consider their most popular combinations as "standards" and will stock at least 10-foot sections of that type of conveyor. If possible, a compromise on the selection of components may result in considerable cost savings and improved delivery.

Gravity rollers use an unground, commercial grade ball bearing referred to as "conveyor grade" bearings. The balls fill the spaces between the inner and outer races and are in contact with each other, which produces some of the noise effect of this type of equipment. However, the full complement of balls also ensures maximum static and low-speed carrying capacity along with shock-loading resistance. The wider manufacturing tolerances of conveyor grade bearings make them more forgiving of variations and alignment tolerances, and allow contaminants to fall through the bearings so as not to jam the balls. Conveyor grade bearings are available in open, shielded, grease-packed, or regreasable designs. In gravity applications, the open or steel shielded bearings are recommended to avoid increased friction in the bearing. Conveyor grade bearings can be used from cold-room applications up to 350°F, but special lubricants should be considered outside the +32 to 150°F range.

Also, felt-type seals should not be used above 180°F, since the felt will char and contaminate the bearing. Steel shields should not be used above 225°F because of distortion in the shield. In high-temperature applications, the load should be spaced on the conveyor and moved quickly to minimize the heat soaking into the rollers. There should also be good air circulation around the rollers to dissipate the heat. Although high temperatures are normally not encountered in the warehouse per se, these conveyors may interface with manufacturing systems where temperature would be a problem. Low temperature is more likely to be a prime consideration in the warehouse. In coolers or areas that interface with the outside, it may be advisable to use galvanized frames and rollers to prevent rusting from condensation and ice buildup on the conveyors.

Depending on the bearing, the tubing, and the manufacturer's standards, bearings are inserted into the tubing by a straight press fit, into a curled end, or swedged into the roller. Adaptor cups are also used to fit smaller bearings and axles into larger-sized rollers. Although the method of assembly is determined by the manufacturer, the user should be aware of the type of assembly, since this may affect whether the bearings are replaceable or the whole roller must be replaced.

The roller capacity is determined by both the basic bearing capacity and the width of the roller. The basic bearing capacity is a capacity determined by empirical formulas and confirmed by laboratory tests. Since these are nonprecision bearings, they do not follow the normal B10 type of rating. The basic bearing capacity is used for narrower-width conveyors, but as the width increases, the roller capacity must be derated because of axle deflection. The clearance built into the conveyor-grade bearings allows approximately 1 degree of axle deflection before the rating is affected. Again, laboratory tests have established roller capacities for various widths based on the combination of basic bearing capacity and the derating based on the width of the roller.

Most conveyor rollers have hexagonal axles to prevent the axles from rotating in the frame rails and to prevent the inner bearing cone from rotating on the axle. Most light- and medium-duty package conveyor rollers have spring-loaded axles. These rollers can be installed or removed from one side of the conveyor. Other axle arrangements are an upset on one end and cotter pin or hog ring on the other end of the rail, and flush axle or drop-in axle construction. With the upset type of construction, the axle must be completely removed from the roller for assembly or disassembly within the frame. This requires clearance next to the other side of the conveyor to remove the cotter pin or hog ring. When assembling longer rollers and frames with this type of construction, it is difficult to feed the axle through the roller and the far bearing and frame rail. When installing rollers with removable axles next to a wall or another conveyor, it is important to install the conveyor with the axle arranged for removal from the side away from the fixed obstacle. Flush axle and drop-in axle construction have flats on the ends of the axles, and the frames are slotted from the top edge. This construction is used for easy replacement of rollers or for safety pop-out in areas where operators may come into contact with rollers in powered applications.

The roller tubing is determined by both the load capacity and the application. The larger-diameter rollers can accommodate larger-capacity bearings. The tubing thickness should be considered in areas of impact to prevent indentation and for abrasion in areas where loads are moved across therollers. Coverings are sometimes used on roller tubing to prevent product marking, deaden noise, or to increase the diameter of the roller (resulting in lower rpm) or to have the roller surface above the frame rail. Roller tubing is available in materials other than steel, such as aluminum for lighter weight and stainless steel for special applications, such as the food industry or environments containing explosives.

The most common frame rails are roll-formed channels, structural channels, structural angles, and flats. Usually, the conveyor frames are the same on both sides, with welded or bolted cross braces between. However, in some applications, the side frame members may not be the same on both sides because of a specific requirement. An example would be at a loading or unloading station where loads must be moved off of and on to a conveyor which, on one side, would have an angle frame with the rollers set high and, on the back side, a channel frame to act as a guide.

Rollers may be set high or low in their frame rail depending upon the axle hole punching (Figure 16.2). If the rollers are set low, the frame rails will contain the product and guard rails will not be necessary. However, wider loads cannot be accommodated on the low arrangement and the conveyor is, therefore, not as adaptable for future applications.

In loading areas, a wear bar may be welded to the frames under the axle hole to prevent the axles from enlarging the holes due to impact on the rollers. Most formed frame rails have standard patterns of axle holes on 1½- or 2-inch centers. The rollers can then be installed on centers that are multiples of the punching patterns. In structural frames, the axle holes are punched to order for the application. Since most manufacturers do not charge for additional punching in structural frames, it is good insurance to punch additional holes, in case rollers need to be added in the future.

A three-frame rail construction is sometimes used in systems to provide additional rollers for better conveyability, capacity, and tracking in

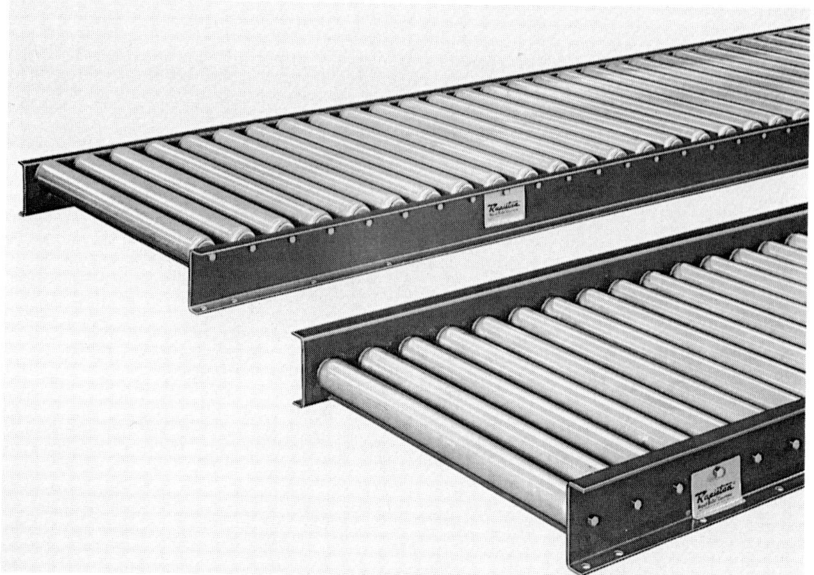

Figure 16.2. Rollers may be set high or low in their frame rails, depending upon the axle hole punching.

curves (Figure 16.3). This construction is also used for a herringbone section for centering loads prior to a sealer or scanner. Another common frame construction is the skewed roller section. This design is used for moving loads to one side of the conveyor prior to them reaching a code reader or pusher.

The capacity of the gravity-roller conveyor depends on the selected components. Most manufacturers provide tables of distributed load capacities of conveyors. This capacity is based on the roller, the frame rails, and the supports for their most popular combinations. To verify the capacity for a particular application, all items to be conveyed must be considered. In figuring roller capacities, a minimum of three rollers should be under the load at all times, and two-thirds of the rollers under the loads should be included in the calculation. All of the rollers are not included in the calculation in order to compensate for uneven load and conveying surfaces. To determine the roller spacing, subtract 1 inch from the load length and divide the number by 3. The next smaller available roller spacing should be used. Checking the roller capacity may indicate that it is necessary to use closer roller centers or a larger-capacity roller. Roller centers for hard-surface items such as castings, steel tubs, or some pallets may be as great as 12 to 18 inches. Roller centers for wooden pallets should not be greater than 6 to 8 inches, and

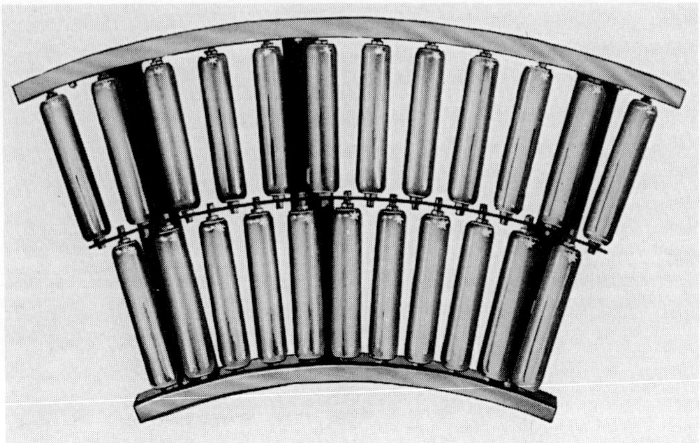

Figure 16.3. A three-frame rail construction.

for cartons not greater than 4½ to 6 inches. Conveyor loading areas will require more rollers with heavier wall construction because of the probable impact. Since impact is difficult to calculate, it is a good practice to double the required calculated capacity in these areas. After determining the roller size and spacing, the frame capacity should be checked. The live load (the total weight of product on the section), the total weight of the rollers, and the frame weight should be compared with the frame capacity. Since the standard length of most conveyor sections is 10 feet, the sections are usually supported on 10-foot centers at section splices. However, for additional capacity, it may be necessary to support the section on 5-foot centers. The frame capacity of a 10-foot section supported on 5-foot centers is approximately four times the capacity of a 10-foot section supported on 10-foot centers.

After checking the frame and roller capacities, the supports should be reviewed. This capacity can be checked based on the number of supports selected in the frame calculation. As mentioned, it is usually desirable to have supports under the spliced joints between sections. In applications where the conveyor is hung from overhead steel, it may be necessary to use additional stringer steel between the roof structure to pick up the conveyor supports. Manufacturers usually supply the hardware for bolting the conveyor sections together and to the supports, but do not supply any additional overhead steel or floor anchors.

As mentioned previously, setting the pitch on gravity conveyor is a compromise between the pitch required to start the load moving from rest and the pitch required to sustain movement. It is also a combination of the size of roller and type of bearing, the weight of the product, the surface condition of the product, and in some cases, the environment.

Experience and testing are the only practical methods for determining the required pitch. However, in estimating the pitch, an average pitch for roller conveyor is approximately 1/2 inch per foot of conveyor length. This pitch must be increased for lighter loads or soft-surface products and decreased for heavier loads or hard-surface items. When both heavy and light loads are mixed on the conveyor, it is difficult to select a pitch that will be satisfactory for safe and reliable movements of both types of load. Most loads reach their average maximum speed of approximately 180 feet per minute within three times their length. Long, uncontrolled runs of gravity should be avoided when handling heavy loads or where it is possible for one load to catch up with another and form a train that will act as a larger load and cause product damage at the end of the run. Speed control devices and retarders can be used to prevent these situations, but they can be costly and are susceptible to problems when there is a large range of products weights.

Gravity Curves. Gravity-roller curves require special consideration in two areas: the width between frame rails or guards and tracking of the conveyed product. For all items except circular ones such as drums, additional conveyor width in the curves will be required because of the cording action of the product. As with the straight sections, it is usually desirable to have 2 to 3 inches total clearance between the product and the frames or guards. A formula for determining the distance between the frames or guard rails (Figure 16.4) is:

$$\text{Distance} = (\text{radius} + \text{package width})^2 + \left(\frac{\text{package length}}{2}\right)^2 - (\text{radius} - 2\text{ inches}) \qquad (16.1)$$

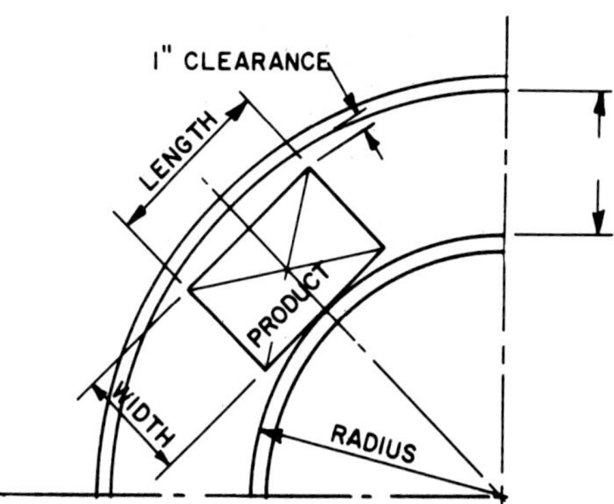

Figure 16.4. Width required between frame rails.

This calculation will determine the width of the balance of the conveyors in the system, since the frame rails on the straight sections and curves should match to avoid product hang-ups.

Curves normally have the same general construction as the straight sections of roller conveyors for the frame, supports, and roller bearings, but consideration must be given to the roller surface for the proper tracking of the product around the curve (Figure 16.5). Since the distance around the outside of the curve is farther than the distance around the inside, the outside conveying surface must turn faster than the inside surface, or the product will rotate on the conveyor. In the case of round articles, such as drums, this rotation will not be a problem. For other products such as cartons or pallets, skewing of the product will be a problem both in the curve and when the product leaves the curve. A tapered roller curve will compensate for this problem, since the taper on the roller face is a cone with the focal point at the center of the radius. Any point on the tapered roller will rotate proportionately faster as the distance increases from the focal point and the roller diameter increases. In using tapered roller curves however, the curve radius selection is limited by the taper manufacturing equipment. Other types of curves that assist proper tracking of the product are wheel curves and three-rail curves. Both allow differential action of the outer conveying surface and assist product tracking.

The inside radius of the roller curve should be greater than the length of the longest item to be conveyed. Curves should not be used for accumulations, since products may wedge together and skew or jam in the curve. Curves should not be connected directly to the end of a belt conveyor, because the greater friction of the belt on the product will force the product to slide across the roller into the outside guard rail

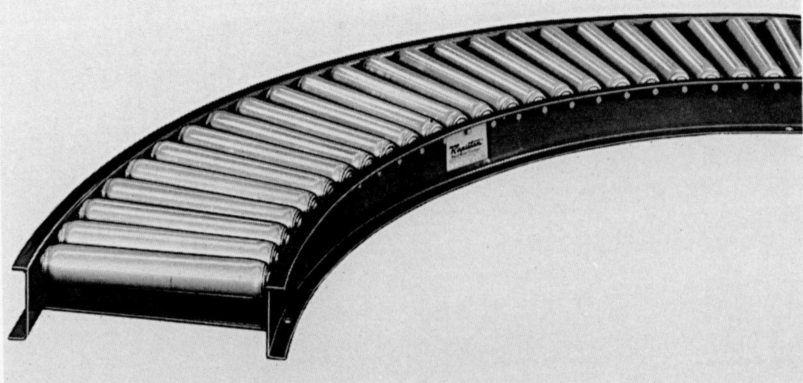

Figure 16.5. Typical gravity roller curve.

and cause product skewing or jamming. A section of straight-roller conveyor at least one-half as long as the longest product should be used between the curve and the belt conveyor. A curve should also not be connected directly to the discharge end of a chute. A section of straight roller at least three times the length of the longest product should be used between the curve and the chute. If the rollers have been set low in the straight conveyor sections and, therefore, in the curve, care must be taken that larger products are not placed on the conveyor, as they may jam in the curve. When the rollers are set high, the product may overhang the rollers, providing the guards have been set back sufficiently far from the curved surface. However, these larger loads may violate the rule of the inside curve radius being larger than the longest product, and the overhang may affect the tracking of the product when it comes out of the curve.

Ball Transfers. Ball transfers consist of a single, large-diameter steel ball riding on a bed of smaller-diameter balls. The large ball is free to rotate in any direction and is used to move hard-surface products both for precise positioning and for transferring from one conveyor to another. Although designed for level mounting with the large ball on top, ball transfers can be tilted up to approximately 30 degrees from horizontal. They should not be used inverted because the principal of the flow of the small balls is upset and the small balls settle down into the clearance around the cup and the large ball.

Ball transfers should be operated without lubrication. When lubricated,they tend to pick up dust and other foreign matter which, when mixed with oil, prevent the balls from rotating freely. Ball transfers should not be used in dusty conditions or where waste products from the process retard the balls and prevent them from rotating freely. Sluggish operation of ball transfers due to glue or carton dust can sometimes be relieved by rubbing paraffin over the large ball.

In operation, ball transfers will mark the running surface on some materials such as brass, soft lumber, highly finished steel sheets, and so on. Ball transfers should not be used for soft-bottom articles, such as soggy cartons or bags, pallets, drums with chimes, baskets, or wire crates. Since they are conveying a hard surface that is usually uneven, good practice suggests that capacity calculation should be based on only three ball transfers carrying the load. Maximum spacing can be determined by dividing the minimum conveying surface dimension by 2.5.

The force required to move the product on ball transfers varies with the weight of the product and the condition of the conveying surface. Hard-surface loads will be easier to push than softer ones. The force required will usually be between 5 and 15 percent of the weight of the load to be moved. Since ball transfers are a multidirectional device, the load will move in the direction it is pushed and may rotate or skew, depending upon the skill of the operator.

Powered Conveyor

The selection of powered conveyor, as with gravity conveyor, depends on the product and the system application. Products with irregular surfaces or loose tags, like mail bags, can only be conveyed on belt conveyors. Spacing, controlled release from accumulation, and accurate positioning on the transport conveyor are also normally done on belt conveyor. However, heavy products are normally only conveyed on live-roller conveyor. Moving products off of or on to the transport conveyor and most types of accumulation conveyor are live-roller types. Therefore, before selecting the type of powered conveyor, complete product information should be gathered and the system application determined.

Belt Conveyors

In addition to uses just cited, belt conveyors are an economical means of horizontal transportation and are used for incline and decline movement of loads. The belt is supported on either rollers or a metal pan called a "slider bed." Roller bed has lower power requirements, longer belt life, and higher capacity. Slider bed is used for loads with irregular bases, conveyor loading areas, and areas where the operators must interface with the conveyors, such as at assembly stations or inspection stations. Slider bed is not recommended for heavy loads or high speeds (above 100 feet per minute).

The rollers or slider bed are set high in the frame with the between-frames dimension 3 inches wider than the belt. For some special applications, the between-frames dimension can be as little as 1 inch wide, but then frame alignment and belt tracking are critical. The belt-carrying rollers should be spaced for a minimum of two rollers under the product at all times, but tall packages should have three rollers under them for additional stability. If the roller spacing is too great, flexing of the belt passing over the rollers causes the package to rock and may cause tumbling. The return-belt idler rollers are spaced on 10-foot-maximum centers.

There are many combinations of belt types, rollers, frames, and drive units, and selection should depend on the product to be conveyed and the system application. The belt type is determined by the belt pull (tension), the environment (oil, water, temperature, etc.), incline or decline (friction surface, rough top, or cleated), and the belt back surface (bare, friction, or slick). Because of the many types of belt available, a belting supplier should be consulted when special conditions exist. The belt selection also affects the conveyor end rollers and drive design, since thicker belts and heavier belting materials require larger pulley diameters. Special consideration must also be given to the crowning of pulleys for certain belts, particularly polyvinyl chloride (PVC) type. If the wrong crowning arrangement is used, the belt will be difficult to track.

The selection considerations for rollers, frames, and supports is the same as those discussed for gravity rollers, except that rollers should have grease-packed or regreasable bearings. If noise is a consideration, one should select bearings with ball retainers and other bearing materials to obtain a lower noise level. In high-speed applications (over 150 feet per minute), precision bearings should be used and, over 250 feet per minute, balanced rollers may be required.

The drive location is dependent on the type of conveyor, the drive type, and the angle of incline or decline. The drive should be positioned such that a minimum amount of return belt is under high tension. If the conveyor direction of travel is reversible, the drive should be located at the center or towards the more heavily loaded end of the conveyor. If the conveyor is single-direction travel, the drive should be located towards the discharge end. On declining slider bed units, the drive should be located on the low end for declines up to 15 degrees and at the high end for declines over 15 degrees. On declining belt on roller conveyors, the drive should be located at the high end. Reversible-belt conveyors require more care in manufacturing and assembly, since the belt is more difficult to track. Also, long (over 50 feet) or very short reversible-belt conveyors are difficult to track. As a general rule, to prevent tracking problems, belt conveyors should not be shorter than three times the belt width.

End drives are used for short conveyors, one-direction travel, and lighter loads. Center drives are used for reversible travel and medium- or heavy-duty applications. Another drive consideration is the conveyor speed. The speed should be as high as practical so that loads are spaced apart, thereby reducing the tension in the belt. A variable-speed drive unit can be used where the delivery rate or speed cannot be predetermined or where the conveyor speed must be relative to another conveyor or piece or equipment. Mechanical variable-speed drives have up to a 10-to-1 speed ratio. Electrical variable-speed drive packages may have as much as a 50-to-1 ratio. When using belt conveyors in the system, each succeeding belt should increase speed approximately 5 feet per minute or 10 percent of the conveyor speed, whichever is greater, to ensure a safe transfer between the conveyors. When a conveyor may start and stop more than eight times per minute such as in an indexing operation, the motor and reducer duty cycle may require special equipment, such as a clutch brake. The manufacturer should be consulted in these applications.

To calculate the effective belt pull and select a drive, use the formulas:

$$\text{BP} = F\,[L + B + R + 0.05(T)\,] + \sin\theta(I) + 0.3(D) \quad (16.2)$$

where BP = belt pull
F = friction (5% for roller tread and 30% for slider tread)
L = live load (total weight of conveyed produce)
B = weight of belt
R = weight of rollers (tread rollers and return rollers)
T = weight of load on tail feed section
θ = angle of incline
I = weight of live load on incline
D = weight of heaviest load to be deflected

$$\text{Effective BP} = \text{BP} \times 1.25 \quad (16.3)$$

This additional 25 percent is for belt flexing and bearing losses.

For motor horsepower use the formula:

$$\text{Motor hp} = \frac{\text{effective belt pull} \times \text{speed in ft/m}}{33{,}000 \times \text{efficiency}} \quad (16.4)$$

Use the efficiency of chain drive (95%) times reducer efficiency (manufacturer's recommendation).

The amount of drift in a conveyor when the power is shut off depends on the drive ratio, the weight of the live load, and the angle of incline. If positioning is important on a horizontal conveyor or if the angle is more than 10 degrees on an inclined or declined conveyor, a motor brake should be used.

Incline belt conveyors are used to raise or lower product at various degrees of slope (Figure 16.6). The maximum angle of elevation is governed by the characteristics and surface of the conveyed product, the type of belt used, and the method of feeding the incline (Figure 16.7). The relationship of the height of the product and its center of gravity to its base length is important in determining the maximum slope. A general rule to follow for a uniform load is to *make the slope such that a perpendicular line through the center of gravity of the package will fall within the middle one-third of the package's base length.* Caution should be used in locating the center of gravity, since not all packages

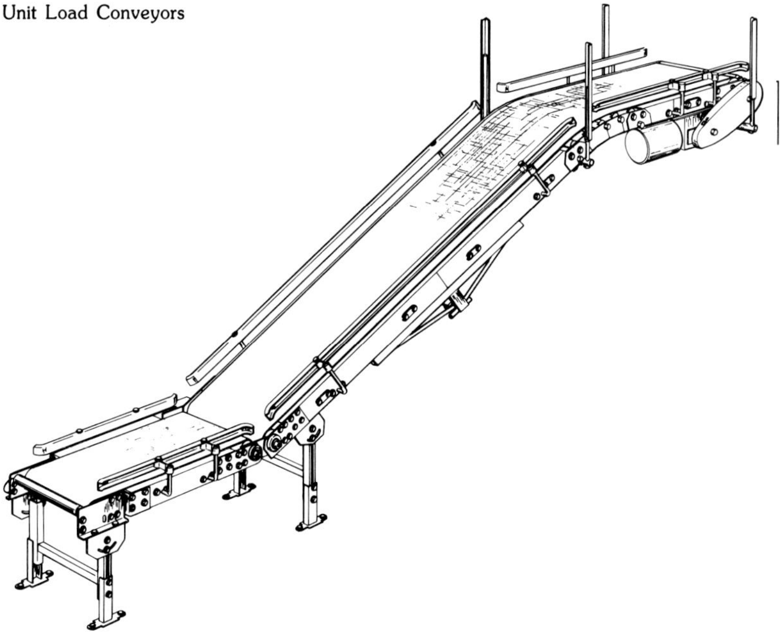

Figure 16.6. Incline belt conveyor.

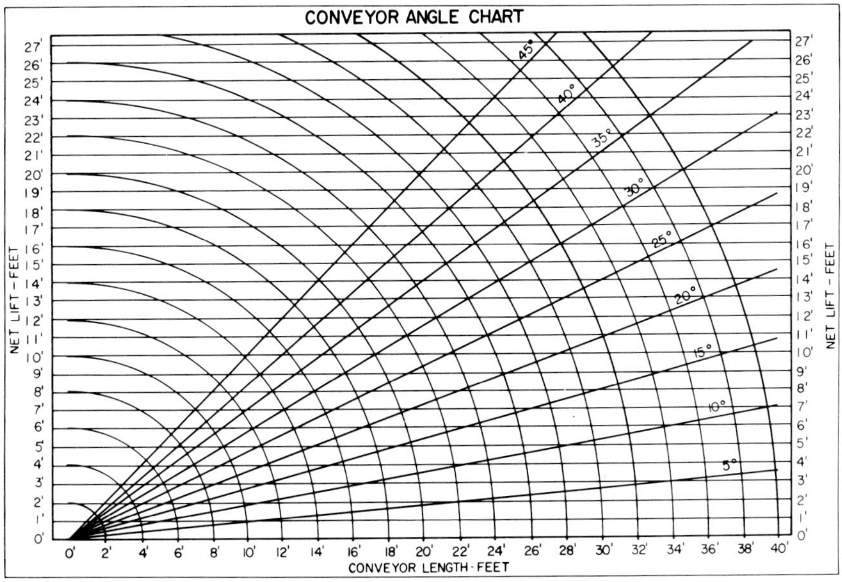

Figure 16.7. Conveyor angle chart.

are uniformly loaded (Figure 16.8). Special consideration must also be given to load stability where an incline belt conveyor might be required to start and stop, causing the load to tumble. In addition to checking the load on the incline, it should also be checked at transfer points, such as the end rollers or transitions to horizontal conveyors.

As mentioned previously, selection of the belt surface requires experience and knowledge of the product to be conveyed. Smooth-bottom plastic tote trays require a special belt on even a 15-degree slope. A slope of 25 degrees was found to be the maximum for conveying most cartons. Some loads may be handled at slopes greater than 30 degrees, but these are special applications and must be given careful consideration.

Up to a slope of 10 degrees and, in some applications, up to a 15-degree slope, loads up to 24 inches long can be transferred from roller or wheel conveyor directly to an incline belt without a powered feed section. Slopes greater than this require a powered feed section, which is a short belt conveyor usually chain-driven from the tail shaft of the incline conveyor. In some cases, a two- or three-pulley device is used where the incline conveyor belt is snubbed down around an arrangement of pulleys, but safety is sometimes a problem in this arrangement. Slave-driven feeder units make it possible to vary the conveyor speed for carton separation, but the rules governing conveyor length versus belt width must be considered to avoid belt tracking problems.

When conveying smaller packages, the transition from one belt conveyor to the next must be checked to see that the package has trans-

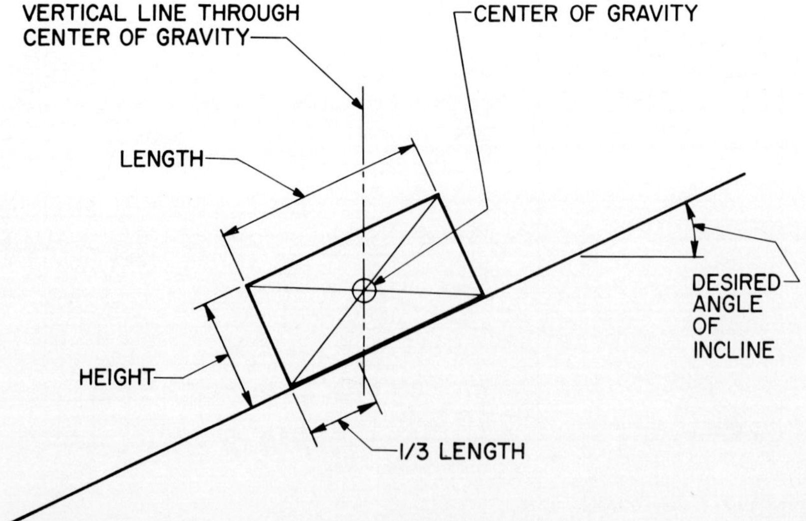

Figure 16.8. Location of center of gravity for a uniform load.

ferred from the one end roller onto the end roller or beyond on the next conveyor. Transition rollers may be required between these end rollers to prevent the package from dipping down between end rollers. These rollers should be of a pop-out construction to prevent injury to operators. Packages making a number of transfers of this type in a system can change orientation on a conveyor; therefore, unless the package orientation can be ensured, always use the smallest dimension as the length of the package when making this check.

In addition to assisting the loads from the horizontal to the incline conveyor, another use of powered feed sections is to space cartons at the transition from gravity conveyor to an incline belt conveyor. Since the speed of loads on gravity conveyor may be two or three times the speed of the same loads on a powered conveyor, the loads may form a train on the gravity conveyor and enter the incline conveyor end to end. The resulting bridging action may damage the loads or even cause them to fall off the conveyor. A solution to this bridging problem is to use a slave-driven tail feeder section and use the sprocket ratio between the horizontal and incline conveyors to effect a slower speed on the feed section, causing carton separation at the transition.

To ensure a smooth load transition from the incline conveyor to the horizontal at the higher elevation, and because of the resulting force on the rollers from the belt tension and the weight of the live load, a nose-over section with heavier-capacity rollers is recommended for inclines over 10 degrees, and is required for inclines over 15 degrees.

Take-ups are required on all belt conveyors to compensate for changes in belt length and to maintain belt tension. The take-up device may be located at any point along the return belt after the drive or at the tail pulley. The most desirable location is immediately following the drive on the slack side of the belt. For rubber-filled belts, take-ups should be designed to provide a minimum of movement of 1 percent of the conveyor length and 2 percent for belts that operate at higher stresses. For stitched canvas or solid woven belts, these figures should be doubled. Gravity take-ups should be used on all belt conveyors for conveyor lengths that exceed the following: 150 feet for rubber-impregnated belting, 70 feet for stitched canvas belting, and 50 feet for woven cotton belting. Gravity take-ups must be used regardless of length on incline conveyors where the drive must be located at the bottom; when slack-side belt tension is critical for drive purposes, as with heavily loaded conveyors; and at installations where there is fluctuating humidity or broad changes in temperatures. On conveyors operating in one direction only, the take-up should be located on the slack side of the drive unit, and the take-up weight must equal twice the required slack-side tension. On reversible conveyors, the take-up weight must equal twice the tension that would normally occur on the right side of the belt. Another consideration is to use two gravity-style take-ups for reversible conveyors, one located on each side of the drive unit with the weight of each take-up being twice the slack-side tension. These take-ups must be provided with stops to limit the movement of the take-up when it is on the tight side of the belt.

Continuous-belt turns are available from 30 to 180 degrees. They are used for many of the same reasons as straight-belt conveyors: soft-bottom packages, irregular conveyor surface, or a wide variety of products. They are available in steel, stainless steel, and molded-frame construction. Although they are more expensive than live-roller curves, the molded construction is less expensive than the steel or stainless steel. Transition rollers and slider plates are used at the transition from the end roller of belt curves to assist the transfer to or from the next conveyor.

Belt curves are also available in a spiral configuration to allow a change of elevations. The effective angles of incline on the centerline are 16 to 20 degrees, depending on the model.

Live-Roller Conveyer

Live-roller conveyors are used for a much wider range of applications than belt conveyors: for accumulation; for diverting on or off the conveyor; for heavy loads; for oily, dirty, or wet conditions; to turn, skew, or move loads on the conveyor; in high or low temperatures; or to eliminate drives. These applications require different types of live rollers, categorized by the type of driving means used to turn the rollers. The most common types are:

1. Flat belt
2. V belt
3. Cable
4. Line shaft
5. Chain
   a. Continuous
   b. Roller to roller
6. Patented accumulation

Flat Belt-Driven Live Roller. Flat belt-driven live-roller construction is very similar to belt conveyor construction, except that the belt is below the carrying rollers and is supported by snub rollers. The selection and spacing of the tread rollers is the same as for gravity-roller conveyor. There should be a minimum of three rollers under the load at all times.

Snub rollers are located between carrying rollers and are adjustable up or down for increasing or decreasing the belt contact with the carrying rollers and, therefore, affecting the driving force on the rollers. At a point on the conveyor where the load may be stopped while the conveyor continues to run, the snub rollers should be lowered for less belt contact with the carrying roller, thus exerting less driving force on the load. A more complete discussion of this and other types of accumulation will follow. In an area where a carton must be diverted from the conveyor, the snub roller should be raised to provide increased driving force on the load. As a general rule, adjust for the minimum belt pressure required to keep the load moving. This will keep belt tension and drive loading to a minimum.

Since the belt width is not related to the actual conveying surface, as with a belt conveyor, a narrower belt width can be used on belt-driven live-roller conveyors. The belt width is selected by determining the effective belt pull and relating that to the belt capacity per inch of width. The maximum belt width is determined by clearances at the end rollers and in the drive unit, as specified by the conveyor manufacturer. The minimum belt width is usually also based on the end roller and drive construction. Most manufacturers use crowned face pulleys to help maintain the belt tracking. The manufacturer will specify a minimum belt width to be used in conjunction with the crowned face pulleys. As mentioned previously, certain belts require a different crowning configuration on the pulleys. Friction-surface, rubber-filled belting is commonly used on belt-driven live roller. The carrying rollers on end rollers and on end drives will be as close as possible to the end of the conveyor. However, the pulleys in these devices will be set in from the end of the conveyor so that the belt does not travel past the end of the conveyor and possibly interfere with the next conveyor. These end carrying rollers, therefore, may not be powered and caution should be used when conveying small articles. If necessary, these rollers can be slave-driven from adjacent rollers by means of O rings.

Belt-driven, live-roller drive, and belt-pull calculations are similar to those for belt conveyors. The effective belt pull can be calculated using the formulas:

$$\mathrm{BP} = F(L + B + R) + \sin\theta(I) + 0.3(D) \qquad (16.5)$$

where BP = belt pull
F = friction (10%)
L = live load
B = weight of belt
R = weight of rollers (tread + snub + idlers)
θ = angle of incline

I = weight of live load on incline
D = weight of heaviest load to be deflected

$$\text{Effective BP} = \text{BP} \times 1.25 \tag{16.6}$$

$$\text{Motor hp} = \frac{\text{effective belt pull} \times \text{speed in ft/m}}{33{,}000 \times \text{efficiency}} \tag{16.7}$$

Use efficiency of the chain drive (95%) times reducer efficiency (manufacturers recommendations).

The maximum recommended incline on belt-driven live rollers is 5 degrees. Greater inclines may be possible, but the products must be tested and the rollers should be on close centers. Declines up to 4 degrees can be considered level in calculating the pull. Over 4 degrees, the belt pull should be calculated two ways: completely empty and completely loaded. The completely empty calculation will be at the belt pull, with horsepower required to run the conveyor empty; the fully loaded calculation will be the belt pull and drive capacity necessary to hold back the load. Caution should be used when matching incline or decline conveyors with level live-roller conveyors. Solid-bottom loads, such as pallets or castings, will cord across the transition and may hang up on the rollers.

V Belt-Driven Live Roller. V belt-driven live roller follows the same driving principle as the flat belt-driven live roller, except that the flat belt is replaced with a V belt and the snub rollers are replaced with snub wheels mounted on one side frame. The drive and end pulleys employ V-belt sheaves.

V belt-driven live roller is used for light loads and short conveyors. Whenever possible, an endless, molded-section V belt is used. Splicing is possible, but unless correctly applied, there is concern for the strength and life of the splice. V belt-driven live roller is ideally suited for curves and spurs since the V belt can flex around the curve radius. Also, the same drive and V belt can power straight sections along with the curve or spur (Figure 16.9). Most manufacturers also offer slave-driven arrangements in which the V belt-powered curves or spurs can be driven from the next belt or belt-driven live-roller conveyor.

Cable-Driven Line Roller. Cable-driven line roller is very similar to the V belt-driven type. The cable is snubbed under the carrying rollers using wheels mounted on the conveyor frame. Different types of cables are employed by various manufacturers. Some cables have a steel intercore with a soft covering for a drive surface on the roller to prevent marking and wearing on the roller. Splicing this type of cable can be a problem because of the flexibility required in the steel core and the soft outer covering. Other types of cables use synthetic materials without the steel core. These are usually easier to splice, but stretching is a problem. Since the stretching is greater than with other types of belts, larger take-up devices must be provided to maintain tension through the drive unit. In extreme conditions, the continued stretching will reduce the diameter of the cable to a point where it loses its driving contact with the carrying rollers. In addition to the obviously lower equipment costs of the components, cable conveyors can be used to eliminate drive units since the cable can drive through corners and straight sections with the same drive unit. This results in not only equipment savings in the drive units, but also electrical controls and field installation savings.

Figure 16.9. V belt-driven curve.

Line-Shaft Conveyor. As with the V belt and the cable conveyors, a major advantage of line-shaft conveyors is the elimination of drive units. The line shaft is mounted on one side of the conveyor frame and can be driven around curves using universal joints. Spurs can also be powered through jackshafts and couplings. The rollers are driven from the line shaft using O rings over the roller and spools on the line shaft. The O rings ride in grooves on the roller to maintain proper alignment and tension. The spool is made from a low-friction material that will slip on the line shaft when the roller rotation is stopped, thus allowing minimum pressure accumulation.

Line-shaft-type conveyors are used for light- to medium-duty applications. They should not be used in oily or wet applications where the friction coefficient between the spool and the drive shaft will be affected.The O rings should not be exposed to continuous direct sunlight or radiation, both of which can cause deterioration. As with the *V*-belt and cable-type live-roller conveyors, splicing O rings in the field requires the proper equipment and materials. In some cases, manufacturers provide additional O rings on the line shaft so that they can be quickly used to replace a broken ring. The O rings are also limited to a temperature range of approximately 32 to 150°F.

In addition to the obvious cost advantages and installation-time advantages of fewer drive units as compared to flat belt conveyors, line shafts are quieter; cleaner, since they do not pick up carton dust and other debris; and safer, because of less contact area between the driving belt and the roller, which could be a pinch point.

Chain-Driven Live Roller. Chain-driven live roller is used in more severe applications, such as heavy loads; oily, dirty, or wet conditions; and high or low temperatures. There are two types of chain-driven live-roller conveyors: continuous and roller to roller. The continuous-chain type has the lower cost but is more limited in application.

Continuous-type chain-driven live roller is a single strand of chain driving a single, welded rack-tooth sprocket on each roller. Since the chain is only in contact with the sprocket teeth on the top of the sprocket, this design should not be used for start-stop applications or with other than moderate weight loads. However, by using side bow chain, it can also be used to power curves or spurs. Minimum roller spacing is affected by sprocket diameter. When close center rollers are required, double-width chain with staggered sprockets or an idler roller between each pair of driven rollers can be used. The drive unit should be located at the discharge end of this type of conveyor.

In roller-to-roller type of construction, two sprockets are welded side by side on one end of each roller. Individual lengths of chain connect-pairs of rollers, alternating side to side along the conveyor. The greater arc of chain and sprocket contact allow larger force to be transmitted. The conveyor length is limited because of cumulative chain pull and slack chain. The maximum number of consecutive chain loops should not exceed 80. By locating the drive in the center of the conveyor, there can be 80 chain loops on each side of the drive, or a total of 160 loops. For moderate applications, the chain can be manually lubricated periodically. For speeds over 150 feet per minute or in higher temperature applications, the chains should be automatically lubricated.

In both continuous and roller-to-roller types of chain-driven live roller, the chain-drive arrangement is covered with a chain box (Figure 16.10). In effect, the rollers are set low on that side of the conveyor. However, the rollers can be set either higher or low on the other side of the conveyor for movement of loads off and onto the conveyor section. The chain box must, therefore, be a concern in locating transfers and spurs on either side of the conveyor. Cross-over arrangements to transmit the driving arrangement from one side of the conveyor to the other through one solid roller are available.

To calculate the drive and chain size for a chain-driven live-roller conveyor, use the formula:

$$\text{CP} = F(L + R + S + C) + \sin\theta(I) + 0.3(D) \qquad (16.8)$$

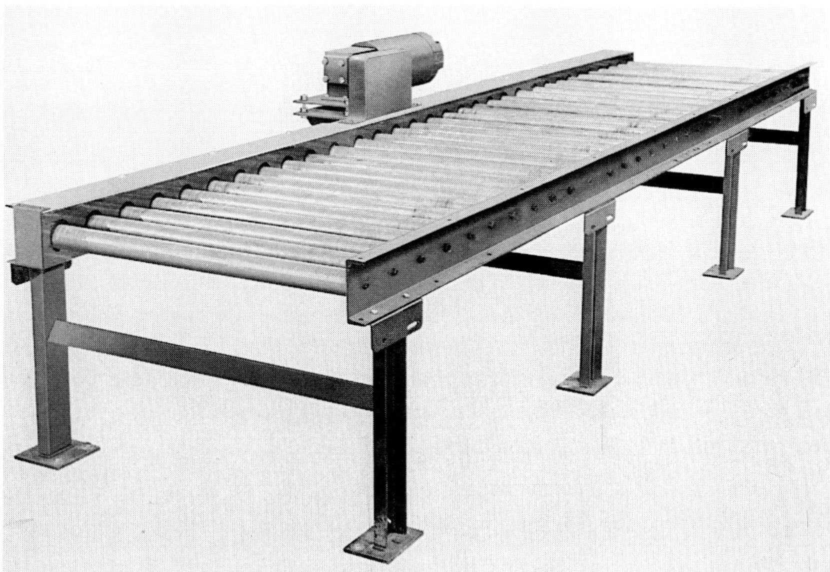

Figure 16.10. In both continuous and roller-to-roller types of chain-driven live roller, the chain-drive arrangement is covered with a chain box.

where CP = effective chain pull
F = friction (6% for continuous chain and 5% for roller to roller)
L = live load
R = weight of rollers
S = weight of sprockets
C = weight of chain
θ = angle of incline
I = weight of live load on incline
D = weight of heaviest load to be deflected

$$\text{Motor hp} = \frac{\text{effective chain pull} \times \text{speed in ft/m}}{33{,}000 \times \text{efficiency}} \tag{16.9}$$

Use efficiency of chain drive (95%) times reducer efficiency (manufacturers recommendations).

Accumulation Conveyors

Two types of accumulation conveyor are available: "generic" (gravity, indexing belt, and kiss-touch live roller) and patented or unique design (zero pressure and zone-type live roller). Gravity-wheel and roller are obviously the least expensive and simplest accumulation conveyor designs. They can be used in many applications with the previously cited guidelines. However, they have the limitations of safety, product damage, and unpredictable movement of product. They should not be used in the main transport line of a system or in controlled release from storage lanes where product movement must take place in a specific length of time or at a certain rate.

Belt conveyors can be used to accumulate by breaking up the accumulation line into several cascade indexing belt conveyors. The product moves onto the first belt conveyor until the tail end of the product is completely on the belt and a sensor stops the conveyor. When the next product arrives, the conveyor again starts and moves until the tail end of that product is on the belt. This continues until the first product reaches the end of the belt conveyor and a sensor indicates that a full slug of product is on the first belt conveyor. This train of product is then moved intact to the farthest empty belt conveyor of the cascade indexing group. Products can be removed from the discharge end of this accumulation line in the same fashion, one at a time or as a complete train. When the discharge conveyor is completely empty, it calls for a train of products from a following belt conveyor.

In this arrangement, product cannot be loaded and unloaded at the same time from the same belt conveyor because of the line-full sensing arrangement. Also, a belt conveyor must be completely empty before a train is conveyed onto it. This accumulation arrangement is, therefore, a compromise between how many belt conveyors are used to transport the trains and how much empty space can be on a discharge conveyor waiting for the final load to be discharged. Another disadvantage is that the entire accumulation line can be empty except for a couple of loads at the input end, but these loads will remain on the input conveyor until a full train is formed. One solution to this problem is that the operator at the discharge can override the indexing controls and call these loads down to the discharge end. The controls can automatically be set up to accomplish this, but then they must also scan the other conveyors in between the input and discharge to make sure that there are no trains in transit. This type of accumulation is often used for products, such as bags, that will not accumulate on live roller or gravity, or where there is a wide variety of products on the same conveyor.

The other generic type of accumulation is kiss-touch live roller. In this arrangement, the pressure rollers that hold the belt up into contact with the tread rollers are adjusted down so that there is a minimum of drive force on the tread rollers. This arrangement does result in line pressure and is sensitive to a large variation of product weights, since the pressure rollers must be set to convey the heaviest products and will, therefore, cause line pressure with all products. One improvement in this design is a conveyor called a "ripple-belt" conveyor. In this arrangement, the pressure rollers are adjusted to provide minimum driving force, and a short, thicker section of belt is laced into the drive belt on 20- to 30-foot centers. When this belt comes through the line, it assists in discharging product. The disadvantage with this arrangement is that, since it is also sensitive to product weight variations, it is impossible to predict if more than one product at a time will be released from the discharge of the line and how long the release must wait for the pad to come to the release position.

Most manufacturers offer their own design of accumulation conveyor, which operates under one of two principals: zoned accumulation or continuous accumulation. In zoned accumulation, the length of conveyor is divided into zones, usually 24 to 30 inches in length. The power to each zone is controlled by a sensor which, when activated, will remove the power from that zone. The first zone of the accumulation line is controlled by an external sensor, usually a line-full sensor or a signal from the system controller. When a product arrives in this first zone and is stopped, it actuates a sensor which then causes the power to be removed from the second zone. When a load arrives in the second zone, it neutralizes the third zone and on back through the accumulation line (Figure 16.11). The release from a zone-type accumulation can occur by either of two methods: individual or slug. Some types of zone accumulation conveyor can only release individual product by applying power to the zone when the sensor on the previous zone has been released. The slug-type accumulation allows the entire conveyor to release by actuating all zones at the same time. The system requirement usually dictates which type of accumulation release is more desirable. When products are being fed into a case sealer or other device requiring individually spaced products, the individual release is more desirable. When the entire slug is required, as at the feed to the palletizer, the slug release is more desirable.

In zone-type accumulation, it is important to compare the maximum- and minimum-length products with the zone size. The zones are usually designed to handle the largest product, but in some cases, a product can overlap two zones. This can result in product drift or line pressure. At the other extreme, two small products may end up occupying one large zone, resulting in an unpredictable release or a significant percentage of the accumulation conveyor being occupied.

In the continuous-type accumulation, products are in contact with one another; the conveyor, therefore, is completely full (Figure 16.12). However, fragile products can be damaged if the line pressure is excessive. The accumulation is accomplished in various ways by different manufacturers' systems. The principle involves removing the power from the

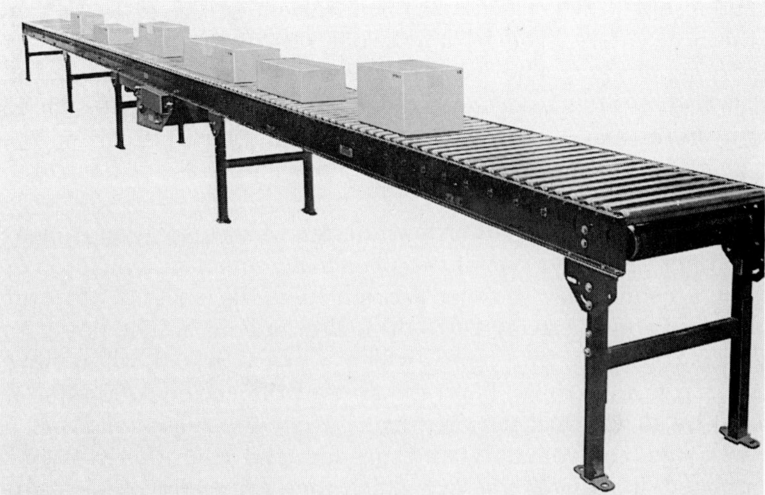

Figure 16.11. Zone-type accumulation.

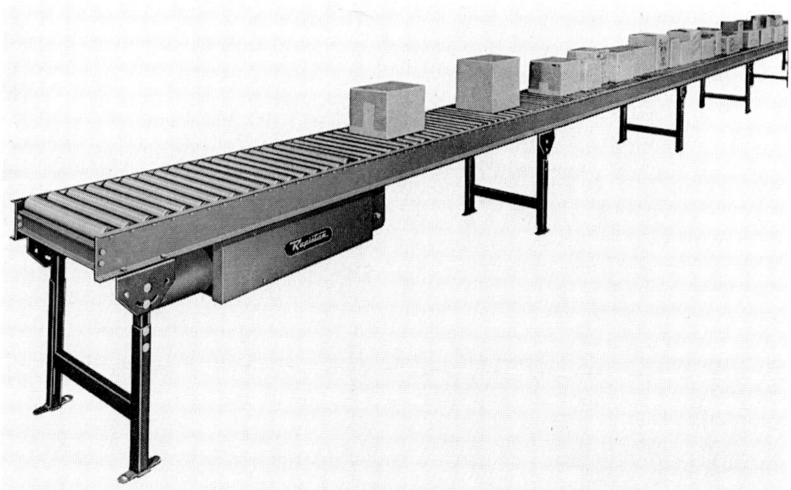

Figure 16.12. Continuous-type accumulation.

conveyor over longer lengths. There is still a minimum amount of driving force, but not sufficient to cause product damage or to overrun the stops at the end of the conveyor. Manufacturers should be consulted for the operating principles of their type of accumulation conveyor and its effect on the product to be conveyed. Also, the products usually must be columnized for this type of accumulation so that they do not accumulate side by side or wedge together.

At the end of accumulation lines, in addition to the sensor-controlled release, other common devices to control accumulation are mechanical stops and brake belts. Mechanical stops are used to ensure that no product escapes from the end of the accumulation line into a transport conveyor. Depending on the product design, it may be difficult to sense a gap between products large enough to raise the stop. For this reason, escapement devices are sometimes used to release one product at a time, or a speed-up section that will pull a gap large enough to read is used in the release belt.

Chain Conveyors

The other major classification of unit load handling conveyors is chain conveyors. There are four general classifications of chain conveyors: sliding, rolling, pusher, and vertical. The type is determined by the application. Chain conveyors are used to transport loads such as tubs, pallets, or other articles that, because of their configuration, must be carried with the runners perpendicular to travel. Chain conveyors are also used for heavy loads, such as large castings, stacks of steel sheets, or steel coils. In many cases, chain conveyors are more economical than other types of conveyors for transporting loads over long distances.

In sliding-chain conveyors, a chain is dragged on a wear bar with the load carried directly on the chain sidebars. Because of the higher friction of this design, it is commonly used for relatively light loads and shorter distances.

There are two types of rolling-chain conveyors: the chain roller on a track and the chain sidebars on a roller track. Rolling-chain conveyors have lower horsepower requirements and wear rates than the sliding-chain design and can, therefore, be used for heavier loads and longer conveyors.

Another variation of the sliding- or roller-chain design is slat or roller flight conveyor. In these designs, a metal slat or roller is mounted between matched pitched chains. The load can be conveyed on the slat or accumulated on the rollers. In the slat conveyor design, fixtures or other special mechanisms can be mounted to the slat for positioning or carrying a load. In the roller flight design, a stop will hold back the load and the chains will continue to move with the rollers turning under the load. The only line pressure will be the resulting force from the friction of the bearings in the rollers. When the stop mechanism is released, the bearing friction will cause the roller to stop turning and the load will be conveyed along with the rollers and chain. Separation or speed-up of the product can also be accomplished on this type of conveyor by moving a section of friction surface material up against the lower surface of the conveying rollers. This results in a load being conveyed at double the speed of the chains.

Vertical-chain conveyors are either of a reciprocating or continuous type. Reciprocating conveyors have limited applications because of a lower throughput capacity (Figure 16.13). Continuous-type chain conveyors can handle a higher rate but usually require more expensive automatic loading and unloading stations. In using either type, the state and local equipment codes must be checked for classification. Some states have ruled that this equipment must meet elevator codes. Although there are numerous court cases on this point, the American Society for Mechanical Engineers and the International Material Management Society have both found that this equipment, considered a vertical conveyor, is in fact covered by ANSI/ASME standard B20.1–1984 Safety Standard for Conveyors and Related Equipment. The purchaser should verify with the manufacturer that the equipment will in fact meet the required code.

In designing a conveyor system, there will be other devices required

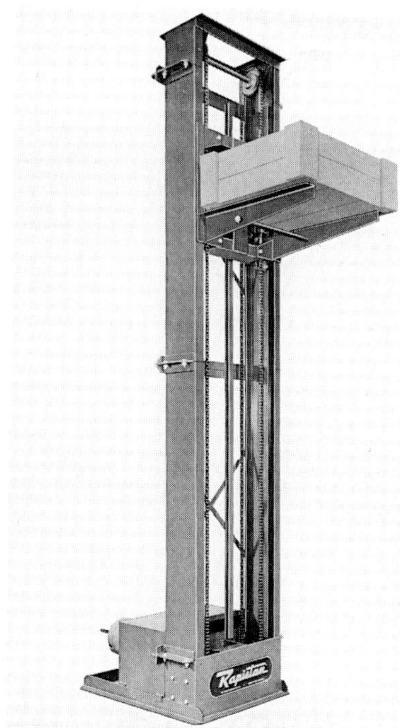

Figure 16.13. Reciprocating vertical-chain conveyor.

which, in most cases, require special design. Such devices as turntables, transfer cars, transfers, diverters, stops, and so on will require the manufacturer's assistance in application because of load capacity and cycle time required in systems.

Turntables

Turntables are used to reorient the product 90 or 180 degrees, or to some other angle for the take-away conveyor or the operation. The turntable consists of a conveyor tread mounted on a bearing surface. The rotation can be either powered or manual depending on the application and the product to be handled. In a powered application, control devices are necessary to ensure that the product is completely on the turntable prior to rotation and that the receiving conveyor has room to receive the load on discharge. Also, when the load is discharged, it must be completely clear of the turntable before the turntable returns to its original position. Turntables are also sometimes used in a conveyor line to reverse the product on the conveyor. The product is conveyed onto the turntable, rotated 180 degrees, and discharged.

Transfer Car

Transfer cars consists of a conveyor tread mounted on a frame with wheels. The tread and travel on the car can be either manual or powered, depending on the application and the product. Transfer cars are used to move loads between lines where the throughput is low and there are several transfer points. There are several methods used for powering the movement of transfer cars: the wheels may be powered, the car may pull itself along on a chain, or a cable mechanism may pull the car forward and back. For short travel, a pneumatic or hydraulic cylinder may be used to pull the car. There are also several types of rails on which the car rides: for heavier applications, industrial rails are recessed into the floor; in lighter applications, an inverted angle is used on one side and a flat steel strip on the other side. In the use of transfer cars, consideration should be given to cross traffic in the area of the transfer car operation. This is particularly important when the car is automatic and may move at any time. The transfer car path should always be fenced in and interlocked with the crossing area to eliminate possible collisions with pedestrians or other traffic.

Sorters

In higher rate systems, the product is moved off the transport line by transfer devices or diverters. Heavier products such as pallets are transferred from the main line using pop-up transfers. In this arrangement, powered chains are raised above the live-roller conveyor and move the load off the transport conveyor onto a receiving conveyor. Diverter design and application is a function of the product and throughput rate. For low to medium speeds and light products, a mechanical arm diverts the product off the main transport line. In higher-speed applications, a positive sorter moves the product off the transport conveyor. There are various other devices using pop-up or skewed wheels or rollers to move the product off the transport conveyor. The manufacturer should be contacted for a recommendation on the choice of the proper type of diverter for the application.

Summary

Although many rules and guidelines for the selection and application of unit load handling conveyors have been given in this section, there is still a certain degree of "art" in applying these rules. Experience is a valuable teacher in making equipment selections and doing system layouts. Although it is important that the user of this equipment understand and use this information, it is still important to benefit from the experience of consultants and manufacturers who can suggest better applications and are informed on the latest state-of-the-art equipment and controls. The size of the project, the risk, and the schedule are some of the criteria for determining if outside help should be used in purchasing a unit load conveyor system.

17
Automatic Guided Vehicle Systems

Adolph Kannewurf

Director of Marketing, Harnischfeger Engineers, Inc., Milwaukee, Wisconsin

Introduction

Automatic guided vehicle (AGV) systems are the foremost integrator of material movement in warehousing. They are extremely flexible systems that have a wide range of vehicles, load transfer techniques, guide path arrangements, and controls.

Multiple-vehicle systems have performance security. If one vehicle in a 10-vehicle system is out of operation, the system is still capable of functioning at 90 percent of maximum capacity.

Systems can begin operation with just enough vehicles to match start-up needs, then add vehicles as the demand builds up. This can be spread out over a number of years and allows a phased capital investment. There is strong economic justification because of the reduction of operators and the fast and efficient handling of material.

Warehousing is a vital part of the automated factory for storing raw material, work-in-process, and finished product. The speed of guided vehicles and the low cost of the guide path increase the choices of warehousing locations associated with manufacturing.

Combining horizontal and vertical load movement and storage with guided vehicles and automated storage/retrieval (AS/RS) systems provides increased productivity in warehousing. Fast automatic load transfer, remote vehicle programming, and interfacing control systems make this possible. Just-in-time material delivery to manufacturing and assembly operations from receiving docks and warehousing by guided vehicles has distinct benefits in inventory reduction.

The types of guided vehicles, controls, and applications are continually expanding. Fork vehicles handle loads at various levels, including floor, conveyor, and pickup and deposit (P & D) stations. Offwire operation for programmed turns and load pickup is increasing. High-lift fork vehicles provide automatic pallet-rack storage. Stock selectors position operators at specified bin locations in small-parts order-selection systems. Computer-controlled systems offer real-time product control by monitoring vehicle status, and on-line material tracking keeps an up-to-date inventory of material in transit.

Guidance

Magnetic guidance is used in most industrial AGVS because of its permanence and reliability, and requires a guide wire embedded in the floor. The flexible stranded wire plus insulation is 1/8 inch in diameter and is energized with a low-current (under 400 milliamps), low-voltage (under 40 volts), low-frequency signal (1 to 15 kilohertz).

The guide wire slot in the floor is sawcut 1/8 inch wide by 1/2 inch deep. Concrete saws need water during cutting, and the process creates a water slurry mixture that must be vacuumed up and removed. Dumping of this slurry should not be done in building water drains.

Sensing coils mounted on the vehicle are activated by the magnetic field of the guide wire. When the vehicle is aligned directly over the wire, the signals in the sending coils are equal and no error signal exists. If there is an imbalance in the sensing coil signals, it will be amplified and fed to a steering motor that will correct vehicle travel in proportion to the error signal. Multiple-frequency guide paths provide an easy means of changing a vehicle from one path to another by switching guidance frequency at decision points.

Optical guidance features a contrasting guide path, such as white tape on a dark floor, a light source on the vehicle to illuminate the guide path, and photocells to read the reflected light and control vehicle guidance. It has often proved to be impractical, except in light industry and office applications, because of difficulties in keeping the guide path clean. Optical guidance is also limited to layout design and communication choices. These drawbacks far overrule the advantage of a taped-down guide path that can be quickly changed.

Chemical guide paths have been used primarily in office buildings with a single vehicle per floor and no traffic control requirements. The guide path is sprayed on the floor or rug and is invisible. It contains fluorescent particles that are activated by an ultraviolet light source on the vehicle.

The use of offwire guidance for programmed turns is increasing. It can simplify guide path installation by using a grid-type layout with guide wires crossing at right angles at intersections. The costly and time-consuming cutting of curves is eliminated. Vehicles make offwire turns leaving one guide wire, running through a turn programmed by an on-board microprocessor, and recapturing the new guide wire.

Vehicles with a short turning radius can provide space savings by using programmed offwire turns to maneuver in tight quarters. A vehicle that can turn on its own axis can make a 180-degree programmed turn and reverse direction in a very limited area, or make a right-angle turn for load pickup in narrow aisles.

Offwire vehicle guidance is expanding beyond programmed turns and can be used to service offpath stations. The refinement of distance measuring devices, exact steering wheel positioning, and on-board microprocessor control will increase this trend in vehicle application. Improved guidance techniques are moving AGV systems closer to the complete elimination of in-floor guide wires.

Types of Vehicles

All guided vehicles are electric-driven and battery-powered. Gas-powered vehicles have been used in the past for heavy-duty applications, but proved to be impractical and were replaced with electrical vehicles with matching capacities.

Tractors. Tractors towing trailers were the first application of guided vehicles in warehousing (Figure 17.1). The driverless tractor-trailer concept was easily understood, because manually driven trailer trains were in widespread use. The theory of operation was proven, and removing the driver provided the economic justification. It was a low-risk system because the tractors could be driven manually as a backup method of operation. Tractor speeds are approximately 250 feet per minute.

The success of guided tractor-trailer trains was furthered by the reasoning that horizontal material movement beyond 300 feet should not be handled by fork trucks and that fork trucks should be assigned to zones, traveling short distances with emphasis on lifting.

Figure 17.1. Tractors towing trailers were the first application of guided vehicles in warehousing.

Towing capacities of tractors range from 10,000 to 50,000 pounds rolling load. Drawbar ratings determine how much a tractor can pull, and there are two ratings: normal and ultimate.

Normal drawbar is the amount of pull in pounds that can be sustained at the towing hitch of a tractor, in a specified duty cycle, without exceeding allowable continuous temperatures for tractor components. It is established by the tractor manufacturer.

Ultimate drawbar is the maximum amount of pull in pounds that can be developed at the towing hitch of a tractor. Duty cycles and allowable component temperatures are not a part of the definition and tractors can sustain this drawbar for only a very short time.

Tractor capacity is also expressed in terms of rolling load, in pounds. This is the total load to be pulled including the loads and the trailers. The drawbar required to pull a rolling load can be calculated by multiplying the rolling load by 2 percent, the coefficient of rolling friction between wheels and dry concrete floor. For example:

$$\text{Rolling load} = 10{,}000 \text{ pounds}$$
$$\text{Drawbar} = 10{,}000 \times 0.02 = 200 \text{ pounds}$$

Ramps increase drawbar requirements dramatically. Calculations for ramp drawbar have two parts: (1) the drawbar to hold the rolling load and the tractor on the ramp and (2) the drawbar to move the rolling load up the ramp. For example for a ramp with a 5 percent incline:

Rolling load = 10,000 pounds
Tractor weight = 4000 pounds

1. Drawbar required to hold load and tractor on the ramp
   (10,000 + 4000) × 0.05 = 700 pounds
2. Drawbar to move the load up the ramp
   10,000 × 0.02 = 200 pounds
   Total drawbar required = 900 pounds

The two examples show that when a 10,000-pound rolling load moves from the level to a 5 percent ramp, the drawbar requirement increases from 200 to 900 pounds.

Some tractor manufacturers allow normal drawbar to be exceeded for short periods of time, such as for a ramp application. The heat dissipation characteristics of the drive motor are a major factor in such decisions.

Early tractor-trailer trains used flatbed trailers that were loaded by fork trucks. Trailers with nonpowered roller decks are used to interface with fixed, nonpowered conveyors using manual assistance for load transfer. Vehicle stopping accuracy of ±3 inches is acceptable.

Trailers with powered roller decks are used in systems with fixed powered-roller conveyors for automatic load transfer. They need power from the tractor battery and data transfer to the tractor controls on load position and destination. Loading and unloading can be done from either side. It is economical to construct these trailers to carry two loads. A data exchange between the trailer and the fixed conveyor, usually optical, ensures that the trailer and load are correctly positioned before load transfer begins. Trailer stopping accuracy should be ±1 inch.

This type of trailer and the associated conveyors are expensive. An alternate solution for systems with a large number of trailers and few load stations uses shuttle transfer tables at the load stations and simple inexpensive trailers with steel-frame decks. Trailers are indexed past the transfer stations one at a time for loading and unloading. The cost of the trailers is approximately one-tenth that of a powered roller trailer.

The maximum number of trailers in a train depends on the trailer size and trailability, the towing capacity of the tractor, and the space available in the aisles at the turns. The first impulse is to have trains longer than are required to meet material movement demands. Long trains create aisle congestion and block cross-aisle movement. The majority of trains are made up of four trailers or less, and trains of more than five are rare.

Trailability of a trailer depends on the type of wheels, wheel location, type of steering, and location of the front and rear hitch. The most common and least expensive trailers have two fixed rear wheels and two front swivel wheels. As these trailers are pulled around a corner, each succeeding trailer moves in toward the center of the turn. Manufacturers' charts show the allowable number of trailers that can negotiate a 90-degree turn between intersecting aisles of various widths.

A four-wheel-steer trailer has four wheels that rotate, and a mechanical linkage between the front and rear wheels rotates the rear wheels opposite to the front. This provides accurate tracking but substantially increases the trailer cost.

A fifth-wheel-steer trailer has two fixed wheels in the rear and a wagon-type arrangement in front; i.e., two fixed wheels on an axle steered by the front tongue and hitch. The bearing and attachment of the front axle to the trailer is termed the "fifth wheel." Their tracking is very good.

Automatic uncoupling of trailer trains is available but is not in widespread use. Automatic uncoupling manually deposits the train to be serviced while the tractor continues productive work. This requires a tractor, eventually, to be recoupled to the train either manually or automatically. Manual interface is simplest, but parts system efficiency in the hands of the operators and good discipline are needed to make this arrangement work.

Automatic coupling increases the system cost because of the need for reverse guidance and increased controls involving remote data gathering and programming. Call buttons connected to the system controller are required to request tractors for train pickup. Accurate positioning of the trailers for automatic pickup is important.

Trailers offer load transfer at one height, which can be a disadvantage, but it is possible to have trailers with different deck heights in the same system. Hand pallet trucks equipped with hitches have been used as trailers and are manually operated to pickup loads at floor level. They have the ability to position loads where required during manual unloading.

Pallet Trucks. Pallet trucks provide an interesting semiautomatic pallet-moving system whereby the trucks are loaded manually and unloaded automatically. These are pallet trucks, not the hand pallet trucks mentioned in the section on tractors (Figure 17.2).

Figure 17.2. Pallet trucks provide an interesting semiautomatic pallet-moving system, whereby the trucks are loaded manually and unloaded automatically.

Standard lifting capacity is 6000 pounds and fork lengths are available up to 96 inches. Most applications use double pallet trucks, and up to four pallets can be carried as long as the total load doesn't exceed the vehicle capacity. Fork length is determined by the size of the pallet. It is absolutely essential that the load wheels are positioned between the appropriate bottom board opening before the load is raised, or the pallet will be damaged. Although the forks are selected for a specific pallet, the vehicle can handle skid loads (no bottom boards) in a broad range of sizes.

A typical round trip begins with an operator manually loading the vehicle. This part of the sequence has not yet been automated because of unreliable quality of the pallets and problems with load wheels moving over the bottom boards. The test is as follows: If a pallet can be loaded without splintering wood, it can be unloaded automatically. Skids do not present the problem because of the absence of bottom boards.

After loading, the vehicle is programmed for the appropriate destination and placed on the guide path. Pallet delivery stations are located on spurs parallel to the guide path. If pallets are being delivered to rack storage, a two-pallet station can be located in a cross aisle at the end of back-to-back racks. This allows easy access by fork trucks for pallet putaway.

As a truck enters a spur, it slows down to creep speed, about 30 feet per minute, and stops, with an accuracy of ± 3 inches. The forks lower automatically, placing the pallets on the floor. The truck restarts, pulls out from the pallets, and proceeds to its next destination. Pallets are placed in storage by fork trucks.

While under guidance, the vehicle speed is 3 miles per hour; but under manual control, the speed is approximately 6 miles per hour. This is important because the vehicle is operated manually every time it is loaded.

A significant feature of the pallet truck is its ability to pick up and deliver loads at floor level. No pickup and deposit stations are required, and the floor is clear and unobstructed.

These vehicles have been used in dry grocery warehouses, meat and dairy coolrooms, drug warehouses, and automotive parts distribution centers.

Platform trucks are similar to pallet trucks, but have the forks replaced with a solid deck or platform that can be raised or lowered. They are ideally suited for handling skid loads automatically because there are no bottom boards to interfere with load wheel movement. Pallets and other loads can also be handled if they are elevated approximately 4 inches off the floor on load rails. This will allow the platform in its lowered position enough room to get under the loads.

Unit Load Carriers. Unit load carriers have expanded the scope of AGV systems by providing individual-load movement flexibility. Load pickup demands can be quickly handled by remotely programming the nearest available carrier to respond. After load pickup, the carrier immediately proceeds to its destination by the shortest route, with no intermediate stops. Both load waiting time and time in transit are reduced compared to tractor-trailer trains, and overall system speed of response is greatly improved. In systems that need individual rather than batch load movement, the unit load carrier is more efficient than tractor trains.

Carriers are usually designed for a single load or double-stacked loads. Other variations include two loads side by side and two loads in tandem. The most popular load capacities are 4000 and 6000 pounds, although capacities up to 16,000 pounds have been used in flexible manufacturing systems. Load decks are between 20 and 30 inches off the floor, and travel speeds range up to 200 feet per minute.

These vehicles are compact and highly maneuverable, with both forward and reverse guidance, and most can rotate 180 degrees in their own length. This feature decreases the space required for guide paths and gives more freedom in system layout.

There are three basic load decks from which to choose:

1. Flat decks that are loaded by fork truck.

2. Lifting decks that raise and lower 4 to 6 inches to pick up loads from nonpowered fixed stands. This is an economical means of automatic load transfer because of the low cost of the load stands (Figure 17.3).
3. Powered roller or chain conveyor decks that interface with fixed powered conveyor stations for automatic power to power load transfer (Figure 17.4).

The cost of powered conveyor load stands is high, and a system that includes a large number of these stands could have a prohibitive price. This may be overcome by using nonpowered roller conveyor stands and a friction drive wheel on the vehicle for load transfer. A powered roller-deck vehicle at a load stand extends a friction wheel to engage the first roller of the stand. Rotation of the friction wheel causes the rollers of the stand to rotate and power-to-power load transfer occurs. This is sometimes called a "parasitic" or "slave" drive.

The successful linking of driverless vehicles with high-rise storage systems can be attributed to unit load carriers more than any other AGV system vehicle. Single-load vehicles are well adapted to interface with AS/RS systems that have nonpowered P & D stands or interconnected front-end conveyor networks. The sizing and weighing of inbound loads can be done while they are in transit on a carrier, using a flush-floor scale and an array of photocells. Rejects can be taken to a special station for inspection and adjustment.

Figure 17.3. Lifting decks that raise and lower 4 to 6 inches to pick up loads from nonpowered fixed stands.

Figure 17.4. Powered roller or chain conveyor decks that interface with fixed powered conveyor stations for automatic power-to-power load transfer.

Unit load carriers are more than a convenient way to interface with AS/R systems; they are an excellent way. The integration of these two systems provides safe and consistent handling of product. AGV systems and AS/R systems are being thought of as one system in the automatic warehouse, controlled by the same computer.

Fork Vehicles. Unit load carriers equipped with forks are the latest vehicles to enter the AGV system market (Figure 17.5). Both straddle and counterbalanced models are available, with lifting capacities to 10,000 pounds and lifting heights to 12 feet. Their primary advantage is that they can handle loads at multiple levels: floor, conveyors, and racks. The freedom to interface with a variety of load heights satisfies a longstanding user need and allows great latitude in system design.

Receiving areas can be arranged for automatic load pickup at floor level. Lanes for pallet placement by manually operated fork trucks need only side markings. There are no precise load positions in a lane and no floor-mounted load position controls. Each lane does have a guide wire.

As lanes are filled, the system controller (the computer control) is notified and the only data required is the lane number. The system controller releases vehicles from a queueing area and, as a vehicle enters the lane, it proceeds until it detects the presence of a pallet by optical sensors in the fork tips. The vehicle slows down, forks enter and lift the pallet, and the vehicle reverses and returns to the main guide path. It proceeds past a scanner that reads a bar code on the load and is remotely programmed by the system controller that contains load destination data. With all lanes empty, the floor of the receiving dock is completely clear and free of any above floor obstructions. Destinations may include floor-level drop-off stations in rack storage areas, P & D stations at an AS/R system, or multiple-high load storage adjacent to assembly areas.

This receiving dock arrangement has been used for just-in-time material delivery in automotive final assembly plants. As many as five pallet sizes have been handled by one standard vehicle.

Automatic closepack floor storage can be accomplished using similar techniques. Lanes can be located as close as load and vehicle clearance will allow. As a vehicle enters an empty lane, it measures the distance it moves and deposits the pallet at the measured end of the lane. Succeeding vehicles deposit loads within a few inches of the last deposited load, controlled by optical sensors in the fork tips. An inventory of loads in storage is maintained by the system controller. This is essentially a single-level AS/R system without random access to loads.

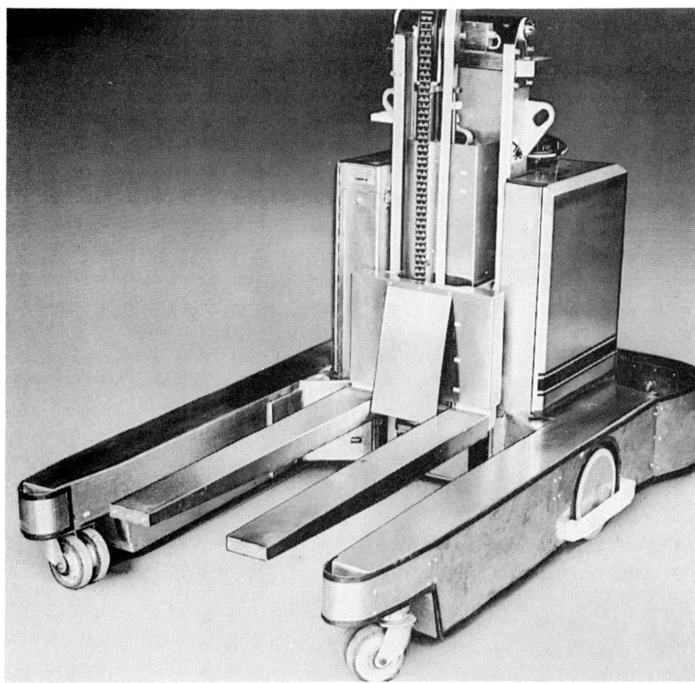

Figure 17.5. Unit load carrier equipped with forks.

Roll handling vehicles with contoured forks can pick up cylindrical loads at floor level. Special forks are available that will automatically position themselves for rolls of varying diameters.

High-lift fork vehicles can be used in AS/R systems where vehicles automatically place and retrieve pallets in rack storage. The vehicles are computer-controlled, have horizontal guidance plus vertical positioning for pallet transfer, and can move easily from aisle to aisle. Initial applications have been small, with one or two aisles 60 to 100 feet long and loads of 2000 pounds stored up to a 20-foot pallet position. Interface with a horizontal AGV transportation system is at floor-level P & D stations at the end of the aisles. Both systems are controlled by the same system computer.

Minimum aisle width depends on the lane size and the type of vehicle. A counterbalanced vehicle with rotating fork or a turret truck can operate in an aisle equal to the vehicle width or load width, whichever is greater, plus 6 inches clearance on each side. Straddle trucks without rotating forks must turn 90 degrees for load transfer, and space must be provided between the floor and the first rack load beam to allow room for the straddle legs.

Stock Selectors. Manually operated stock selectors have been retrofitted with guidance controls for more than 20 years. The guidance was originally mechanical, using floor or rack-mounted guide rails. This allows a stock selector to operate in narrow aisles, with 4 to 6 inches clearance on each side of the vehicle, without damage to product, vehicle, or racks. It also increased operator efficiency because vehicle speed between picks could be increased.

Wire guidance is now used in most guided stock-selector applications because it reduces installation costs (in-floor guide wires are less expensive than guide rails), reduces maintenance, and improves housekeeping (no debris collecting behind guide rails). The increased cost of wire guidance on the vehicle over mechanical guidance is offset by the savings of guide wire installation compared to guide rails.

Guidance packages are available in kit form to be added to existing vehicles and provide straight-line guidance in the selecting aisles with no positioning controls. Movement of the vehicle and locating it for product selection is under manual control.

Wire-guided and computer-controlled stock selectors have been used effectively in small-parts handling and order selection. This "brings the operator to the part" type of picking features microprocessor-controlled vehicles that receive instructions from a central computer control.

Each vehicle has an operator, and transmitted picking instructions are arranged in correct sequence by on board controls prior to entering an aisle. Automatic positioning of the vehicle and elevating the operator's platform locates the picker adjacent to the desired bin. A spotlight illuminates the correct picking side, either left or right. A CRT displays the part name and number, the bin number, quantity desired, and control number.

When an item is picked, the operator keys in its control number. If it does not match the number on the CRT, the error must be corrected before work can continue. The number of issue routing documents required is keyed in and the TASK COMPLETE button is pressed. The documents are printed on board and attached to the material picked. The operator handles the paperwork as the vehicle proceeds to the next location. The major benefits of this order selection system are accuracy in parts picking, improved speed of response to high-priority items, and immediate inventory update.

Batteries

It is important to have guided vehicles powered by batteries of correct ampere-hour capacity to ensure proper operation throughout the designed duration of usage before requiring recharging. Vehicles operating with a low battery charge are a potential source of frustrating malfunctions. In most cases, vehicles can be equipped with enough battery capacity to run two shifts, with the third shift providing sufficient time for recharging.

The number of ampere-hours required for a battery can be calculated very accurately if the loads and distances traveled are known. Battery manufacturers are the best source for battery sizing. A rule of thumb for estimating battery capacity is to allow 120 watthours per ton mile of material moved. This should include the weight of the vehicle and battery. Be sure to account for vehicles running without loads if that is part of their normal duty cycle. For example:

Total rolling load 14,000 lb = 7 ton
Travel 5 at 2 mph = 10 mi
Ton·miles = 7 ton × 10 mi = 70 ton·mi
Watthours = 70 ton·mi × 120 wth/ton·mi = 8400 Wh

Divide this figure by the battery voltage to get battery capacity.

8400 Wh/24 volts = 350 Ah

Batteries should never be completely discharged, so the calculated figure should be increased by at least 20 percent.

Actual battery capacity = 350 Ah
× 1.2 = 420 Ah

Three shift operations will require two batteries per vehicle, allowing one to be charged while the other is in use. Battery changing should be done on a regular, daily schedule to make sure no batteries miss a charge.

Battery discharge indicators that activate a light to alert operators that a battery needs recharging should be avoided if possible. The problem is one of discipline, because it is all too easy for an operator to ignore the visual request and let the next operator handle the responsibility.

A much better method is to have the battery discharge indicator automatically report the condition to the system controller as a part of vehicle monitoring. The system controller can respond by dispatching the vehicle to the battery charging area. An exception might be if the vehicle were performing a high-priority task, which it would be allowed to complete before proceeding to the charging area. The most popular voltages for guided vehicle batteries are 24, 36, and 48 volts.

Guide Path Data

Positions along the guide path need to be identified to vehicles much the same as drivers need road signs on highways. The road signs of the guide path identify decision and stopping points, and vehicle functions such as speed up, slow down, change guide frequency, sound horn, reverse, or lift and lower load deck.

Magnets embedded in the floor and read by reed switches mounted on vehicles are one of the most popular methods used to supply data concerning the guide path. The magnets are approximately 1 inch in diameter, 3 inches long, and are positioned vertically. They can be located in one position adjacent to the guide path and counted sequentially by a single-reed switch on the vehicle. A disadvantage to this technique is that all magnets look alike to the vehicle, and if the magnet counting gets out of sequence, the vehicle is lost. A home base must be established where magnet counting is reset to zero, and when vehicles are added to the system, it must be done at a home base location.

It is more desirable to create unique floor information, and this can be done by using multiple magnet positions across the width of the vehicles. The wider the vehicle, the more magnet positions available, and a vehicle knows exactly where it is on the guide path as it reads each magnet. The possibility of missing a magnet and getting out of sequence is eliminated, and vehicles can be added to the system at any point.

A restriction to the single-magnet unique code is the limited number of magnet positions available. The number of codes can be increased substantially by using one- and two-magnet codes, and this should provide more than 150 codes. Additional codes can be obtained by using a double row of magnets spaced approximately 1 foot apart along the guide path.

Another form of unique floor codes is microwave code plates. They are small, battery-powered units installed in the floor and are excited by a microwave transmission from passing vehicles. This triggers a microwave response that is decoded by the vehicle. These units are more expensive and contain more data than magnet codes, and can be reprogrammed.

In multiple-frequency systems, in-floor wires can be arranged adjacent to the guide path, and can carry a different frequency to provide location information and vehicle instructions. These wires are read by a side antenna on the vehicle, and distance measuring devices verify unique arrangements. Vehicles being added to the system must know their location on the guide path before they are started. This can be obtained by use of an on-board terminal or a remote fixed terminal connected to the system controller. Some systems using these methods allow vehicles to be added only at designated areas.

Vehicles move along the guide path and recognize information in the floor in various forms. At decision points, i.e., where paths diverge, a choice is made based on the shortest path to destination. This choice is in memory for each decision point and destination, either on board the vehicle or in the central controller.

Communications

Computer-controlled systems need a means of communicating with vehicles for programming and traffic control. Four types of communications are available:

1. Radio
2. Data transmitted on the guide wire
3. Optical infrared
4. Inductive loops

Radio communication provides a continuous two-way data link with vehicles and involves a fixed, multichannel unit in the central controller and single-channel units on each vehicle. Frequencies are in the 460 megahertz range. Some testing may be required to determine if there are any dead spots in the system that would inhibit radio transmission and to aid in determining the number, type, and location of antennas.

Vehicles are monitored approximately once a second, and normal interrogation involves vehicle ID, location, and destination. These exchanges are brief but can be extended by the vehicle if more than the requested data is on hand, such as alarm conditions, low battery, emergency bumper stop, or lost guide wire signal. On-board microprocessors manage this data, receive and decode messages from the central controller, and arrange and encode vehicle responses to the controller.

Radio provides maximum flexibility in system control. Vehicles can be programmed "on the fly," and system speed of response to changing load movement demands is improved. It is independent of the guide wire, which is important for systems employing offwire turns and maneuvers.

Data transmitted on the guide wire by the guide line driver provides almost the same flexibility as radio, with the exception of vehicle movement off the wire. Since the distance between the guide wire and the on-board responders is constant, there are no transmission dead spots, as there may be with radio. The techniques to accomplish this type of data link are not widespread.

Optical infrared communication is highly reliable but has the disadvantage of not being continuous: it is point to point. Vehicles must be stopped during data exchange, and this usually occurs at load stations where fixed and mobile units are aligned and in close proximity. Distance between the units can be up to several feet.

Vehicles are usually not dispatched from a communication point unless the path to the next destination is free of traffic, and in large systems this could present a problem in meeting throughput. Alarm conditions cannot be reported as they occur. This type of communication is suited for small systems with few vehicles and load stations.

Inductive loops are another means of point-to-point communication. In-floor wire loops are located adjacent to the guide wire and connected to the central controller for data transmission. They are usually 3 to 10 feet long and must be located at every point communication with vehicles is desired. This is an inexpensive but limited method of data transfer. Some systems using this method do not require vehicles to stop while receiving data from inductive loops.

Controls

Traffic Controls. Multiple-vehicle systems prevent collisions by means of traffic or blocking controls. Guide paths are divided into zones and only one vehicle is allowed in a zone, the size of which can vary from a vehicle or train length to several hundred feet, depending on the blocking techniques used.

One of the simplest blocking methods uses magnets on vehicles to activate in-floor reed switches connected to fixed controls that energize blocking signals. These signals are usually carried by in-floor wire loops adjacent to the guide path. On-board receivers recognize these blocking signals and stop vehicles as long as the signal is present. This method is sometimes called "fixed blocking."

As a vehicle passes a zone boundary, a blocking signal is energized at the entrance to that zone, and the blocking signal at the entrance to the zone just vacated is deenergized. It is a latch-unlatch operation and the fixed controls are wire-connected to accomplish this.

Care must be taken when manually removing vehicles from a system using this type of blocking to avoid locking up the system. If a vehicle is removed from a zone, the blocking signal remains energized and the system acts as if the vehicle is still in the zone. The result is a phantom vehicle lock-up. In areas where this is likely to occur, a manually operated switch should be provided to release the blocking signal.

A more flexible and expensive blocking method employs 40- to 200-kilohertz transmitters and receivers on vehicles, and continuous in-floor wire loops along the guide wire. Transmitters send a blocking signal to the in-floor wire and, at blocking zone entrance, this same wire is crossed to the other side of the guide path and arranged in a short holding loop. The receiver on a following vehicle senses a holding signal in this loop as long as there is a vehicle in the zone ahead, and stops. When the vehicle ahead leaves the zone, the holding signal disappears and the following vehicle restarts.

This method, called "continuous blocking," eliminates phantom vehicles in the system because, when a vehicle is manually removed from a zone, the holding signal from its transmitter is also removed. No fixed equipment or overhead interconnecting wire is required. Both fixed and continuous blocking methods may need additional controls for intersections and merging paths.

Computer blocking offers the greatest flexibility and potential for efficient system operation. Blocking instructions do not come from in-floor devices but are issued from the central controller, and a communication link between vehicles and the controller is required.

The central controller contains a table of all blocking zones in the system and the rules that govern vehicle movement in each zone. It also maintains an up-to-date record of all vehicle locations. Vehicle movement can be prioritized according to status of activity and the zone conditions en route to the destination.

Computer blocking generally permits a wider variety of blocking zones in terms of length, location, and complexity. This should result in improved vehicle efficiency and constant product flow. Installation is faster and costs less than either fixed or continuous blocking because no fixed equipment, interconnecting wiring, or extensive in-floor wiring other than the guide wire is required.

On-Board Programming Controls. Those involve selector panels for manually choosing vehicle destinations. Toggle switch panels provide a switch for every vehicle destination but do not have the memory to arrange them in the sequence in which they were selected. They are limited to simple guide paths, under 50 destinations, and decision points for path-changing requires a course selector switch. Use of these panels is primarily for single-destination or point-to-point operations. Thumbwheel selector switches also fall into this category.

Push-button programmers usually include a microprocessor and have a memory that records the sequence in which destinations are entered. Special functions to be performed at each destination, such as "pickup load at trailer position 4," can be included. Up to 10 destinations can be entered into vehicle memory, and an operator display reveals them one at a time. The display can be stepped up or down to check all programming, and changes can be made by deleting and inserting destinations. Once a vehicle reaches a station and performs the desired functions, the command is erased from memory. When no programming remains in memory, the vehicle automatically returns to a queueing area. It can also circulate on a predetermined route and be available to respond to fixed, manually operated, empty-vehicle stop switches. Push-button programmers provide sophisticated manual system control, especially for tractor trains and pallet trucks.

Computer Controls. These provide a more precise and efficient use of guided vehicles. The central controller can perform the following functions:

1. Program and dispatch vehicles from queueing stations or while in motion

2. Monitor vehicle location and provide data for graphic CRT panel
3. Maintain traffic control
4. Receive data from fixed operator call stations and store FIFO
5. Initiate special functions such as "every fourth load from station 10 goes to inspection"
6. Provide real-time material tracking and verification of load delivery
7. Maintain system inventory
8. Flag priority tasks
9. Respond to vehicle alarm conditions
10. Interface with other material handling systems computer controls
11. Interface with host computers

Vehicles equipped with microprocessors have these capabilities:

1. Receive remote programming commands and store in sequence
2. Report location and load data, receive traffic commands
3. Report destination
4. Remember special functions to be performed at unique command, such as recirculating on a special route when vehicle is empty
5. Monitor alarm conditions such as:
   a. Low battery
   b. Loss of guide signal
   c. Emergency bumper stop
   d. Emergency stop button activated
   e. Invalid programming
   f. Load not correctly positioned
   g. Vehicle placed on guide path backwards
   h. Trailer malfunction
   i. Loss of traffic control signals

The General AGV System Control Diagram (see Figure 17.6) illustrates most of the controls associated with guided vehicle systems.

1. *Operator interface.* CRT and keyboard for manually entering data in system controller. Can be used as manual backup to operate system and to interrogate vehicles. CRT can display vehicle data. Printer can be included.

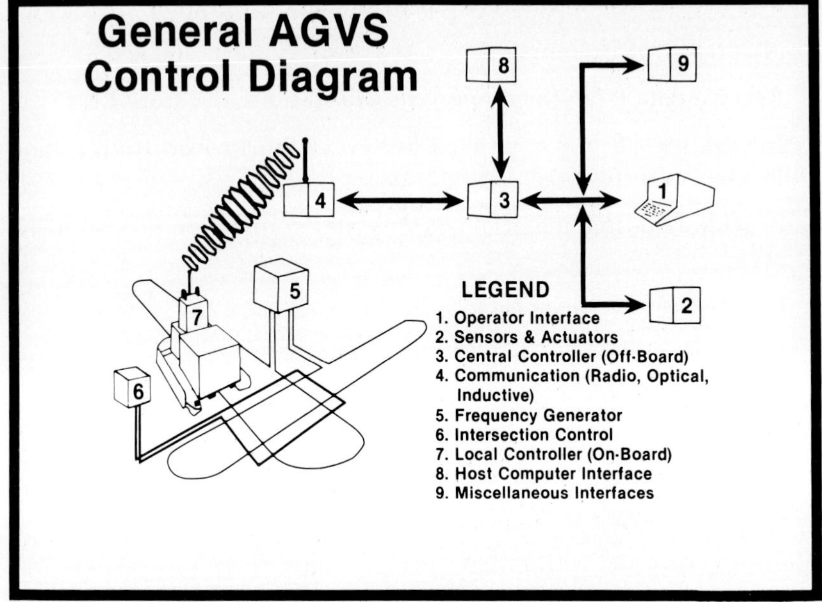

Figure 17.6. General AGV system control diagram. (*Conco-Tellus Inc.*)

2. *Sensors and activators.* Load sensing switches at P & D stations, signals from fire door controls, manually controlled call boxes.
3. *Central controller (off-board).* System computer control.
4. *Communications (radio, optical, inductive).* Data links between central controller and vehicles.
5. *Frequency generator.* Unit that provides the guidance signal to the guide wire.
6. *Intersection control.* Units usually required in addition to normal blocking techniques to control traffic at intersections.
7. *Local controller (on-board).* Usually includes a microprocessor to handle on-board programming, remote programming and interrogation, and to keep track of vehicle location data from floor codes and alarm monitors.
8. *Host computer interface.* Can provide load movement demand that the central controller uses to direct vehicle actions. Inventory can be updated.
9. *Miscellaneous interfaces.* Other material handling system controls, such as AS/RS systems and conveyors.

Safety and Warning Features

The safety record of guided vehicles has been outstanding since their inception, because safety has always been considered an item of major importance by vehicle developers and a key to AGV system acceptance. Providing a failsafe means of rapidly stopping a vehicle when it makes contact with an object in its path was of high priority for early AGV system designers. The answer was an emergency bumper mounted on the front of each vehicle that caused it to stop abruptly when the bumper was activated.

The distance required for this type of stop depends on the vehicle speed, the total rolling load, and the resistance between the braking wheels and the floor. It is not always possible to bring a vehicle to a stop within the distance between the vehicle frame and the bumper, which is usually 12 to 18 inches. Heavy loads with light vehicles may cause the maximum braking resistance to be exceeded and the braking wheel to skid. Individual vehicle manufacturers are the proper source for braking data.

Types of emergency bumpers are:

1. Double-leaf. Two metal strips, usually stainless steel and at least 3 inches wide, arranged one inside the other. When pressure causes the leaves to touch, the vehicle stops.
2. Single-leaf with photocells on the vehicle directed to reflective spots on the bumper. When pressure on the bumper moves a spot out of a photocell's view, the vehicle stops. Single-leaf bumpers can be metal or plastic.
3. Single-leaf and spring-loaded cables connected to microswitches. When bumper movement eases cable tension, a microswitch is activated and the vehicle stops.

Unit load carriers that travel in both forward and reverse direction have bumpers on both ends of the vehicle.

Sonic and optical infrared devices are used as look-ahead object detectors. They complement the emergency bumpers by sensing objects ahead of the bumper and cause a speed reduction or stop prior to bumper contact. These units are directional and adjustable and lessen the demand for rapid bumper stops.

Large mushroom-type stop buttons are readily accessible from both sides of the vehicle. A warning light is activated whenever a vehicle is in automatic operation. It is usually red or amber and can be either rotating or a high-intensity flash. Vehicles stop automatically with loss of guidance signal. Horns can be sounded and vehicle speeds reduced at blind corners and intersections. Different tones or horn patterns can be used for reverse guidance. Down-ramp speeds are controlled to prevent runaway vehicles.

Mechanical wheel bells that sound whenever a vehicle is in motion in both manual and automatic mode are an effective warning device in noisy areas. Fire door controls stop oncoming vehicles when fire doors close. Controls for doors that are automatically opened and closed by vehicles will stop an incoming vehicle if a door does not open. Traffic controls prevent collisions in multiple-vehicle systems.

System Planning

System Objectives. The first step in system planning is to define the system objectives, and a database is needed before they can be stated. Find out how much of what is going where. Begin with the load characteristics:

Length

Width

Height

Weight: average _____ maximum _____

Stability

Type of load bottom: pallet _____ skid _____ other _____

(Multiple load sizes may affect the vehicle choice.)

Next, look at the load activity. How many loads move to and from specific load stations and in what time frame? How fast must the system respond to load pickup and delivery demands? This information gathering is one of the toughest parts of system planning, but it is a key element in formulating the objectives.

The type and height of load stations must be identified. Is there freedom to choose the type of stations, or are they already established? Are the loads on the floor, on nonpowered stands, or on powered conveyors? Is load transfer to be manual or automatic? If automatic, then what is the source of destination programming information? If this is not known, a decision must be made on how to get it and incorporate it into the system controls. Perhaps it is available from the host computer. It will not do to ask for computer control if the proper information is not available. Do not overlook operators as data sources even if load transfer is automatic. Manually operated call buttons and automatic load sensing switches at P & D stations can supply valuable load movement requests to a central controller.

Are there other material handling systems to integrate with for load transfer and control interface, such as AS/RS systems and conveyors?

A layout drawing of the area to be serviced should be on hand at the time system planning starts. It should show aisle locations and widths, and all P & D stations. The scale should not be smaller than 1 inch = 16 feet. Look out for tight spots and narrow aisles that might interfere with vehicle movement. If the building already exists, these conditions may be difficult to change.

A tentative guide path that passes all the P & D stations should be drawn on the layout, and the direction of travel should be indicated with arrows. Guide paths are normally laid out with 8-foot-radius turns for vehicle speeds of 3 miles per hour. The radius of turn depends on vehicle size, wheel arrangement, and speed. Reducing speed by one-half should allow the radius of turn to be reduced by a similar amount.

Try to stay away from path segments with two-way travel unless it is absolutely necessary. In general, one-way travel is better for material flow, and the system controls will be reduced. The first consideration for any back-tracking in the system should be the shortest recirculating path. The extra travel involved is usually a better trade-off than tying up a portion of guide path with two-way travel. The challenge is to arrange the guide path in its simplest form and still fulfill the system demands.

The data layout now on hand should be sufficient for setting down the system objectives. They should outline what is to be accomplished in terms of load movement and control.

Choice of Vehicle. Is the system best served by load movement in batches (tractor trailers) or in single loads? If it is tractor trailers, base the selection on proper towing capacity.

If it is to be pallet trucks or unit load carriers, base the decision on controls and load transfer heights. Pallets to be handled at floor level and operators available for vehicle loading and programming would be a good application for pallet trucks. Pallets at floor level to be delivered to conveyor stands with automatic load and unload and remote vehicle programming could be handled nicely by fork vehicles. Carriers with lifting load decks are a good choice for picking up pallets from P & D stands at an AS/RS system and delivering them to stations of equal height and design.

Determining the Number of Vehicles Required. In simple systems with a single guide path loop, it is very easy to determine the number of vehicles required. For example:

Guide path length = 2000 ft
Volume of loads = 40/h

Vehicles are tractors pulling three trailers. A round trip consists of automatically loading all three trailers at one station, unloading single loads at three stops, and traveling the entire guide path. Time for a train to make one round trip:

Loading, 30 sec per load	1.5 min
Unloading, 30 sec per load	1.5 min
Travel time, 2000 ft/200 (ft)(min)	10.0 min
Add 20 percent for delays, traffic controls	2.0 min
Round-trip time	15.0 min

Loads moved per train per hour:

$$15\text{(min)(trip)}/60\text{ min} \times 3\text{ loads per trip} = 12$$

Number of vehicles required:

$$12\text{(loads)(vehicle)(hour)}/40\text{(loads)(hour)} = 3.33$$

Use 4 vehicles.

Rounding the calculated number to the next higher number adds a small amount of vehicle capacity, but in systems of 10 vehicles or more, serious consideration should be given to adding spare vehicles.

Few systems are as simple as the example above. As guide paths become complex, it is more difficult to establish a round-trip distance and an educated guess may have to be made. Look out and adjust for imbalances, such as high volume on long runs.

The load movement in many systems demands that vehicles move from point to point; they do not follow round-trip paths. A detailed analysis is required and a table should be constructed to aid in handling the data in the following steps:

1. List all load movement per hour between individual pickup and deposit stations. Include empty container movement.
2. List the distances, in feet, between all stations identified in step 1.
3. Multiply the totals from steps 1 and 2 to get total distance traveled

for all load movement. Analyze the data for vehicle deadheading and, if present, increase the total distance traveled by an estimated percent.

4. Determine the time required for all load movement by dividing the total distance from step 3 by the average vehicle speed in feet per minute.
5. Determine the time required for all load pickups and deposits. If load transfer is automatic, it should be in the range of 20 to 30 seconds.
6. Add steps 4 and 5 to get the total time required for load pickup, deposit, and movement.
7. Add 20 percent to the step-6 figure to account for delays. This represents the total running time required for all vehicles during a 1-hour period.
8. Divide the total time from step 7 by 60 minutes to get the number of vehicles required.

This method of analysis can be quite an ordeal for large complex systems, and computer simulation should be seriously considered. It can determine the number of vehicles required and test the system throughput after design is complete. Potential bottlenecks can be identified and removed. There is a practical limit to the number of vehicles that can operate in a system before it becomes saturated. Some paths are more heavily traveled than others and they must not be allowed to be overloaded. The rush-hour traffic jams must be avoided, and alternate routes can be used effectively in smoothing out the peaks and valleys of load movement. Layout changes can be tested to reduce travel time, and vehicle speed and load pickup and deposit procedures should be reviewed. Any manual interface should be suspect for improvement. Users should agree on the time required for manual interface and be responsible for it.

Other items not to be overlooked in system planning are:

Fire doors: Locate on layout.

Automatic doors that must be opened and closed: Locate on layout.

Ramps: Indicate length and slope in percent.

Elevators: If part of system.

Drawbridges: If part of system.

Floors, type and condition: Location of expansion joints, drains that might interfere with the guide signals. Be realistic; wood-block floors subject to water and buckling are not going to be held in place by guide wires.

Freezers, coolers, outdoor operation: Heaters in control cabinets and appropriate lubricants may be required. Traction outdoors in northern areas could be a problem.

Review of the AGV System Advantages

Guide paths can be easily installed in new and existing buildings.

Floor is clear—no obstructions.

Unlimited number of stopping points available.

Guide paths can be expanded and revised, and stops added or deleted.

Vehicles can be added to increase system capacity; allows phased capital investment.

Multiple-vehicle systems have failsafe security.

Manual backup operation available.

Safe and consistent handling of product; less damage to vehicles.

Strong economic justification; reduction of operators.

Can operate on ramps, elevators, and drawbridges, and cross railroad tracks.

Can operate in cool rooms, freezers, and outdoors.

Improved material control. Real-time tracking of product movement provides the flexibility for changing production needs.

Improved inventory control.

Interface with other material handling systems controls and host computer.

Interface with AS/RS system with automatic load transfer.

Interface with robots or carry on-board robots for load transfer.

The foremost integrator of material movement in warehousing.

Well-proved, reliable, and capable of precise control with any degree of flexibility you may need.

18 Overhead Cranes

Michael S. Erwin

Manager, Marketing, Harnischfeger Corporation, Milwaukee, Wisconsin

Types of Cranes

The two major types of overhead traveling crane are the top-running crane and the underhung crane. The top-running crane is designed and built to cover a greater range of capacities (to 500 tons and greater); longer, unsupported spans between runways; and higher-speed applications than underhung cranes. However, underhung cranes have advantages in terms of economy and versatility.

Top-Running Bridge Cranes

Top-running overhead traveling bridge cranes are one of the most commonly used pieces of material handling equipment found in warehouses handling heavy loads. They are used to transport loads through the air anywhere in a warehouse. The use of an overhead traveling hook crane allows transporting loads within close proximity to the sides and ends of a building without having to worry about machinery or other large obstacles mounted on the floor. There are two categories of overhead traveling cranes used in warehousing today: single-girder and double-girder.

Single-Girder Cranes. Single-girder, top-running cranes consist of a single girder mounted on top of two end trucks that span the width of a building and have a hoist running on the lower flange of a structural shaped girder (Figure 18.1). These cranes normally have capacities up to 10 tons and spans up to 60 feet. The design of the hoisting mechanism and trolley travel mechanism are similar to those found on monorail-type cranes. Single-girder, top-running cranes are normally operated from the floor by a pendant station that travels with the hoisting and trolley mechanism across the span of the structural shape girder. The single-girder, top-running crane is a very economical crane; however, it should be kept in mind that it is normally used in light to moderate service.

Double-Girder Cranes. Double-girder, top-running cranes, unlike the single-girder crane, have a trolley mounted above the crane girders. The trolley traverses the span of the girders on crane rails attached to the top of the crane girders. This design places the crane hoist as close to the roof trusses of a building as possible, thereby obtaining the highest possible lift for a given building. Top-running, double-girder cranes are operated by various means (Figure 18.2). In a high-production warehousing operation, one would normally operate the crane from a fixed or traveling cab requiring a full-time crane operator. Another method of operation would be the same as used on single-girder, top-running cranes; i.e., by using a pendant station suspended from either the crane trolley or from an independently mounted festoon system spanning the length of the crane. A third method of operating the crane is by the use of radio control. This allows the crane operator standing on the crane floor to walk anywhere in the building independent of the crane and still be able to operate the crane.

As previously mentioned, the underhung crane is the other of the two major types of overhead traveling cranes (Figure 18.3).

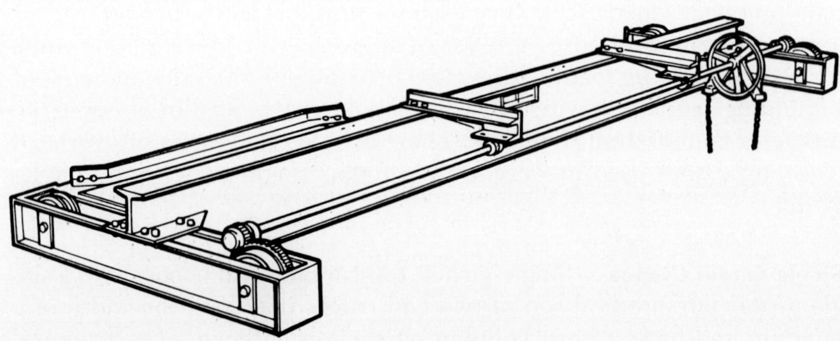

Figure 18.1. Single-girder, top-running overhead bridge crane.

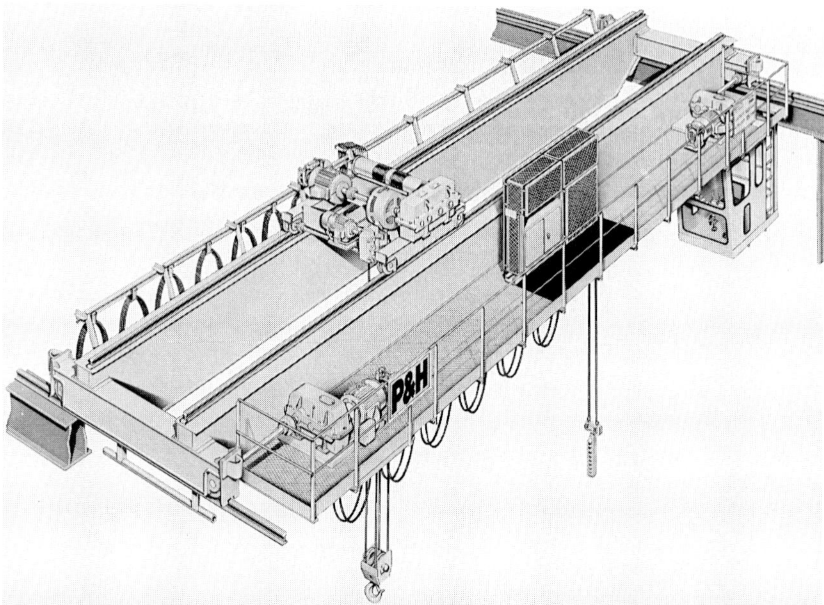

Figure 18.2 Double-girder, top-running overhead bridge crane. (*Harnischfeger Corp.*)

Construction. Lightweight, highly durable underhung cranes and runways are constructed from specially designed and fabricated hardened track rail. This rail is fabricated from a flat-tread, high-carbon, specially rolled bottom T, continuously welded to an upper T section. The upper T section is normally fabricated from steel plate. The advantages of this rail are in the T and the high "strength-to-weight" ratio. The flat-tread bottom T permits easier crane/carrier movement because it generates less friction and promotes longer wheel life. The high carbon content gives much longer life than a conventional I beam and prevents peening, which can quickly destroy a rail. The high strength-to-weight ratio allows use of a shallower, lighter beam that can span greater distances between support points than an I beam can. This decreases both the loading on the building structure and the installation cost.

Basically, an underhung crane bridge consists of two or more parallel rails or runways that are suspended at the same level and a constant distance apart. Across this distance, or span, is another rail (or rails) which is called a "bridge." Attached to the ends of the bridge are end trucks that contain wheels that run on the lower flanges of the runway rails. Suspended by trolleys from the lower flange of the bridge beam is the hoist or lifting mechanism.

In contrast to the top-running crane, which is suspended from brackets attached to the building columns, the underhung crane runway is suspended from the roof structure. Also, whereas the top-running bridge is bolted to the top of the end trucks, which run on top of rail heads fastened to the top side of the runway beams, the crane bridge is hung *between* the runways and bolted to the underside of the end trucks. The end trucks run on the bottom flange of the runways. Because the underhung crane runs suspended under its runway rails, the crane bridge can extend beyond the runway rails, thereby extending the hoist/load travel distance.

Advantages. Because of the underhung crane's features, the cost of the total installation can be reduced through savings in equipment and building costs, and the underhung system provides greater load handling flexibility and efficiency than a top-running crane system.

Savings in the cost of the installation can be achieved primarily in two areas:

1. Savings in the costs of the crane bridge and runways. The use of specially designed and fabricated hardened track beams with their high strength-to-weight ratio as compared to conventional structural shapes and I beams results in lighter-weight, less expensive cranes and runways.
2. With a wide variety of suspension clamps and fittings available, underhung crane runways can be installed without major building modifications, thus saving the expense of these modifications.

Through-the-air material handling with an underhung crane gives load handling versatility that cannot be achieved with lift trucks or conveyors. Six advantages that underhung cranes have over other types of material handling equipment are:

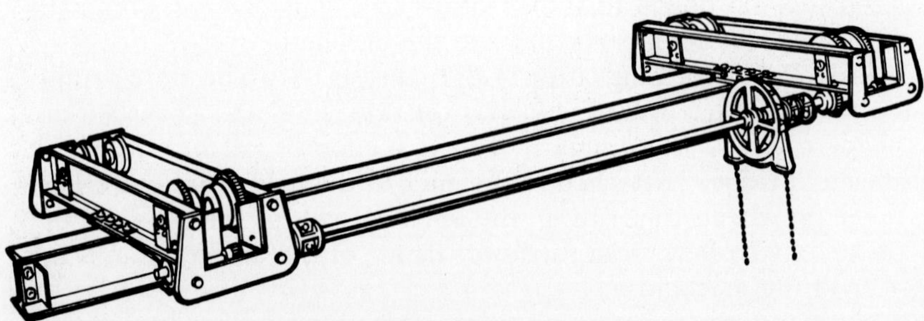

Figure 18.3 Typical underhung bridge crane.

1. Better floor coverage by use of through-the-air material handling equipment. The hoist can cover almost every square foot of floor space and travel from point to point by the shortest route—a straight line.
2. The low-profile design of an underhung crane installed up close to the roof trusses gives maximum hook lift and maximum valuable, vertical warehouse storage space under the crane.
3. Wide bay service is possible with a low-cost, lightweight, low-profile underhung crane bridge through the use of multiple runways. It is not unusual to have three, four, or more runways spanning distances to 120 feet or beyond.
4. Through-the-air material handling cuts down on the number and width of aisles requires for proper load handling, thus freeing up valuable floor space in a warehouse.
5. Overhead material handling permits positioning of the lifting device (hoist) directly over the load to allow precise load positioning, thus cutting down on load handling damage.
6. Overhang construction allows the hoist to pass under the runways for greater floor coverage than possible with top-running cranes. This permits hoist and load to be transferred by means of interlocks to cranes of the same construction in adjacent bays, or onto a fixed spur track or monorail system for increased loading handling versatility.

Underhung Crane Variations. There are a number of underhung crane variations available to fit most any material handling requirement. Underhung cranes are grouped into the following types.

1. Single-Girder
   a. Hand-pushed
   b. Hand-chain-driven
   c. Motor-driven
2. Double-Girder
   a. Motor-driven

The problem is which to choose for a given application. In general, there are several key questions that help make the right decision. These questions are:

- How much is the load weight?
- How high does it have to be lifted?
- How far does the load have to travel?

- How fast does the load have to travel
- How accurately does the load have to be spotted?
- How often will the crane be used per hour, hours per day, and days per week?

Single-Girder Cranes. The first underhung type is the *single-girder, hand-pushed* crane. This unit is the most economical to purchase and is normally available in capacities to 2 tons and spans to 30 feet. It is recommended that the distance from the operating floor to the crane not exceed 20 feet. These limitations are placed on a hand-pushed crane because the amount of effort required to propel the crane is a direct function of span, load being moved, coefficient of friction, and elevation of the crane.

To propel a hand-pushed underhung crane, with or without a load, it is necessary to pull on the hook. A 2-ton-capacity, 30-foot-span crane with a 20-foot elevation would require approximately 50 pounds of horizontal effort to get the load started, and half that to keep it moving. Moving loads heavier than 2 tons requires a good amount of work, and it is difficult to control the spotting of a load that requires an excessive amount of physical effort.

Since the underhung crane can be at any elevation, the pendulum action from the hoist to the load can greatly affect the amount of physical effort needed to move the load. As the operator starts to pull on the load, the load tends to curve upward so that he or she is not only pulling on the load, but also lifting it slightly. In effect, the higher the crane, the harder it is to pull and control. Therefore, it is recommended that in most hand-pushed applications the maximum height of the crane not exceed 20 feet.

The hand-pushed underhung crane is designed to accept a hand-chain hoist (Figure 18.4). This type of crane is most often used where material activity is very slight and low cost of equipment is an important factor.

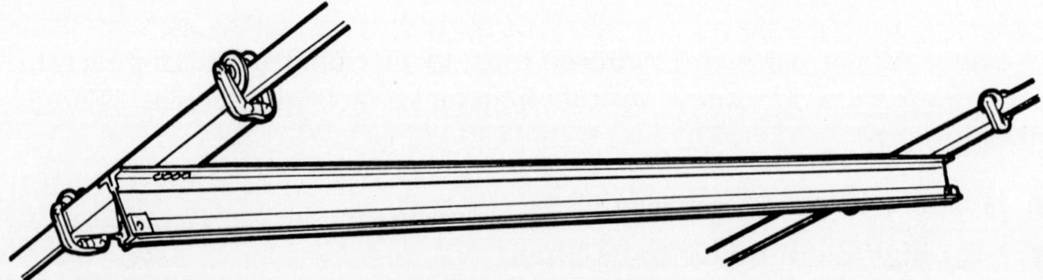

Figure 18.4. Hand-pushed underhung bridge crane.

Once the material handling activity increases or the required capacity exceeds 2 tons, the *single-girder, hand-chain-driven crane* becomes useful. This type of crane can be used in capacities up to 5 tons and spans to 30 feet, and can be used with either a hand-chain or electric motor-driven hoist.

Hand-chain-driven underhung cranes should be used only where the service is relatively light or where spotting a load is extremely critical. Runway travel required for normal load handling should typically not exceed 50 feet. Even when the crane is unloaded, it is necessary to use the chain drive to traverse the crane. The chain wheel-to-drive shaft ratio that makes traversing of the loaded crane easier causes slow movement of the bridge crane. Other disadvantages of hand-chain-driven cranes include the fact that, because the hand chain on the crane is in a fixed position, it is necessary to keep an aisle clear so the hand chain is accessible to the operator. Also, because the hand chain operating the crane is in a fixed position but the hoist is free to move back and forth across the crane bridge, the operator must change positions to handle the load. In general, hand-chain-driven cranes should be considered for standby or infrequent service where accurate load spotting is required.

The next type of underhung crane is the *single-girder, motor-driven bridge.* An electric motor drive is added to a crane bridge to eliminate the labor required to propel it without the disadvantages of hand-pushed or hand-chain-driven cranes. This type of crane is normally used for capacities to 15 tons and spans to 60 feet.

Two of the primary considerations in selecting an underhung, single-girder, motor-driven crane are in the speed and type of control. Control will be covered in detail later on in this section.

For floor-controlled, motor-driven cranes it is recommended that the travel speed not exceed 150 feet per minute. In effect, the slower the crane traverses, the easier it is to control. A good minimum speed would be 50 feet per minute and a very good top speed would be 100 feet per minute. These speeds are also recommended because a comfortable walking speed for an operator is approximately 125 feet per minute.

Quite often the length of a crane runway can be misleading, and a crane can be provided with a travel speed too great for proper transportation and spotting of the load. In most cases, even though a runway is 200 feet long, a crane transports the load on the runway for only a short distance. The need for the crane to travel from one end to the other of the runway, either loaded or unloaded, is generally infrequent. At the recommended speeds, it would take only a few seconds longer than, say, a speed greater than 200 feet per minute would take. This would be a very minor disadvantage compared to the increased difficulty of controlling the load that the increased speed may cause.

Most hoists used on motor-driven cranes are motor-driven with motor-driven carriers (Figure 18.5). Because the travel distance across the bridge is short, usually 60 feet or less, a fast hoist carrier traverse speed is not necessary and can be most objectionable.

A single-girder, motor-driven, underhung crane will do most everything a double-girder, motor-driven crane will do, except it will do it for less money. However, a single-girder, motor-driven crane will require more headroom. The hoist on this type of crane is suspended from the bridge girder, which is in turn suspended from the crane end trucks. This puts limitations on how high off the operating floor the hoist can be suspended. When greater lift, greater capacity, or a crane that takes up a very narrow envelope of space is required, a double-girder crane is required.

Double-Girder Cranes. With the *double-girder, underhung crane* bridge construction, there is air space between the two bridge girders, which allows the hoist to be placed up between the girders. This provides a better hook lift and requires a narrower envelope of space for the crane. Double-girder cranes are usually built in spans to 60 feet and capacities to 30 tons. The same rules governing bridge and carrier traverse speeds for the motor-driven, single-girder cranes also apply to the double-girder cranes.

Power and Control Options. Underhung cranes with motorized drives must have a means to provide power and control to the moving crane and/or hoist. There are three major types of power and control conducting systems available for use with underhung cranes:

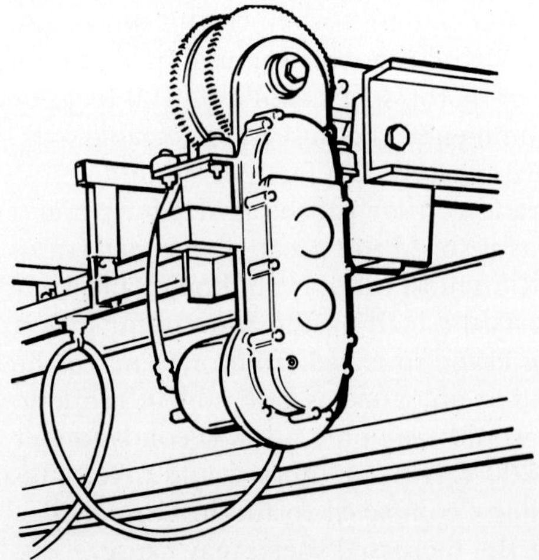

Figure 18.5. Typical motor-driven carrier.

1. *Cable reels,* which can be used on short-span crane bridges or runways. Reels should normally not be used when the length of the crane bridge or runway exceeds 20 feet of cable reach. Excessive pull developed by the spring tension of the reel and the weight of the cable are the limiting factors. A ratchet on the reel should always be considered.
2. *Festooned cable* can be used on either crane bridges or runways; however, it is more commonly used on bridges. The cable is carried by messenger trolleys suspended from either a steel cable or with wheels running in a track. The steel cable-supported system is most economical, but is limited to a maximum length of 30 feet. The track-supported systems are commonly used to 60 feet and beyond.
3. The third type is a *shielded rigid bar conductor* that is a conductive metal bar or shape that is covered on three sides by a nonconductive cover. The open side makes contact with a spring-loaded sliding collector shoe. This conductor can be used on very long-span cranes and runways.

Motor-driven cranes and carriers have a variety of controls and controllers available for proper load control and positioning. There are two basic types of control used with underhung cranes: one-speed control, for crane traverse speeds to 100 feet per minute and two-speed control, for speeds in excess of 100 feet per minute. Two-speed control gives a top-end speed for traversing a long distance and a low-end speed for better load control. A typical two-speed control would give a top speed of 150 feet per minute and a low speed of 50 feet per minute. Coupled with the controls are either a ballast resistor or solid-state soft start device for smooth acceleration and deceleration of the crane during traverse. The ballast resistor has the advantage of low cost, while the solid-state units work best on heavier-duty applications, because they do not generate the heat that the ballast resistors can.

On floor-controlled motor-driven cranes, trolleys, and hoists, control of the motor-driven motion is usually from a push-bottom pendant station. The pendant station can be fixed and suspended from a point on the crane bridge. This is best used on short-span cranes because the operator cannot control the crane and move with the load. The pendant station can also be suspended from the moving hoist and move with the hoist and load. This is required in applications where the operator must accompany the load for proper handling and positioning. Some applications may require the operator to move with the load as it is traversed across the bridge, but due to the size of the load or the type of material being handled, the operator must also maintain a safe distance from the load. In this case, a pendant station suspended from a festooned cable carried in a messenger track is ideal. This allows the operator to move back and forth across the bridge independent of the hoist, allowing him or her to maintain proper load control while maintaining a safe distance from the load, if necessary.

Two other types of control are cab and radio. Operator control cabs are usually used on high-speed, heavy-duty, double-girder cranes. The operator rides in the crane bridge suspended cab and controls the motions by means of push-button pendant station or master switches. Radio control can be used to control floor-controlled cranes in areas that would be difficult or dangerous for the operator to walk through, or to send a crane and control of that crane from one operator to another in long bay applications.

Monorails

A monorail is a single track containing one or more trolleys, with the pickup and setdown points located directly under the centerline of the rail. It is different from a crane system in that it has an unlimited sense of direction and therefore, can be "snaked" through a warehouse. Monorails are sometimes used in conjunction with a crane bridge system through the use of an interlocking device. A monorail is most economically supported from existing building steel, since floor supports can involve a great deal of superstructure and, therefore, be quite costly.

The main disadvantage of a monorail is that the pickup and setdown stations must be located under the centerline of the track. Consequently, some flexibility of movement throughout is lost because of its predetermined path.

Monorails usually contain a combination of curves and switches; however, they can be as simple as a straight line with end stops at either end. A monorail is made up of many short sections of track spliced together to form one continuous track.

Monorail Components. A monorail system can be made up of a combination of the following components:

1. The hardened *track* is a specially designed and fabricated steel beam with a flat-tread, high-carbon bottom T running surface. This provides long wear and ease of traverse motion by trolleys and tractors due to a low coefficient of friction and a high strength-to-weight design that permits spanning greater distances between support points with a lighter, shallower beam, as compared to an I beam or structural shape. The high-carbon, flat-tread bottom T gives greater beam life and helps prevent the peening that may occur with I beams. The track may be directly

bolted to the overhead building steel or suspended by means of a flexible suspension system comprised of hanger clamps and steel suspension rods.

2. Monorail *track curves* can be obtained with various radii and bends to meet the needs of the application. Curves are used to change the direction of travel of the monorail system or to go around permanent obstructions.

3. *Trolleys* can have two, four, or eight wheels, depending on the requirements of the load. The trolleys run on the bottom flange of the track and most are self-centering, so when not in motion, the load exerts equal loading on both sides of the track. Most trolleys are provided with flat-tread wheels which, when used with the flat-tread rail, have a low coefficient of friction and are much easier to move.

4. *Drive tractors* are available in hand-geared or motor-driven versions for easier movement of heavier loads (2 tons or greater) through a system. The drive tractor is trolley-suspended and obtains its drive traction through the use of a rubber drive tire that exerts pressure to the underside of the track by means of an adjustable spring.

5. To maintain complete flexibility in monorail systems, the manufacturers developed several types of *switches:* tongue, sliding or glide (Figure 18.6), cross-track, and turntable. The *tongue switch* was so named because it resembles a tongue. It is fixed at one end by the hinge. The other end swings free like a gate to select the direction of flow. The free end is fitted with a positive latch device for alignment. Safety stops lock the open end of the rail when the switch is thrown. The chief advantage is that its simplicity makes it the least expensive of all the switches. Offsetting this advantage are some limitations: tongue switches

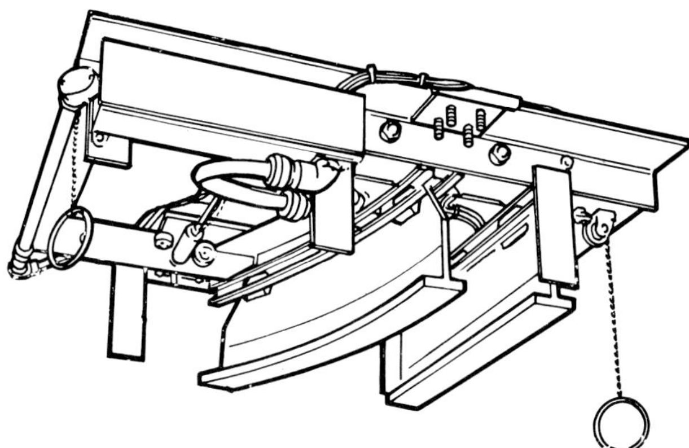

Figure 18.6. Monorail track switch.

are more difficult to electrify, require more layout room because they cannot turn as tight a corner as a sliding switch, and the trolley transition is not as smooth as with the sliding switch. Tongue switches can be used in right-hand, left-hand, Y, and three-way switching operations.

The *sliding* or *glide switch* performs the same duties as the tongue switch. This switch operates with a *movable* inner frame sliding within a *fixed* outer frame. Short sections of curved and straight track are mounted on the inner frame. The inner section glides at right angles to the flow of the material.

This switch is superior in design to the tongue switch. Its construction leads to smoother trolleys operation through the curved portion of the switch. This is achieved by mounting a portion of the curve to the inner frame of the switch. The sliding switch can be more easily electrified and is more compact than the tongue switch, allowing for tighter corners. This compactness better suits tighter layout situations. Because of its superior design, the cost of this switch is higher than that of the tongue switch.

The *cross-track switch* is used when it is necessary to cross the path of two individual monorails. The cross-track switch should never be operated with a load on the moving section. The construction of the cross-track switch involves a frame within a frame, with the inner frame being capable of rotating 90 degrees on a central bearing. Connecting tracks are secured to the switch plate by fixed hangers similar to those utilized on the glide and tongue switches. The track is notched to fit locking lugs on the switch hangers. Safety latches and stops are similar to those incorporated on the tongue and sliding switches. This switch cannot be electrified, and the best method of support is to bolt it directly to the superstructure, thus ensuring rigidity. The *turntable* is very similar in design to the cross-track switch, except that is is normally designed to be operated with *a load on the moving section.*

6. *Lift sections* are special, separate sections of track on which a trolley or load can be positioned. This independent track section can be raised or lowered by a hoist. A lift section is similar to an elevator in that the hoist is mounted on top of a shaft or structure that raises the live section of the lift from one elevation to the next. This can be used to raise a hoist with load from one floor level in a warehouse to another without rehandling the load.

A *drop section* is usually designed *without* an elevator-type shaft and generally lowers the load no more than a few feet. Drop sections are used for permanently fixed lowering operations and for transporting a large number of loads to several predetermined locations. It operates by moving a free trolley onto the live portion of the drop section. The live section drops down to hook onto a load and raises back to the track level. Safety trolley stops release, allowing the loaded trolley to move to its next location.

7. Monorails with motor-driven hoists or tractors must be provided with a means to provide *power and control* to the moving crane and/or hoist. The three major types of power and control conducting systems available for use with monorail systems are the same found on underhung cranes.

8. Motor-driven hoists and carriers have a variety of *controls and controllers* available for proper load control and positioning. There are two basic types of controls used in monorail systems: *one-speed control* for traverse speeds to 100 feet per minute and *two-speed control* for speeds in excess of 100 feet per minute. *Two-speed control* will give a top end speed for traversing a long distance and a low end for better load control. A typical two-speed control would give a top speed of 150 feet per minute and a low speed of 50 feet per minute. However, due to the normally short travel distances encountered in a monorail system and the need to negotiate switches and curves, a slower traverse speed of approximately 60 feet per minute is recommended.

9. The monorail system is fastened to the building roof structure one of two ways. The first method, *direct bolt* or *clamping,* saves money on suspension hardware and results in a better hook lift. However, because the rail is direct-bolted, there is little allowance for runway flexibility to compensate for building expansion, contraction, or shift. The second method, flexibly suspending the rail by means of hanger clamps and steel rods, is more expensive than direct bolting and may reduce hook lift. However, *flexible suspension* allows for ease of monorail releveling and adjustment in the event of building shift.

Gantry Cranes

Like overhead traveling cranes, gantry cranes use either an underrunning or a top-running trolley. Gantry cranes consist of either single- or double-girder design with either one or two shear legs. A gantry crane with one shear leg is referred to as a "single-leg gantry." The *single-leg gantry* has an end truck running on a runway supported from the building structure and one or two girders spanning a predetermined distance. These are connected to a shear leg, which in turn is connected to a second end truck that runs on a rail mounted on the operating floor (Figure 18.7). The *double-leg gantry* is of similar design; however, it is completely supported from the operating floor using two rails running either

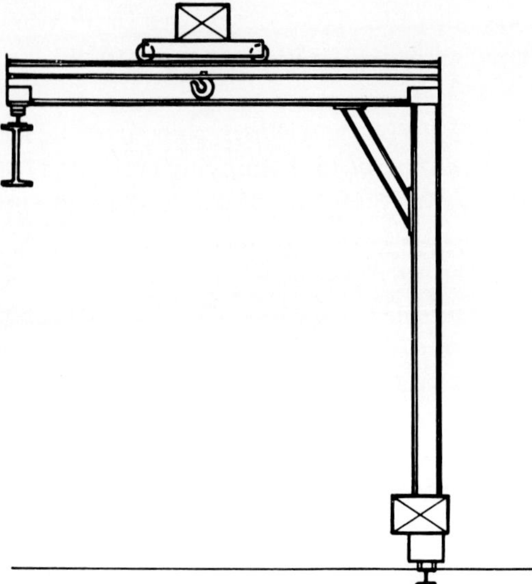

Figure 18.7. Single-leg gantry crane.

the full or partial length of the building, whichever is desired. Gantry cranes inside an enclosed warehouse are normally used to supplement the overhead crane. Quite often they are of the single-leg type, spanning either one-fourth or one-half the entire crane bay, adding flexibility to the material handling. This allows through-the-air movement of material with two cranes independent of each other. The double-leg gantry design is more commonly used for outdoor warehousing, such as steel storage or receiving and unloading (Figure 18.8).

Stacker Cranes

Stacker cranes are another form of overhead traveling crane that add the ability to rotate a load 360 degrees. In addition to being able to rotate a load 360 degrees by the use of a turntable mounted on the crane trolley, the stacker crane consists of a telescoping rigid mast suspended from the crane trolley. This allows more precise spotting of loads. Stacker cranes are becoming more and more popular in warehousing because of this ability. The operator's cab on a stacker crane can be mounted from either the overhead crane bridge or the telescoping mast, or travel up and down independently from the stacker mast. This allows an operator to place loads into storage bins that are approaching

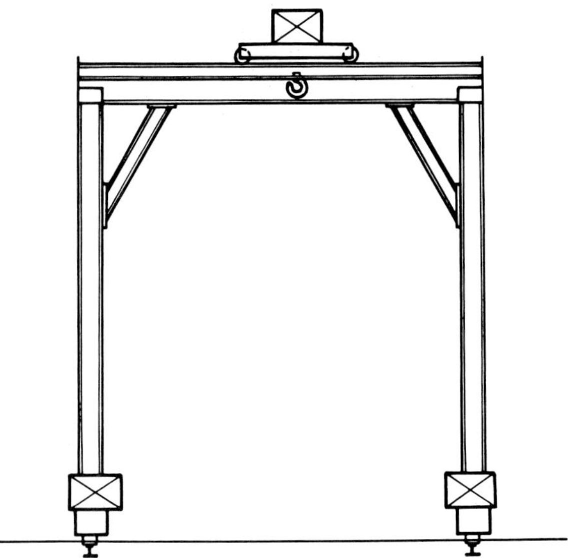

Figure 18.8. Double-leg gantry crane.

the bottom of the crane girder. Because the stacker crane has a rigid telescoping mast, it lends itself to automation, which is becoming more popular in the warehousing of products (Figure 18.9).

Hoists

The hoist is the backbone of all through-the-air material handling equipment discussed in this chapter. Hoists have been termed the second greatest invention (after the wheel). There are many types and styles of hoists, with most major manufacturers' product lines containing 2000 to 15,000 models. For the sake of general warehouse planning, we will identify the three primary types and general features.

The *manual chain hoist* is exactly as its name implies (Figure 18.10). Its operation is accomplished by pulling a wheel-suspended hand chain, which in turn drives a gear reduction directly connected to a chain pocket wheel. The rotating pocket wheel drives the load chain, which is connected to the hook block, resulting in directional movement. The manual hoists may be hook- or trolley-suspended. They are designed for portability and infrequent service. Their warehouse use would be centered around service areas utilizing manual, single-girder cranes. Capacities for this product range from 1/2 to 60 tons. Typical vertical lifts start at 8 feet and can go as far as 100 feet.

Figure 18.9. Telescopic mast overhead stacker crane. (*Harnischfeger Corp.*)

Figure 18.10. Manual chain hoists. (*Harnischfeger Corp.*)

The next category, the *electric hoist* (Figure 18.11), is the most widely used hoisting system for bridge crane and monorail applications. It uses two distinct lifting mediums:

1. Wire rope (cable)
2. Chain (welded link or roller)

Electric hoists range in capacity from 1/8 to 500 tons. Typical warehousing applications range from 5 to 50 tons.

When used with cranes on monorails, the electric hoist may be one of the following varieties:

1. Top-running, double-girder trolley hoist
2. Underrunning, double-girder trolley hoist
3. Underrunning, single-girder; jib; or monorail trolley hoist

Electric hoists are available for lifts ranging from 10 to 500 feet. Normal warehouse crane lifts range from 20 to 40 feet. On monorail and jib cranes found in warehouse areas, lifts range from 10 to 40 feet. The speeds in electric hoists are also very flexible and tend to range from a slow 10 feet per minute to a high speed of 100 feet per minute. The typical warehouse service application ranges from 25 to 60 feet per minute. Typical operational features found in electric hoists are:

1. High-torque reversing service motors
2. Electric motor brake
3. Block travel limit switch
4. Gear drive system
5. Rope drum or chain pocket drive wheel
6. Control system

Electric hoists can be found in both the standard-headroom and low-headroom (profile) models. Headroom is a critical consideration for bridge cranes and monorails, and wasted under-beam space is costly to a warehouse. Standard-headroom hoists are normally parallel-mounted to the crane or monorail and are designed to bring the hook up under the machinery. Low-headroom hoists are normally perpendicular to the crane bridge or monorail beam and are designed to bring the hook up in front of the machinery, thus taking up less space. Hoists are rated by either the Hoist Manufacturers Institute or the Crane Manufacturers Association of America. Please refer to these specifications for exact details.

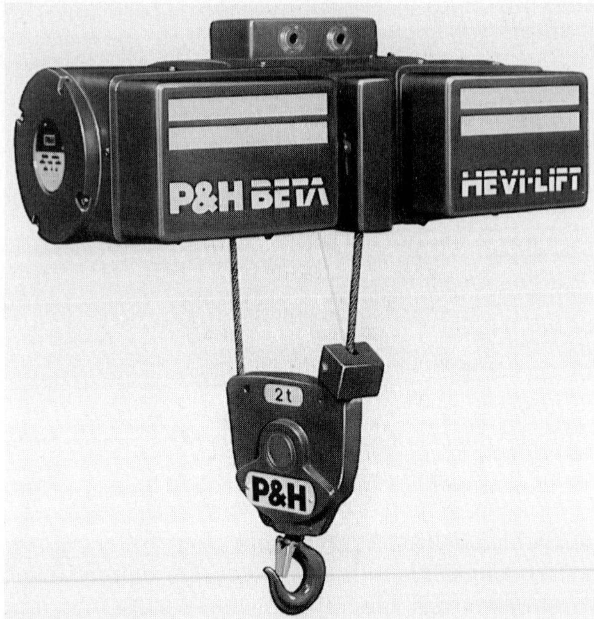

Figure 18.11. Overhead electric hoist. (*Harnischfeger Corp.*)

The final style is the *air-powered hoist.* It, in many ways, is similar to the electric hoist but has certain limitations. The typical capacity range is from ½ to 15 tons, with speeds that range from 10 to 100 feet per minute. Air hoists have the chain and wire rope lifting mediums, as well as similar mounting arrangements. For a variety of reasons, air hoists are primarily found in high-production manufacturing facilities where compressed air is plentiful and in hazardous locations where electrical sparks would ignite combustible material found in the area. They are seldom used in warehousing environments.

For typical applications of various hoist classifications see the Hoist Duty Service Classification, Table 18.1.

General Selection Guidelines for Overhead Cranes

Selecting the proper overhead crane for an application is of utmost importance. Table 18.2 describes six crane service classifications, but by itself does not completely define how to select a crane. A determination must also be made as to what crane speeds will be required. As a guide

Table 18.1. Hoist Duty Service Classification Chart

Classification and application			Operational time rating @ $K = 0.65$			
			Uniformly distributed work periods		Infrequent heavy work periods	
Hoist class	Typical areas of application	Hoist B10 bearing life at $K = 0.65$, hours	Maximum on-time minutes per hour	Maximum number of starts per hour	Minutes	Starts
H1	Powerhouse and utilities, infrequent handling. Hoists used primarily to install and service heavy equipment, where loads frequently approach hoist capacity, with periods of utilization being infrequent and widely scattered.	1250	8	75	30	100
H2	Light machine shop and fabricating industries and service and maintenance work, where loads and utilization are randomly distributed with capacity loads infrequently handled, and where total running time of equipment does not exceed 10 to 15% of the work period.	2500	8	75	30	100
H3	General machine shop, fabricating, assembly, storage, and warehousing, where loads and utilization are randomly distributed, with total running time of equipment not exceeding 15 to 25% of the work period.	5000	15	150	60	200
H4	High-volume handling in steel warehousing, machine shops, fabricating plants, mills, and foundries. Manual or automatic cycling operations in heat treating and plating operations. Total running time of equipment normally approaches 25 to 50% of work period, with loads at or near rated capacity frequently handled.	10,000	30	300	Not applicable	Not applicable
H5	Bulk handling of material in combination with buckets, magnets, or other heavy attachments. Equipment often cab-operated. Duty cycles approaching continuous operation are frequently necessary. User must specify exact details of operation, including weight of attachments.	20,000	Up to continuous	600	Not applicable	Not applicable

Table 18.2. Crane Service Classifications

2.2 Class A (stand-by or infrequent service)
This service class covers cranes which may be used in installations such as powerhouses, public utilities, turbine rooms, motor rooms, and transformer stations, where precise handling of equipment at slow speeds with long, idle periods between lifts are required. Capacity loads may be handled for initial installation of equipment and for infrequent maintenance.

2.3 Class B (light service)
This service covers cranes which may be used in repair shops, light assembly operations, service buildings, light warehousing, etc., where service requirements are light and the speed is slow. Loads may vary from no load to occasional full-rated loads with two to five lifts per hour, averaging 10 feet per lift.

2.4 Class C (moderate service)
This service covers cranes which may be used in machine shops or papermill machine rooms, etc., where service requirements are moderate. In this type of service, the crane will handle loads which average 50 percent of the rated capacity with 5 to 10 lifts per hour averaging 15 feet, not over 50 percent of the lift at rated capacity.

2.5 Class D (heavy service)
This service covers cranes which may be used in heavy machine shops, foundries, fabricating plants, steel warehouses, container yards, lumber mills, etc., and standard-duty bucket and magnet operations where heavy-duty production is required. In this type of service, loads approaching 50 percent of the rated capacity will be handled constantly during the working period. High speeds are desirable for this type of service with 10 to 20 lifts per hour averaging 15 feet, not over 65 percent of the lifts at rated capacity.

2.6 Class E (severe service)
This type of service requires a crane capable of handling loads approaching a rated capacity throughout its life. Applications may include magnet, bucket, magnet/bucket combination cranes for scrap yards, cement mills, lumber mills, fertilizer plants, container handling, etc., with 20 or more lifts per hour at or near the rated capacity.

2.7 Class F (continuous severe service)
This type of service requires a crane capable of handling loads approaching rated capacity continuously under severe service conditions throughout its life. Applications may include custom-designed specialty cranes essential to performing the critical work tasks affecting the total production facility. These cranes must provide the highest reliability with special attention to ease-of-maintenance features.

SOURCE: Courtesy of Harnischfeger Corp., Milwaukee, Wisconsin.

to aid you in this selection, refer to Table 18.3. If a specific duty cycle must be achieved, then a complete study involving the material handled, the distances traveled, and the amount of material that has to flow through the plant can be formulated to determine the speeds that will be necessary for production. The type of hoist that is selected is determined not only by the classification of the crane, but also by the amount of downtime that is acceptable to a particular warehouse. The following types of issues must be carefully analyzed to ensure the proper crane is selected for the application:

1. Capacity (i.e., the heaviest load to be handled)
2. Type of system
   a. Top-running crane (double- or single-girder)
   b. Underrunning crane (double or single-girder)
   c. Jib crane
   d. Monorail system
3. Runway or monorail length
4. Service or duty (see Duty Chart, HMI and CMAA categories)
5. Type of power
   a. Manual
   b. Electric
   c. Air
6. Loads to be handled
7. Speed (when motor-driven)
   a. Bridge

Table 18.3. Suggested Operating Speeds, feet per minute

Capacity, in tons	Hoist			Trolley			Bridge		
	Slow	Medium	Fast	Slow	Medium	Fast	Slow	Medium	Fast
Floor-controlled cranes									
3	14	35	45	50	80	125	50	115	175
5	14	27	40	50	80	125	50	115	175
7.5	13	27	38	50	80	125	50	115	175
10	13	21	35	50	80	125	50	115	175
15	13	19	31	50	80	125	50	115	175
20	10	17	30	50	80	125	50	115	175
25	8	14	29	50	80	125	50	115	175
30	7	14	28	50	80	125	50	115	150
35	7	12	25	50	80	125	50	115	150
40	7	12	25	40	70	100	40	100	150
50	5	11	20	40	70	100	40	100	150
60	5	9	18	40	70	100	40	75	125
75	4	9	15	40	70	100	30	75	125
100	4	8	13	30	60	80	25	50	100
150	3	6	11	25	60	80	25	50	100

Table 18.3. *(Continued)*

Cab-controlled cranes									
3	14	35	45	125	150	200	200	300	400
5	14	27	40	125	150	200	200	300	400
7.5	13	27	38	125	150	200	200	300	400
10	13	21	35	125	150	200	200	300	400
15	13	19	31	125	150	200	200	300	400
20	10	17	30	125	150	200	200	300	400
25	8	14	29	100	150	175	200	300	400
30	7	14	28	100	125	175	150	250	350
35	7	12	25	100	125	150	150	250	350
40	7	12	25	100	125	150	150	250	350
50	5	11	20	75	125	150	100	200	300
60	5	9	18	75	100	150	100	200	300
75	4	9	15	50	100	125	75	150	200
100	4	8	13	50	100	125	50	100	150
150	3	6	11	30	75	100	50	75	100

NOTE: Consideration must be given to length of runway for the bridge speed, span of bridge for the trolley speed, distance average travel, and spotting characteristics required.
SOURCE: Courtesy of Harnischfeger Corp., Milwaukee, Wisconsin.

   b. Trolley
   c. Hoist
8. Lift required
9. Type of atmosphere
10. Span of crane girder or jib boom
11. Floor or control-cab operated
12. Clearances for machinery
    a. End approaches
    b. Hook approaches
13. Optional below-the-hook devices
    a. Grabs
    b. Electromagnets
    c. Special customer-engineered attachments

Conclusion

The material presented in this chapter is provided as a general insight tool. Specific warehouse planners should always engage the assistance of a crane or monorail systems application engineer.

The following are sources for the most currently available standards, specifications, and regulations (addresses of organization follow):

Consensus of the National Electrical Code, CMAA

Consensus of the National Electrical Code, HMI

Considerations in Specifying Underhung Cranes and Monorail Systems, MMA

Crane Operator's Manual, MHI

National Electric Code (NEC), NFPA

Overhead and Gantry Cranes (Top-Running Bridge, Multiple Girder), ANSI B30.2.0-1976

Overhead and Gantry Cranes (Top-Running Bridge, Single-Girder, Underhung), ANSI B30.17-1980

"Overhead and Gantry Cranes," *Federal Register,* OSHA Pt. 1910.179

Overhead Crane Inspection and Maintenance Checklist, CMAA

Safety Standards for Hooks, ANSI B30.10-1982

Safety Standard for Monorail Systems and Underhung Cranes, ANSI B30.11-1980

Safety Standard for Overhead Hoists, ANSI B30.16-1981

Safety Standards for Slings, ANSI B30.9-1971

Specifications for Electric Overhead Traveling Cranes, CMAA no. 70-1983

Specifications for Electric Overhead Traveling Cranes for Steel Mill Service, AISE no. 8

Specifications for Top Running and Under Running Single Girder Electric Overhead Traveling Cranes, CMAA no. 74-1974.

Specifications for Underhung Cranes and Monorail Systems, ANSI MH 27.1-1981

Standard Specifications for Electric Chain Hoists, HMI 400

Standard Specifications for Wire Rope Hoists, HMI 100-74

Underhung Cranes and Monorails, MMA

"Walking-Working Surfaces," *Federal Register,* OSHA Pt. 1210.21-24

The following is a list of addresses where these standards, specifications, and regulations can be obtained:

AISE	Association of Iron & Steel Engineers Three Gateway Center, Suite 2350 Pittsburgh, PA 15222
ANSI	American National Standards Institute, Inc. 1430 Broadway New York, NY 10018
CMAA	Crane Manufacturers Association of America, Inc. 1326 Freeport Rd. Pittsburgh, PA 15238
HMI	Hoist Manufacturers Institute 1326 Freeport Rd. Pittsburgh, PA 15238
MHI	The Material Handling Institute, Inc. 1326 Freeport Rd. Pittsburgh, PA 15238
MMA	Monorail Manufacturers Association 1326 Freeport Rd. Pittsburgh, PA 15238
NFPA	National Fire Protection Association Batterymarch Park Quincy, MA 02269
OSHA	Occupational Safety & Health Administration U.S. Department of Labor Washington, DC 20210 (or Regional Offices)

19 Automatic Identification Systems

Richard D. Bushnell

President, Bushnell Consulting, Chalfont, Pennsylvania

Introduction

In considering the use and application of automatic identification, a variety of questions should be raised. These questions include: What is automatic identification? How can it be employed? Why would it be used? When does it fit? Automatic identification should be evaluated broadly because the potential benefits are not limited. *Always think of the big picture even if the scope, initially, seems small.*

The fundamental purpose for automatic identification is to provide discrete information about a person, place, or thing with little or no human intervention. *The benefit of the ability to quickly and accurately gather information is limited only by the potential use of that information.* We are, as indicated in all the magazines and news coverage, becoming a more information-based society. What this means is that decisions that have been made based on generalities, average consensus, and assumption are now made in a prescribed manner based on specific, factual information. To make these decisions, we need to have individualized information that is now more and more readily available because of the use of information handling equipment, such as computers.

Since the cost of computers has come down dramatically, more and more people are able to employ them; and this is where the information spiral begins. Since computers can act on a variety of inputs and make calculations so rapidly, they thrive on quantities of discrete information. *The important thing is to provide that information in an accurate and reliable form.* The ability to manipulate information provides the user of that information base tremendous power. The user can evaluate a variety of different solutions to a problem and then execute the one that seems best, in his or her estimation. If all of the variables for possible action can be determined, then even the decision-making process can be programmed and executed by the machine.

Some people reading this chapter may come from a management information systems (MIS) background and are truly unaware of the impact that their decisions, right or wrong, have on the physical movement of goods in a manufacturing plant or warehousing. Too often, the classic approach has been for information-oriented people to dwell in the abstract and overlook the fact that forklift drivers earn overtime as a result of a miscalculation or that a small army of clerical people may be required to handle problems arising from things being sent to the wrong department or customer. *The MIS department must be involved in the use of information provided in the form of automatic identification.*

People involved in the physical movement of goods have too often thought of things only in physical terms. They have solved problems by actually moving, queueing, storing, and retrieving the items and have overlooked the possibility of manipulating the information rather than manhandling the product. *With more information, warehouse personnel can handle less product.* Knowledge about what has to be moved can not only reduce the amount of inventory, but also reduce the number of times an item has to be handled.

Automatic identification is nothing more than information acquisition that minimizes or eliminates human operator involvement. In years gone by, this information had to be entered by operators using some type of keypad. Automatic identification bypasses the requirement for keypads; hence, this technique has been referred to as "key-entry bypass." Keystrokes generally result in one error in 50 strokes or characters. Bar code entry is less than one error in 3 million.

The reason for the interest in automatic data acquisition is twofold: it eliminates the requirement of having an individual present to enter the information and it tremendously increases the validity of the information being entered. *The strongest reason to employ automatic identification is to guarantee the validity of data.* As we see more and more automation, we see that automation both provides and requires predictability. It is this predictability that yields the greatest benefit to system managers, because it allows them to be in control of the system and make the necessary decisions to handle changes in priority and even emergencies as needs arise. From a manageability perspective, the reason to automate is to guarantee performance; and guaranteed performance can only be based on valid information.

There are a variety of ways to enter information automatically into a control system which will eliminate the need for operator key entry. These fall into three main categories:

1. *Radio frequency.* This is based on a device's ability to transmit a radio frequency which, in turn, invokes a response from a transponder. This type of equipment may have beneficial application by providing information about pallets and locations without requiring line of sight or physical contact as do the optical forms.
2. *Magnetic.* This involves the application on a card of a magnetically encoded film or strip, which is read by a sensing head using digital circuitry.
3. *Optical systems.* These employ light, visible or invisible, that is reflected from a printed pattern and sensed by a light-sensing element and then decoded.

This chapter will deal with optical automatic identification techniques, specifically bar coding. All of the automatic identification techniques are valid and carry with them a variety of benefits. *We will deal solely with bar coding because it is the least expensive and most broadly applicable technique and, therefore, widely used in warehouses.*

In the realm of optical systems, there are also a variety of techniques, but the wide-narrow bar code provides greater reliability, flexibility, and low-cost reader availability than other techniques. It can be read by hand-held or automatic scanners, and at distances, without critical alignment. Bar code symbols have a lower substitution error rate than does optical character recognition (OCR). They are also easier to print and less susceptible to partial destruction in the industrial environment.

When developing or employing an automatic ID system, the user must recognize the interdependence of the various elements. These elements are:

1. Function
2. Scanning
3. Printing
4. Symbology

All of these elements must work together, in concert, if the system is to be successful.

Function

The most basic question that has to be answered is, what is the system to do? There are three basic scanning system functions: to provide information, to cause action, or both (information/action).

Information. In this type of system, the scanner reads the bar code and transmits the number that it sees to other computer-related hardware. The information could be product number, serial number, customer order number, job number, location, and so on.

Action. In an action system, the local logic section, with its interface, causes action to occur based on predetermined programming held in electronic memory at the scanning location. This programming can be set in via thumbwheel switches or toggle switches, or by downloading from other computer devices. The identifying number itself can carry the action command. For example:

- The bar code representing the number 2 means divert this product at lane 2, or
- The scanner could be programmed with bar code 197 = divert lane 2.

Information/Action. In these systems, both of the previously mentioned functions occur when an item passes the scanning head. This can result from two different code patterns on the same box. One code creates the action and the other code provides information. This can also occur by matching the coded number to internal memory, which causes the action and simultaneously transmits data to a supervisor.

Scanning

There are many different types of scanners and scanning techniques that can be employed. The dynamics of the system and the parameters that are established will aid in the selection. It must be recognized that *system performance will be depend upon proper scanner selection based on the symbol and printing harmony.*

Scanner Overview

The bar code symbol contains information encoded in wide and narrow bars and spaces. The bars absorb the light and the spaces return the light, which is directed onto the symbol. The scanner is the device that converts the reflected light to a digitized signal, and then converts that into a meaningful number that is usually transmitted from the scanner in ASCII form. *Every scanner relies on this reflected light concept and uses a method that scans the entire symbol.* The scanning action responds to time, and this equates to the electronically perceived wideness and narrowness of the bars and spaces.

Different wavelengths of light can be used. The wavelength depends on the light's source, and there may be some advantage in spectral response depending on the color of the printing and its background. Furthermore, certain specifications call out the wavelength of light to be used with a given symbol and printing technique.

Basically, three wavelengths are used in scanning. They are 633, 800, and 900 nanometers. The 633-nanometer wavelength is most common, since that is used by scanners employing helium-neon (HeNe) gas-filled tubes. This red beam is seen at grocery store scanners and in virtually all of the industrial scanners in use today. The same wavelength is available from light emitting diodes (LEDs), which are used in hand-held wand scanners. The 800- and 900-nanometer wavelengths are in the infrared area of the spectrum and are invisible to the human eye. They have become popular because they provide the light at low energy, thus enabling the use of laser diodes for 800-nanometers wavelengths and gallium arsenide in the 900-nanometer range. The symbol specification may indicate which wavelength is to be used, and this should be matched against the scanner specifications. It should also be recognized that *various printing techniques provide different spectral responses,* and it may be necessary to describe the printing technique and examine its specifications to ensure that the scanner will be in harmony.

Scanning systems are optically based and rely on a focal point and resolution to determine the bar and space differential. This means that *the scanner must be able to be "focused"* in such a way that it will be able to distinguish the sharp edge of the bar as related to the space adjacent to it. This focusing relates to the size of the scanned beam and that beam's attenuation over distance. Where the scanning element comes in actual contact with the symbol, this focusing can be factored by the size of the aperture. In dynamic scanning situations in which the beam is being swept across the symbol at some distance, this focusing equates to depth of field or operating range over which the scanner will recognize code patterns.

To be able to harmonize the scanning, printing, and symbology elements, the system planner-designer should determine whether the size and distance will require a low-, medium-, or high-density symbol, as follows:

Low—greater than 0.025 inches

Medium—0.011 to 0.025 inches

High—less than 0.010 inches

The higher the density, the more characters can be encoded in an inch; but the narrower the bars, the more difficult to read over distance. The amount of space required for the data is also related to the symbol and its construction.

Scanning performance is based on the interrelationship of the scanning device, its technique, and the symbol's density and printing technique. The "bottom line" is: How successful is the operator at an attempt to scan a symbol? This is called "first-read" rate and is presented as a percentage. Typically, *first-read rates of 98% are desirable and attainable.* The operator's first-read rate does depend to some degree on familiarity with the equipment, although most operators find that the initial technique takes less than 10 minutes to master and a day of scanning generally makes an operator expert.

Another term commonly referred to when evaluating scanning is "substitution error." This is the situation in which the scanner reports an erroneous number. For example, if the number that was encoded was 1234 and that symbol were reported as 1235, there would be a substitution error. The statistical probability of this occurring with Code 39 (symbology for encoding alphanumeric characters) is 1 in 3 million characters read. With a fixed-length Interleaved 2 of 5 symbol with a calculated check digit (for numeric characters only), the statistical probability approaches the same number. (Symbology is discussed in greater detail in "Commonly Used Symbols," later in this chapter.) *The possibility of error occurs more frequently with poor printing,* and once again the interdependency of the printed symbol and the scanning technique is seen.

Scanning Equipment

Scanners are categorized by hand-held, fixed mount, contact, or noncontact. Further categorization goes into wavelength of light, resolution, depth of field, and fixed beam or moving beam.

Hand-Held Wands. The most commonly used and least expensive scanner is the hand-held wand. This device is approximately the size of a large marking pencil and is held in the operator's hand while it is passed over the entire symbol, from the clear area before the symbol to a similar clear area following the symbol. Scanning wands are usually provided with an aperture set for high-density or medium-density symbols and, depending on the aperture setting, can read symbols from 0.006 to 0.040 inches. The label is illuminated by an LED which can be either infrared or visible. A variety of tips are used, including metal, plastic, and industrial sapphire. Since the tip of the scanning wand does come in actual contact with the label, it is important to recognize that the scanning activity can, in fact, damage the symbol.

Contact. In addition to the scanning wand, two other types of scanners are available. One is the size of a small pistol and fits neatly into the palm of the operator's hand. It is drawn across the symbol, employing approximately the same technique as the scanning wand. Another type of contact scanner is static in nature. This device, which looks like a safety razor, is placed with the scanning head, which is dimensionally about the same size as the razor's head, over the entire symbol. A diode array inside the head then scans the illuminated symbol while the operator simply holds the scanner steady over the coded area.

Noncontact. This type of scanner can have a fixed beam (nondynamic) or a moving beam and can be provided with a laser diode or a gas-tube laser. The laser diode emits light in a wavelength of 900 nanometers and may not be acceptable to all types of inks and printing systems. The more adaptable and widely used gas-filled laser is more expensive to produce and requires more power to operate. Most of the hand-held moving-beam scanners are of the gas-filled type, which operate in the 633-nanaometer range.

The advantage of the moving-beam scanner is that it automatically repeats the scanning activity approximately 40 to 100 times per second. The fixed-beam variety, however, requires the operator to create the scanning motion and, should the first attempt fail, he or she will need to traverse the symbol again to obtain a scan. In some situations, the increased productivity of the automatic sweeping beam can be of value. There is one potential disadvantage, however. The distance of the dynamic sweep is a function of the number of mirrors and other mechanical scanning techniques. Typically, this is somewhere around 7 to 8 inches. If a symbol is longer than the overall sweep of the beam, the moving-beam scanner cannot read the symbol. On the other hand, the advantage of the fixed-beam scanner is that the length of the sweep is controlled by the operator, just as with the wand scanner. It will sweep the area as directed by the operator's hand and, therefore, can traverse a symbol significantly larger than can the other type.

Fixed-Mounted. Fixed-mounted scanners can be fixed-beam or moving-beam. Since their *position* is fixed, the scanning motion occurs as the label is passed in front of the scanner. One version illuminates the label with LEDs and then images the symbol through an aperture. The other version illuminates the label with light from an infrared laser diode and collects the reflected light. The beam can be circular, rectangular, or elliptical. The elliptical beam can provide better read capabilities where deficiencies in printing occur.

The most common fixed-station, moving-beam laser scanner employs the helium-neon 633-nanometer-wavelength light source, although some of the fixed laser diode scanners are now becoming available. These scanners generally provide scan rates from 40 to 500 scans per second, and some approach 1000 scans per second. The price is directly proportional to the scan speed. Typically, the beam sweeps in one continuous direction, since the scanning action is caused by a rotating polygon. Another technique is to use a vibrating vein, which causes the beam to oscillate back and forth to generate the sweeping action. When the scanning action occurs from floor to ceiling, the symbol is presented to it so that the bars look like the rungs of a ladder. This is referred to as a "ladder code." When the scan direction is parallel to the floor, the bars of the symbol must be presented perpendicular to it, somewhat like a picket fence. In the picket-fence configuration, since the beam is at a fixed point when the symbol is presented, only one small area of the symbol is evaluated. To avoid potential problems in reading the symbol, which may have a minor flaw in it, several techniques, including rastoring and beam tilting, are used.

The same situation does not exist when the symbol is presented in the ladder position. Since these scanners provide the sweep in only one plane, they will not read a symbol presented to them at a 90-degree rotation to the norm. The length dimension of the bar cannot be parallel to the sweep of the beam. To overcome this problem, some applications use scanners set so that the two scanning heads present a beam in an X pattern, whereas other scanners provide omnidirectional scanning by sweeping a variety of beams at a variety of different angles tangent to one another.

Vision-Camera. These systems employ a charged coupled device (CCD) to detect the reflected light, which is provided by a flash tube. The flash tube's strobe, in effect, freezes the object's motion. The image is received through a lens system onto the CCD array. A CCD consists of a series of points that respond to the reflector light. A microprocessor examines each point and sets up an electronic image, which is then processed and decoded. The advantage to this technique is that it uses no laser or moving parts.

Scanning Considerations

When discussing scanners, it is important to know the following things:

1. Scan rate: the minimum and maximum number of scans per second that the reader can provide
2. Resolution: the minimum and maximum bar and space widths, referred to as "X dimension," which it will resolve
3. Symbols: the symbols the scanner will read (e.g., USS-39, USS I 2 of 5, and UPC) and whether it will read several simultaneously
4. Depth of field: the variation in distance at which the symbol is to be scanned, i.e., 9 to 24 inches
5. Information handling capabilities and memory size of the scanner itself
6. Communications: baud rate, parity, message configuration, RS232 or EIA current
7. Machine control outputs available: TTL or relay
8. Wavelength of light source

These items all have strong influence on the symbol, scanner, and system function. They must be evaluated in concert to provide the most reliable system considering operational trade-offs.

Printers and Printing

As there are a number of scanning techniques, so are there a number of printing techniques. They include ink, thermal, and laser. The technique may affect the size of the bar and its color. In addition, some techniques take longer, while still others have costly consumables. Finally, some require substantial investment, and whether to print on site or to buy from an off-site supplier must be considered. To start, let's review some simple capabilities.

The most obvious difference is in the bar-width resolution each technique can produce. The high resolution available in one printing technique may not be necessary for the overall bar width required because of other system parameters. But as a rule of thumb, we can divide the printing resolution into high resolution (0.010 inch or less), medium resolution (0.011 to 0.025 inches), or low resolution (above 0.025 inches). Resolution is not only the ability to print a fine line and the space between lines, but also to hold the specified tolerance. This tolerance is perhaps best expressed in percentage of the narrowest element, either bar or space, which, as previously mentioned, is sometimes called the X dimension. Most commercially available scanners can tolerate an X variation of ± 20 percent. The variation in the tolerance has to do with the symbol and the wide-to-narrow ratio. Each symbol has a formula used to calculate the tolerance and should be employed when the symbol is specified. For example: If the nominal dimension is 0.020 inches and the ratio is 2 to 1, the wide bar would be 0.040 inches. The tolerance would be 20 percent of 0.020 inches, which equals 0.004 inches. So, the printing technique must be able to provide that narrow or wide bar space with no greater than a 0.004-inch variation.

Before selecting a printing or scanning technique, evaluate the function of the label and symbol that is required. Information that must be changed frequently will require that the printer be available at the site of the operation. It is not always desirable to print "in house," and the requirements can sometimes be met by the use of preprinted labels, each carrying an individual and different number. These labels can be affixed to the product and matched to a cross-referenced table in a mini or microcomputer. Keep in mind that *you must specify not only the printer, but the label stock and the adhesive as well.* You must be sure that ink and paper are compatible, and that the adhesive will stick to the surface.

When considering labels, *you must think about both the symbol and the human-readable information.* Printers available today can vary not only the information, but the entire label format. They include expanded character sets so that large, human-readable information as well as bar code information can be provided. The system planner and designer must also establish in-house quality control and quality assurance measures to guarantee that labels throughout their life are readable by machines and humans. Ink-bleed and distortion may not be detectable at the time of printing but may render the labels useless after some period of time. *Label "life" evaluation must be taken into account during planning.*

Incoming inspection and life testing must certainly be considered. Labels' costs, whether produced in house or purchased outside, must be put in true perspective; any cost-saving program related to labels should be fully evaluated. Realizing that label costs can go from a few mils to several cents each and that use volumes can go to hundreds, thousands, or millions per year, there is a natural instinct to fixate on these costs and reduce them. When you realize the value-added cost of the product on which the label is applied or the total cost of the information systems that it serves, there can be little advantage to skimping on label quality to save costs.

Printing Techniques

As mentioned earlier, there are a variety of techniques that can be employed to generate bar codes. We will explore on-site techniques and off-site techniques, and provide some of the reasons for selecting one method over another.

On-Site Bar Code Printing.* On-site bar code printing can provide you with a viable alternative to purchasing bar codes printed offsite. The advantages include:

- Reduction in lead time
- Elimination of need for film masters and printing plates
- No minimum ordering requirements
- Increased flexibility to produce various label formats and comply with multiple industry regulations

The on-site printing alternatives can reduce the inventories associated with purchasing and storing all the various label formats and cartons that a company needs. Inventory requirements are reduced to a "generic" label or carton, and the unique information associated with a given product can then be printed as needed. In one instance, the purchase of a dot matrix label-printing system reduced label inventory from approximately 700 different label formats to just one generic label. The label formats are stored on floppy disks and are produced as required—not purchased and stored months in advance. This also eliminates the need to scrap labels that have become obsolete or require minor copy changes.

On-site printing also eliminates the long lead times associated with purchasing off site. Depending on the type of printing being done, lead time can range from two to six weeks, although some service bureaus can provide quick turnaround at a premium. You can print your cartons or labels as you need them, eliminating the hold-up on shipping or manufacturing due to labels not being delivered on time.

Most off-site printing techniques require the additional cost of a film master and printing plate for producing bar code. With the marriage of a microprocessor or computer to many of the techniques discussed in this chapter, the need for film masters and printing plates is eliminated.

In many cases, the quantity required for any given bar code label or mark is small, on the order of 10 to 500. Those are below the minimum ordering requirements for most off-site printing. The excess labels are

* The author would like to thank Richard Fox of Matthews International, Pittsburgh, Pennsylvania, for his contributions to this topic.

either discarded or saved for some future use. On-site printing allows you to print only the labels you require, thereby eliminating the inventory buildup and the loss associated with discarding the labels.

And finally, on-site printing provides you with the flexibility to change variable information and label layouts, meet changes in production schedules, and comply with the multitude of bar code industry requirements. In most systems, all of the above can be satisfied with a few keystrokes into the computer.

The label printing techniques discussed here are:

- Wet ink
- Direct thermal
- Thermal transfer
- Character impact
- Bar impact
- Dot matrix
- Hot stamp
- Laser page

Table 19.1 presents a relative comparison of features of the various printing techniques.

Wet Ink Printing. This is perhaps the type of printing that comes most quickly to mind. It employs a rubber or plastic mat sometimes referred to as a "plate," which is produced by a photographic etching process. The plate is affixed to a roller and wet ink is applied. It is then used to "kiss" the label stock, which is pressed against it. Since each different label requires a different plate, change-over time and plate storage must be considered.

Direct Thermal Label Printing. The direct thermal label printing process produces an image by selectively heating and coating small elements in a thermal print head that is in contact with a coated paper. The paper discolors when heated, providing the contrast for the bar codes.

The heating elements are microprocessor-controlled, thereby providing almost unlimited flexibility with respect to character and bar code selection. Reverse printing, four-way information orientation, graphics, and sequential numbering are easily accomplished. The thermal printer has very few moving parts, operates very quietly, and can print at relatively high speeds (greater than 3 inches per second).

The limitation of direct thermal label printing is that the thermal label stock degrades and discolors when subjected to high heat conditions and ultraviolet light. Typical sources of ultraviolet light are the sun and

Table 19.1. Relative Comparison of the Various Printing Techniques

	X Dimension (X = 0.001)	Speed	Print stock	Noise level	Other consumable material	Interface	Flexibility
Wet ink	7.5	300 labels/min	Paper Vinyl Polyester	Low	Plate Ink	No	None
Direct thermal	10	2–3 in/sec	Coated stock	Very low	None	Yes	High
Thermal transfer	7.5	1 in/sec	Smooth stock	Very low	Ribbon	Yes	High
Character impact	7.5	40–100 labels/min	Paper Vinyl Polyester	High	Ribbon	Yes	Limited
Bar impact	10	2 in/sec	Paper Vinyl Polyester	High	Ribbon	Yes	Limited
Dot matrix	10	60–100 labels/min	Paper Vinyl Polyester	High	Ribbon	Yes	High
Hot stamp	10	115 labels/min	Leather Plastic	Medium	Film master Foil Die	No	None
Laser page	7.5	12* pages/min	Paper	Low	Toner	Yes	High

*The durability of the label and the image after printing must be considered. There are so many variables that this point must be discussed on an individual basis.

some industrial lighting systems. Inappropriate matching of the label stock with the bar code scanner can result in labels that cannot be scanned. Label stock is available for laser, visible red, and infrared scanning devices. It is important that this be addressed when installing a system based on direct thermal label technology.

Thermal Transfer Printing. The thermal transfer printing technique is a marriage of direct thermal printing and hot stamp printing. A thermal print head comparable to the one used in direct thermal printing selectively transfers ink from a single-pass film ribbon to the label. Many thermal transfer printers have the option of printing directly on thermal paper without the ribbon. The advantage of this process over direct thermal is the ability to print on standard smooth paper label stock. This allows for bar code labels that are not susceptible to deterioration from ultraviolet rays and high heat environments. One limitation of most of the printers utilizing this process is that the transfer ribbon moves in concert with the label stock. This tends to increase the amount of waste and costs when printing labels with a large unprinted area.

Character Impact Printing. The preformed character impact printer consists of a rotating print drum and a hammer mechanism. The bar code and/or characters to be printed are reverse-etched onto the drum, much like with a typewriter. A single-pass film ribbon and the label stock are situated between the drum and a hammer. Printing is accomplished by the hammer striking the rotating drum when the selected character is aligned with the hammer. The ink is transferred from the ribbon to the label stock.

The entire bar code character or alphanumeric character is produced with one strike of the hammer. This requires that the character sizes and bar code symbology be fixed for a given print drum.

Bar Impact Label Printing. The bar impact label printer consists of a combination dot matrix print mechanism and a single bar print mechanism. The dot matrix print mechanism consists of a single row of 15 wire needles for printing alphanumeric characters. The bar print mechanism consists of a single bar of a fixed height (3/8 to 1/2 inch) and a width corresponding to the bar code *X* dimension, from 10 to 13 mils. The bar code is produced by a microprocessor controlling both the movement of the label *past* the bar print mechanism and the activation of the solenoid *in* the bar print mechanism. Wide bars are produced by successive bar strikes as the label moves by the head. The dot matrix print mechanism prints the human-readable interpretation line below the bar code and additional alphanumeric information to the right or left of the bar code. The bar impact technology employs a multiple-pass, carbon-coated film ribbon for printing on paper, vinyl, and polyester. The printer produces labels at approximately 2 inches per second, with a maximum label height of 1 inch.

Dot Matrix Printing. The dot matrix printer provides almost unlimited flexibility with respect to label size, character size, character placement and orientation, and bar code formats.

There are basically two types of dot matrix printing technologies being used for printing bar codes: serial-wire matrix printers and line-wire matrix printers.

The serial-wire matrix printer consists of a seven- or nine-wire print head that reciprocates on a shaft the entire width of the web. These wires are driven by solenoids that are activated as the print head moves by the location to be printed on the paper. A multiple-pass fabric ribbon is situated between the print head and the paper stock. As the wires are activated, they strike the ribbon and paper, thus transferring the ink from ribbon to paper.

Another popular dot matrix technology being used for printing bar codes is the line printer. The line printer consists of a row of solenoid-activated wires across the paper web. The number of wires across the print mechanism can range from 17 to 34. When printing, the entire print mechanism reciprocates approximately 3/8 inch. The solenoids are activated and strike the ribbon and paper to produce the mark. The result is precise dot placement on the paper and very good bar codes.

Hot Stamp Label Printing. The hot stamp printing process consists of a hot etched metal die that transfers ink from a foil onto the label. The label stock and single-pass foil are transported between the hot metal die and a support base. Printing is accomplished by the die pressing the foil to the paper. The heated image areas of the die transfer the ink to the label stock.

Production of the image on the metal die is accomplished by a film master of the bar code and alphanumerics to be printed. As a result, the process has little flexibility with respect to random information changes and sequential numbering. The hot stamp equipment available can provide additional die areas for adding colors or other information to the label; any information changes on the label require new die and film masters.

Laser Page Printing. Laser page printing technology utilizes a technology very similar to the standard office copying machine. The process involves a rotating belt that accepts and transfers an image to a sheet of paper. The process begins as the belt passes through a cleaning and corona conditioning section that prepares the surface of the belt for laser imaging. The laser imaging station consists of a microprocessor-controlled helium-cadmium, argon-ion, or helium-neon laser that is rapidly turned on and off to generate on the belt positively charged dots that correspond to the image. Next, a negatively charged toner is spread over the belt. The negatively charged toner adheres to the positively charged dots and is transferred to corona-conditioned paper. The toner is either heat-fused or pressure-fused to the paper. The belt is subsequently cleaned and conditioned for the next laser image. The laser page printer can print from 12 to 120 pages per minute. Because the laser imaging station is microprocessor controlled, the equipment can provide various character fonts, character sizes, and sequentially numbered bar codes.

Off-Site Bar Code Printing.* Off-site printing is subject to the same restrictions and considerations as in-house printing. Vendors vary in their abilities to print high-density images, handle more than one symbology, and produce high-quality labels. The reasons to consider off-site suppliers may include:

1. Equipment cost
2. Production staff
3. Quality control

The off-site techniques include:

1. Flexographic and offset
2. Letterpress
3. Silk screen
4. Laser
5. Ion deposition
6. Photocomposition

Flexographic and Offset Printing. Designed for printing on packaging materials, these are among the dominant methods for printing on corrugated containers and for printing high-quality multicolor labels. These methods require a photographic master from which to produce a printing plate. The minimum recommended X dimension (the average of the narrow-bar, narrow-space measure) is 0.020 inches for corrugated and 0.0075 inches for label stock or package material. These printing methods do not provide for great variability of information, although non-variable human-readable characters and other artwork can be printed to nearly any specification. These processes are mandatory for multicolor labels whether or not variable information will be printed else-

* The author would like to thank Ivan Jeanblanch of Moore Business Forms, Glenview, Illinois, for his contributions to this topic.

where. Given the proper substrate and quality control, flexographic and offset can produce medium-density Code 39 (9.8 CPI) accurately and economically.

Letterpress Printing. Quality depends more on the experience and knowledge of the printer and the film master producer than on the process itself. Letterpress does not provide for great flexibility in variable human-readable characters because it is essentially a formed-font process. Non-variable characters can be printed to suit the user. Letterpress printing can produce medium-density Code 39 with proper control.

Silk Screen Printing. Although slow compared to other off-site printing methods, it is used to print on a variety of shapes and surfaces, such as wood, glass, plates, and fabric. Quality for medium-density Code 39 can be as good as letterpress, though information cannot be varied without preparing a new screen.

Laser Printing. Off-site equipment uses the same basic technology as the smaller, in-house units available, but works at speeds far greater than those attainable by smaller units. Flexibility is good; quality and density are both high.

Ion Deposition Printing. This patented, microprocessor-based, electrographic, nonimpact imaging process is capable of printing bar codes and other information on a variety of substrates, such as paper, vinyl, polyester, and tags, at speeds of up to 30 inches per second. It provides excellent flexibility and can handle both discrete and continuous codes. The density is in the medium to high range (7 to 9 CPI for Code 39).

Photocomposition. Using a light source, a microprocessor, and photosensitive stock (whether paper or metal), this method is very flexible and can produce sequentially numbered bar codes, both discrete and continuous. Quality is very high. It can produce bar codes with an X dimension of 0.004 to 0.005 inches (up to 14 CPI for Code 39). This method is relatively expensive because of substrate costs and is most often used to produce very durable labels or tags that will be subjected to high temperature and/or abrasion from harsh chemicals.

Cost Factors. From the analysis of label requirements and printing methods, the field of viable options should have been narrowed. For the final evaluation of whether an on-site system or outside purchase will be preferable from an operation standpoint, the cost factor becomes important. There are five cost factors that need to be considered to arrive at an ultimate "cost per label" figure.

Length of Run. This consideration is essentially one of volume. For standard labels, the condition would be primarily one of finding the price from an outside vendor. For applications requiring random data, on-site production is mandatory. In many cases, labels need not contain anything other than a product identification number and human-readable characters. In this case, on-site cost is determined mostly by the price of blank label stock and necessary print equipment.

However, for applications involving unique variable information combined with some form of standard or corporate artwork, an evaluation must be made of the cost differential between short-run, totally preprinted labels and lot-run, "generic" (partially printed) labels imprinted with unique information in house. In most cases, the generic approach will prove most cost-effective.

For example, a company that manufactures and needs to identify 100 different products or parts may purchase 100 different labels in lots of 100,000, for a total of 10 million labels. It may also purchase generic labels with standard information preprinted, and print them on site with different product information and bar codes. Since generic labels may typically cost 25 percent less than preprinted labels, the difference can be significant.

Inventory Costs. A second economic consideration is inventory carrying costs. The cost of keeping a supply of labels on hand for all products or parts is usually figured at 30 percent of the purchase price. If a company needs 100 different preprinted labels a year and carries an inventory of 100,000 of each kind at a cost of $20 per thousand (a $200,000 total investment), the inventory costs can be figured at $60,000.

Using a more generic label, however, will not only cost less in label materials, but also require less inventory to be kept on hand to ensure sufficient stock. If the label costs $15 per thousand and only 5 million must be purchased during that year, the investment will be $57,000. Inventory costs (30 percent of the investment) will be $22,500.

Previously mentioned with regard to the advantages of on-site printing is the issue of label obsolescence. If product number, unit of use, or other encoded information changes, existing stocks of preprinted labels or packages would have to be scrapped. This could represent a significant cost factor in operations that maintain high levels of label or package stock.

Additional Production Costs. Purchasing labels from an outside supplier may also involve the cost of a film master for each bar code or product type. Film masters cost about $20 each, which means that for 100 different products or items, the total cost is about $2000. If the encoded information does not change, this is a one-time investment. However, each change requires a new film master.

Ribbons for printers must be replaced regularly to produce codes with an acceptable print contrast signal (PCS). The cost of ribbons and frequency of replacement vary from method to method, as does the cost of label stock.

Quality Assurance. On-site printing may require a quality control program to ensure that good codes are being printed. Use of manual or automatic quality control methods should be considered as a part of the on-site printing costs.

Equipment and Maintenance Costs. On-site equipment costs vary widely, ranging from the relatively inexpensive dot matrix printers up through high-speed laser printers or etching equipment. Reliability and maintenance costs of the various technologies must also be weighed against initial cost.

Symbol Selection

Symbol selection, much like printing technique, can be the subject of an entire study. It is important to recognize that the selection of a symbol is based upon certain parameters that carry the true personality of the system. Basically, there are two fundamental questions that need to be answered: What is the type of information that must be contained in the symbol? and How much room is there to produce the symbol? These two factors generally lead to a symbol selection as well as a printing technique. The printing technique may be already given because of the *X* dimension provided by that certain technique. This may then also determine the selection of one symbol over another.

Commonly Used Symbols

The following bar code symbols are commonly in use in warehouse operations today.

Interleaved (I) 2 of 5. The Interleaved 2 of 5 symbology is designed for numeric data only and offers a relatively high character density within the symbol. No check characters are specified for this symbology, and the code has been designed for applications in which the symbols have a fixed number of characters. The potential for read errors is increased if symbols with varying numbers of characters must be read. The user is advised that, whereas a check digit for validation is always a good idea, it is mandatory if variable-length messages are employed.

Code 39. The Code 39 symbology permits encoding of uppercase alpha characters plus the numeric digits. This expanded character set requires more space per character than Interleaved 2 of 5, resulting in significantly lower character densities in the symbol. No check digit is required in Code 39 symbology, although one can be employed.

Codabar. The Codabar symbology offers six special characters plus the numeric digits. Character densities for this symbology lie in between those for Interleaved 2 of 5 and Code 39. Codabar also offers four different start and stop characters that can be used to define the context of the data within the label. No check digits are required.

Code 93. Code 93 is one of two popular symbologies featuring all 128 ASCII characters, which can be used to define the context of the data within the label. No check digits are required.

Code 128. Code 128 also offers the full 128-character ASCII subset featuring very high density for the numerics. This symbology also features code select characters, plus three different start characters for data context definition. One check character is required.

UPC/EAN. Originally developed for the food industry, the UPC/EAN numeric encoding symbology was developed to permit reliable reading of numeric bar codes printed in a wide variety of forms. Standard forms of this symbol include a 6- and a 12-digit format. A single check digit is always included in the symbol.

It differs from the other symbols in that its bars dimensions in a given symbol can be X, $2X$, $3X$, and $4X$; where the others always have only two different dimensions, i.e., X and $2.5X$ or X and $3X$.

Autodiscrimination of Symbologies

Labels may carry more than one symbol, and merchandise from different sources carries different symbologies. Because of this, a growing trend in the industry is to require that equipment be able to read more than one type of symbology, as well as symbols with a varying number of characters. The manufacturers of reading equipment, therefore, are providing systems that will read any of the common symbologies. In general, it is possible to provide reading equipment that can autodiscriminate among all six of the common symbologies discussed.

The utility of autodiscriminating readers is becoming more important as the use of bar code labels expands. Several industries have developed guidelines that call for the use of I 2 of 5 and Code 39, interchangeably. To ensure accurate reading, the I 2 of 5 symbol is fixed with a calculated check digit.

Interdependency of All Elements

Having just described the elements of function, scanning, printing, and symbology, it is now time to tie them all together, since, ultimately, *all of these elements must work together in concert if the system is to be successful.* This simple statement can neither be understated nor said too many times.

To further understand how all the elements must be balanced, consider the analogy of an airplane. For an airplane to fly in a straight line, the nose and tail sections must be level, and both wings must be level. Too much weight at the front will cause the plane to "nose down"; too much weight on the left wing will cause the plane to turn left. So, to fly straight, all elements—right wing, left wing, nose, and tail—must be balanced.

If we now construct an airplane with printing technology at the nose and scanning technology at the tail, we have the fuselage of our airplane. The wing assembly is made up of the symbol on the left wing and the function on the right wing. Obviously, if all we have is fuselage (scanning and printing), our plane cannot fly, because it has no wings. Similarly, if we only have wings (symbol and function defined), our plane cannot fly, because there is no fuselage to tie the wings together. So, even though the elements balance one another in their respective structure, they must still play totally together to provide an entire airplane.

The symbol is most closely related to the data to be encoded and the numeric coding system. We must recognize the importance of the symbol, since it must be printed reliably and scanned reliably and exist within a certain amount of space. But the symbol is also closely related to the function—information, action, information/action.

The printing technique is selected after evaluating the symbol, its size, and the relative bar widths. It is empirically reviewed by the scanner each time a label passes by. The scanning techniques must be linked to the symbol through the printing technique. Poor printing will result in the scanner's inability to read the data and to cause the functions to occur. The functions of the automatic identification system are the baseline upon which the entire system is evaluated. The functions provide the demonstrative action that the system users have requested of the system planners.

20 Containers and Packaging

David C. Morrison

Offset Program Manager, Frito-Lay, Inc., Dallas, Texas

Introduction

In today's highly competitive market where profit margins have narrowed, competition is tougher, and the consumer is more demanding, it is an appropriate time for many companies to take a close look at their organization's costs. One of the best methods for dealing with that competition is to offer the best-quality product at the lowest possible price. Management styles, productivity, information systems, raw materials, current use of technology, and even container cost are all proper areas for examination. Many of these areas are ripe for new and innovative improvements.

In light of the present economic and industrial environment, this chapter will examine the area of containers and packaging and will attempt to point out potential cost-saving opportunities.

In general, warehouse managers and employees are excellent "fire fighters." They solve many problems on a day-to-day basis and always seem to get the product out the door, regardless of labor shortages, equipment failure, or material shortages. But many warehouses have been slow to change or react to new market conditions, new technologies, and innovations that are available to them. For many warehouses to maintain the competitive edge that they have experienced in the past, they must improve on their ability to make change. When it comes time to make a change in the package or container, the warehouse organization is one of the last to have input into any design changes. Yet the warehousing function is just as important as marketing, sales, manufacturing, legal, or any others.

In some respects, the fields of warehousing and packaging are similar to the computer industry. Many new technological improvements have been introduced in the last 10 years, the cost of that technology has decreased, and all warehouses, including the competition, have access to this new technology. Even with many technological changes in the field of materials handling, a person walking into an average warehouse is likely to find forklift equipment, wooden pallets, and corrugated boxes. In many industries, the technology of warehousing has changed very little in the last 25 to 30 years.

This chapter is intended to help the reader see and understand packages and containers from some different points of view. It is expected that this higher understanding will help the reader find, sell, and implement some new cost savings ideas in the packaging area.

All products (with the exception of some bulk commodities) are packaged in some form. A typical consumer goods packaging system may consist of a primary package, which touches the product, and an intermediate or secondary package such as a folding carton, which contains a high number of individual packages and typically carries the advertising message and proper identification for the enclosed contents. This chapter will deal mainly with the intermediate or secondary package.

It should be pointed out that, even though this chapter will focus on packaging and container costs, the point must be made that any time packaging changes are made, the total warehousing system must be examined and the impact on the total system measured. Many warehousing and distribution managers have a low opinion of packaging design engineers and vice versa. One reason might be that cartons do not perform well in the materials handling and distribution system. But is it the carton or the system? The blame many times is put on "the other person." But, for any organization to be adaptable and to stay profitable, all participating functions must be involved in changes. This ensures that the total systems impact is considered and that decisions are made to enhance the total system, not just warehousing or distribution or the package.

This chapter will approach the subjects of packaging and containers and examine the materials handling system in the following manner:

Macro			Micro	
Customer needs	Transportation/ distribution needs	Internal material handling needs	Packaging/ container	Product needs/ requirements

It is not the intent of this chapter to go into great detail about new technologies, because it is felt that vendors are best at discussing and presenting their particular products. But, this chapter can give some general direction for possible cost-saving opportunities as they relate to the container and how that container is used in a particular materials handling system.

Advantages and disadvantages of different technologies will be examined. By identifying one possible cost-saving opportunity, this chapter should give a tremendous return for the reading time invested.

A Macro View of Containers and Packaging

Looking at an object from many points of view can enable an individual to get much more insight into a situation than merely taking at face value what is first perceived. To get some insight into possible improvement areas for containers, different points of view will be taken in looking at containers and packaging. It should be noted that rarely will anyone look at containers and not be concerned about "costs," whether it be the customer for the finished product or the manufacturer of the container. It will be pointed out that cost is a common concern regardless of which point of view is taken.

The Customers Point of View of Containers and Packaging

As a customer views a product, the impression of quality is often conveyed more by the container than by the product itself. Our logic tells us that you can't judge a book by its cover, but for many items that are bought on impulse, this logic tends to be forgotten. This fact is especially true for the primary package. Most food items and personal items would fall into this category. Most grocery store shoppers will avoid picking up a damaged container, even though the contents are not exposed and are of equal quality to the contents of a nondamaged container.

Sales and marketing people many times have legitimate concerns about the appearance of a package when it reaches the customer's shelf. Portraying a quality image has many implications and impacts on a container design and the distribution system.

Containers must properly identify their contents. For many secondary containers, it is necessary to identify the contents on all sides of the package. Extra printing can result in extra cost, even though printing cost is typically low in comparison to total package cost. Some exceptions might be where several colors are used or high contrast is required by marketing. Opportunities may exist to decrease the cost of printing by examining the number of colors used, the necessity of having high versus low contrast and/or printing on all sides, or the possibility of eliminating stickers or visual add-ons that identify the product. Due to the cost of printing typically being a low percentage of total carton cost, opportunities to save large dollar amounts by eliminating, simplifying, or reducing printing are not easily found.

Customers can view a package as adding value to their purchase. Containers are expected to protect the contents, not allow for contamination, and be easily disposed of after use. There exist many opportunities to have the container add value for the customer. For example, having a container that is easily opened or requires no special tool for opening is a customer benefit. Identifying product age or shipment date can aid in stock rotation. One string manufacturer shipped a large ball of string in a corrugated box. This box not only protected the string and kept it clean and dry, but also had a cutting blade attached, which was viewed very favorably by the customer. Many examples of value-added packages exist. The use of reclosable and reusable containers has increased over the last few years. Asking oneself "How might we add value to the package? " may lead to innovative improvements to packaging as viewed by the customer.

Many times customers tell manufacturers how they view a particular product via customer complaints. Examining customer complaints closely and probing for possible problem areas can prove rewarding in discovering opportunities for improvement. It is not uncommon for customer complaints to reveal not only problems related to a product, but also problems related to the packaging of that product.

One issue that a customer always considers is the value of the product obtained for the expenditure made. Few customers know the cost of the container for a particular product, and very few customers are even concerned with the container cost. On the other hand, almost all customers are concerned with the total cost of the product. Therefore, it is the responsibility of the manufacturer to provide packaging for the product that adequately meets the customer's needs at the lowest possible cost.

A Transportation/Distribution Point of View

In examining a container from a transportation or distribution point of view, one can determine that many cost trade-offs exist among various aspects of a distribution system. In trying to examine or measure these trade-offs, one might consider examining some of the following factors:

- Time of delivery or time in the distribution system
- Condition of load upon arrival or damage cost
- Total cost of delivery

In trying to determine how a package will perform in a distribution system, one of the best indicators or measures may be the cost of damage. If damage did not exist, the cheapest possible package would be used and all distribution efforts would be directed towards cutting time of delivery and using the cheapest possible mode of transportation. But in reality, damage does exist. The author suggests that the relationships between cost and damage, as exhibited in Figures 20.1, 20.2, and 20.3, can help one understand some of the trade-offs that must be considered when searching for productive cost-saving areas. These relationships are thought to be generally true, but exceptions can be found.

Figure 20.1 suggests that, as more money is spent on the packaging

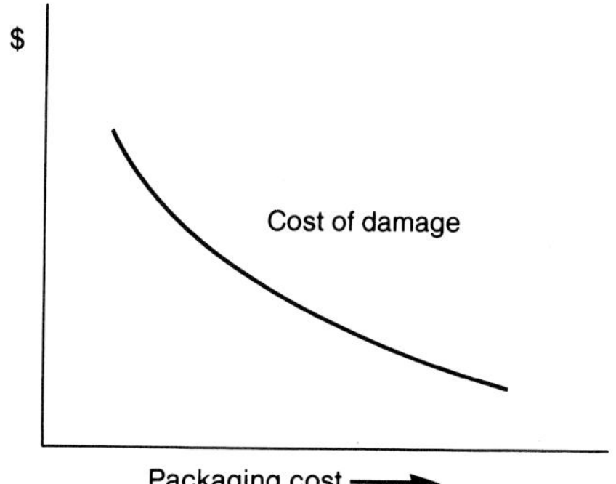

Figure 20.1. As more money is spent on the packaging container, the cost of damage should decrease.

container, the cost of damage should decrease. The range of types of containers includes everything from metal or wooden crates all the way to plastic bags. The important factors that typically dictate what type of container is used are:

- The cost or value of the product
- The product's susceptibility to damage
- Government regulations (e.g., child-proof containers)

For example, computers or other high-value items would typically be shipped in very strong wooden or corrugated containers with firm-fitting packing material that provide a high degree of protection from various elements of the distribution system. Another example at the other extreme would be a product like a pillow or beanbag chair, which is not susceptible to damage and is typically shipped in just a plastic bag to keep the product clean and dry. The curve in Figure 20.1 indicates that the cost of damage could be greatly decreased if packaging costs were greatly increased or, conversely, that the cost of damage would greatly increase if the cost of packaging were greatly decreased.

Other packaging cost areas that one might examine to find either damage reduction or cost reduction opportunities are:

- Corrugated dividers
- The mullen strength of corrugated used
- The amount of empty space at the top of the secondary package caused by the vibration or movement of product during transit
- The internal support provided by the product
- Moisture barriers
- Types of dunnage both inside and outside the container
- Stackability of the product in the box
- The size of carton flaps and how the carton is sealed, i.e., glue, tape, or other adhesives.

The key point is to know how much damage costs and to know that each component of your package is paying for itself.

Figure 20.2 suggests that the more a particular product is moved, the greater the potential for high damage costs. Thus, by eliminating unnecessary moves in a distribution system, the cost of both distribution and damage can many times be reduced.

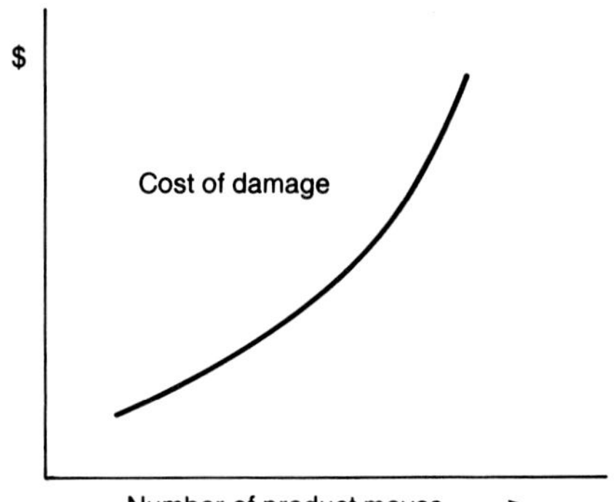

Figure 20.2. The more a particular product is moved, the greater the potential for high damage cost.

Figure 20.3 suggests that the cost of damage might be decreased by increasing the cost of the distribution method or type of distribution. For example, one could add a large amount of shipping dunnage to a particular load and decrease the amount of damage, but at the tradeoff of an increase in distribution cost for the dunnage. Various distribution modes, such as rail and truck shipments, have various costs associated with them and can have an impact on the amount of damage experienced. Some examples of options that cost more but can result in reduced damage are:

- Using bulk heads
- Using improved suspension systems

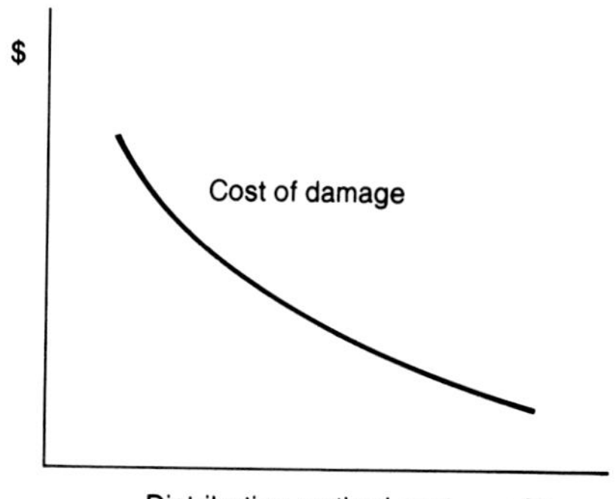

Figure 20.3. The cost of damage might be decreased by increasing the cost of the distribution method or type of distribution.

- Having the shipper rather than the carrier load and unload
- Having exclusive use of equipment
- Selecting a longer, smoother route over a shorter, rougher one, or route around a particular switching yard
- Adding more and/or better dunnage
- Limiting the stack height of product in transit or during hot, humid months

If an individual could collect the information necessary to determine the cost trade-offs as exhibited in Figures 20.1, 20.2, and 20.3, then minimizing the cost of damage in relation to packaging cost or the distribution method would be simplified. Due to the fact that these costs and these systems are dynamic, determining the relationships is a difficult task. Many companies do not do a thorough job of tracking damage costs. But if a database can be established, many of the variables associated with damage costs can be examined and methods for minimizing the total cost of distribution can be determined.

Many insights can be gained by examining the environment to which most containers are exposed. A number of factors in our environment are not easily controlled, such as humidity, heat, and cold. But if these factors are at least identified, recognized, and dealt with, many possible cost-saving ideas are possible. For example, oftentimes a person who purchases cartons for a nationwide company purchases an identical container for all areas of the country. But, it is a fact that different geographical areas experience different humidity levels and different temperature levels. It is possible for a carton to perform well in one section of the country and for that same carton to perform poorly in another section of the country. Often in a situation like this, the carton is upgraded to satisfy the needs of one geographic area, and that change is rolled out to all areas, even though the change is not needed. Varying carton characteristics based on the area in which that carton is distributed and the changing elements, such as humidity and temperature, to which the carton will be exposed over the course of the year may provide opportunities for cost savings.

An excellent source of information to determine how a carton performs in various environments is the carton manufacturer or vendor. Most carton manufacturers have access to packaging labs that can conduct controlled experiments for their customers (or potential customers) and provide a great deal of data on how a particular carton will react in various environments. Information that is more valuable, but a little more difficult to obtain, deals with how that carton will perform with your product inside it. Many carton vendors are willing to help their customers conduct tests of a particular package design, which will yield valuable insights into carton performance. It is also possible to test a carton at a relatively low cost in a real-live warehousing and shipping test. Warehouse stack tests can be conducted using various types of cartons. Factors such as temperature and humidity can be observed or recorded during these tests. Shipping tests to examine various types of containers can also be conducted at a relatively low expense. As with warehouse tests, "live shipments" can be tested, which will yield realistic data and reduce the cost to test various types of cartons. Taking pictures before, during, and after tests can aid in actually seeing what changes take place to the carton during the duration of a test. Instruments such as humidity and temperature recorders are available to collect or observe on a continuous basis many of the conditions that may affect carton performance.

An Internal Material Handling Systems Look at Containers

The greatest area providing cost reduction opportunities related to containers and packaging is typically one's own internal materials handling system. The reason is that this is the area that one typically has the most control over and can most rapidly change. Taking a close look at your own internal material handling system should help you identify many cost-saving opportunities.

Most warehouses handle individual cases in the form of a unit load. A *unit load* is defined as a material handling unit made up of numerous individual cases that is moved and stored to increase handling efficiency.

Unit Load Dynamics. The following factors relating to unit loads should be considered or examined closely to ensure that a particular unit load is capable of being efficiently and effectively handled:

1. *The unit load size should be one that fits all modes of transportation, such as trucks, railcars, and sea-vans.* The most standard unit load dimension in industry is 48 by 40 inches. The unit load size should allow enough clearance so that a loader can quickly load or unload that unit.

   a. If unit loads are too large:

      (1) Space utilization might be sacrificed due to not being able to stack two to three high or two wide when in transit.

      (2) Handling efficiency might decrease due to lack of maneuverability.

      (3) Damage might increase.

b. If unit loads are too small:
   (1) Space utilization might be sacrificed.
   (2) Handling efficiencies might be low due to a small quantity moved per trip.
   (3) Damage might increase due to load shifts in transit.
   (4) Shipping cost might be excessive due to the cost of excess dunnage required.

2. *Uniformity in unit load sizes is desirable, especially when various brands or types of product are shipped together on the same load.* Improved space utilization typically results from handling uniform-size loads. Uniform load sizes also increase the chance that unit loads will mesh with other handling systems besides the home-base system. Odd-size unit loads can cause problems farther down the distribution systems if they do not fit rack openings or row widths.

3. *Unit load length and width are particularly important if pallets are used in the materials handling system.* Unit loads that overhang the pallet can cause some individual cases to be damaged, as shown in Figure 20.4. Note that the vertical sides of cases support much of the weight or stress caused by upper layers or upper unit loads of product. If the vertical sides of a unit load are not supported, much of the vertical stacking strength is lost. Figure 20.5 demonstrates another reason why unit load overhang can result in increased damage. As a forklift approaches a load for pickup, the forks make contact with the product first. Also, as product is loaded or put away, the point of contact is the

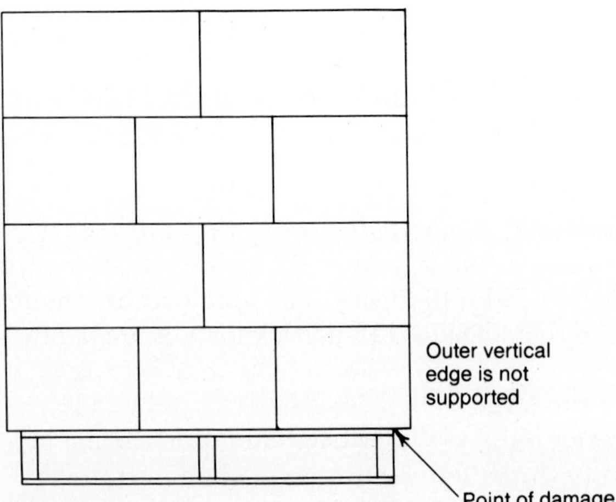

Figure 20.4. Unit loads that overhang the pallet can cause some individual cases to be damaged.

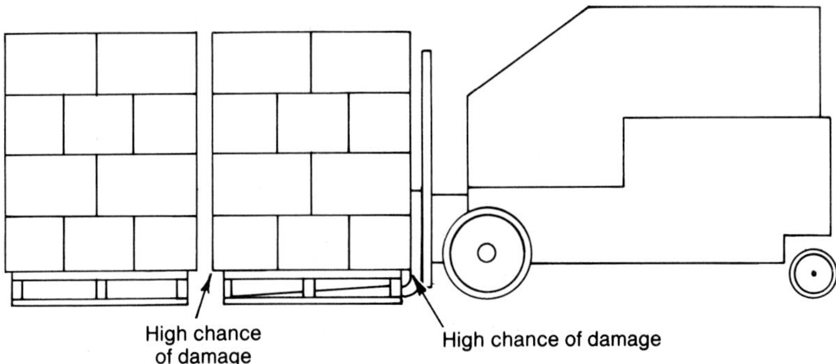

Figure 20.5. Unit load overhang can result in increased damage when forklift makes contact with product first.

lower edge of the unit load if the load is tilted. If a unit load's length and width are smaller than the pallet size, this underhang can cause poor utilization of space and possible unstable warehouse stacks, as shown in Figure 20.6.

4. *Unit load height is important to ensure efficient cube utilization of both warehouse space and transportation equipment.* It may be possible to make minor changes in the height of an individual case to improve

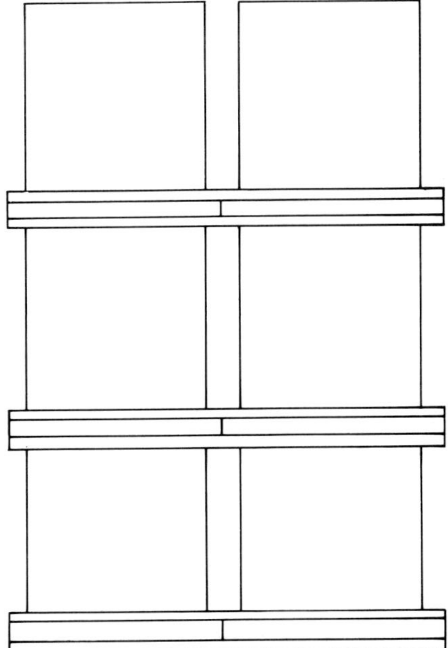

Figure 20.6. Under-utilization of space.

cube utilization of either the warehouse or the transportation equipment, or both. If one additional layer of product could be stacked in the warehouse, in a truck, or in a rack system, cube utilization and handling efficiency would be improved to a great degree. Consistency in unit load height is an important factor in eliminating product shifting in transit. It has been observed that when unit load heights are not consistent, the tall unit loads should be placed near the front of a trailer and the shorter unit loads placed near the rear of the trailer. This loading procedure eliminates product shifting to the front of the truck as the truck applies brakes to stop. When loading railcars, even more care must be taken because the railcar front-to-back orientation can change during transit. It is important in loading railcars that the entire load is secured both front to back and side to side. Having uniform load heights eliminates the need for this extra care when loading.

5. *The stacking pattern of the individual cases that make up the unit load can have a major impact on the dynamics of that unit load.* Two basic stacking patterns exist. An interlocking stack pattern is shown in Figure 20.7. An *interlocking stack pattern* is accomplished by alternating every other layer by 180 degrees. The advantage of an interlocking pattern is that it tends to tie the unit load together by bridging cases and may prevent or reduce a unit load's tendency to flair or separate at the top. The disadvantage of the interlocking pattern is that it is sometimes a little more difficult to form and it does reduce the vertical stack strength of a unit load. Figure 20.8 shows a columnar stack pattern. A *columnar stack pattern* is formed by stacking cases from the various layers directly over the top of a case of the next lowest layer. Note in Fig-

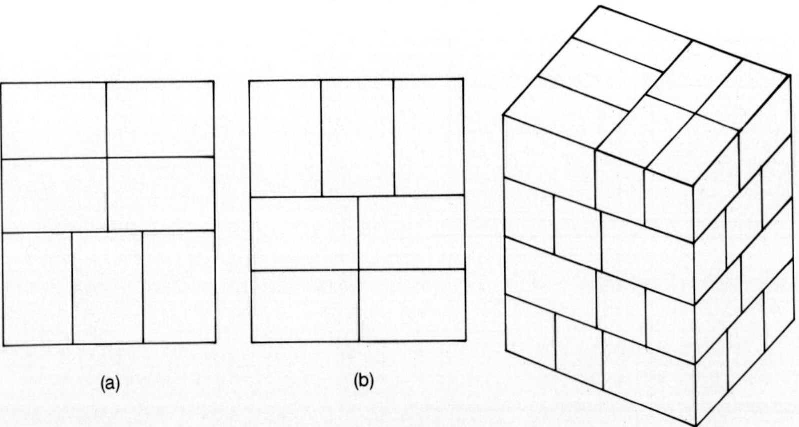

Figure 20.7. Interlocking stack pattern. (*a*) **First layer; (*b*) second layer.**

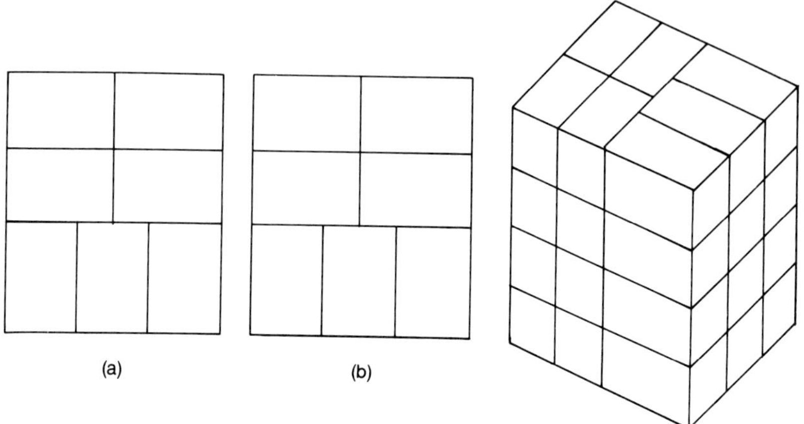

Figure 20.8. Columnar stack pattern. (*a*) **First layer;** (*b*) **second layer.**

ure 20.8 that each layer is assembled the same way and is not rotated 180 degrees as in the interlocking stack pattern. A columnar stack pattern allows for a stronger unit load capable of supporting greater vertical forces than an interlocking load, because the vertical walls of each case are aligned. Figure 20.9 shows the importance of having vertical walls properly aligned, particularly when a columnar stack pattern is utilized. Columnar loads have a tendency to flair or separate at the top and are not as stable as an interlocked load. This can cause problems as forklift trucks turn corners or slow down.

6. *The weight of a unit load has many effects on the materials handling system.* The weight of an individual case is made up almost entirely of the weight of the product. But cases can be added to or taken away from a unit load to affect the total unit load weight. The weight of the unit load has an impact on the following areas of a materials handling system:

a. Materials handling equipment capacity must be capable of handling the unit load weights.

b. The use of warehouse racks is affected by unit load weight due to rack weight capacities.

c. Vertical stack heights are affected by unit load weight and individual case weight. The mode of transportation equipment used is influenced highly by unit load weights. For example, many times it is more economical to ship extremely heavy products by rail, rather than by truck.

d. A unit load's weight dictates the type and quality of support used; i.e., for heavier unit loads a pallet might be used instead of a pallet board, or a higher grade of pallet might be used instead of a cheaper grade.

Unit Load Stabilization. Unit load dynamics have been improved considerably in the past 10 years due to many of the new and improved unit load stabilization methods. Stabilization methods in use today include steel strapping, polypropylene strapping, stretch wrapping, shrink wrapping, stretch netting, adhesives, and industrial rubber bands. Many of the advantages that can be obtained from various stabilization methods include:

- Improved load stabilization
- Less product damage
- Improved space utilization in warehouse and transportation vehicles
- Less pilferage
- More efficient handling due to more flexible and faster product movement
- Extended carton life
- Improved vertical strength
- Improved product appearance

Disadvantages associated with many of the unit load stabilization methods can include:

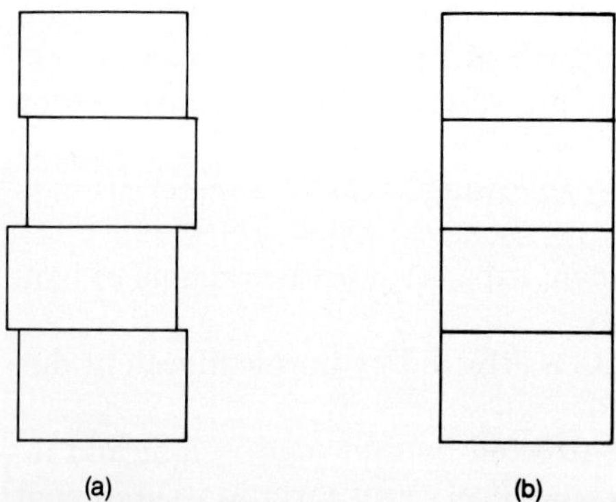

Figure 20.9. The importance of having vertical walls properly aligned, particularly when a columnar stack pattern is utilized. (*a*) **Stacking strength is decreased due to misalignment; (*b*) aligned cases allow for maximum utilization of the strongest component of a corrugated case.**

- Each stabilization method requires material to be purchased at some cost.
- Labor and time are required to apply the stabilization method.
- When the unit load is broken apart, the product used to stabilize must be disposed of.
- Equipment to apply stabilization material can be expensive, can take up space, usually requires energy usage, and must be maintained.
- Storage space is required in which to put stabilization material.
- Corner crushing of cases can result with some stabilization methods.

The lists of advantages and disadvantages are general and do not hold true for each method of stabilization. Some of the more popular methods of stabilization will now be discussed in detail. An estimated cost table for various stabilization methods is provided in Table 20.1. In comparing various stabilization methods, the inherent advantages and disadvantages of each method must be examined in addition to the cost of that particular method.

Stretch Wrapping. Stretch wrapping can be described as the process of stabilizing product loads by stretching a plastic film around the unit loads. Stretch wrapping was introduced in the early 1970s and is becoming one of the most popular stabilization or unitization methods. Figure 20.10 shows a popular stretch-wrapping machine equipped with a prestretch film system. Today, more than 10,000 stretch-wrap units are in

Figure 20.10. Popular stretch-wrapping machine equipped with a prestretch film system. (*Lantech, Inc.*)

Table 20.1. Cost Comparison of Load Stabilization Methods*

Load height, inches	Steel strapping†	Shrink-wrap‡	Polypropylene strapping§	Conventional stretch-wrap¶	Nonpowered prestretch¶	Powered prestretch¶
30	$0.28	$0.65	$9.16	$0.31	$0.21	$0.13
40	0.28	0.77	0.16	0.43	0.28	0.17
45	0.28	0.83	0.16	0.51	0.34	0.21
50	0.28	0.89	0.16	0.55	0.36	0.22
55	0.28	0.94	0.16	0.58	0.39	0.24
60	0.28	1.00	0.16	0.66	0.44	0.27
65	0.28	1.06	0.16	0.70	0.46	0.28
70	0.28	1.12	0.16	0.74	0.49	0.30

* Pallet size = 40 by 48 inches.

† Steel strapping price: one strap to unitize all load heights; ½-inch by 0.020-inch steel strapping at $50/cwt or $0.170/foot; one clip.

‡ Shrink film price: C-fold bag, 3-mil protection at $0.65/pound end-user price.

§ Polypropylene strapping price: ½-inch with 750-pound breading strength; 5–14 coil at $0.0089/linear foot; one clip.

¶ Stretch film price: one to two pallet-load price of $34/5000-foot roll.

operation using an estimated 110 million pounds of stretch-wrap film annually. Growth projections indicate an increase in use of about 100 percent by the late 1980s. Stretch-wrap film can be applied either by hand or by semiautomatic or fully automatic machine.

Some of the particular advantages of stretch-wrap film are:

- Stretch-wrap provides an excellent moisture barrier around corrugated cases. This moisture barrier enables corrugated cases to maintain their strength over a longer period of time.
- The entire four-sided surface of the load can be held in place by the forces of the stretched film, sometimes called the "rubber band" effect.
- Stretch-wrap provides a barrier around cases to keep them clean and free from outside contaminates.
- The product can be seen through transparent stretch-wrap film; therefore, identification of damage and/or pilferage is readily visible.
- Odd-shaped loads can be stretch-wrapped easily.
- Stretch wrapping allows for the removal of one product container at a time without destroying the unitizing integrity of the remaining load.
- Refrigerated and hazardous environment applications are feasible. Stretch films require no heat source and can be mechanically applied in subzero atmospheres.
- The test strength of corrugated cardboard or the weight and/or number of multiwalls in bags may be reduced without sacrificing durability in transit because of the additional protection provided by the encapsulation.
- Some types of stretch-wrap film can be recycled or reextruded into construction film. When burned properly, some films break down into harmless hydrocarbons.
- Stretch wrapping a load around a pallet will aid that load in staying in position over the pallet.
- Prestretch film delivery systems allow stretch film to be stretched to high stretch levels economically, yet the film can be applied with low force on the load.

Some of the disadvantages associated with stretch wrapping include:

- Stretch-wrap film and the necessary equipment do have associated costs, as demonstrated in Table 20-1. But, it should be noted that in many instances the cost advantages far outweigh the material and equipment costs.

- Equipment cost to apply stretch-wrap ranges from approximately $50 for a hand-held unit to over $200,000 for fully automatic machines and the necessary conveyors.
- Stretch-wrap film must be disposed of after use. In some cases, it may be possible to recycle stretch-wrap film to recover some of the costs of disposal.
- The disadvantages associated with any equipment apply, i.e., equipment takes up space, must be maintained, and uses energy.

Shrink Wrapping. Shrink wrapping can be defined as the process of stabilizing product loads by draping or covering a unit load with a plastic material and by then applying heat to that material, thereby allowing it to shrink around the load, conforming to the shape of the load. Figure 20.11 shows a shrink-wrap machine with infeed and outfeed conveyor. Shrink wrapping offers many of the same advantages as stretch wrapping, even though the two processes are entirely different. The advantages of shrink wrapping include:

- Shrink wrapping protects a load from moisture, dirt, dust, and other contaminants.
- Shrink wrapping keeps cartons aligned for greater vertical strength.
- Shrink-wrap shrinks and/or molds tightly around any shape of unit load. Figure 20.12 shows a nonuniform load of farm machinery parts that are unitized with shrink-wrap.

Disadvantages of shrink-wrap are as follows:

- The cost associated with shrink-wrap is shown in Table 20.1. Please note that the cost advantages of shrink-wrap often far outweigh the cost of purchasing equipment and materials.
- Shrink-wrap does not allow for good product visibility.
- Due to the heat required in the shrink-wrapping process, energy costs can be high.
- The cost of shrink-wrap equipment can vary from approximately $50 for a hand-held heating gun to over $150,000 for a fully automated shrink system, including conveyors.

Unit Load Banding. The stabilizing of a unit load by banding is carried out by placing a band around one or more layers of the unit load to tightly hold the given layers together. The banding of unit loads is one of the oldest forms of stabilization. The most common type of banding material is a steel band. Other types of banding material, such as polypropylene, are available. The most common band widths range from 1/2 to 1 1/4 inches, although other band widths are available as well. Banding of unit loads is often used in conjunction with corner board material to fully tie the unit load together. Some of the advantages of banding unit loads are as follows:

- Banding material is extremely strong.
- Banding is one of the cheapest alternatives for load stabilization.
- Banding allows for almost full visibility of the product.
- Banding can be applied manually or automatically.

Figure 20.11. Shrink-wrap machine with infeed and outfeed conveyor. (*Lantech, Inc.*)

■ Banding can be applied to unit loads either vertically or horizontally to fully secure a unit load to a pallet.

Some of the associated disadvantages of banding units loads are as follows:

■ Unless bands are applied to every product layer or corner boards are used, the load will not be fully unitized as with stretch-wrap or shrink-wrap methods.

Figure 20.12. Nonuniform load of farm machinery parts that are unitized with shrink-wrap. (*a*) **Loads of 4500 lb being stored outside at Beall Mfg. Co., Division of Varlen Corp., East Alton, Illinois, which utilized the Bell System for formed steel replacement parts for farm machinery. The Bell III replaced a pallet box and extensive ¾" steel binding;** (*b*) **close view of single load.**

- Applying bands to a unit load manually is very labor-intensive.
- Damage to cases can result from using narrow bands, especially on corner cases.
- The cutting and disposal of bands can cause safety concerns due to the tension of the bands and their sharp edges (on metal bands).

Stretch Netting. The stretch-netting method of stabilizing units loads consists of pulling a net material tightly around the unit load to secure the cases or contents on the unit load. Stretch netting is typically made of polyethelene. Stretch netting is applied in a manner similar to stretch-wrap material. The advantages are as follows:

- Stretch netting can stabilize an entire load from top to bottom.
- Stretch netting allows air to circulate around a load.
- Stretch netting allows for good visibility of the product.
- Stretch netting can be applied both manually and mechanically.
- Stretch netting conforms to the load shape.
- Stretch netting can be cut off as needed to access the load, allowing for the remainder of the load to maintain its stabilization.

Some of the disadvantages of stretch netting are as follows:

- Stretch netting does not protect the load from moisture or dust.
- The disadvantages associated with equipment remain true for stretch netting in that equipment takes up space, requires maintainence, and uses energy.
- Stretch netting requires disposal after it is used.

Adhesives Used for Unit Load Stabilization. In the past few years, adhesives have been used to glue individual cases together, forming an entire unit load stabilized with glue. The adhesives are typically applied to the top of a case or bag and, as the unit load is formed, the layers are glued together. When the unit load is to be separated, the seal that has been formed by the adhesive can be broken by simply bumping or pulling on the case or bag. The advantages of using an adhesive for stabilization purposes are as follows:

- Adhesives are an extremely low-cost stabilization method.
- Automatic equipment that can apply the adhesives is inexpensive (a fully automated system starts at under $2000).
- Adhesives can be applied to virtually any surface.

- Adhesives perform in any environment.
- Application equipment can be mounted on existing conveyors.
- Adhesives dry clear and do not distract from case appearance.
- Adhesives maintain load integrity even after the load is partially broken down.

Some of the disadvantages associated with adhesives used for stabilization purposes are:

- Once an adhesive is broken, it does not reseal.
- Adhesives do not lock the cases or bags to the pallet.
- Adhesives are only used for stabilization and do not protect the load from moisture, dirt, dust, or other contaminants.

Industrial Rubber Bands. Industrial rubber bands can be described as large circular rubber bands that are used to secure a load by placing bands around various layers of product on a particular unit load. These rubber bands come in various widths, thicknesses, and lengths. Rubber bands act much like the metal or polyethelene bands that were described earlier. Rubber bands can be purchased either in a circular form or in lengths that can be cut and joined by a metal clip, thereby allowing the user to make any size rubber band needed.

The advantages of industrial rubber bands include the following:

- Bands are reuseable.
- Bands can be used in conjunction with corner boards.
- Bands work particularly well on lightweight cases.

Disadvantages of industrial rubber bands include the following:

- Bands are expensive unless they are used numerous times.
- Bands are hard to apply to lower levels of a unit load unless they are applied as the load is formed.
- Because of the band's stretchability, its strength factor is low.

Unit Load Support Methods. The most common method of supporting a unit load is with the use of a pallet. Pallets have provided a useful service in industry since the fork truck was developed. They have withstood the test of time and allow for ease and efficient movement of unit loads by forklift truck.

Pallets are produced in various sizes and designs. They are made of various materials such as wood, metal, corrugated paper, and plastic. Various types of pallets will be discussed in detail.

Pallets provide a very useful function in many materials handling systems, but they do have some inherent problems. When considering what unit load support method to use, one should be aware of the following concerns when considering pallets:

- Pallets are costly. The price for a 48- by 40-inch hardwood, four-way entry pallet ranges from $5.50 to $21, depending on where it is purchased, time of year, and quantity purchased.
- Unless pallets are only used internally, getting pallets returned once they are shipped out is sometimes difficult.
- Pallets are hard to clean and hard to keep clean.
- Pallets provide an excellent harbor for insects and rodents.
- Most pallets are made of flammable materials and present a potential fire hazard when in storage and not in use.
- Pallets take up space that could be used for product in the warehouse and in transit.
- Empty pallets take up warehouse space.
- Damage to pallets can cause product damage and unstable stacks.
- Repair and maintenance of pallets can be costly.
- Pallets add extra weight to pallet stacks and product shipment (40 pallets shipped in a truck load can add over 2000 pounds to the load weight).

Wooden Pallets. Wooden pallets are the pallets most commonly used in industry. The following information about wooden pallets should help when considering what type of pallet to use:

- Wooden pallets are readily available in almost any geographic area of the United States.
- Most pallet manufacturers produce to meet any customer's specifications, such as sizes, styles, and types of wood used.
- Wooden pallets can be repaired in house when damaged.
- Wooden pallets are strong and can bridge a span on the warehouse rack. Therefore, if pallets are used, cheaper warehouse racks can be utilized.
- Used wooden pallets can usually be sold to a local buyer (albeit at a small fraction of the purchase price).

- Green wooden pallets (pallets made from freshly cut lumber) can give off a very pungent odor if not dried properly.
- Four-way entry pallets can only be used four ways by a lift truck. Pallet jacks typically do not enter the slots on the long side of a four-way pallet.
- Pallets should be checked upon delivery to ensure they meet purchasing standards. Manufacturers can cut their costs by using narrow slats and runners, which are not easily detected by the buyer.
- The type of fastener or nail used to assemble a wooden pallet can be critical. A blunt-ended nail is preferable to a sharp-pointed nail to eliminate splitting of boards. A knurled nail is preferable to a smooth-shaft nail because a knurled nail is less likely to work its way out of the wood. Nail heads that stick up are a common cause of product damage when pallets are used.
- Rough lumber can cause problems related to splinters.
- The fewer the knots in the wood used, the stronger the pallet. As the wood dries out, knots can fall out of a slat, thereby reducing the strength of that slat.

Plastic Pallets. In recent years, the use of plastic pallets as an alternative to wood has increased. Plastic pallets are five to ten times as expensive to purchase as wooden pallets. Therefore, their use tends to be justifiable only if they are used solely for internal purposes. Among the advantages of plastic pallets are:

- Plastic pallets are more durable than wooden pallets.
- Plastic pallets are typically cleaner to use than wooden pallets.

Some of the disadvantages of plastic pallets include the following:

- Plastic pallets are not as strong as wooden pallets, particularly when they are needed to bridge or support a load in racks. Plastic pallets have been observed to bow and warp when supporting a heavy load in a rack structure.
- Many insurance companies will not allow plastic pallets due to the gases given off when plastic burns.

Corrugated Pallets. Another alternative to wooden pallets, corrugated pallets are available in sizes that can handle up to 4000-pound loads. The advantages of corrugated pallets include the following:

- Corrugated pallets can be a cheaper alternative to wooden pallets, especially when shipped one way.
- They can be purchased broken down and erected as needed, reducing the amount of space they occupy when not in use.
- If the pallets have plastic feet and can nest, they require only a small amount of space when not in use.
- Corrugated pallets can be purchased in various sizes and designs.
- Some corrugated pallets have a high compression strength.
- Corrugated pallets are lightweight, allowing for them to be moved easily, and they do not add greatly to the overall load weight.

Some of the disadvantages of corrugated pallets are:

- Corrugated pallets typically will not take much abuse and are damaged easily.
- Corrugated pallets do not hold up well if a twisting motion is applied to the pallet.
- If a pallet that has small feet is used, all of the weight of the unit load is concentrated on a small area, which can damage cases the pallet is sitting on.
- Due to the ease with which corrugated pallets are damaged, one could only expect to use this type of pallet once or twice.
- Since they are made of paper, they are more of a fire hazard than other materials.

Pallet Boards. Pallet boards are often used to support a load. A pallet board is a solid, flat board approximately the size of the unit load base and is usually ½ to 1 inch thick. Pallet boards are typically made of wood or a combination of wood and metal. Wooden pallet boards are usually made of either compressed particle board or plywood. Pallet boards tend to work very well on roller conveyors. The flat, smooth underneath surface of a pallet board rolls straighter and more smoothly on conveyors than the slats of a wooden pallet. Pallet boards must be placed on a stand when they are set down due to the absence of built-in space available for the board to be picked up with a fork truck. For this same reason, pallet boards cannot be used in product stacks in a warehouse. Pallet boards that are not in use require only a small amount of storage in a warehouse.

Slipsheets. Slipsheets are gaining in popularity as an alternative to pallets. Typically made of either paper or plastic, they are flat sheets approximately the size of the unit load base and have either one, two, three or four flaps, approximately 4 inches long, that extend beyond the base of the unit load. This flap allows for a load to be pulled onto a platform by a mechanical mechanism so that the load can be transported. Using slipsheets requires that a mechanism, called a "pull-pac," be attached to a lift truck.

Slipsheets range in price from about $0.5 up to $4. Good-quality slipsheets that are reusable can be bought for under $1. Slipsheets tend to be an excellent alternative to pallets when one-way shipments are made. Some of the advantages of using slipsheets include the following:

- Slipsheets are a low-cost load support method.
- Slipsheets require very little storage space when not in use.
- Slipsheets take up practically no space when in use, allowing for greater cube utilization of the warehouse or transportation equipment.
- Slipsheets can be used in conjunction with other load support methods, such as pallets or pallet boards.
- Any size slipsheet can be ordered to fit the unit load.
- Stacking stability can be improved due to the placing of a flat surface of one unit load against the flat surface of another unit load.
- Many slipsheets are reusable.
- Slipsheets can be bought with lips on all sides, allowing the load to be addressed from any direction.
- Due to the pull-pac equipment, slipsheets, unlike pallet boards, can be used in product stacks.

Some of the disadvantages of slipsheets include the following:

- The use of slipsheets requires additional equipment to be put on each lift truck (pull-pac attachments cost approximately $2000).
- A higher skill level is required by the lift-truck operator.
- If a slipsheet lip is torn off the slipsheet, the load must usually be hand-stacked off to another slipsheet, unless the load can be addressed from another side.
- Slipsheets will not support a load in a rack.
- Some insurance companies have concerns about using slipsheets because the product is put close to the floor. With only a slipsheet between the floor and the product, high-water damage would be expected in the event the floor is flooded.

A Micro Look at Packages and Containers

Package/Container Needs

The cost impact that cartons have on an organization's profitability may be more staggering than would be expected. The carton selected to contain, protect, advertise, and identify your product has impact on all of the following areas:

- Package cost
- Packaging labor
- Damage levels
- Product image
- Customer acceptance and complaints
- Product identification (advertising)
- Rework/repack costs
- Warehousing costs
- Transportation costs

The cost of an individual carton may be low in comparison to the total cost of the product. But, this fact does not mean that cartons are not a prime opportunity area for making major cost improvements. Due to the high volume of cartons that are typically used, a $0.01 savings per carton can yield large dollar savings. In examining just what carton should be used for your product, there are many trade-offs that must be evaluated. The cost of a carton should be as low as possible without sacrificing or offsetting other major cost improvement efforts, such as warehousing costs, packaging costs, damage reduction, and so on. How a carton is stored, erected, filled, closed, and warehoused can have a major impact on the labor costs, maintenance costs, and energy costs of the warehouse. The cost implications of the advertising message displayed on a case are hard to measure. If one does not think the message printed on a carton has a value, then just ask marketing to change the message on a case. Marketing will very quickly demonstrate the importance of their efforts and why the carton says what it does .

Some of the factors that affect the cost of a corrugated carton are:

- Size
- Strength and type of corrugated material used
- Type and complexity of cut

- Order quantity
- Number of folds, creases, and perforations
- Type of joint
- Type of closure
- Printing

Some of the factors that contribute to the design characteristics and have a high impact on the cost factors mentioned are as follows:

- The amount of internal strength provided by the product or primary package has an impact on the strength needed for a secondary carton.
- The environmental conditions to which a corrugated case are exposed have an impact on the material and strength characteristics needed. The following conditions have an impact on corrugated material:

  Humidity

  Heat

  Cold

  Abrasiveness

  Handling method

  The use of load stabilization methods, such as stretch-wrap

  Vibration

  Vertical and horizontal stresses applied

  Weight placed inside of the carton

  Whether the case is a one-way or returnable carton

  Time span that the carton will be needed

  Anticipated appearance needs of the carton

  Handling method used to move the carton

  Past and current damage rate of the product

  Value of the product

  Chance of damage to the product

  Chance of pilferage to product

  Ability of the manufacturer to control the distribution system

  What your competitors are using

  Specialty control and closure needs (e.g., for pharmaceuticals)

Processing needs of the carton (e.g., Will the carton be automatically erected? Will the carton be glued or taped? To what degree will the carton be automatically processed?)

Method in which the product is placed in the case (i.e., depending on how the case is filled, the case might require internal spacers)

Product Needs

Protection and containment are probably the most important needs that a product has of a carton. If a product has a high value, more protection will be required to protect the product from damage and pilferage. Also, the more susceptible to damage a product is, the more protection will be required by the primary and secondary package. In searching for cost improvement opportunities in the area of product protection, first determine what you are protecting the product from, then determine the frequency and cost of no protection, if possible. If protection must be given at any cost (e.g., the government's regulations to prevent tampering with drugs), then search for the cheapest, most reliable form of protection. Some of the most common elements from which products must be protected are:

- Temperature
- Dust
- Moisture
- Air
- Tampering
- Light/darkness
- Theft
- Handling
- Vibration
- Fingerprints or oil

Once you determine reasons for protection, the area or time span when protection is needed should be examined. It is sometimes possible to protect the product better and less expensively by protecting an entire unit load or secondary package instead of the primary package. This fact is especially true if product containment is the problem.

Other product needs of a container include:

- Product identification, i.e., brand name (and content information)

- Instructions as to how to properly use the product
- Product visibility
- Customer appeal, which could include presenting a certain image, such as high quality, clean, or classic
- Added value from the container, such as a no-drip spout or resealable top
- Providing an advertising or promotional medium, such as coupons for family products
- Low cost

For many of the product needs listed above, the marketing function is the resource and driver. The marketing functions often take a different view of packages and containers than manufacturing and warehousing functions. To select the best designs or methods for handling product, all functions' viewpoints must be considered.

Conclusion

Due to the economic environment, the need to change at a faster rate exists. When making change to control costs, packages and containers provide one area of opportunity. Technology has improved at a faster rate than most warehouses or businesses have changed their methods of handling. Therefore, an opportunity exists to modernize or update many of our present systems.

There are many ways to approach or look at change. The more points of view you take, the more possible ways you have of seeing improvement ideas (i.e., a customer looks at a package and what that package does much differently than a warehouse person or a marketing person). Each point of view can give you more insight into ways to improve the package or container. In this chapter, packages and containers were examined from the following points of view or "need" areas.

Macro			Micro	
Customer needs	Transportation/ distribution needs	Internal material handling needs	Packaging/ container	Product needs/ requirements

When looking at a package or container from an internal materials handling point of view, understanding the unit load dynamics of a load can offer many insights into improvements. Technology has advanced unit load stabilization methods to the point that many cost-saving methods that did not exist 5 or 10 years ago are now available.

The cost of damaged product is higher than many people expect. Getting a handle on your damage cost is a first step in justifying changes to your present materials handling system or package designs. A thorough examination and understanding of the environment your containers are exposed to might yield many opportunities for improvements to that container. Talking with vendors and exploring the new packaging technology can also yield many ideas for improvement.

21
Warehouse Computer Systems

Raymond A. Nelson

President, Raymond Nelson Distribution Consultants,
Stamford, Connecticut

Introduction

The power of the computer should be integrated with most warehousing operations, not only for order processing and record keeping, but as a major *operating* tool for the warehouse. The computer can be integrated with the physical operations of the warehouse to assist warehouse employees in their functions of:

- *Receiving* material into the warehouse and updating inventory records.
- *Inspection and quality control* of inbound material to ensure that the proper quality and quantity of material are received.
- *Storage and location of material.* Determination of the location of material and maintaining proper inventory records.
- *Cycle counts* of inventory to ensure accuracy of inventory and location records.
- *Order entry and preparation of proper picking documents and shipping labels.*
- *Scheduling of work in the warehouse* using standards for each operation.
- *Replenishment of forward picking lines,* if appropriate, for the physical operation of the facility.

- *Inspection of customer or end-user shipments* for accuracy.
- *Scheduling of outbound delivery vehicles* or common carriers.
- *Development of load plans* for outbound shipments.

as well as providing performance reports for the warehousing operations in terms of:

Productivity of personnel.

Utilization of space.

On-time shipment performance.

Fill-rate performance. Line items shipped complete.

Quality assurance of order fulfillment and material transfers through the warehouse.

Costs. Performance against budget for labor, occupancy cost, and other operating costs.

The computer, when combined with data entry devices, such as CRTs, data scanning equipment, optical scanning equipment, and other equipment, can eliminate much of the paperwork that is inherent in the warehousing operations.

In addition, the computer can be used to control physical equipment, such as automated storage/retrieval (AS/RS) systems (either for pallets or tote boxes), conveyor sortation and delivery systems, automatic or mechanized picking systems, palletizers, depalletizers, forklift truck or high-rider picking systems, automatic guided vehicle (AGV) systems, or other warehousing equipment to eliminate the need for manual controls over this equipment. Even in the smallest warehouse, the computer can be utilized to provide operating controls and assistance for the warehousing personnel to make their jobs easier, more accurate, and more productive.

Power of the Computer

The computer, when combined with proper data entry equipment and output devices, can provide the warehouse with:

- *On-line information* for storage locations, status of inventory, order requirements, status of carriers or delivery vehicles, and so on. The key here is that the warehouse personnel can inquire of the computer via a CRT about the work requirements of the operations with which they are involved.

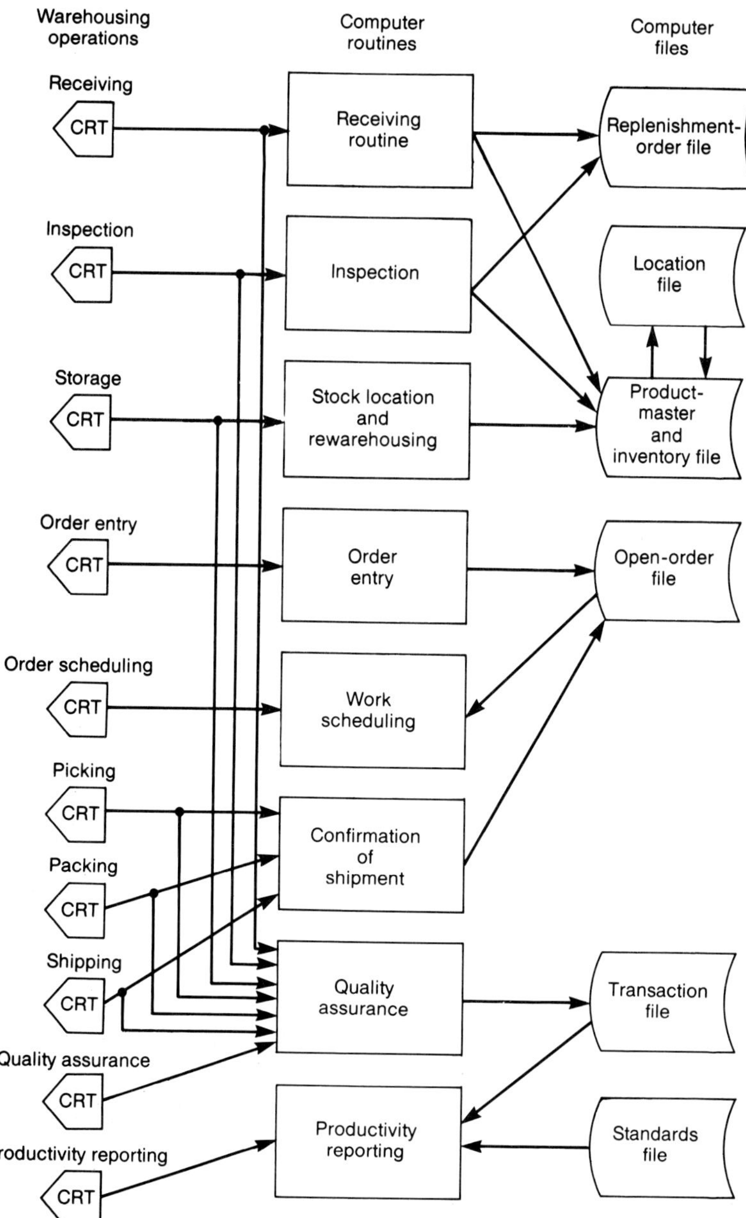

Figure 21.1. Computer-controlled warehouse system. (*Raymond A. Nelson Distribution Consultants, 1983.*)

- *Real time information.* The computer can be updated *when* a transaction occurs so that inventory files, orders, receipts, storage locations, and so on are up to the minute to give warehouse operating personnel the information necessary to do their jobs.

In addition, the computer has the capability of providing the information necessary in any warehousing operation to make decisions regarding proper storage locations; manpower requirements for receiving, storing, picking, packing, and shipping; and the scheduling of receipts to and withdrawals from the warehouse.

The cost of computers and peripheral equipment has decreased dramatically in the past few years, and should continue to decrease due to the technological strides being made and the competitive nature of the computer business.

Total Warehouse Computer Control System

Figure 21.1 illustrates the total computer control system and shows the major files and routines that are necessary for a typical warehouse. CRTs or data entry or output devices can be installed at each of the operating areas or functions in the warehouse, as follows:

- *Receiving:* for the entry of material into the warehouse
- *Inspection:* for the confirmation of quality and quantity of receipts
- *Storage:* for the locating of material to be put away, rewarehoused, or cycle counted
- *Order entry:* for the receipt of orders
- *Order scheduling:* for the scheduling of orders to meet customer delivery needs, availability of outbound delivery vehicles, and availability of manpower
- *Picking:* for the physical dissemination of order information, locations, and quantities of material
- *Packing:* for dissemination of container size or load configurations
- *Inspection:* for the inspection of final orders shipped to customers or users of the warehouse
- *Shipping:* for confirmation that the material has been shipped with carrier or delivery information

The computer routines that are necessary for a totally computerized warehousing system are:

- Receiving routine
- Inspection routine
- Stock location and rewarehousing routine
- Order entry routine
- Picking, packing, and outbound delivery scheduling routines
- Confirmation of shipment routine
- Transaction reporting routines for material movements through the warehouse to provide an audit trail for all transactions and to provide the information for determining the productivity of the warehouse

The files that must be maintained in a computerized warehouse are:

- Replenishment order file for purchased or production shipments that will be received in the warehouse.
- Location file for the location of material in the warehouse.
- Inventory file for the inventory status of material in the warehouse.
- A product master file to include the necessary information for each stockkeeping unit (SKU) to be maintained in the warehouse. (This can be incorporated in the inventory file for some warehouses.)
- Open order file of all orders that have not been filled by the warehouse.
- Transaction file to contain the transactions that occur as material moves through the warehouse.
- Standards file to maintain the standards for warehouse performance for each of the warehousing operations.

The outputs of the computer system are CRT screens for:

- Inbound purchase orders or production releases for receiving and inbound quality control
- Inventory locations
- Orders for picking, packing, and outbound inspection
- Scheduling the manning of the warehouse
- Inventory items and status reports that can be used by the warehouse for inquiry purposes as well as for data input either by key entry, light pens, or data scanning equipment

Hard-copy outputs of a computer system can be:

- Move tickets for storage of material
- Inventory locations for cycle counting
- Picking documents for manual picking
- Orders for inspection purposes
- Picking labels
- Carrier bills of lading or manifests and packing lists

The objective should be to minimize the amount of paperwork by integrating the computer with the operations under consideration and allowing the collection of data by automatic, rather than manual, methods.

Order Entry System

The computer should be used for order entry so that the order information is entered only once. The order can be entered into the computer manually as it is received from the customer or user, or orders can be entered automatically from a customer's or user's computer system. The elements that must be considered for an order entry system are:

- Confirmation that the customer or user is valid. A customer file or authorization file can be used to check that the order has been signed by a bona fide and authorized user of the warehouse material. A credit check is generally included in commercial warehouses.
- Availability of inventory to meet the customer order. This interface with the inventory file must be accomplished to ensure that the warehouse can complete the order. Backorders, if allowed, can be prepared by the computer.
- Confirmation that the item desired by the customer is the item in the warehouse. This is necessary in maintenance and supply warehouses, where the user might not have the proper identifying number of the item wanted.
- Allocation of inventory to the customer order. This is necessary in almost all warehouse computer systems. As the item is entered, the inventory (and perhaps the location of the inventory) is allocated to that specific customer's order. This is called "prepicking" the order

and ensures that, when the order is released to the warehouse for picking, the material will be there.

- Confirming the shipping date to meet the customer's or user's needs.

As we can see, the order entry routine must be interactive with a customer file (if appropriate), the inventory file for inventory availability, the location file, and the open order file. This interactivity is important in the design of the computer system.

Order Scheduling

The single most important function of the warehouse is to ship orders to meet the customer's or end user's needs. This is accomplished by the order scheduling routine that can incorporate standards for picking and packing into the order. This application of standards for the order generally consists of time elements for:

- *The order.* These are time elements that are directly related to the handling of the order. For example, in an order-by-order picking system, travel time for the picker or picking mechanism to traverse the picking line would have to be included no matter what the size of the order.
- *The line items.* Search and confirmation of pick time is dependent on the number of line items in the order. These elements are based on the physical requirements for finding the location of the item and for confirming that the pick was made.
- *Picking the stockkeeping unit.* Some items can be picked very quickly; others require a longer physical time for picking. The times associated with each SKU must be determined and are generally maintained in the inventory file.

These time elements can then be summated for each order to provide the warehouse with the standard times for picking the order. The picking scheduling routine can then summarize the standard minutes required for picking, and the warehouse manager can allocate the manpower to fill the orders.

Most warehouses should be scheduled in short intervals throughout the day. The computer can prepare a batch of orders to be picked that could require three people in the morning and two in the afternoon, depending upon the delivery times for the orders, the manning levels of the warehouse, and, of course, the availability and schedule of outbound delivery vehicles.

Once the orders have been scheduled, the output of the order scheduling routine will be:

- Picking documents or computer data for the people or picking mechanisms
- Picking labels or shipping labels
- Bills of lading for orders
- Manifests for combined shipments

Confirmation of Shipment

The confirmation of shipment can be accomplished when the order is picked, inspected, packed, placed in the shipping accumulation area, or physically shipped, depending on the physical operations of the warehouse. The confirmation of shipment can be accomplished by:

- CRT entry from the picker, inspector, packer, or shipper to indicate that the order has been picked complete, and that all line items and quantities have been confirmed as picked correctly.
- Data scanning equipment that will confirm that the order has been transferred from the picking area to the shipping area. This system works well when machine-readable picking or shipping labels are placed on the container and information is transferred via the data scanning equipment to the computer.

Weight of the outbound shipment can be determined during the confirmation of shipment routine, if necessary, for bill of lading or billing purposes, as follows:

- Synthetic determination of weight. Each SKU can be weighed and the data maintained in the inventory file (or product master file). As orders are entered, the computer can calculate the weight of the order by multiplying the quantity on the order by the weight of the SKU package, and total the order.
- Actual weighing of the shipment. This can be accomplished mechanically at the shipping dock with the scale providing the actual weight directly to the computer, which could then print out the bill of lading or documents for the particular shipment.

Where cube is of importance, the computer can also calculate the cube of the shipment by having the dimensions of the SKU in the inventory file and calculating the total cube of the particular shipment. This could be important for warehouses that utilize a contract or private delivery service.

Transportation costs, if required, can be calculated by the computer if the rate schedule is maintained in the computer. For UPS, parcel post, or a small customer base, this is simple for the computer. However, if shipments are made to many destinations, the maintenance of a rate file can be costly, and it would be wiser, unless the warehouse is very large, to use a rate service bureau to provide the outbound transportation rates.

Carrier or outbound delivery scheduling can be incorporated into the computer system by integrating the outbound order requirements with the scheduling system for outbound shipments. As the orders are received, a file, in terms of cube or weight, can be established for the outbound movements by location of carrier. As demands build up, carriers can be scheduled to meet these requirements. Pooling or consolidation of outbound small shipments is a good example of this computer routine for the warehouse.

Inventory Status

A warehouse is responsible for the receipt, storage, and release of material contained in the warehouse. One of the most important computer applications for a warehousing operation is the maintaining of inventory records for each stockkeeping unit in the warehouse. The inventory status system must have a record for each SKU that shows:

- Inventory on hand
- Inventory allocated to customer orders

And for a more elegant system:

- Expected receipts: quantity and expected receipt date
- Allocation of receipts to backorders

The inventory status is maintained in an inventory file which must be interactive on a real-time basis with the receipts entry, inspection of outbound material, storage routines to add inventory, and the shipment confirmation to reduce inventory. The inventory status system must also interface with the order entry system for the allocation of inventories to customer's or user's orders.

Receipts Control

The receiving function can be computerized by having a CRT on the receiving dock for direct entry of receipts into the inventory system. It should be noted that, if there is a quality control check, material cannot be received into inventory until that quality control check is made.

The interface between open purchase orders (POs) or production requisitions (PRs) (if the warehouse is being supplied from a production plant) should be computerized to allow the receiver to call up the actual purchase order or production requisition to:

- Confirm that the material to be received is a valid receipt. (Some vendors have been known to ship material to a warehouse without a valid order and then attempt to get payment because of the proof of receipt.)
- Provide the items and quantity ordered to ensure that what was ordered was received.
- Allow a data entry or light pen confirmation of the receipt.

The receipts routine, therefore, will be interactive with the:

- Open purchase order (or production receipts) file for updating the open order with the actual receipt
- Inventory file, to indicate that the material is now in the warehouse and available for orders
- Backorder or open order file to allocate the received material to backorders

This procedure allows the receiver to know what has been ordered, to report the receipt electronically (rather than writing a receiving report), and to have the inventory and the order file updated at the time of receipt. This eliminates the writing and searching for paperwork on the receiving dock.

Inspection and Quality Control

Maintenance repair parts and vendor-supplied production or assembly parts for a manufacturing facility often require very vigorous inspections for inbound parts. Here, the computer can be used to display on a CRT an inspection checklist and the actual specifications, eliminating the inspector's having to refer to checksheets or drawings. Light pens or key entries can be made on line by the inspector as the item is inspected.

After the inspection process, on-line entry can be made to update the purchase order or production requisition file to show that the proper material and quantity have been received. The inventory file is, of course, also updated with the proper quantity.

Location Control and Space Utilization

Inventory location control is a major necessity for most warehousing operations. Locations for storage can be either in designated storage systems (such as a forward picking line) or a random location system (for reserve storage). The computer can be used for either type of system and can include the inventory in each of the storage locations.

A location *matrix* is necessary for computer control of inventories. Each aisle as well as each storage cell along the aisle must be identified. The storage matrix can look like:

Aisle	Spot	Tier	Subtier	Cube available	Cube utilized	Percent utilization

The dimensions of each of the cells must be obtained and entered into the computer so that the cube of the cell can be determined. As material is put into the storage cell, the identification of the SKU and the cube of the SKU can be obtained from the inventory file or product master file. The cube within the cell can then be computed and compared with the total cube in the cell. From this, a percent utilization of the storage cell can be computed. Reports can then be made of the utilization of space for each cell, type of cell, aisle, or total warehouse and, if necessary, by type of product. These reports can show where space is misused, the number of empty cells, and other factors. More importantly, the storer can ask the computer for the locations of empty cells to determine where to put material; the locations of partially used cells for rewarehousing material from partially used large cells to smaller cells to increase space utilization; or obviously, the location or locations of a particular SKU in the warehouse for cycle counting or inventory control purposes.

The location file will be interactive with:

- The storage routine for material put-away
- The order entry routine for allocation of customer orders to inventory locations
- The picking or confirmation or shipment routine for withdrawing inventory from a location

- The replenishment or rewarehousing routine for withdrawing inventory from one location and placing it into another location

The location matrix can also be used to determine the actual travel distances for storing and for picking orders to provide realistic time standards for storage, withdrawal, order-picking, and movement to outbound accumulation areas.

Inventory Control

The computer is ideal for inventory control in a warehouse. The inventory *status* system keeps track of the amounts of inventory in the warehouse. The inventory *control* system, however, also has the mission of:

- Indicating when the inventory reaches a level for reordering or replenishing the material
- Placing an order for the required reorder quantity using an interface with the production scheduling or the purchasing system
- Forecasting demands for the item and determining reorder points and quantities based on historical information

Many small warehouses need this type of system to eliminate the tedious review of inventory cards. The computer can be programmed to search for all of the items ordered from a particular source when a scheduled order point is reached. This allows the replenishment of a number of items at the same time.

Storage and Replenishment of Forward Picking Lines

The computer can assist the storer in determining the proper location of material to be put away. If the warehouse is set up with a random location system, the computer can assign the storage locations by providing the storer with a list of cells that will contain the cube to be put away. The storer would enter the SKU number and quantity and request a storage location. The computer would compute the cube of the material by referring to the SKU dimensions contained in the product master or inventory files, then search the location file for a suitable location. The storer would then put the material away and confirm that the material had been put away in the proper location. In a designated storage system, the computer would indicate the aisle-spot-tier-subtier location for the storer. Move tickets could be prepared by the computer at the time of receiving or quality control inspection to notify the storer of the proper location to which to move the material. The storer could then confirm that the material was put away by key entry or light pen scanning of bar codes on the package and the storage location.

Transaction Reporting and Quality Assurance

Each movement of material through the warehouse can be reported to the computer to maintain an audit trail of the material movements and to maintain tight controls over the warehouse operation. The order of movement would be as follows:

1. *Receiving.* Input to the purchase order or production requisition file that material has been received. Noted in inventory file.
2. *Inspection.* Input to the purchase order or production requisition file that material is now in the warehouse and available for picking.
3. *Rewarehousing.* Transfer of material from one location to another in the warehouse to provide good space utilization.
4. *Replenishment of forward picking lines.* The reporting of transfers of material from reserve storage to forward picking lines.
5. *Picking.* The confirmation that the item and quantity desired by the customer was, in fact, picked.
6. *Packing.* The confirmation that the order was packed.
7. *Shipping.* The confirmation that the shipment was, in fact, shipped and the identification of the delivery vehicle.

As can be seen, the computer can maintain running balances of the inventory in each function of the warehouse, transferring the responsibility for the material from warehouser to warehouser. The inbound shipment is transferred from the inbound carrier or delivery system to the receiver. The receiver then has the responsibility for the material until it is transferred to the inspection function or storage. The inspection function receives the material from the receiver and has responsibility for the material until transferred to the storage function or disposition is made of under- or off-spec material. The storer has the responsibility for the material until it is picked or replenished to a forward picking line. Picking the material transfers the material from storage, either in reserve or in a forward picking line, to an order. The order then moves through inspection for verification that the material picked is correct, through packing, and finally to the shipping dock where the material, now a customer order, is the responsibility of the shipper, until it is transferred to the delivery system. This procedure provides a record of the responsible warehouser for each function. It also can minimize or eliminate errors in reporting the movement of material. The transaction file when run in conjunction with the standards file can give a report on the performance of each function in the warehouse.

Warehouse Standards

The computer can be used to process standards for work scheduling in the warehouse and for the after-the-fact reporting on the performance of the warehouse. Standards can be developed for each of the functions of the warehouse, recognizing that the major elements of time used in the warehouse are:

- *Travel time.* The movement of people, either on foot or on equipment, either loaded or unloaded, through the warehouse.
- *Search time.* The time spent looking for an item or location.
- *Paperwork or control time.* The time spent in reading or writing, inquiring of a CRT, or keyboarding data into a computer.
- *Work time.* This is the actual work performed in a warehouse and can include picking up or dropping a pallet, picking a line item, packing an order, counting out pieces, and so on.

For each of the warehouse operations of receiving, storage, inspection, picking, packing, and shipping, standards can be developed considering the time elements of travel, search, paperwork, and work. These standards can then be run on a daily basis against the transaction file, which shows the actual movement of volumes and actual travel distances, to provide the standard time to perform work. This can then be compared with the actual work minutes and used to provide a performance report for each of the operations in the facility.

Performance Reports

Feedback or performance reports for the warehouse operations should be included in the computer system. This is important in the day-to-day operation of the warehouse for both the operating personnel and for management purposes. Performance reports that are generally used are:

- *On-time performance.* The number of orders (or line items) shipped on schedule to meet end-user or customer needs.
- *The fill rate.* The line items shipped complete from inventory. The reason for items not being shipped should be indicated.
- *Productivity of each warehousing operation.* The standard hours versus actual hours for each operation.
- *Accuracy reports.* Line items picked incorrectly as a percent of total line items picked.
- *Space utilization.* Percent of cubic space available used for storage. This is very important during peak inventory times.
- *Budgeted cost versus actual costs.*

Performance reports can be by shift or by day so as to provide immediate feedback on performance of the warehouse operating groups. Weekly and monthly summaries are necessary to detect trends of both good and bad performance. Implicit in any performance report is the standard or goal that the performance is measured against. Standards, therefore, should be established for each area of performance measured.

Interfaces with Materials Handling Equipment

The warehouse computer can be used to operate or control storage and handling equipment in the warehouse. Examples of computer-controlled equipment are:

- *Automated storage/retrieval systems.* Mechanical equipment is used to store and retrieve material either in large pallet loads or smaller tote boxes. When the material is to be placed into storage, the identification and quantity are entered into the computer either by key entry or bar code scanning. The computer then determines the storage location (generally random), the material is stored, and the location is remembered so that when the item is needed the computer can locate the material. When the material is to be retrieved, the stacker mechanism moves to the proper location and the pallet or tote box is retrieved.
- *Conveyors and diverting equipment.* Material must be identified by bar code scanning or key entry as it passes a point on the conveyor; then, by the proper programming, the conveyor will move the material to the proper diverting channel or location for movement of the material off the conveyor.

- *Palletizers and depalletizers.* These can be computer controlled by having the tier and pallet pattern in memory. This equipment automatically creates unit loads (palletization) or singularizes unit loads (depalletization).
- *Automated picking machines.* An AS/RS system is an automated picking machine for pallets or tote boxes. Cartons or individual pieces can also be picked using automated equipment. Here, the computer will have a file of items to be picked that can be supplied to the picking control system. When the items are located, solenoid pushers or other devices are actuated to release the item in the proper quantity to a take-away conveyor.
- *Forklift truck controls.* The computer can control the operations of forklift trucks by maintaining a file of work to be accomplished using the location matrix and directing the forklift truck to and from the location by:

  Hard-copy move tickets

  Radio dispatch verbally from a dispatcher to the drivers

  Radio from the computer to a CRT mounted on the lift truck

  Directly by radio to control the movement of the forklift truck
- *Automated guided vehicle systems.* The computer can control the movement of mobile equipment from location to location in the warehouse.

The computer system must be integrated into the operating system of the warehouse, tieing in with automated or mechanized equipment, transferring instructions to the equipment from the computer, and verifying that the instructions were accomplished via feedback from the equipment to the computer.

Employee Job Enrichment

A major advantage of using the computer in warehouse operations is that it improves the working conditions of the warehouse operating personnel. The computerized system allows the warehouse personnel to use the computer to assist them in their tasks in the warehouse and, if designed properly, to:

- Eliminate paperwork
- Allow inquiry into the status of inventories, storage locations, open orders, and so on

- Provide the information that will allow the employee to do a better job and to make the employee's job more interesting and rewarding

The computer, therefore, should be considered as a way to enrich the work content of the employees. The employee-user should, therefore, be considered in the design of the system regarding:

- What information the employee needs to do his or her job
- How to make it easy for the employee to communicate with the computer

Warehouses that have installed computers for the use of the operating personnel have found that the employees have more interest in their particular job, errors are reduced, productivity is increased, absenteeism is lower, and turnover of personnel is reduced.

Implementation of a Computer Warehouse System

The implementation of a computerized warehousing system must consider advanced materials handling equipment, both mobile and storage, prior to the computerization of the activities of the warehouse. The computer can, of course, be integrated with existing operating procedures and equipment, but the power of the computer makes possible modifications or changes to the operating procedures that will allow reduced costs and more efficient physical operations. The accounting and financial reporting requirements for inventories, order processing, and billing and budget procedures for the warehousing operation must also be incorporated into the warehouse computer system.

Once the warehouse operating, financial, and accounting requirements have been defined, the system's design and operating procedures can be firmed up for the warehouse. These will include:

- *Input data requirements.* The data that will be required for entry into each of the computer files associated with the warehouse.
- *The file formats* for each of the files involved: open order, inventory, stock location, transaction, standards, and so on.
- *The output requirements* for hard copy, such as picking documents, labels, and performance reports, as well as data requirements for accounting and financial purposes that can be directly transferred from the warehouse computer.
- *Screen formats.* The screen formats are the interfaces between the

operating personnel and the computer system. No system should be implemented without user approval and understanding of the screen formats.

Once the screen, file, input, and output formats have been defined, the quantities of data transactions that will occur can be forecast. Then the determination of the computer system requirements can be developed, to include:

- Number of CRT or input stations, including data scanning equipment.
- Size and number of files that will be required to define the computer memory requirements.
- Number of transactions that will occur to define the power required for the central processing unit (CPU). This will also indicate any need for redundant computer power to ensure no interruptions in the work load.
- Communications equipment requirements for interfaces with the warehouse work stations and any outside computers.

The computer system, including hardware and software requirements, should now be defined and *documented* with the users of the system as well as with the accounting and financial operations. Approval must be given by all parties concerned. The procurement of equipment and programming for each warehouse function can then be accomplished. The major effort will be in selecting the proper computer and peripheral equipment. Once this is accomplished, programming can commence using off-the-shelf packages where appropriate and modifying existing programs if economically feasible.

A task force should be used to schedule and control the implementation activities. This task force should include operations personnel as well as the systems or computer personnel involved in the project. Scheduled progress meetings should be held to ensure that all activities are integrated and that all personnel are aware of any changes or modifications made to the original system. The final computer system should be installed and then operated along with the existing system until the debugging process and the training of the workers in the new system have been *fully* accomplished. It will require time to get the new system operating satisfactorily.

22

Requirements of a Warehouse Operating System

William Wrennall, C. Chem., CMC

President, The Leawood Group, Ltd.; Partner, Muther International; Director, Invotek, Inc., Leawood, Kansas

Introduction

The warehousing function is an integral part of the manufacturing industry. The requirements of a warehouse operating system vary. What constitutes the optimum system depends on the special circumstances within each organization. Factors such as organization style, economic needs, and material characteristics are also influenced by environmental considerations. The above and other factors are in a state of continuing change. The warehouse manager must influence this evolutionary process.

This chapter surveys the warehouse operational process. The facets of warehousing as presented are not exhaustive, but comprehensive. The newcomer to warehousing management is provided with an overview. Other chapters in this volume are provided for those who need more detail on specific topics.

History

Old Concepts

The term "warehousing" was not used very much until about 25 years ago. One of the earliest references was by Brech in 1953. Storekeeping had been the more common term for warehousing. Stores were the place where materials were stored.

Top management of the manufacturing industry regarded the storage of materials as a nuisance or necessary evil. The manufacturing manager reluctantly allocated spare factory space for storage until it was needed for production. As demand for production space grew, materials in storage were displaced into some other space.

This attitude, typical of manufacturing management, blamed the need for material stocks on the incompetence of the procurement function and the unreasonable demands of the marketing function.

The space used for storage was a general-purpose space. It certainly was not planned for the special purpose of warehousing. Today, warehousing and warehouse management are recognized as important specialist activities in industry.

Materials Management

In the late 1960s, attention was focused on the importance of materials control as a total concept. Large industrial organizations in the United States, such as General Electric, are associated with the development of what is now known as "materials management."

The concept resulted in organization structures with a materials manager controlling materials procurement, warehousing, materials handling, production planning, and distribution. Ericson in 1974 considered that the approach was equally useful for commercial applications. He also described the European development of "material administration and logistics" as comparable with the materials management concept in North America.

Because of the increasing emphasis on materials management, warehousing and warehouse management are now recognized as even more important industrial activities.

Recent Developments

In the 1970s, automated high-rise warehouses were popular. Automated storage/retrieval systems, AS/RS systems as they were known, were an essential part of the automated factory. The warehouses were often high-rise structures with precision racking and sometimes rack-supported structures. The warehouse grew into a sophisticated, computer-controlled materials handling and storage system, and a professional warehouse manager was needed.

In the 1980s, the zero stock philosophy emerged. Shingo (1982) considered "stocks as a necessary evil." Stock had been used classically to uncouple supply from demand. With the high cost of money, stock (as a necessary evil) was challenged. Ironically, the challenge came from Japan, where interest rates and, thus, inventory costs were much lower than in Western nations.

The Toyota Production System is a recent development that has received a lot of publicity. Mr. Toyota is reported to have asked his colleagues *why inventory was necessary* at all. After due consideration the following reasons were submitted:

- Sales forecasting is not always accurate and inventory is necessary to ensure that the customer's requests are quickly met.
- Manufacturing processes do not operate at the same rate and inventory is necessary as a buffer to compensate for the lack of balance.
- Workers and machines do not always produce good parts and inventory is needed to replace defective ones.
- Machines sometime break down and inventory is required to allow time to repair them before subsequent operations are affected.
- Suppliers cannot deliver parts in the precise quantities and times that they are required by the assembly lines. Inventory compensates for these differences.
- Suppliers are not always reliable in their delivery schedules. Sometimes parts are defective and we, therefore, need inventory.

Mr. Toyota then asked his colleagues to eliminate these reasons. He saw that *each reason for maintaining inventory compensated for a problem that should be eliminated.* Inventory is a means of compensating for defects in the production system. When the defects are corrected, inventory becomes unnecessary.

The main feature of the Toyota Production System is the concept of "nonstock." The first necessary step is to acknowledge "stock" correctly (Shingo 1982). Stocks are considered in two groups: stocks that occur and necessary stocks.

Because both groups reduce profits, it is, therefore, necessary to consider eliminating them. However, zero inventory may, in practice, be neither attainable nor desirable.

Toyota and other companies have aimed for zero stock with spectacular results. These companies are not typical of industry in general, but they have certainly drawn to our attention the possibilities of improving our management of materials. The effect of the Toyota concept is to provide a challenge to manage our materials better. This means we need to be better warehouse managers.

In summary, warehouse operations, as an integral part of materials control, has become very important recently because:

1. The materials management concept worked for the total materials cycle.
2. High interest rates have drastically raised inventory carrying costs.
3. The Toyota company has successfully controlled inventory levels and developed the concept of "just-in-time" delivery.

The Range of Warehouse Operating Requirements

Warehouse Operations

The decision regarding which functions are included in warehouse operations is an organizational one. There is a tendency to include functions within the warehousing management scope over and above that of just storekeeping. This is consistent with the total materials cycle concept.

Warehouse operations include the following:

Receiving — Inspecting
Unpacking/repacking — Holding
Accepting — Rejecting
Storing — Consolidating
Order-picking/kitting — Packing/crating
Issuing — Shipping
Handling — Cycle counting
Physical inventory counting and recording

Some of these functions imply physical action to the materials. They modify unit loads by size, mix, container, and location. Other functions are information- and control-related. Information about the materials is essential for tracking as well as for asset management.

Considerations in Warehousing Scope

Warehousing is a part of the total materials cycle. It begins when materials are transferred from suppliers to purchasers, and ends with the shipping of materials (products) to the distributor, retailer, or user.

The warehousing process is characterized by changes in ownership among:

- Vendor
- Purchaser
- Customer

The Purchasing/Receiving Interface

Receiving/Acceptance

The receiving and acceptance function is the interface between supplier (vendor) and customer (user). Usually ownership changes at this point. It may have changed earlier with F.O.B. or other agreed terms. In any case, provisional acceptance occurs at the receiving dock.

It is necessary to check for whom the goods are intended, where the materials are to be dispatched, and whether they were delivered to the intended customer at the correct location.

Conditional acceptance is formalized by documentation, usually at the physical transfer of materials onto the warehouse receiving dock. The deliverer usually obtains a signature for receipt on a delivery note. The receiving staff may receive a copy of the delivery note or they may raise a "goods received note."

Initial acceptance is based on the fact that:

- The goods were ordered and there is an authorization (purchase order) to buy them.
- The particular goods correspond in whole or in part to what was ordered.
- The count and quality corresponds to the order and delivery note (as far as can be seen by an initial check that they are apparently in good condition).

It is not usually possible to give unconditional acceptance immediately after delivery because:

1. The receiving staff may not have sufficient knowledge of the materials.
2. Counting may not be possible except for bulk items.
3. The matching of specifications against goods received may be a lengthy procedure.
4. Testing may not be possible on the receiving dock.
5. Unpacking may be a specialized task that cannot be performed by the receiving staff.
6. It is impractical to carry out complete inspection.
7. The turnaround of vehicles at the receiving docks would be too slow.

Receiving Inspection. This may or may not be under the control of the warehouse manager. Even when the inspection function is performed by the staff of the quality assurance department, the warehouse manager must retain the initiative on material movement. Unnecessary delay between receiving and the inspection proccss must be avoided. Equally important, pressured acceptance of unchecked goods by user departments must be avoided.

A feature of the Toyota system (the just-in-time concept) means delivering the necessary parts in the necessary quantities at the right time. It also implies the correct quality. If the supplier has delivered the correct-quality goods, further inspection can be considered unnecessary. If the quality function is performed properly at the source, then the receiving acceptance cycle becomes much shorter. Acceptance of vendor quality assurance is not new; neither is its use widespread.

In some instances (especially with a proven, reliable vendor), materials may be delivered directly to point of use. In these cases, the receiving and inventory control functions may be purely "information paperwork" transactions with little or no physical handling of the materials within the warehouse.

Storage Units. The warehouse is the place where unit quantities may be changed. After product reaches the warehouse, the packaging necessary for intersite transfers may no longer be necessary for storage and on-site handling. Removal of packaging or detrashing before moving the items to storage may remove a lot of bulk, but this may also remove protection. The packaging, because of its bulk and weight, may require special material handling and space considerations.

Determination of the optimum storage unit is vital to an efficient warehouse operation. Space utilization may be improved and handling made easier by reducing the size of storage units and transferring items to more suitable containers.

Warehouse Count. Verification of accurate counts of quantities received into or issued from storage may not be easy or cost-effective. For this reason, with small parts and fasteners, the supplier count is often accepted. A sample check may be carried out to establish consistency of container quantity.

Weigh counting can also be used. The newly delivered container is weighed and the content count calculated from knowledge of the weight of a known quantity after deducting the container weight.

Standard container weight checks at intervals are important. Errors due to changes in container and content unit weights can be very costly.

Vendor Returns. Items damaged in transit and items that failed inspection procedures will be held as unacceptable. They cannot be taken as inventory.

Before financial adjustments can be made, isolation and count of identifiable items is advisable. The place where suspect or defective items is generally held is known as "vendor returns."

The administrative process in dealing with unacceptable materials can be quite lengthy. Discussions between the purchasing department and the supplier are carried out to decide disposition and financial arrangements. The vendor may wish to carry out repairs or corrections on the customer site. Sometimes the goods are accepted at a lower price; sometimes they are returned to the supplier. It is important that vendor-return items be kept secure. In the event of production item shortages, it is not uncommon for rejected materials from vendor returns to be issued without authorization. Some useful components or subassemblies of items may have been removed, then when the time comes to return the goods to vendor, they are either missing or incomplete.

Material Identification

It is necessary to identify materials received, materials in storage, and materials issued or shipped. Identification at receiving is necessary to correlate what is received against what was ordered.

After acceptance of the materials, the company records need to reflect what was purchased. The new material assets are added to inventory for financial accounting purposes as well as for materials control.

For materials control, verbal descriptions are difficult to process. *Unique identifiers in code form are easier to use.* The code may be numeric or alphanumeric. The identifier codes provide a basis for material management, and are also used to retrieve materials for issuing and shipping. Retrieval is facilitated when the inventory system includes identifier as well as quantity and location of each item in stock. With a uniform, industry-wide identification system, coding and recoding are minimized.

Identification Methods

The code used to identify the material can be on the container(s), the part or product, or the storage location. When containers or storage locations are dedicated to a particular use, they may be permanently coded. The part, subassembly, or product code may have information additional to the part number. The batch number, date of manufacture, and shelf life may be added to facilitate selection priorities such as first in, first out (FIFO). Identification can be extended to include instructions such as process routing or capital project allocation.

Automatic Identification

The traditional printed label or stenciled identification on a carton or drum has been extended to include automatic identification media, such as:

- Magnetic ink character recognition (MICR)
- Optical character recognition (OCR)
- Magnetic stripes
- Bar codes

Automatic identification of an item arriving at a dock, in storage, or moving through a warehouse allows information about the item to be captured and its movement to be tracked. To complete the process, an automatic reading device or scanner is needed. This inputs the coded information into the computer inventory data system. Bar codes are currently considered to be the more useful automatic identification medium in warehousing.

Types of Bar Code Scanners. Bar code scanners can be stationary on-line devices or portable devices with self-contained memory. Scanners may be hand-held or be fully automatic, as in the scanning of containers on a conveyor. Types of scanners include:

1. *Wand readers*: Wand readers are hand-held light pens. They are inexpensive and easy to use for on-line or portable applications.
2. *Fixed-beam scanners*: These scanners are fixed units and require the items bearing the symbol to be moved past them.
3. *Laser scanners*: Bar code laser scanners range from small, hand-held devices to fixed-location scanners. Omnidirectional laser scanners will read the bar code irrespective of the orientation of the bar code to the scan. The orientation of the item or container to the scanner is thus less critical.

Implications of Automatic Identification. Automatic material identification is significant to the warehouse manager because:

- It extends the scope of his or her work.
- It automates inventory control.
- It provides for an integral part of the automatic factory system.
- It may require bar code printing as an additional function.
- It allows the vendor to supply precoded containers.
- It provides the warehouse manager with more accurate information, thus allowing him or her to exercise improved warehouse control.
- It allows the sharing of data between supplier and user and extends the concept of manufacturing requirements planning (MRP) into distribution requirements planning (DRP).
- It enables the warehouse manager to look at a bigger inventory picture in real time.

The Receiving/Storage Interface

Once goods have been received and accepted for inventory, taken on charge, coded, and are in the approved storage unit, they are ready to transfer into storage. At this point, information must be transferred to purchasing, accounting, and possibly the user department. This will update inventory, authorize payment to the vendors, and trigger use schedules.

Containerization

This is the term given to the design and provision of containers in which items are moved or stored. Containers additionally:

- Protect materials
- Prevent contamination
- Give regular shape and facilitate stacking
- Standardize handling and storage methods
- Provide an easier count
- Facilitate labeling or identification
- Convert materials into stockkeeping units (SKUs)
- Require storage space themselves

Storage

This is the part of the facility where materials are physically located. The warehouse will probably have several storage modes. Materials may be floor-stored, solid-stacked, or in racks. Rack storage may be of several types: pallet, flow-through, drive-thru, or cantilever racks. Small parts may be stored in tote pans or special bins, on miniloaders, on shelves, or in cupboards.

Pallet Storage Methods

The consideration of pallet storage method selection includes:

- Ease of storage
- Ease of retrieval
- Ease of location
- Security of location
- Low risk of damage
- Good use of cubic space

- Cost of storage equipment
- Cost of handling equipment
- Cost of operations

There are, of course, cost of operation conflicts when choosing alternatives. Deciding between floor and rack storage for items held in large quantities is a common example. A typical warehouse design includes several storage methods.

Rack storage is advantageous for ease of storage and retrieval. Pallet racks are used for pallet loads that are not stackable. They are also preferable when the volume per item is too low to justify floor stacking and selective retrieval is important.

Racking can also be used for storage of irregular-shaped items up to the limits of rack opening sizes and dimensions. The irregularity of the item loses its importance if the item is placed on a pallet in a rack. Racks are regular-shaped storage locations that can be used for a variety of materials. The spaces need not be used for the same materials all the time. With rack storage it is not necessary to store similar items in neighboring storage positions.

Floor storage is the method by which the materials are floor-supported.They may be on pallets or independent. Floor-stored items may be stacked or single-tier stored. Materials contained in bags (sacks) can be floor-stacked. The stability of the stack is sometimes increased by using the building walls as supports. The difficulty with floor stacking of bags is that they cannot be easily retrieved except by manual methods.

There are many advantages of the floor storage method. Irregular shapes, such as pieces of machinery, can be floor-stored. The size and shape do not cause a storage problem. The weight of the item to be stored is limited only by the floor strength and the area over which the weight is distributed.

Floor stacking is suitable for high-volume items that are stackable. Regular-shaped or contained items can be stored to give good utilization of three-dimensional space (cube).

When the materials are pallet loaded, overhang is usually not a problem with solid stacking. A simple building can be used for floor stacking. Stack sizes can be adjusted to suit quantity in store. Fewer aisles are needed with this method, and aisle locations can be easily changed.

There are disadvantages. First in, first out is not always possible. In addition, the stack edges are not protected and there is a tendency for damage by material handling equipment.

Stack tidiness depends on the material handling operator and the stability of the unit loads. Unstable stacks are all too familiar. Unfortunately, many accidents are caused by collapse of stacks. With combustible items, size of stack is often limited. Insurance companies usually specify the maximum height or size of stack. Distance below overhead sprinklers may also be a factor.

Floor stacks tend to become untidy, and retrieval of a particular unit can require multiple moves. Stack stability of pallet loads can be increased by positioning the pallet with the longest side facing the aisle.

Too many rows are inadvisable. The increase in floor space utilization is negligible. Truck and storage utilization are also reduced.

The following "rules of thumb" can be used in floor stacking:

1. Allow at least two rows for each item.
2. Vary row capacity.
3. Use double-faced pallets or slipsheets to spread the load.
4. Use pallet supports or post pallets for fragile loads.
5. Leave a clearance for truck mast (minimum of 8 inches) under the roof.
6. Limit stack to free under-roof height (below ducts, sprinklers, etc.).

Location Concepts

Location Systems

Location systems are used to enable the storage locations of items to be known. For this purpose, it is necessary to label each storage location. Materials may be stored in random locations or in special or dedicated locations in the warehouse. This allows materials to be identifiably stored under appropriate titles. When the time comes to withdraw from stock, the materials can be readily retrieved.

The whole warehouse may be divided into zones, with a unique storage location code for each storage space. The code will have a three-dimensional feature to fix the point in space. It is easier to code rack spaces than positions in solid floor stacking.

Random Location Systems. With a good location system, the best utilization of rack space can be obtained with a random storage system. That is, any item may be stored in any available position. Simulation studies have shown that random storage systems can save up to 35 percent of travel time and up to 30 percent of storage space when compared to dedicated systems (Goetschalckx and Radcliffe, 1983). This is true, providing all openings are sized to hold the largest possible item.

Dedicated Location Systems. In a dedicated location system, there is a specific place allocated for each item. If the volume is large, the dedicated areas may be more than one storage position per item. Dedicated locations may be chosen for the following reasons:

1. The location is most suitable for that item; e.g., storing packaging materials near the packing department.
2. The location is selected to suit the material size or weight.
3. Storage conditions are critical for the storage of that item; e.g., pharmaceuticals, such as antibiotics, require temperature-controlled conditions.
4. Flammable material stocks need to be limited in height to meet fire codes and insurance standards.
5. Management or other policies dictate that items be kept separate from others; e.g., service parts must be segregated in an enclosed area; raw chemicals must be kept apart from finished pharmaceutical products.
6. To give high visibility.
7. To reduce hazard, such as fire, explosion, and so on.
8. To facilitate retrieval; location can be memorized.
9. To secure critical items.

Zoning

Zoning is a method by which stored items are allocated to suitable zones within the warehouse. Zoning may be by different areas of the warehouse or different levels within a rack section. For instance, heavy items may be located on the lower level, light-weight items located in the higher positions, irregular shapes located in the lower levels for ease of location and retrieval, and small-parts storage separated from large items.

Other examples are:

Few varieties, high volume—Floor block storage

Many varieties, low volume—Pallet racks

High volume, not stackable—Drive-in racks

Small parts, great variety—High-density storage

Small volume—Shelves

Splits and combines are extensions of the zoning concept such that the zones may be physically split or in separate locations. Typically, warehouses contain features that are split for some materials and combined for others.

An example of splitting or separating materials is storing packaging materials in a separate area from product components. An example of combining is storing work-in-process items with incoming materials.

Inside or Outside Storage

A warehouse operation does not have to be in an enclosed building. Outside storage can be used more extensively in good climates. Some items, such as inert bulk items, sand, and gravel do not need the protection of a building. Mobile equipment, for example, is generally stored outside.

Outside storage is low cost and easy to move. Security can be maintained by fencing. When some protection from the elements is necessary, this can be provided by temporary cover or simple roof structures.

Centralized or Decentralized Storage

Sometimes it is beneficial to hold most of the inventory in a central warehouse from which the satellite warehouses are supplied. Often the central warehouse is combined with one of its satellites.

The advantage of such an arrangement is that there is only one safety stock. The needed stock, is "pulled" to the point of use, as and when required.

With *point-of-use storage,* we have the ultimate in decentralization. One disadvantage of total decentralization is possible loss of control. The materials are located not in the warehouse, but in production space, and manufacturing staff are not always the best custodians of stores items. As one moves nearer to the point-of-use concept, materials accountability is dispersed. With *decentralized storage,* there is also a tendency to accumulate safety stocks at each location.

Reasons for Centralizing

Storage can be centralized for the following reasons:

1. Easier control when all materials are in one location
2. Economies of warehouse staff
3. More efficient use of space possible
4. Gives a focused operation
5. Opportunities for increased utilization of material handling equipment

Reasons for Decentralizing

The grouping of stores items into specialized or separate locations depends upon the compatibility of the materials. It may be natural to group items because of physical and chemical characteristics. Bases for grouping or separating may be:

- Liquids, solids, or gases.
- Regular or irregular shapes.
- Large or bulky versus small.
- Valuable versus low value.
- Inflammable or inert.
- Toxic, edible, or noxious.
- High control required with substances such as radioactive isotopes, controlled drugs or medicines, explosives, top-secret documents, or new inventions.
- Where different methods of handling or care and attention are required. Easily damaged items, such as glassware or electronic components, should be separated from building maintenance items, such as doors, cement, ducting.
- Where product identification is critical and requires special knowledge.
- Items that have infrequent and restricted use, such as accounting documents that have been archived or long-term maintenance safety spares.
- Items that require controlled atmospheric conditions to avoid damage, such as freezing.
- Dirty versus clean items, such as carbon black and paper.
- Packaging materials are heavy and bulky and are best separated from small, easily damaged components used in assembly operations.

- Service parts are often kept separate from product components. One reason may be organizational rivalries.
- Incoming from outgoing items. Finished product may be transferred to sales department charge or control.
- To spread risk. A locked area for safety stock items critical to company operations may be worthwhile. In the extreme, it may be advisable to move part of the warehouse to another building or even to another site.
- Work in process is sometimes stored in the manufacturing environs when the storage time is short and the warehouse location is remote.

Stock Consolidation or Rationalization

After a warehouse has been operating for some time, the utilization of storage space may decrease. This can occur for several reasons. Full cases may be received, stored, and issued; part cases may be returned to stock from manufacturing. It may be necessary to keep items in separate batches for quality control reasons. Previous high-use items may have become obsolete, but are stored in small quantities as spare parts to service old product models.

Periodically, capital or special-project items are stored in the warehouse. They are "one off" items. Once issued, this space is either available for other use or may still hold residues that have no regular or obvious use.

Warehouse space may be occupied by items resulting from purchasing mistakes where:

- The specification was incorrect.
- That "bargain buy" has become a burden.
- The quality is not what it seemed to be.
- The buyer or company officer became a speculator.
- That wonderful new gadget does not work.

Other materials may have accumulated for other reasons:

- They were damaged in the warehouse.
- They have exceeded their shelf life.
- Dies and fixtures used on old products are needed for service parts.
- Procrastination on disposition.

- Awaiting credit clearance.
- Custom-built items never accepted by customer.
- Old machines and equipment that might be useful one day.
- Satellite plant or associate company closed down and stores transferred.
- Company merger followed by closure of operations and warehouses.

To improve space utilization, consolidation of stock into concentrated locations is needed. This is a task that should be done regularly, rather than as a periodic "blitz."

Decisions to remove some slow-moving items from the main warehouse may have to be made. Sale, scrapping, or removal to off site or low-cost, leased warehouse space may be worthwhile.

Security

Secure storage means protection from theft, fire, flooding, terrorism, vandalism, and industrial espionage. *The warehouse manager is the custodian of the materials and equipment held in storage.* He must ensure that what is authorized for vendor payment was authorized for purchase; and that the goods were correct, of acceptable quality, and were in fact received. He must take all reasonable steps to guard against unauthorized issue or theft, known politely as "stock shrinkage."

The ability to operate securely is enhanced when security has been designed into the facility and its operations. The warehouse manager should, therefore, be involved in the planning stage of the facility.

The Warehouse/Customer Interface

This interface may be between the warehouse and:

- Another department of the organization
- Another division or company within the group
- An outside company
- A supplier
- A finisher who is performing a service, such as metal plating

This interface is significant because:

- There will be a change of ownership or responsibility.
- There may be a change of container.
- The transaction will be preceded by order preparation or order-picking.

There is also an information interface with:

- Accounting department, for the necessary financial or cost transactions
- Inventory control to update stock levels
- Shipping department, for transport arrangements and preparation of the necessary insurance and export/import documents

Order Filling

The process of withdrawing materials from stock to complete an issue order is known as "order filling." Items are picked to fill orders. The interface between the warehouse and the user is known as the "order entry/shipping interface."

Order filling is the operational purpose of the warehousing function. Traditionally, the pulling, sorting, compiling, and packing of warehouse items into accurate orders are costly and critical activities. There may be high labor costs, and the consequences of errors may be expensive.

Filling Arrangements

There are numerous order-filling systems to choose from, varying in complexity from hand-cart to advanced technology systems. Basically, there are three filling arrangements: *internal picking, external picking, and automatic picking*. In an internal picking arrangement, the order filler moves to the storage area; conversely, the product moves to the order filler in an external pick arrangement. Automatic picking eliminates the individual order filler, but the device needs to have its low-volume storage frequently replenished. The replenishment is usually performed manually.

The order-filling system can be a pick-by-order or pick-by-article system. Pick-by-order systems are the most common; the order picker fills one order at a time.

In a pick-by-article system, the order filler picks one article at a time for all orders or a batch of orders. Two operations are added when picking by article: customer orders must be sorted by item, and picked items must be sorted by customer.

For each of the order-filling arrangements, there are alternative levels of automation to choose from. Figure 22.1 summarizes the arrangements.

Conventional Systems

Conventional systems include low-level internal picking systems and high-level systems using elevating order-picking trucks and order-picking stacker cranes. Also considered conventional is the manual retrieval, external picking arrangement.

Three techniques used to improve the performance of conventional order filling systems are:

1. *Zoned pick locations*: Zones are arranged by volume of individual items. Items with the highest pick volume are located close to the order fill destination. Zones reduce the overall travel time of order fillers.
2. *Computer scheduling*: Computers are used to sort the listed items into a sequence of shortest travel for the order picker to follow. Computers are also used to determine work standards based upon picking location, unit size, weight, shape, and quantity.
3. *Wage incentive programs*: Time standards are a basis for control and incentive payment plans for order pickers. Successful incentive systems require sound work standards and accurate information systems.

Mechanized Systems

Mechanized systems reduce the fatiguing manual work in order-filling tasks, such as order-filler travel time. In an internal-picking, mechanized, loose-pick system, the order is brought to an operator in a picking zone; the order moves on when filled. In some systems, lights located above parts bins indicate which parts are to be picked for the current order.

In a mechanized batch-pick system, all of the items for a batch of orders are picked, and a conveyor then takes them to an external sorting area.

External picking by automated retrieval systems is another form of mechanized order filling. The operator's physical involvement is usu-

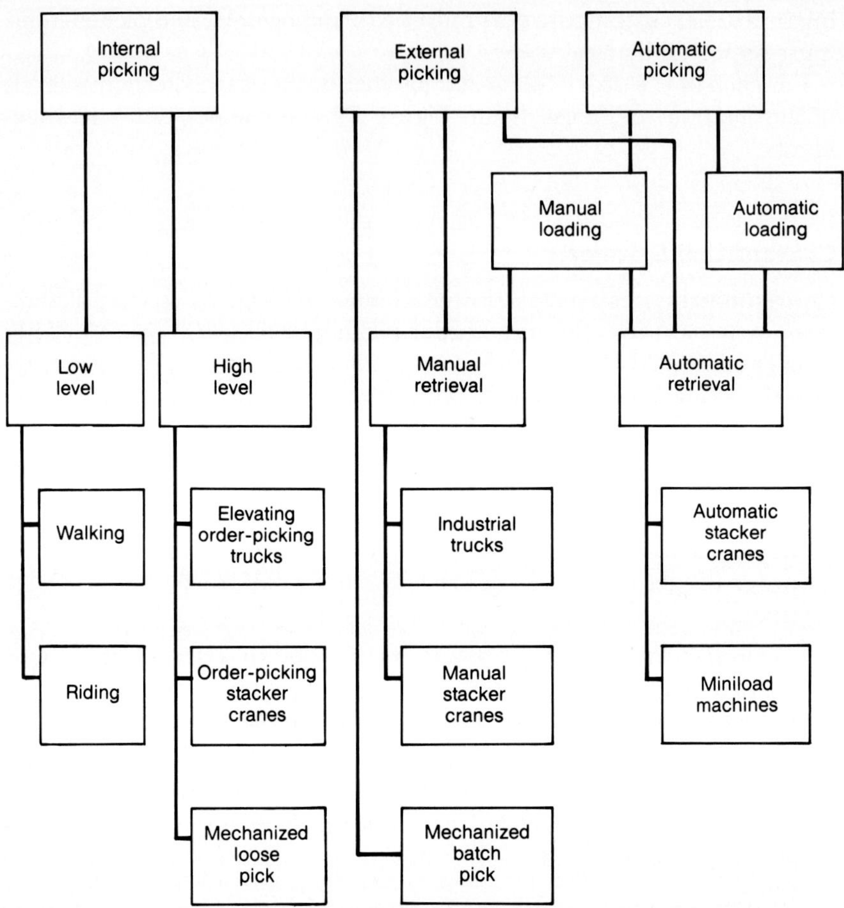

Figure 22.1. Order-filling arrangements. *Note*: **All alternatives except mechanized loose pick and mechanized batch pick are valid for picking by order and picking by article.**

ally limited to handling articles at the external location and keying in data to the miniload or automatic stacker crane system.

Automated Systems

Automated systems eliminate the human element from the order-picking function. Typical automated systems have low storage capacities. A person is necessary in most systems to load the picking machine either from an automated or manual retrieval system. To make a system fully automated, a robot would be used to pick from an automated retrieval system and load the order picker.

Large-scale, fully automated (unmanned) systems may be difficult to cost-justify. When hazardous materials are involved, however, it may not be possible to use personnel in the system.

The more complex order-filling systems require computer support. The benefits of labor reduction in a complex system are offset by the maintenance and computer support costs. However, improvements in speed, accuracy, security, and flexibility of an automated system may be overriding considerations.

Picking, Packing, and Crating

At this stage in the warehouse process, unit loads and containers may be changed again. This may depend on the user location. If the issue is made to a neighboring department, the storage containers may be used for shipping. Shipping of materials to an outside processor is also usually made in the same container. When containers are changed, provision for a supply of new containers as well as storage space for the originals are required.

Materials issued in kit form have a much bigger transformation. Kits of mixed items may be issued to internal user departments or they may be shipped to outside customers. The implication for the warehouse manager is the complexity of picking and packing or crating. The complexity is also extended into the documentation.

Packing and crating may or may not be part of the warehouse management function. If it is, materials for shipping and crating, as well as personnel with packing and crating skills are required. Crating materials can be bought as lumber, or prefabricated crates can be purchased and held in stock.

The packing and crating department is the interface between picked items for shipping and their shipping containers. At this point, items such as product literature and spare parts may be added. They are often provided from organizationally different storage areas. The transition from manufacturing to marketing and customer influence becomes evident.

Reporting Systems

Reporting Rationale

Reporting is required for accounting and control purposes. Reporting systems vary from mimimal to comprehensive. The reporting system is the window for viewing what is happening to materials received, stored, issued, and shipped.

Reporting can be manual (clerical) or electronic (computer). The data are the same whatever the process. Differences are speed, accuracy, and the ability to integrate the information system with a control system.

A computer-based warehouse with automated storage and retrieval is an essential part of an automated factory.

Warehouse reports are an integral part of the management information system (MIS). These reports are for inventory accounting and control. Warehouse managers also need reports for their own use in controlling the warehouse operations. Data for the MIS include materials received, accepted, returned to vendor, shipped, in stock, and scrapped.

This information allows management to account for its receipts. For example:

- What did the company receive?
- What did they accept?
- Were they ordered?
- What was returned to vendor?

Accuracy of information enables the accounting department to ensure that they pay vendors for authorized, acceptable materials only. Accounting can also invoice customers for materials shipped or allocate costs to departmental customers for materials issued to them.

Reports for Warehouse Control

Warehouse managers need reports that enable them to control their operations, over both the short and long term. They need to know how well they use the resources at their disposal in the short term, and to plan what resources they will require in the longer term.

They need to know:

- Truck arrivals per day
- Amount unloaded
- Time to unload or load
- Number of trucks loaded per day
- Number of items shipped per day
- Number of stores issued per day
- Average size and weight of issue

- Time taken per issue
- Utilization of storage space
- Labor performance
- Inventory levels
- Inventory turns
- Warehouse operating costs
- Product and component changes
- Business policies and plans that will affect the warehousing operation

Reporting Points

In order to track materials, reporting is made on receipt, when accepted into stock, and when the goods leave the warehouse.

Goods Receiving. At the incoming point at which there is a financial commitment and there is an addition to the company's assets, the following records are necessary:

- What is received?
- How much?
- When was it received?
- Was it accepted into inventory?
- Were there any rejects?
- How many?
- Where are they?

This information is the basis for adjusting inventory and approving vendor invoices.

Warehousing. The reporting of materials within the warehouse is required for accounting purposes as well as for material and production control purposes. The recording of quantity in stock of each item by approved identifier—name, description, part number, supplier, delivery date, batch number, shelf life—is fundamental to establishing inventory held. The quantity by item received with identifier and the location in the warehouse allows for updating of inventory levels.

Shipping. When materials exit the warehouse, ownership passes to another company or to another department's charge. There are thus external company contractual obligations as well as internal accounting requirements. The basic information required for accounting is:

- Quantity by item issued, scrapped, or returned to supplier, with identifier
- Name and address of the customer
- Order number or document reference that authorizes shipment
- Common carrier information
- Bills of lading

This information is then used to raise transfer documents, customer invoices, and common carrier payment authorization.

The reporting system reports all receipts, items stored, and details of issues. The inventory control system will update stocks after each receipt and issue. The conversions of quantities to values are part of the materials control function, but not usually part of the warehousing function.

Inventory Checks

The count accuracy of inventory needs to be verified periodically by physical check and reconciled with the information system. Physical inventory checks can be made in different ways. The first way is to stop all material transactions and check each stock item and record the inventory level. This method is considered by some to be the most accurate. The pressure to get the job done quickly and resume operations can cause inaccuracies to occur. Costs can also be quite high with this method because the physical inventory is planned for weekend or vacation time when penalty wage rates have to be paid.

An alternative method of taking physical inventories is cyclical counting, sometimes known as the "continuous inventory method." An item for checking is selected at random. The count is made and compared with the recorded inventory, and adjustments are made to correct the record.

With the continuous inventory method, disruption to operations is minimized. Difficulties in counting and reconciling the inventory do occur, however, because items are being moved in and out during the checking process.

The purpose of "stock taking" is to establish, as accurately as possible, what materials the company holds in stock. Following the inventory count, the records are adjusted to correspond with the physical count.

The reasons for periodic stock checks are:

1. Legal: for financial accounting of the company's assets
2. Operational: so that the managers of the company's operations can plan with realistic numbers

The minimum frequency of stock checks may be determined by law, company auditors, or corporate policy.

It is good practice, at the discretion of the warehouse manager or the controller, to vary the inventory count procedure, counting, perhaps, more frequently or at irregular or unexpected times.

Inventory Control

Inventory costs money. The materials have value, and they have a carrying cost. To minimize inventory costs, organizations try to optimize their rate of stock turnover.

Stock turnover is the number of times per year materials pass through the inventory system. If materials in stock equal one month's average usage, then the stock turnover is 12 per year.

Turnover can be measured in two ways:

1. By item count
2. By value

The first method indicates the ability of the firm to use items of stock efficiently from a time standpoint. The second method is a measure of how efficiently an organization uses the money it has invested in materials.

There has been a much greater emphasis on inventory control in the last few years. By efficient material control and reduced inventory, cash is released for other uses. When the cost of money is high, self-financing is very attractive.

Data Processing

Uses and Advantages

Data processing or computer aids can be applied to virtually all stages of warehousing. Some reasons for having a data processing system in the warehouse are:

- Provides fast and accurate information handling within the warehouse and with other departments in the organization
- Simplifies information entry for material control
- Provides an efficient means for warehouse management to control operations
- Makes possible the integration of the warehouse into the automated factory

Uses of data processing in the warehouse include:

- Materials planning
- Automated material identification
- Bills of material
- Inventory costing
- Stock locating
- Inventory records
- Order information
- Picking information
- Decision support
- Warehouse labor efficiency reporting
- Priorities setting
- Stock disposition recording
- Mathematical modeling
- Control of warehouse equipment
- Information interchange between warehouse and customers and suppliers
- Access to company database
- Report generation

In summary, the uses of computers are:

- Material information processing and reporting
- Control of warehousing operations
- Decision support systems

Examples of material information processing and reporting are:

- Number of transactions per day
- Number of truck arrivals per day
- Storage space utilization

Control of warehousing operations examples include:

- Automated identification and tracking of materials
- Automated sorting
- Automated storage and retrieval

The computer extends the manager's ability to improve his or her performance by providing a decision support system. He or she can:

- Carry out "what if" exercises
- Determine if it is economical to consolidate stocks
- Determine the cost effect of relocating stock
- Simulate material handling advantages with different warehouse layouts

Selection of Data Processing Equipment for the Warehouse

Once the extent of computer support to the warehouse management or operation manager has been decided, the means of doing it can be advanced. All the capabilities may be attempted using the same system, or the work can be shared between computers. An important consideration is, should the computer be dedicated to the warehouse function or should the warehouse share the use of the company computer. There are advantages to both alternatives.

A special-purpose computer will generally provide better response time and greater "up time." The shared computer may require less capital by utilizing excess capacity, thus lowering operating costs due to a sharing of staff. Choice of method to adopt should be based on the consequences of the disadvantages. The method that has the least disadvantages should be chosen. A support staff is required for a dedicated computer, while intermittent communication interruptions with the central computer can be expected with time-sharing.

Even if a dedicated computer is selected, the company's central computer may be relied on for order information. If it is necessary to rely on a computer at a distant location and/or shared with many other functions, a backup system should be provided. After the special-purpose versus time-sharing decision has been made, make a list of the disadvantages of the system selected, then prepare contingency plans to deal with the problems that might occur. Do this in the planning stages instead of waiting until implementation.

The warehouse manager needs to consider what kind of backup to have if the computer fails. If the information system suffers a temporary failure, the organizational impact will be minimized by planning for the "worst-case" scenario. A manual backup, which allows operations to continue while the computer is down and data is later being restored, may be adequate. All the procedures need to be written down and the necessary forms for manually recording transactions need to be in place, along with procedures for recording the data when the system recovers. If the computer is very crucial to the operation, a spare (redundant) computer may be necessary. Special procedures are necessary to preserve system data. Daily transaction records and file status must be transferred to permanent storage media each day. User involvement is the key to informed system selection and procedure development.

To ensure a successful warehouse operating system, it is necessary to install a data processing system that is compatible with the warehousing requirements. The best way to ensure this is involvement in the original planning of the system and by periodical updating. Consider future trends. In the future your warehouse computer may be networked with your vendor's and with automated systems.

Conclusions

The historical transition from storekeeping to warehouse operating systems has been a remarkable one. There is no reason to believe that the recent rapid rate of change will slow down. The shift in emphasis from "just a place to store something" to real-time asset management can be expected to prevail.

Managers responsible for warehousing have an opportunity to make a major contribution to the efficiency of their organization's operations. To do this, they need to keep abreast of technological advancements in all aspects of material control.

Bibliography

Ackerman, Kenneth B.: *Practical Handbook of Warehousing,* 1st ed., The Traffic Service Corp., Washington, 1983.

Ballou, Ronald H.: *Business Logistics Management,* Prentice Hall, Englewood Cliffs, New Jersey, 1973.

______: *Business Logistics Management,* Prentice Hall, Englewood Cliffs, New Jersey, 1978.
Bowerson, Donald J.: *Logistical Management,* 2d ed., Macmillan, New York, 1978.
Brech, E. F. L., (ed.): *The Principles and Practice of Management,* Longmans, Green, London, 1953.
Compton, H. K.: *Storehouse and Stockyard Management,* Business Books, London, 1970.
Davis, Grant M. and Stephen W. Brown: *Logistics Management,* Lexington Books, Toronto, 1974.
Ericson, Dag: *Materials Administration,* McGraw-Hill, London, 1974.
Goetschalckx M. and H. D. Ratliff: "Shared Versus Dedicated Storage Policies," Georgia Institute of Technology PDRC Report 83-08.
Heinlein, Ronald: Automated Order Selection, Proceedings 5th ICAW, Atlanta: IIE, 1983.
Monden, Yasuhiro: *Toyota Production System,* Industrial Engineering and Management Press, Atlanta, 1983.
Shingo, Shigeo: *Study of 'Toyota' Production System from Industrial Engineering Viewpoint,* Japan Management Association, Tokyo, 1982.
Tompkins, James A. and Jerry D. Smith, (eds.): *Automated Material Handling and Storage,* Auerbach, Pennsauken, New Jersey, 1983.
Weisz, Howard P.: *Warehouse Management and Operations,* H. P. Weisz, Media, Pennsylvania, 1983.

23
Receiving Systems

James M. Apple, Jr.
Partner, Systecon, A Coopers & Lybrand Division, Duluth, Georgia

Randall M. Ballard
Consultant, Systecon, A Coopers & Lybrand Division, Duluth, Georgia

Receiving System Overview

Receiving can be defined as that activity concerned with the orderly receipt of all materials coming into the warehouse, the necessary activities to ensure that the quantity and quality of such materials are as ordered, and the disbursement of the materials to the organizational functions requiring them.[1] The primary objectives of a receiving system are[1]:

1. Safe and efficient unloading of carriers
2. Prompt and accurate processing of receipts
3. Maintaining accurate records of activities
4. Disbursing receipts to appropriate locations for subsequent use

Accomplishing the objectives of a receiving system requires concentration on an efficient procedure to complete each of the following primary functions[1]:

1. Analysis of documents for planning purposes, including:
   a. Determining approximate dates of arrival in terms of type and quantity of material
   b. Scheduling carrier arrivals as much as is practicable
   c. Furnishing carrier or incoming traffic controller with spotting information
   d. Preplanning temporary storage locations
2. Unloading carriers and clearing bills of lading or carrier responsibility
3. Unpacking goods as necessary
4. Identifying and sorting goods
5. Checking receipts against packing slips and other documentation
6. Marking records to call attention to unusual actions to be taken
7. Recording receipts on receiving slip or equivalent
8. Noting overages, shortages, and damaged goods
9. Disbursing goods received to appropriate location for subsequent use
10. Maintaining adequate and accurate records of all receiving activities

"Systems" Design Approach

A "systems" approach must be utilized in designing a receiving system. The systems approach will provide an overall look at the entire operation of a business in order to tie in the receiving function to all other functions. The receiving operation should not be established as a "kingdom," but rather as a smoothly operating segment of a planned warehouse distribution system—a chain of carefully, interconnected activities.[1]

The following functions within an organization should be considered when designing a receiving system.[2] Each function has a significant interrelationship with receiving that must not be overlooked in a systems design approach.

Purchasing. Purchasing is the link between receiving and the vendor. When possible, purchasing, in cooperation with handling and packaging experts, should furnish vendors with packaging instructions to spell out details of:

1. Packing
2. Packaging

3. Labeling (standardization)
4. Palletizing (including pallet size and patterns)
5. Proper identification
6. Instructions on carrier loading
7. Required *date* of delivery

Receipt of goods that are over- or under-packaged can be avoided through careful planning in the initial stages of the receiving system design, thereby eliminating unnecessary labor and reducing the number of damaged goods receipts.

Vendors. There are several important benefits to be gained from a closer cooperation between distributors and their suppliers. Many of these will result from working with the vendor in designing containers that will make the product:

1. Easier to pack
2. Easier to load
3. Easier to unload
4. Easier to handle
5. Easier to inspect
6. Easier to store
7. Easier to disperse

The container may even be designed specifically for reuse as a shipping container. Even though a new package design might exceed the present cost, the savings are often many times the cost differential. In addition to container design, the vendor should be requested to label the package accurately and in the proper location on the package.

Carriers. Scheduling carriers can prevent congestion during peak times, thereby decreasing the carrier turnaround time.

Material Handling. One goal of the receiving system function is to get goods in, through, and out as fast as possible. Planned and/or mechanical handling is one way of ensuring that this will happen.

Quality Control. A common goal of the quality control function of both the vendor and purchaser is to ensure that the received goods meet the quality agreed upon. The quality control function can be of great assistance in helping receiving to set up records for collecting accurate information for use in the receiving operation and in designing testing programs to determine the adequacy of packaging and packing.

In manufacturing plants, with the current pressure to reduce inventories, it is critical that the quality of parts in the warehouse be ensured. Discovering quality problems at the time of use is very costly.

Data Processing. More often than not, paperwork creates the greatest delays in material movement. Therefore, the data processing function becomes an important one in the systems link with receiving. Since three major goals of the receiving operation are to (1) provide access to material as soon as possible for order filling, (2) make it easy to put material away, and (3) facilitate paying the bills, those responsible for initiating the information flow in receiving must:

1. Get sufficient data (not too much)
2. Get accurate data
3. Report information promptly
4. File information promptly and accurately

The receiving system function must utilize efficient information flow to clear receipt of goods without delay. Delays in finding purchase order data and recording receipts must be eliminated. The expedient reporting of material clearances is important to good material flow. The availability of data must be timely to avoid delays in locating material or checking efficiency of buyers, vendors, and carriers.

Traffic. Receiving can utilize purchase order information to verify that shipment was made by the classification requested. This is frequently a source of unrecognized savings opportunities. Lack of awareness of ICC requirements for paying bills can lead to problems and losses due to errors or misunderstandings. A close contact with the traffic function can help to avoid these problems.

Shipping. Since the shipping function is often physically close to the receiving function, their operations must be planned so that the two activities can work very closely together in such areas as space utilization, scheduling, and manpower and equipment sharing.

Personnel. Good personnel should be rotated among the receiving activities to add to their experience and prepare them for new or better jobs. Extra effort should be expended to motivate receiving personnel, since they are often in remote areas of the building and often must work alone. Training of these persons should emphasize the importance of the receiving operation to the success of the organization. Instruction in material handling, work simplification, and even "information flow" should pay dividends.

Receiving System Design Principles

To provide effective designs for both the physical layout and equipment for receiving and the information control system, the following basic principles should be observed[3]:

1. Utilize carrier driver for unloading function.
2. Concentrate as many functions as possible at one work station.
3. Balance carrier load at dock.
   a. Schedule carriers.
   b. Shift some time-consuming receipts to off-peak hours.
   c. Spot trailers.
4. Arrange activities to permit straight-through flow.
5. Minimize or eliminate walking.
   a. Flow material past work stations.
   b. Arrange activities according to relationships.
6. Schedule manpower for peaks to keep material moving.
7. Provide efficient flow for exceptions.
8. Consider returnable container staging.
9. Provide easy access to receiving data:
   a. Purchase orders.
   b. Labels.
   c. Destinations.
   d. Storage locations.
10. Plan for small vehicles and small receipts.
11. Except when using the carrier's vehicle as an operating storage location, turn trucks around quickly.
12. Redistribute (cross docking) whenever possible to eliminate unnecessary material handling and storage between receiving and shipping.

Data Requirements for Design

The collection of important data on the receiving operation is essential to a design that will meet the objectives most efficiently. In order to segregate the most important data required, several factors must be considered. The following list provides a starting point for factors to be considered in a receiving system design process.[1] The list is intended not to be comprehensive, but rather a beginning point for the analysis of a problem.

A. Materials received
   1. Type or types
      a. Raw materials
      b. Purchased parts
      c. Operating supplies
      d. Nonproductive materials, such as maintenance and prototype parts
      e. Scrap and waste (outbound)
   2. Physical characteristics
      a. Dimensions
      b. *Shape*
      c. Weight
      d. Machine handleability
      e. Palletization capability
      f. Crush resistance
      g. Perishability
      h. Unusual characteristics
   3. Receipts
      a. Number
      b. Volume: normal, peak, or seasonal
      c. Frequency
      d. Schedule
      e. Degree of containerization
      f. Sizes of receipts
      g. Carrier characteristics
      h. Number of carriers
      i. Vendor/user restrictions
      j. Need for repacking
      k. Issuing units or order-picking units
      l. Condition of receipts
      m. Pieces per receipt
      n. Weight per receipt
      o. Quarantine or holding requirements
B. Space
   1. External
      a. Yard
      b. Approach

- *c*. Apron
- *d*. Dock
- *e*. Auxiliary buildings: sheds, garages

2. Internal
   - *a*. Ramp
   - *b*. Dock
   - *c*. Unloading
   - *d*. Inspection
   - *e*. Sorting
   - *f*. Temporary storage
   - *g*. Office
   - *h*. Equipment storage
   - *i*. Amount of space available

C. Building Characteristics
1. Size, shape
2. Dimensions
3. Clear height
4. Structural design
5. Construction type
6. Floor level
7. Floor load capacity
8. Overhead conditions
9. Floor conditions
10. Elevators, ramps
11. Doors: number, size, locations
12. Docks: number of openings, size, location, height
13. Lighting
14. Column spacing
15. Transportation facilities: existing, proposed
16. Unloading facilities
17. Location on site
18. Main aisle locations
19. Logical direction of expansion
20. Orientation: exposure to wind and rain

D. Space Layout
1. Space requirements (see B.2.)
2. Equipment space requirements
3. Activity interrelationships
4. Material flow direction
5. Handling methods
6. Control points
7. Environment(s) required
8. Aisle requirements: number, type, location, width

9. Flexibility
10. Expansion potential

E. Equipment
   1. Handling and movement
      a. Quantities
      b. Frequencies
      c. Distances
      d. Handling units
      e. Traffic
      f. Running surfaces
   2. Storage (see A.)
   3. General
      a. Investment costs
      b. Operating costs
      c. Intangibles

F. Operations
   1. Handling methods
   2. Storage methods
   3. Information system transactions
   4. Manpower requirements
   5. Separate or combined receiving and shipping
   6. Need for more than one location of either
   7. Location in relation to other activities
   8. Effective utilization of labor and equipment

Forms of Data Collection

The first logical step in developing receiving requirements is to analyze available data or begin collecting useful data. An efficient form of data gathering for the receiving function is to utilize a form to collect (1) the most important data first and (2) other helpful data for use in refining the receiving plans or operations. The data can be collected by using a form similar to the receiving log shown in Figure 23.1.[4]

The receiving log requires each operator to document each receipt according to the types of loads received. The log may be used without actual times. Standard motion and movement times can be utilized for setting standards. The data, when tallied, will provide a distribution of the load types received and the quantities received of each load type. These numbers are then utilized to develop standards for each type of receipt. Standards will provide a planning tool for manpower requirements and also a useful tool for daily operation. The study required to apply standards to the motions will also force the observer to ask "why"

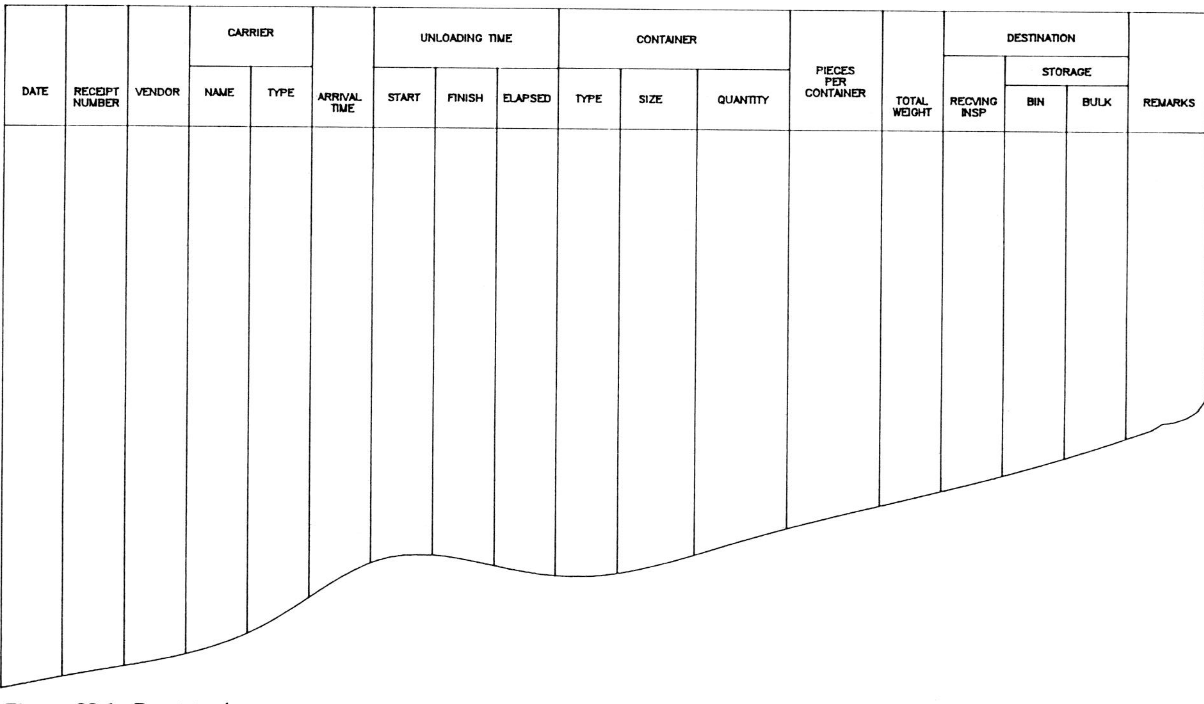

DATE	RECEIPT NUMBER	VENDOR	CARRIER		ARRIVAL TIME	UNLOADING TIME			CONTAINER			PIECES PER CONTAINER	TOTAL WEIGHT	DESTINATION			REMARKS
															STORAGE		
			NAME	TYPE		START	FINISH	ELAPSED	TYPE	SIZE	QUANTITY			RECVING INSP	BIN	BULK	

Figure 23.1. Receiving log.

for each motion. Subsequent actions could eliminate unnecessary motions and movements. The types of loads that may be received in a shipment may include pallets, cartons, coil stock, sheet stock, crates, drums, and slipsheets. Each of the loads is unloaded and prepared for receipt in a different manner. A receiving log will provide the necessary information to design an effective receiving system around these types of receipts.

The vendor and carrier columns of the receiving log will provide insight for scheduling opportunities, based on the distribution of receipts for each vendor and by each carrier. The unloading times will provide the data necessary to estimate manpower requirements and to consider the benefits of scheduling carriers. Comparison of receipt types to estimated unloading times will help to identify scheduling opportunities. The container information should be used to determine unloading equipment requirements and staging area requirements. The weight of each container is also required for equipment planning. The destination column will provide the information necessary to estimate the necessary manpower to transport receipts to the selected location, or to provide the necessary equipment for automated delivery.

The data collected using the receiving log should be translated into a usable form for planning and operating a receiving system. The following items can be extracted from the data:[4]

1. General characteristics of goods received
2. Quantities of each type of goods, package, or container
3. Distribution of sizes of packages, containers, unit loads, and so on of goods received
4. Distribution of weights of loads and shipments received
5. Distribution of number of shipments received per time periods throughout the day, week, month
6. Distribution of pieces per shipment received
7. Number of receipts by each carrier
8. Number of receipts required to complete an order
9. Unloading method and time required

These kinds of information will be critical in determining the following design parameters for a receiving system:[4]

1. Workloads
2. Unloading methods and facilities
3. Dock requirements

4. Receiving inspection needs
5. Temporary staging facilities
6. Handling methods and equipment
7. Space requirements for receiving activity
8. Carrier schedules

An example of a distribution of receipt weights is shown in Figure 23.3.[4] Such a chart might indicate:

1. Unloading methods and equipment needs
2. Handling methods and equipment needs
3. Need for requesting fewer but larger packages and/or shipments
4. Need for convincing suppliers to ship in unit loads
5. An opportunity to reduce congestion by scheduling carrier arrival

Although it is desirable to make the receiving operations as efficient as possible, it is important not to lose sight of the fact that this function is only part of the total distribution system. Making the best use of each inventory dollar may dictate extra effort in receiving. This extra effort should be viewed as a valuable service to the rest of the organization and not as an inconvenience or imposition.

Another method of graphically portraying receiving data is to plot the following data:

1. Arrivals
2. Waiting time
3. Spotting time
4. Unloading time
5. Volumes unloaded from each carrier

This form of data will show activity levels and provide insight concerning peaks to be expected and planned for, or possibly leveled out, by working with vendors and/or carriers. Figure 23.2 shows carrier activity at a dock for one day, indicating arrival time, unloading time, and departure. Occurrences of facility and system overload are easily spotted.

Productivity Measures

The collection of information from a receiving system can be utilized to measure the productivity of the system. This analysis can prove to be

Truck	Time in	Time out	Received
AF	8:30 a.m.	8:35 a.m.	16 Cartons
AF	8:42 a.m.	8:50 a.m.	10 Pallets
UPS	8:52 a.m.	9:24 a.m.	105 Cartons
CC	9:10 a.m.	10:20 a.m.	7 Bundles
FE	9:12 a.m.	9:15 a.m.	2 Packages
PU	9:35 a.m.	9:45 a.m.	Equipment
CC	9:53 a.m.	10:20 a.m.	4 Pallets
CC	10:50 a.m.	10:56 a.m.	5 Cartons
CC	11:10 a.m.	11:25 a.m.	1 Carton
CC	11:30 a.m.	11:40 a.m.	1 Bundle 13 Cartons
CC	12:30 p.m.	1:00 p.m.	34 Rolls
LV	12:30 p.m.	12:36 p.m.	17 Cartons
CC	12:37 p.m.	12:52 p.m.	4 Pallets
CC	1:27 p.m.	1:34 p.m.	8 Cartons
CC	1:37 p.m.	1:39 p.m.	2 Cartons
CC	1:47 p.m.	1:56 p.m.	1 Bundle
CC	2:34 p.m.	2:57 p.m.	2 Pallets
CC	2:40 p.m.	2:53 p.m.	2 Pallets
CC	2:55 p.m.	2:57 p.m.	1 Pallet

Key
AF = Air Freight; CC = Common Carrier; UPS = United Parcel Service; FE = Federal Express; LV = Light Van; PU = Pickup Truck.

Figure 23.2. Daily dock activity.

invaluable in a day-to-day operation of the system and as a planning source for continuous improvement of the receiving operation. A daily effort of documenting the receiving system operations will provide the data necessary to track operational efficiency. A difficulty in obtaining productivity measures for receiving is determining which ones to use from among the many possible measures. The following list comprises a summary of productivity measures that may be utilized for tracking a receiving system operation[5]:

1. Pounds, pallets, cubic feet, dollar value, trailer loads, lines, cases, and/or units received per day
2. Cartons, pallets, or receipts per manhour
3. Daily pallet/carton turnover in receiving
4. Daily payload utilization of inbound carriers
5. Daily cube utilization of inbound carriers
6. Dock to stock time for individual receipts

Weight of receipts	Number of packages									
	1	2	3	4	5	6–10	11–25	26–50	51–100	Over 100	Total receipts
Less than 25 lb											
25–50 lb											
51–100 lb											
101–500 lb											
501–1000 lb											
1001–2000 lb											
Over 2000 lb											
Total receipts											

Figure 23.3. Distribution of receipts.

Incidentally, a more global measure of total organizational productivity would reflect the success of coordinating receipts into usage or demand and can be expressed in the percentage of receipts that are sent directly to production operations or transshipped to customers. This objective is relevant to both wholesale and retail distribution and to manufacturing operations.

Receiving Control Systems

The receiving function is primarily one of information processing rather than physical handling. Consequently, it is desirable to plan and concentrate the information-related tasks into as few steps as possible. Accomplishing this requires on-line accessibility to receiving information and real-time interaction with the database.

Information Processing

Receiving tasks might be thought of as a series of questions to be answered regarding each item that crosses the dock. The basic questions, which should be built into a control system for each receipt, are listed below. Yes answers indicate straight-through flow with little cause for delay. A no answer requires resolution or exception processing, and usually interruption of flow. It becomes obvious that the best improvements in receiving operations are a direct result of ensuring that the answers will be yes. Receiving process questions:

1. Am I expecting a shipment from this company on or before this date?
2. Do the cartons/pallets match the freight bill?
3. Does the merchandise appear to be undamaged?
4. Are the items on the packing slip included on open purchase orders?
5. Do the items and quantities in the shipment match the packing list?
6. Is the merchandise in good condition, and do the parts match the purchasing specifications?
7. Is the merchandise received needed by production or a customer now, and what are the destinations?
8. If it is not needed immediately, where should I store it?

If these questions are portrayed as a series of decisions in a system design diagram, the branching and resolution related to no answers can also be shown. Figure 23.4 is a simplified receiving control system diagram illustrating two no branches.

Physical Handling

The information processing requirements are used to generate a physical handling system. Each of the decision points should be reviewed to determine which ones can be performed at a single station. The consolidation of information processing tasks into groups should be based on the following three principles:

1. Simplify workplace
2. Maximize utilization of manpower
3. Minimize material movement

There are several issues that affect the design of a physical handling system. These include load size, degree of quality inspection required, and peak work-load requirement.

A shortcoming of many receiving systems is the distance between the merchandise and the documentation required to perform the receiving functions. It is not uncommon to have the receipts spread out in a staging area while the first steps are undertaken. Excessive walking, waiting, and locating are symptoms of a poor design (or more likely, a nondesign). The most effective receiving systems use layout and handling equipment to permit material to *flow* through or past a receiving station. Here, as many of the tasks as possible, including exception processing, should be done at one time.

Figure 23.5 illustrates a receiving system design that facilitates "straight-through" processing. The arrangement of the equipment and positioning of the operators for information processing force a straightforward flow.

Pallets of receipts are placed on accumulation conveyor sections when they are unloaded from a carrier. The system is designed to allow each operator work station to process any load receipt. Therefore, it is not necessary to select a specific accumulation lane based on any variable other than availability.

After the shipment has been unloaded and queued on the accumulation conveyor, the container count per pallet is verified. The operator also performs a routine inspection to identify obviously damaged loads.

When the pallet load indexes to the operator work station, the operator begins to remove the cartons and verifies the pallet piece count. The operator also performs the required quality inspection for each re-

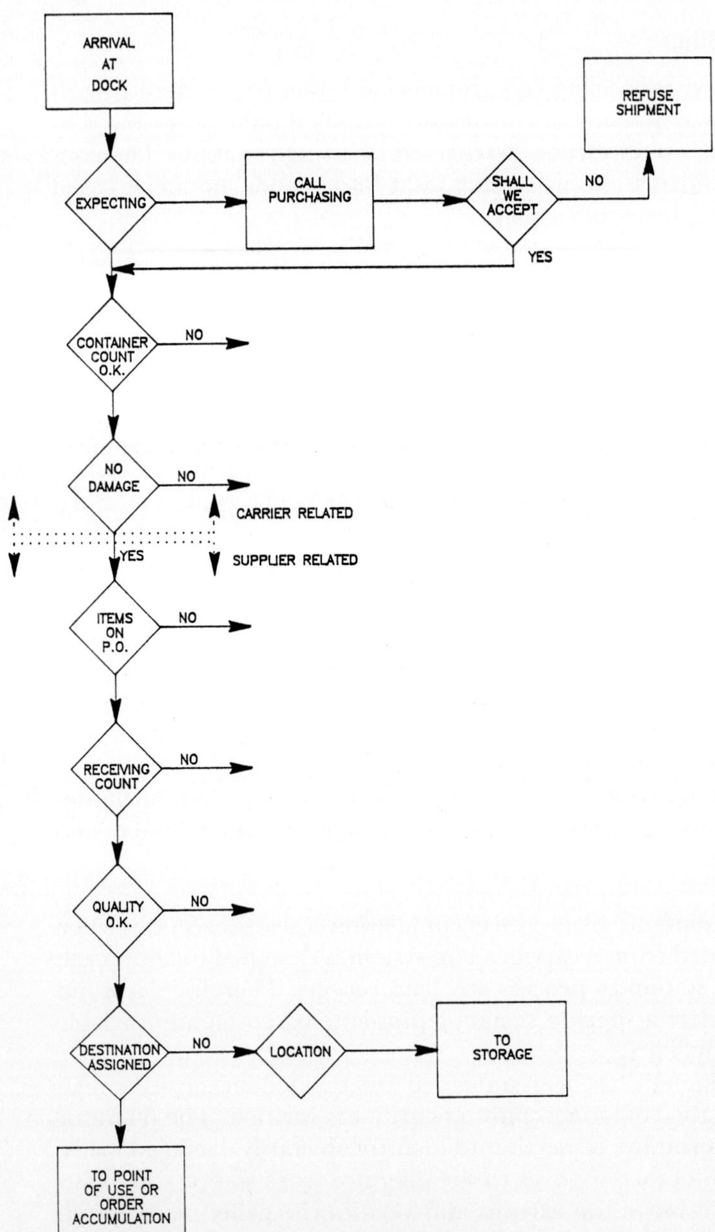

Figure 23.4. Receiving control-system diagram.

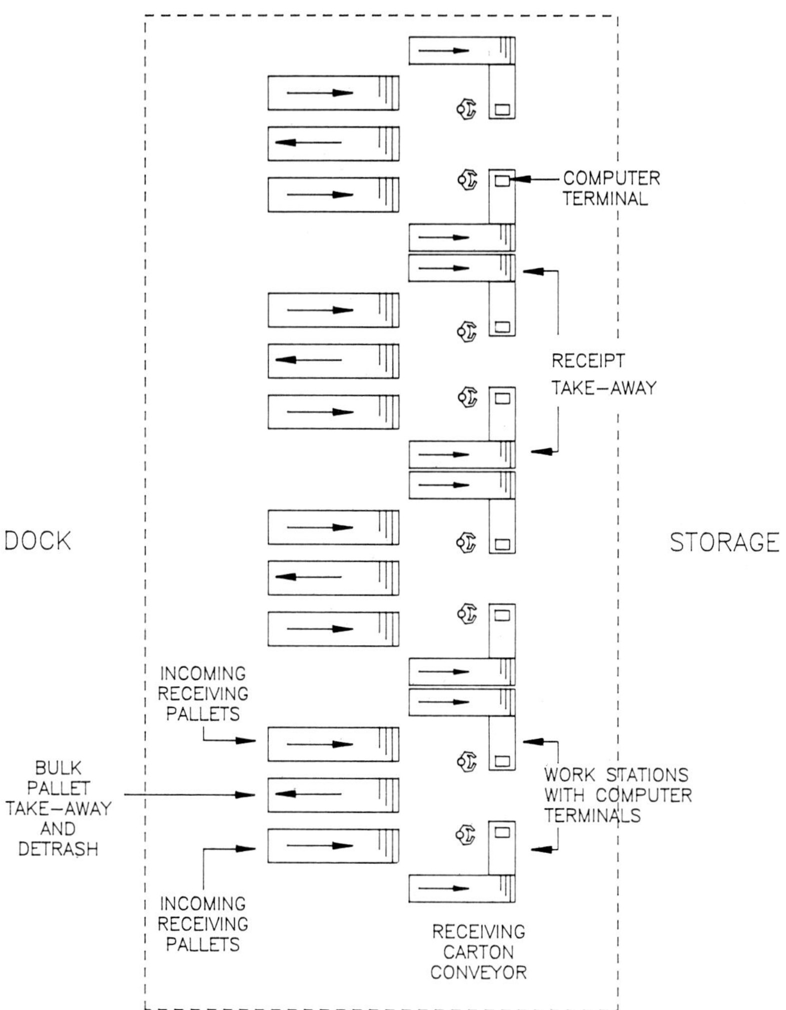

Figure 23.5. Receiving system layout.

ceipt. Each work station is equipped with a computer terminal for access to purchase orders and instructions for quality inspection requirements. As noted previously, each work station and operator is equipped to inspect any type of receipt. If the receipt is acceptable, the operator assigns a storage location and places the carton on the receiving carton conveyor. The carton flows to the end of the conveyor section from which it may be transported to the appropriate storage location.

The system design provides a high degree of flexibility for staffing requirements. Based on the receipt volume, operators are assigned to the different functions. If the volume is low, one operator may be able to unload a truck, place the pallet on the accumulation lane, verify shipment count, depalletize the load, verify carton count, inspect, assign storage location, and store the load. As the area becomes busier, additional personnel can be added at the induction point, inspection point, or storage point. The system design includes only two points of information processing. The first point is at the initial induction point onto the accumulation queues, and the second point is at operator work stations.

Figure 23.6 illustrates a receiving system design that includes additional equipment to provide the flexibility desired. The transfer car acts to integrate each of the pallet conveyor accumulation lanes with the inspection work stations. Unlike the previous system shown in Figure 23.5, each of the work stations in this system is dedicated to a group or family of part types. For example, one work station may be equipped for inspection of electrical component parts and an adjacent work station may be equipped to process only mechanical parts. The transfer car provides the flexibility for a pallet in any accumulation lane to be transferred to any work station. Therefore, the total capacity of the queueing pallet conveyor can be utilized. If the pallet conveyor sections were directly linked to a work station, each conveyor section would have to be sized for the maximum anticipated surge of loads received for the part family of the particular work station. As with the previous system design,

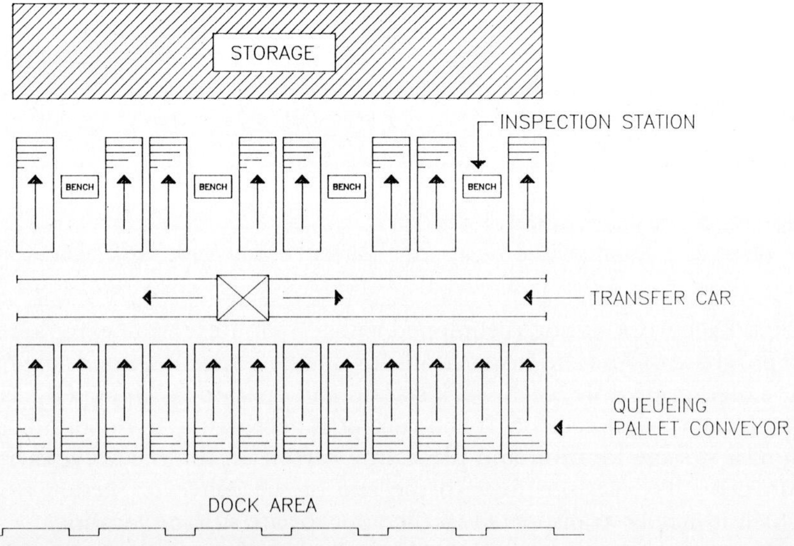

Figure 23.6. Receiving system layout.

this layout includes only two information processing points: one at the initial induction point and one at operator work stations.

Dealing with Roadblocks

Two major obstacles must be overcome for this type of flow-through receiving to be possible:

1. Immediate availability of information
2. Capacity to handle peak demands

Solving the first problem usually speeds up the process so much that capacity is no longer a problem. Having immediate availability of information will eliminate wasted time by personnel searching for the information. Most of the delays in the receiving process result from lack of correct or adequate information. Easy access to information will also reduce the need for staging space.

Centralized computer databases with on-line terminals would appear to be the logical solution; and, indeed they are. When the computer is up, the response time is short and the data is all there. For years, large central mainframe computers have forced us to grow accustomed to batch processing of data and long response times—approaching, or even exceeding, a minute for a reply to a command. Data processing systems designers felt successful when they were able to consistently respond within three seconds. However, recent studies have indicated that *subsecond* responses provide a dramatic increase in productivity at computer terminal operations.

With today's computer costs falling, availability and response time are frequently addressed with a processor dedicated to the warehouse or even just the receiving function. Data completeness and accuracy result from a truly integrated system design that requires data relevant to receiving be in place in the files before purchase orders can be released.

Working in conjunction with computers, automatic identification systems also play a vital role in speeding data entry, maintaining system integrity, and facilitating automatic operations. It is common for documents, containers, and even individual parts to be labeled with a code.

Receiving System Software

There are many packaged software systems on the market today that include a receiving module as part of the package. The functions most often performed by receiving software are receipt notification, receipt verification, receipt scheduling, and serial/lot number control.[6] The majority of available software packages will perform these functions. While this implies that there is software designed specifically for receiving, in reality, available software packages do not stop with just the receiving function. Receiving functions are most often integrated into broader software packages.

The probability of finding a software system that will perfectly match specific receiving system requirements is very slim. The issue, then, is whether you modify the software package or modify the system design. Although most packaged software does allow a certain degree of tailoring, it is not the recommended solution. Where possible, packages should be used without modification. Modifications can be very expensive since the software is customized. A modified software package also does not have the same degree of reliability as a developed, commercially available package. There are other problems associated with a modified software package. The system start-up will, in most cases, not be as smooth as with a package system. Also, the support, after installation, of a commercially available package is better than that of a customized package. It is of extreme importance to review *all* available packages in order to find the best match for the requirement.

References

1. James M. Apple, "Receiving Is Where It All Begins," *Warehouse Distribution,* March 1973.
2. James M. Apple, "Look to Others for Receiving Efficiency," *Warehouse Distribution,* April 1973.
3. James M. Apple, "How to Document Your Receiving System," *Warehouse Distribution,* May 1973.
4. James M. Apple, *Plant Layout and Material Handling,* 3d ed., Ronald Press, New York, 1977.
5. John A. White, "Operating Efficiency: Receiving and Shipping," *Yale Management Guide to Productivity,* Eaton Corp., Philadelphia, 1979.
6. "Software Speeds the Flow at the Receiving Dock," *Modern Materials Handling,* March 1985.

24
Warehouse Control Systems

Donald G. Reid

Principal, Donald Reid and Associates, San Francisco, California

This chapter is devoted to the control of material with warehouse control systems. We will discuss why material should be controlled, how material should be controlled, and some techniques for controlling material.

What Is a Material Control System?

It is axiomatic that control of material requires a good material control system. But what is a material control system? In this chapter, a *material control system* is defined as a control system that tracks materials that flow in a warehouse and keeps track of material locations and inventory levels. Material control systems generally interface with inventory management systems, the functions of which are to control the ordering and levels of inventory. Techniques of planning inventory levels, such as distribution requirements planning (DRP) and "just in time" (JIT) are not discussed in this chapter. However, without good material control systems, inventory management systems would not function.

The material control system should be sophisticated enough to accomplish the desired control, but simple enough to be managed by the people involved. The range of systems are varied—from manual systems for companies with a small volume and limited number of stockkeeping units (SKUs) to larger and more sophisticated systems that utilize computerized warehousing techniques, automated guided vehicle systems, automated storage/retrieval (AS/RS systems), bar code scanning systems, and others.

Is Total Material Control Necessary?

Each individual company has to evaluate the extent of material control that can be economically achieved. Total material control implies many things. While automation is not required, without some aspects of automation, material control is difficult. Automation is frequently the tool that permits the desired level of material control.

What Happens If Control Is Lost?

There are many indications that a warehouse is out of control. Evidence is seen when the ratio of unfilled line items to total lines allocated for picking is on the rise. Material is misplaced at least temporarily. The result is that orders are lost because line items cannot be filled even though material is in the warehouse. Returns from customers due to damaged shipment or shipment of the wrong item is on the upswing. Not only does this cause additional double handling or loss of productivity, but customer goodwill is damaged.

If the warehouse is "full" and receiving is backed up, but a walk through shows empty cubes, control is lacking. If material is received and stored in the wrong type of location, cube utilization is reduced. Minimum-height pallet loads should be stored in reduced rather than full-height openings. If high-volume items are not stored for easy access, productivity is reduced.

An increase in inventory write-off or a high percentage of inaccurate inventory locations are signs of a lack of control. Another indication is the advanced picking of stock for priority customers to ensure availability. Without adequate material control, errors that cause computer reruns or costly error correction routines are introduced into the system.

How Is Control of Material Lost?

The following are a few examples of how control of material is lost:

1. Goods are lost in the warehouse.
   a. A warehouse worker stores a pallet in an empty location and writes down the wrong location.
   b. Less than pallet loads of material are added to locations of a different item.
   c. Items are rewarehoused and location records are not updated.
2. Wrong items or quantities are shipped.
   a. Worker picks too many items. The customer takes the excess items without notifying shipper.
   b. Substituted items are not entered as an exception.
3. A warehouse converts to a more sophisticated system and loses control because the personnel involved were not properly trained and the implementation was not well planned. The problem might be the lack of training, too much sophistication for the personnel involved, or a system that is just ill conceived.

How to Control Material

The following sections describe some of the key elements of a good material control system.

Track Item Inventory in All Locations. The ideal system has the flexibility of controlling a stockkeeping unit in multiple locations. Each location is identified on a file by date, lot number, quantity, or other application-required information. Normally there is only one SKU per location, although some applications, such as kitting for manufacturing, may require multiple SKUs per location. By controlling material in all locations, the system produces the following advantages:

1. Companies that have an obsolescence or dating problem can easily order-pick or retrieve using first-in, first-out (FIFO) strategies.

2. Companies can utilize random storage locations with potential increase in inventory accuracy and reduction in shortages.

3. Companies can utilize optimum picking and stocking strategies for productivity or cube utilization improvement. These strategies frequently require controlling material at each location.

Control Material as Soon as It Is Received. Received material should be promptly entered into the system. The system can check for backorders. Backorders can be filled without the material being stored, thus reducing handling and expediting the backorders. Items that are stored are available for order selection sooner. Inventory levels are reduced for the same level of service.

Track Material as It Flows from Receiving to Storage, Storage to Shipping. A lot or container can be labeled with a bar code. As the container or lot moves, it can be manually or automatically scanned and its movement tracked. By recognizing material that has been allocated to storage but not physically stored, a higher order fill rate is achieved. The system will know that there is material in the process of being stored and will schedule the order selection procedure to retrieve the in-process material.

Record Material Movement on a Timely Basis. As material flows through a warehouse, it should be tracked on a timely basis. An AS/RS system will automatically update the location when the item is stored. Likewise, in a computer-directed system, material is stored with a conventional fork truck. Terminals mounted on the trucks can record the storage. In both of these approaches, the material is immediately available for picking.

Record Discrepancies on a Timely Basis. As a control system becomes more automated, discrepancies are less likely to occur. However, they will still occur, even under near-optimum conditions. With terminal-mounted fork trucks, any discrepancies can be entered into the system as they occur. If a fork truck operator is directed to put away an item in a location that contains another item, the operator immediately records the discrepancy. The item to be stored is rerouted to another location. The item "found" at the previous location is available for order-picking. This approach can be used with terminals attached to other systems, such as carousels. In the same manner, exceptions are entered on a timely basis.

Warehouse Functions

Let us examine the control of material in terms of the traditional functions of warehousing as they are typically performed: receiving, storage of material, retrieval of material or order selection, order accumulation, shipping, and record keeping.

Receiving. Typically, material that is received in a controlled system first requires inspection, then identification to the system. In most companies, 80 to 90 percent of the shipments coming from suppliers cause no problems. Purchase order numbers and the count received can be verified with the original documents or processed by on-line terminals. But the other 10 to 20 percent cause problems, such as the following:

- Material arrives with little or no paperwork for proper identification.
- Backordered material stays on the receiving dock as unchecked material.
- Decisions have to be made regarding over- or under-shipments.
- Goods are damaged in shipment.
- Required inspections and how they should be accomplished have to be determined.

How can a material control system interface with the functions of receiving?

Identifying Receipts. Material arriving at the receiving area is normally accompanied by a packing slip, manufacturing move order, or similar document containing purchase order number, item number, and quantity. The receiving clerk enters the purchase order number or manufacturing move order number into the receiving terminal. Details of the purchase order are displayed on the terminal. At this time, discrepancies should be resolved.

It is a test of the sophistication of the receiving system as to whether the receiving clerk can resolve most of the discrepancies. For instance, if the paperwork is missing or incomplete, it may be necessary to identify a receipt by one of the following pieces of information: item number, item name, quantity, supplier number, supplier's own part number, or some other reference number. In some cases, receiving will have to ask for help from purchasing. The objective of the information flow is to enter the information into the system as quickly and error free as possible.

Any receiving identification documents can be automatically prepared at this time to accompany the items if the application warrants. Information, such as part number, description, quantity, and date received, would be available for put-away or to be stored with the item. In other applications, an identifying bar code label can be printed and affixed to pallet loads, containers, or lots. This bar code will be used for tracking and will increase control as material flows throughout the warehouse.

Inspection. The system should determine whether items must be inspected or whether inspection can be by-passed. The purchase order number might contain a quality assurance code, or the computer terminal might display an inspection notification. The system should then track the items through Q/A.

Receipt Location. If possible, material should flow immediately to storage. However, if material has to remain at the receiving location for some time, the system should maintain the location and status so that items are not lost or mislaid and so that inquiries as to status can be made at all times. Palletized material that has passed inspection and is awaiting storage can be located in a location grid. Less than pallet-load or case-load material can be located by batch awaiting zone put-away.

Since the system knows the status and location of all received material, material can be issued directly for backorder filling.

Storage of Material. Once an item is properly identified, the control system will determine where the item should be stored. At this point in the design of a material control system, serious thought should be given to the type of location control system. There may be several alternatives for a particular warehousing environment, and the final decision may be controversial.

Location Control. A principle of good location control is that no location is ever associated permanently with a given item number. There are, of course, excellent dedicated storage systems in existence. These dedicated systems could have advantages in terms of employee training, simplicity, and productivity in certain applications. But, in general, a random storage system controlled by a computer has advantages over the dedicated storage system in most cases.

This flexibility of not having fixed locations offers the following advantages:

1. Better utilization of cube. Empty locations can be filled with any item that physically can be stored in those locations.
2. Items can be controlled on a first-in, first-out basis.
3. Items can be controlled by lots or dates.
4. Change in the mix of items (new versus obsolete) are easily handled.
5. New locations can be picked to expedite picking productivity.

6. Changes in inventory levels are accommodated by additional locations per item rather than increased bin sizes.
7. Increased control due to the ability to provide a "free" inventory count every time a location has a zero count.

The free inventory count is a powerful advantage. As the number of items in a location becomes zero, that location becomes available for new receipts. If, in fact, a discrepancy exists and there are items in the location, those items are found when the system tries to put a new receipt in that location. Likewise, shortages are found when the system tries to pick the remaining items in a location. Both overages and shortages are recorded on a timely or on-line basis. Thus, the result of a zero location is a free cycle count; and since locations become zero periodically throughout the year, inventory accuracy is increased. One major company that implemented a random storage system along with a semiautomated picking system reduced its inventory write-off at year end by 90 percent. As a result, their auditors have eliminated the need for an annual inventory.

To properly assign receipts to their storage destinations, the material control system must know the item's characteristics. Such information would include:

- Dimensions, space occupied, or size of pallet
- Weight
- Frequency or volume of movement
- Shelf life
- High pilferage indication
- Special storage requirements
- Quantity and pack information
- Item class or customer ordering information

The control system locates the item based on a predetermined algorithm. The decision rules of the algorithm are based on the type of business, physical constraints, and management's priorities. The following are typical system design questions:

1. When should items be added to existing items versus storing items in new locations?
2. Does the type of material handling picking system dictate storing like items together, in the same aisle, or in different aisles? Like items

are normally stored together. However, many times fast-moving items in a multiaisle AS/RS system or order-picking vehicle system should be stored in different aisles in order to reduce congestion and ensure access.

3. Does class of customer dictate storing classes of items together? Some companies have DEM products as well as retail products. If customers order by product class, the products should be stored by zones to increase productivity.
4. Should the season dictate changes in the storage rules? For instance, snow tires should be stored in the back of the warehouse during off months.
5. When should items be stored in bulk, as floor stock, or in primary picking positions?
6. Should items be stored without regard to backorders, or should backorders be picked from receiving?

Once the control system has "picked" the appropriate storage location for the item, that location is allocated for that item. In some systems, the receiving operator has the ability to override the decision and can pick locations from a list of available locations.

Control of Movement. The inventory in a location should not be updated until the item is actually put away; but the movement of material to that storage location should be controlled. A pallet might be moved by a fork truck, conveyor, or automated guided vehicle system. The fork trucks could be equipped with bar code readers. When the operator stows a pallet, he or she would scan a bar-coded location. The on-board terminal would check the validity of the location. Radio data terminals would transmit the completed transaction to the material control system computer. Conveyable items or pallets would be identified by laser scanners, which would transmit arrivals at put-away locations. If the storage location is in an AS/RS system, the control system can be automatically updated. Of course, any exceptions or errors are entered into the system as they occur.

Retrieval of Material or Order Selection. We have discussed the functions of receiving, identification, and storage. In our opinion, these functions are the most important for material control. The methodology for controlling material during the retrieval or order selection cycle should have been considered when the storage or put-away cycle was designed. However, because the number of picks in a typical warehouse usually exceeds the number of stows, picking systems are sometimes designed without regard to the productivity or control of the replenishment system. The ideal system should consider the total warehouse in terms of productivity and material control.

It has been estimated that the cost of an order selection error ranges from $10 to $30 for each occurrence. These costs accrue for various reasons:

- Inventory write-off from shipping overages and wrong items
- Additional handling from returns and second shipments
- Loss of future customer business
- Cost to correct errors in paperwork and computer systems

How can order selection errors be minimized?

- Develop an effective stock locator system.
- Use a clear picking document with identifiable items for hand-picked items.
- Develop sound decision rules.
- Make exception reporting timely and systematized.
- Automate to minimize human errors.

Effective Stock Locator System. An effective stock locator system should be easy to understand while keeping control on a location basis. In an AS/RS system, the computer or programmed controller can automatically move the storage/retrieval machine to the correct location. In a computer-directed or manual system, the locator system should allow the worker to easily understand how to move from one location to another, and once at the location, the worker should easily be able to verify that it is the correct location.

Bar code scanning equipment can aid the verification process. The operator would bar code scan the location address which might contain six digits, such as 11-23-05, where 11 is the aisle number; 23 is the bay, bin facing, or stop in the aisle; and 05 is the height or specific pallet opening. The computer would then verify that the operator had picked from the correct location.

Clear, Identifiable Picking Document. Item descriptions should be standardized so that the order, package label, and shelf label all contain the same description. If the material control system computer generates all the documentation, then standardization is simple. The picking quantities should relate to the physical items. Items received packed 10 to a box require a clear standard unit of issue.

Sound Decision Rules. Order selection methodology must be determined by the priorities of the warehouse. Decision rules for the control system must not be taken lightly. The rules should be well thought out. Without specific instructions, workers are apt to make their own decisions.

An actual example from a parts depot in the automotive industry illustrates a point. The decision was made to force the computer to allocate a pick from a location that contained at least the required number of items to be picked. Thus, if a quantity of 50 were required and location A contained 60, location B contained 30, and location C contained 20 of an item, the computer would allocate 50 items to be picked from location A. After some time when productivity started to drop, a post-installation audit revealed that the "full" warehouse had many partially filled storage locations. The decision rule was changed so that the computer first allocated stock from locations that had *equal to or less than* the required number of items. The warehouse cube utilization increased and productivity rose. This parts depot could have picked on a FIFO basis (oldest location first). This decision rule would have also helped the cube problem.

Timely Exception Reporting. The timely recording of discrepancies or exceptions is an important in picking as in storing. In an order-picking system in which the number of picks exceeds the number of stows and high productivity is required, exception reporting has to be timely yet simple enough for the personnel involved. Most exceptions are repetitive and can be systematized. In an AS/RS system, the warehouse worker performing the order selection can enter exceptions via a computer terminal. In a computer-directed system or a batch-updated system with terminals on material handling equipment, the operator can also enter exceptions.

A well-designed system that gives the operator terminal access will have simple responses for exception reporting. Table 24.1 is an example from one firm's procedure manual for stow exceptions.

Automate to Minimize Human Errors. A well-designed automated system will increase productivity while providing a higher level of material control. Small-parts picking is a particular problem. However, there are systems available that automatically pick the required items and sequence the items to the correct order. These systems have been found to be more accurate and productive than the manual systems they replaced.

Order Accumulation. Many order-picking systems do not pick complete orders. What this means is that each line on an order is picked independently and assembled with the rest of the lines into an order. In ad-

Table 24.1. Exception Codes

Exception Code Procedure

Date	Section name	Section	Page	Title	Objective	Responsibility	Action
12/03/82	Exception procedures	4.4.10	1 of 1	Responds to stow exceptions.	This procedure describes the proper vehicle code input and actions required for vehicle and AS/R system terminals for stow exceptions.	Warehouse worker	1. If exception occurs while stowing, enters the correct exception code. 2. If quantity is required with exception code, enters quantity. 3. Takes action defined below.

Exception Codes and Actions Required

Code	Name	Explanation	Action
1	Wrong item in from location.	Receiving location does not contain correct item.	Keys in code. Leaves item in receiving location.
2	Wrong quantity in from location.	Receiving location contains wrong quantity.	Keys in code. Leaves item in receiving location.
3	Wrong item in storage location.	Storage location contains different stock number.	Keys in code. Keys in quantity put away. Stows items in terminal-directed location.
4	Location full.	Storage location cannot hold all additional items.	Keys in code. Keys in quantity put away. Stows remainder in terminal-directed location.
5	Movement not performed.	Task not completed. Movement requeued.	Keys in code. Returns material to receiving section.

dition, stock numbers are batched for multiple orders (batch picking), then assembled to the correct order. There are several reasons to use a picking system that requires order accumulation:

- Higher picking productivity is frequently obtainable.
- Long travel distances.
- Multiple types of storage/retrieval systems.
- Decreased picking congestion by keeping pickers in constrained zones.

Material control is extremely important when batch or zone picking. Many methods have been devised for controlling material during batch picking. Material can be identified by order and assembled at pack stations or shipping areas. Cases or containers can be bar coded for automatic order assembly. Line items to be picked can be grouped by routes or destinations.

Some manual systems attempt to control the material by physically segregating the picking by schedule. However, computer-controlled systems can more easily control the assembly. Since the material control system can keep track of and control order-picking batches, the schedule is more flexible and productive.

Shipping. A well-designed material control system recognizes the cost and control factors in shipping. The following are several questions that can be analyzed.

- Can we increase the flow of material and reduce congestion in the shipping area by picking in waves or other schedules?
- Can we combine pick tickets and shipping labels?
- Can we pick into modules or onto pallets that can be shipped directly to the customer?
- Can we prepare automatic bills of lading or manifests?

The key is not only to optimize the transportation and shipping function, but to optimize the total warehouse functions while controlling material. Like the receiving and picking systems described, shipping systems should record exceptions and confirmations on a timely basis. In this way, material is controlled from receipt to shipment.

One company verifies shipment to their stores on their own trucks by scanning bar code labels that are prepared for each order. The drivers load their own trucks and scan the bar codes. A shipping manifest is then automatically printed.

Record Keeping. Most good material control systems use a computer system for the control and record keeping. However, there are computer "warehousing packages" that do not provide the elements to track and control material; i.e., the systems may be oriented around accounting or management of inventory levels. However, the best planning and forecasting systems are of limited value if adequate control is unavailable in the warehouse. A summary of the characteristics of a good computerized control system is a summary of the elements discussed in this chapter.

25 Order-Picking Systems

John R. Huffman, Ph.D., P.E.
President, John R. Huffman, P.E., Glendale, California

Order-Picking System Overview

Definition

An order-picking system consists of:

1. A physical subsystem comprised of order-picking personnel or mechanical picking equipment and the related material handling equipment required to pick, check, pack, and ship an order
2. Data processing subsystems that provide the information required to operate the physical system

In many warehouses, there are additional data processing subsystems that assist warehouse supervision to plan and control operations.

Physical Subsystems

Warehouses in which the picking operation is performed by an order filler are called "manual warehouses." Picking personnel walk or ride a vehicle; picking instructions are provided to them by documents or visual displays.

Mechanical systems release merchandise from each picking position in the quantity and at the times specified by a computer executing stored picking instructions. The balance of the order-picking system, in either case, consists of the workstations, methods and procedures, and material and information handling equipment required to check, pack, and ship an order.

Data Processing Subsystems

The Primary Data Processing Subsystem. The primary data processing subsystem processes orders against the customer and item files. Its outputs are:

1. Instructions to order fillers or mechanical order-filling equipment, checkers, packers, and shipping dock personnel
2. Information to the customer about items ordered, but not picked, or partially picked
3. Information for invoicing
4. Cost and/or selling price information to the customer, when necessary
5. A separate packing list, when necessary
6. Shipping labels, when necessary

Since order processing updates item inventories, it also provides information for purchasing and inventory control.

Picking Position Replenishment Subsystems. When orders are picked mechanically or picking positions are confined to flow rack, shelving, or pallet-rack positions reachable by a walking picker, the order-picking system includes an informal or formal subsystem for replenishing picking position inventories from reserve stock. The output of a formal replenishment subsystem is usually one or more picking documents, but may include displays; it may also include random picking position assignments.

Operations Planning and Control Subsystems. The information required to prepare the outputs of the primary data processing subsystem can be used by other data processing subsystems which:

1. Determine the mode of shipment: UPS, common carrier, or captive truck

2. Plan deliveries by captive trucks
3. Estimate picking, packing, checking, shipping, and replenishment staffing requirements by shift
4. Prepare a daily, short-interval schedule for these operations and estimate the staffing required by each one during each schedule period

The outputs of these subsystems are documents not required to pick orders; the subsystems are usually interactive.

Order-Picking System Design

The design of an order-picking system depends primarily upon the manner in which order integrity is treated during picking and subsequent operations. Order integrity may be:

1. Maintained during the picking, checking, packing, and staging of an order for shipment
2. Destroyed during picking, but restored during order assembly on the shipping dock

When order integrity is maintained, there is one order-picking system. It usually consists of mobile equipment, such as a picking cart, and a location-sequenced picking list. As the order is picked, it is assembled for packing, checking, and shipping. The computer maintains one inventory and one picking position per stockkeeping unit (SKU). It frequently does not distinguish between repack and full-case picks of the same item.

When order integrity is destroyed and restored, the warehouse layout includes several order-picking systems that occupy separate areas. An order is picked simultaneously in each area by the order fillers assigned to it. Typically, one group of order fillers picks repack with a picking list, another picks conveyable cases with labels, and a third uses mobile equipment and labels to pick nonconveyable merchandise. Mechanical order-filling equipment may replace the repack picker, the conveyable case picker, or both. Conveyors move repacked merchandise and conveyable cases to the shipping dock, where they are sorted and merged with any nonconveyables to restore order integrity.

When order integrity is destroyed and restored, the computer distinguishes broken-case picks from full-case picks of the same item. It maintains separate picking positions and picking position inventories and provides different documents for picking from them. The physical and data processing subsystems and the operating methods and procedures of the order-picking system must be designed simultaneously to provide the desired warehouse throughput and level of customer service.

Picking Instructions

Picking instructions are created by a computer. They are presented to the order filler as:

1. Printed documents, i.e. picking lists or picking labels
2. Visual displays

Printed documents have been used in both walk-and-pick and ride-and-pick warehouses for many years; visual displays are a recent development.

Printed Documents

Picking Labels. Labels are used to pick shippable full cases, shippable individual pieces, and repacked merchandise.

Because labels used to pick shippable pieces are also shipping labels, they should be pressure sensitive. If a warehouse supplies independent customers or ships via common carrier, each label should bear the following minimum information (Figures 25.1 and 25.2):

1. Picking instructions
2. Digits that identify each piece for sorting and order assembly on the shipping dock
3. All necessary order and invoice numbers
4. A unique identification number or numbers for inputting picking exceptions and restarting interrupted printing operations
5. The data and scheduled picking period to facilitate merging pieces astray in the warehouse with the balance of the order
6. The name and address of the customer and warehouse for identification of individual pieces after they leave the warehouse

Picking and order assembly operations will be most efficient if items 1 and 2 are readily distinguishable from each other and the balance of the information on the label; picking instructions should be printed at the top or bottom. Items 3, 4, and 5 should be inconspicuous, because

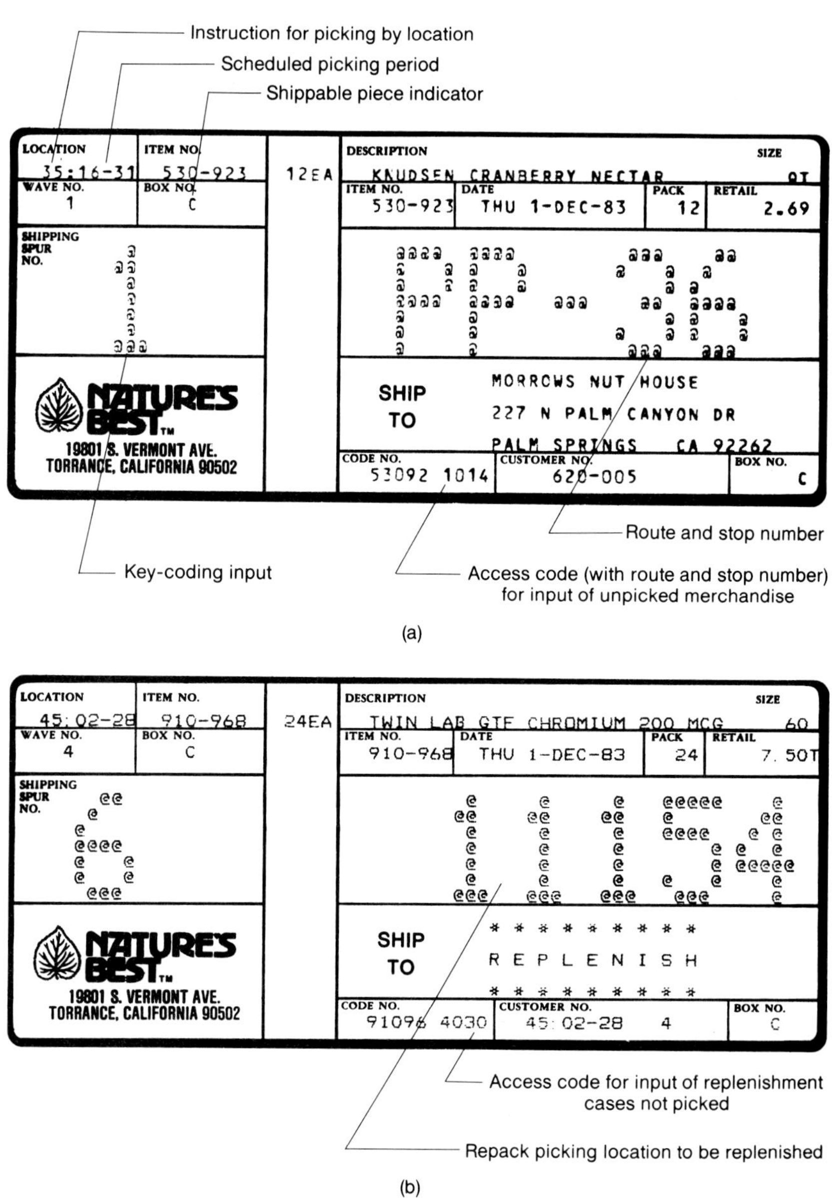

Figure 25.1. Packing labels for sortation by key coding. (*a*) **Conveyable case/nonconveyable piece picking/shipping label; (*b*) label for picking a conveyable case to replenish a repack picking position. (*Nature's Best*.)**

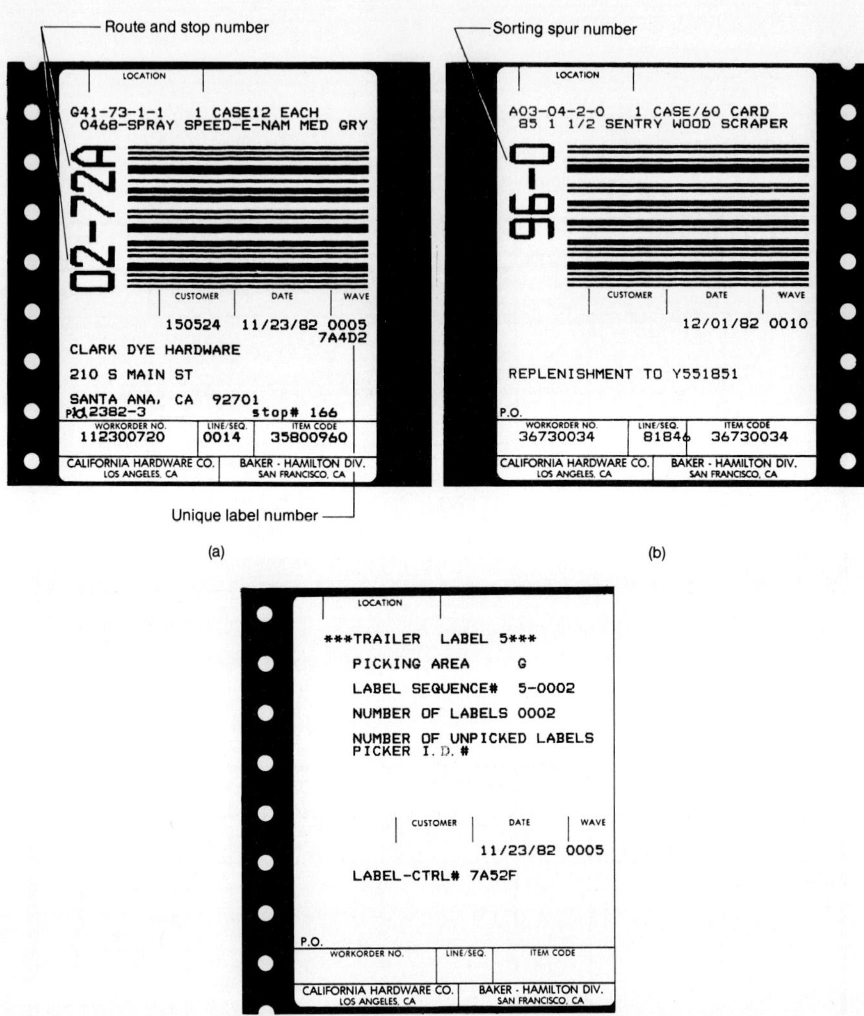

Figure 25.2. Picking labels for sortation by scanning and trailer label. (*a*) **Conveyable case picking/shipping label;** (*b*) **label for picking a conveyable case to replenish repack;** (*c*) **trailer label.** (*California Hardware Co.*)

reference to the information they contain is infrequent. The names and addresses (item 6) should be prominent.

When orders are assembled manually, the order assembly code can be a route and stop number printed in either matrix format (Figure 25.1) or expanded digits (Figure 25.2). When the piece picked is conveyable and mechanically sorted after key-coding or scanning:

1. The route and stop number should be preceded by matrix-printed or expanded digits to be input by the key-coder, if the route number will not serve this purpose (Figure 25.1), or
2. A scannable code should be added to the label (Figure 25.2).

Usually, the latter represents the sorting spur number, but in systems under consideration it will represent other information that will control sortation and provided positive confirmation of picking as a basis for invoicing.

There is one label per piece, sack, or bundle shipped except:

1. When one or two each of loose pieces, such as a shovel, a spade, and a pitchfork, are picked with separate labels but shipped in one bundle.
2. When pallet loads are picked with labels; two to four labels are commonly printed for each load.

Labels are printed in location sequence for bulk picking or picking by order.

Label Design Variations. The label in Figure 25.4 shows how much the design of conveyable case picking labels varies. It does not include a prominent route or stop number because sortation by spur, or lane, is all that is necessary to assemble the one order assigned to each spur during each wave. The orders filled by the warehouses using these labels:

1. Consist of pallet loads which are taped or stretch wrapped after assembly at the end of the spur and manually identified for loading, or
2. Are truck loads in which case-picked pieces are loaded from the spur into the truck.

The highly reliable scanning systems employed require very infrequent reference to the batch, spur, and shipping door numbers, which effectively define an order picked by these labels.

Figures 25.2, 25.3 and 25.4 show the three available scannable codes. Selection of the sorting code and scanner should recognize that:

1. The codes in Figures 25.2 and 25.3 can be read omnidirectionally by scanners with a greater depth of reading and tolerance for mis-

alignment to the horizontal than the code in Figure 25.4. It also requires placing the label on each piece within ±10 degrees of a predetermined orientation because it is read by a line scanner.

2. Omnidirectional scanners read a higher percentage of the labels scanned than line scanners.
3. A printer will produce picking labels bearing the codes in Figures 25.3 and 25.4 much more rapidly than labels with the bar code shown in Figure 25.2.

If the customer price-tickets the loose pieces and the merchandise in the cartons, 12 tickets can be added to labels, like those shown in Figures 25.1, 25.2 and 25.3. The picker folds the tickets under the plain carrier backing portion of the label before applying it to the piece; this prevents damage to the tickets. For each 12 ticketed units per case, the order filler must affix an additional label—plainly marked "Do Not Pick"—to the case or insert it inside if the case is small. Other labels with price tickets leave them exposed.

When used to pick nonconveyable merchandise, the label in Figure 25.2 does not include a scanning code. An enlarged route and stop number occupies the area previously devoted to the bar code. A label of different design—without bar code—replaces the one in Figure 25.4.

Design Considerations: Labels to Pick Repack. The repack picking document is comprised of labels printed in picking location sequence:

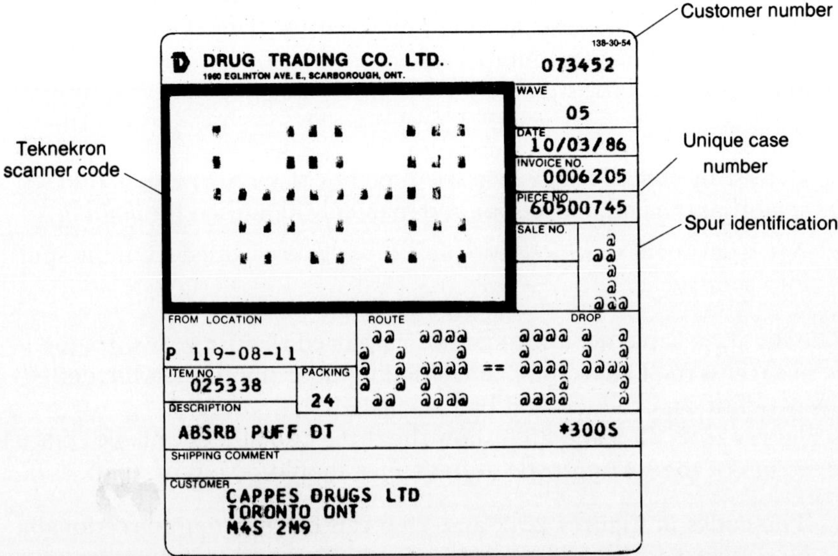

Figure 25.3. Picking label for sortation by scanning. (*Drug Trading Company, Ltd.*)

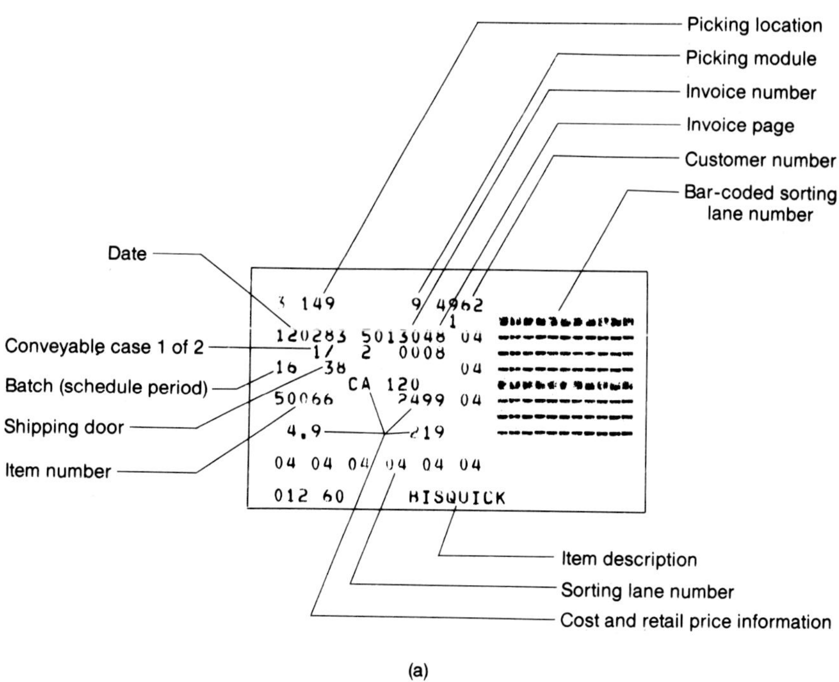

(a)

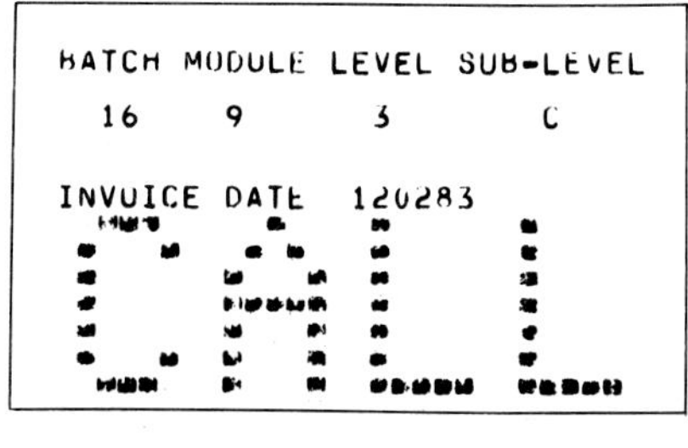

(b)

Figure 25.4. Scanner-coded label for picking conveyable cases. (*a*) **Bar-coded label for picking conveyable cases;** (*b*) **batch identification.** (*Certified Grocers of California.*)

1. When individual items, such as nuts, bolts, and small parts, are not readily identified by the customer
2. In mail-order houses

When labels are used to pick merchandise that cannot be identified readily, they must not only provide the picking location, item identification, and order number, but also remain with the product as long as the customer requires. For these reasons, and to reduce label costs, the labels are as small as possible with dimensions determined by each application. Labels may be pressure sensitive for application to plastic envelopes containing small parts or to the parts themselves, or they may be printed on card stock for insertion in the envelope before it is sealed.

Some warehouses, particularly those in manufacturing plants, include the bar-coded item number on the label. Systems under development in these and other warehouses where items identification is extremely critical contemplate bar coding both the picking and picking *location* labels. They anticipate that the picker will carry a portable bar code reader that will emit a unique tone if the two do not match.

In a mail-order warehouse, the bar code controls a tray sorter, which deposits bulk-picked merchandise in the packing station designated for each order included in the pick. The labels, which are printed on heavy pressure-sensitive paper, are placed on cartons, on the plastic in which the merchandise is packaged, or on a paper sack in which loose merchandise is sealed. The scanner reads the code even if the label is wrinkled.

Label Control. For positive control over the issue and return of labels, each group should be followed by a trailer label (Figures 25.2 and 25.4), which identifies the order or bulk pick. Each label often indicates the number of labels to be picked and provides space for the picker to record the number of attached labels not picked and his or her identification number. Start and completion times are sometimes recorded manually or time stamped by the picker for the calculation of worker productivity. The label batch identification in Figure 25.4 is supported by systems and procedures that accomplish these purposes.

A label control sheet that identifies and lists, by wave, each group of labels to be picked provides a record of label issues and returns. Groups of labels may be identified by the trailer label number; their return is verified manually and by the computer when the label control number is input.

Picking Lists. Computer-prepared picking lists were a logical outgrowth of the accounts receivable, billing, and inventory control systems, which were the initial applications of the computer in warehouses. Because these systems required input to the computer of all picking results and because a picking list printed by the computer prior to order-filling appeared to offer many advantages, there was a widespread effort to develop order entry systems that would make such a document possible.

As these systems were developed, computer-prepared picking lists became common. The order entry systems reduced clerical costs by combining order writing or typing with keypunching. The computer-prepared picking lists reduced picking labor costs and picking omissions by presenting the picking task in location sequence. The location numbers and computer-printed "standard" item descriptions reduced the number of picking errors, and, therefore, the number of returns. These benefits and the possibility that a picking label could also be used as a shipping label were the impetus for the development of picking/shipping labels.

Overall Design Considerations for Repack Picking Lists. The medium on which a repack picking document is printed and the number of copies printed depend upon:

1. Whether or not the document includes price tickets
2. Whether the order is prebilled or postbilled
3. Whether copies of the pick document are used for other purposes

Most repack picking documents are printed on forms (Figure 25.5) or computer paper (Figure 25.6); price tickets are printed separately. If the orders are prebilled, there are always at least two picking-list copies. The amount invoiced is adjusted manually for picking discrepancies on both copies. Then one combination invoice/packing list copy goes

Route and stop number
Pressure-sensitive shipping label
Picking zone
Header

WAVE	DATE
0005	11/23/82
166	02-72A

150524 CLARK DYE HARDWARE
210 S MAIN ST
SANTA ANA, CA 92701
P/O# 112382-3

WORK ORDER NO. 112300720
PAGE 1

LOCATION	MANUFACTURER NO. & DESCRIPTION	QUAN. ORD.	UNIT	QUAN. SHIP	ITEM CODE	LINE
Y-12-10-1-2	B231 3/4" BLK SCRU BMPR BOX100	1	BOX		21236005	0009
Y-18-16-2-2	W216 1/2 SCREW EYE 100 PER BOX	6	BOX		19708189	0010
Y-24-05-6-2	5B GENERAL CIRCLE CUTTER	3	EACH		25535089	0011
	END OF ORDER					

LOCATION
025 72A TOTE PAGE 1 Y

02-72A

CUSTOMER	DATE	WAVE
150524	11/23/82	0005

CLARK DYE HARDWARE
210 S MAIN ST
SANTA ANA, CA 92701
112382-3 stop# 166

WORK ORDER NO	LIN/SEQ	ITEM CODE
112300720	1	

CALIFORNIA HARDWARE CO. LOS ANGELES, CA — BAKER HAMILTON DIV SAN FRANCISCO, CA

Figure 25.5. Repack picking document. (*California Hardware Company.*)

to accounting personnel who input the discrepancies for the issuance of credits and file the documents; the second copy accompanies the shipment.

Order-picking productivity will be improved if the picking document consists of one copy that is the source for both a postbilled invoice and packing list. At most the picker should deal with a two-part document.

When pressure-sensitive price tickets are combined with the pick document, they are printed on a form comprised of pressure-sensitive labels (Figure 25.7) or a sheet of labels. If the order is postbilled, the picking document may also be the packing list.

Conventional Picking-List Formats. The format of a repack picking document depends on the preceding and:

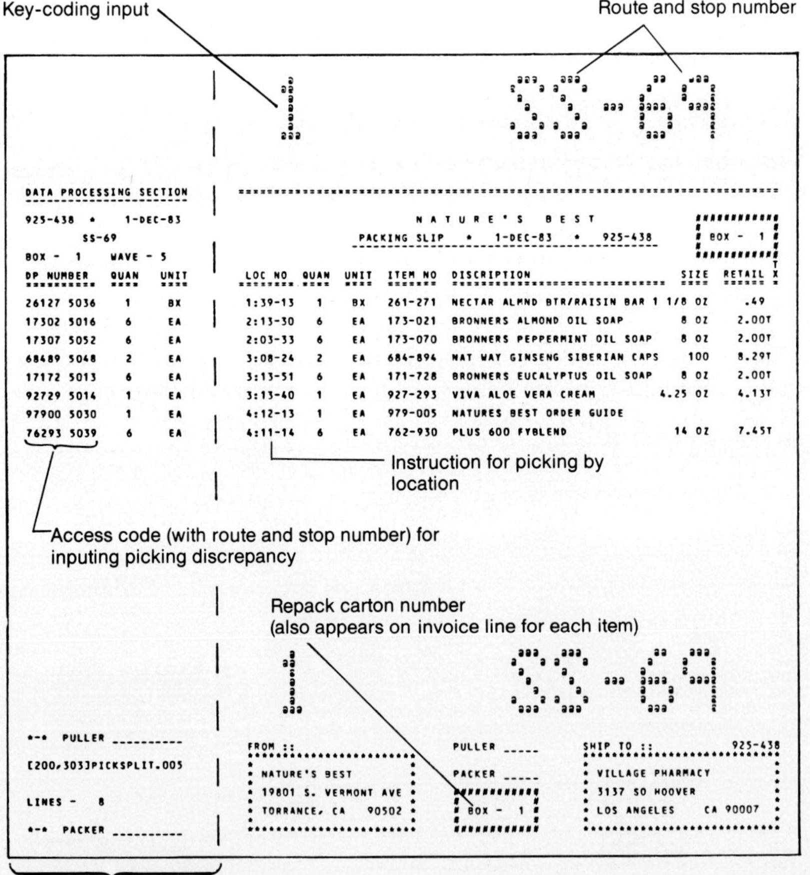

1 SS-69

DATA PROCESSING SECTION

925-438 • 1-DEC-83

SS-69

BOX - 1 WAVE - 5

NATURE'S BEST

PACKING SLIP • 1-DEC-83 • 925-438

BOX - 1

OP NUMBER	QUAN	UNIT	LOC NO	QUAN	UNIT	ITEM NO	DISCRIPTION	SIZE	RETAIL	TX
26127 5036	1	BX	1:39-13	1	BX	261-271	NECTAR ALMND BTR/RAISIN BAR	1 1/8 OZ	.49	
17302 5016	6	EA	2:13-30	6	EA	173-021	BRONNERS ALMOND OIL SOAP	8 OZ	2.00	T
17307 5052	6	EA	2:03-33	6	EA	173-070	BRONNERS PEPPERMINT OIL SOAP	8 OZ	2.00	T
68489 5048	2	EA	3:08-24	2	EA	684-894	NAT WAY GINSENG SIBERIAN CAPS	100	8.29	T
17172 5013	6	EA	3:13-51	6	EA	171-728	BRONNERS EUCALYPTUS OIL SOAP	8 OZ	2.00	T
92729 5014	1	EA	3:13-40	1	EA	927-293	VIVA ALOE VERA CREAM	4.25 OZ	4.13	T
97900 5030	1	EA	4:12-13	1	EA	979-005	NATURES BEST ORDER GUIDE			
76293 5039	6	EA	4:11-14	6	EA	762-930	PLUS 600 FYBLEND	14 OZ	7.45	T

1 SS-69

- PULLER __________

[200,303]PICKSPLIT.005

LINES - 8

- PACKER __________

FROM ::
NATURE'S BEST
19801 S. VERMONT AVE
TORRANCE, CA 90502

PULLER _____

PACKER _____

BOX - 1

SHIP TO :: 925-438
VILLAGE PHARMACY
3137 SO HOOVER
LOS ANGELES CA 90007

Figure 25.6. Repack picking list.

1. The information required by the picker, other warehouse and office personnel, and the customer
2. Warehouse operating methods and procedures

An effective format (Figure 25.5):

1. Sparates the body of the picking list into:
   a. "Header" information referenced by the picker but used extensively by others.
   b. The lines to be picked.
   c. Space for recording the picker and packer identification and the number of totes or cartons to be shipped.
   d. Shipping labels if they are part of the document.
2. Presents the information about each item to be picked on one line in the sequence that will:
   a. Maximize the productivity of the picker and the personnel inputting picking exceptions.
   b. Segregate the information required by the customer and arrange it in a convenient order.
3. Supports warehouse operating methods and procedures by printing multiple pick lists for one order. There may be:
   a. One list per picking zone.

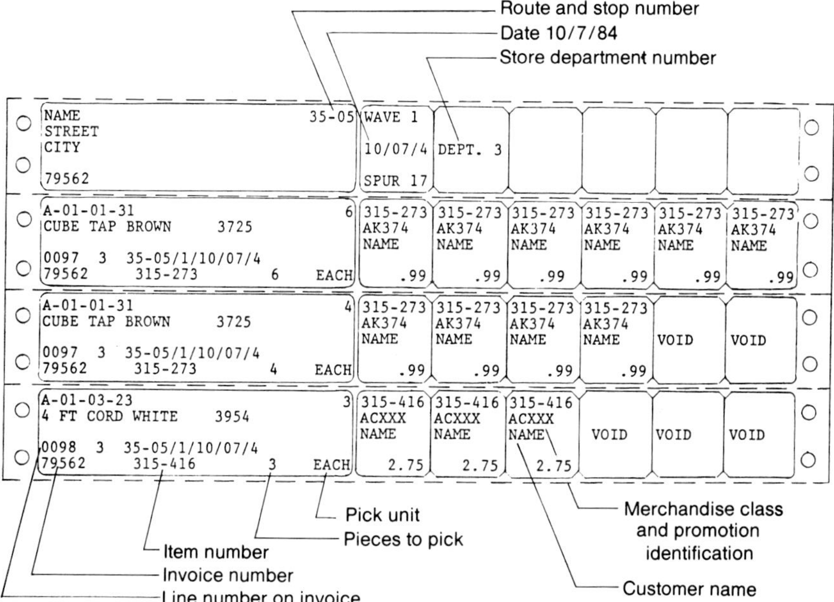

Figure 25.7. Repack picking document comprised of labels.

b. One list per repack shipping container with the merchandise specified on each list limited to a merchandise cube or weight maximum for each size tote or carton.

If a picker must identify the merchandise by reading its description before picking, the picking line shown in Figure 25.5 maximizes order-filling productivity. The picker refers only to the information up to the "Quan. Ship"; this information is in the sequence the picker requires. He or she records picking results in the "Quan. Ship" column. Personnel inputting picking exceptions refer to the "Quan. Ship" and "Line" columns and the order number in the document header. The item number provides computer-item file access to those investigating picking discrepancies and other questions.

When merchandise is picked by location, the picking location should appear first, followed by the quantity ordered, the picking unit, the quantity picked, and the item number and description. The order line number should be last, but custom results in placing it ahead of the location number. The right-hand portion of the picking list in Figure 25.6 follows this format generally. Unit prices, costs, and invoice amounts should appear at the right of the document, as in Figure 25.6.

Formats for Documents Providing Price Tickets. Figure 25.7 shows one document utilized when the customer tickets the merchandise. If only three pieces must be picked, three of the six tickets per row shown in Figure 25.7 are blank. If more than six tickets are required, successive rows of tickets are used; the picking location and other information appear on the item identification label in each row. The picking list for one order is the packing list. It may be printed:

1. As one long document which is torn apart so each piece can be placed in the tote or carton containing the merchandise picked
2. As a number of documents, one per picking zone
3. As a number of documents, each specifying the merchandise that will not exceed the weight or cube of a shipping carton

When merchandise is picked and ticketed simultaneously, the picking document consists only of price tickets. The picking location is printed at the top of each ticket; other necessary information appears below it. Tickets are printed in location sequence across each row. Orders are separated by blank tickets and others identifying each order. A separate packing list is necessary.

Visual Displays

Visual displays replace the picking document with direct communication between a computer and the order filler. This change is a step toward a "paperless warehouse" with lower warehousing costs because:

1. Picking productivity increases.
2. Errors in reporting picking results decrease.
3. Controlling the issue and return of picking documents and the inputting of picking results require less clerical effort.
4. The computer will calculate productivities.

Displays can reduce picking of the wrong merchandise or incorrect quantities if supplemented by bar coding and bar code readers. Mobile displays will also facilitate lower-cost receiving and stocking operations. The savings generated by these improvements require initial investments in data processing equipment, hard wiring, or communications equipment and programming.

Fixed Displays. Permanently located displays provide instructions to order fillers picking merchandise from flow racks, shelving, and carousels (Figure 25.8). The equipment consists of:

1. A controller or bay indicator/controller that displays the number of the order being picked.
2. A bay indicator that lights up when there is a pick in a flow rack bay, shelving unit, or carousel bin.
3. Picking location displays that indicate the items to be picked by their locations and the quantities to be picked by the number each displays. Carousel indicators light up as soon as the desired location or locations are positioned for picking. A button for inputting picking results is part of this display; pressing the button turns off the picking location display and both other displays when all picks from a flow rack bay or carousel section have been completed.
4. A microcomputer-based data processing system that receives picking instructions from a host computer and controls the displays and carousel; it also stores picking results for transmission to the host. The micro system can provide information for planning daily operations, the current status of operations, worker productivities, and other information, limited only by the ingenuity of the programmer and the capabilities of the hardware. The displays are hard-wired to the microcomputer system.

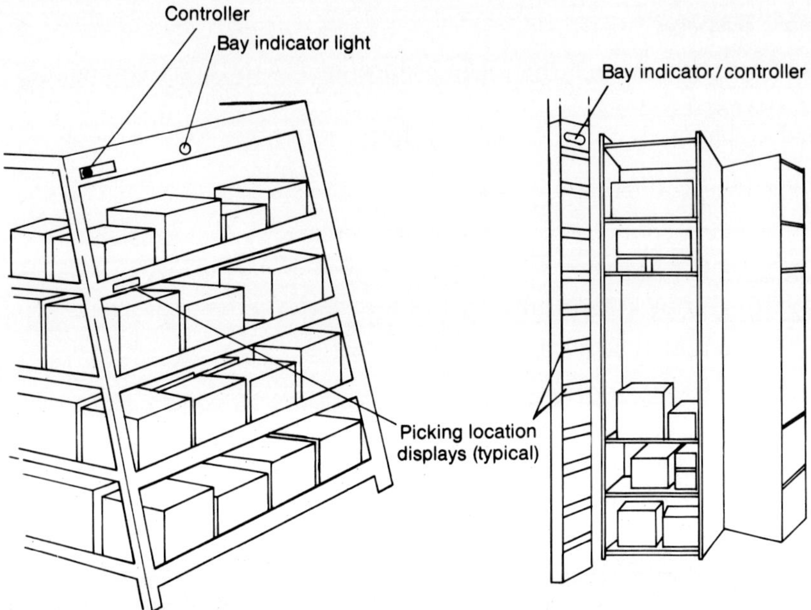

Figure 25.8. Fixed visual display (*Adapted from Ref. 1, Courtesy of* **Modern Materials Handling,** *by Cahners Publishing Company, Division of Reed Holdings, Inc., 1983.*)

Mobile Displays. Mobile picking instruction displays are mounted on vehicles such as forklifts and order pickers. The display is part of a terminal (Figure 25.9) that includes a microprocessor, memory, a keyboard, connections for bar code or OCR reader input and printed output, and an FM transceiver or data port. When equipped with a transceiver, the terminal is "on line" to a base station transceiver, which is linked to a host computer by a microprocessor interface. Picking instructions, including the item description when desired, are transmitted one at a time and displayed by the picker or automatically on an LED or vacuum fluorescent display which can be scrolled to show the contents of the several-hundred-character receiving memory. After picking the merchandise, the order filler inputs picking results and presses the transmit button. As soon as the base station receives the information, it transmits the next instruction. One base station, which requires a Federal Communications Commission (FCC) license, will support a maximum of 20 mobile terminals; each installation must be preceded by a survey that establishes the limitations, if any, on radio communication within the warehouse.

When equipped with a data port instead of a radio, the mobile terminal is "off line." Picking instructions in predetermined sequence are stored by the host computer and loaded into the memory of the terminal via the port. Picking proceeds in the same manner as when the unit is equipped with a radio, but the picking results are stored for unloading to the base computer via the data port after picking has been partially or fully completed.

Picking Hardware

Picking hardware falls into these categories:

1. Equipment for the order filler:
   a. Picking with a document
   b. Picking from visually displayed information
2. Equipment for manual picking:
   a. When order integrity is maintained
   b. When order integrity is destroyed and restored

Equipment for the Order Filler

The equipment required by the order filler depends on the document being used and not how order integrity is treated. If the document is a picking list, the picker requires:

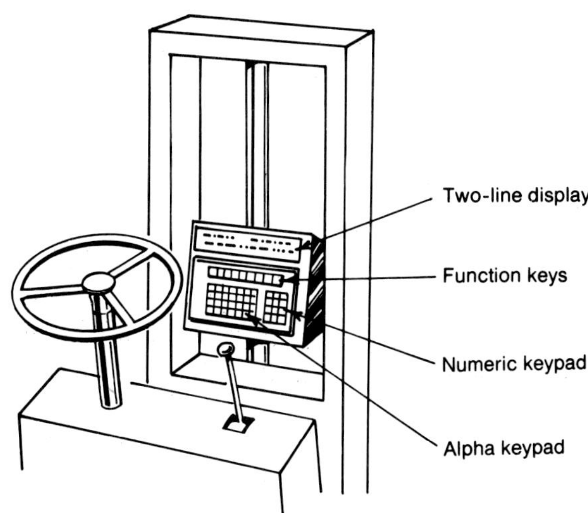

Figure 25.9. Mobile visual display. (*LXE, a division of Electromagnetic Sciences, Inc.*)

1. A clipboard that minimizes document handling time
2. An apron with arm loops that convert it to a carrying pouch and pockets for pencils, pens, markers, and note pads
3. Totes or shipping cartons

A dispenser for one-up labels is desirable when they comprise the picking documents. Case pickers should have a hand dispenser for pressure-sensitive tape to reseal cartons.

Visual displays make the clipboard or label dispenser unnecessary, but frequently require that a wand for reading bar or OCR code be available to the picker.

Equipment for Manual Picking

Order Integrity Maintained. When order integrity is maintained in a walk-and-pick warehouse, the picking equipment consists of carts, pallets, and pallet jacks. Pigeonhole carts are used to pick multiple repack orders simultaneously with the risk of missorting the picked product. A cart equipped with a mobile display and sorting lights would minimize this risk and improve productivity. The equipment in a ride-and-pick warehouse ranges from forklifts and mobile order pickers to man-aboard picking cranes.

Order Integrity Destroyed and Restored. Order integrity is destroyed and restored primarily to gain the increased picker productivity possible when additional picking hardware—usually conveyor—is installed. While the picker now uses documents in practically all warehouses, visual displays will become more common.

In a typical walk-and-pick warehouse, repack is picked from flow rack, carousel, or shelving, any of which can be equipped with visual displays. The order filler places the merchandise in a tote or carton pushed along a gravity conveyor or moved via cart. Filled containers are placed on a take-away conveyor above which are two conveyors: one supplying empty totes or cartons, the other removing trash. Conveyable full cases are transferred from picking positions accessible to the walking pickers to a facing take-away belt or picked to a cart and subsequently transferred to a belt. All take-away conveyors terminate in a sorting system (on the shipping dock) that sorts repacked cartons and full cases for order assembly, and full cases only to replenishment accumulation spurs in the repack picking area.

If there is nonconveyable merchandise, it is picked to a pallet transported by a manual or powered jack or a forklift and transported to the dock. Forklifts may be equipped with mobile displays, particularly if they are also used to store receipts.

There are some ride-and-pick warehouses in which repack and/or full cases are picked separately. The picker rides a man-aboard crane or vehicle and deposits the repacked cartons or conveyable cases on take-away conveyors. In such warehouses, the labor savings resulting from the substitution of visual displays for picking documents should be substantial, especially if the picked cases are bar coded.

Data Processing Subsystems for Picking Position Replenishment

Manual and computer-supported subsystems provide replenishment for repack picking positions and pallet positions from which conveyable full cases and nonconveyables are picked.

Repack Picking Position Replenishment Subsystems

Manual Systems. Informal systems for replenishing repack rely upon picking personnel to replenish each position as the inventory is exhausted or during a specific period at the end of the shift. These systems are used in warehouses that maintain order integrity and those that destroy and restore it.

Computer-Supported Systems. Formal replenishment systems are usable in warehouses when order integrity is destroyed and restored, because they provide separate repack and full-case picking or reserve positions. Formal systems separate replenishment and picking operations by assigning specific personnel to each.

There are two common formal systems requiring different levels of computer support. In the system requiring the least computer support, replenishment personnel inspect picking positions—some once a day, some twice a week, others weekly or biweekly—according to a schedule based upon the replenishment frequency as required by the capacity of each position and the rate of use of the merchandise it houses. The number of an item to be replenished is input to a remote order entry device by keying or wanding a bar-coded label at the position; the replenish ment quantity is keyed in. The computer creates a picking list or replenishment case picking labels.

In a more sophisticated replenishment system, the computer database includes the capacity of each position and its replenishment order point. The computer maintains the inventory in each position. When it falls below the order point, the computer creates replenishment case picking labels automatically.

Full-Case Picking-Position Replenishment Systems

Manual Systems. Manual systems to replenish pallet positions from which conveyable full cases and nonconveyable merchandise are picked rely upon a multiple-copy pallet tag prepared when the replenishment pallet is stored. Both copies of the tag include the reserve storage and picking position; one copy is filed by picking location or at the picking location.

When a pallet is almost empty, a picker removes the few remaining pieces and places them aside. A forklift driver notes the empty pallet, obtains the tag for the oldest position, and transfers the pallet to the picking position. This informal system is suitable for warehouses that maintain or destroy and restore order integrity.

Computer-Based Systems. Computer-based systems for replenishing full-case picking positions are possible only when order integrity is destroyed and restored. The computer maintains:

1. The picking location of each SKU
2. The inventory in that location
3. The location of reserve pallet loads and the inventory on each one
4. A list of empty picking locations

When the inventory in a picking position reaches zero, the computer issues instructions to remove it and adds the location to an empty picking-position list after the removal has been confirmed. The computer issues an instruction to transfer a pallet from a reserve location to the first location on the empty picking-position list or one selected randomly from a group meeting specific criteria.

Sample Order-Picking System Application

Company XYZ distributes health foods from a Los Angeles warehouse to customers in Northern and Southern California.

In the 100,000-square-foot warehouse, order integrity is destroyed and restored. The design of the conveying system that transports full cases and repacked cartons and sorts them for order assembly requires that each picking shift be divided into periods, or "waves," during which a specified group of orders is picked, assembled, and loaded into trucks or trailers.

Overall Operating Plan. Almost all merchandise is picked and loaded into captive trucks or trailers, one route per vehicle, during an evening shift; each vehicle departs in time to deliver its load during the next day. A few orders are shipped by common carrier.

To be competitive, Company XYZ accepts orders until one hour prior to the start of the picking shift. If the computer attempted to process all the orders for a shift during this interval, it could not print any picking documents. To provide picking documents at the start of the shift, the orders from customers on one, two, or three routes are assigned to successive waves and processed one wave at a time. Picking documents are printed after each processing.

The formal picking-position replenishment system relies on the computer to generate replenishments. The schedule for picking and stocking replenishments reflects the short interval between order entry cutoff and the start of picking operations.

Operations During a Wave. An order filler, using a single-copy picking/packing list, picks repack from flow rack and shelving pick positions into a shipping carton as he or she pushes it along a gravity-roller conveyor. Picking discrepancies are recorded on the body of the picking/packing list and the data processing stub. When the contents specified by the computer for a carton have been picked, the order filler places the document in the carton and transfers it to a powered take-away conveyor, which delivers it to packers. The packers spot check picking accuracy and remove the data processing stub. They then pack the merchandise with plastic "peanuts"; close the carton; seal it; and fasten the picking/packing list to the carton with the spur, route, and stop numbers at the top of the document on top of the carton, and the balance of the document on the carton's side. The packed carton travels by conveyor to a key-coding station.

A walking order filler picks conveyable full cases by:

1. Affixing a case picking/shipping label to the case so the spur number is visible from the top, and the route and stop number are visible from the side
2. Transferring the case from a pallet or hand stack position to a powered take-away conveyor system that ultimately merges the cases with repacked cartons flowing to the key-coder

These picking operations destroy order integrity.

Key-coding initiates the restoration of order integrity. It activates pushers that sort: (1) repack replenishment cases onto conveyors leading to the repack area and (2) conveyable pieces for predetermined routes and stops onto two or three of the five sorting spurs available. Pallets identified by route and stop number are located on both sides of the two or three spurs. Shipping personnel restore order integrity by transferring each piece from a sorting spur to the pallet identified with the route and stop number appearing on the piece.

Nonconveyable pieces are bulk picked to a pallet moved by a jack and delivered to the appropriate pallet by the picker. Before moving the loaded pallets in delivery stop sequence to each truck for loading, order assembly personnel verify the piece counts by route and stop number against a route manifest. While the orders comprising one wave are being assembled and loaded, personnel place pallets around the sorting spurs not in use and identify them with the route and stop numbers of the customers whose orders will be filled during the next wave.

Order Processing and Document Printing. As it processes a single, consolidated order for each route and stop assigned to one wave past the item file, the computer:

1. Classifies each line by type of pick: repack, full-case, repack and full-case, or nonconveyable.
2. Decreases the inventory in the fixed repack or nonconveyable picking position or the randomly assigned conveyable case picking position.
3. Determines the replenishment required for each picking position.
4. Specifies the contents of each tote that comply with a maximum weight or cube specification.

5. Determines the number of pieces, the cube, and the number of staging pallets required for each stop.
6. Specifies the placement of pallets in stop sequence within route around successive spurs.
7. Prints a loading manifest by stop within route for each spur. If the weight or cube of the load exceeds the capacity of the vehicle normally assigned to the route, a larger one is assigned.
8. Prints picking/shipping labels for bulk picking, picking/packing lists for picking by order, and loading manifests.

Picking-Position Replenishment. The computer generates a repack picking-position replenishment order when the position inventory falls below a minimum level. Labels to pick the necessary conveyable cases are merged with the labels to pick the full cases for shipment during the wave.

The hour between the end of order entry and the start of picking permit only the full-case picking-position replenishments required to meet unusual customer demands. For this reason, full-case picking positions comprised of pallet loads facing belt conveyors house the number of pallets of each item required by a predetermined daily demand level. At the end of order processing for each day, the computer prints an empty pallet pickup list; the pallets are removed during the next day shift. It also prints a list of pallets that must be transferred from specific reserve locations to belt pick positions to rebuild the inventory of each SKU to the predetermined level. A forklift operator moves each pallet to an open position and, after removing the empty pallets, records its location for input to the computer.

If unusually large demands deplete the case-picking inventory of an SKU at a belt, the computer prints emergency replenishments. These replenishment pallets are moved to a number of adjacent picking locations assigned one location number. The order filler checks the merchandise description before picking from one of these locations.

Reporting Picking Results. Because Company XYZ combines all orders for one customer, it does not indicate its invoice number and the customer's order numbers on picking documents; they appear on the post-billed invoice that accompanies each shipment. The route and stop number and the codes on the repack picking list stubs and picking labels provide access to computer files for adjusting invoices when merchandise ordered is not picked.

Bibliography

"Computer-aided Orderpicking: Paperless Picking That's Accurate and Very Fast," *Modern Materials Handling,* September 6, 1983, pp. 44–47.

"Computer Integrated Warehousing—Advanced Controls Boost Productivity 40%," *Modern Materials Handling,* February 5, 1982, pp. 48–53.

26

Stock Location and Inventory Control

Richard E. Ward, Ph.D., P.E.

Director of Education, Material Handling Institute, Charlotte, North Carolina

Introduction

A warehouse exists for the purpose of storing inventory. This is a rather redundant statement to be making in Chapter 26; one would think that those reading this handbook may have learned that lesson by now. Yet, it is so central to the point of this chapter that it is worth repeating, and as many times as necessary to drive the point home. The point is: The warehouse manager is charged with the responsibility to manage inventory, and not just to manage a building with racks, aisles, and material handling equipment. Therefore, the manager's performance will be judged largely on the decisions being made and the policies being adopted that can affect the control of inventory within the warehouse. This part of the handbook looks at some of the policies that can be followed and some of the decisions that can be made by the warehouse manager that can either make or break the manager's reputation.

There are, of course, many decisions to be made that impact on the inventory to be warehoused. Quite a few of these decisions are typically made outside the influence of the warehouse manager, such as the determination of lot sizes, order quantities, customer service levels, safety stock levels, whether to pursue price discounts, and so on. The warehouse manager can no doubt perform his or her job better if it is understood how these decisions are made, but it is certainly not a pivotal issue. On the other hand, there are several decisions and operational policies for which the warehouse manager is often held directly accountable. One set of decisions in this category relates to matters of space utilization, equipment selection, equipment utilization, and the like. Another set relates more to the handling of inventory transactions and keeping track of items stored in the warehouse. The focus of this chapter is on the latter set of decisions and policies. Among the issues to be raised in this chapter are the following:

- The degree of discipline present within the warehouse organization regarding the timely and accurate handling of inventory transactions
- The process to be used whereby it can be determined where specific items are to be stored within the warehouse
- The process to be used whereby one can find exactly where an item has been stored within the warehouse
- The process to be used whereby a physical inventory (count) can be periodically taken on all items normally stored in the warehouse

Poor decisions related to any of the above general sets of decisions, including space utilization, equipment utilization, the handling of transactions, and so on, undoubtedly increase indirect operating expenses; make an organization less competitive; and, therefore, provide ample motivation for wanting to study this handbook in detail. However, in the latter set of issues dealing with inventory transactions, there is much more than just a cost accounting viewpoint to be reckoned with. For example, when it comes to maintaining inaccurate or accurate records of what is currently being stocked in the warehouse, your choice can make the difference between shutting an entire plant down or keeping it operating. Just try to operate a business (ergo a warehouse) on the basis of what you think is in stock (according to the records) versus what is actually in stock. The same catastrophic result can be achieved if, even though you know for certain that an item is in stock, you cannot find it. Now that is motivation!

Anatomy of the Warehouse Cycle

For the purposes of this chapter, the *warehouse cycle* is defined as the sequence of all activities related to the handling and storage of a stock-keeping unit (SKU) in a warehouse. Once the activities have been defined, subsequent discussion in this section will deal with applicable principles that can be used to guide the manager's planning for and execution of these activities. Not all of the activities taking place during the warehouse cycle are discussed in detail in this chapter. Therefore, to the extent that certain of the activities are emphasized elsewhere in this handbook, appropriate reference is made.

The warehouse cycle begins with the receipt of an item (SKU) either individually or as part of a larger lot or order, and ends with the item being shipped to a customer or dispatched to the shop floor, again, either on its own or as a part of a larger lot, order, or production kit. The warehouse is held accountable for that item from the time it hits the receiving dock to the time it leaves the shipping area. During this period of time, the item is under the control of warehouse policies and procedures, and it is expected that these policies and procedures are such that (1) warehouse personnel know that they have the item at all times and (2) they know where it is.

A number of things happen to an item or lot during receiving that make it awfully easy to lose track of SKUs at that point in time:

1. Items may be counted for the purpose of verifying orders.
2. Items may be inspected for the purpose of verifying quality.
3. Different items within the same order or shipment may be sorted and staged for subsequent transportation to a permanent storage location.

The receiving area itself is characterized by a lack of permanence in the items to be found there. It is a very dynamic place, the scene of a great deal of material handling (mostly manual), and it is subject to a great deal of confusion if not properly planned in terms of adequate space or the layout of that space (see Chapter 6 for more discussion on this topic).

The same sorts of things can be said about shipping. In some instances, the items to be shipped arrive at the shipping location already kitted or ready to be shipped; in other instances, much more activity is likely, as follows:

1. Items may arrive at shipping individually and then require subsequent consolidation to form a single order.
2. Items may be sampled for the purpose of verifying quality.
3. For customer delivery off site, as opposed to lots destined to the shop floor, orders may require packaging, labeling, weighing, and so on.

4. Orders will have to be merged and staged for subsequent pickup and delivery to common destinations.

There is no less opportunity for confusion in the shipping area than in the receiving area, once again due to the amount of material handling taking place. Adequate space is needed for all the various subactivities, and it must be well laid out and well marked, especially in the staging area, lest an order should find its way to the wrong destination.

In between receiving and shipping, there is still ample opportunity to lose track of SKUs. One of the more common causes can be attributed to a poorly designed or informal locator system, or worse yet, having no locator system at all. More will be said about locator systems in a subsequent section. However, suffice it to say at this point that if you do not know where an item is to be stored once it has been processed through receiving, the longer that item(s) will remain on the floor in free space until such a decision is made, if ever; and the greater the likelihood that the item(s) will be lost in the shuffle.

A corollary to this observation is that the more rapidly an item can be advanced through the first half of the warehouse cycle, from receiving to permanent storage, the greater the degree of control to be expected over individual items. This leads one to the conclusion that material handling can play a significant role in the control of inventory in a warehouse. More precisely, reference is made to both the choice of material handling systems and the utilization of such systems, whether they are manually driven forklifts or more automated transporters. Specific decisions that can affect the outcome involve matters of:

1. Matching a system's capability and versatility to the needs and handleability of the items to be transported
2. System sizing with regard to throughput capacity and load carrying capacity
3. Equipment and personnel scheduling relative to both transportation requirements and resource availability

Clearly, what has been said about material handling on the storage side of the warehouse cycle applies equally well to the retrieval side. The speed with which a system can locate, retrieve, and carry needed items to shipping is just as important as how rapidly storage can be affected; only in this case the objective is different. In the former case, clearing items from the floor is the driving force. In the latter case, the objective is customer service and the need to coordinate the movement of material from retrieval all the way down to its pickup at the staging area and delivery to the final destination.

The issue of an appropriate locator system is also as important to the retrieval function as it is to the storage function and provides added reason to carefully plan, not only where items will be stored, but also how to determine where items are stored.

This section has reinforced what may have been picked up in other chapters: that in order to be a successful warehouse manager, one must realize that, at least in part, the control of inventory in the warehouse has as much to do with layout planning and material flow as anything. Not to appreciate this fact will mean that much else of what you know or learn will do you little good. Of course, to think that this is all there is to know can be equally as damaging. Let us consider, then, other aspects of the problem.

Anatomy of the Stockkeeping Unit

Another way to approach the control of inventory in a warehouse and to understand more about how things can go wrong is to consider how a person knows whether or not an item is in the warehouse. First, one must accept the fact that an item assumes two identities upon entering the warehouse. Both have to be recognized and dealt with in order to achieve high performance expectancies.

The first identity is an item's physical identity: its size, weight, handleability, and other distinguishing characteristics. Because of its physical identitiy, an item can be seen and an item can be counted, which is one way of knowing whether or not it is in the warehouse, and how many are in stock.

In the preceding section, the physical attributes of an item were seen to influence the selection of appropriate material handling equipment. Consideration of size (and volume) also plays another important role in the control of inventory in a warehouse. Reference is made in this instance to the planning for adequate storage capacity. The extent to which space planning has not been given proper attention is the extent to which, in all likelihood, operation of the warehouse will be daily faced with having to resolve space shortages.

Most countermeasures employed to combat inadequate space will result in some loss of control over inventory in the warehouse, even with the best of locator systems. The worst scenario is one in which stock is forced to be left sitting in the aisles or in other open areas where it is far more susceptible to being eventually misplaced, not to mention the increased risk of damage or pilferage. Another scenario involves having to split a lot among several locations, possibly having to co-locate two or more items in the same physical location. This does not have to be all that bad, depending on the detail allowed in the locator system. However, such remedial action does increase the risk of (1) items not being found and (2) human error associated with retrieving the wrong parts. It definitely increases the retrieval time to complete an order. This risk increases in direct proportion to the distance between multiple locations, and is at its worst when the same item is stored in separate buildings, even if they are adjacent.

The second identity that an item possesses is its paper identity, which for all intents and purposes is dimensionless. Reference is made more specifically to all the paperwork, tags, and records that are associated with an SKU. An item's paper identity also permits warehouse personnel to determine whether or not an item is currently in the warehouse. In practice, an item's paper identity, ergo its stock record, is used more frequently to determine stock-on-hand balances than for an actual physical check at the known stock location(s).

The most important point to be raised concerning the difference between these two identities is the fact that they generally follow entirely different paths through the warehouse. The physical item follows the material handling paths and is found on the floor or in storage bins. The paper item, with the possible exception of a tag, follows a path that eventually leads to its being stored as part of a record in a file drawer, computer database, or some other convenient information storage and retrieval system.

This difference in flow is a recognized fact, and there is little one can do to change that. The real issue, however, is not so much the flow as it is the timeliness of the flow and the subsequent updating of records. Take, for example, the receipt of a new lot of items, and then its subsequent placement in storage bins. When they reach the storage bin, items in the lot are conceivably available for filling an order. This will be true only if (1) the paperwork accompanying the newly received lot makes it to data processing in an equally expeditious manner and (2) the information on the paperwork gets transcribed to the permanent record, almost without delay. Should this not occur, the newly binned items will not exist as far as the system is concerned. The results vary, depending on the time lag present. About the worst thing that can occur will be a reordering of items when they are not needed, eventually resulting in an overstocking.

A similar lag in the handling of paperwork and records can have even more serious repercussions when items are being withdrawn from the warehouse. In this instance, a lag in subtracting items from the record will result in the system thinking it has more in stock than it really does.

The result is accepting customer orders that cannot possibly be filled (at least not in time), or shutting down an assembly line for lack of needed parts.

So far, mention has not been made of human error associated with the dual identity of an SKU. This certainly is a problem to be reckoned with, as warehouse personnel can certainly affect real-time stock record accuracy. Whether a stock handler is writing down stock withdrawals on a card or a data processing operator is entering withdrawals at a computer terminal, there is the possibility of making a mistake. The result can be just as bad as not updating records in a timely manner.

Policies and Procedures for Inventory Records

Any number of things can help achieve improved, real-time, inventory record accuracy, such as the following:

1. Establish a climate of high expectations within the warehouse organization.
2. Measure record accuracy frequently.
3. Report results for all to see.
4. Reward improvements and the maintenance of high levels of performance.
5. Discuss ways of improving performance with affected employees.
6. Do not simply use accuracy checks to correct the records; use information gained to search for and correct the causes of errors.
7. Establish formal procedures and policies for the handling of paperwork such that all persons involved know *how* information is to be communicated regarding inventory transactions; *who* is to initiate communication; *from whom* and *to whom* information is to flow; and *when* it is expected to take place.
8. Standardize and simplify all paperwork used within the warehouse that is associated with the flow of material into or out of stock.
9. Train all personnel on the use of the system.
10. Provide adequate training, with periodic refresher sessions, on warehouse policy, on the use of all forms, and on the correct execution of established procedures.

Types of Stock Locator Systems

The merits of a workable locator system have been established for the purposes of both storing and retrieving stock. However, what works well in one environment may not work so well in another. For the purposes of discussion, three broad types of locator systems are outlined below, along with some idea of what can be expected when each is used in a particular setting. The three systems are generally known as:

1. Informal systems
2. Random-location systems
3. Fixed-location systems

Informal Systems. Such systems may vary somewhat in implementation, but they basically rely on two operating premises:

1. Inventory will be stored wherever there seems to be space, and
2. The ability of those in the warehouse to remember where they stored the items.

An informal system implies that no records are kept, which only works (although seldom well) when everything about the environment in which it is operating is small:

- A relatively small number of different SKUs, and
- A relatively small number of different storage locations

This is imposed by simple human limitation and the inability to remember too many facts. A further restriction on such systems is that the number of persons required to store and retrieve stock must, by necessity, be low. More than one person can work in the same storage area so long as they communicate well and the means for doing so are in place. Of course, that is an ideal view of reality. One quickly learns that as soon as someone is charged with retrieving an item that someone else has stored, the informal system shows signs of deterioration. Therefore, the practical realities of an informal system pretty much dictate that only one person work as a stock handler in a given storage area.

In certain ways, an informal system may be seen to operate as a random location system, where material can be stored anywhere there is room. The truth of the matter is, so long as the smallness criteria is met, the stock handler should be capable of remembering where like items are stored and will use this knowledge to store additional items so long as there is space. Short of space, the stock handler is likely going to add the new stock to an available stock location closest to the first one, and so on. While there may well be some rhyme and reason to a stock handler's action, it is all quite informal, and little or no documentation exists to help others locate items in the warehouse.

Random-Location Systems. In a strictly random system, there is no rhyme or reason to the choice of stock location other than current availability of space; nor does it matter much since formal records are kept that identify every location currently occupied by a given stock item and the quantity to be found at each location. Whether the record system is operated manually or whether it is computer-based, its success or failure depends totally on the discipline exhibited by those working in the warehouse. Such a system demands timely and accurate updating of the records following the replenishment and withdrawal of stock.

In its simplest form, a manual stock-item record might appear similar to the example illustrated in Figure 26.1. Entries are made on the record in chronological fashion. Eventually new cards (records) are needed to replace those that have become outdated or have run out of space on which to record transactions.

It is quite likely that a given application might also require that the record be designed with space to record additional information, such as the condition of the items received, the quantity of items per case or package (if they are prepackaged), the date they were packed, the type of package, and the like. In a formal inventory system, additional records will be maintained for each stock item, such as an overall stock balance; the names, addresses, and telephone numbers of vendors (if the item is purchased); the unit price; discounts available; expected lead time; economic lot size; and so on.

Random-location systems may vary somewhat in application, mostly depending upon the degree to which additional decision rules might be applied to guide or bias the selection of a storage location. However, in general, a random-location system will work along the following lines, with some possible variations as noted:

1. When an item is received, the stock location records for the given item are pulled (either manually or at a computer terminal) in order to determine whether the item is currently in stock, and if so where it can be found (most warehouses will employ a location numbering system that allows the operator to immediately identify the location by bay, aisle, side of aisle, and bin).
2. Assuming that a location exists with a current balance of the given item and that sufficient space remains, the newly received units are

Location no.	Primary		Location cube		Item description	Stock no.
	Bulk		Case cube			
			Case count			

Transaction date	Order number	Quantity received	Quantity withdrawn	Location balance	Item balance

NOTES:
1. One card for each location (Primary and Bulk) occupied by a given item.
2. Records stored in stock number order.
3. A new bulk location card is inserted for each new location.
4. A bulk location card is removed from the file when the location is emptied.
5. Item balance maintained on Primary location record only.

Figure 26.1. Model format for a manual location locator record.

assigned the same storage location and the location record updated to reflect the new balance.

a. If multiple locations exist, the assignment might be made on a totally random basis, or, for example, a decision rule might be implemented that results in assignments requiring the least amount of travel in order to store the items.

3. If no location exists (an out-of-stock condition) or if there is insufficient space in the current location, the newly received material is placed in any available storage location. The degree of sophistication possible at this point varies greatly.
   a. In a computer-based system, an additional record might be maintained on every stock location, with the current available space being the primary piece of information contained in the record.
   b. Storage locations might be searched (via the computer) in certain sectors of the warehouse only; or, as another example, storage locations might be searched on the basis of their proximity to any existing location already containing the item in question. Subsequent picks could then be accomplished in the least amount of time.
4. As before, once a new assignment has been made, the stock location record must be updated by recording the address (based on the specific warehouse numbering system) of the storage location and the quantity added to that location.
5. When retrieval of a certain quantity of an item is required, the stock location record for the item is pulled (again, either manually or via a computer terminal) for the purpose of finding the storage location(s) (address) where the item can be found. As before, variation is possible.
   a. For example, if a location can be emptied or nearly emptied, this location might be chosen for the pick in order either to reduce the remaining number of locations where an item can be found or to lessen the likelihood that subsequent replenishments of other items would have to be split between multiple locations.
6. Once the availability of the material is confirmed and the storage locations selected for the pick, the correct quantity is removed from the location(s) and the stock location record is updated by adjusting the stock balance at the storage location.

If properly designed (with simple, easy-to-read records) and properly maintained (in a timely and accurate fashion), a random-location storage system can generally result in a very high utilization of space. It is particularly well suited to computer-based implementation, especially if additional decision rules are to be employed to facilitate meeting multiple objectives, such as minimized travel time.

Fixed-Location Systems. In such systems, the location of every item is always known. This is brought about by requiring that every stock item be assigned a specific and unique location in the warehouse. In theory, no other item may be stored in a location assigned to another item, even if the location is currently empty.

As discussed previously, unless the warehouse is small, a formal record system is required to keep track of all items and all locations. Even in a relatively small facility, one will experience personnel turnover, absenteeism, and the like, all of which requires some way of informing those unfamiliar with the system where things are stored and the numbering system employed to address specific locations within the warehouse.

The choice of specific location assignments can make a definite difference in warehouse efficiency, as measured by the time it takes to store and retrieve items. Ideally, high-volume items, for which there is a relatively large number of transactions in a given period of time, should be located close to the point of usage. Low-volume, low-throughput items can be assigned storage locations that are further from the point of use. In a distribution warehouse, the *point of use* is defined as the receiving and shipping areas.

A fixed-location assignment pattern in common use is one in which stock items are stored in stock number sequence. There are two reasons for wanting to consider such an assignment:

1. The volume and frequency of transactions for all items are fairly evenly distributed. If this is not the case, throughput will likely suffer for the high-volume item.
2. If the need to refer to stock location records is eliminated, the warehouse could conceivably eliminate such records, and thereby eliminate the expense of maintaining a formal record system.

The primary disadvantage of the fixed-location system as compared to the random system is that it makes poor use of space, since each location has to be designed to accommodate the maximum number of items to be stored at one time. In practice, when insufficient space is available, stock handlers often begin to make decisions on the floor, and they start storing overflow items in locations previously assigned to other items. Nothing will cause a warehouse manager to lose control of inventory faster than that.

How to Control Access and Shrinkage

Shrinkage is a natural occurrence when items are stored. It can be attributed to obsolescence, deterioration, and damage. However, a warehouse manager has some control over this phenomena. The obvious thing to do is to move material out of the warehouse as quickly as possible, since exposure to shrinkage is directly proportional to the time spent in the warehouse. Therefore, the control over the flow of material will be on a first-in, first-out (FIFO) basis, and both replenishments (storage) and retrievals must reflect this policy.

Adherence to a number of other policies will also serve to minimize shrinkage:

1. Make certain that all units have an assigned storage location, random or fixed.
2. Move material through receiving and shipping as rapidly as possible.
3. Get all material off of the floor and into assigned storage locations as rapidly as possible.

Shrinkage is also a more polite way of saying theft. The immediate reaction to rising theft is to lock the warehouse; however, the motivation for doing so is often wrong. Specifically, it should not be for the purpose of keeping thieves out. If theft is on someone's mind, a way will be figured out, even with locked doors. What really needs to be done is to control access (entry and exit points) to the warehouse storage area, so that those entering and leaving will be known and their reason for being there can be confirmed if necessary. Access can be controlled without having to resort to a locked warehouse.

Other actions that can be taken to help minimize pilferage include the following:

1. Screen personnel during the hiring stage and require some form of references for all job applicants.
2. Design a reward system and group benefits that recognize improvements in shrinkage or continued maintenance of high standards.
3. Limit access to the warehouse to only those persons authorized to store and retrieve stock.
4. Institute a policy that does not permit items to be moved, placed in storage, or withdrawn from storage without valid written instructions.

How to Measure Performance

There are two primary reasons for measuring performance, regardless of what is being measured. The first is to demonstrate that one means what one says, and to help create the air of expectation mentioned earlier in the chapter. Nothing helps more to improve performance than simply to let others know that it is being measured. The second reason is to help identify where problems lie so that action can be taken to correct these problems.

There are three critical measures of performance in the warehouse over which the manager has some control. They are throughput, order-filling accuracy, and record accuracy. *Throughput* refers to the volume of transactions (storage and retrieval) that can be handled in a given unit of time. *Order-filling accuracy* refers to shipping the correct order in terms of items and quantity. *Record accuracy* refers to knowing stock-on-hand balances and their locations—exactly, and at all times.

The first two performance issues are reasonably easy to measure and track, particularly the second, since incorrectly delivered orders will almost always invoke an irate phone call. Of course, if production shuts down because of an incorrect order being sent to the shop floor, one is likely to get more than an irate phone call.

The measurement of record accuracy is far more difficult, simply because of the large number of items being stored, all of which have to be counted at one time or another, and because of the sheer effort required in going out into the warehouse and physically counting inventory.

The traditional opportunity for taking a physical count (most commonly called just a "physical") is at year end, an exercise long required by the accountants for the purpose of financial reporting. In most cases, this way of going about a physical requires the shutting down of the entire operation, particularly if the warehouse supports a manufacturing facility. The reason for this is twofold. First, it is nearly impossible to get an accurate count if material is still flowing. Clearly, shutting down the plant freezes all transactions. Second, the annual physical is generally a monumental undertaking, requiring every available person in the plant if it is to be done in the shortest possible time. Sometimes, in order to shorten the counting period even more, it is necessary to hire temporary help.

The annual physical is generally of no value to anyone except the accountants, who have an obligation to report the year-end stock-on-hand balance to the corporation stockholders and the tax people. Typically, if there are discrepancies (errors) between what the records show and what they physical turns up, the records are corrected and the discrepancy written off as a loss.

Chances are that if there are discrepancies at the end of the year, there have been discrepancies throughout the year. Waiting until the end of the year to discover where these discrepancies are and exactly how bad they are is of no help to the operation, and is small consolation to those trying to reduce inventories or to those who have been plagued by material shortages throughout the year.

A growing awareness of the shortcomings of the annual physical has led to the wide acceptance of a more frequent physical, which has come to be known as "cycle counting." Clearly, no operation can stand the cost and disruption of counting all stock items any more frequently than once a year. The solution has been that only a small percentage of the items are counted frequently (say, once every three months), a greater percentage may be counted less frequently (say, once every six months), and the rest only once a year. Because of what has already been said, one must conclude that those items still being counted once a year represent items which are either (1) not very critical to the mission or operation or (2) account for a relatively small percentage of the total dollar-volume of inventory on a yearly basis. It must also be concluded that those to be counted most frequently are those that are extremely critical and/or relatively high dollar-volume movers.

Putting all of this in the context of control, the warehouse manager will want to exert the hightest control (which translates to more than just frequent counting) on the most important stock items, and the least control on the less important items. How many degrees of control and how many degrees of importance might exist in any given warehouse are matters to be agreed upon by both the warehouse manager and the other levels of management within the organization. No two warehouses are exactly alike; therefore, one should not expect a pat answer to the question. Some operations can justify as few as two levels of control and two categories of inventory; others may have the need to go to as many as six.

The most traditional breakdown of inventory control found in textbooks is that of three categories. That is fine for illustration purposes, so long as the reader does not get the idea that this is the way it always is or the way it should be. The three categories just referred to are classically known as A, B, and C categories. Subsequent discussion in this chapter will be restricted to an ABC classification scheme.

Reporting Inventory Record Accuracy

Record accuracy is defined as the degree of agreement between what the records say is in stock and what the physical count actually turns up.

When reporting warehouse performance, one should always attempt to report record accuracy rather than record error. It is believed that for psychological reasons and employee motivation a manager should stress the goodness in the operation rather than the badness.

In arriving at inventory record accuracy figures, however, one must first calculate the relative error. The following formula applies:

$$\text{Relative error, \%} = \frac{\text{physical count} - \text{record balance}}{\text{physical count}} \times 100 \qquad (26.1)$$

The difference shown in the numerator is the absolute difference. A common mistake is to use the record balance in the denominator. The physical count represents the true balance and is the correct value to use. Getting it reversed will distort the conclusion in most cases. For example, if the physical balance is 500 units and the record shows only 300 units, there is a discrepancy (error) of 200 units. The correct relative error is:

$$\text{Correct relative error} = \frac{500 - 300}{500} \times 100 = 40\% \qquad (26.2)$$

An incorrect measure of relative error is given below, and would lead one to conclude that things are far worse than they really are:

$$\text{Incorrect relative error} = \frac{500 - 300}{300} \times 100 = 67\% \qquad (26.3)$$

The correct value to be used as a measure of a record accuracy is simply the complement of relative error:

$$\text{Accuracy, \%} = 1 - \text{relative error, \%} \qquad (26.4)$$

Experimentation with different values for the physical count and record balance will confirm that the relative error, as it has been defined, will range from a possible low of 0 percent to a high that can theoretically approach positive infinity. Accuracy will range from a possible high of 100 percent to a theoretical low of negative infinity. Should accuracy ever drop below 0 percent, it might be better to switch to reporting relative error, thereby avoiding the use of negative numbers.

It is sometimes useful to report accuracy for a group of items (for example, a group of B items) instead of reporting on an item-by-item basis. This might be done, for example, to measure how well a given person is controlling inventory in the area assigned to him or her. In this case, one can use a simple average of the individual B-item accuracies, or a weighted average to reflect the volume of transactions. Another approach would be to have preestablished accuracy goals that are agreed to as being acceptable; for example, 95 percent of all B items in a given storage area. One can then count the number of items that meet or exceed the goal. The correct expression for accuracy would become:

$$\text{Accuracy, \%} = \frac{\text{number which pass}}{\text{total number of items}} \times 100 \tag{26.5}$$

The accuracy calculated in this way (using counts) may also be weighted to reflect the volume of transactions or any other weight.

Implementing a Cycle Counting Program

In a given cycle, a prespecified number of A, B, and C items will be counted. The length of the cycle, for example one week, will depend on the number of items to be counted and the standard time required to count and record balances. It will also depend, as will the number of persons required to do the counting, on the total number of items in inventory in each class and the yearly frequency of count for each class of items. A certain percentage of the time allocated to every cycle should be reserved for recounting a few items from the previous cycle. The reason for this will be brought out in the following discussion.

Cycle counting programs may be implemented somewhat differently in different organizations. However, to provide some idea of the possibilities, the following model is outlined. The model is adapted from a news note written by Hal Mather of G. W. Plossl & Co.:

1. Select the items that are to be counted by one person in the next cycle, say one week. If the warehouse supports a manufacturing operation, one would expect to find some finished goods, parts for assembly, subassemblies, raw material, and even repair parts among the items to be counted.
2. Go out into the warehouse or stockroom and count the actual stock-on-hand balance and compare these counts against the record.
3. If there is no discrepancy for a given item or if it is within acceptable limits, take no action other than to report the results.
4. If an unacceptable discrepancy is observed, make note of it, but do not change the record, at least not yet.
5. On the first occurrence of a discrepancy, one might first assume that it is due to a poor count.
6. Items noted above may then become part of the items assigned for counting in the very next cycle. This is why a certain amount of time is reserved each cycle for recounts.

7. If a discrepancy reappears on the second count, one makes a second note of this, but still does not authorize a correction of the records.
8. On the second occurrence of a discrepancy one might now assume that the counter did not locate all the parts or that some others were counted along with the right ones.
9. Items with a second note may again become part of the items assigned to the next cycle.
10. If discrepancies persist during the third cycle, one might now reasonably assume that all units were found and that their count was good.
11. Now is the time to adjust (correct) the record to agree with the last cycle count.
12. The same item should be assigned for counting again in the subsequent (fourth) cycle.
13. Now, any discrepancies between the count and the records are probably not due to the counting exercise, but are due to the system that maintains the records.
14. Since only one cycle has gone by since the record was adjusted, there should be only a few transactions entered. It should be far easier to track down the cause of the discrepancy following only a few transactions than following many.
15. This is, after all, the primary reason for conducting frequent counts—discovering the source of the errors and correcting them.
16. Items for which records have now been adjusted and for which the causes of the errors have been corrected may now be assigned for counting, yet again, to the next cycle. The purpose in so doing would be to ensure that the corrective action accomplished what it was intended for and that there was not some other source of error as yet undiscovered.
17. Such a reassignment might continue until an item passes two successive cycles within acceptable accuracy levels.

One might ask what it costs to operate in this manner. A more appropriate question would be what it cost *not* to operate in this manner, in terms of customer dissatisfaction, lost sales, and/or disrupted production. In fact, cost is one of the reasons for not wanting to jump in and correct the records when a discrepancy is first found. Correcting the records involves a cost, particularly if records are computerized and if future production schedules have already assumed the current record balance. Likewise, searching for a cause of errors, even if only a few transactions have been entered, will involve costs.

Summary

A few highlights of this chapter in the form of key words and phrases would include: (1) use formal and standardized systems to control inventory in the warehouse, regardless of size, (2) document the flow of material and the flow of paperwork within the warehouse, (3) keep material moving, off of the floor, and in properly designated and identified storage areas, (4) maintain discipline within the warehouse with respect to following standard procedures, (5) measure and report performance, and (6) do not just white-out errors and mistakes; take steps to correct them and take every reasonable precaution to ensure that they will not reoccur.

In the warehouse, documentation of procedures and the flow of paperwork is probably the single most important principle to be applied to help discover and correct discrepancies in the records. If discrepancies are present and documentation does not exist, your first step should be to take the time necessary to go out on the floor and "flowchart" the path of all paperwork and activities originating from the receipt of an order and the initiation of a withdrawal. This exercise alone, even if it is done as a matter of record, will likely suggest improvements that can be made in the warehouse to improve the control over inventory.

Bibliography

"Cycle Inventory Counting," Training Aid, American Production and Inventory Control Society, Washington, 1974.

Norman, H. Vanasse, "Parts Bank Locator Concepts," *Production and Inventory Management,* 4th quarter, 1982, pp. 68–86.

27
Shipping Systems

Robert B. Footlik
Executive Vice President, Footlik & Associates, Evanston, Illinois

Introduction

In any given endeavor, it is the last 10 percent of the effort involved that will make or break the project or endeavor. This is especially true when it comes to shipping goods from a warehouse. This is the last contact that you will have with the goods, and it is the one point where everything focuses and culminates. All the other activities that have taken place are there solely to support the shipping function. If this job is performed properly, you will have the opportunity of checking on the success of the other 90 percent of the operation. Receiving, storage, handling, order-picking, and packing all directly affect the shipping process, and in turn, the methods employed for these functions can be dictated by shipping.

Where to Start

Before making any improvements or changes, or even developing a shipping department, the first step is the determination of the common carriers or private carriage means by which the goods will be shipped. There is a vast menu of available shipping methods, including couriers, taxicabs, vans, minivans, straight trucks, semitrailers, sea/land containers, air-freight packages, air-freight containers, air-freight charters, railroad cars, barges, ships, U. S. postal service, United Parcel Service, and a host of other shipping methods. From this vast menu, a selection must be made based on the physical characteristics of the products, the quantities to be shipped, the quality of service desired and, of course, the costs.

All other things being equal, for a given commodity there will be a relatively short menu of available shipping methods. For example, a 10,000-pound machine tool is not going to be sent via United Parcel. This means that product characteristics and quantities will provide you with the first and simplest selection factor, but beyond this, to narrow down the field between individual carriers, the three "Ss," service, security, and savings, are of prime importance.

An examination of service must include such factors as the speed of delivery, scheduling flexibility, consistency of service, reliability, and cooperation. Security should be examined not just in terms of direct loss through theft, but also security from the environment. If one carrier has an open loading dock and another carrier has an enclosed truck terminal, then it is clear who would have the edge in terms of product protection in inclement weather. The third factor of savings has to be examined in the larger context of your overall shipping program. Direct cost of the service is only one component in the overall environment. You must also look at savings of space on the loading dock area, potential cost sharing and savings sharing, and the savings that you would have from peace of mind, i.e., knowing that your goods are secure and will be consistently delivered in good condition. These factors are tangible and intangible. One carrier may have lower costs, but it may not really be worth the aggravation of dealing with drivers who provide no cooperation; or, alternatively, the cost may be lower in terms of the direct expense paid to the carrier, but considerably higher if that particular carrier's drivers steal from you.

Innovation Saves Time, Money, and Manpower

Part of the selection process should also include some time spent with the common carrier to devise innovative methods of shipping. There is a great deal of cooperative effort that can be expended that will have major savings for each partner in the shipping process. Typically, less-than-load (LTL) freight (i.e., less than 500 pounds) is a losing proposition for most freight companies. If, however, you can develop a pallet exchange program so that LTL pieces are presented to the carrier on a pallet to save rehandling, then ideally you should be able to negotiate a much more favorable rate than what otherwise would be available. Similarly, a carrier who is willing to drop off a trailer every day at no charge, in reality, may be offering you an extra 320 square feet of staging area that will greatly reduce congestion and confusion in your facility. Keep in mind when negotiating with the carrier that if your freight volumes are not steady, you should be looking at either an averaged or, preferably, a fluctuating freight rate that goes down as your volume increases. Rates such as this were not possible under a regulated system but are possible now, since the rates are set by a free market.

Another area for cutting down your freight costs, particularly to distant points, is to contact other similar companies in your area who will help you in consolidating your freight with theirs. For example, if you have a shipment that will occupy one-half of a sea/land container and the company next door can fill up the other half, you both can effect excellent savings by consolidating your freight and shipping it at one time. A good warehouse manager or freight dispatcher will continually strive to pull together a cooperative unit to take advantage of this type of shipping. This also opens up the doors to alternative shipping methods by which two of you can charter your own vehicle or vessel and generate some handsome savings in the process.

Above all, do not overlook the nontraditional methods that are available to you. Companies that service a rural area should contact the local dairy or newspaper and tap into their existing delivery services, which are geared to consistent overnight delivery with door-to-door service. There are many small- to medium-size cities where delivery services such as this are already in place and can be utilized to cut everyone's costs while raising the level of service available to the customer. Interurban bus companies are another nontraditional mechanism available for the up-to-500-mile shipment of freight, provided you can meet their requirements and, perhaps, show them how they can service you.

Private Carriage

One special area of carrier involvement is to have your own delivery vehicles. This offers a great deal of flexibility, which can save you time and space if properly utilized. Company trucks can be either purchased or leased, and the drivers may be on your payroll or on the payroll of the leasing company. In either case, it is still in everyone's best interest to utilize these vehicles at minimum costs. Driver route books or logs can be very valuable in developing economical routing for customer service on a regular basis. A considerable amount of time can be saved through the use of such logs to help a new driver find the customer and plan his or her route intelligently. Similarly, installation of citizen band radios can help your drivers draw on the expertise of other drivers in finding customer locations. Having the information available not only cuts down on the time required to break in a new driver, but also can produce major savings in time and fuel by allowing you to plan your schedule around the real-world environment. Routes can be set up in a linear or a circular pattern, depending on which will gain the maximum benefits and get the delivery truck back to your facility in the shortest possible time.

There are two drawbacks, however, to having your own vehicles. The first is security: the necessity for implementing controls on the driver's use of the vehicle, the goods that will be transported, possible collusion, and so on. The problems here can be addressed by periodically spot-checking loads or by spot-checking the drivers themselves by riding with them or by waiting for them on your customer's dock. A good warehouse manager knows that if you want to talk to drivers, the best place to do it is in the cabs of their vehicles. The privacy and intimacy available may encourage the drivers to point out security breaches to you, while cementing your own managerial relationship.

The second drawback to having your own vehicles is that delivery services will be abused unless specific rules are set up and adhered to. Order cutoff times, accommodation pickups, moving of the boss's furniture, and a host of other tasks can be imposed on your own company vehicle to the detriment of warehouse operation costs, flexibility, and delivery service. The only way around this is to develop a uniform set of rules for any vehicle you use and top management's backing for adhering to these procedures. The salesman who holds back a truck to add on a few more pieces for the customer who called in late is doing the other customers a disservice, particularly if this happens regularly. Company truck use must be controlled very tightly, because the expenses associated with it are frequently charged against the warehouse.

Vehicle Loading

After the shipping method has been selected, the next area to look at is how these vehicles will be loaded. In part, this will be dictated by quantity, physical characteristics, and distances the product will be moved. Materials that are delivered from one side of town to the other, every single day, and always between point A and point B should definitely be palletized, unitized, or on some type of transfer vehicle. One-way shipments for long distances, however, may require an entirely different method of vehicle loading. Therefore, these determinations are made on a case-by-case basis with a large measure of common sense. Typically, truck loading is done by one of four methods: handstacking on the floor, palletization or unitization, "inner bodies," or mass loading.

Floor loading of the truck is most commonly performed on vehicles that will be making a one-way run over a long distance, especially if the product characteristics are light weight and high cubic volume. Under these conditions, the trailer will be filled long before it reaches maximum weight, and at the opposite end, your customers' receiving will be performed fairly fast because of the large size of the individual pieces. The fallacy here, of course, is the amount of manual labor that is required at both ends. Floor loading could have been accomplished at the shipping point using a clamp type of lift truck, but you are only going to move the problem to your customer's loading dock because the unloading process will definitely be labor-intensive, particularly if the load has shifted in transit.

For this reason, products that are relatively heavy, bulky, or come in small units should normally be palletized. The pallets utilized can be special disposable pallets that are "thrown away" by shipping them to the customer. If your receiving department is generating pallets from your vendors, it may be possible to recycle these pallets and save on scavenger costs by shipping them to your customers. This may not look as professional as having a consistent uniform pallet for shipment, but it certainly is cost-effective. The whole point of palletizing or unitizing loads is to create as large a unit as possible, consistent with handling at both ends. Shrink-wrap, stretch-wrap, stretch-net, strapping, or taping can all be used to secure the load against movement in transit and ensure that your customer will have an easier time receiving the merchandise.

If you are shipping consistently between two standard points on a vehicle that makes a round trip, a third method of shipment that can be particularly advantageous is the use of an inner body, such as a cart, collapsible pallet, or container that can be continually recycled. Uniform inner-body devices consistently save labor at both the shipping point and the receiving point, and generate additional profitability throughout the entire distribution system. Large triple-wall corrugated cartons can frequently be used for this function and are readily obtainable from any company that uses plastic injection molding equipment. A 40- by 40- by 40-inch (1 by 1 by 1 meter) triple-wall container is standard for the bulk shipment of plastic resins, and frequently this is thrown away by plastic molding companies. If purchased, these boxes may be relatively expensive, but if they are already being generated elsewhere in your own company, something that is today a loss may become a profitable item.

The fourth method of truck loading is based on automatic or semiautomatic equipment to mass load the entire vehicle at one time. Devices to accomplish this have been under development for more than

20 years and include air flotation of the goods, chain-type conveyors both on the dock and in the delivery vehicle, and various types of hydraulic "pushers" to push the goods into the trailer on a quasi-continuous basis. Generally, most of these systems share one flaw, and that is that the vehicle and the dock must be compatibly equipped. To date, no common carriers have uniformly equipped their fleets of vehicles to accommodate any specific system.

Designing a Staging Area

The truck loading method will, in turn, dictate the layout and utilization of the staging area where goods will be held prior to their being placed in the common carrier's vehicle. *Ideally, the warehouse manager should strive to totally eliminate the staging area.* This can be done by having your carrier dropship the vehicle so that order-picking, packing, and truck loading can be accomplished on a continuous basis, or alternatively, orders would not be assembled prior to the arrival of the delivery vehicle. This can be especially helpful in improving and controlling will-call pickups. Any time the delivery vehicle can be loaded directly without utilizing the staging area, you will be operating at lower costs and with better labor and space utilization.

For the unfortunate majority, however, two words would seem to characterize the staging area: necessary and evil. The necessary part should always be questioned, and the evil part should always be turned around. If it is, indeed, necessary to stage, then by all means do so in the most expedient manner possible, via segregating the materials into specific areas by common carrier, portion of route, or any similar subdivision that will allow you to maximize the space utilization while minimizing the amount of time required for hunting of merchandise. In the Occupational Health and Safety Act, Section 1910.144, there's a statement that a line shall be painted on the floor or put on the floor with tape to designate aisles and specific areas in the facility. Not only is this the law, but it is also excellent practice and represents the only method for ensuring nonchaotic loading docks. Without having definite lines on the floor, it is impossible to ensure the consistent placement of goods in the right area. Further segregation and space utilization can be achieved by placing pallet racks in the staging area to take advantage of the height available in the space, while simultaneously further subdividing and segregating the goods. Typically, the staging area is a low-ceiling-height function, but it is frequently in a high-ceiling-height area. Pallet racks are one method of utilizing the cube and returning it to storage. It is also possible to use a freestanding mezzanine above the staging area to hold plant services, offices, storage, assembly, packing, dispatching, or other similar low-ceiling-height operations. The minimum height requirement to do this comfortably would be 16 feet 0 inches (4.8 meters). Significant advantages in terms of tax savings, accelerated depreciation, and the flexibility of being able to move and reuse this mezzanine would all point to using a mezzanine to take advantage of available cube.

Transportation from Staging to Delivery Vehicle

Moving the goods from the staging area into the delivery vehicle will, of course, be a function of the loading method. Typically, if goods can be staged on pallets or on inner bodies, they can be moved directly into the vehicle and either shipped in their staged format or, alternatively, off-loaded directly in the vehicle. Depending on the common carriers involved, it may be possible to have the driver do this unstacking, instead of tying up your own personnel. Palletized or unitized loads or materials that are excessively heavy or bulky should be moved in and out of the trailer using mechanical equipment. A dock leveling device (dockboard) will greatly expedite the movement of materials by mechanical means, such as a forklift, hand pallet jack, or even a simple two-wheel hand truck. For continuous flows of goods, however, a skate wheel, flexible roller, or powered conveyor may be the ideal material handling equipment. Conveyors are commonly used as the output side of a packing line or may be connected directly to a sortation system as part of a larger materials handling and conveying system. Smaller operations especially will find significant advantages in by-passing staging in favor of direct conveyance into the truck or railcar. United Parcel Service and the U.S. postal service will, upon request, drop trailers for their larger customers, and these can be loaded directly from packing via a conveyor that extends into the truck or container.

Schedule for Flexibility

One of the most important aspects of shipping that is frequently overlooked is the necessity for proper scheduling of outbound shipments. As a shipper, you have much greater control over when the vehicle will arrive than you do as a receiver. With this in mind, it is important to schedule your outbound materials so that the shipping department operates on the basis of a continuous flow, rather than a "feast and famine" sporadic type of movement. This is an important factor in the selection of your key common carrier or carriers because it minimizes the extra labor that has to be on hand to cover peaks in the shipping period. If the shipping and receiving docks are located adjacent to each other, you will have greater flexibility through the reapportionment of time and manpower.

Scheduling is important to both you and the common carrier because it ensures that the delivery vehicle can be turned around in the minimum amount of time possible. Scheduling can allow two loading docks to function as four by making sure that the docks are utilized 100 percent of the time; but, scheduling is not merely limited to working with the common carrier. There are other ways of scheduling to improve the shipping functions.

Take advantage of the normal ebb of traffic in any urban area by scheduling trucks to leave at off times. For example, your own delivery vehicles could be leaving at 7:00 a.m. to miss the traffic if they have been preloaded or if your shipping crew is available from 5:00 a.m. until 7:00 a.m. In a similar vein, many of your customers would be quite comfortable in receiving shipments after the "normal" business hours. A quick poll of your customers may be able to pinpoint exactly who would be willing to receive a 9:00 p.m. shipment of materials. Doing this will allow you to miss traffic, and at the same time, get better utilization of the truck and driver. In many cases, part-time drivers can be engaged specifically for this run and paid a fraction of what a normal driver, who must also have considerable fringe benefits attached to his wage, would cost.

Branches of your own operation can be serviced at off hours, using a relay system by which a driver leaves your premises with a fully loaded truck and exchanges it for an empty truck at the branch, bringing back the empty so that it can be refilled, serviced, checked, and sent out again on an ongoing basis. Doing this at night using part-time personnel means lower costs, higher vehicle utilization, and a very reliable method of delivery. For this to succeed, however, both ends must be using the same type of delivery vehicle and mechanisms have to be in place for supervising the exchange at each end; alternatively, very reliable individuals must be engaged as drivers.

Scheduling is not the only way of getting greater truck turnaround. Considerable improvements in dock utilization can also be gained by painting lines on the floor of the truck well or dock area and continuing these lines up the wall of the building so that drivers have a reference point to look at in their mirrors while backing up. Similarly, posting of "No Parking" signs directly opposite the loading dock will increase the truck maneuvering area and decrease the amount of time spent by truck drivers in backing up. Keep in mind that a recessed indoor truck well typically has lighting in the neighborhood of 20 footcandles. During a bright summer day, the outdoor lighting may be in excess of 4000 footcandles. This means that a truck driver who is backing into your facility is virtually blind upon entering the loading dock. Therefore, mounting lights in the truck area that can be seen by the driver or at least painting obstructions a bright color will go a long way towards reducing the dangers and the time required for a driver to back in.

Security Considerations

The shipping dock is a major area for security improvements. This is a place where outsiders regularly interface with your personnel, and it is the easiest spot for collusion to take place between your people and truck drivers. There is no real way to prevent this, but it can be reduced by establishing some clear-cut, simple rules about how the drivers are to be treated, along with lines of responsibilities.

When drivers arrive at your facility, instead of just walking in, they should come through a door or press a doorbell to be let into a specific caged area. An interior cage will keep drivers out of the weather while you deal with the paperwork of their arrival. In this manner, instead of having outsiders wandering through your facility, you have drivers in one specific area until they can be dealt with and dispatched.

Once you are ready to let a driver in, make sure both of you know who is responsible for loading, who will tie down the load, who will count the load, and who will ensure that the driver signs the necessary documentation. Typically, this is the province of one or two individuals, and should remain with as few people as possible. In this manner, if you see anyone engaging in a long conversation with an outside driver, you will be in a position to investigate and check on what the problem is and why it is occurring—if indeed it is a problem.

Outside drivers are not your only security leak at this point. No employee vehicles should be parked near the shipping dock. Preferably, they should be located in a separate area, with the truck maneuvering area and loading dock totally fenced off from outside traffic. Management personnel, salespersons, and others who have no business in the shipping area should be barred from the dock. Many companies have greatly improved security by establishing a badge or identification system for anyone who comes to the warehouse, and this is particularly important at the shipping dock where it is a simple matter for someone to get goods out of the warehouse by putting an extra carton or two on a vehicle.

With your own company vehicles, periodic spot-checking of individual loads or touring with the driver should greatly improve security. You can also police this by taking both a weight and a count of all goods shipped. Many common carriers prefer this, and it certainly is a good practice in any operation where you suspect a security leak.

Nothing Moves Without Paper

Documentation of individual shipments will be dependent upon the requirements of the common carrier, your own organization, and any governmental bodies that are involved. Specific procedures for documentation of outbound goods should be established and posted for all shipping department individuals and truck drivers. No goods should leave the facility without having complete and total documentation as to the type of materials, their destination, weight or size, and so on. A uniform bill of lading is the most common document, but it may not provide the kind of detail that you need to expedite tracing of shipments or fulfill government requirements. Therefore, review all documentation regularly to see whether it can provide you with further information that will help expedite the shipping function in the future. Many warehouse managers find that a stamp (time in and time out) on the common carrier's bill of lading can be used to spot collusion and as a bargaining point at the rate negotiating table. Proving that the common carrier vehicle is back on the road in minimum time is an important point in obtaining the lower rate on all freight.

Keep the Goods Moving

In the normal flow of goods, everything should move from receiving through storage and out through shipping. If you do this right, the shipping function will operate at minimum cost and maximum efficiency. The ideal shipping department is a hole in the wall where the goods can move out continually, without being touched again. The closer you can come to this ideal, the greater will be your efficiency and the better will be your operation.

28

Warehouse Maintenance

William L. Morton

Manager, Ernst & Whinney, Washington, DC

Introduction

Starting up a new warehouse in this age of automation necessitates that a well-planned maintenance program be implemented. Organizing the maintenance department prior to start-up requires more than hiring a few technicians and providing certain tools and equipment. Though it is possible to survive the new facility start-up without good advance planning, this generally results in higher costs than would normally be expected. Furthermore, bad work habits established in this period will remain to plague future operations. If initial planning is not done at facility start-up, all is not lost. However, time is money, and it is difficult to explain why a multimillion-dollar investment is sitting idle because no plan for maintenance was formulated, and subsequently, a critical component failed.

Maintenance planning should embrace all activity necessary to plan, control, and record work in a facility to maintain an acceptable level of service. Additionally, a comprehensive maintenance program should consider corrective maintenance and planned overhaul for sophisticated handling equipment, maintenance material management, equipment history compilation, spare parts forecasting, and labor control. In a fully controlled situation, only the time spent on emergency work is "unplanned" and this could be less than 10 percent of available service hours in the maintenance department. The basic responsibilities of warehouse maintenance operations are deceptively simple:

- Keep material handling equipment in operation.
- Maintain buildings, grounds, utilities, plumbing, heating, air conditioning, and similar assets.

If a maintenance department can handle 90 to 95 percent of equipment component failures with tools, parts, and personnel skills on hand or purchased immediately at reasonable cost from a vendor, then the operation is probably cost-effective. To ensure a cost-effective operation, three basic requirements are:

- A program of maintenance activity for buildings and equipment
- A means of ensuring that the above program objectives are fulfilled
- A method of recording performance and assessing results

These requirements have traditionally been handled manually through card systems for inventory and labor control and the manual manipulation of work orders. However, facilities are now frequently larger in size, equipment is more sophisticated and expensive, and labor rates for maintenance technicians have soared. Manual methods may no longer be economically attractive.

A variety of computer systems have been developed for the management of maintenance operations. A range of features typically offered includes the ability to record equipment history, work order management, staffing allocation, maintenance material management, cost allocation by maintenance account, and analysis of feedback and cost. Traditionally, these systems have been based on mainframe computers, which were also employed for a variety of other purposes. The task for management was to select an appropriate software product to facilitate maintenance information management. However, the use of corporate mainframe computers gave rise to delays, with the maintenance department low in the order of priority for computer time, especially when large financial programs were scheduled for processing.

The ideal computer system for maintenance control is one which is interactive, dynamic, and dedicated. *Interactive* means that it can be queried on an as-needed basis for information internal to the system. *Dynamic* means that it gives a fast response to data input and changes. *Dedicated* means that it is always available to the maintenance department for data entry or for instant retrieval of data for planning or management. These requirements can be most satisfactorily met by an on-line computer system. This can be accomplished with a mainframe, but with the associated penalties for operating in a timesharing environment. Therefore, potential users looked at the dedicated minicomputer as an acceptable alternative. However, the cost still was beyond the grasp of many medium to small maintenance groups. Fortunately, the desktop microcomputer has come onto the scene. Although prices vary significantly, these systems are well within the grasp of even the smallest maintenance operation.

Preventive Equipment Maintenance

Preventive equipment maintenance (PEM) programs are complex and, frequently, difficult to "sell" to management because there is no immediate dollars-and-cents payback; a *two-year delay before the benefit signs appear is not unusual.*

Preventive equipment maintenance means different things to different people. Management frequently sees it as "overhead that may or may not be of value"; production people usually consider it to be "something that prohibits scheduled product delivery"; line mechanics place it somewhere between corporal punishment and management stupidity. In general, their attitudes are summed up by: "The machine is working fine, why work on it?" However, a PEM program can be a big weapon in the battle to keep critical equipment in operation.

Basically, the prime objective of a PEM program is to expose component weaknesses before machinery fails and causes stoppages. On the average, maintenance departments with good PEM programs expend about 15 percent of their total effort on equipment breakdowns; this figure jumps to well over 70 percent in departments without PEM programs.

Management must review the overall facility operating procedure and conditions, analyze company goals, and then decide whether to:

1. Continually operate all facilities and equipment at maximum capability, shutting down only for emergency repairs, or
2. Employ a PEM program on a firm, regular schedule, perhaps reducing daily output slightly, but, in turn, practically eliminating costly shutdowns.

Normally, when attempting to start a PEM program, it is relatively easy to overcome the usual obstacles with a little diplomatic effort and extensive planning. One point is clear: management will be receptive to any well-planned cost reduction program, so the best approach for a PEM program presentation to management is one that emphasizes dollar savings.

PEM is expensive. However, in the long-run, an effective PEM program will return many more dollars than are spent on it. Most warehouses and distribution centers will not require sophisticated and complex PEM programs, although some degree of PEM should be practiced. A warehouse may have many different types of equipment. It is not uncommon for a facility to have a combination of docks with levelers and door attachments, storage racks, conveyors, lift trucks, automated storage/retrieval (AS/RS) systems, automated guided vehicle (AGV) systems, automatic identification equipment, containers, packaging equipment, palletizers and depalletizers, communications equipment, computer systems, and auxiliary equipment of many types.

It is obviously not cost-effective to treat every piece of equipment in a facility equally. Some components wear faster than others. Some are more critical to continuous operations. The literature is filled with examples of sophisticated methods for failure analysis, predicting failures, and the like. While these methods have merit when attempting the final 10 percent realization of maintenance expenditures, it is getting the initial 90 percent realization that is the major concern of managers today.

Preventive Equipment Maintenance Misconceptions

A number of underlying misconceptions exist about what a PEM program will accomplish. The following are some of the most common ones:

1. *PEM can be done using the present maintenance work force.* If a maintenance technician already has a full workload, then additional tasks cannot be handled without neglecting some existing assignments. Maintenance personnel have long been regarded as nonproductive overhead. Therefore, management has tended to trim the maintenance work force to an absolute minimum. A logical solution may appear to be the reassigning of existing personnel; however, the reassigning of personnel can lead to other problems. The normal backlog will continue to grow as a result. PEM inspectors will add new repair orders that should be handled promptly to avert equipment breakdowns. This combination of a significantly *increased* workload and a *decreased* repair crew will rapidly create a four-step chain reaction:

   a. PEM requests for preventative repairs will be ignored.
   b. PEM inspectors will stop turning in repair requests.
   c. As repair foremen fall behind, they will be siphoning PEM inspectors from their assigned work and place them into the breakdown repair crews.
   d. At this point, the program degenerates to a "paperwork PEM program." Management discovers this and terminates the program.
2. *PEM will reduce maintenance cost.* This is not so. If a PEM program is working effectively, maintenance *material and labor costs* must *increase.* These costs can be justified because machines being repaired "now" would have lasted only a few weeks. At the same time, *today's* breakdowns are being repaired.
3. *PEM will reduce overall operating costs.* It will, if adequate personnel are employed for a long enough period to produce results. This is the primary justification for any PEM program. The availability of all material handling equipment will allow the shipment of more orders which will result in more profits.
4. *Repair crews can do PEM inspection while awaiting breakdowns.* This does not seem unreasonable at first glance in that it would mean greater utilization for an occasionally idle work force. However, there are major drawbacks to this approach. A major problem is that the maintenance technician may be unreachable when needed most on short notice. This results in a maintenance supervisor simply not ordering key personnel out on PEM inspections. It would not be unusual for critical equipment to be given a "paperwork PEM" inspection in this situation.
5. *PEM inspection is not different from normal maintenance inspection.* When equipment breaks down in an automated warehouse, all operations may cease, At the very least, they will be greatly impaired. When the maintenance technician arrives to perform repairs, the pressure will be great to accomplish the task quickly. In many cases, the repair will be a hurried temporary correction. Often, within a few hours, days, or possibly weeks, the equipment will experience another breakdown that will be repaired in a similar way. If this happens with frequency, a PEM program should be strongly considered because one of the phenomena of today's complex material handling equipment and other systems is that the *obvious* cause of a breakdown rarely seems to be the cause of the breakdown. A technician cannot be expected to search for the true causes of breakdowns while assigned to an emergency breakdown repair crew. PEM repairs must be performed while machines are idle, such as during a third shift or on weekends.

PEM Program Justification

As stated earlier, costs will show slight increases in the start-up of a PEM program. This increase can be attributed to the expense of starting a new program while the old emergency repair system is still in effect. It is necessary to continue emergency repair work until equipment is worked into the new PEM program. This could take up to 12 months.

Because of this initial negative appearance of PEM programs, it is necessary to show the long-run benefits. This can best be done by preparing charts, graphs, tables, and so on that show: (1) the actual costs for the two years immediately preceding introduction of the PEM program, and (2) projected costs for the two years following start-up of the program. These visual displays will serve two basic functions. They will be an invaluable aid in showing what the program can do and they will provide the plant engineer with a budget reduction goal.

Program projections must be realistic, however. If the figures are too extreme, management may simply elect to kill the program before it even gets started. The initiator of the plan must thoroughly understand the potential benefits of the program before approaching top management.

One last group must be convinced of the overall value of an effective PEM program—the maintenance personnel themselves. Maintenance mechanics frequently offer the most resistance to such a program, because, too often, the philosophy of "reaction" type maintenance has been thoroughly taught, and mechanics fully advocate the thinking that equipment should not be touched as long as it is still running.

The best approach for convincing maintenance personnel is the proof-by-results methods. *Proof-by-results* is a broad and somewhat misunderstood term, but it may be described as a visible and unquestionable happening, wherein the end observations show mathematical evidence of time and/or money savings. Often, improvements in the quality of work life can help sell the program. In most cases, the most skeptical maintenance person will quickly offer support when it is proven that his or her job can be made easier by planned and scheduled downtime.

Organize PEM Data

Any successful PEM program requires a workable method of organizing information. One approach involves separate maintenance forms for various inspection frequencies: daily, weekly, monthly, bimonthly, and annual. A specific list of tasks may be printed on the back of each sheet. The tasks are grouped by functional headings, such as drives, conveyors, and flow control devices. Typical tasks that apply especially to powered conveyors are presented in the section, "Basic Conveyor PEM Procedures."

The front of each sheet should contain a unit code number and corresponding unit description symbols, along with numbered columns that correspond to the task categories on the back. There should also be a column for the maintenance worker's initials, one for the supervisor's initials, and one for comments. Each sheet, with the exception of the daily one, should be identified by a work-week number. Thus, maintenance work is detailed for every week of the year.

Plan the Work Year

The one-year time frame permits inclusion of every necessary PEM task in a written program. Although writing the program takes time, once completed, it will pay for itself both as a monitor of equipment or system performance and as a permanent record of the equipment's condition.

One of the best ways to develop an efficient schedule is to "walk through" the system, identifying all components requiring PEM and mapping out a logical pattern. This exercise helps to coordinate the movement of maintenance personnel and equipment (such as lubrication carts) with the physical configuration of the system. Each component is assigned a unit number and grouped according to inspection/maintenance frequency. At this point, unit numbers can be transferred to the maintenance sheets. At the same time, they should be stenciled on or near the individual components for rapid identification.

Plan the Size of the Maintenance Staff

Staffing requirements for any PEM program are directly related to the size and complexity of the system. Some general guidelines can be developed, however, on the basis of many good years of experience with preventive maintenance in both manufacturing plants and warehouses.

The following example has been devised to illustrate the rationale used in preparing a staff plan. The hypothetical conveyor system consists of 200 to 250 power units. It is assumed that 80 percent of the equipment is at elevations from 10 to 30 feet above the floor. With such a system, operating one shift, five days a week, two maintenance workers are required for the PEM program only. These workers should be considered to be two-thirds of the total personnel required, because an additional person should be designated for emergency repairs. For a seven-day-a-week schedule, a multiplier of 1.4 should be applied.

The number of workers needed for emergency backup should be multiplied by the number of shifts per day. Safety requirements and common sense dictate that some maintenance jobs be done by two people, so some additional personnel should be accounted for. Summing up then, the system described in the example would require:

- Two workers—assigned to preventive maintenance only
- One worker—added for backup and emergency repairs (2/3 rule of thumb)
- One worker—added for safety considerations (80 percent of equipment 10 feet above floor or higher)

The basic complement of maintenance people would be four. The number of workers assigned to backup or emergencies would be multiplied by the number of shifts the plant operates.

A final consideration involves those factors that inherently impede the efficiency of preventive maintenance. They can include plant operations that preclude PEMs being carried out on schedule, or any of a number of policy issues. In such cases, it is advisable to apply a further multiplier of 1.3 to the original baseline number.

Keep Repair Records

Repair maintenance is another area that involves record keeping. Most organizations have maintenance logs tailored to their own operations. The size and design of the system to a large extent determine the methods used. However, the following items should be incorporated into any repair maintenance log:

- The date and time that the repair call is received, along with the identity of the person taking the call
- A brief description of the trouble
- A record of the repair assignment, including personnel assigned to the repair and the date and time of the assignment
- Identification of the equipment involved in the repair and a list of any parts used
- A record of the completion of the work, with a brief description of what was done and a sign-off by the repair crew

Some plant engineering departments keep repair and maintenance records that go beyond these minimum requirements. They may even maintain a computerized history of every power unit in the system. A program this extensive often can be justified on the basis of avoiding costly downtime.

In most cases, the maintenance log is kept in the maintenance shop, where it is conveniently available to maintenance personnel. Another effective procedure is to attach an envelope to each power unit in the envelope. A maintenance person called to service a unit then has the historical record at the work site.

Beyond the paperwork, a successful PEM program needs two additional ingredients: commitment and discipline. When they are present, there is also a high level of confidence that the warehouse system will run smoothly.

Set Up a Training Program

A maintenance crew should be named before installation and should begin training while installation is under way. The training timetable depends on the size and complexity of the system and the corresponding size of the maintenance crew. In most cases, a minimum training period should be included as part of the system contract. Obligations of the conveyor supplier must be clearly spelled out. Documents such as layout drawings, wiring diagrams, bills of materials, service manuals, parts catalogs, recommended spare parts lists, and lists of safety precautions are all essential.

A detailed training program ought to be agreed upon before the contract is signed. The program should provide for both hands-on and classroom instruction.

The hands-on phase develops familiarity with individual system components. Usually conducted by the system supplier, this training should be organized, direct, and personal. It is especially during this phase that maintenance personnel can be motivated with a sense of accomplishment and confidence. That confidence should then be reinforced through the classroom phase. The ultimate goal is to develop competency and self-sufficiency in each member of the maintenance team.

Throughout the training cycle, trainees should be encouraged to ask questions. One technique that usually helps stimulate the question-answer exchange is having the maintenance supervisor set the stage by asking questions. Because the supervisor will probably have some advance experience with the system, he or she is better able to anticipate those aspects that are apt to present difficulties for the trainees. The example set by the supervisor can help overcome reluctance on the part of other workers to speak up and ask questions.

Training must be approached one step at a time. The object is to avoid instilling awe or fear of the system. Regardless of its complexity, a system is made up of individual components.

Keep the Program Alive

Just as important as preliminary planning and organization is a firm commitment to maintaining an ongoing PEM program. If procedures and schedules have been well thought out, and if the maintenance team is adequately staffed, execution of the program should be smooth. Downtime surprises will be minimized or eliminated, and a detailed history of the system's performance will be automatically generated through the maintenance records. The records themselves can provide the basis for further fine tuning of the program.

After extended service, certain segments might require closer attention or more frequent inspection as a result of changing system demands. Such patterns can be readily recognized if maintenance records are accurate and complete.

Consistent records can also be instrumental in identifying people problems that are at the root of the apparent equipment problems. An example might involve repeated jam-ups in a certain area. If trouble calls are evenly distributed over all shifts in a 24-hour period, the problem is probably an equipment malfunction. If, on the other hand, records show that calls are registered only at certain times or on a particular shift, the reason can probably be found among the operators instead of the equipment. Another essential aspect of keeping the PEM program alive is retraining. Retraining is necessary because of normal turnover and changes in the physical configuration or operating conditions of the system.

An example that illustrates the point is a system designed to convey parts through a merging or sorting operation at a rate of 40 per minute. Over the years, however, the required rate shifts to 55 or 25, and some kind of adjustment becomes necessary.

A common error is to conclude that the adjustment will take the form of a change in equipment to speed up or slow down the operation. However, all that may be needed is a change in stock location or personnel allocation, or modification of a computer program.

Most material handling systems are based on a balanced-flow concept, whereby throughputs from various sectors of a system balance out, one against another. Many factors that affect this balance may not be directly related to equipment.

Contract Maintenance

Contract maintenance can vary from very slight usage by the owner to complete usage. A warehouse or distribution center could contract its roofing, painting, and maybe other minor items, such as grass cutting, or contract 100 percent of its maintenance, including supervision. In some cases, facilities use contract maintenance involvement in order to "buy" the know-how that is brought to the facility by the contractor. To have this full range of alternatives, the warehouse must be in a favorable geographic location where the capabilities exist to furnish these services.

More rather than less involvement appears to be most attractive to new facilities, since contracting all or all significant maintenance would not include changing an existing system. Under these circumstances, both the owner and the contractor develop procedures during the start-up phases of the operation. Certainly, from a practical standpoint, contract maintenance in general is more applicable to a new facility, particularly if the owner is thinking in terms of total contract maintenance. Existing union agreements, present laws, and court and National Labor Relations Board (NLRB) rulings may make it highly unlikely that an owner can find a set of circumstances in which total contract maintenance can realistically be considered in an established facility. With this framework, the following alternatives are available:

1. Owners can have their own maintenance forces performing all maintenance work—both day-to-day and peak-loads requirements. Until recently, this alternative accounted for the great majority of plants and warehouses.

2. Owners can use their own maintenance forces for all day-to-day requirements, but bring in contractor forces to handle major peaks. In this case, the contractor forces would be working under specific terms and conditions.

3. Owners can have their own minimum maintenance forces perform only part of the day-to-day requirements and use contractor maintenance forces to do the balance of the day-to-day work and to handle peak requirements.

4. Owners can elect to have no maintenance working personnel of their own and rely entirely on contract forces to provide all maintenance personnel for normal and peak maintenance needs.

The Advantages of Contract Maintenance

1. The ability to fluctuate staffing to exactly meet day-to-day needs permits expending less man-hours per year to perform a given amount of work. This eliminates employment of full-time personnel to handle peaks and reduces the tendency for built-in featherbedding. It permits scheduling certain work, such as painting, to take advantage of seasonally good weather.
2. A facility can meet the extraordinary personnel needs for start-up without overstaffing for normal operations and should work less overtime during start-up.
3. Since contract labor already has the basic skills of their craft, they require less training than the typical maintenance employee to reach a given level of efficiency.
4. If the owner elects, responsibility can be passed on to the contractor for essentially all or a significant part of facility maintenance. This can leave more of the owner's key personnel with more time to concentrate on process operations. This does not mean that maintenance will be forgotten or become a stepchild, because maintenance contractors have a real economic incentive to do a good job—any maintenance project is part of their bread and butter.
5. The owner can draw on the contractor for additional help for services over and above normal maintenance work. The contractor—if he or she is the right one—can provide additional supervision as needed. The contractor can also provide intermittent supervision in specialty areas, such as rigging, critical equipment inspection and repair, and so on. The owner can use additional spot help for activities such as take-off, estimating, sketching, and buying, and still keep company personnel at a constant level.
6. One advantage that is often talked about is that the owner can reduce the investment in facilities, buildings, tools, and equipment. This is not a significant advantage. Over a period of time it appears that locker rooms, offices, and other space for contract personnel approach the norm for the owner's people. Shops of various types can be kept minimal, and the larger, infrequently used equipment is available for rent by the owner from the contractor or others, regardless

of contract versus in-house maintenance. There may be some savings on investment in tools if the contractor supplies them, but this is not substantial.

7. The owner can shift essentially all responsibility for labor relations with maintenance personnel to the contractor.

To summarize the advantages of contract maintenance in just a few words, we can say that the owner has a "wide degree of flexibility," substantially more so than that enjoyed with a typical, in-house maintenance force.

Battery Selection Considerations and Maintenance

Batteries for electric truck motors are usually lead-acid, traction-type, industrial-grade units. Voltages range from 12 volts (typical for powered walkie trucks) to 24, 36, and 48 volts for average-sized rider fork trucks, and up to 72 volts for heavy-duty units.

Battery capacities are expressed in ampere-hours. Selecting the proper size battery is important because the idea is to have the battery last for a full eight-hour shift. Factors that influence the battery selection decision include truck weight, average and maximum load weight, trips per hour and average length of trip, lifts per hour, utilization percentage of truck per shift, number of shifts per day, and number and slope of ramps in the facility.

One possible way of giving electric trucks new life may be through new batteries. New lower-maintenance batteries appeared in the marketplace during the early 1980s. One of the ways that this limited-maintenance feature evolved was through the hanging of the alloy in order to reduce or remove certain alloying materials from the battery grid. The result of this replacement is a battery that has a higher on-charge voltage than conventional batteries.

The effect of having higher on-charge voltage batteries is that these limited-maintenance batteries require a charger matched to their specific characteristics. Also, in order to keep these batteries healthy, it is necessary to increase the voltage of the charger in order to fully charge the battery.

The objective of battery maintenance is to ensure that fresh batteries are always available for all battery-powered vehicles, even when a nominal number are down for repairs. Batteries for these vehicles should be in a ratio of slightly more than two batteries per vehicle.

Every organization with battery-powered vehicles should recognize the importance of proper battery maintenance. Several principles have emerged over the years; these include:

- Battery maintenance cannot be a part-time responsibility delegated to maintenance technicians on a basis whereby this task is only accomplished when resources are available. A good battery maintenance program demands trained, experienced personnel whose sole responsibility is to maintain and repair batteries.
- A well-equipped battery repair shop must be provided. Facilities should have the capability to replace bad cells.
- Record keeping is an essential part of any program intended to provide optimum battery utilization and ensure maximum battery lift. Records permit programming the use of the battery throughout its entire life.
- Low-voltage operation of trucks must be eliminated. Such operation can negate much of the careful attention accorded by battery maintenance personnel, and can be prevented by utilization of a monitoring device (voltage meter) that does not require a qualitative decision by equipment operators.
- A program of equipment operator education is necessary. Such a program should acquaint operators with the effects of low-voltage operation and help them to understand the need for and mechanics of protection equipment installed to prevent such operation.

If a battery is not performing properly, it should be brought immediately to the repair shop for a discharge test. If the battery is found to be in basically good condition, it should be uncased and demossed, or have any other required repairs made. Repairs may include installing new separators, replacing a cell, and/or releasing. If the general condition of the battery is questionable, the record of the battery must be analyzed, and a decision made either to return the battery to service or scrap it.

Record keeping is a key part of the battery charging operation. When a battery is changed, a record should be completed for the removed battery. Information in this record relates to the timing and repairs performed during the cycle. Records should be maintained for each battery and include information on how many cycles have been performed, the trucks on which these cycles took place, specific gravity readings, and number and type of repairs.

Battery charging rooms should be arranged and equipped so that equipment drivers are accommodated with minimal downtime. A small bridge crane is best for removing old discharged batteries. A new, freshly charged battery can then be installed, plugged in, and the driver back in service with minimal interruption.

A reasonable target objective is to bring equipment in for a battery change when battery specific gravity has dropped to about 1150. At this point, truck operating efficiency will still be high, and only about five or six hours will be required to bring the battery back to full charge. On the other hand, a specific gravity drop to 1100 will produce sluggish performance, and the truck may be damaged. Operation of a truck in a low-voltage condition is irresponsible, can burn out a motor, damage wiring and commutators, and cause fuses to blow. A battery brought in for charge at a specific gravity of 1100 will require about 11 or 12 hours for recharge. Charging under a rundown condition will cause considerable heat to be developed in the battery, contributing to battery deterioration. Moreover, the battery cannot be returned to service until it has cooled.

Low-voltage operation can be prevented by the installation of battery protectors. New equipment purchases should be specified with the protectors as OEM equipment. These devices eliminate the guesswork on battery change-out.

At some time in the battery's life, a decision will be made to assign it exclusively to light duty. Reassignment should be to equipment required to perform only two or three work cycles per week. In this service, a battery can be expected to last one or two more years. At the end of its life, the battery will have performed approximately 1300 to 1500 work cycles.

Conveyor Maintenance

In order to keep a conveyor system operating as originally specified, a well-planned preventive maintenance should be implemented and sustained. The PEM program should be designed specifically to meet a particular vendor's requirements. However, there are some general rules that almost all programs can incorporate.

The program should include a daily formal, but brief, check of key system components, such as bearings and power delivery components. An evaluation of the critical components in the system should be made. Some components will be relatively more critical than others. Some conveyors will be relatively straightforward, operating only at standard speeds. In some cases, multiple units may be operated in such a way as to back each other up so minor breakdowns will not cause total facility breakdowns.

Many conveyor systems are custom-designed, one-of-a-kind systems. When these systems experience a failure, the entire facility usually experiences a failure. The frequency and depth of PEM for these systems should obviously be greater than for standard systems.

A general rule for standard systems is that under "normal" operating conditions, conveyor components should be inspected thoroughly and serviced at one- to two-month intervals. Critical components, those absolutely essential to overall system performance or that operate at high speeds, should be inspected and serviced at intervals ranging from once a week to every day.

Finally, adequate time should be allocated in warehouse operating schedules to allow for thorough, general lubrication of the entire system once per year. This lubrication program should include oiling, grease changing, and so on. The vendor should provide detailed lubrication instructions.

Basic Conveyor PEM Procedures

The basic conveyor PEM procedures listed below are based on inspection intervals of one month, two months, and one year. If preprinted forms are used for the PEM program, it is convenient to list the specific tasks to be performed at each interval. These guidelines are especially applicable to conveyor systems having powered units.

Some of the tasks vary depending on the type of conveyor involved. Examples include powered belt, live roller, powered curve, slider bed, and accumulation conveyors. General tasks are summarized below, organized by inspection level.

A. Daily inspection
   1. Observe all belts while the unit is running.
      a. Check for proper belt tension. It should be tight enough to prevent slippage between the belt and drive pulley under full load.
      b. Check for damaged or frayed belts that could cause interference or jam-ups.
      c. Look for shredded belt droppings which indicate belt or roller misalignment.
      d. Replace any frayed V belts.
      e. Listen for excessive noise from bearings, reducers, motors, or a chain-and-drive sprocket drive.
   2. Manually check all mechanical controls and see that they operate freely.
      a. Check oil level in oiler of air system.

   b. Check drain in air system.
   c. If system has hydraulic circuitry, check oil level in reservoir. Also check for leakage.
   d. Look for noisy rollers.
   e. Check linkages and springs.
   f. Check for sticky sensors.
   g. Check cams.
   h. Observe quality of housekeeping.
   i. Make sure belt lacing is intact.
   j. Check end pulley alignment.
   k. Check O rings (or replace) in skewed wheel diverters.
   l. Check air lube system.
   m. Check for air leaks.
   n. Secure all setscrews.
   o. Check for loose bolts or nuts.
3. Inspect material flow control devices while equipment is operating.
   a. Make sure photocells are operating.
   b. Check air pressure and pressure regulator.
   c. Check oil in mist lubricators; adjust for proper level.
   d. Drain all water traps.
   e. Oil moving parts.
   f. Look for broken or missing O rings.
   g. Check timing belt tension.
   h. Make sure limit switches are operating.
   i. Make sure safety devices are operating.
   j. Check and clean filters on air system.
4. Observe product flow while equipment is operating.
   a. Make sure guards are properly aligned.
   b. Look for soft spots.
   c. Check for excessive line pressure.
   d. Check operation of accumulation lines.
   e. Report nonconveyable items.

B. One-year frequency
1. Perform basic maintenance on drives.
   a. Change oil in gear case and hydraulic unit.
   b. Grease bearings.
   c. Check for oil level and leaks in hydraulic and air power units.
   d. Remove and clean drive chains.
   e. Change filters on hydraulic units.
2. Clean and lubricate conveyor components.
   a. Clean and grease rollers.
   b. Grease all bearings with jerks.
   c. Check and clean return rollers.

3. Check and adjust material flow control devices.
   a. Change all photocell bulbs.
   b. Check and replace burned or dirty contacts in cabinets.

Bibliography

Alsentzer, John: "Lift Truck Economics—Gas vs. Electric," *Plant Engineering Library—Material Handling,* Technical Publishing Company, Barrington, Illinois, 1979, pp. 19–22.

______ :"Lift Truck Economics—Buy, Lease, or Rent," *Plant Engineering Library—Material Handling,* Technical Publishing Company, Barrington, Illinois, 1979, pp. 23–25.

Ames, John A. and George J. Havens: "A Battery Maintenance Program that Works," *Plant Engineering Library—Material Handling,* Technical Publishing Company, Barrington, Illinois, pp. 28–30.

Anderson, Lee: "Establishing an Effective PM Program," *Plant Engineering Library—Maintenance,* Technical Publishing Company, Barrington, Illinois, pp. 5–20.

Cooling, W. Colebrook: *Simplified Low-Cost Maintenance Control,* rev. ed., AMACOM Book Division, American Management Associations, New York, 1983.

Gill, Norman: "Floor Coatings: A Guide to Selection and Application," *Plant Engineering and Maintenance,* vol. 6, no. 3, June 1983, pp. 48–49.

Husband, T. M.: *Maintenance Management and Terotechnology,* Saxon House, Teakfield Limited, Westmead, Farnborough, Hampshire, England, 1976.

Mann, Lawrence, Jr.: *Maintenance Management,* Lexington Books—D. C. Heath, Lexington, Massachusetts, 1976.

Morton, William L.: "Five Steps in Selecting Maintenance Control Software," *Plant Engineering and Maintenance,* vol. 5, no. 7, December 1982, pp. 20–25.

Pomponio, Henry: "Managing Maintenance to Improve Your Investment" *Material Handling Engineering,* vol. 36, no. 5, May 1981, pp. 70–75.

Romero, Max E.: "Automatic Fire Protection—A Review of Fixed and Portable Specialized Systems," *Plant Engineering,* Technical Publishing Company, Barrington, Illinois, vol. 37, no. 14, July 7, 1983, pp. 65–69.

Quinlan, Joe: "It's Time to Bet on Energy Savings in Material Handling," *Material Handling Engineering,* vol. 37, no. 2, February 1982.

White, E. N.: *Maintenance Planning, Control and Documentation,* Gower Press, Teakfield Limited, Westmead, Farnborough, Hampshire, England, 1976.

White, John A.: *Yale Management Guide to Productivity,* Industrial Truck Division, Eaton Corp., 1979.

29
Loss Control

Thomas F. Cecich

Manager of Safety, Health & Environmental Affairs, Glaxo, Inc., Research Triangle Park, North Carolina

Introduction

A modern warehouse may contain a huge investment in raw materials, in-process manufactured parts, and finished products. The value of the stored materials alone can easily run into many millions of dollars. The building structure and equipment can also be a significant investment. Thus, the warehouse with its contents represents a link in a process that helps bring about a product or service that will eventually result in a profit.

Warehouses may store key raw materials in short supply as a buffer to offset anticipated future shortages due to strikes, disasters, or unanticipated volumes. Such key materials may not have a significant dollar value on their own; however, an entire manufacturing process may be dependent on ready access to that material. Loss of such key resources could create a significant business interruption.

Much attention is given to the procurement, tracking, handling, and distribution of materials and products in warehousing operations. However, particular attention should also be given to the preservation and protection of such materials just as with any other company property. Loss of such assets can impose severe operating and financial costs to a company.

Prudent organizations develop loss control programs in an attempt to eliminate or at least minimize the impact of unexpected losses. In this chapter, the losses that are most likely to be incurred and possible control techniques will be discussed. Losses from (1) fires and explosions, (2) accidents, (3) theft, and (4) various forms of inventory damage will be covered. The final section of this chapter will deal with the ways in which a company manages against the possibility of a loss. The section will introduce the concept of risk management and discuss the tools available to individuals assuming the role of risk managers.

Fires

Background

Of the variety of losses that can be experienced in warehousing operations, a major fire poses the greatest threat. Although the other types of losses can be quite severe, the possibility of a devastating fire is always present. As a result, fire-loss prevention and control activities must receive constant attention. Any relaxation of the necessary vigilance can have disastrous consequences.

The severity of most warehouse fires is not high. The majority are discovered at the incipient stage and are extinguished rapidly by personnel using portable fire extinguishers. As a result, very little product or structural damage is incurred.

Some fires progress past the incipient stage due to delayed detection or the rapid combustion of the stored materials. Such fires are usually too extensive to extinguish with portable extinguishers, and large fire hoses or automatic fire suppression systems are needed to combat the fire.

When operating effectively, automatic fire protection systems and hose streams can adequately suppress a fire. However, in each case, the fire will have progressed to the point that considerable fire damage is sustained. In addition to the damage directly attributed to the heat and smoke, damage from water or other extinguishing agents can be significant. In many cases, experience shows that the extinguishing agent (usually water) may cause more damage than the fire itself.

Of course, the ultimate objective in fire-loss control is to prevent the warehousing facility from experiencing a catastrophic fire that could result in the total loss of the facility. An example of such a loss occurred in West Germany in October 1977. In this fire, which involved an automotive parts warehouse, over $100 million in losses were incurred.

In addition to the direct loss of the building and stored materials, a company may also sustain significant business interruption losses. Such losses may ultimately be larger than the direct cost of the material itself. A warehouse storing subassemblies or hard-to-obtain components with long lead times may directly impact many operations that depend on rapid accessibility to raw materials or parts.

A fire-loss control program consists of two major components: fire prevention and fire protection. Each of these is essential to reduce the potential for fire.

Fire Prevention

An effective fire-loss control program begins with a management commitment to implement a fire-prevention plan. Fire prevention includes a number of activities to identify and eliminate, or at least control, potential fire hazards. Many can best be implemented when planned during the initial construction phase of the warehouse. However, as in many times the case, it may not be possible to predict during the design phase of a general-purpose warehouse exactly what types of operations will ultimately be performed there. As a result, many fire-prevention plans are developed after the building is occupied.

Even when a fire-prevention plan is carefully prepared prior to occupancy, continuous vigilance is required to ensure that all fire risks are minimized. An audit or inspection program designed to identify high-risk areas is essential. Such audits should be conducted periodically by trained loss-control specialists associated with the company, insurance carrier, or another interested third party. Consultants often are utilized to perform independent loss-prevention reviews.

In addition to a formal audit program, frequent inspections are necessary to identify conditions that can have immediate fire potential. Such inspections are particularly important where personnel are not routinely present. Inspections are commonly performed during off-hours by security personnel as part of their normal building tours. It is important that security officers be properly instructed so as to be able to identify hazardous conditions.

Although fire prevention can take on many forms, only four activities will be discussed in this chapter: (1) control of ignition sources, (2) housekeeping, (3) occupancy, and (4) arrangement of storage.

Control of Ignition Sources. Ignition sources must be controlled in a warehouse. Unfortunately, a variety of conditions generate sufficient heat to cause ignition. Many ordinary combustible materials that are stored in warehouses have ignition temperatures of less than 500°F. Considering that a match burns at greater than 2000°F and a smoldering cigarette may reach 1000°F, a significant threat of a fire can exist from one unauthorized smoker.

In addition to careless smoking, many other potential sources of ignition are present. Welding and cutting operations have accounted for a number of severe fires. The hazards associated with these jobs should be clearly recognized and strict controls be placed in areas where welding or cutting must be performed. Particular attention should be given to welding contractors to ensure that they abide by strict safety requirements.

A formal permit system is essential to ensure that management is informed of the need for a welding or cutting job. Only after the job is carefully analyzed and appropriate safeguards taken should management give approval for welding or cutting operations. Once started, these operations should be properly monitored by a designated fire watch equipped with a fire extinguisher. The fire watch should continue during all break periods and for 30 minutes after the completion of the job.

There are a variety of additional ignition sources associated with warehousing. Electrical equipment, which accounts for nearly 25 percent of all industrial fires, is always present. Material handling equipment, such as forklift trucks, are also potential sources of ignition. Particular attention should be given to electrical equipment and motorized vehicles when operated near or around potentially hazardous environments. Areas where flammable liquids or combustible dusts are stored require special precautions.

Housekeeping. Housekeeping-related problems are the easiest fire-prevention measures to identify and, perhaps, the most difficult to control. The basis of a continuing housekeeping problem usually results from a lack of management commitment. Management must recognize that poor housekeeping not only affects the fire-prevention effort, but also has a negative impact on areas such as safety, quality, and employee morale. The management techniques that work effectively to control low productivity, poor quality, and labor-related problems should also be applied to correct housekeeping difficiencies.

Poor housekeeping impacts the fire-prevention program in several ways. Modern warehousing and distribution facilities contain combustible materials that will more readily ignite when loosely divided. When housekeeping is poor, these fuels are often configured so as to be easily ignited. Once ignition occurs, rapid flame spread and greater fire damage are likely.

Occupancy. A key factor that determines the fire risk of a particular building is its occupancy. The occupancy of the building is the type of operations or materials that are stored or used in the building. A steel-fabricating facility is normally less hazardous than a chemical processing plant. In addition to the occupancy of the building, it is important to determine the fire loading of the building. The *fire load* is defined as the amount (weight) of combustibles per square foot. A building that contains large amounts of combustible materials will be characterized as having a high fire loading.

Warehousing operations are generally considered to be relatively low-hazard occupancies from the standpoint of potential ignition sources. However, because of the large amounts of materials stored, the fire loadings are usually quite high. Safety and fire-protection engineers must carefully analyze the types of materials stored and what the fire properties of those materials are.

In the automotive parts warehouse discussed earlier, two occupancy changes were major factors that contributed to the loss. The first change was the temporary storage of a large quantity of motor oil. A flammable storage area existed but, because of a temporary overflow condition, motor oil was stored in the main warehouse. The severity was compounded when the oil was placed in an aisle because rack space was also limited.

The storage of the motor oil illustrates an all-too-common problem. Nearly all warehouses, at one time or another, are confronted with the need to provide temporary storage. All other options should be explored before materials are allowed to accumulate beyond the volumes originally specified. When temporary storage conditions are truly temporary and no other choices are available, then the warehouse should be carefully analyzed by fire-protection personnel to determine what measures can be taken to safeguard the facility.

It may be possible to provide some form of temporary fire protection for the duration of the overflow condition. Another option may be to provide additional guard inspection service to limit employee access as well as to provide more rapid fire detection. One additional measure may be to enact strict precautions that restrict possible ignition sources during the exposure period.

All of the temporary precautions just mentioned are only a compromise when temporary storage conditions are absolutely necessary. Of course, the conditions may be such that certain types of temporary storage can never be permitted no matter what extra precautions are taken. This should have been the case in the illustration of the motor oil mixed with the auto parts.

The other occupancy change that impacted the auto parts warehouse was more subtle than the motor oil. When the warehouse was originally constructed in the late 1960s, automobiles were constructed primarily of metal. During the following decade, more and more auto parts were made of different forms of plastic. The switch from metal to plastic may have lowered the unit cost of the individual components as well as reduced overall car weight; however, plastic parts increased the risk of fire.

Plastics are derived from petroleum and are at least as combustible as wood; in many cases, far more combustible. In addition to the ease of ignition and the amount of heat generated, most plastics release large amounts of toxic gases. While it is true that all burning materials will generate some toxic combustion products, many plastics release significantly greater amounts.

In the auto parts warehouse cited, the occupancy of the warehouse changed gradually but significantly during a 10-year period, as the materials used to construct automobiles changed. Because the occupancy change was gradual, no changes were made to upgrade the fire protection.

The widespread use of plastic materials in our society has created a number of fire-related concerns for warehouses. Not only must the basic product being stored be considered, but also the packaging materials protecting the product. Common packing materials such as styrofoam and polyurethane foam can present significant fire exposures. In addition to the fuel contribution to the fire, various packing materials give off differing toxic materials while burning. Styrofoam can release significant amounts of phosgene gas, whereas tests show that polyurethane foam decomposes to form excess amounts of hydrogen cyanide gas. Since both gases are considered to be highly toxic, when these gases are combined with the other fire gases generated, a deadly combination exists.

Arrangement of Storage. The arrangement of stored goods in warehouses receives close scrutiny by fire inspectors. During the last 25 years, considerable research has been devoted to the effect of storage configurations on fire prevention and control. The storage of rubber tires, rolled paper, flammable and combustible liquids, and plastics, among other materials, has been studied in detail. Storage on racks also has been thoroughly studied. As a result of both fire research and loss experience, the National Fire Protection Association (NFPA) has developed standards for recommended indoor storage practices.[1,2]

Storage height is a key variable that has significant impact on the way a fire behaves. Fire tests show that fire intensity varies with the square of the storage height. Storing materials on racks introduces additional problems. Depending on rack configuration, ceiling sprinklers may not be able to provide sufficient coverage for fires occurring within the structure of the rack. Where rack storage is used, fire codes often call for in-rack sprinkler protection. The variables that determine if in-rack sprinklers are required include storage height, shelving, and whether single or double racks are used.

Another variable that affects ceiling sprinkler performance is the distance that material is stored below the sprinkler head. Fire codes require at least an 18-inch clearance between the bottom of the sprinkler head deflector and the stored material. This allows an effective water discharge pattern from the sprinkler head. If there is not adequate sprinkler-pattern coverage, the fire may be more difficult or impossible to extinguish.

Fire Protection

Effective warehouse loss control must give high priority to fire prevention. Nevertheless, management must also ensure that adequate means are available to extinguish a fire should one begin. An effective fire-protection program evaluates the potential for a fire and then determines what measures are necessary to limit and extinguish the fire. The following fire-protection measures will be discussed throughout the remainder of this section: (1) portable hoses and extinguishers, (2) automatic sprinklers, and (3) fire-fighting organizations.

Portable Hoses and Extinguishers. However large the end result, all fires begin small (with the exception of an explosion). The first five minutes of a fire has been defined as the critical time for fire fighting. It is during the beginning or the incipient stage of the fire that it can be rapidly extinguished with little or no damage. Once beyond the incipient stage, the fire progresses very rapidly with the corresponding buildup of heat and smoke.

In order to effectively combat fires during the incipient stage, it is important that portable equipment be readily available and in proper working condition. Where searching is necessary or an inoperable extinguisher is found, precious seconds have been wasted. Portable fire extinguishers should be matched to the type of fire that they will be used to combat. They should also be in close proximity to the hazard. Travel distance should be no greater than 75 feet for ordinary combustibles or 50 feet for flammable or combustible liquids.

Automatic Sprinklers. Automatic sprinkler systems are the main line of defense against fire loss. The National Fire Protection Association estimates that over 95 percent of the automatic sprinkler systems that have been used have exhibited satisfactory performance in extinguishing fires. Most warehouse operations have at least some degree of sprinkler protection, since properties without sprinkler protection may have insurance rates that are five times greater than those with sprinklers.

An automatic sprinkler system serves three functions: it detects the fire, it sounds an alarm, and it extinguishes or controls the fire. Essentially, sprinklers are interconnected systems of piping that are filled with water or air. The sprinkler water flow is controlled by a number of devices or heads that are set to open at a predetermined temperature. "Wet" pipe systems that are filled with water at all times are the most common. However, where freezing may be a problem, "dry" pipe systems that use compressed air can be utilized. Normally, wet pipe systems would be preferable, since they give immediate water flow when activated.

When sprinklers are installed, they are designed for a specific building and occupancy. Usually, the initial design and any changes or modifications must be approved by the insurance carrier or representative. Any changes to the original design, such as a reduction in the volume or pressure of the water supply, can have a serious impact on the capability of the system to properly extinguish a fire.

To ensure that sprinklers are in proper operating condition, a thorough maintenance and inspection program should be implemented. The single most frequent cause of sprinkler failure is closed water-control valves. An effective inspection program combined with a system to electronically monitor or otherwise lock control valves open can virtually ensure that these critical valves remain in service. Other common sprinkler failures are caused by frozen systems, slow operation due to painted or corroded sprinkler heads, inadequate water supplies, or change of occupancy classification without a corresponding upgrade of the sprinkler system.

Fire Walls. A major fire-protection strategy is to limit the spread of a fire should one occur. To accomplish this, buildings are divided by walls that are resistant to the effects of fire for a specified time period. These fire walls are designed to limit the extent of damage in the event of a large fire.

Fire walls are usually designed and constructed when the warehouse is initially built. Retrofitting fire walls is usually not economical or effective. However, where walls are installed, it becomes the responsibility of the occupant to ensure their integrity. The most frequent problem involves wall openings.

In warehousing operations, materials often must be physically transferred from one area of the building to another. This movement may be done by forklift truck, conveyor, crane, or other material handling equipment. Such transportation usually requires doors or other openings in the fire walls. In the event of a fire, the openings must either be automatically closed or an alternate means of protection, such as a water curtain, must be provided. Self-closing fire doors may be actuated by a fusible link or smoke detector or both.

The rapid operation of the fire door is critical in the event of a fire. If the door does not close completely when triggered, there may be no limit to the spread of heat and smoke in the building. Thus, a program should be in place to regularly inspect and test all fire doors to ensure their proper activation in an emergency. All doors should be given an actual test annually to determine if they will properly close. The cause of failures may be apparent, such as damage from being struck by material handling equipment. Unfortunately, the door may fail because of poor lubrication or loss of spring tension, both of which cannot be recognized by a visual inspection.

Fire-Fighting Organizations. As already mentioned, the first five minutes of the fire are the most critical. It is important that some plan be established for handling such emergencies. The Occupational Safety and Health Act (OSHA) sets standards for minimum requirements for employee fire brigades. Where such volunteer brigades exist, the employer must prepare an organizational statement outlining what the responsibilities of the fire brigade are. The employer must also provide a program of education and training for all members.

Whether or not an employer elects to form a fire brigade, there should be an employee evacuation plan. The warehousing operation should also be coordinated with the local fire department. Such planning will acquaint the fire department with the layout of the facility and will allow them to become familiar with any unique fire hazards, such as the storage of flammable liquids or plastics.

Inspections

A key element in any fire prevention and control program is effective inspection. Fire-protection equipment must be inspected periodically to ensure that it is fully operational if needed. Some inspections are mandated by federal, state, or local codes, whereas others may be required by an insurance carrier. All inspections should be documented and discrepancies quickly corrected.

In addition to inspecting fire-protection equipment, fire-prevention inspections or audits should also be performed. Such inspections should examine such things as storage practices, housekeeping, possible heating sources, and handling of flammable liquids.

Safety

Work-related losses are accepted by many managers as a cost of doing business. It is important, however, that managers recognize the true magnitude of these costs. All states have workers' compensation laws that require employees to be fairly compensated for work-related injuries. Compensation usually consists of the payment of medical expenses, weekly disability payments, and lump-sum payments for death or permanently disabling injuries. Worker's compensation costs are usually referred to as the direct or insured cost of accidents. The actual dollar value of the accidents are easily tracked through insurance company records.

The cost of worker's compensation insurance premiums is usually directly associated with the accident experience of the company. The higher the accident frequency, the greater the premium. However, there are a number of costs associated with accidents that are not so easily recognized. These are usually referred to as the indirect or uninsured costs of accidents.

The indirect accident costs are those that are associated with the accident but may be difficult to measure. Grimaldi and Simonds[3] identify 10 different indirect costs that may be incurred by an accident:

1. Cost of wages paid for working time lost by workers who were not injured.
2. The net cost to repair, replace, or clean material or equipment that was damaged.
3. Cost of wages paid for working time lost by injured workers, other than worker's compensation payments.
4. Extra cost due to overtime work necessitated by the accident.
5. Cost of wages paid supervisors while their time is required for activities necessitated by the injury.
6. Productivity loss due to decreased output of injured worker after return to work.
7. Cost of learning period for new worker to replace injured worker.
8. Uninsured medical costs borne by the company.

9. Cost of time spent by higher management and clerical workers on investigations or in the processing of compensation applications.
10. Miscellaneous costs.

Although some of the indirect costs, such as equipment damage, can be easily measured, other costs are very difficult to accurately account for. The cost of management time assigned to accident investigation and report writing represents an opportunity cost of not having management personnel available for other profit-making tasks. Likewise, measurements of reduced productivity or training costs are generally only an approximation. Nevertheless, these are accident-related costs that will sap a company's resources.

Past studies have attempted to determine the relationship between the direct and indirect cost of accidents. Although the results vary, it seems that the indirect costs of an accident are usually three to four times greater than the direct cost. Therefore, to get an approximation of total accident costs, it would be necessary to multiply the direct or insured costs by a factor of 3 or 4. Although not exact, this figure would allow upper management to see the actual impact of accidents and injuries.

Manual Material Handling

The National Safety Council states that 20 to 25 percent of all work injuries result from material handling accidents. That figure is an average for all industries. However, material handling accidents account for a significantly higher percent of injuries in warehousing operations, since that is the nature of the business. In general, material handling accidents can be divided into two types: manual and mechanical.

Manual material handling accounts for more than 20 percent of the disabling injuries suffered in accidents. Back injuries resulting from strains and sprains have long been recognized as a serious problem. A significant amount of research has been devoted to the problem of reducing the incidence and severity of these injuries. Unfortunately, little if any progress has been achieved. Manual material handling injuries continue to plague employees and employers.

In an attempt to reduce manual material handling injuries, old methods and techniques are being closely examined. Traditionally, the lifting method that has been recommended is the "straight-back" technique. This method seems to work well when compact loads are being lifted. However, in reality, such loads are the exception and not the rule. In the work environment, employees find themselves in a position to make a variety of lifts involving differing sizes and weights of materials.

Although many modern warehouses are highly automated, a significant number of operations are performed by hand. Many unloading, uncrating, sorting, and packing operations require human intervention. These operations may involve random as opposed to routine lifts. Such nonroutine lifting is difficult to plan and thus may require a person to lift a load to which they are unaccustomed. The traditional approach has been to train warehouse personnel to recognize potential lifting problems and use the correct lifting method.

The straight-back lifting method has been taught to workers for years, but that training has not yielded promising results. The National Institute for Occupational Safety and Health (NIOSH) has published a document entitled *Work Practice Guide for Manual Lifting*.[4] Among other things, this document examines the role of training in reducing manual material handling injuries. It indicates that the effect of training is probably overstated, since employee training programs have failed to reduce back injuries.

Where training in manual material handling is conducted, the following guidelines are recommended:

1. Lift comfortably.
2. Avoid unnecessary bending.
3. Avoid unnecessary twisting.
4. Avoid reaching out.
5. Avoid excessive weights.
6. Lift gradually.
7. Keep in good physical shape.

It is interesting that the current guidelines do not emphasize lifting with a straight back. Indeed, there may be times when attempting to use the straight-back lift may put greater stress on the back. During manual lifting, the further the person must hold the object away from the front of the body, the greater the stress to the spine. The closer the object's center of gravity is to the spine, the shorter the moment arm, which results in a torqueing action on the structure of the back.

Using the straight-back method of lifting minimizes the moment arm when the load is small. However, when a larger load is being lifted, the straight-back lift tends to create a larger moment around the spine, since the arms must reach out to the object.

The most impressive reduction of back-related injuries has resulted from modifying the job through engineering changes. Where lifting tasks are somewhat routine, mechanical aids can be used to improve the task for the worker. Eliminating the need to lift is by far the most effective means of eliminating costly back injuries. Lifting aids and other mechanical devices may require some investment of capital funds, but normally if one back injury is prevented, the expenditure is justified.

Ergonomics is the discipline that examines a person's relationship to his or her work in an attempt to maximize productivity and quality while trying to minimize injuries and employee dissatisfaction. Ergonomic improvements begin by studying a particular task that has resulted in a large number of injuries, has low productivity, or has received a number of employee or management complaints. It may then be determined in what manner the job can be altered to be more compatible with the capabilities of the human operator. A number of reference texts identify key parameters, such as workbench height, chair height, strength requirements, and other data regarding large populations of people.[5,6,7]

Mechanical Handling Equipment

Studies indicate that 5 to 10 percent of worker's compensation–related accidents result from material handling equipment. In warehousing operations, it can be expected that mechanical handling equipment can account for a much higher percentage of accidents. Mechanical material handling equipment includes forklift trucks, conveyors, and hoists, as well as a number of specialized lifts and cranes. Such equipment can be manually driven or automatically controlled. In addition, many warehousing and distribution centers are utilizing robots to handle packing or loading operations. Robotic operations can present unique exposures that may require specialized safeguarding.

An analysis of past data shows that plant and industrial vehicles account for over two-thirds of all the mechanized material handling injuries. Hoisting apparatus, conveyors, and packaging or wrapping machines are responsible for the majority of the remaining accidents. Almost half of all the injuries occurred when employees were struck by or struck against some piece of material handling equipment.

In general, all accidents are caused by unsafe conditions or the unsafe actions of people. The same relationship holds for accidents involving materials handling equipment. Unsafe equipment can usually be eliminated by periodic inspection and preventive maintenance. Both the inspection and the maintenance schedule will vary according to the equipment. Many such inspections are recommended or required daily. In the case of powered industrial trucks, OSHA requires that prior to each shift they be inspected for mechanical defects. Where conditions are found that would adversely affect the safety of the truck, OSHA requires that it not be operated.

The majority of accidents associated with mechanized materials handling equipment are due, however, to the unsafe actions of an operator or pedestrian. A major effort should be devoted to the training and retraining of the operators of material handling equipment. Although OSHA requires that only trained individuals be permitted to operate powered industrial trucks, the law does not specify the content of the training program. As a result, operator training programs vary considerably from one hour to the National Safety Council's recommended five-day program.

Whatever the length of operator training, the program should be designed to ensure that the operators are fully equipped to perform the variety of tasks they may be asked to do. It is essential to provide some sort of training with the equipment as well as in a classroom. It is also important to have the trainee demonstrate a degree of proficiency with the type of equipment that he or she will be expected to operate.

Occupational Health

New research findings and recent court decisions have focused on occupational disease as a serious problem in many workplaces. Although warehousing operations ordinarily do not have the exposure that manufacturing industries may have, some potential health hazards exist. All warehouses using equipment with internal combustion engines face the threat of overexposure to carbon monoxide. Most occupancies are vented sufficiently to prevent the accumulation of hazardous levels of carbon monoxide; however, should the engines be used for a considerable time period in an enclosed space, an overexposure is possible.

Acid in storage batteries is another possible health-related exposure in warehouses. Care should be taken to prevent the liquid from splashing onto the skin and eyes. Thus, where batteries are handled and acid added, an eyewash and safety shower should be present in the case of accidental contact from splashing. The area should also be adequately ventilated to prevent the buildup of hydrogen gas or acid vapors.

Each warehouse operation should also be examined for unique health hazards. Insulation on the walls and ceiling should be inspected for asbestos content. Where there is doubt, qualified professionals should be contacted for an evaluation.

In addition to the existing equipment and building, the material stored in the facility should be inspected for leaks or spills that could be creating a health hazard by exposure. The hazardous properties of the materials stored in the warehouse should be noted in the event that a spill or fire occurs involving those materials.

Security

For the most part, the types of losses that have been discussed in the previous sections can be considered to be unintentional. This section will analyze losses that result from willful intent. An effective loss-control program must recognize the various types of security exposures that may exist and implement programs that will minimize those risks. This section will examine three types of security exposures as they relate to warehousing operations: (1) theft, (2) vandalism, and (3) arson.

Theft. Although every warehouse faces some threat of theft, the magnitude of the theft problem is determined by the value and configuration of the product stored in the warehouse. A product that has little commercial value, such as bales of cotton or steel columns, requires a lower level of security. Whereas, a product like food, clothing, or tools, with high appeal and resale capability need considerably more stringent security controls.

When designing a security program, it is important to determine where the facility is most vulnerable. It should be recognized that the theft exposure can be from either the general public or the employees. Employee theft can many times be characterized as pilferage. Although pilferage may not be seen as serious as felonious larceny, it can amount to a greater loss to the company. Once again, the degree of employee pilferage will be determined by the value and the configuration of the product. Even though a microwave oven would have considerable value, such a large, bulky item would be rather difficult for an employee to smuggle out.

There are a number of measures that can be implemented to control both employee and nonemployee theft. Restricted access to the warehouse and to sensitive areas within the warehouse would be considered the first line of defense. A security plan should be developed that will restrict outside access via perimeter fencing. A well-constructed fence will discourage all but the most determined thieves. Where fences are impractical or where the inventory is so valuable as to anticipate fence penetration, additional levels of security must be provided.

In addition to the fence, access into the building must also be restricted. Well-designed door and window fixtures will discourage or at least delay intruders. An effective program must also be developed to ensure tight control over the distribution of keys.

Another method of protection would be some form of surveillance. Surveillance includes both direct security guard services and various types of electronic monitoring using remote devices. Video cameras, motion detectors, and intruder alarms can all be effective in the remote monitoring of high-security areas.

Vandalism. Vandalism, the willing destruction of property, can take many forms, ranging from writing on walls to arson. All forms of vandalism incur some repair costs and may result in large financial losses.

It is difficult to characterize the personality or the motive of the vandal. Such a person may feel vengeful toward a specific company or the actions may be completely random. Many times, the vandalism may be largely due to the location of the warehouse. Inner-city facilities are more prone to be affected by random vandalism than those in suburban locations.

Protection against vandalism varies. Access control will minimize damage within a building. Fencing and other forms of isolation will help to restrict access and also prevent exterior damage. Security patrols, lighting, remote monitoring, and increased police surveillance are also possible solutions.

Arson. Although both theft and vandalism can be a serious drain on company resources, neither compares to that of arson. Not only does the arsonist threaten the building and its contents, but also the lives of the building's occupants. Although some facilities are more likely to be the target of an arsonist, no operation is immune.

As with the vandal, the motives of the arsonist are diverse. The random pyromaniac is always a threat, but normally this threat can be minimized by limiting personnel accessibility. Agitated customers have also been the source of fires in certain industries, but, once again, by restricting access their threat is minimal.

A more serious arson threat comes from disgruntled or recently terminated employees. This type of individual is particularly dangerous because of his or her knowledge of the facility. It may also be difficult to restrict the access of a person with knowledge of the facility. Personnel procedures should ensure that employees are escorted from the warehouse site immediately after termination. Discharged employees should be profiled to determine whether possible threats are merely idle or whether they should be taken seriously. Many small fires are intentionally set by employees in order to get management's attention. The employees do not intend to cause severe damage, but rather to have management recognize that the employees want to be heard.

Unfortunately, it may be impossible to eliminate all intentional fires. It is too easy for an employee to drop a match into a trash container in a rest room. There are, however, several critical measures that must be taken to eliminate the risk of a severe fire. First, employees must be restricted to areas that are considered necessary to the requirements of the job. When employees are allowed to wander, it becomes very difficult to exercise control measures. Where employees have unrestricted access, they can find the areas most vulnerable to a fire.

The second protection against arson is the installation and maintenance of an automatic fire-protection system. Even if an arsonist strikes and a fire starts, an effective fire-protection system will detect and control the fire. It is of primary importance that the potential arsonist not be able to disable or circumvent the fire-protection systems.

The prevention of loss from theft, vandalism, and arson presents a unique challenge to warehouse operations. A security plan should be developed and carefully analyzed for each location. Various contingencies should be anticipated in order to minimize such losses. All managers should recognize that loss control and asset production are line responsibilities for which they are accountable.

Damage Control

Another type of loss that can be incurred in warehousing operations is product damage. Product damage takes on many forms. The type of damage depends on the type of warehousing, but can include spoilage, contamination, rodent damage, sunlight, or water damage.

Controls for the prevention of product damage are as diverse as the cause of the damage. As a general statement, it is the responsibility of management to assess the vulnerability of the product being stored and to determine how best that product can be protected. Many of the problems, such as spoilage and contamination, may be related to the shelf life of the product.

Many times product damage occurs when adequate warehousing space is not available and temporary or improvised storage facilities are utilized. Prudent action would require the existing inventory to be analyzed to determine if any storage can be considered surplus. When overflow conditions exist, surplus or storage of a lower quality should be the first to be removed to less secure quarters.

In addition to damage that is unique to specific products, there are certain types of losses that can affect all types of warehousing operations. Losses due to various forms of natural disasters present threats to all facilities. Although it may be difficult to prevent such losses, proper planning can minimize damage and downtime should such an emergency occur.

Natural disasters include severe conditions, such as hurricanes, tornados, and floods, but also include more common conditions, such as snowstorms, severe lightning and hailstorms, and power failures. Potential threats from fires, explosions, and chemical spills and releases have already been described.

Planning for an emergency is a task that should be undertaken by all warehousing and distribution facilities. Not only should all possible contingencies be planned for, but available emergency resources should be identified prior to being needed. An effective emergency action plan should identify management responsibilities in the event of an emergency as well as establishing the communication network to be used.

Of course, having an organization on paper is no guarantee that such an organization will function properly should an emergency occur. As a result, it is important to conduct drills and training sessions on all aspects of the plan. Such drills may help to identify weak spots in the plan. In addition, drills help to ensure that all employees with emergency control responsibilities understand what these are.

Product damage takes on many forms. It can occur slowly, as in the case of rodent infestation, or rapidly, as in the event of a tornado. In either event, it is management's responsibility to anticipate and control the conditions that create the product damage. Where such conditions cannot be controlled, management must develop a plan to limit potential damage and outline resources to be used to restore operations as quickly as possible.

Risk Management

From the previous sections, it can be seen that the possibilities for a large loss are numerous. This final section will discuss methods that can be used to manage the losses that may be encountered. Although no profitable organization wants to incur such a loss, it would be irresponsible if no planning were conducted prior to a loss occurring. The modern term of "risk manager" is applied to those individuals who manage such losses in their organizations.

In a sense, everyone is a risk manager. Every individual performs risk management activities in his or her personal life. All of us must examine our assets, such as cars, houses, and boats, and determine the most effective way to protect them against loss. In many cases, insurance is the major portion of the answer. Insurance can protect us against some of the losses we can incur, but certainly not all. Of course, before we purchase insurance, we must weigh the cost of the insurance against the probability of a loss.

Auto insurance is a good example of how we manage our personal risks. Very few people would buy a new car and drive without some collision insurance. However, 100 percent insurance coverage is usually prohibitively expensive. Therefore, we decide to accept a portion of the risk and obtain collision insurance with a deductible portion that we must pay before the insurance becomes effective. As our car becomes older, its value drops and we may elect to eliminate our collision coverage altogether. In our own way, we are electing to be risk managers of our own assets.

In the same way, every organization must have a formal plan for evaluating its assets against possible loss. In a small organization, the president or the owner usually handles this responsibility. In larger organizations, however, the protection of company assets is usually delegated to an individual who may have the title of risk manager, insurance administrator, or director of property protection. This person's function is to recommend to top management the most cost-efficient method to manage company risks.

The risk manager must examine all aspects of the company's business and should initially determine the large-loss risks to which the company may be vulnerable. Variables such as construction, occupancy, exposures, water availability, and public fire protection among others must be evaluated to determine loss potential. Once the existing company assets are reviewed, the risk manager must analyze the company's financial data to determine the overall effect of the loss on the facility. The dollar loss of a building may not be particularly high, but the potential business interruption may represent a staggering loss from which the organization may not be able to recover.

Once the information on possible risks is accumulated, the risk manager must make recommendations as to how those risks are best managed. Generally, there are three methods to manage risk: (1) retention, (2) self-insurance, (3) insurance. *Retention* is a way of dealing with a loss as a means of normal business. This approach would tend to accept losses as they occur and deal with them as appropriate. Although retention may have some benefit for small losses, it can be a dangerous practice where the potential is present for a large loss. The loss due to employee pilferage may be accepted as part of normal business; however, the loss from a major fire may be impossible to absorb. *Self-insurance* is a method whereby an organization sets up a special or internal fund to pay for large losses. One advantage of self-insurance is that the company may save a significant amount of money that would ordinarily go to an insurance company in the form of premiums. If a self-insured company achieves a good loss record, the organization enjoys a direct economic gain, since it does not have to pay insurance premiums. In the event of worker's compensation payments, the company is required to establish a permanent fund that workers will have access to in the event of occupational injury and disease claims. Nevertheless, organizations with good loss records can achieve significant savings if self-insured.

As is the case with retention, however, a catastrophic loss could potentially bring financial disaster to an organization. Before the decision to self-insure is made, the overall financial impact to the entire company should be assessed. A large company may be able to absorb such a large loss with only temporary effects; whereas a smaller company with fewer assets could be financially ruined. *Insurance* is a method of transferring the risk to a third party or a number of parties. In most cases, the risk is transferred to an insurance company. For accepting the risk, the insurance company receives payment in the form of a premium. The greater the dollar value of the property and the greater the risk, the greater the cost of the insurance.

Many organizations use a combination of options to manage their risks. In many cases, fire and disaster insurance may include a sizable deductible that the company would incur. This lowers the overall insurance premium because the insurance company only becomes responsible for high-value losses. Insurance programs with deductibles encourage company loss prevention because small losses are absorbed directly by the company.

Companies may obtain coverage from one or many insurance companies. For high-value facilities ranging into the millions of dollars, insurance companies may elect to have different levels of coverage. A facility valued at $100 million may be self-insured for the first million, insured by one company from $1 to $10 million, and another from $10 to $20 million. Finally a third company may provide the extra coverage from $20 to $100 million. This multiple coverage allows the insurance companies to transfer some of the risk so that one company would not be forced to underwrite a catastrophic loss.

The specifics of the insurance process are very complex and far beyond the scope of this section. It is safe to say, however, that many of the loss-control activities outlined earlier in this chapter are the most effective methods of minimizing insurance rates. Where company assets may reach billions of dollars, effective loss prevention may save several million dollars in premiums alone. Thus, loss prevention becomes a very important part of the risk management process.

Although most companies have elected to carry some form of insurance coverage for protection of assets, it is important to recognize what the shortcomings of insurance are. Even when a company has full protection, there are many aspects of the business that insurance cannot cover. Many intangibles, such as loss of customers, loss of key employees, and loss of community goodwill, cannot be insured against. The National Fire Protection Association has indicated that only 29 percent of businesses suffering a major fire loss will reopen and still be in business three years later.

Risk management and loss-prevention activities cannot always prevent losses. However, a comprehensive loss-prevention program will keep losses to a minimum, and effective risk management will provide the best protection for the minimum price. Both functions can play a vital role in maintaining the economic health of a company.

References

1. Indoor General Storage, NFPA Code 231. National Fire Protection Association, Boston, Massachusetts.
2. Rack Storage of Materials, NFPA Code 231C, National Fire Protection Association, Boston, Massachusetts.
3. John V. Grimaldi and Rolin H. Simonds, *Safety Management,* Richard D. Irwin, Homewood, Illinois, 1975.
4. *Work Practices Guide for Manual Lifting,* DHHS (NIOSH) Publication No. 81-122, 1981.
5. John D. Benson, "Ergonomics and Safe Lifting," *Professional Safety,* vol. 29, no. 2:33-36, 1984.
6. *Ergonomic Design for People at Work,* vol. 1, Lifetime Learning Publications, Belmont, California, 1983.
7. E. Grandjean, *Fitting the Task to the Man: An Erognomic Approach,* Taylor and Francis, London, 1981.

Index